Dear NFT Reader,

Don't believe the east coast partisan propaganda. There is a functional mass transit system in Los Angeles, nd we'll show you how to use it. But the other side of the country does get one LA stereotype right: we emain a city in love with the internal combustion engine. It's not a reciprocal romance—your car won't plan the date by itself, and it assuredly never pays for anything while continuing to suck your bank account dry. But NFT can wing for you. As usual, the Not For Tourists guide to LA is designed to fit snugly under the driver's seat, and be easily retrieved while watching the road. When you're parked in 405 traffic, you can thank us for the reading material.

But NFT isn't just for drivers. It's for anyone who wants to make this somewhat maddeningly designed, palm tree-peppered concrete jungle a home. We invented sprawl, y'all, and it's well nigh impossible to nd one's way around without good leads. When the Bruins, the Hollywood Bowl, and the Academy Awards bottleneck traffic, we'll show you alternate routes. When you find yourself trapped in the tangled Downtown freeway plug, we'll show you how to unclog yourself. And when you don't feel like driving (or, heaven forbid, your car is in the shop), we'll show you the bank branches, grocery stores, and cheap hangouts that have been hiding out in your neighborhood this whole time.

"It's a nice place to live," said Mark Twain, "but I wouldn't want to visit." That's why, even if you're just in ere for the weekend, we want you to see Los Angeles through the eyes of savvy Angelenos y Angelenas. here's a lot to see, and it's not all bucolic beaches, bottle-blondes, and lettuce lunches. If LA is a materialist mecca and the world's most prolific illusion factory, it's also the globe's most "global" metropolis and we ent some of the smartest, most curious, most hype-resistant people we know to sup, drink, dance, listen, learn, browse, play, exercise, relax, shop, visit, mingle, and report on the melting pot within the melting pot.

Without fail or pause, Los Angeles changes. Thus, while this book is the essence of our mission, we're pretty sure this computer thing isn't a fad, and we also work hard and late to stay current at www.notfortourists.com. If your favorite art gallery folds, or you finally find a place in this town with a good deep-dish, please let us know. NFT never sleeps. As a complement to the book and the website, we've launched our very own swank iPhone apps. The books and the apps are not mutually exclusive—there are some things that this book will do best for always, but the iPhone app will serve as our evolving, ready-reference take on city life. It will geo-locate you anywhere in Los Angeles, and allow you, dear NFT user, to kvetch to us, directly, instantly, about anything.

Like we always do about this time, we'd like to thank our contributors for their work. Another flash of the movie-star smile goes to the office staff, for making it happen. And a final thanks to you, dear reader, for exploring Los Angeles with us.

Happy navigating,
Jane, Scott, Meg, et al.

The Valley
42 Chatsworth
43 Granada Hills/ Northridge
44 Mission Hills/ North Hills
45 Canoga Park/ Woodland Hills
46 Reseda
47 Van Nuys
48 North Hollywood
49 Burbank
50 Burbank East/ Glendale West
51 Glendale South
52 Tarzana/ Woodland Hills
53 Encino
54 Sherman Oaks West
55 Sherman Oaks East
56 Studio City/ Valley Village
57 Toluca Lake
Griffith Park
PAGE 182
West Side & the Beach
1 Beverly Hills
2 West Hollywood
3 Hollywood
4 Los Feliz
5 Silver Lake/ Echo Park/ Atwater
6 Miracle Mile/ Mid-City
7 Hancock Park
8 Korea Town
9 Downtown
10 Baldwin Hills
11 South Central West
12 South Central East
13 Inglewood
14 Inglewood East/ Morningside Park
15 Pacific Palisades
16 Brentwood
17 Bel Air/ Holmby Hills
18 Santa Monica
19 West LA
20 Westwood/ Century City
21 Venice
22 Mar Vista
23 Rancho Park/ Palms
24 Culver City
25 Marina Del Rey/ Westchester West
26 Westchester/ Fox Hills/ Ladera Heights/ LAX
LAX
PAGE 250
Central LA
27 El Segundo/ Manhattan Beach
28 Hawthorne
29 Hermosa Beach/ Redondo Beach North
30 Torrance North
31 Redondo Beach
32 Torrance South
South Bay
Pacific Ocean
East Side & Pasa
33 Eagle Rock/ Highland Park
34 Pasadena
35 Pasade East/ San Mari
36 Mt Washington
37 Lincoln Heights
38 El Sereno
39 Alhambra
40 Boyle Heights
41 City Terrace/ East LA
405
170
5
210
101
134
2
110
10
710
105

Table of Contents

Map 1 • Beverly Hills

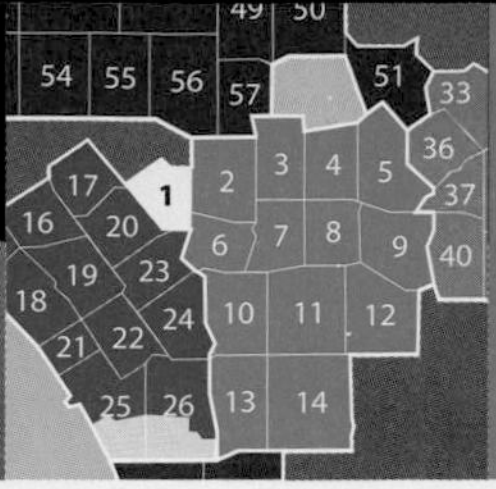

When the outside world pictures Los Angeles, it often defaults to well-lit images of Beverly Hills: palm trees, 23 broad avenues, nice cars, snappy rich folk. Shopping Rodeo Drive is high-stakes fun, but locals avoid it. To store the best BH memories, visit during the holidays, when the decorations above Wilshire Boulevard beam their glitzy charm. And there's one mental-health practitioner per 100 residents! If you're just visiting, enjoy the town's only freebie: two hours gratis in a public parking lot.

Landmarks

- **Academy of Motion Picture Arts & Sciences** • 8949 Wilshire Blvd
310-247-3000
Brake for red carpets and klieg lights! Many premieres are held here.
- **Beverly Hills Civic Center** • Santa Monica Blvd & N Rexford Dr
310-285-1000
Infrastructure for the rich and famous.
- **The Beverly Hills Hotel** • 9641 W Sunset Blvd
310-276-2251
Legends have stayed at the Pink Palace.
- **Four Seasons Beverly Wilshire** • 9500 Wilshire Blvd
310-275-5200
Pretty Woman stayed here.
- **Greystone Mansion** • 905 Loma Vista Dr
310-285-6830
Formerly the Doheny Mansion, now part of a lovely public park.
- **Greystone Park** • 905 Loma Vista Dr
310-285-6830
Amazing views of Beverly Hills at this public mansion estate. Luke and Laura got married here, and you can too.
- **Paley Center for Media** • 465 N Beverly Dr
310-786-1091
Where reruns of old sitcoms are considered art.
- **Prada** • 469 N Rodeo Dr
310-385-5959
Architect Rem Koolhaas gives BH something else to look at.
- **The Witch's House** • 516 Walden Dr
Fairytale haunt straight out of Hansel and Gretel.

Nightlife

- **Bar Noir** • 140 S Lasky Dr
310-281-4000
Très petit hotel bar serves mondo martinis.
- **The Blvd** • 9500 Wilshire Blvd
310-275-5200
Hotel bar with clubby feel.
- **The Club Bar** • 9882 S Santa Monica Blvd
310-551-2888
Classy hotel bar.
- **Livello Lounge** • 9291 Burton Way
310-278-3344
Sophisticated and elegant, the perfect spot for an intimate redezvous.
- **Oliverio** • 9400 W Olympic Blvd
310-407-7791
Mid-century modern poolside cocktails.
- **Trader Vic's** • 9876 Wilshire Blvd
310-276-6345
Polynesian institution. Recently relocated.

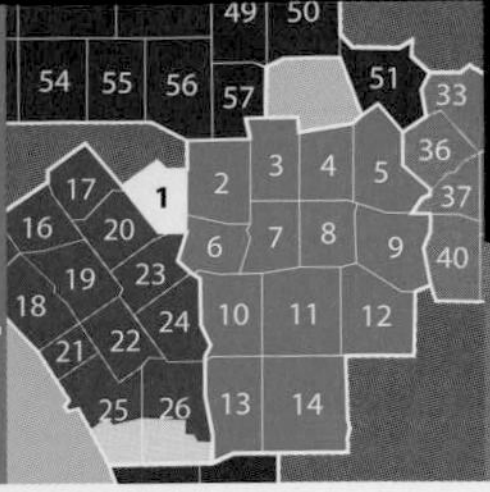

Beverly Hills

Restaurants

- **Barney Greengrass** • 9570 Wilshire Blvd
310-777-5877 • $$$
An LA icon.
- **The Belvedere** • 9882 Little Santa Monica Blvd
310-975-2736 • $$$$
Upscale hotel dining.
- **The Blvd** • 9500 Wilshire Blvd
310-275-5200 • $$$$
Pretty Woman in us all.
- **Boa** • 9200 W Sunset Blvd
310-278-2050 • $$$$
Steaks on the Sunset Strip.
- **Bouchon Bistro** • 235 N Canon Dr
310-271-9910 • $$$$$
Bev Hills stereotypes eating French classics.
- **Brighton Coffee Shop** • 9600 Brighton Way
310-276-7732 • $$
Comfort food.
- **Café Talesai** • 9198 W Olympic Blvd
310-271-9345 • $
Thai specialties with a twist.
- **Crustacean** • 9646 S Santa Monica Blvd
310-205-8990 • $$$$
High-end Vietnamese.
- **Da Pasquale** • 9749 Little Santa Monica Blvd
310-859-3884 • $$$
Neighborhood Italian.
- **The Farm of Beverly Hills** • 439 N Beverly Dr
310-273-5578 • $$$
Yeehaw darlings! Farm-fresh salads and entrees.
- **The Grill on the Alley** • 9560 Dayton Way
310-276-0615 • $$$$
Hollywood power lunch spot.
- **La Scala** • 434 N Canon Dr
310-275-0579 • $$$$
Classic Italian.
- **Le Pain Quotidien** • 9630 S Santa Monica Blvd
310-859-1100 • $$
Classy French sandwich shop.
- **Mastro's Steakhouse** • 246 N Canon Dr
310-888-8782 • $$$$$
Great steaks; don't miss the upstairs piano bar.
- **Maude** • 212 S Beverly Dr
310-859-3418 • $$$$$
Heady, inspired ever-changing tasting menus in intimate setting.
- **Mulberry Street Pizzeria** • 240 S Beverly Dr
310-247-8100 • $$
Thin-crust pizza.
- **Mulberry Street Pizzeria** • 347 N Canon Dr
310-247-8998 • $$
Thin-crust pizza.
- **Nate 'n Al's** • 414 N Beverly Dr
310-274-0101 • $$
New York-style deli.
- **Nic's** • 453 N Canon Dr
310-550-5707 • $$$$$
Oysters and martinis—need we say more?
- **Oliverio** • 9400 W Olympic Blvd
310-277-5221 • $$$$
Poolside cocktails…very LA.
- **The Polo Lounge** • 9641 W Sunset Blvd
310-887-2777 • $$$$$
The Grande Dame of hotel dining.
- **Spago Beverly Hills** • 176 N Canon Dr
310-385-0880 • $$$$$
Flagship restaurant that begat the airport food court empire.
- **Sprinkles Cupcakes** • 9635 S Santa Monica Blvd
310-274-8765 • $
LA's version of Magnolia bakery.
- **Trader Vic's** • 9876 Wilshire Blvd
310-276-6345 • $$$$
Old-school Polynesian-themed restaurant; fruity drinks and fried appetizers.
- **Xi'an** • 362 N Canon Dr
310-275-3345 • $$$
Healthy and delicious Chinese in a BH atmosphere.

Beverly Hills

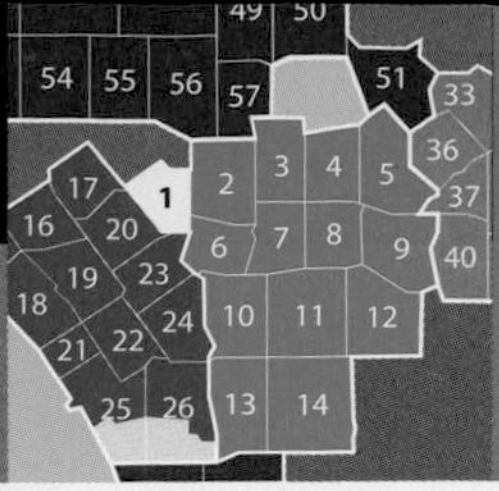

Map 1

Rodeo Drive is a theme park, complete with sky-high price tags, throngs of tourists, and annoying parking. Rodeo is surprisingly not always a reliable place to gawk at the *beau monde*—you're better off trying a restaurant like **Bouchon**. To get closer to earth, try Beverly Drive south of Wilshire—get lunch at **The Farm** and browse art books at **Taschen**.

Shopping

- **Anthropologie** • 211 S Beverly Dr
  310-385-7390
  Unique, super-feminine clothes and accessories. Goldmine clearance.
- **Barney's New York** • 9570 Wilshire Blvd
  310-276-4400
  Upscale department store. It's not shopping—it's investing.
- **Chanel Boutique** • 400 N Rodeo Dr
  310-278-5500
  You can channel Coco here.
- **The Cheese Store of Beverly Hills** • 419 N Beverly Dr
  310-278-2855
  High-quality cheese, even better olives. Also wine counseling.
- **Fritelli's Doughnuts & Coffee** • 350 N Canon Dr
  310-276-1408
  Fancy donuts in fancier digs.
- **Gearys** • 351 N Beverly Dr
  310-273-4741
  The place for wedding gifts and now wedding rings.
- **Giorgio Armani** • 436 N Rodeo Dr
  310-271-5555
  It's Rodeo Drive, baby.
- **Gucci** • 347 N Rodeo Dr
  310-278-3451
  Ignore the imitations; this is the original.
- **Mrs. Beasley's** • 255 S Beverly Dr
  310-276-6516
  How most Hollywood assistants' holiday weight is gained.
- **Neiman Marcus** • 9700 Wilshire Blvd
  310-550-5900
  High-end department store.
- **Prada Epicenter** • 337 N Rodeo Dr
  310-278-8661
  The conceptual Rem Koolhaas-designed store.
- **Ron Herman** • 325 N Beverly Dr
  310-550-0910
  Home of the "Citizens of Humanity" jeans.
- **Saks Fifth Avenue** • 9600 Wilshire Blvd
  310-275-4211
  Chi-chi department store.
- **Sprinkles Cupcakes** • 9635 S Santa Monica Blvd
  310-274-8765
  Cupcakes with intimidating pedigree.
- **TASCHEN** • 354 N Beverly Dr
  310-274-4300
  For all your art and fetish needs.

Map 2 • West Hollywood

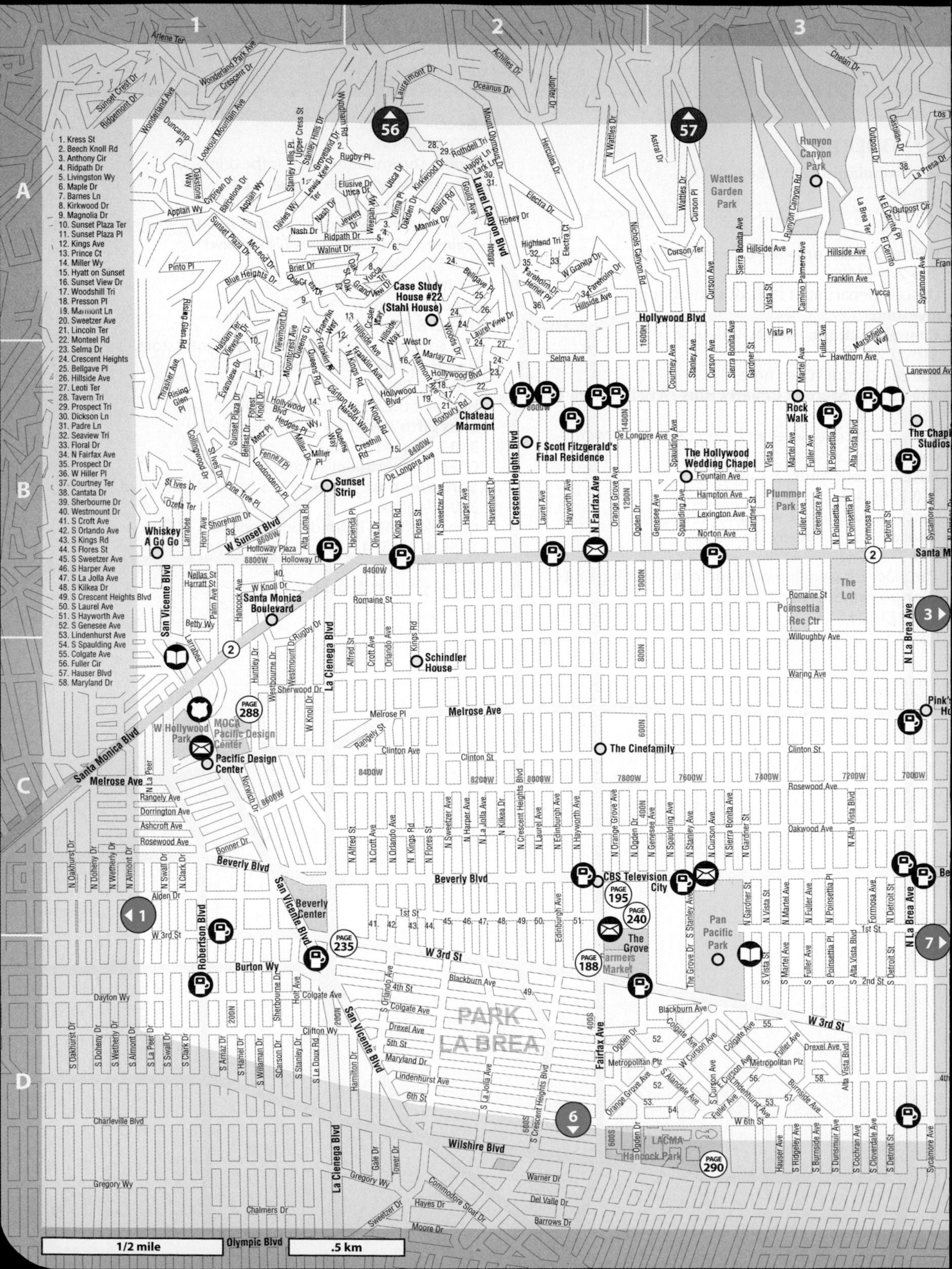

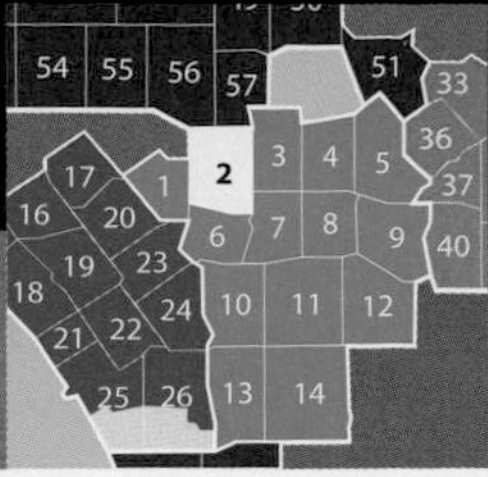

Fun fact: While it is, in many ways, the heart of Los Angeles—featuring some of the area's most ubiquitous locations, from the Sunset Strip to Chateau Marmont—West Hollywood is technically its own city. It's also the center of all things gay in Los Angeles. Don't miss the spectacular costumes (and ogling masses) of the Halloween parade.

oLandmarks

- **Case Study House #22** • 1636 Woods Dr
Pierre Koenig's architectural triumph that sums up the whole spirit of late twentieth-century architecture.
- **CBS Television City** • Beverly Blvd & N Fairfax Ave
323-575-2458
Wanna be on *The Price is Right*? Come on down!
- **The Chaplin Studios** • 1416 N La Brea Ave
Charlie Chaplin's charming English Tudor-esque studios, now the Jim Henson studio.
- **Chateau Marmont** • 8221 W Sunset Blvd
323-656-1010
Chic hotel where John Belushi died.
- **The Cinefamily** • 611 N Fairfax Ave
323-655-2510
Only the ticket prices will remind you that it's the 21st century.
- **Pacific Design Center** • 8687 Melrose Ave
310-657-0800
Nicknamed "The Blue Whale" for obvious reasons.
- **Pan Pacific Park** • 7600 Beverly Blvd
323-939-8874
It's a storm drain! We mean, it's a park!
- **Pink's Famous Hot Dogs** • 709 N La Brea Ave
323-931-4223
A line around the block; it's that famous.
- **Rock Walk** • 7425 W Sunset Blvd
323-874-1060
Mann's Chinese has John Wayne, the Rock Walk has Slash.
- **Runyon Canyon Park** • Franklin Ave & N Fuller Ave
Once Errol Flynn's estate, now a very popular off-leash hiking trail.
- **Santa Monica Blvd** •
Santa Monica Blvd & N La Cienega Blvd
The heart of gay West Hollywood.
- **Schindler House** • 833 N Kings Rd
323-651-1510
A desert camp inspired this brilliant creation by architect Rudolph Schindler.
- **Sunset Strip** • W Sunset Blvd & N Doheny Dr
Its clubs are still the center of LA's (bridge and tunnel) nightlife.
- **Whisky A Go Go** • 8901 W Sunset Blvd
310-652-4202
Music venue for legendary bands of yore.

Nightlife

- **The 3rd Stop** • 8636 W 3rd St
310-273-3605
Beer bar.
- **The Abbey** • 692 N Robertson Blvd
310-289-8410
Mix, mingle, and make out in this West Hollywood gem.
- **Andaz Lounge** • 8401 W Sunset Blvd
323-656-1234
Raw vegetables and groundbreaking cocktails. Try a Mr. Plant.
- **Bar 1200** • 1200 Alta Loma Rd
310-358-3720
So mellow, the star at your shoulder ain't no thing.
- **Bar at the Standard** • 8300 W Sunset Blvd
323-650-9090
This trendy spot is anything but standard.
- **Bar Lubitsch** • 7702 Santa Monica Blvd
323-654-1234
The vodka flows at this Russian bar.
- **Barney's Beanery** • 8447 Santa Monica Blvd
323-654-2287
A low-rent (but fun) LA institution.
- **Club 7969** • 7969 Santa Monica Blvd
323-654-0280
Ravers rejoice! This place is all about the dance.
- **The Comedy Store** • 8433 W Sunset Blvd
323-650-6268
See Jeffrey Ross's signature. Two-drink minimum.
- **The Dime** • 442 N Fairfax Ave
Unassuming yet hip watering hole.
- **El Carmen** • 8138 W 3rd St
323-852-1552
Among the best margaritas in LA.
- **Factory** • 652 N La Peer Dr
310-659-4551
Wildly popular gay dance club.
- **The Fat Dog** • 801 N Fairfax Ave
323-951-0030
Solid beer list and addictive spicy rosemary almonds.
- **Fiesta Cantina** • 8865 Santa Monica Blvd
310-652-8865
Sticky floor worth the best drink deals in town.

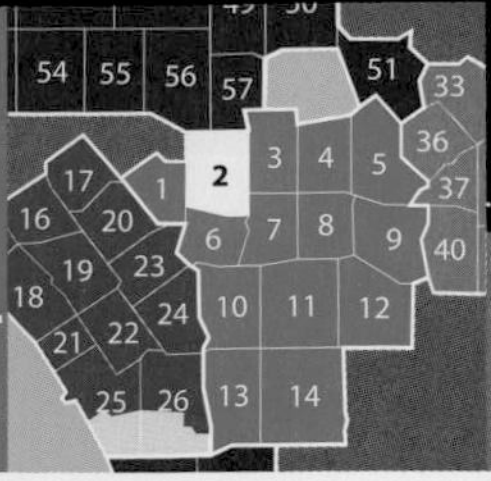

West Hollywood

- **Formosa Café** • 7156 Santa Monica Blvd
  323-850-9050
  Train car drinks and rooftop bar. Avoid the food.
- **Fubar** • 7994 Santa Monica Blvd
  323-654-0396
  Cutest gay hipsters west of Avenue A.
- **Genghis Cohen** • 740 N Fairfax Ave
  323-653-0640
  Acoustic music and Chinese food.
- **Gold Coast Bar** • 8228 Santa Monica Blvd
  323-656-4879
  Cheap, low-key gay bar.
- **Hollywood Improv** • 8162 Melrose Ave
  323-651-2583
  Most of the big names stop here. Two-drink minimum, natch.
- **House of Blues** • 8430 W Sunset Blvd
  323-848-5100
  Big(ger) acts on the Sunset Strip.
- **The Improv Comedy Lab** • 8156 Melrose Ave
  323-651-2583
  Experimental offshoot of the Improv with sketch and stand up.
- **Kibitz Room** • 419 N Fairfax Ave
  323-651-2030
  Divey McDive Bar with lots of live music.
- **Largo** • 366 N La Cienega Blvd
  310-855-0350
  Jon Brion on Friday nights: a perfect LA experience.
- **Laugh Factory** • 8001 W Sunset Blvd
  323-656-1336
  Nightly comedy shows featuring local and mainstream talent.
- **Lola's** • 945 N Fairfax Ave
  323-654-5652
  Birthplace of the apple martini.
- **Melrose Umbrella Company** • 7465 Melrose Ave
  323-951-0709
  Smart cocktails within well-appointed, umbrella-bedecked interior.
- **Micky's** • 8857 Santa Monica Blvd
  310-657-1176
  Drag queens and hot go-go boys every Monday.
- **Molly Malone's** • 575 S Fairfax Ave
  323-935-1577
  The ultimate neighborhood pub.
- **Mondrian Skybar** • 8440 W Sunset Blvd
  323-848-6025
  Excuse me, you're standing on my Manolos…
- **Monsieur Marcel** • 6333 W 3rd St
  323-939-7792
  Parisian wine bar in the Farmer's Market.
- **Plaza** • 739 N La Brea Ave
  323-939-0703
  Drag queens and ranchero music…ay yi yi!
- **Rage** • 8911 Santa Monica Blvd
  310-652-7055
  Hard-bodied boys cram the soft-rubber dance floor.
- **Rainbow Bar and Grill** • 9015 W Sunset Blvd
  310-278-4232
  Those who rock will be saluted at this hairband hangout.
- **The Roger Room** • 370 N La Cienega Blvd
  310-854-1300
  Elegant drinks if you can get through the crowd.
- **Rosewood Tavern** • 448 N Fairfax Ave
  323-944-0980
  Get your Anchorman on with scotchy scotch scotch.
- **The Roxy** • 9009 W Sunset Blvd
  310-276-2222
  A bastion of the Sunset Strip.
- **Snake Pit Ale House** • 7529 Melrose Ave
  323-653-2011
  Fairfax District's version of a Hollywood dive.
- **St Nicks** • 8450 W 3rd St
  323-655-6917
  Great westside dive, complete with stocked jukebox.
- **The Surly Goat** • 7929 Santa Monica Blvd
  323-650-4628
  Westside beer-snob Mecca. They've always been nice to us.
- **The Tar Pit** • 609 N La Brea Ave
  323-965-1300
  Old-timey vibe and drinks. New-timey prices.
- **The Tower Bar** • 8358 W Sunset Blvd
  323-654-7100
  Restaubar in mobster Bugsy Siegel's old pad.
- **Troubadour** • 9081 Santa Monica Blvd
  310-276-6168
  Legendary club where Tom Waits got his start.
- **The Viper Room** • 8852 W Sunset Blvd
  310-358-1881
  After Johnny fled to France, scensters say it lost its bite.
- **Windows Lounge** • 300 S Doheny Dr
  310-273-2222
  Elegant hotel bar.

West Hollywood

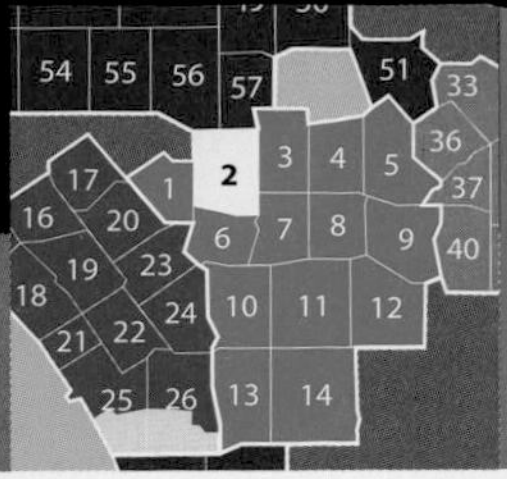

WeHo boasts some of the most cohesive and walkable mini-neighborhoods in town (e.g., Third Street west of Fairfax, the demographically amorphous area of Melrose between Doherty and La Brea, or Fairfax north of Beverly). You can generally avoid the Grove—one of those big, cookie-cutter shopping complexes—unless you're there for the foods of the **Farmers Market**. Don't miss the weekend movie + party events at the **Silent Movie Theatre**.

Restaurants

• **Ago** • 8478 Melrose Ave
323-655-6333 • $$$$
High-end Italian.

• **Amalfi** • 143 N La Brea Ave
323-938-2504 • $$$
Rustic, authentic Italian, good for groups.

• **Andre's Italian Restaurant** • 6332 W 3rd St
323-935-1246 • $
Italian cafeteria complete with plastic flowers. Since 1963.

• **Animal** • 435 N Fairfax Ave
323-782-9225 • $$
Amazing dishes out of unheralded, and sometimes, frankly, gnarly parts.

• **AOC Wine Bar** • 8022 W 3rd St
310-859-9859 • $$$$
Little plates, big wine selection, and savvy servers.

• **Basix Café** • 8333 Santa Monica Blvd
323-848-2460 • $$
Popular breakfast spot.

• **Beverly Hills Juice** • 8382 Beverly Blvd
323-655-8300 • $
Drink this juice. Your intestines will thank you.

• **BLD** • 7450 Beverly Blvd
323-930-9744 • $$$
Stands for breakfast, lunch, and dinner—so good you'll want to try all three.

• **Blu Jam** • 7371 Melrose Ave
323-951-9191 • $$
Terrific brunch and coffee bar.

• **Bossa Nova** • 7181 W Sunset Blvd
323-436-7999 • $$
Savory Brazilian dishes. Open til 4 am.

• **Café Angelino** • 8735 W 3rd St
310-246-1177 • $$
Flaky thin crust pizzas.

• **Canter's Deli** • 419 N Fairfax Ave
323-651-2030 • $$
Classic deli with swinging lounge attached.

• **Chateau Marmont** • 8221 W Sunset Blvd
323-656-1010 • $$$$
Celeb-heavy scene, cuisine-light menu.

• **Chaya** • 8741 Alden Dr
310-859-8833 • $$$$
Great food in a schmoozy setting.

• **Dan Tana's** • 9071 Santa Monica Blvd
310-275-9444 • $$$$
Old H'wood glamour…if you can get a table…

• **Dialog Cafe** • 8766 Holloway Dr
310-289-1630 • $$
Lunch spot with salad bar. A little on the pricey side.

• **Ed's Coffee Shop** • 460 N Robertson Blvd
310-659-8625 • $
Home-cookin'.

• **Fish Grill** • 7226 Beverly Blvd
323-937-7162 • $
No-frills, super-fresh fish.

• **Flavor of India** • 9045 Santa Monica Blvd
310-274-1715 • $$$
Dolly Parton likes the chicken tikka masala.

• **Fogo de Chao** • 133 N La Cienega Blvd
310-289-7755 • $$$$
An orgy of meat cooked Brazilian churrasco-style.

• **The French Crêpe Co.** • 6333 W 3rd St
323-934-3113 • $
Even the crepe snobs love it.

• **French Quarter** • 7985 Santa Monica Blvd
323-654-0898 • $$
Food for everyone, especially night owls.

• **Gardens of Taxco** • 1113 N Harper Ave
323-654-1746 • $$
Odd little fixed-price institution with verbal menu.

• **The Golden State** • 426 N Fairfax Ave
323-782-8331 • $$
Bang-up burgers. Try the curry ketchup.

• **Greenblatt's** • 8017 W Sunset Blvd
323-656-0606 • $
Kosher deli and wine shop.

• **The Griddle Café** • 7916 W Sunset Blvd
323-874-0377 • $$
Brunch with the stars—of the WB.

• **The Gumbo Pot** • 6333 W 3rd St
323-933-0358 • $$
Best Cajun in LA.

• **Hamburger Mary's** • 8288 Santa Monica Blvd
323-654-3800 • $$
LA's worst kept secret.

• **House of Blues** • 8430 W Sunset Blvd
323-848-5100 • $$$
Saucy Cajun. Try Sunday's Gospel Brunch.

• **Hugo's** • 8401 Santa Monica Blvd
323-654-3993 • $$
Power brunches.

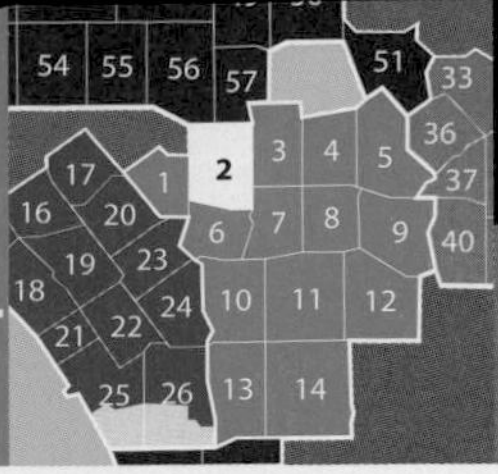

West Hollywood

- **Ikemen** • 1655 N La Brea Ave
  323-800-7699 • $
  Good dip-style ramen with unexpected flavors…and, oddly, fries.
- **ink.** • 8360 Melrose Ave
  323-651-5866 • $$$$
  Creative dishes; lower-case menu.
- **Irv's Burgers** • 8289 Santa Monica Blvd
  323-650-2456 • $
  Classic burger joint. NFT fav.
- **The Ivy** • 113 N Robertson Blvd
  310-274-8303 • $$$$
  Broker a deal over traditional American fare.
- **Jar** • 8225 Beverly Blvd
  323-655-6566 • $$$$
  Upscale comfort food.
- **Joan's on Third** • 8350 W 3rd St
  323-655-2285 • $$
  Foodies can eat-in or carry out.
- **Joey's Cafe** • 8301 Santa Monica Blvd
  323-822-0671 • $$
  Fresh and delicious breakfast and lunch.
- **Jon and Vinny's** • 412 N Fairfax Ave
  323-334-3369 • $$$
  All-day pizza-pasta casual spot from Animal dudes.
- **Jones** • 7205 Santa Monica Blvd
  323-850-1726 • $$
  Pizza and pasta in leather pants. With cocktail in hand.
- **La Conversation** • 638 N Doheny Dr
  310-858-0950 • $$
  Popular and très mignon brunch and lunch bistro. A good place to eat and be seen.
- **La Paella** • 476 S San Vicente Blvd
  323-951-0745 • $$$
  As authentic as you'll find this side of Barcelona.
- **Le Pain Quotidien** • 8607 Melrose Ave
  310-854-3700 • $$
  Classy French sandwich shop.
- **Little Next Door** • 8142 W 3rd St
  323-951-1010 • $$$
  Delightful French food with a great brunch and pastries.
- **Los Tacos** • 7954 Santa Monica Blvd
  323-848-9141 • $
  Cut your hangover off at the pass with the best Mexican in WeHo.
- **Loteria Grill** • 6627 Hollywood Blvd
  323-465-2500 • $
  Muy fresicita.
- **Lucques** • 8474 Melrose Ave
  323-655-6277 • $$$$
  Chez Panisse-style cooking in LA.
- **M Cafe** • 7119 Melrose Ave
  323-525-0588 • $$
  Contemporary macrobiotic. Only in LA.
- **Mandarette** • 8386 Beverly Blvd
  323-655-6115 • $$
  Chinese fusion.
- **Millions of Milkshakes** • 8910 Santa Monica Blvd
  310-652-1118 • $
  Like if DQ only served Blizzards and had vegan options.
- **Murakami Sushi** • 7160 Melrose Ave
  323-692-1450 • $$
  Good, relatively cheap sushi, but skip the rice-heavy bowls.

West Hollywood

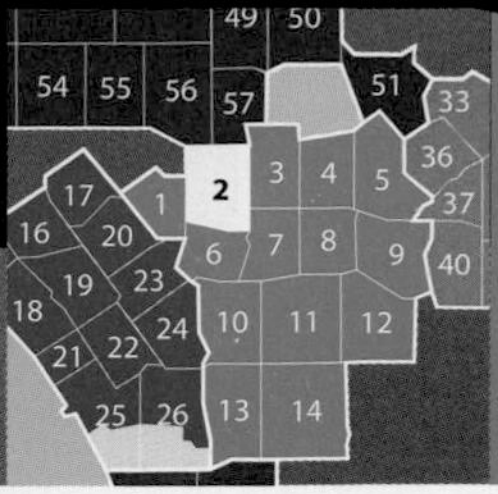

It sounds like a terrible marketing cliché, but this area really does have something for everyone (unless you hate fun). You can grab your pooch for a hike in Runyon Canyon, check out the great author events at **Book Soup**, or scope out music at the notorious venues of the Sunset Strip (and keep an eye out for the West Hollywood Jesus wandering the streets). Looking for food or drink? Brunch is at **BLD**, burgers with a delightful drawing are courtesy of **Irv's**, and **Comme Ca**'s penicillin is a cocktail worthy of poems.

- **Night + Market** • 9041 Sunset Blvd
  310-275-9724 • $$
  Thai street food. More good than gimmick.
- **Odys + Penelope** • 127 S La Brea Ave
  323-939-1033 • $$$
  Meat-forward, grill-friendly cuisine in wide-open space.
- **Petrossian** • 321 N Robertson Blvd
  310-271-6300 • $$$$
  Little nibbles of caviar and other conspicuous bites.
- **Quality Food & Beverage** • 8030 W 3rd St
  323-658-5959 • $
  Dog-friendly brunch hangout.
- **Real Food Daily** • 414 N La Cienega Blvd
  310-289-9910 • $$
  One of the healthiest-tasting restaurants in town.
- **Republique** • 624 S La Brea Ave
  310-362-6115 • $$$$
  Modern French-European amid vaulted architecture.
- **Robata Jinya** • 8050 W 3rd St
  323-653-8877 • $$
  Get the spicy ramen or the tasting menu. Slurp!
- **Saddle Ranch** • 8371 W Sunset Blvd
  323-656-2007 • $$
  Late-night chophouse with a mechanical bull.
- **Singapore's Banana Leaf** • 6333 W 3rd St
  323-933-4627 • $
  Where the President of Singapore chows down when in LA.
- **Son of a Gun** • 8370 W 3rd St
  323-782-9033 • $$$
  Seafood rebels. The shrimp toast is mandatory.
- **Sweet Lady Jane** • 8360 Melrose Ave
  323-653-7145 • $$
  Decadent desserts to die for.
- **Swingers** • 8020 Beverly Blvd
  323-653-5858 • $
  Classic late-night diner, both loved and hated.
- **Tart** • 115 S Fairfax Ave
  323-556-2608 • $$$
  Farmer's Daughter restauraunt offers down-home food for WeHo types.
- **Taste** • 8454 Melrose Ave
  323-852-6888 • $$$
  Trendy Cali-fusion, Melrose-style.
- **Tiago Espresso Bar + Kitchen** • 7080 Hollywood Blvd
  323-466-5600 • $
  Chorizo breakfast burritos, good coffee, and standard lunch fare.
- **Toast Bakery Cafe** • 8221 W 3rd St
  323-655-5018 • $$
  Great for celebrity spotting while you brunch.
- **Toi** • 7505 W Sunset Blvd
  323-874-8062 • $$$
  Late night, hard rock Thai.
- **Ulysses Voyage** • 6333 W 3rd St
  323-939-9728 • $$$
  Outdoor ouzo oasis.
- **Urth Caffé** • 8565 Melrose Ave
  310-659-0628 • $$
  All organic lunch place, plus coffee and sweets.
- **The Village Idiot** • 7383 Melrose Ave
  323-655-3331 • $$$
  Bustling British pub with surprisingly good food.
- **Vinoteque** • 7469 Melrose Ave
  310-860-6060 • $$$
  Small plates, big wines.

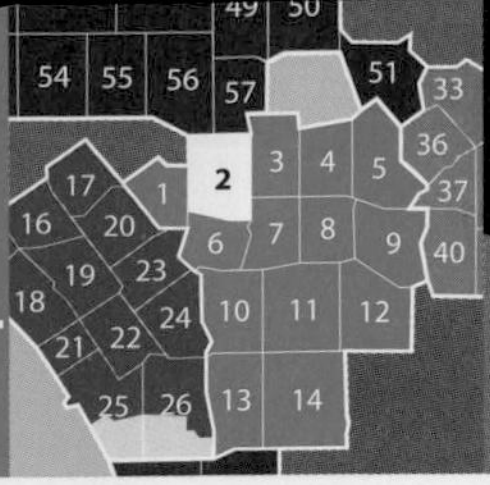

West Hollywood

Shopping

- **Agent Provocateur** • 7961 Melrose Ave
  323-653-0229
  Sexy undies annually contribute to Hollywood's baby boom.
- **American Apparel** • 802 N San Vicente Blvd
  310-659-0373
  Simple clothing: sweatshop-free, but still scandalous.
- **American Rag** • 150 S La Brea Ave
  323-935-3154
  Trend-setting designer and vintage looks at a price.
- **Anya Hindmarch** • 118 S Robertson Blvd
  310-271-9707
  So many fancy bags. Plus some dresses.
- **Beauty Collection** • 8951 Santa Monica Blvd
  310-858-8838
  Eclectic beauty supply.
- **Beige** • 7274 Beverly Blvd
  323-549-0064
  Colorful boutique with an impressive designer palette.
- **Ben Sherman** • 8500 Beverly Blvd
  310-657-3400
  Tailored contemporary duds for those with a British persuasion.
- **Blick Art Materials** • 7301 Beverly Blvd
  323-933-9284
  Corporate but comprehensive. Good selection of art magazines.
- **Book Soup** • 8818 W Sunset Blvd
  310-659-3110
  The Roxy of LA bookstores.
- **Bristol Farms** • 7880 W Sunset Blvd
  323-874-6301
  Upscale grocery. Newest and biggest of its kind.
- **Crate & Barrel** • 189 The Grove Dr
  323-297-0370
  There's never too many crates or barrels on your registry.
- **Decades** • 8214 Melrose Ave
  323-655-1960
  Discover the history…and future…of fashion.
- **Denim Doctors & Hollywood Trading Company** • 7383 Beverly Blvd
  323-964-0080
  They'll sell you vintage jeans or fix the ones you've already got.
- **Denmark 50** • 7974 Melrose Ave
  323-653-9726
  Stare-worthy Danish mid-century furnishings.
- **DNA** • 8000 W Sunset Blvd
  323-882-8464
  Shhh…this tiny designer outlet is a big secret.
- **EM & Co.** • 7940 W 3rd St
  323-782-8155
  Well-curated fashions from local and international designers.
- **Ethel Boutique** • 8236 W 3rd St
  323-658-8602
  Great women's clothing, indie brands.
- **I. Martin Bicycles** • 8330 Beverly Blvd
  323-653-6900
  They cater to both serious racers and the training wheels crowd.
- **Jet Rag** • 825 N La Brea Ave
  323-939-0528
  Vintage; Sunday is $1 sale day in the parking lot.
- **Keep** • 523 N Fairfax Ave
  323-655-1010
  Shoes and home decor. Why not.
- **Kiehl's** • 106 N Robertson Blvd
  310-860-0028
  No more mail-order. NY-fave beauty products.
- **Light Bulbs Unlimited** • 8383 Beverly Blvd
  323-651-0330
  Every bulb under the sun.

West Hollywood

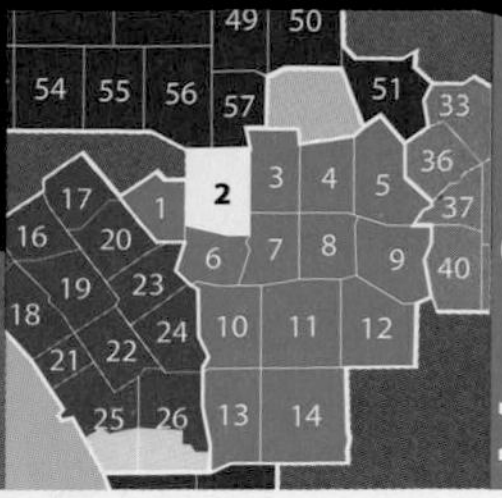

Lean in to catch the latest hushed gossip and receive pitches at **Lucques**. Meanwhile over on Fairfax, **Animal** has rock stars in the kitchen and the dining room, while a few doors down, historic **Canter's Deli** rocks the cheesecake and the self-published Guns 'N Roses memoirs. It's not true that Orson Welles ate 18 hot dogs in one sitting at **Pink's** but we dare you to match the feat.

- **Madison** • 8745 W 3rd St
  310-275-1930
  Beautiful clothes for beautiful people.
- **Mama's Secret Bakery** • 8316 W 3rd St
  323-424-3482
  Pieces of fabulousness, all for sale.
- **Marc Jacobs** • 8400 Melrose Pl
  323-653-5100
  Marc Jacobs has arrived. Say "hi" to Winona if you see her.
- **Mashti Malone's** • 1525 N La Brea Ave
  323-874-0144
  2,500 year old Persian ice cream.
- **Melrose Trading Post** • 7850 Melrose Ave
  323-655-7679
  Get your bartering on and benefit boho teens' school.
- **Milk** • 8209 W 3rd St
  323-951-0330
  Stylish fare, but prepare (yes) to be milked.
- **Necromance** • 7220 Melrose Ave
  323-931-2997
  Morbid and eclectic, this boutique sells taxidermy and natural curios.
- **Nordstrom** • 189 The Grove Dr
  323-930-2230
  Awesome shoe department.
- **Plastica** • 8405 W 3rd St
  323-655-1051
  All things trendy and plastic. So LA.
- **The Pleasure Chest** • 7733 Santa Monica Blvd
  323-650-1022
  Our cleanest, best managed, most famous sex shop.
- **Politix** • 8500 Beverly Blvd
  310-659-1964
  Best mens' shoes in LA.
- **Pulp** • 456 S La Brea Ave
  323-937-3505
  For people who still write letters (or wish they did).
- **Rehab Vintage Interiors** • 7609 Beverly Blvd
  323-935-8438
  Industrial furniture for steel lovers.
- **Ron Herman** • 8100 Melrose Ave
  323-651-4129
  There's something wrong with selling peasant skirts for $308 dollars.
- **Russh Mode** • 352 S Robertson Blvd
  323-920-6738
  One more temple for the cult of denim.
- **Sam Ash Music** • 7360 W Sunset Blvd
  323-850-1050
  Like the nearby Guitar Center, but far less intimidating.
- **Samy's Camera** • 431 S Fairfax Ave
  323-938-2420
  The only place to go to for cameras in LA.
- **South Willard** • 8038 W 3rd St
  323-653-6153
  For the cultured gentleman.
- **Susina Bakery & Cafe** • 7122 Beverly Blvd
  323-934-7900
  Not just a bakery...yummy chocolates, focaccia sandwiches, and beautiful cakes.
- **Sweet 9** • 7631 Melrose Ave
  323-655-1196
  Stylish cuts in a funky locale.
- **Tarina Tarantino** • 7957 Melrose Ave
  323-651-5155
  Jewelry for pink ladies.
- **TenOverSix** • 8425 Melrose Ave
  323-330-9355
  A whole store dedicated to shoes, jewelry, bags (etc.).
- **Trashy Lingerie** • 402 N La Cienega Blvd
  310-652-4543
  Trashy, yes, but they also sell high-quality custom-fitted lingerie.

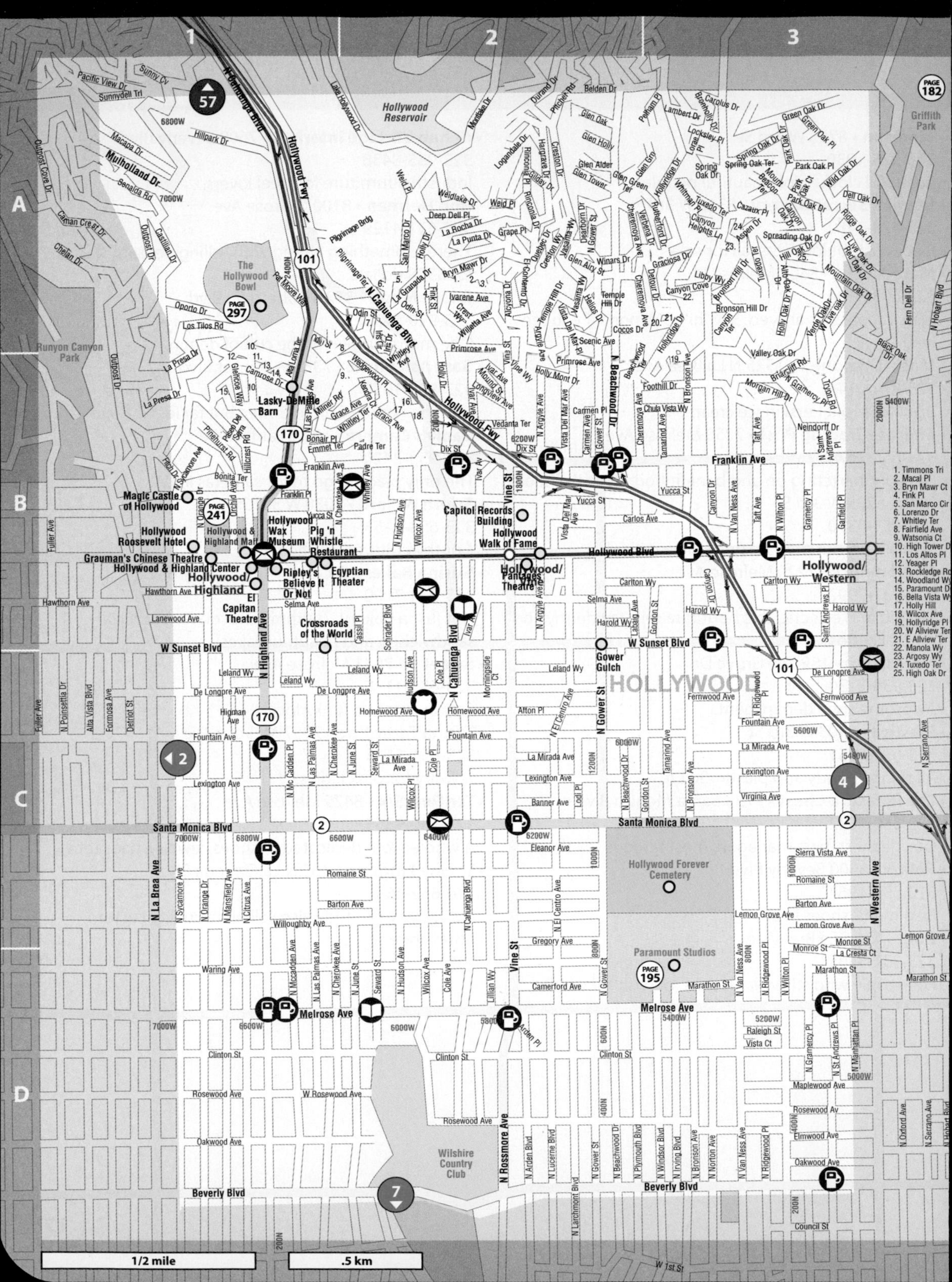
N
1
2
3
A
B
C
D
Hollywood Reservoir
Griffith Park
Runyon Canyon Park
The Hollywood Bowl
Mulholland Dr
Hollywood Fwy
N Cahuenga Blvd
Lasky-DeMille Barn
Magic Castle of Hollywood
Hollywood Roosevelt Hotel
Grauman's Chinese Theatre
Hollywood & Highland Center
Hollywood & Highland Mall
Hollywood/ Highland
El Capitan Theatre
Hollywood Wax Museum
Pig 'n Whistle Restaurant
Ripley's Believe It Or Not
Egyptian Theater
Crossroads of the World
Capitol Records Building
Hollywood Walk of Fame
Hollywood/ Vine
Pantages Theatre
Gower Gulch
HOLLYWOOD
Hollywood/ Western
Hollywood Forever Cemetery
Paramount Studios
Wilshire Country Club
Franklin Ave
Hollywood Blvd
W Sunset Blvd
Santa Monica Blvd
Melrose Ave
Beverly Blvd
N Highland Ave
N La Brea Ave
Vine St
N Gower St
N Western Ave
Beachwood Dr
Fountain Ave
De Longpre Ave
Lexington Ave
Romaine St
Willoughby Ave
Waring Ave
Clinton St
Rosewood Ave
Oakwood Ave
N Rossmore Ave
PAGE 297
PAGE 241
PAGE 195
PAGE 182
1. Timmons Trl
2. Macal Pl
3. Bryn Mawr Ct
4. Fink Pl
5. San Marco Cir
6. Lorenzo Dr
7. Whitley Ter
8. Fairfield Ave
9. Watsonia Ct
10. High Tower Dr
11. Los Altos Pl
12. Yeager Pl
13. Rockledge Rd
14. Woodland Wy
15. Paramount Dr
16. Bella Vista Wy
17. Holly Hill
18. Wilcox Ave
19. Hollyridge Pl
20. W Allview Ter
21. E Allview Ter
22. Manola Wy
23. Argosy Wy
24. Tuxedo Ter
25. High Oak Dr
1/2 mile
.5 km

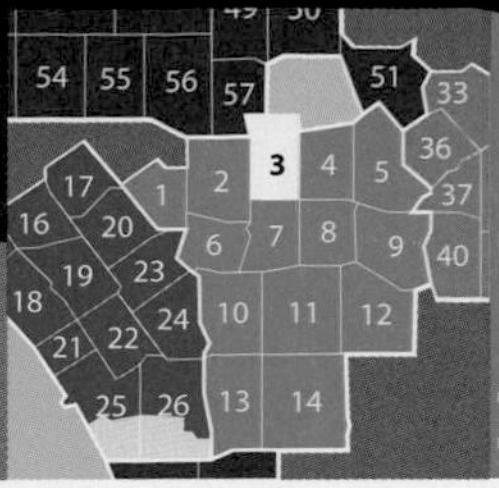

Though Hollywood has cleaned up its act in the last few years, it's still a hodgepodge of neighborhoods. Ethnic enclaves like Thai Town and Little Armenia provide the most fun and best food, but tourists still flock to the Hollywood and Highland area, where they're happy to be ripped off by Supermen and Jack Sparrows. Still, they clear out at night to make room for Hollywood's new "elegant" clubs, where velvet ropes open for anyone willing to pay for bottle service.

oLandmarks

- **Capitol Records Building** • 1750 Vine St
  323-462-6252
  Designed to look like a stack of records—remember those?
- **Crossroads of the World** • 6671 W Sunset Blvd
  323-463-5611
  Former 1930s shopping center with a nautical theme, now deemed a cultural landmark.
- **Egyptian Theater** • 6712 Hollywood Blvd
  323-461-2020
  The beautiful home of American Cinematheque features an eclectic variety of features, shorts, and documentaries.
- **El Capitan Theatre** • 6838 Hollywood Blvd
  818-845-3110
  Live shows with movies in opulent historic theater.
- **Gower Gulch** • W Sunset Blvd & N Gower St
  Studio-adjacent intersection where cowboy extras used to congregate. Now a Western-themed strip-mall.
- **Grauman's Chinese Theatre** • 6925 Hollywood Blvd
  323-464-6266
  See how your shoe size measures up against Sylvester Stallone's.
- **Hollywood & Highland Center** •
  6801 Hollywood Blvd
  Sterile, touristy mall that houses the Oscars.
- **Hollywood Bowl** • 2301 N Highland Ave
  323-850-2000
  Eclectic music and picnicking under the stars.
- **Hollywood Forever Cemetery** •
  6000 Santa Monica Blvd
  323-469-1181
  The only place in LA where you can still see Douglas Fairbanks and Tyrone Power.
- **Hollywood Roosevelt Hotel** • 7000 Hollywood Blvd
  323-466-7000
  Recently renovated and rumored to be haunted by Marilyn Monroe.
- **Hollywood Walk of Fame** •
  Hollywood Blvd & N Gower St
  323-469-8311
  Tourists love this shrine to often-mediocre celebs.
- **Hollywood Wax Museum** • 6767 Hollywood Blvd
  323-462-5991
  Celebrities in wax. Greeeat.
- **Lasky-DeMille Barn** • 2100 N Highland Ave
  323-874-2276
  The birthplace of the Motion Picture Industry and now the Hollywood Heritage Museum.
- **Magic Castle** • 7025 Franklin Ave
  323-851-0800
  Spend the night or catch a show—if you know a member.
- **Pantages Theater** • 6233 Hollywood Blvd
  323-468-1770
  Go for the big Broadway shows.
- **Paramount Studios** • 5555 Melrose Ave
  323-956-5000
  The last movie studio actually IN Hollywood.
- **Pig 'n Whistle** • 6714 Hollywood Blvd
  323-463-0000
  Hollywood watering hole and restaurant dating back to the golden era.
- **Ripley's Believe It or Not** • 6780 Hollywood Blvd
  323-466-6335
  More oddities, less exhausting than *Guinness Book*.

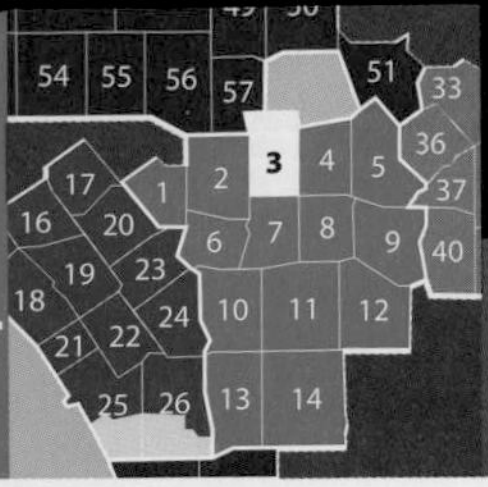

Hollywood

Nightlife

- **The 3 Clubs** • 1123 Vine St
  323-462-6441
  Low-key Hollywood hangout.
- **ArcLight Café Bar & Balcony** • 6360 W Sunset Blvd
  323-464-1478
  Discuss the film over martinis and fried raviolis.
- **Avalon** • 1735 Vine St
  323-462-8900
  Old Palace, now Oakenfold and the Streets.
- **The Bar** • 5851 W Sunset Blvd
  323-468-9154
  Formerly Raji's, now rocker bar/lounge.
- **Bardot** • 1737 Vine St
  323-462-1307
  Smallish club with a quiet bar room.
- **Birds** • 5925 Franklin Ave
  323-465-0175
  Unpretentious restaurant/bar favored by the carefully disheveled.
- **The Blue Boar Pub** • 1615 N Cahuenga Blvd
  323-465-1750
  Never too crowded, never too douchey. Go grab a pint.
- **Blue Palms Brewhouse** • 6124 Hollywood Blvd
  323-464-2337
  Well-curated beer bar/gastropub. Taps change regularly!
- **Boardner's** • 1652 N Cherokee Ave
  323-462-9621
  Quiet watering hole becomes dance club.
- **Burgundy Room** • 1621 N Cahuenga Blvd
  323-465-7530
  If Johnny Rotten and Blondie had a kid. And the kid was a bar.
- **The Cat & Fiddle** • 6530 W Sunset Blvd
  323-468-3800
  Pub plus patio draws Brits in search of better weather.
- **Catalina** • 6725 W Sunset Blvd
  323-466-2210
  New location, same groovy jazz.
- **Cinespace** • 6356 Hollywood Blvd
  323-817-3456
  Movies, music, food, cocktails, and huge smoking room.
- **Covell** • 4628 Hollywood Blvd
  323-660-4400
  Hollywood's friendliest wine bar, converting noobs into oenophiles.
- **Dillon's Irish Pub** • 6327 Hollywood Blvd
  323-957-1667
  Brave the sometimes douchey crowd for great $3 pints.
- **Dragonfly** • 6510 Santa Monica Blvd
  323-466-6111
  Alcoholics-in-training dance the night away in one of two rooms.
- **El Floridita** • 1253 Vine St
  323-871-8612
  Salsa club (with lessons!).
- **El Scorpio** • 6679 Hollywood Blvd
  323-464-3026
  Trying to escape the Hollywood club wasteland? Head to this dive.
- **Frolic Room** • 6245 Hollywood Blvd
  323-462-5890
  Where Spacey searched his soul in *LA Confidential*.
- **The Hotel Café** • 1623 N Cahuenga Blvd
  323-461-2040
  New York-style acoustic club draws a crowd.
- **iO West Theater** • 6366 Hollywood Blvd
  323-962-7560
  California outpost of the improv brand that brought you the Harold.

Hollywood

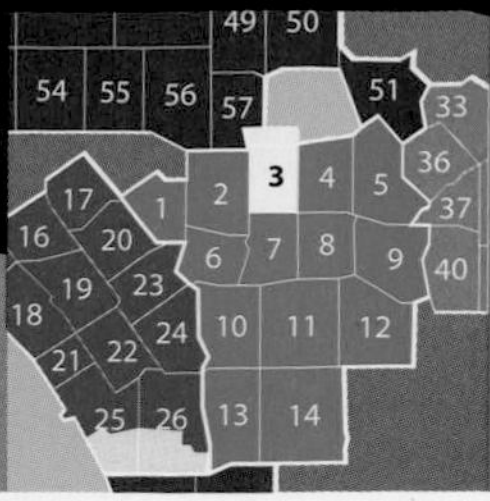

The star-marked length of Hollywood Boulevard will, it seems, always remain somewhat seedy—although it's nothing like it was in *Pretty Woman*. Today it's tacky souvenir shops, hooker-shoe stores, bumpin' clubs, and a few surprisingly good restaurants and bars. For the best time in Hollywood, get off the Boulevard itself—but don't miss its great **Sunday farmers market**. In the summer, catch a flick among the corpses at the **Hollywood Forever Cemetery**.

- **Joseph's Cafe** • 1775 Ivar Ave
  323-462-8697
  Where Britney met K-Fed.
- **King King** • 6555 Hollywood Blvd
  323-960-9234
  Live music, rotating DJs, very few jerks per capita.
- **La Velvet Margarita Cantina** • 1612 N Cahuenga Blvd
  323-469-2000
  Imagine a gothic circus in Tijuana…
- **M Bar** • 1253 Vine St
  323-856-0036
  Liberace would have loved the interior.
- **Musso & Frank Grill** • 6667 Hollywood Blvd
  323-467-7788
  Hollywood's oldest bar with spectacular martinis.
- **No Vacancy** • 1727 N Hudson Ave
  323-465-1902
  Speakeasy-style place that's ridiculously over the top.
- **The Parlour Room** • 6423 Yucca St
  323-463-0609
  Cocktails. Chandeliers. Velvet. Pure swank.
- **Penthouse Billiards** • 1810 Wilcox Blvd
  323-465-1413
  Kinda seedy and totally amazing pool hall.
- **Power House** • 1714 N Highland Ave
  323-463-9438
  Dive bar favorite.
- **The Room** • 1626 N Cahuenga Blvd
  323-462-7196
  Once a hip-hop dive, now just as glossy as the rest of the boulevard.
- **Sassafras** • 1233 Vine St
  323-467-2800
  Delightfully aged cocktails and old-timey bands.
- **The Well** • 6255 W Sunset Blvd
  323-467-9355
  Daddy's owners draw up a similar watering hole.

Restaurants

- **101 Coffee Shop** • 6145 Franklin Ave
  323-467-1175 • $$
  Famous diner with yummy sweet potato fries.
- **Al Wazir Chicken** • 6051 Hollywood Blvd
  323-856-0660 • $
  Great chicken and all the other usual Mediterranean business.
- **Ammo** • 1155 N Highland Ave
  323-871-2666 • $$$
  Trendy California comfort food.
- **Astro Burger** • 5601 Melrose Ave
  323-469-1924 • $
  Tasty meat-free burgers.
- **Baroo** • 5706 Santa Monica Blvd
  323-819-4344 • $$$
  In which crazy things happen fermentationally and with non-meat items.
- **Beachwood Cafe** • 2695 N Beachwood Dr
  323-871-1717 • $$
  Brunch: Yes. But stay away from way-annoying bingo night.
- **Big Wangs** • 1562 N Cahuenga Blvd
  323-469-2449 • $$
  Texas brings good 'ol beer and wings to LA. Karaoke Wednesdays.
- **Birch** • 1634 N Cahuenga Blvd
  323-960-3369 • $$$
  British food reimagined in Hollywood; check out the Sunday Roast.
- **Bricks & Scones** • 403 N Larchmont Blvd
  323-463-0811 • $$
  Afternoon tea, a study area…how civilized.
- **Butchers & Barbers** • 6531 Hollywood Blvd
  323-461-1464 • $$$
  Well-crafted, seasonal, curated comfort food.
- **Cactus Taqueria** • 950 Vine St
  323-464-5865 • $
  Cheap, fast, good tacos and more.
- **California Chicken Café** • 6805 Melrose Ave
  323-935-5877 • $
  Popular cop hangout: the safest chicken in town.
- **California Donuts** • 5753 Hollywood Blvd
  323-871-0778 • $
  Cake or yeast, the best damn donuts in LA.

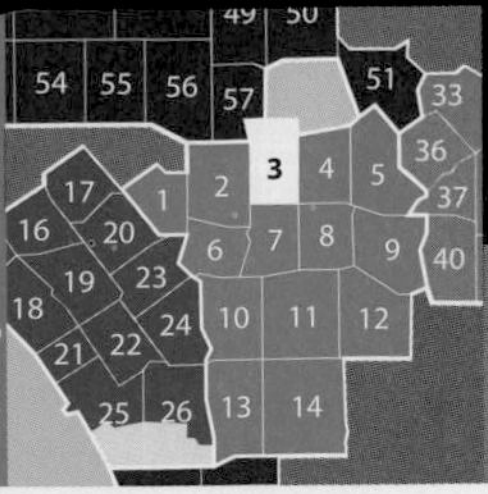

Hollywood

- **Chan Dara** • 310 N Larchmont Blvd
  323-467-1052 • $$$
  Huge Thai portions served by tiny Thai women.
- **Crispy Crust** • 1253 Vine St
  323-467-2000 • $$
  Great delivery, a truly crispy crust.
- **Delphine** • 6250 Hollywood Blvd
  323-798-1355 • $$$$
  Classic French in not-at-all classic Hollywood.
- **Fabiolus Café** • 6270 W Sunset Blvd
  323-467-2882 • $$
  Dine in, deliver, or take-away Italian.
- **Franklin & Company** • 5923 Franklin Avenue
  323-463-1552 • $$
  Sandwiches are meh, but the beer selection is always great.
- **Frog Frozen Yogurt Bar** • 1550 N Cahuenga Blvd
  323-462-3764 • $
  Tasty, independently owned Pinkberry-style business.
- **Geisha House** • 6633 Hollywood Blvd
  323-460-6300 • $$$$
  Sushi, sake, and maybe get Punk'd.
- **The Hungry Cat** • 1535 Vine St
  323-462-2155 • $$$
  Seafood and hip cocktails. Killer bleu cheese burger.
- **La Poubelle** • 5907 Franklin Ave
  323-465-0807 • $$$
  Gallic gourmet dining and '80s music.
- **Larchmont Deli** • 5210 Beverly Blvd
  323-466-1193 • $
  Try the pastrami.
- **Le Oriental Bistro** • 1710 N Highland Ave
  323-463-4747 • $
  Chinese for real.
- **Lexington Social House** • 1718 Vine St
  323-461-1700 • $$$
  Classy, high-visibity dining in arty surroundings.
- **Los Balcones del Peru** • 1360 Vine St
  323-871-9600 • $$
  Peruvian entrees & ceviches.
- **Magnolia** • 6266 W Sunset Blvd
  323-467-0660 • $$$
  Familiar yet delicious bistro fare at new Hollywood hotspot. Try the mac-n-cheese.
- **The Mercantile** • 6600 Sunset Blvd
  323-962-8202 • $$
  Cute space, cute food, unlikely location for such.
- **Miceli's** • 1646 N Las Palmas Ave
  323-466-3438 • $$
  Classic Hollywood Italian since 1949 (warning for the easily annoyed: singing waiters here).
- **Murakami Sushi** • 1714 N Wilcox Ave
  323-467-8181 • $$
  Good, relatively cheap sushi. Skip the bowls—too much rice.
- **Musso & Frank Grill** • 6667 Hollywood Blvd
  323-467-7788 • $$$
  Old-fashioned American. Go once. It's a legend.
- **Off Vine** • 6233 Leland Way
  323-962-1900 • $$$$
  Romantic Californian.
- **Osteria La Buca** • 5210 Melrose Ave
  323-462-1900 • $$
  Sophia Loren would eat at this tiny Italian ristorante.
- **Osteria Mozza** • 6602 Melrose Ave
  323-297-0100 • $$$
  Worth the wait and the price—and you'll learn what real Italian food is.
- **Palms Thai** • 5900 Hollywood Blvd
  323-462-5073 • $$
  Thai Elvis impersonator!
- **Petit Trois** • 718 N Highland Ave
  323-468-8916 • $$$$
  French bistro, Hollywood style, with cocktails.
- **Pig 'n Whistle** • 6714 Hollywood Blvd
  323-463-0000 • $$$
  Dine in "bed" or people-watch from a comfy booth.
- **Pizza Bella** • 1900 N Highland Ave
  323-876-5961 • $
  Good NY pizza (at least for LA).
- **Pizzeria Mozza** • 641 N Highland Ave
  323-297-0101 • $$$$
  Ridiculously good designer pizza.
- **Providence** • 5955 Melrose Ave
  323-460-4170 • $$$$$$
  Super-fancy seafood tasting menus.

Hollywood

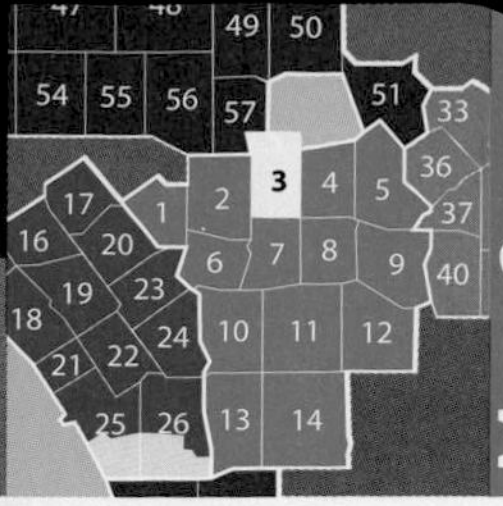

Musso & Frank Grill has been in the martini business since before Hollywood was even Hollywood. Brit expats especially enjoy a pint at **The Cat & Fiddle**. Get a drink and pick a table that takes advantage of one of the best views of Los Angeles at **Yamashiro** in the Hollywood Hills. **El Floridita** is a fun salsa club in a shady strip mall on Fountain and Vine. And **The Hotel Café** is LA's best loved acoustic venue.

- **Roscoe's House of Chicken 'n Waffles** •
  1514 N Gower St
  323-466-7453 • $$
  Southern-fried bonanza.
- **Skooby's Hot Dogs** • 6654 Hollywood Blvd
  323-468-3647 • $
  Tasty dogs with homemade chili.
- **Sqirl** • 720 N Virgil Ave
  323-284-8147 • $$
  Breakfast and lunch from a damn good jam-maker.
- **Stout Burgers & Beer** • 1544 N Cahuenga Blvd
  323-469-3801 • $$
  Burgers and beer till 4 am.
- **Sushi Ike** • 6051 Hollywood Blvd
  323-856-9972 • $$$
  Good sushi in the last strip mall you'd expect it.
- **Tamarind Ave Deli** • 1471 Tamarind Ave
  323-960-2451 • $
  Solid sandwiches and a spiffy soda selection. Cheerwine! Blenheim's!
- **Trois Mec** • 716 N Highland Ave
  323-468-8915 • $$$$
  Ticketed multi-course tasting menu in former strip mall pizza joint.
- **Truly Vegan Restaurant** • 5907 Hollywood Blvd
  323-466-7533 • $$
  Thai without the meats on sticks.
- **Village Pizzeria** • 6363 Yucca St
  323-790-0763 • $
  Hoppin' pizza place.
- **Xiomara** • 6101 Melrose Ave
  323-461-0601 • $$$$
  Upscale Cuban with revolutionary mojitos.
- **Yamashiro** • 1999 N Sycamore Ave
  323-466-5125 • $$$$
  Romantic Japanese with a view.

Shopping

- **Amoeba Music** • 6400 W Sunset Blvd
  323-245-6400
  Cavernous music store…used CDs, DVDs too. A dangerous place to carry your wallet.
- **The Conservatory** • 1900 N Highland Ave
  323-851-6290
  Gorgeous, minimalist floral creations.
- **The Daily Planet** • 5931 Franklin Ave
  323-957-0061
  Books, magazines, and unusual gifts.
- **Dawson's Book Shop** • 535 N Larchmont Blvd
  323-469-2186
  Rare books on the American West.
- **Domaine LA** • 6801 Melrose Ave
  323-932-0280
  Friendly wine store with super-knowledgeable staff.
- **Frederick's of Hollywood** • 6751 Hollywood Blvd
  323-957-5953
  Lingerie that keeps nothing secret.
- **Hollywood Toys & Costumes** • 6600 Hollywood Blvd
  323-464-4444
  Quality medieval armor.
- **Home Depot** • 5600 W Sunset Blvd
  323-461-3303
  Reliable for all things home and garden.
- **Larry Edmunds Bookshop** • 6644 Hollywood Blvd
  323-463-3273
  Need to find a movie still from the '30s? It's here.
- **Locali** • 5825 Franklin Ave
  323-466-1360
  Organic and local, with bitchin' vegan (and non-vegan) sandwiches.
- **Mel Pierce Camera** • 5645 Hollywood Blvd
  323-465-2191
  Friendly local source for cameras, papers, printers, etc.
- **Native Boutique** • 5915 Franklin Ave
  323-962-7710
  Indie designers grace the famous Franklin strip.
- **The Oaks Gourmet** • 1915 N Bronson Ave
  323-871-8894
  Part sit-down restaurant, part wine, cheese, and deli offerings.
- **Panpipes Magickal Marketplace** •
  1641 N Cahuenga Blvd
  323-462-7078
  One-stop shopping for all your magickal needs.
- **Space 15 Twenty** • 1520 N Cahuenga Blvd
  323-465-1893
  Like a mall, if malls were cool.
- **The Tropics** • 7056 Santa Monica Blvd
  323-469-1682
  Greenery galore.

Map 4 • Los Feliz

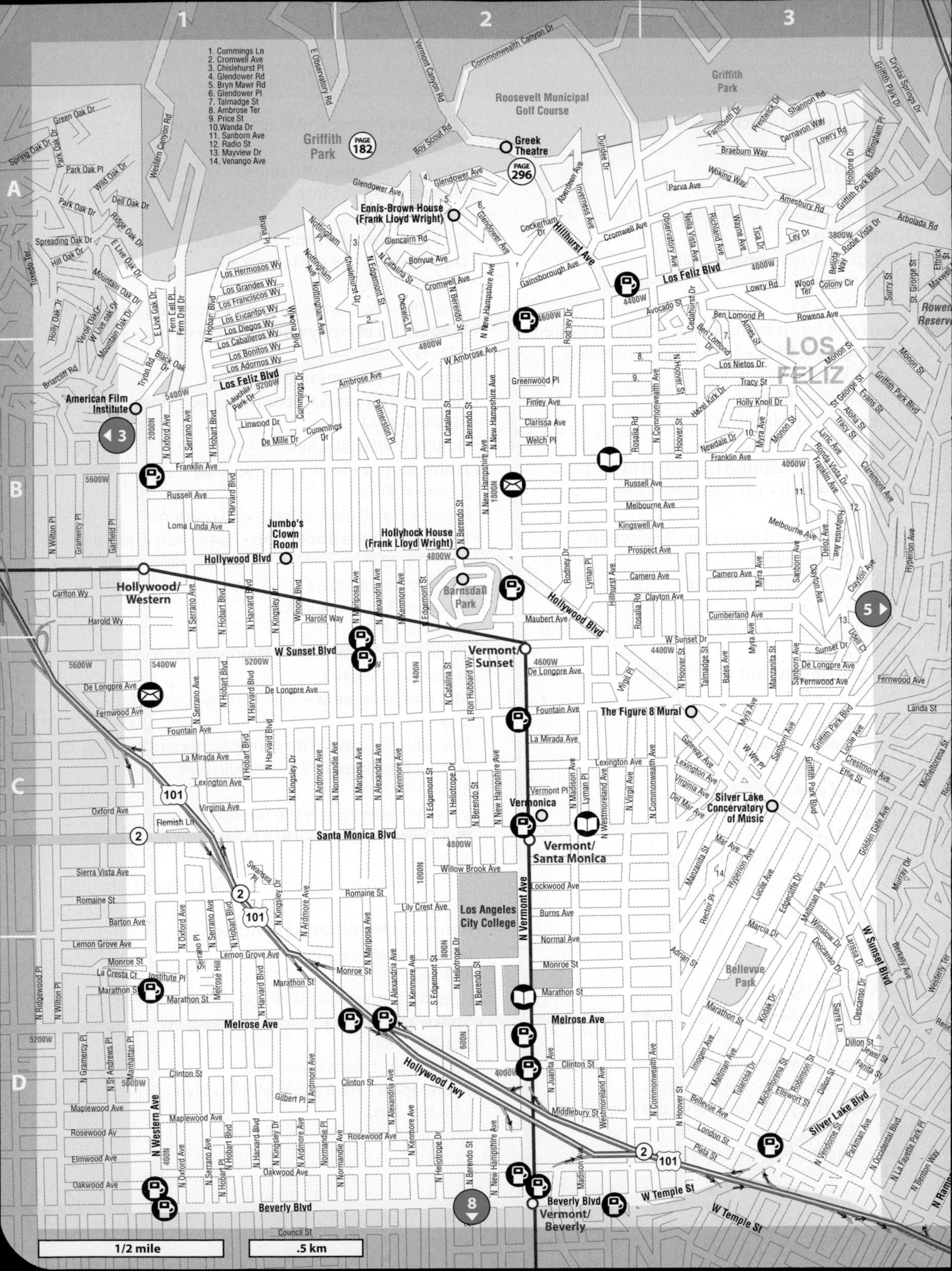

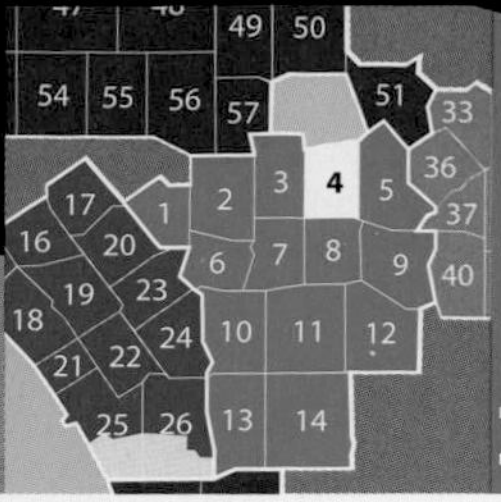

Los Feliz perseveres despite the burden of being America's most hyped neighborhood. It continues to have ample room for everyone—from grannies wearing old cardigans to hipsters wearing...old cardigans. You'll find multimillion-dollar playpens on the hill, as well as crowded studio apartment buildings lining Vermont and Hillhurst Avenues. Los Feliz is home to some of LA's most beloved and relevant attractions—**Griffith Park**, the Los Angeles Zoo, and the **Greek Theater**—proving that, even in Los Angeles, sometimes you really can believe the hype.

oLandmarks

• **American Film Institute** • 2021 N Western Ave
323-856-7600
The next David Lynch might be honing his craft here right now. Or not.

• **Barnsdall Art Park** • 4800 Hollywood Blvd
323-660-4254
Griffith Park may get all the glory, but Barnsdall Art Park is a great place to wander around on a lazy Sunday.

• **Ennis-Brown House** • 2607 Glendower Ave
323-660-0607
Frank Lloyd Wright's version of a Mayan temple.

• **The Figure 8 Mural** • 4334 W Sunset Blvd
Former cover art, this mural is now a tribute to departed indie fave Elliott Smith.

• **Greek Theatre** • 2700 N Vermont Ave
323-665-5857
A more intimate alternative to the Hollywood Bowl.

• **Hollyhock House** • 4800 Hollywood Blvd
323-644-6269
Another brilliant Frank Lloyd Wright design, open for public tours, love the fireplace.

• **Jumbo's Clown Room** • 5153 Hollywood Blvd
323-666-1187
Seedy strip club where Courtney Love first exposed her "celebrity skin."

• **Silverlake Conservatory of Music** •
3920 W Sunset Blvd
323-665-3363
Neighborhood music school and hang-out courtesy of Chili Pepper Flea.

• **Vermonica** • Santa Monica Blvd & N Vermont Ave
Quirky display of LA streetlamps from various eras.

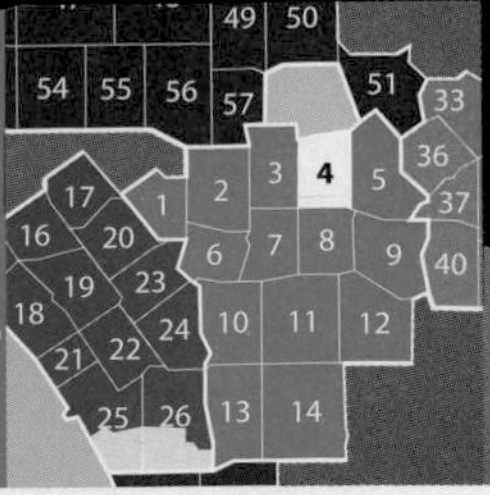

Los Feliz

Nightlife

- **Akbar** • 4356 W Sunset Blvd
  323-665-6810
  Your friendly neighborhood homo/hetero hangout.
- **Blipsy Barcade** • 369 N Western Ave
  323-461-7067
  Dive bar/arcade? Yes please. Do the Playboy pinball.
- **Blu Monkey** • 5521 Hollywood Blvd
  323-957-9000
  Middle Eastern vibes in deep Hollywood.
- **Drawing Room** • 1800 Hillhurst Ave
  323-665-0135
  Tiny strip-mall dive, no pretense, TV 'n' locals.
- **The Dresden** • 1760 N Vermont Ave
  323-665-4294
  Home of Marty & Elayne's famed lounge act.
- **Eagle LA** • 4219 Santa Monica Blvd
  323-669-9472
  The place to meet the leather-daddy of your dreams.
- **Faultline** • 4216 Melrose Ave
  323-660-0889
  An irresistable trifecta of beer, bears, porn.
- **Good Luck Bar** • 1514 Hillhurst Ave
  323-666-3524
  Confucius say: hook-ups likely.
- **Harvard and Stone** • 5221 Hollywood Blvd
  323-466-6063
  Craft cocktails near Thai Town.
- **Hemingway's** • 6356 Hollywood Blvd
  323-469-0040
  Cool Hollywood hideaway inspired by tough-guy lit.
- **Jay's Bar** • 4321 Sunset Blvd
  323-666-1898
  A lovely li'l gastropub.
- **Jumbo's Clown Room** • 5153 Hollywood Blvd
  323-666-1187
  The seediest little joint in Hollywood.
- **La Descarga** • 1159 N Western Ave
  323-466-1324
  Old Havana nightclub on a scary stretch of Western Ave.
- **Rockwell** • 1714 N Vermont Ave
  323-669-1550
  Weird crowd, but food better than would be expected.
- **Smog Cutter** • 864 N Virgil Ave
  323-660-4626
  Hole-in-the-wall karaoke.
- **Tiki-Ti** • 4427 W Sunset Blvd
  323-669-9381
  Fortify yourself with a famous Blood of the Bull.
- **Whitehorse Inn Cocktail Lounge** • 1532 N Western Ave
  323-462-8088
  Serious drinking with Bukowski's ghost.
- **Ye Rustic Inn** • 1831 Hillhurst Ave
  323-662-5757
  If ye want pink drinks, get thee the hell out.

Los Feliz

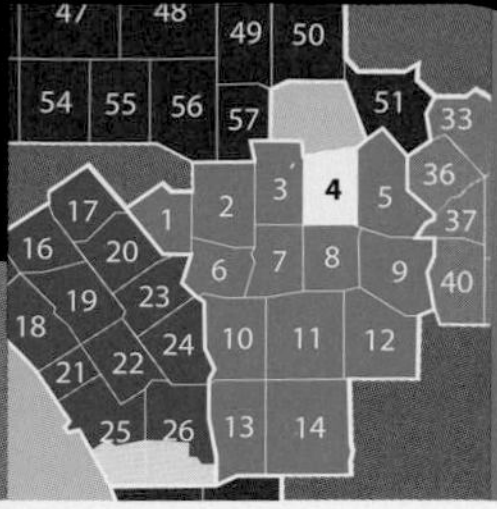

With the **Griffith Observatory** twinkling down on the neighborhood, Los Feliz reminds us that the stars are among us, even where you least expect it. There's a democratic quality to hedonistic pursuits here, and it's not uncommon to see your favorite celebrity catching a film at the **Vista** or grabbing a bite on Hillhurst. Whether you're enjoying the world's best breakfast dish (the smoked salmon stack at the **Alcove Café**), or enjoying a divey round of dirty photo hunt at the **Drawing Room**, Los Feliz is the perfect place for brunch, booze, and the pursuit of happiness.

Restaurants

- **Alcove Cafe & Bakery** • 1929 Hillhurst Ave
323-644-0100 • $
Brunch, lunch, gourmet food market, beautiful patio out front.
- **The Black Cat** • 3909 W Sunset Blvd
323-661-6369 • $$$
Another French-inspired food and cocktail spot. Meow!
- **Blossom** • 4019 W Sunset Blvd
323-953-8345 • $$
Feel good pho in a slightly upscale atmosphere.
- **Café Los Feliz** • 2118 Hillhurst Ave
323-664-7111 • $
Neighborhoody gem. Exquisite tarts and cinnamon rolls.
- **Cafe Stella** • 3932 W Sunset Blvd
323-666-0265 • $$$$
Trendy French bistro and wine bar.
- **Casita Del Campo** • 1920 Hyperion Ave
323-662-4255 • $$
It's all about the margaritas.
- **Cha Cha Cha** • 656 N Virgil Ave
323-664-7723 • $$$
Caribbean food and sangria.
- **Cliff's Edge** • 3626 W Sunset Blvd
323-666-6116 • $$
Cal-Euro tapas, upscale bohemian digs, and Silver Lake's swankiest patio.
- **The Deli at Little Dom's** • 2128 Hillhurst Ave
323-661-0088 • $$
Unassuming gem, adjacent to popular eatery.
- **El Cid** • 4212 W Sunset Blvd
323-668-0318 • $$$
Spanish dinner and a show!
- **Electric Lotus** • 1739 N Vermont Ave
323-953-0040 • $$
Hip Indian disco.
- **Flore** • 3818 W Sunset Blvd
323-953-0611 • $$
Seitan himself must be responsible for this sinfully delicious vegan fare.
- **Forage** • 3823 W Sunset Blvd
323-663-6885 • $$
Local produce making modern deli salads and desserts.
- **Fred 62** • 1850 N Vermont Ave
323-667-0062 • $$
Retro-styled diner with surprising menu.
- **Good Microbrew & Grill** • 3725 W Sunset Blvd
323-660-3645 • $$$
Overpriced comfort food tempered by mucho bottled brews.

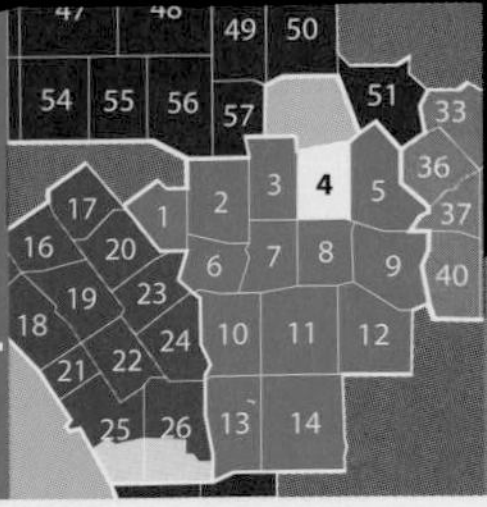

Los Feliz

- **Home** • 1760 Hillhurst Ave
323-669-0211 • $$
No place like this outdoor eatery. Try the waffle fries.
- **The Kitchen** • 4348 Fountain Ave
323-664-3663 • $$
Late-night comfort food.
- **Little Dom's** • 2128 Hillhurst Ave
323-661-0055 • $$$
Cheap? Not really. Tasty? Yes, indeed.
- **Lucifers Pizza** • 1958 Hillhurst Ave
323-906-8603 • $
Famous for the gothic decor and the Veggie Supremo.
- **Madame Matisse** • 3536 W Sunset Blvd
323-662-4862 • $$
Matchbox-sized and mellow French Café packed with regulars. BYOB.
- **Malo** • 4326 W Sunset Blvd
323-664-1011 • $$$
Yummy Mexican for the hipster cheapskate.
- **Marouch** • 4905 Santa Monica Blvd
323-662-9325 • $$$
Not a joke: the Chef's Special really is.
- **Mexico City** • 2121 Hillhurst Ave
323-661-7227 • $$$
Arty Tex-Mex cantina.
- **Night + Market Song** • 3322 W Sunset Blvd
323-664-1011 • $$$
Fun all-in-the-family Thai food experience.
- **Pa Ord Noodle** • 5301 Sunset Blvd
323-461-3945 • $
Cheap, delicious Thai with legit, face-melting spice.
- **The Palace** • 2112 Hillhurst Ave
323-667-1595 • $$$
Good Chinese food and those tasty, elusive appetizers, crab rangoons!
- **Paru's** • 5140 W Sunset Blvd
323-661-7600 • $$
Delicious South Indian food with lots of happy-smiley service.
- **Pazzo Gelato** • 3827 Sunset Blvd
323-662-1410 • $
Because gelato is the best of all frozen treats.
- **Ruen Pair** • 5257 Hollywood Blvd
323-466-0153 • $$
So good chefs come here after work.
- **Sanamluang** • 5170 Hollywood Blvd
323-660-8006 • $
Huge plates of noodles at 3 am.
- **Sapp Coffee Shop** • 5183 Hollywood Blvd
323-665-1035 • $
Not only coffee, but Thai boat noodles. Anthony Bourdain liked it.
- **Scoops** • 712 N Heliotrope Dr
323-906-2649 • $
Amazing vegan and non-vegan daily ice-cream.
- **The Trails** • 2333 Fern Dell Dr
323-871-2102 • $
Comfort food esconced in pastoralia.
- **Trattoria Farfalla** • 1978 Hillhurst Ave
323-661-7365 • $$$
Inexpensive, reliable Italian.
- **Umami Burger** • 4655 Hollywood Blvd
323-669-3922 • $$
Dig those crazy burgers. Still one of LA's best.
- **Yai's on Vermont** • 1627 N Vermont Ave
323-644-1076 • $$
Kinda greasy but still divine. Comfy booths and great patio.
- **Yuca's** • 2056 Hillhurst Ave
323-662-1214 • $
A busy shack serving luscious Yucatan-style burritos and tacos.
- **Zankou Chicken** • 5065 W Sunset Blvd
323-665-7845 • $
Palm-licking, Beck-serenaded chicken.

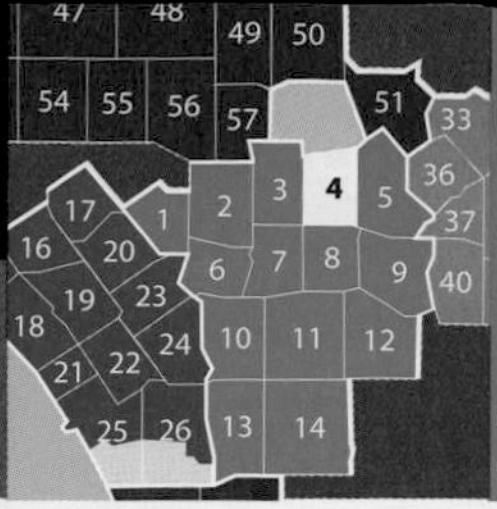

Los Feliz

Figaro Bistrot on Vermont squeezes in thirsty hipsters. **Malo** on Sunset has an industrial-looking, surprisingly intimate outdoor seating area with heating lamps. **The Dresden Room** solidified its fame with a cameo in 1996's prerequisite LA film *Swingers*, and comes with its very own lounge act. **Paru's** is a bounty of all-veggie Indian fare, but don't forget the local outpost of **Zankou Chicken**, the Armenian mini-chain with the most delectable poultry you will ever have the privilege of fingerlicking.

Shopping

- **Bar Keeper** • 3910 W Sunset Blvd
  323-669-1675
  From spirits to shakers, everything you need for fancy cocktailery.
- **Bicycle Kitchen** • 4429 Fountain Ave
  323-662-2776
  Non-profit community bicycle workshop.
- **Blue Rooster Art Supplies** • 1718 N Vermont Ave
  323-661-9471
  Everything for the starving artist, except food.
- **Casbah Café** • 3900 W Sunset Blvd
  323-664-7000
  Café featuring gifts and home décor stuff a la Marocaine.
- **The Cheese Store of Silver Lake** •
  3926 W Sunset Blvd
  323-644-7511
  High-quality cheese and a great selection of cured meats, olives, and gourmet teas.
- **Glory** • 4659 Hollywood Blvd
  323-644-5679
  '50s Americana, cycles, and oddities.
- **Gipsy** • 3915 W Sunset Blvd
  323-660-2556
  Ponchos, Che tees, Mexican silver, and assorted funkiness.
- **Lark Cake Shop** • 3337 W Sunset Blvd
  323-667-2968
  Succulent rum cakes.
- **Le Pink & Co.** • 3820 Sunset Blvd
  323-661-7465
  Girly gifts, olde-time candy treats.
- **McCall's Meat & Fish Co.** • 2117 Hillhurst Ave
  323-667-0674
  Fancy groceries for the carnivores among us.
- **Ozzie Dots** • 4637 Hollywood Blvd
  323-663-2867
  Vintage clothes, costume rentals, loads o' fun.
- **Pacific Auto Service** • 4225 Santa Monica Blvd
  323-666-7689
  Jimmy may be a little eccentric, but he knows how to fix a car.
- **Panty Raid** • 1953 Hillhurst Ave
  323-668-1888
  Tell your boyfriend/girlfriend about their frequent lingerie sales.
- **ReForm School** • 3902 Sunset Blvd
  323-906-8660
  Awesome gifts and housewares with a school theme.
- **Secret Headquarters** • 3817 W Sunset Blvd
  323-666-2228
  Embrace your secret comic book obsession here.
- **Squaresville** • 1800 N Vermont Ave
  323-669-8464
  A staggering collection of vintage clothing, including high-end labels like Gucci and Pucci.
- **Una Mae's** • 4651 Kingswell Ave
  323-662-6137
  The going designer threads & killer discounted vintage rack.
- **Wacko / Soap Plant** • 4633 Hollywood Blvd
  323-663-0122
  Books, tchotchkes, party favors, and obscure tees.
- **Y-Que Trading Post** • 1770 N Vermont Ave
  323-664-0021
  Gifts, trinkets, "Pluto: Never Forget" T-shirts.

Map 5 • Silver Lake / Echo Park / Atwater

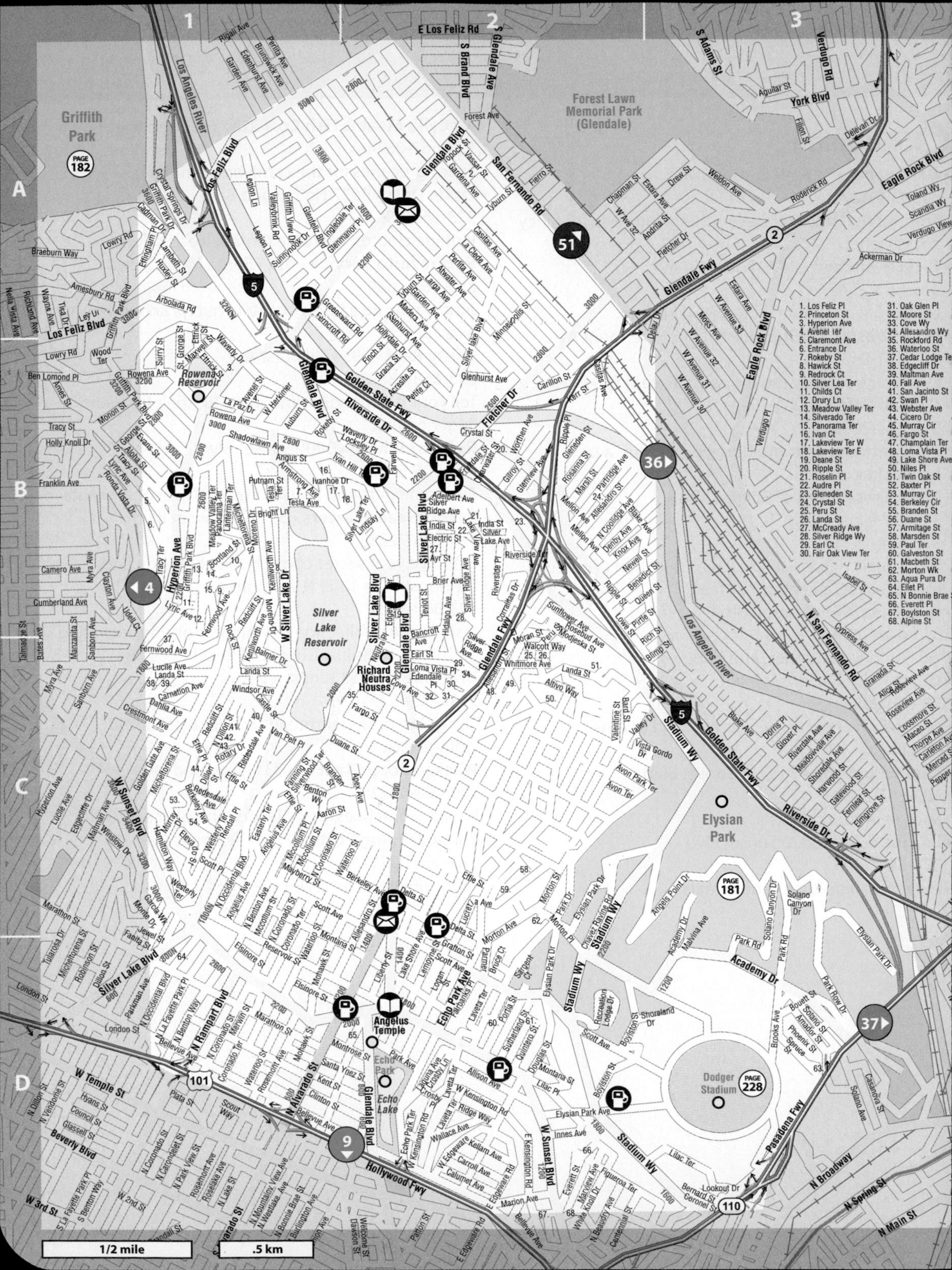

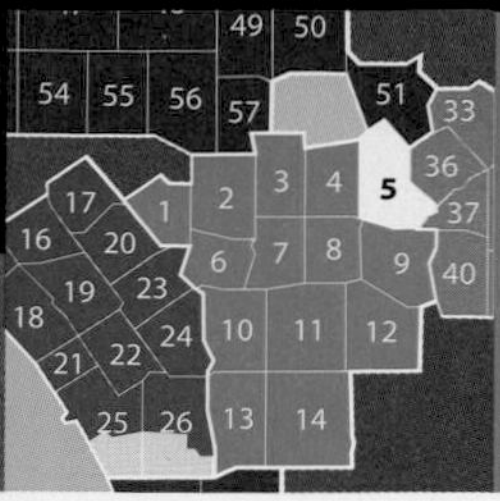

A few years on, and still the coolest neighborhood in Los Angeles. The hip kids are becoming slightly wealthier adults, with retail following the trendy money: **Sunset Junction** is now home to the longest meals in town, fancy salons, local designer boutiques, and enough specialty stores to fill a giant supermarket, from cheese to spices. But don't grow up too fast—there's still plenty of fun nightlife, from live music venues to cool cocktail lounges.

oLandmarks

- **Angelus Temple** • 1100 Glendale Blvd
  213-816-1109
  Founder claimed the Lord led her to the site.
- **Dodger Stadium** • 1000 Elysian Park Ave
  323-224-1507
  With a view like this, who needs luxury boxes?
- **Echo Park** • Glendale Blvd & Park Ave
  The paddle boats alone are worth a trip.
- **Elysian Park** • 835 Academy Rd
  213-485-5054
  LA's oldest park, crisscrossed with hiking trails.
- **Richard Neutra Houses** • 2200 Silver Lake Blvd
  A can't-miss for architecture buffs.
- **Rowena Reservoir** • Hyperion Ave & Rowena Ave
  This strategically landscaped reservoir contains 10 million gallons of water and cost a few more million to build.
- **Silver Lake Reservoir** • Silver Lake Blvd & Duane St
  Take a jog, a stroll, and a dog! There is an off-leash dog park at the reservoir's base.

Nightlife

- **55 Degree Wine** • 3111 Glendale Blvd
  323-662-5556
  Tasting room and shop. Surly service; good selection.
- **Bigfoot Lodge** • 3172 Los Feliz Blvd
  323-662-9227
  It's too bad boy scouts don't drink.
- **Club Tee Gee** • 3210 Glendale Blvd
  323-669-9631
  Dependable watering hole since 1946.
- **The Echo** • 1822 W Sunset Blvd
  213-413-8200
  Eastside hipster haven for DJ electronica and dancing.
- **Gold Room** • 1558 W Sunset Blvd
  213-482-5259
  Looks scarier from the outside than it is.
- **The Griffin** • 3000 Los Feliz Blvd
  323-644-0444
  Casual-yet-classy spot for whiskey and beer.
- **Hyperion Tavern** • 1941 Hyperion Ave
  323-665-1941
  Ex-S&M bar. Current boho hub. Offbeat entertainment. No liquor.
- **Little Joy Cocktail Lounge** • 1477 W Sunset Blvd
  213-250-3417
  Hipsters have the hegemony on this one; Sunday open mics showcase scribes & neo-Elliott Smiths.
- **MJ's** • 2810 Hyperion Ave
  323-660-1503
  Rage's hairier Eastside cousin.
- **Pins and Needles** • 1623 Allesandro St
  323-313-9449
  Awesome old pinball machines. BYOB!
- **Red Lion Tavern** • 2366 Glendale Blvd
  323-662-5337
  Year-round Oktoberfest, plus schnitzel.
- **The Roost** • 3100 Los Feliz Blvd
  323-664-7272
  Cheap drinks, free popcorn, no frills.
- **The Satellite** • 1717 Silver Lake Blvd
  323-661-4380
  Formerly Spaceland, currently housing the live (indie) rock.
- **The Short Stop** • 1455 W Sunset Blvd
  213-482-4942
  Cool dive bar, seasonally packed with Dodger fans.
- **Silverlake Lounge** • 2906 W Sunset Blvd
  323-663-9636
  Silver Lake's holy church of rock 'n' roll salvation.
- **Sunset Beer** • 1498 W Sunset Blvd
  213-481-2337
  Buy bottle by the beer, drink there or take away.
- **Tam O'Shanter** • 2980 Los Feliz Blvd
  323-664-0228
  Me want prime rib and beer. Grrr.
- **Thirsty Crow** • 2939 W Sunset Blvd
  323-661-6007
  Cool, calm whiskey bar on the retro-Prohibition tip.

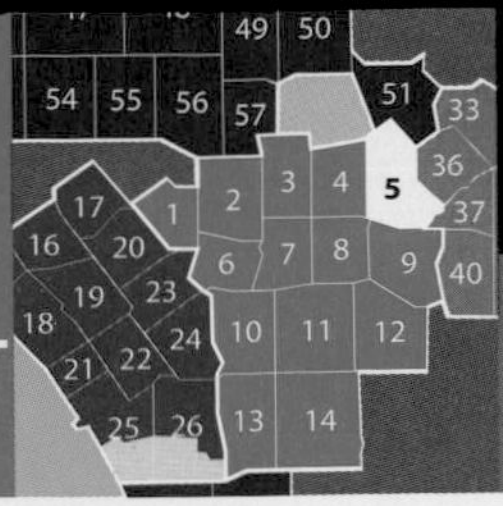

Silver Lake / Echo Park / Atwater

Restaurants

- **Alimento** • 1710 Silver Lake Blvd
  323-928-2888 • $$$
  Italia via Los Angeles.
- **Astro Family Restaurant** • 2300 Fletcher Dr
  323-663-9241 • $
  Relaxed '50s modern diner.
- **ATX by Kitchen12000** • 3245 Casitas Ave
  323-522-3488 • $$
  Good food almost makes up for the dumb name.
- **Baracoa Cuban Café** • 3175 Glendale Blvd
  323-665-9590 • $
  Home-style Cuban cooking.
- **Barbrix** • 2442 Hyperion Ave
  323-662-2442 • $$
  Affordable Euro-wine and food in LA? Yup, it's true.
- **Black Hogg** • 2852 W Sunset Blvd
  323-953-2820 • $$$
  Another "New American" place, but this one's good. Chicken liver!
- **Blair's** • 2903 Rowena Ave
  323-660-1882 • $$$$
  Silver Lake's premier eatery.
- **Canele** • 3219 Glendale Blvd
  323-666-7133 • $$$
  European farm-to-table.
- **Dusty's** • 3200 W Sunset Blvd
  323-906-1018 • $$$
  Eclectic French bistro.
- **Edendale Grill** • 2838 Rowena Ave
  323-666-2000 • $$$$
  Former fire station serves American favorites…dine in or dine out.
- **Elf Cafe** • 2135 W Sunset Blvd
  213-484-6829 • $$
  No sign, just look for the line. Miranda July frequently holds court.
- **Giamela's Submarine Sandwiches** •
  3178 Los Feliz Blvd
  323-661-9444 • $
  When you need a reliably good sub: Giamela's.
- **Gingergrass** • 2396 Glendale Blvd
  323-644-1600 • $$
  Upscale Vietnamese food for a gringo palate.
- **Gobi Mongolian BBQ** • 2827 Sunset Blvd
  213-989-0711 • $$
  Fill up the bowl, throw it on the grill.
- **The Griffin** • 3000 Los Feliz Blvd
  323-644-0444 • $$
  Standard gastropub fare in a space fit for plotting.
- **Hard Times Pizza** • 1311 Glendale Blvd
  213-413-1900 • $$
  Sicilian- and Neopolitan-style pies to take out or eat in.
- **India Sweets and Spices** • 3126 Los Feliz Blvd
  323-345-0360 • $$
  Vegetarian delicacies, Indian groceries, and Bollywood hits under one roof.
- **Leela Thai** • 1737 Silver Lake Blvd
  323-660-6100 • $$
  Inexpensive, delicious, friendly.
- **Los Angeles Police Revolver & Athletic Club Cafe** •
  1880 Academy Dr
  323-221-5222 • $
  Dine with the cadets.
- **Mae Ploy** • 2606 W Sunset Blvd
  213-353-9635 • $$
  Home-style Thai food served with a smile.
- **Masa of Echo Park** • 1800 W Sunset Blvd
  213-989-1558 • $
  Neighborhood bakery and pizza house run by Patina vets.
- **Nicky D's Wood Fired Pizza** • 2764 Rowena Ave
  323-664-3333 • $$
  Friendly local spot for NYC-style pies. Try the Garlic Clam pizza.

Silver Lake / Echo Park / Atwater

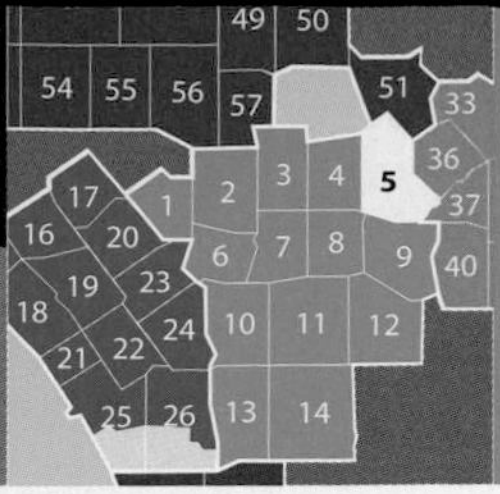

OK—let's stop rambling on about how this area is oh-so-hip and discuss all the great things to do. Feel like a king (or at least a baron) drinking in the castle-like interior of **The Griffin**, get beautiful views (and make your legs burn) walking the stairs in the hills near the reservoir, or catch some comedy and music at **The Echo**. Oh, and that **Silversun Liquor**? That's where the Pickups got their name.

- **Pazzo Gelato** • 1910 W Sunset Blvd
  213-353-9263 • $
  It's creamy. It's delicious. Get the salted caramel.
- **Rambutan Thai** • 2835 W Sunset Blvd
  213-273-8424 • $$
  Trendy but good Thai favorites.
- **Red Lion Tavern** • 2366 Glendale Blvd
  323-662-5337 • $$
  Go for the German brats.
- **Sage Organic Vegan Bistro** • 1700 W Sunset Blvd
  213-989-1718 • $$
  Large-menu vegan spot. Perfect for a pre-Echoplex bite.
- **Silverlake Ramen** • 2927 Sunset Blvd
  323-660-8100 • $
  A perfect cool-weather evening: ramen, then Thirsty Crow.
- **Spain** • 1866 Glendale Blvd
  323-667-9045 • $$
  Sangria and paella without the airfare.
- **Taix** • 1911 W Sunset Blvd
  213-484-1265 • $$
  Say "Tex" and check out "Two-fer Tuesdays" for double the wine at this French standard.
- **Thank You For Coming** • 3416 Glendale Blvd
  323-648-2666 • $
  Ever-changing experimental restaurant with cool residency program.
- **Tomato Pie Pizza Joint** • 2457 Hyperion Ave
  323-661-6474 • $$
  East coast-style pizza for expatriates & those sick of vegan fare.
- **The Village Bakery and Cafe** • 3119 Los Feliz Blvd
  323-662-8600 • $$
  Solid sandwiches and utterly delightful pastries.

Shopping

- **A Runner's Circle** • 3216 Los Feliz Blvd
  323-661-8971
  A great place to get fitted for running shoes.
- **Echo Country Outpost** • 1930 Echo Park Ave
  323-667-9606
  For pretending you live in the woods.
- **Echo Park Time Travel Mart** • 1714 W Sunset Blvd
  213-413-3388
  Everything you need before you take a road trip through the fourth dimension.
- **Little Knittery** • 3195 Glendale Blvd
  323-663-3838
  Cozy and friendly knitting store with fun classes.
- **Potted** • 3158 Los Feliz Blvd
  323-665-3801
  Tiles, fountains, wrought-iron furniture, enthusiastic advice from "exterior decorators."
- **Rockaway Records** • 2395 Glendale Blvd
  323-664-3232
  5000 square feet of used vinyl and CDs.
- **Say Cheese** • 2800 Hyperion Ave
  323-665-0545
  Great smelly cheese tastings.
- **Silver Lake Wine** • 2395 Glendale Blvd
  323-662-9024
  Snacks and hors d'oeuvres served with tastings at this convivial wine store.

Map 6 • Miracle Mile / Mid-City

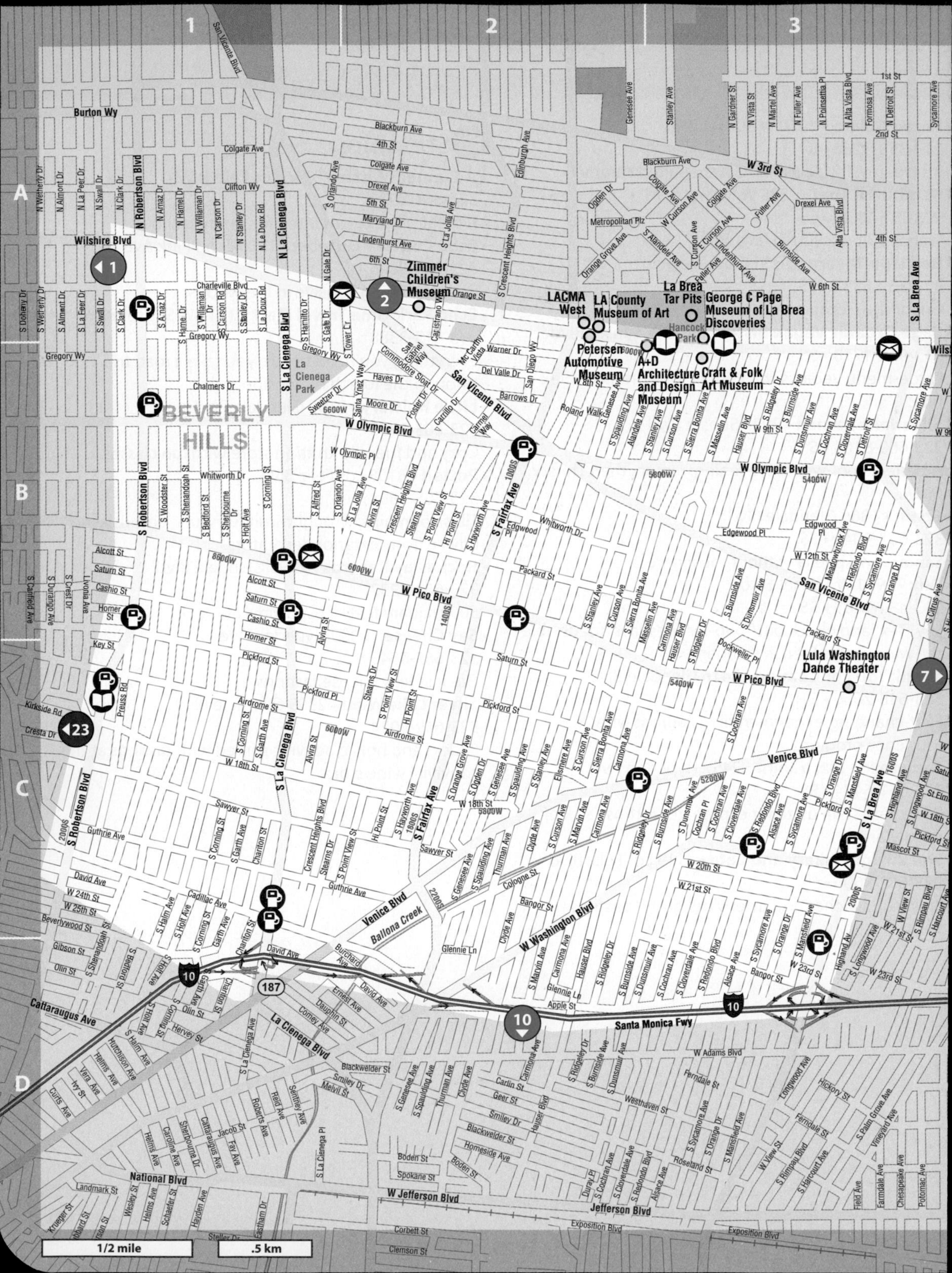

"Miracle Mile" is the stretch of real estate on Wilshire Boulevard between La Brea and Fairfax Avenues. Once a snappy, Art Deco-influenced shopping destination, this area has become a bit scruffy with age. You can still see the Art Deco, but now Miracle Mile draws traffic for its Museum Row, including the **La Brea Tar Pits**, the **Peterson Automotive Museum**, and the **Craft and Folk Art Museum**. Check out the **LA County Museum of Art**, recently renovated and expanded and now officially a world-class attraction.

Landmarks

- **A+D Museum** • 6032 Wilshire Blvd
  323-932-9393
  All things architecture—check it out here.
- **La Brea Tar Pits** • Wilshire Blvd & S Curson Ave
  323-934-7243
  It's just a big pool of tar, yet it continues to fascinate us.
- **LACMA West** • 6067 Wilshire Blvd
  323-933-4510
  This Art Deco building used to be home to the May Co. Department Store.
- **Los Angeles County Museum of Art** •
  5905 Wilshire Blvd
  323-857-6000
  From King Tut to Jasper Johns, this museum covers it all.
- **Lula Washington Dance Theatre** • 5041 W Pico Blvd
  323-292-5852
  Renowned African-American dance company with classes and residencies.
- **Page Museum at the La Brea Tar Pits** •
  5801 Wilshire Blvd
  323-934-7243
  Don't miss the La Brea Woman exhibit.
- **Petersen Automotive Museum** • 6060 Wilshire Blvd
  323-930-2277
  Like you don't see enough cars in LA. Mediocre.
- **Zimmer Children's Museum** • 6505 Wilshire Blvd
  323-761-8984
  Learning place for kids to explore.

Nightlife

- **El Rey Theatre** • 5515 Wilshire Blvd
  323-936-6400
  Diverse musical lineup.
- **The Joint** • 8771 W Pico Blvd
  310-275-2619
  Former Jazz club, new renovation hosts wide array of music and scenesters.
- **Little Bar** • 757 S LaBrea Ave
  323-937-9210
  Beer and wine only at this friendly BYO food spot.
- **The Mint** • 6010 W Pico Blvd
  323-954-9400
  Casual acoustic venue with smokin' sound system.
- **Tom Bergin's** • 840 S Fairfax Ave
  323-936-7151
  Guinness and fifty years of paper shamrocks.

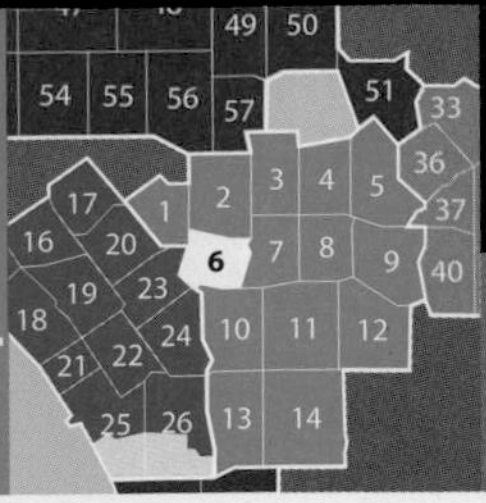

Miracle Mile / Mid-City

Restaurants

- **Black Dog Coffee** • 5657 Wilshire Blvd
  323-933-1976 • $
  Friendly and tasty. Breakfast, lunch, coffee, dog biscuits.
- **Caffe Latte** • 6254 Wilshire Blvd
  323-936-5213 • $$
  California-style coffee and breakfast shop.
- **Crazy Fish** • 9105 W Olympic Blvd
  310-550-8547 • $$$
  Insanely popular sushi joint.
- **Fu's Palace** • 8751 W Pico Blvd
  310-271-7887 • $
  Crispy, spicy, sweet, and sour aromatic shrimp.
- **Kate Mantilini** • 9101 Wilshire Blvd
  310-278-3699 • $$$
  Boxing-themed upscale bistro with knockout desserts.
- **Lucy's** • 1373 S La Brea Ave
  323-938-4337 • $
  A 24-hour tacos, chili dogs, burgers, and anything else bad for you.
- **Luna Park** • 672 S La Brea Ave
  323-934-2110 • $$$
  Cocktails, tasty food, lively scene. LA outpost of San Francisco original.
- **Merkato** • 1036 S Fairfax Ave
  323-935-1775 • $
  Eat with your hands at this Ethiopian joint.
- **Natalee Thai** • 998 S Robertson Blvd
  310-855-9380 • $$
  Popular Thai food.
- **Rahel Ethiopian Vegan Cuisine** • 1047 S Fairfax Ave
  323-937-8401 • $
  Most vegan restaurant in Little Ethiopia.
- **Red Medicine** • 8400 Wilshire Blvd
  323-651-5500 • $$$$
  They have a restaurant "manifesto," but it shouldn't deter you.
- **Rosalind's** • 1044 S Fairfax Ave
  323-936-2486 • $$
  Local favorite, Ethiopian.
- **Roscoe's House of Chicken 'n Waffles** •
  5006 W Pico Blvd
  323-934-4405 • $$
  Cheap Southern soul food chain.
- **Tagine** • 132 N Robertson Blvd
  310-360-7535 • $$$
  An eating experience with set menus of small plates.
- **Versailles** • 1415 S La Cienega Blvd
  310-289-0392 • $$
  The LA institution's garlicy Cuban grub will stay with you.
- **Wi Jammin** • 5103 W Pico Blvd
  323-965-9809 • $
  A tiny hole-in-the-wall Carribbean restaurant where the local hairdressers hang out.

Miracle Mile / Mid-City

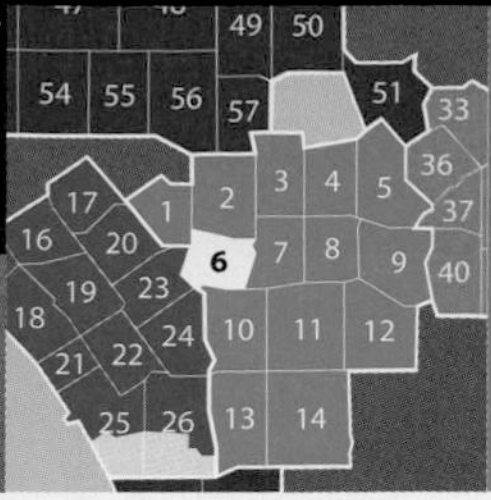

We hesitate to tell you this, because we don't want to see it overrun, but Saturday night trivia at the bring-your-own-food **Little Bar** is a nearly perfect way to spend a weekend evening. Where should that BYOF come from? **Versailles** has crazy good garlic chicken. Not feeling trivia? Look to **The Mint** for a night of music or comedy.

Shopping

- **99 Cents Only Store** • 6121 Wilshire Blvd
  323-939-9991
  99-cent cell phone charger or a half gallon of soy milk.
- **Ace Gallery** • 5514 Wilshire Blvd
  323-935-4411
  Established in 1940, this up and down gallery showcases mostly local Los Angeles artists.
- **Albertson Chapel** • 5318 Wilshire Blvd
  323-937-4919
  Wanna get married NOW? Civil and Catholic services available.
- **City Spa** • 5325 W Pico Blvd
  323-933-5954
  Body wraps, massages, and steam rooms galore.
- **Feldmar Watch Co.** • 9000 W Pico Blvd
  310-274-8016
  From Timex to Rolex, they've got it all.
- **Hansen's Cakes** • 1072 S Fairfax Ave
  323-936-4332
  Wedding cake central and imaginative birthday creations.
- **It's a Wrap** • 1164 S Robertson Blvd
  310-246-9727
  Clothes previously worn by your favorite TV stars.
- **Marinello School of Beauty** • 6111 Wilshire Blvd
  323-938-2005
  A full-service beauty school with facials at half the going rate.
- **Pearl Art and Craft Supplies** •
  1250 S La Cienega Blvd
  310-854-4900
  Art supplies for everyone from the career artist to the scrapbook hobbyist.
- **Tom Bergin's** • 840 S Fairfax Ave
  323-936-7151
  Guinness and fifty years of paper shamrocks.

Map 7 • **Hancock Park**

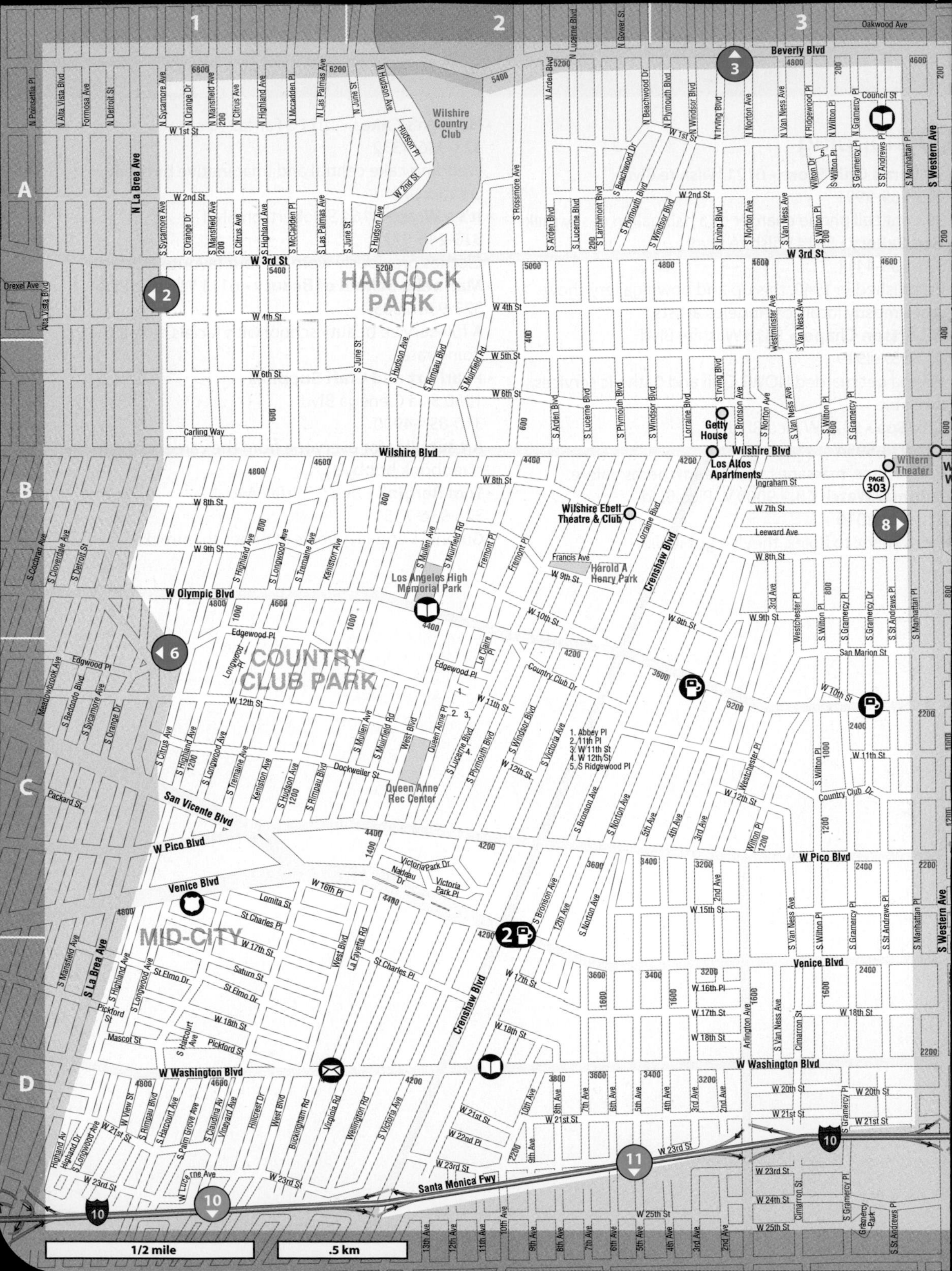

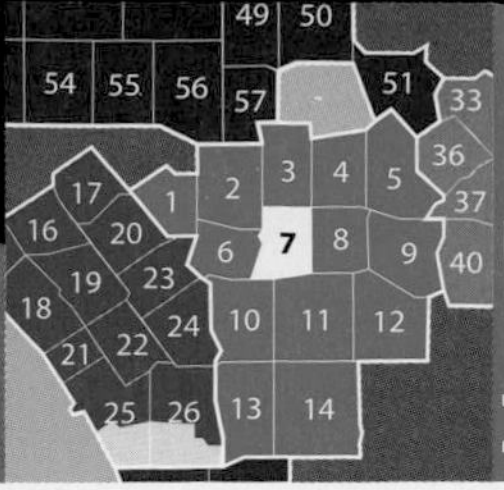

Hancock Park was once LA's most desirable neighborhood, and now that it's surrounded by the best of the city (Koreatown, the calmer side of Hollywood), it may well be again. The houses are magnificent enough to warrant a stroll through the neighborhood, and on Sunday the **Larchmont Farmers Market** is the place to be for newly minted stroller pushers.

Landmarks

- **Getty House** • 605 S Irving Blvd
  323-930-6430
  The home that LA's mayors use to par-tay.
- **Los Altos Apartments** • 4121 Wilshire Blvd
  There is a waiting list for apartments in this historic Spanish-style building.
- **Wilshire Ebell Theatre** • 4401 W 8th St
  323-939-0126
  Renaissance-style buildings used mainly for private events.
- **Wiltern Theater** • 3780 Wilshire Blvd
  213-380-5005
  Cool Art Deco building attracts equally cool, eclectic musical acts.

Nightlife

- **Jewel's Catch One** • 4067 W Pico Blvd
  323-734-8849
  Think Madonna's "Material Girl" days.

Restaurants

- **Girasole** • 225 N Larchmont Blvd
  323-464-6978 • $$
  Tiny, cozy, delicious osso buco.
- **Kiku Sushi** • 246 N Larchmont Blvd
  323-464-1323 • $$
  All-you-can-eat sushi.
- **Le Petit Greek** • 127 N Larchmont Blvd
  323-464-5160 • $$$
  How about a nice dollop of whipped caviar?!
- **Noah's New York Bagels** • 250 N Larchmont Blvd
  323-466-2924 • $
  Bagels and schmear with an NYC theme.
- **Prado** • 244 N Larchmont Blvd
  323-467-3871 • $$$
  Spicy Latin-Caribbean.
- **Village Pizzeria** • 131 N Larchmont Blvd
  323-465-5566 • $
  Might be LA's best NY-style pizza.
- **Z Pizza** • 123 N Larchmont Blvd
  323-466-6969 • $$
  Thin-crust deliciousness. A handful of sidewalk and indoor tables.

Shopping

- **Above the Fold** • 226 N Larchmont Blvd
  323-464-6397
  Good selection of newspapers and magazines.
- **Absolute Tickets** • 144 N Larchmont Blvd
  323-957-6699
  Tickets to just about everything, if you've got a few bucks to spend.
- **Center for Yoga** • 230 N Larchmont Blvd
  323-464-1276
  Classes, clothing, books, incense, sticky mats, and deep breaths.
- **Chevalier's Books** • 126 N Larchmont Blvd
  323-465-1334
  Great children's section.
- **Hans Custom Optik** • 212 N Larchmont Blvd
  323-462-5195
  Great selection of frames.
- **Kicks Sole Provider** • 141 N Larchmont Blvd
  323-468-9794
  Lots of stylin' sneaks.
- **Landis Gifts & Stationary** • 138 N Larchmont Blvd
  323-465-7003
  A little bit of EVERYTHING. The stationery department is especially good.
- **Larchmont Beauty Center** • 208 N Larchmont Blvd
  323-461-0162
  Arguably the best beauty supply store in the city.
- **Larchmont Village Wine, Spirits, & Cheese** •
  223 N Larchmont Blvd
  323-856-8699
  When Two-Buck Chuck just won't do. Amateurs are just as welcome as oenophiles.
- **Picket Fences** • 214 N Larchmont Blvd
  323-467-2140
  Juicy Couture, Cosa Bella undies, Kaminski hats, cute gifts.

Map 8 • Korea Town

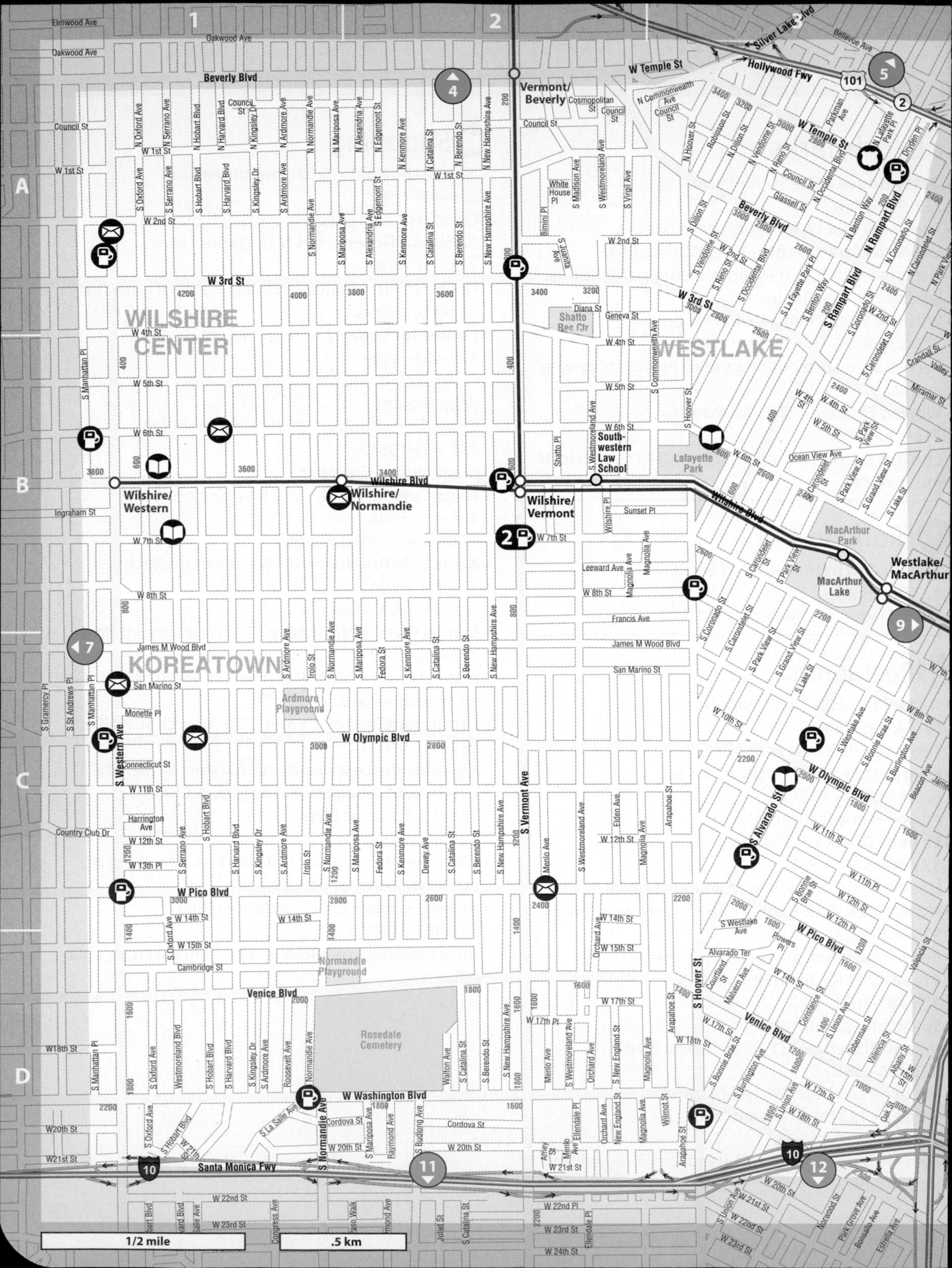

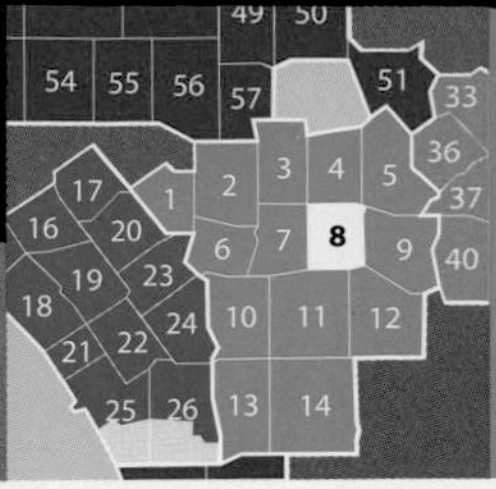

Home to one-third of the US Korean population, Korea Town is a bustling epicenter of nightlife and restaurants nestled against Wilshire Boulevard's business district. If a non-Korean Angeleno were to free associate about K-Town, three things would probably immediately come to mind: reasonable rents, karaoke, and barbecue. And although the Korean population has given way to a rising Hispanic majority in recent years, many of the storefronts and signs remain in Korean and the culture is imprinted on every corner.

Landmarks

- **MacArthur Park** • Wilshire Blvd & S Alvarado St
  Avoid at night, or you'll be melting in the dark!
- **Southwestern Law School** • 3050 Wilshire Blvd
  213-738-6700
  Legendary Art Deco department store turned law school.

Nightlife

- **Caffe Brass Monkey** • 3440 Wilshire Blvd
  213-381-7047
  One of the best of K-town karaokes, enter in back.
- **Frank N Hanks** • 518 S Western Ave
  213-383-2087
  Beloved K-town hole in the wall.
- **HMS Bounty** • 3357 Wilshire Blvd
  213-385-7275
  Nautical-themed old man bar patronized by the new kids.
- **Medusa Lounge** • 3211 Beverly Blvd
  213-382-5723
  For all your Satanic ritual needs.
- **The Prince** • 3198 W 7th St
  213-389-2007
  Smokin' waitresses, undercover celebs, cool.
- **Q's Billiard Club** • 11835 Wilshire Blvd
  310-477-7550
  Brentwood's pool bar. A great place to find locals to do coke with.
- **R Bar** • 3331 W 8th St
  213-387-7227
  Mellow K-Town dive. Check the 'net for the password.
- **Rosen Music Studio** • 3488 W 8th St
  213-387-0467
  The K-Town karaoke legend.

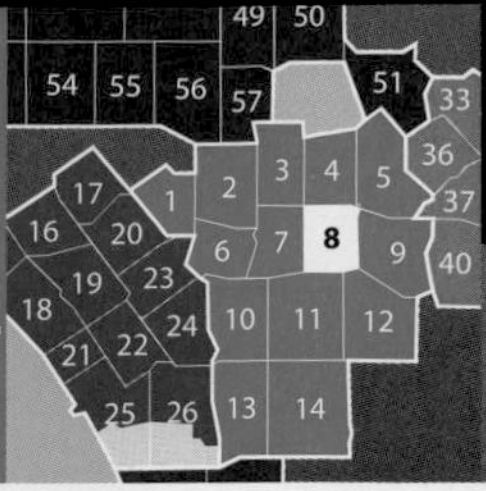

Korea Town

Restaurants

- **Beverly Soon Tofu Restaurant** • 2717 W Olympic Blvd
  213-380-1113 • $$
  Top food-centric spot specializing in soft tofu soups.
- **Chunju Han-il Kwan** • 3450 W 6th St
  213-480-1799 • $$
  All the homey classics.
- **Dong Il Jang** • 3455 W 8th St
  213-383-5757 • $$
  Upscale Korean barbecue, also serving sushi.
- **El Cholo** • 1121 S Western Ave
  323-734-2773 • $$
  Long time favorite Mexican chain.
- **El Farolito** • 2737 W Pico Blvd
  323-731-4329 • $
  Chicken enchiladas.
- **Guelaguetza** • 3014 W Olympic Blvd
  213-427-0608 • $$
  Warm, informal, authentically Mexican dining experience.
- **Gui Il Bun Ji BBQ** • 3055 W 7th St
  213-380-6606 • $$
  Meat smoke gets in your eyes.
- **Ham Hung** • 3109 W Olympic Blvd
  213-381-1520 • $$
  Korean for Koreans…and outsiders.
- **Hodori** • 1001 S Vermont Ave
  213-383-3554 • $
  24-hour Korean restaurant with killer barbecued beef.
- **Jun Won** • 3100 W 8th St
  213-383-8855 • $$$
  Korea Town brilliance.
- **Kyochon** • 3833 W 6th St
  213-739-9292 • $
  Korean fried chicken. Different from the Colonel.
- **Langer's** • 704 S Alvarado St
  213-483-8050 • $$
  Great Jewish deli in MacArthur Park. Try the pastrami sandwiches.
- **Literati Cafe** • 12081 Wilshire Blvd
  310-231-7484 • $$
  Bring your laptop so you can work on that screenplay you'll never sell.
- **M Grill** • 3832 Wilshire Blvd
  213-389-2770 • $$$
  Authentic Brazilian, sleek interior.
- **Mama's Hot Tamales** • 2122 W 7th St
  213-487-7474 • $
  An amazing selection of tamales from all over Central and South America.
- **Oo-Kook** • 3385 W 8th St
  213-385-5665 • $$
  All the delicious meat you can (literally) stomach.
- **Palomino** • 10877 Wilshire Blvd
  310-208-1960 • $$
  Strong menu, solid happy hour.
- **Papa Cristo's** • 2771 W Pico Blvd
  323-737-2970 • $
  Greek market and deli serving delicious gyros and souvlaki.
- **Pharaoh Karaoke Lounge** • 3680 Wilshire Blvd
  213-383-8686 • $$
  Fusion fare with private karaoke rooms.
- **Park's BBQ** • 955 S Vermont Ave
  213-380-1717 • $$
  Do your Korean BBQ here. Seasoned special pork belly!
- **Pipers** • 222 N Western Ave
  323-465-7701 • $
  Dependable 24-hour diner.
- **POT** • 3515 Wilshire Blvd
  213-368-3030 • $$$
  Gateway Korean with young creative flair.
- **Soot Bull Jeep** • 3136 W 8th St
  213-387-3865 • $$$
  Brilliant, smoky Korean BBQ; get the Spencer Steak.
- **Ssing Ssing** • 709 S Vermont Ave
  213-382-6099 • $
  Family-run Korean with delivery.
- **Taylor's Steakhouse** • 3361 W 8th St
  213-382-8449 • $$$
  Old-fashioned steak house.
- **Tommy's** • 2575 Beverly Blvd
  213-389-9060 • $
  Their burgers are renowned.

Korea Town

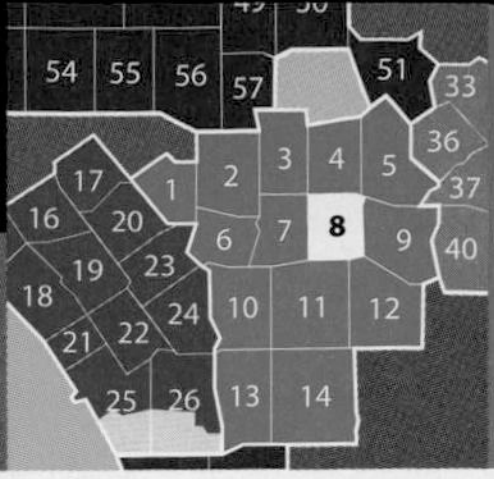

Going out for a night on the K-Town? Here's a handy equation: Korean BBQ + karaoke = good times. Try **Soot Bull Jeep** for a no-frills dining experience with a few friends. Follow a feast of kimchi and short ribs with generous portions of sake and awfulsome '80s tunes at **Orchid Karaoke** or **Rosen Music Studio**. Both offer private party rooms and drinks—Orchid even serves dinner—so you can satiate after slaughtering "Don't You Want Me." Decompress with a few soju cocktails and swear you'll do this every weekend.

Shopping

- **Han Kook Supermarket** • 124 N Western Ave
  323-469-8934
  Korean supermarket.
- **Koreatown Galleria** • 3250 W Olympic Blvd
  323-733-6000
  Best Korean market around.
- **Koreatown Plaza** • 928 S Western Ave
  213-382-1234
  Mall with an amazing food court.
- **Light Bulbs Unlimited** • 2309 Wilshire Blvd
  310-829-7400
  Every bulb under the sun.

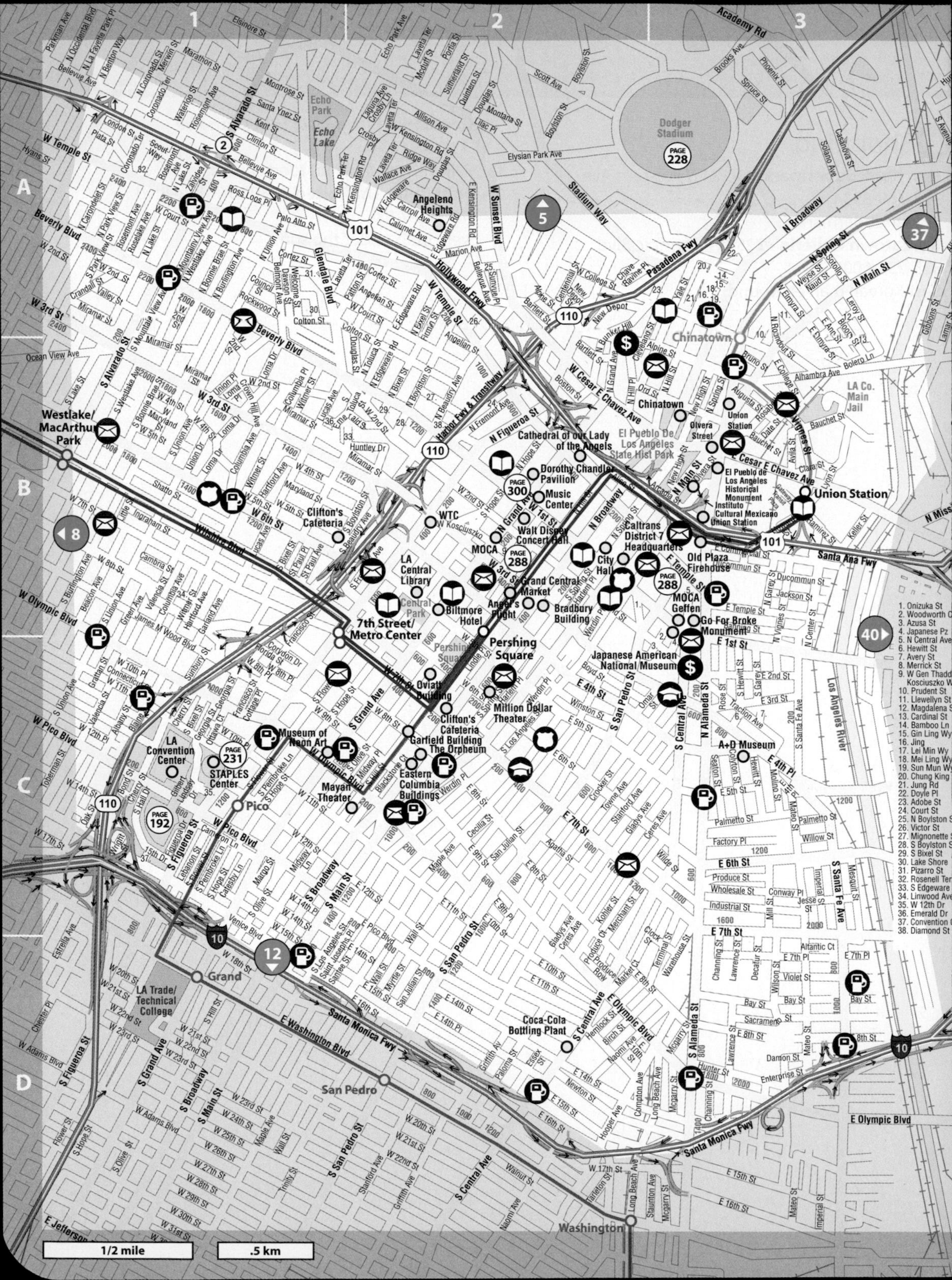
1
2
3
A
B
C
D
Dodger Stadium
PAGE 228
Echo Park
Echo Lake
Angeleno Heights
Chinatown
LA Co. Main Jail
Westlake/ MacArthur Park
Cathedral of our Lady of the Angels
El Pueblo De Los Angeles State Hist Park
Dorothy Chandler Pavilion
PAGE 300
Music Center
Union Station
El Pueblo de Los Angeles Historical Monument
Instituto Cultural Mexicano
Union Station
Olvera Street
Clifton's Cafeteria
WTC
Walt Disney Concert Hall
MOCA
PAGE 288
Caltrans District 7 Headquarters
City Hall
Old Plaza Firehouse
LA Central Library
Central Park
Biltmore Hotel
Angel's Flight
Grand Central Market
Bradbury Building
MOCA Geffen
Go For Broke Monument
7th Street/ Metro Center
Pershing Square
Japanese American National Museum
Oviatt Building
Clifton's Cafeteria
Million Dollar Theater
Museum of Neon Art
Garfield Building
The Orpheum
Eastern Columbia Buildings
Mayan Theater
A+D Museum
LA Convention Center
PAGE 231
STAPLES Center
PAGE 192
Pico
Grand
LA Trade/ Technical College
San Pedro
Coca-Cola Bottling Plant
Washington
Hollywood Fwy
Harbor Fwy & Transitway
Pasadena Fwy
Santa Ana Fwy
Santa Monica Fwy
Los Angeles River
1. Onizuka St
2. Woodworth C
3. Azusa St
4. Japanese Pz
5. N Central Ave
6. Hewitt St
7. Avery St
8. Merrick St
9. W Gen Thadd Kosciuszko W
10. Prudent St
11. Llewellyn St
12. Magdalena S
13. Cardinal St
14. Bamboo Ln
15. Gin Ling Wy
16. Jing
17. Lei Min Wy
18. Mei Ling Wy
19. Sun Mun Wy
20. Chung King
21. Jung Rd
22. Doyle Pl
23. Adobe St
24. Court St
25. N Boylston S
26. Victor St
27. Mignonette S
28. S Boylston S
29. S Bixel St
30. Lake Shore
31. Pizarro St
32. Rosenell Ter
33. S Edgeware
34. Linwood Ave
35. W 12th Dr
36. Emerald Dr
37. Convention C
38. Diamond St
1/2 mile
.5 km

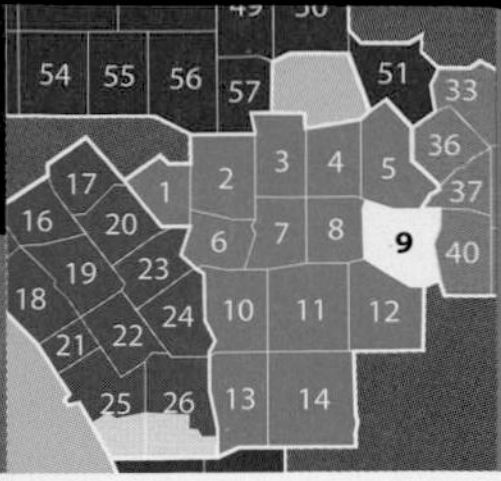

Downtown's revitalization has placed Skid Row residents on the doorsteps of yuppie loft dwellers—a juxtaposition that is (amazingly) working. Head south to find portfolio-toting FIDM students and the Fashion District, or explore Little Tokyo and Chinatown's galleries and restaurants to the north. From Downtown's epicenter, visit Gehry's **Walt Disney Concert Hall** and the **MOCA**; stroll the Jewelry District for wholesale goodies; stock up on veggies at **Grand Central Market** and (for you early birds) don't miss the vibrant **Flower District**.

oLandmarks

- **A+D Museum** • 900 E 4th St
  323-932-9393
  All things architecture—check it out here.
- **Angeleno Heights** • Carroll Ave & W Kensington Ave
  Enclave of Victorian homes. Some lavished with astonishing TLC, some not.
- **Bradbury Building** • 304 S Broadway
  Eclectic and dramatic Victorian masterpiece that was featured in *Blade Runner*.
- **Caltrans District 7 Headquarters** • 100 S Main St
  A solar behemoth that is as energy-efficient as it is commanding.
- **Cathedral of Our Lady of the Angels** •
  555 W Temple St
  213-680-5200
  Architectural Catholicism for the post-Y2K generation.
- **Central** • 630 W 5th St
  213-228-7000
  Grand downtown library.
- **Chinatown** • N Broadway
  It may not sound like much, but the slippery shrimp at Yang Chow can't be missed.
- **City Hall** • 200 N Spring St
  213-485-2121
  Got a gripe? Here's the place to start.
- **Clifton's Cafeteria** • 648 S Broadway
  213-627-1673
  Tri-level cafeteria with a woodsy theme and fake animals since 1931.
- **Coca-Cola Bottling Plant** • 1334 S Central Ave
  213-746-5555
  Designer Robert Derrah's all-American Streamline Moderne chef d'oeuvre.
- **Dorothy Chandler Pavilion** • 135 N Grand Ave
  213-972-0711
  The Oscars are gone but the LA Opera is still here.
- **Eastern Columbia Buildings** • 849 S Broadway
  Hulking turquoise Art-Deco monument.
- **El Pueblo de Los Angeles Historical Monument** •
  200 N Main St
  213-485-6855
  The real LA story, but with Mexican and Native American influence.
- **Garfield Building** • 403 W 8th St
  Another Art Deco monument from LA's past. Check out the lobby.
- **The Geffen Contemporary at MOCA** •
  152 N Central Ave
  213-626-6222
  Formerly known as the "Temporary Contemporary," the museum is still going strong.
- **Go For Broke Monument** • 160 N Central Ave
  Honoring Japanese-Americans who fought with the allies in WW2.
- **Grand Central Market** • 317 S Broadway
  213-624-2378
  Mexican specialties and more.
- **Instituto Cultural Mexicano** • 125 Paseo de la Plaza
  213-417-8384
  Dedicated to the cultural exchange between American and Mexican cultures.
- **Japanese American National Museum** • 369 E 1st St
  213-625-0414
  Chronicling the Japanese experience in the US.
- **LA Convention Center** • 1201 S Figueroa St
  213-741-1151
  The building's green glass exterior is visible for miles.
- **The Mayan** • 1038 S Hill St
  213-746-4674
  Spooky and cool. Check out the lobby if you can.
- **Millennium Biltmore Hotel** • 506 S Grand Ave
  213-624-1011
  First lady of Downtown hotels, testament to LA's architectural heritage.
- **Million Dollar Theater** • 307 S Broadway
  213-617-3600
  Historic theater; now homes and offices. Check out the pharmacy downstairs.
- **MOCA** • 250 S Grand Ave
  213-626-6222
  Received much well-deserved attention for its wildly popular Andy Warhol retrospective.
- **The Music Center** • 135 N Grand Ave
  213-972-7211
  Four music venues in one.
- **Old Plaza Firehouse** • 134 Paseo de la Plaza
  213-625-3741
  LA's oldest firehouse; haunted by Dalmatians.

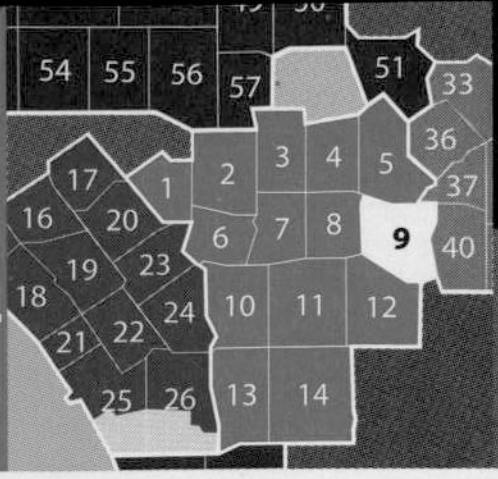

Downtown

- **Olvera Street** • Olvera St
An authentic Mexican marketplace in the heart of downtown LA.
- **The Orpheum** • 842 S Broadway
877-677-4386
Former Vaudeville house, now hosts assortment of live events.
- **Oviatt Building** • 617 S Olive St
213-379-4172
Art Deco treasure. Be sure to sneak a peek inside.
- **STAPLES Center** • 1111 S Figueroa St
213-742-7100
If the Staples folk could find a way to play baseball inside the arena, they'd lure the Dodgers too.
- **Union Station** • 800 N Alameda St
213-625-5865
Makes you wish people still traveled by train.
- **Walt Disney Concert Hall** • 141 S Grand Ave
323-850-2000
Gehry's architectural masterpiece.
- **The Westin Bonaventure Hotel** • 404 S Figueroa St
213-624-1000
John Portman's shiny, often-filmed towers.
- **World Trade Center** • 350 S Figueroa St
213-489-3337
Far less impressive than its former NY namesake, but a vital part of Downtown nonetheless.

Nightlife

- **1642 Beer & Wine** • 1642 W Temple St
213-989-6836
Usually chill beer and wine bar. Impress your date here.
- **Angel City Brewery** • 216 Alameda St
213-622-1261
Small DTLA brewery makes deliciously bitter beers.
- **Bar 107** • 107 W 4th St
213-625-7382
Kitschy hangout for jaded Hollywood outcasts and downtown dwellers.
- **Bona Vista Lounge** • 404 S Figueroa St
213-624-1000
Secret microbrewery, packed happy hour.
- **Bootleg Theater** • 2220 Beverly Blvd
213-389-3856
This cramped venue gets some big names.
- **Bordello** • 901 E 1st St
213-687-3766
Food, cocktails, jazz, blues, burlesque…
- **Broadway Bar** • 830 S Broadway
213-614-9909
Celebrating the glamorous side of cocktailing.
- **Cana Rum Bar** • 714 W Olympic Blvd
213-745-7090
Yo-ho-ho and more than 100 varieties of rum.
- **The Edison** • 108 W 2nd St
213-613-0000
Experience the roaring 20s with dancing flappers, hot jazz, and killer cocktails.
- **Elevate Lounge** • 811 Wilshire Blvd
213-623-7100
21st-floor dance party.
- **Gallery Bar and Cognac Room** • 506 S Grand Ave
213-612-1562
Specialty drink's the Black Dahlia: champagne + Guinness.
- **Golden Gopher** • 417 W 8th St
213-614-8001
Outdoor smoking alley, chandeliers, gold gopher lamps.
- **Hop Louie** • 950 Mei Ling Way
213-628-4244
Popular w/ the art crowd, cheap bevs.
- **La Cita Bar** • 336 S Hill St
213-687-7111
Rock out to indie tunes under twinkle lights.
- **Las Perlas** • 107 E 6th St
213-988-8355
Creme de cacti. Scorpion honey. Tequila. They've got it.
- **The Mayan** • 1038 S Hill St
213-746-4674
Salsa club with strict dress code, call for required attire.
- **Redwood Bar & Grill** • 316 W 2nd St
213-680-2600
Pirate-themed hangout - perfect for finding booty.
- **The Rooftop** • 550 S Flower St
213-892-8080
Make an entrance upstairs, then stumble to your room.

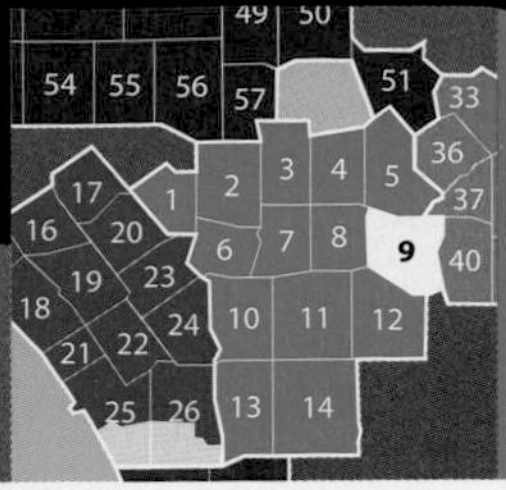

Downtown is in a weird state of transition: its restaurants and bars are some of the city's best, but residents only relatively recently got their first grocery store. Unless you're celebrating a special occasion, skip the awesome but dress-coded **Edison** and instead head to the friendly, good-beer-serving **Golden Gopher**. **Daikokuya** is your spot for the city's best ramen—just get there early to avoid the rush—and **Wurstkuche** stays at the delish forefront of the sausage-and-beer trend.

- **Seven Grand** • 515 W 7th St
  213-614-0736
  Whisky and pool tables. Enough said.
- **The Smell** • 247 S Main St
  All ages, no booze, but underground music.
- **Tony's Saloon** • 2017 E 7th St
  213-622-5523
  Nowhere location, but the drinks you'll remember.
- **Villains Tavern** • 1356 Palmetto St
  213-613-0766
  Goth-noir decor and cocktail-culture hedonism. This joint owns Halloween.

Restaurants

- **24/7 Restaurant** • 550 S Flower St
  213-892-8080 • $$$
  24-hour diner menu, post-party or in your room.
- **B.S. Taqueria** • 514 W 7th St
  213-622-3744 • $$
  Stylish, farm-fresh taqueria.
- **Baco Mercat** • 408 S Main St
  213-687-8808 • $$$
  Menu begins with the "Baco" flatbread; add an umlaut for flavor.
- **Bar Ama** • 118 W 4th St
  213-687-7000 • $$$
  Inspired-from-the-kitchen Sonoran-American comfort food.
- **Bestia** • 2121 E 7th Pl
  213-514-5724 • $$$
  Modern Italian in chic industrial setting.
- **Blossom** • 426 S Main St
  213-623-1973 • $$
  Fresh authentic Vietnamese in "blossoming" downtown neighborhood.
- **Bottega Louie** • 700 S Grand Ave
  213-802-1470 • $$$
  Fantastic space. Food's fine.
- **Broken Spanish** • 1050 S Flower St
  213-749-1460 • $$$
  Four-star Mexican cuisine.
- **Brooklyn Bagel** • 2217 Beverly Blvd
  213-413-4114 • $
  Five-decade old authentic bagelry.
- **Café Pinot** • 700 W 5th St
  213-239-6500 • $$$$$
  Downtown's classy French bistro.
- **Casa La Golondrina** • 17 W Olvera St
  213-628-4349 • $
  A historic setting for classic Mexican food complete with serenading Mariachis.
- **Checkers** • 535 S Grand Ave
  213-624-0000 • $$$$
  Upscale downtown pre-theater dining.
- **Chego!** • 727 N Broadway
  323-380-8680 • $$
  Roy Choi's fun Chinatown rice bowl spot.
- **Cicada** • 617 S Olive St
  213-488-9488 • $$$$
  California Italian.
- **Clifton's Cafeteria** • 648 S Broadway
  213-627-1673 • $
  Tri-level cafeteria with a woodsy theme and fake animals since 1931.
- **Curry House** • 123 S Onizuka St
  213-620-0855 • $$
  Japanese comfort food that will leave you fat, full, and happy.
- **Daikokuya** • 327 E 1st St
  213-626-1680 • $$
  Not your college ramen.
- **Empress Pavilion** • 988 N Hill St
  213-617-9898 • $$
  Specialty salads, sandwiches, and coffees.
- **Engine Co. No. 28** • 644 S Figueroa St
  213-624-6996 • $$$$
  Good firehouse-inspired eats.
- **Fickle** • 362 E 1st St
  213-628-1888 • $$
  Sandwiches by day, fancier at night. Confusing but good.
- **The Gorbals** • 501 S Spring St
  213-488-3408 • $$$
  Here, Top Chef fame = weird food.
- **Homegirl Cafe** • 130 Bruno St
  213-617-0380 • $$
  Staffed by recovering gangbangers. Now open for dinner.

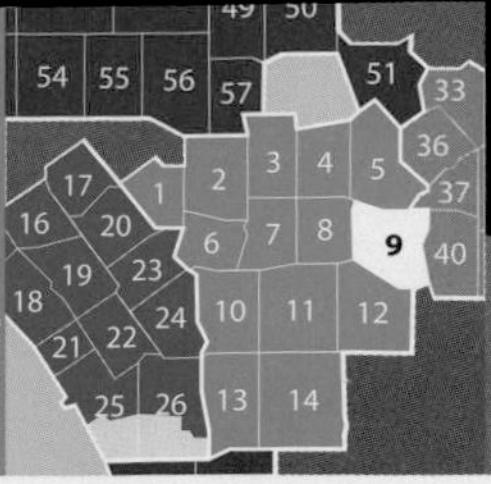

Downtown

- **Hop Li** • 526 Alpine St
  213-680-3939 • $$
  Inexpensive Chinese.
- **Hygge Bakery** • 1106 S Hope St
  213-995-5022 • $
  Danish pastries. So very buttery.
- **Johnny Rockets** • 445 S Figueroa St
  213-488-9186 • $$
  You know what you're getting, and it's going to be cheap.
- **Lazy Ox Canteen** • 241 S San Pedro St
  213-626-5299 • $$$
  Fusion defined, and almost all perfect.
- **Ledlow** • 400 S Main St
  213-687-7015 • $$$
  The young creative's diner; pastas, entrees in their comforty goodness.
- **Men Oh Tokushima** • 456 E 2nd St
  213-687-8485 • $
  When the Daikokuya wait is long, head here.
- **Mendocino Farms** • 444 S Flower St
  213-627-3262 • $$
  Perhaps the best sandwiches in the world.
- **Mikawaya** • 118 Japanese Village Plz Mall
  213-624-1681 • $
  Delicious, sweet Japanese treats! Gelato mochi is the best.
- **Nick & Stef's Steakhouse** • 330 S Hope St
  213-680-0330 • $$$$$
  Old-fashioned steaks in an ultra-modern downtown setting.
- **Noe** • 251 S Olive St
  213-356-4100 • $$$$
  Omni Hotel's upscale Japanese-American.
- **Oomasa** • 100 Japanese Village Plaza Mall
  213-623-9048 • $$
  Cozy, late-night, traditional Japanese fare.
- **Original Pantry Café** • 877 S Figueroa St
  213-972-9279 • $
  All-American diner open 24 hours since 1924.
- **Orsa & Winston** • 122 W 4th St
  213-687-0300 • $$$$
  Affordable Japanese-Italian tasting menus defying obvious Marco Polo tropes.
- **Pacific Dining Car** • 1310 W 6th St
  213-483-6000 • $$$$
  Steak all day, all night.
- **Patina** • 141 S Grand Ave
  213-972-3331 • $$$$
  French-Californian fusion.
- **Pete's Café & Bar** • 400 S Main St
  213-617-1000 • $$$
  Great bar, big drinks, tasty American fare.
- **Philippe the Original** • 1001 N Alameda St
  213-628-3781 • $
  The best French dips in town. Totally awesome.
- **Pitfire Artisan Pizza** • 108 W 2nd St
  213-808-1200 • $
  Local ingredients for discerning locals.
- **Plum Tree Inn** • 913 N Broadway
  213-613-1819 • $$
  Delicious Chinese.
- **R23** • 923 E 2nd St
  213-687-7178 • $$$$
  Stylish sushi in the LA arts district.
- **Redbird** • 114 E 2nd St
  213-788-1191 • $$$$
  Sharp, stylish, to-the-point ecumenical cuisine.
- **Saffron** • 505 S Flower St
  213-488-9754 • $
  Serving straightforward Indian dishes to the downtown lunch crowd.
- **Señor Fish** • 422 E 1st St
  213-625-0566 • $
  Tacos de fish.
- **Suehiro Café** • 337 E 1st St
  213-626-9132 • $$
  Comfort food, Japanese-style, with comic books.
- **Sushi-Gen** • 422 E 2nd St
  213-617-0552 • $$
  Excellent sushi favored by locals.
- **Syrup Desserts** • 611 S Spring St
  213-488-5136 • $
  For your sweetest tooth.
- **TOT** • 345 E 2nd St
  213-680-0344 • $$
  Good lunch spot for affordable Japanese. Try one of the tuna bowls.

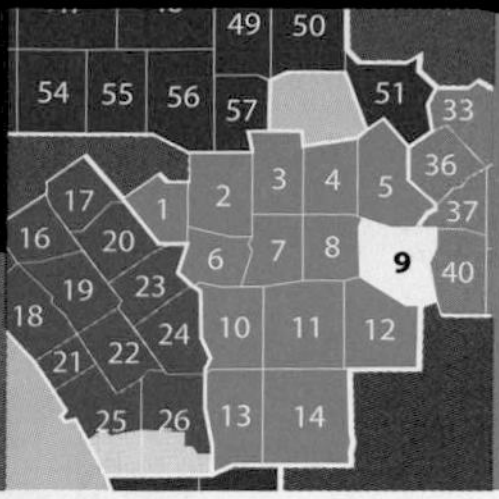

Philippe the Original serves its famous French dip sandwiches at long tables on a sawdust-covered dining room floor. During the inevitable exodus from a Staples Center event, don't pass up the **Original Pantry Café**, a 24-hour diner that claims to have never closed its doors. **Lazy Ox** offers scrumptious and hearty food from around the world, on plates both small and large. In Little Tokyo, **Sushi-Gen** can't be beat.

- **Traxx** • 800 N Alameda St
  213-625-1999 • $$
  As elegant and exquisite as Union Station itself.
- **Tribal Café** • 1651 W Temple St
  213-483-4458 • $
  Filipino friendliness.
- **Via** • 451 Gin Ling Way
  213-617-1481 • $
  Small Vietnamese café mostly occupied by young artists and gallerists.
- **Water Grill** • 544 S Grand Ave
  213-891-0900 • $$$
  Expense-account dining to impress. And it's delicious.
- **Wurstkuche** • 800 E 3rd St
  213-687-4444 • $$
  Have some bier with your sausage.
- **Yang Chow** • 819 N Broadway
  213-625-0811 • $$
  Popular Chinese chain.
- **Zip Izakaya** • 744 E 3rd St
  213-680-3770 • $$
  Fusion sushi in the heart of the Artists' District.

Shopping

- **American Apparel** • 363 E 2nd St
  213-617-7222
  Simple clothing made sweatshop-free.
- **American Apparel Factory Store** • 747 Warehouse St
  213-488-0226
  Find irregular or overstock items at a fraction of retail price.
- **Berger Beads** • 413 E 8th St
  213-627-8783
  More vintage beads than you could possibly imagine.
- **California Market Center** • 110 E 9th St
  213-630-3600
  Gift, home accent, and fashion showrooms, as well as a handful of restaurants.
- **Fig at 7th** • 735 S Figueroa St
  213-955-7150
  Downtown's only real shopping mall.
- **Grand Central Market** • 317 S Broadway
  213-624-2378
  An LA legend since 1917 with produce, fish, meat, and ice cream all under one roof.
- **Los Angeles Flower Market** • 766 Wall St
  213-627-3696
  Say it with flowers, cheaply.
- **Michaels** • 219 Glendale Blvd
  818-291-0944
  Pipe cleaners, felt, and puff paints galore!
- **MOCA Store** • 250 S Grand Ave
  213-621-1710
  Museum store's a haven for design.
- **Moskatels** • 733 San Julian St
  213-689-4590
  Massive craft and flower store.
- **Ooga Booga** • 943 N Broadway
  213-617-1105
  Cool store featuring LA artists.
- **popKiller Second** • 343 E 2nd St
  213-625-1372
  When you"re in Little Tokyo and you need a with-it belt buckle…
- **Pussy & Pooch** • 564 S Main St
  213-438-0900
  Pethouse and Pawbar—grooming and gifting for the Angeleno animal.
- **The Santee Alley** • 210 E Olympic Blvd
  310-203-0101
  The perfect place to find convincing "kate spate" or "Prado" handbags.
- **Shan Fabrics** • 733 Ceres Ave
  213-891-9393
  They carry Vlisco (the Dutch rolls royce of African wax resist fabric!!).
- **Welcome Hunters** • 454 Jung Jing Rd
  213-687-9905
  Happy-to-help fashion consultation for happenin' youth.

Map 10 • Baldwin Hills

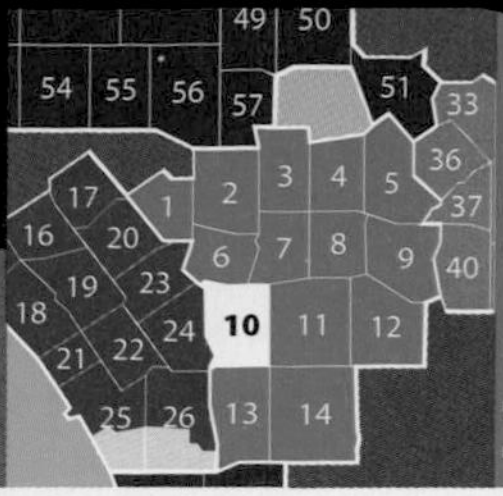

Baldwin Hills is a well-to-do African American community whose first claim to fame was hosting the world's first Olympic Village in 1932. Post-Olympics, this mid-city swath of rolling hills became the gilded, exclusive enclave of the rich and famous—called the "Black Beverly Hills." Today's roster of homeowners now includes more doctors, dentists, lawyers, and other professionals than top entertainment and sports stars.

Landmarks

- **Kenneth Hahn State Recreation Area •**
  4100 S La Cienega Blvd
  323-298-3660
  Most people only think of this park as they're driving to LAX. That's a mistake.

Nightlife

- **Café Fais Do-Do** • 5257 W Adams Blvd
  323-931-4636
  Cajun food, eclectic music.
- **The Living Room** • 2636 Crenshaw Blvd
  323-735-8748
  Cocktails and live music.
- **Mandrake** • 2692 S La Cienega Blvd
  310-837-3297
  Think art students talking theory bar.

Restaurants

- **JR's Barbeque** • 3055 S La Cienega Blvd
  310-837-6838 • $$
  One of the top LA BBQ spots; Memphis style.

Shopping

- **Berbere World Imports** • 3049 S La Cienega Blvd
  310-842-3842
  Old world furniture and accessories from all corners of the Mediterranean.
- **Graphaids** • 3030 S La Cienega Blvd
  310-204-1212
  If you're not an artist, this store will make you wish you were.
- **Normandie Bakery** • 3022 S Cochran Ave
  323-939-5528
  A Parisian oasis.
- **Tokidoki** • 5655 W Adams Blvd
  323-930-0555
  Toys, skateboards, bags for anime fiends.

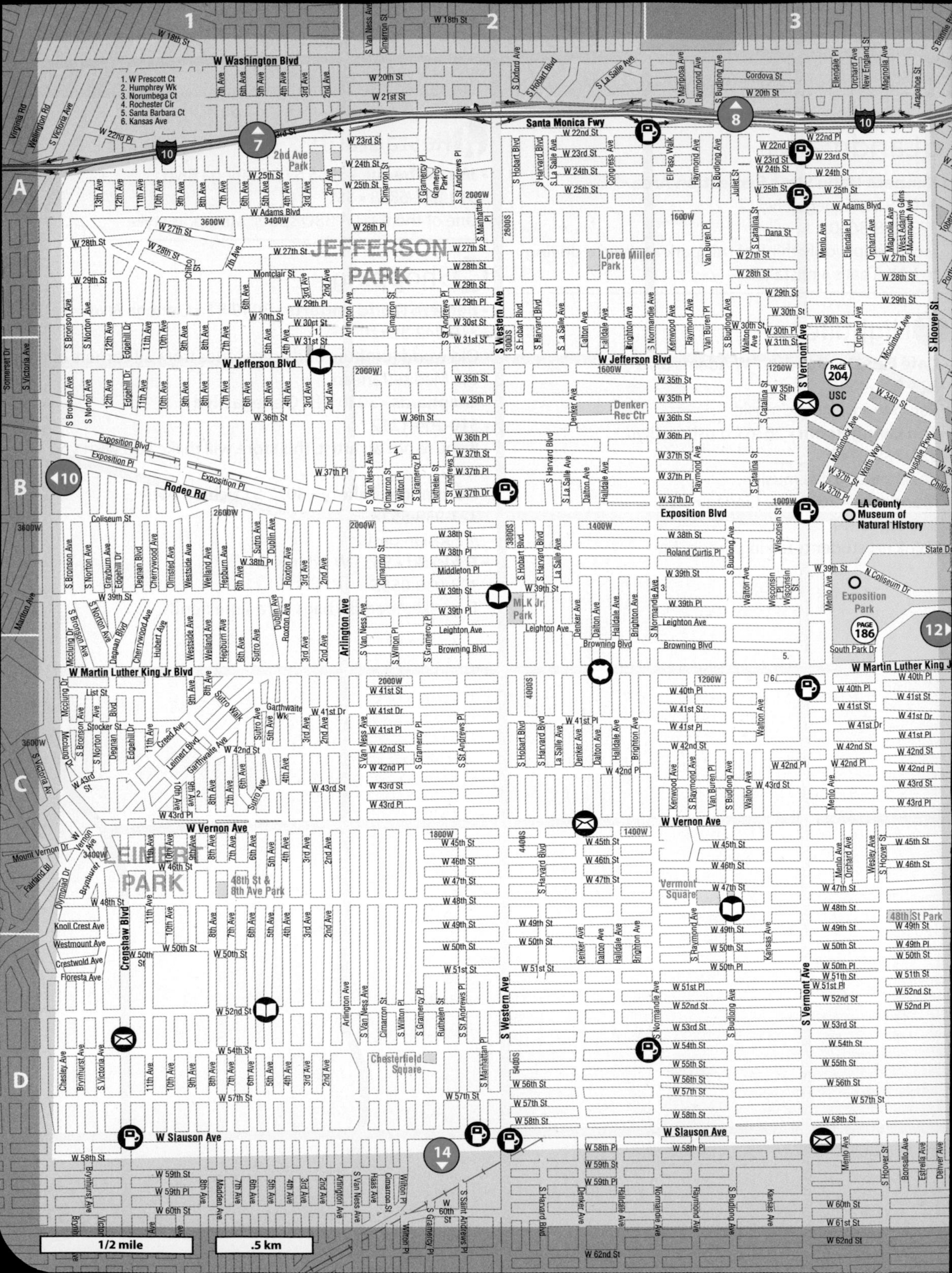
N
1
2
3
A
B
C
D
W Washington Blvd
1. W Prescott Ct
2. Humphrey Wk
3. Norumbega Ct
4. Rochester Cir
5. Santa Barbara Ct
6. Kansas Ave
Santa Monica Fwy
10
7
8
2nd Ave Park
JEFFERSON PARK
Loren Miller Park
W Jefferson Blvd
W Adams Blvd
S Western Ave
S Vermont Ave
S Hoover St
S Normandie Ave
Arlington Ave
Crenshaw Blvd
USC
PAGE 204
Denker Rec Ctr
Exposition Blvd
Exposition Pl
Rodeo Rd
LA County Museum of Natural History
Exposition Park
PAGE 186
MLK Jr Park
W Martin Luther King Jr Blvd
W Vernon Ave
LEIMERT PARK
48th St & 8th Ave Park
Vermont Square
48th St Park
Chesterfield Square
W Slauson Ave
14
12
1/2 mile
.5 km

This area gets congested during college football season, when drunken cardinal-and-gold-bedecked USC fans cheer on the Trojans. There's plenty to do on campus, whether or not you're enrolled, including cheap movies, free concerts, elevated lectures and the surprisingly entertaining science center. On the southwest side, the Leimert Park arts and shopping district is a low-key area, excellent for rare finds.

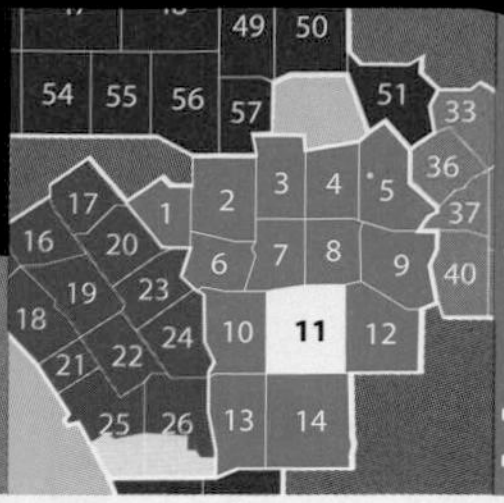

Landmarks

- **Exposition Park** • 700 Exposition Park Dr
  213-765-5369
  Forget the Coliseum and check out the Rose Garden. Or not.
- **Natural History Museum of Los Angeles County** •
  900 Exposition Blvd
  213-763-3466
  Kids just love the dinosaur fossils.
- **University of Southern California** •
  S Vermont Ave & Exposition Blvd
  213-740-2311
  Cardinal and gold private option, since 1880.

Nightlife

- **Babe's & Ricky's Inn** • 4339 Leimert Blvd
  323-295-9112
  Blues music.

Restaurants

- **Aunt Rosa Lee's Mississippi Soul Food** •
  2781 S Western Ave
  323-733-8586 • $$
  Real soul food.
- **Harold & Belle's** • 2920 W Jefferson Blvd
  323-735-9023 • $$$
  Great Cajun food.
- **La Barca** • 2414 S Vermont Ave
  323-735-6567 • $$
  Mexican.
- **Phillip's Barbecue** • 4307 Leimert Blvd
  323-292-7613 • $$
  Southern-style ribs in southern LA.
- **Pizza Moon** • 2619 S Western Ave
  323-733-2222 • $
  Pizzas, burgers, Mexican dishes, etc., for sit-down, takeout, or delivery.

Shopping

- **Zambezi Bazaar** • 4334 Degnan Blvd
  323-299-6383
  African-American specialty store.

Map 12 • South Central East

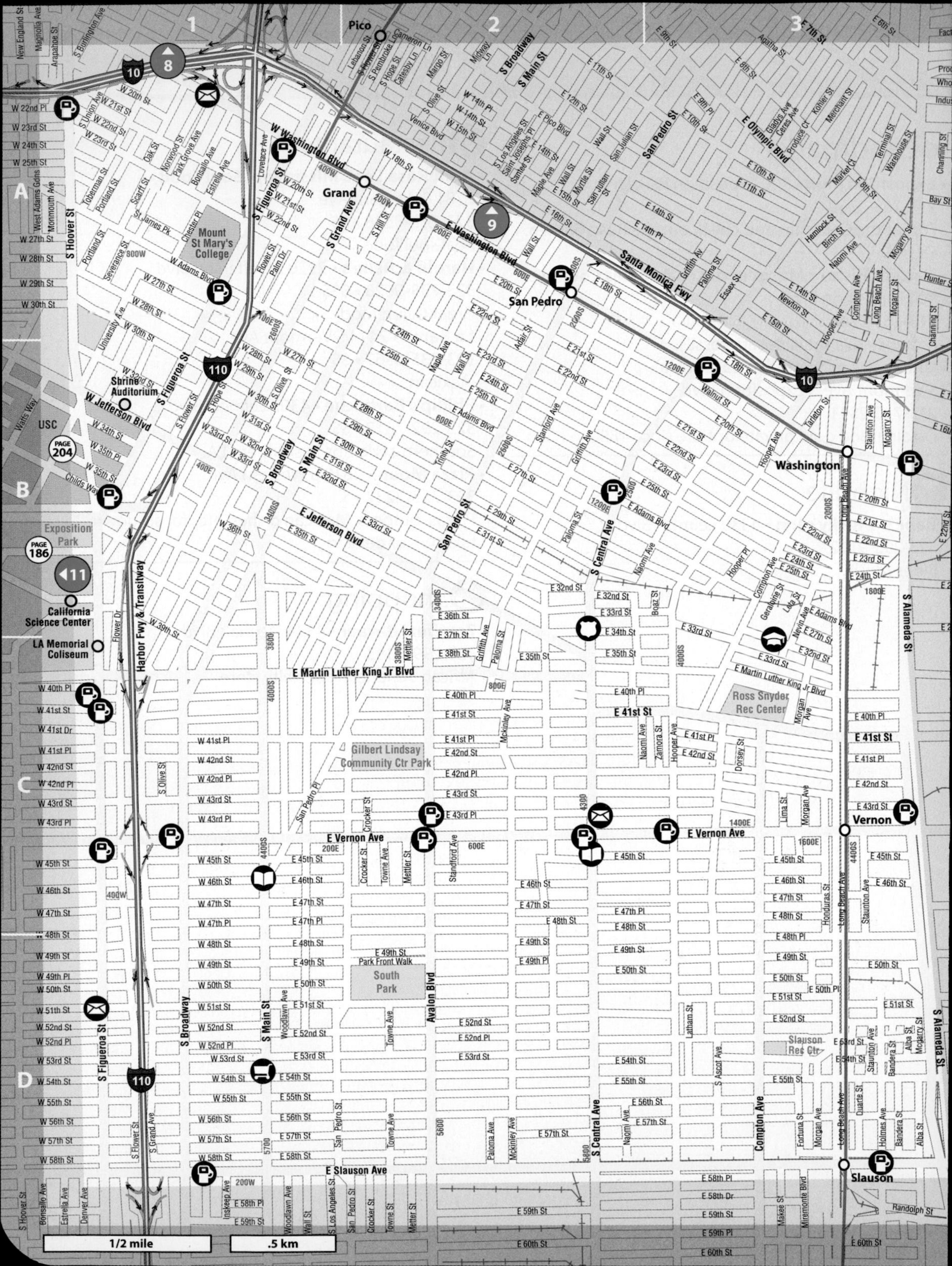

South LA. Once known as South Central LA. Perhaps you've heard of it. Crime and poverty persist here, next door to one of the nation's most high-status universities. Still home to a predominantly African-American and Latino population, this area has nevertheless felt downtown's encroaching development, and the uneasiness of shifting demographics. Watch your back after dark, but give it up for the charities and activists working to make things more peaceful.

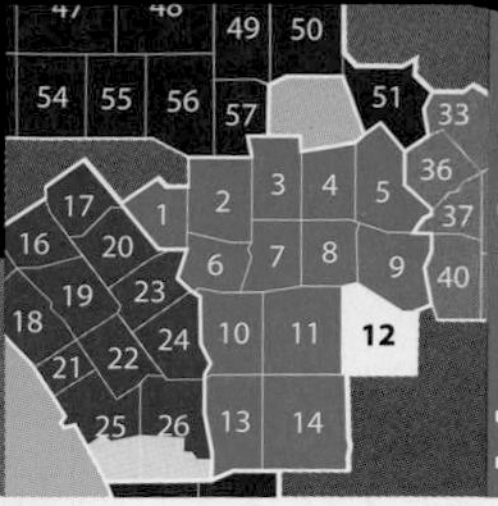

oLandmarks

- **California Science Center** • 700 Exposition Park Dr
  323-724-3623
  Come for the exhibits and high-wire bicycle acts.
- **LA Memorial Coliseum** • 3939 S Figueroa St
  213-747-7111
  We're still waiting for that LA football team…
- **Shrine Auditorium & Expo Hall** •
  665 W Jefferson Blvd
  213-748-5116
  The mosque design makes it one of the neighborhood's most visible buildings.

Restaurants

- **29th Street Café** • 2827 S Hoover St
  213-746-2929 • $$
  The spot in South Central for brunch.
- **Chano's Drive-In** • 3000 S Figueroa St
  213-747-3944 • $
  Drive-in to dive into authentic Mexican food.
- **Pasta Roma** • 2827 S Figueroa St
  213-742-0303 • $
  University student hangout for cheap Italian.

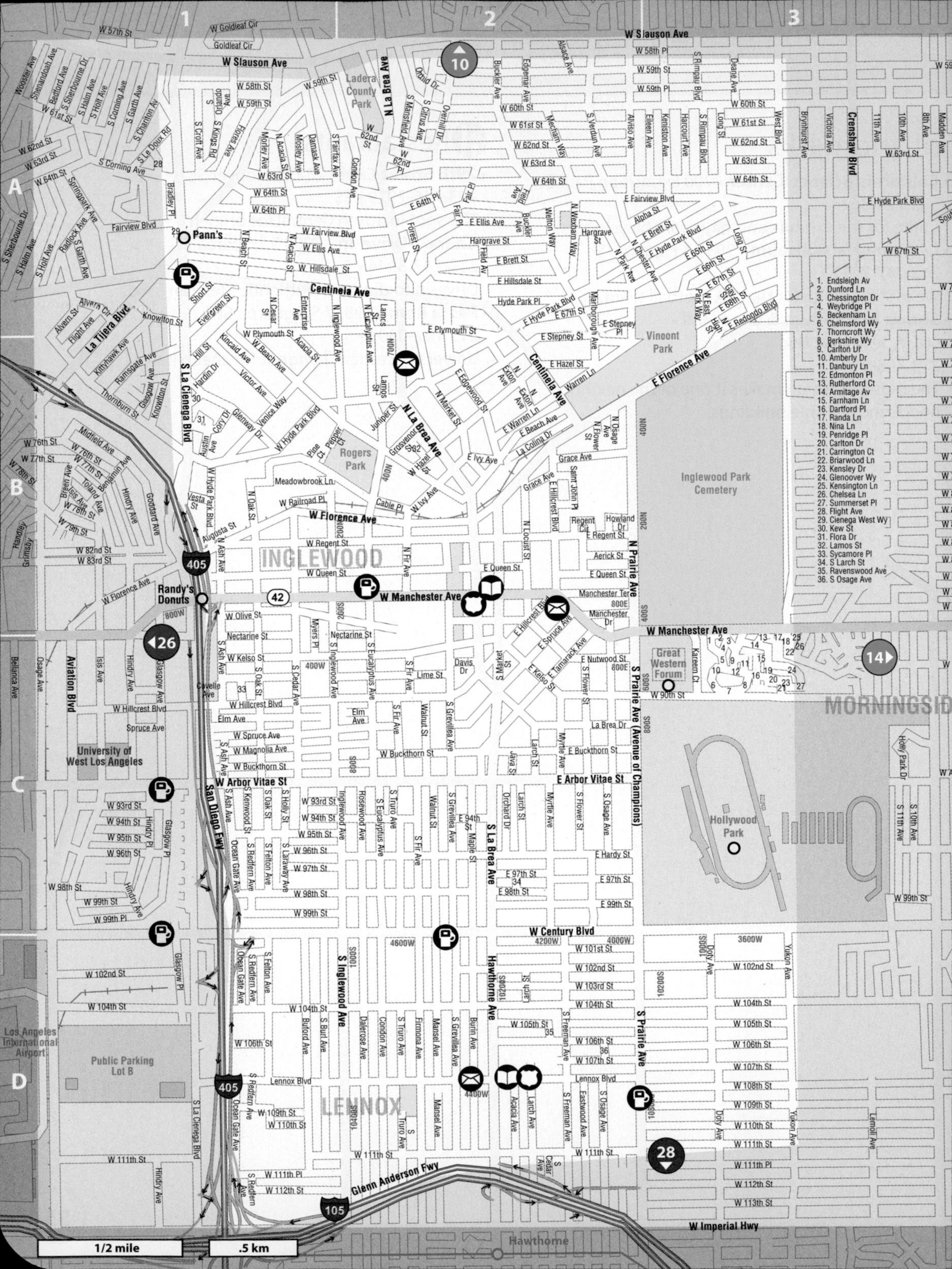
N
1
2
3
A
B
C
D
10
26
14
28
405
105
42
W Slauson Ave
W Goldleaf Cir
Goldleaf Cir
W 57th St
Ladera County Park
N La Brea Ave
W 58th St
W 59th St
W 59th Pl
W 60th St
W 61st St
W 62nd St
W 63rd St
W 64th St
W 64th Pl
Fairview Blvd
Pann's
W Fairview Blvd
W Ellis Ave
W Hillsdale St
Centinela Ave
La Tijera Blvd
Knowlton St
W Plymouth St
E Plymouth St
Hyde Park Pl
E Hyde Park Blvd
E Stepney St
Vinoont Park
E Florence Ave
E Hazel St
Warren Ln
S La Cienega Blvd
W Hyde Park Blvd
Rogers Park
Inglewood Park Cemetery
Meadowbrook Ln
W Railroad Pl
Cable Pl
W Florence Ave
W Regent St
INGLEWOOD
E Queen St
W Queen St
Randy's Donuts
W Manchester Ave
Manchester Ter
W Olive St
Nectarine St
W Kelso St
Lime St
Davis Dr
Great Western Forum
W 90th St
MORNINGSIDE
Aviation Blvd
W Hillcrest Blvd
Spruce Ave
University of West Los Angeles
Elm Ave
W Spruce Ave
W Magnolia Ave
W Buckthorn St
E Buckthorn St
W Arbor Vitae St
E Arbor Vitae St
La Brea Dr
S Prairie Ave (Avenue of Champions)
Hollywood Park
San Diego Fwy
S La Brea Ave
W 93rd St
W 94th St
W 95th St
W 96th St
W 97th St
W 98th St
W 99th St
W 99th Pl
E Hardy St
E 97th St
E 98th St
E 99th St
W Century Blvd
W 101st St
W 102nd St
W 103rd St
W 104th St
W 105th St
W 106th St
W 107th St
W 108th St
W 109th St
W 110th St
W 111th St
W 111th Pl
W 112th St
W 113th St
Hawthorne Ave
S Inglewood Ave
Crenshaw Blvd
Los Angeles International Airport
Public Parking Lot B
Lennox Blvd
LENNOX
Glenn Anderson Fwy
W Imperial Hwy
Hawthorne
1/2 mile
.5 km
1. Endsleigh Av
2. Dunford Ln
3. Chessington Dr
4. Weybridge Pl
5. Beckenham Ln
6. Chelmsford Wy
7. Thorncroft Wy
8. Berkshire Wy
9. Carlton Dr
10. Amberly Dr
11. Danbury Ln
12. Edmonton Pl
13. Rutherford Ct
14. Armitage Av
15. Farnham Ln
16. Dartford Pl
17. Randa Ln
18. Nina Ln
19. Penridge Pl
20. Carlton Dr
21. Carrington Ct
22. Briarwood Ln
23. Kensley Dr
24. Glenoover Wy
25. Kensington Ln
26. Chelsea Ln
27. Summerset Pl
28. Flight Ave
29. Cienega West Wy
30. Kew St
31. Flora Dr
32. Lamos St
33. Sycamore Pl
34. S Larch St
35. Ravenswood Ave
36. S Osage Ave

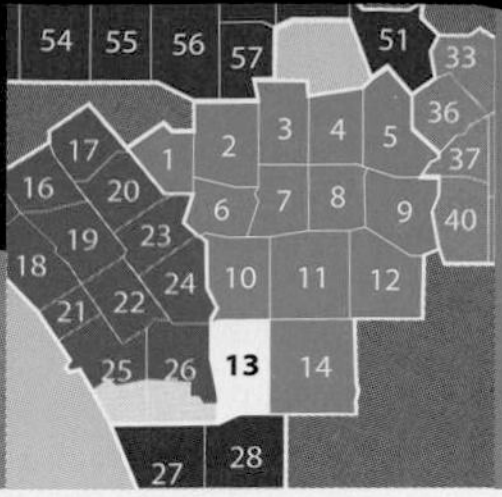

While North Inglewood's charming, sylvan avenues played stunt double for the Yourtown, Midwest backdrop of Wayne's World, much of the city's residual grittiness reflects the loss of its adored Lakers to the Staples Center (Map 9). But if Laker great Magic Johnson has his way, Inglewood will be just fine. Johnson gets the assist for bringing a burst of commercial energy to the area. Grabbing a selection from **Randy's Donuts** before you hop on your plane at LAX is the best way to show whoever you're visiting that you care (about tasty breakfast sweets). True friends make sure at least one is maple-frosted.

oLandmarks

- **Betfair Hollywood Park** • 1050 S Prairie Ave
  310-419-1549
  When you've just got to play the ponies…
- **Great Western Forum** •
  S Prairie Ave & Manchester Terrace
  310-330-7300
  The Lakers' and Kings' former home is now the Faithful Central Bible Church. There's irony for you.
- **Pann's** • 6710 La Tijera Blvd
  323-776-3770
  One of the best remaining examples in the country of '50s coffee shop design—and they serve a down-home tasty breakfast.
- **Randy's Donuts** • 805 W Manchester Blvd
  310-645-4707
  Giant donut perched on top of this beloved donut stop.

Nightlife

- **Betfair Hollywood Park** • 1050 S Prairie Ave
  310-419-1549
  Race track, nightclub, live music, games, etc.

Restaurants

- **Ibex Ethiopian Restaurant** • 630 N La Brea Ave
  310-673-3392 • $$
  Traditional Ethiopian cuisine, like we'd really know.
- **La Costa Mariscos** • 597 S La Brea Ave
  310-672-2083 • $
  Latin-styled fast food with the accent on seafood.
- **La Perla** • 10623 S Prairie Ave
  310-677-5277 • $$
  Ernestina Murillo's kitchen serves up Latin American cuisine.
- **Little Belize** • 217 E Nutwood St
  310-674-0696 • $$
  Get your Belizean fix on at this inexpensive spot.
- **Pann's** • 6710 La Tijera Blvd
  323-776-3770 • $$
  One of the best remaining examples of '50s coffee shop design.
- **Thai Plate** • 10311 Hawthorne Blvd
  310-412-0111 • $$
  This neighborhood-style restaurant's specialty is Northern Thai cuisine.

Shopping

- **Zahra's Books & Things** • 900 N La Brea Ave
  310-330-1300
  African-American bookstore that hosts great readings and events.

Map 14 • Inglewood East / Morningside Park

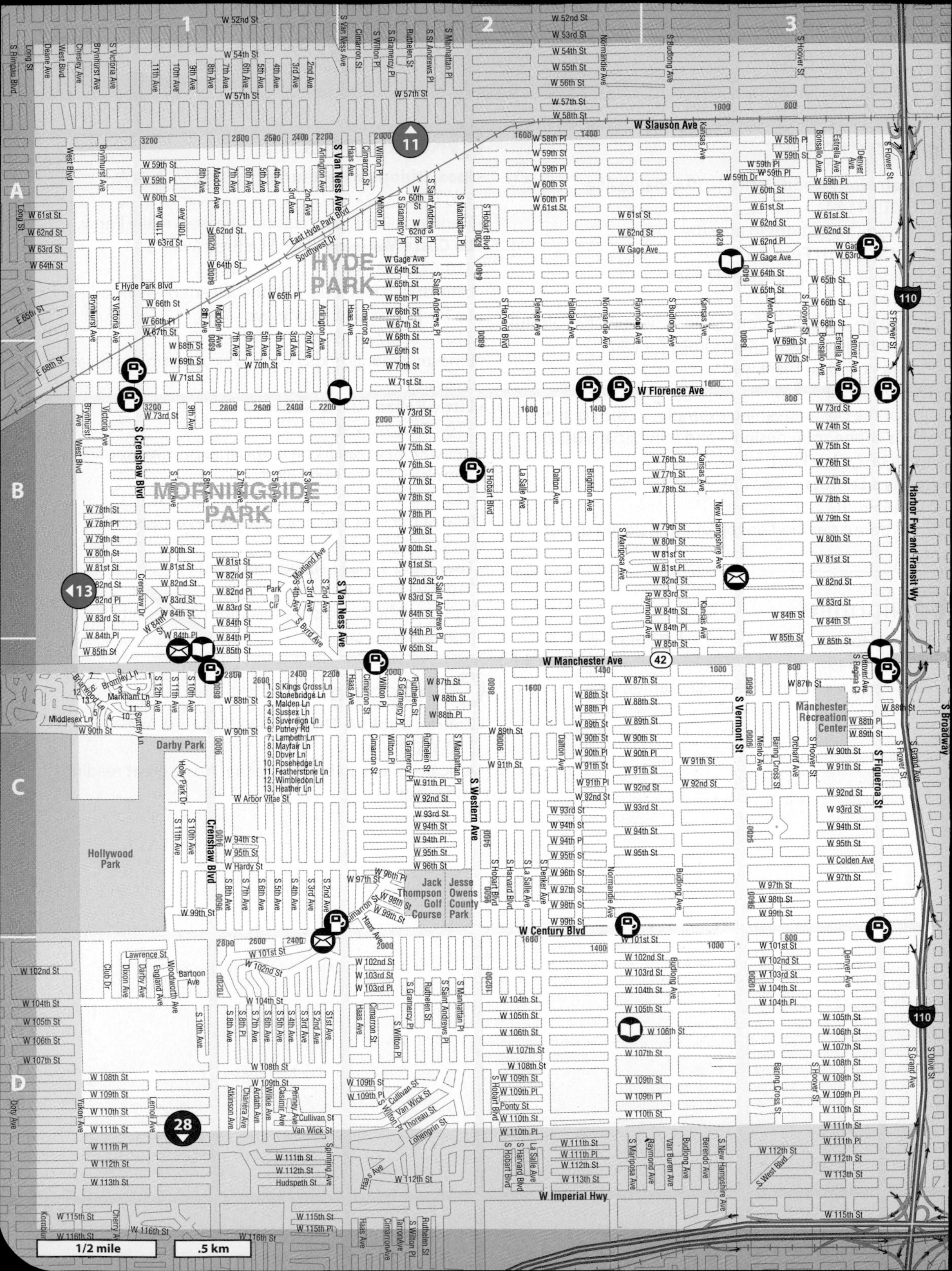

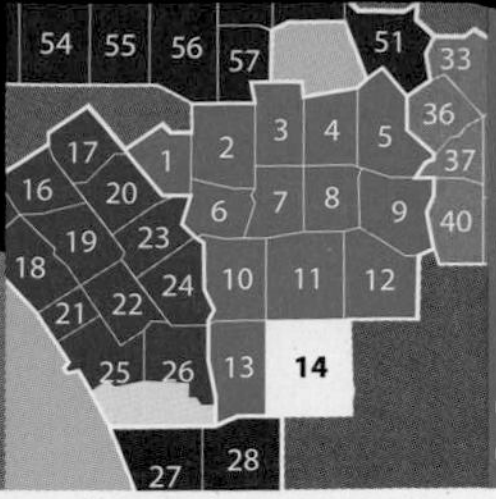

Over time, Morningside Park has shed its inner-city vibe and become more like the neighboring communities in the South Bay. Residential areas here are bisected by commercial throughways filled with shopping centers anchored by big-box retailers like Costco. That said, these mini-malls still make room for the local mom-and-pop businesses.

Restaurants

- **M&M Soul Food** • 3300 W Manchester Blvd
  310-673-5031 • $$
  Consistently delicious.

Shopping

- **Costco** • 3560 W Century Blvd
  310-242-2777
  Buy it in bulk.

N
1
2
3
A
B
C
D
Topanga State Park
PAGE 200
Will Rogers State Historic Park
Temescal Canyon Rd
Rustic Canyon Channel
Sullivan Fire Rd
Farmers Fire Rd
Bayliss Rd
N Westridge Rd
W Boca De
Hilltop W
Melhill Way
Old Ran
Alta Mura Rd
San Onofre Dr
Capri Dr
San Remo Dr
Umeo Rd
Amalfi Dr
Sorrento Dr
Monaco Dr
16
D Este Dr
Lucca Dr
Fermo Dr
Romany Dr
Pavia Pl
Jonesboro Dr
Evans Rd
Will Rogers State Park Rd
Oracle Pl
Paskenta Rd
Marinette Rd
Chautauqua Blvd
Goucher St
Berea Pl
Monument St
Mckendree Ave
Rimmer Ave
Whitfiled Ave
Bestor Blvd
Temescal Canyon Park
Albright St
Charm Acres Pl
Embury St
Fiske St
Galloway St
Iliff St
Kagawa St
N Villa Woods Dr
S Villa Grove Dr
Villa View Dr
Villa Grove Dr
Rivas Cyn
W Sunset Blvd
Rustic Canyon Rd
Ravoli Dr
Napoli Dr
Minorca Dr
Corsica Dr
Spezia Pl
Riviera Country Club
Toulon Dr
Luna Vista Dr
Shadow Mountain Dr
El Hito Cir
Lachman Ln
Chamel Ln
Tellem Dr
Las Pasas Rd
Las Lomas Ave
Anoka Dr
Bienveneda Ave
Maroney Ln
Glenhaven Dr
Enchanted Way
Jacon Way
Akron St
Muskingum Ave
El Medio Ave
Palisades Dr
Via Santa Ynez
Marquez Ave
Baylor St
Las Casas Ave
Almar Ave
Junaluska Wy
Antioch St
Bashford St
Carey Rd
Hartzell St
Drummond St
Galloupe Pl
Bowdoin St
Radcliffe Ave
Haverford Ave
Northfield St
Temecula St
Wildomar St
Miami Way
Pamela Ave
Lake Shrine Temple
PACIFIC PALISADES
Livorno Dr
Berry Pl
Marquez Pl
Mantua Rd
Arno Wy
Trino Wy
Trino Club Dr
Adero Wy
Pintoresca Dr
Grenola St
Muskingum Pl
Puerto Del Mar
Ysidro Pl
Seabec Cir
Erskine Dr
Asilomar Blvd
Carthage St
Temescal Canyon Park
Via De La Paz
Swarthmore Ave
Hampden Pl
Patterson Pl
Ocampo Dr
Toyopa Dr
Palisades Park
Chapala Dr
Frontera Dr
El Cerco Pl
Pampas Ricas Blvd
Alma Real Dr
Almoloya Dr
Borgos Pl
Greentree Rd
Ranch Ln
Brooktree Rd
Rustic Creek Ln
Latimer Rd
Haldeman Rd
Rustic Canyon Rec Center
Hightree Rd
Alisal Ct
Parma Pl
Gale Pl
San Vicente Blvd
Woodacres Rd
Esparta Wy
Ermont Pl
Mesita Wy
San Lorenzo St
Kingman Ave
Dryad Rd
Attilia Rd
Entrada Dr
Stassi Ln
Adelaide Pl
Adelaide Dr
18
Georgina Ave
Brentwood Ter
Carlyle Ave
Marguerita Ave
15th St
16th St
17th St
12th St
11th St
10th St
9th St
7th St
6th St
5th St
4th St
3rd St
2nd St
Lincoln Blvd
Montana Ave
Idaho Ave
Washington Ave
California Ave
Wilshire Bl
Ocean Ave
Palisades Beach Rd
Alta Ave
Palisades Ave
Santa Monica Steps
Ocean Way
Mabery Rd
Channel Rd
Sage Ln
Sumac Ln
Spoleto Dr
Upper Mesa Rd
Mesa Rd
Sycamore Rd
Vance St
Eames House
Mar Rd
W Channel Rd
E Rustic Rd
W Rustic Rd
Hillside Ln
Chautauqua Blvd
Alva Dr
Camarosa Dr
La Cumbre Dr
Ramos Pl
Corona Del
Altata Dr
Earlham St
Lombard Ave
De Pauw St
Mount Holyoke Ave
Beirut Ave
Friends St
Via De Las Olas
Palisades Park
Pacific Coast Hwy
Will Rogers State Beach
Terrace Dr
Seaview Dr
Tahiti Ave
Bali Ln
Aloha Dr
Copra Ln
Samoa Wy
Vista Ter
1. Drift Wood Dr
2. Drift Wood Pl
3. Terrace Pl
4. West View Ln
5. Ocean Vw
6. Pacific Pl
7. Kontiki Wy
8. Coco Pl
9. Kiki Pl
10. Haney Pl
11. Dobbins Pl
12. Channel Ln
13. Short St
14. La Cruz Dr
Pacific Ocean
1/2 mile
.5 km

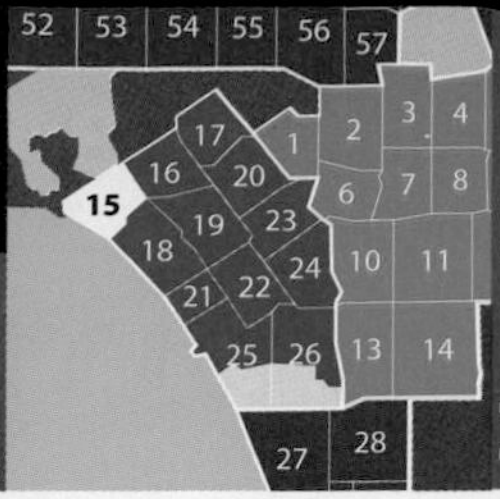

With streets meandering lazily through the hills, sweeping ocean views that cover the waterfront, and jaw-dropping canyons, Pacific Palisades earns its sticker-shock asking price. It's peopled with celebrities, executives, and a lot of high-fiving real estate agents. This close-yet-removed enclave is spooned between the Pacific Ocean and Topanga State Park, and couldn't be better for a romantic after-dinner stroll.

oLandmarks

- **Eames House** • 203 Chautauqua Blvd
  310-459-9663
  Iconic house that influenced modern architecture in the 'burbs.
- **Santa Monica Steps** • 4th St & Adelaide Dr
  Climbing these is the most LA workout you can ever hope to have.
- **Self-Realization Fellowship Lake Shrine Temple** • 17190 W Sunset Blvd
  310-454-4114
  Stunning gardens.
- **Will Rogers State Historic Park** • Sunset Blvd
  310-454-8212
  Hiking, picnicking, and polo. Yes, polo.

Nightlife

- **Pearl Dragon** • 15229 W Sunset Blvd
  310-459-9790
  Cocktail lounge from Voda owners, full liquor license.

Restaurants

- **Il Ristorante di Giorgio Baldi** • 114 W Channel Rd
  310-573-1660 • $$$$
  Memorable Tuscan cooking.
- **Kay 'n Dave's** • 15246 W Sunset Blvd
  310-459-8118 • $$
  Healthy Mexican with a family-friendly atmosphere.
- **Marix Tex Mex Café** • 118 Entrada Dr
  310-459-8596 • $$$
  Perfect for post-beach margaritas and tacos. Sandy patrons OK.
- **Modo Mio Cucina Rustica** • 15200 W Sunset Blvd
  310-459-0979 • $$$
  Oddly office-like outside, quiet, authentic, well-executed Italian inside.
- **Patrick's Roadhouse** • 106 Entrada Dr
  310-459-4544 • $$
  Quintessential place for breakfast at the beach.
- **Robeks** • 15280 Antioch St
  310-230-3991 • $
  Juice, salads, sandwiches.

Shopping

- **Bentons the Sport Shop** • 1038 Swarthmore Ave
  310-459-8451
  Beach clothing and equipment.
- **Canyon Beachwear** • 106 Entrada Dr
  310-459-5070
  Bathing-suit-a-rama.
- **Elyse Walker** • 15306 Antioch St
  310-230-8882
  When you want to dress cool. But not too cool.
- **Gelson's The Super Market** • 15424 W Sunset Blvd
  310-459-4483
  When Trader Joe's won't cut it. Excellent foreign foods.
- **Gift Garden Antiques** • 15266 Antioch St
  310-459-4114
  Fine gifts from a smattering of decades.
- **The Prince's Table** • 863 Swarthmore Ave
  310-573-3667
  Gifts and original paintings.
- **Puzzle Zoo** • 1041 Swarthmore Ave
  310-454-8648
  Toys to educate or palliate.
- **Vivian's Unique Boutique** • 875 Vía De La Paz
  310-573-1326
  Vivian hands out free earrings with purchase.

Map 16 • Brentwood

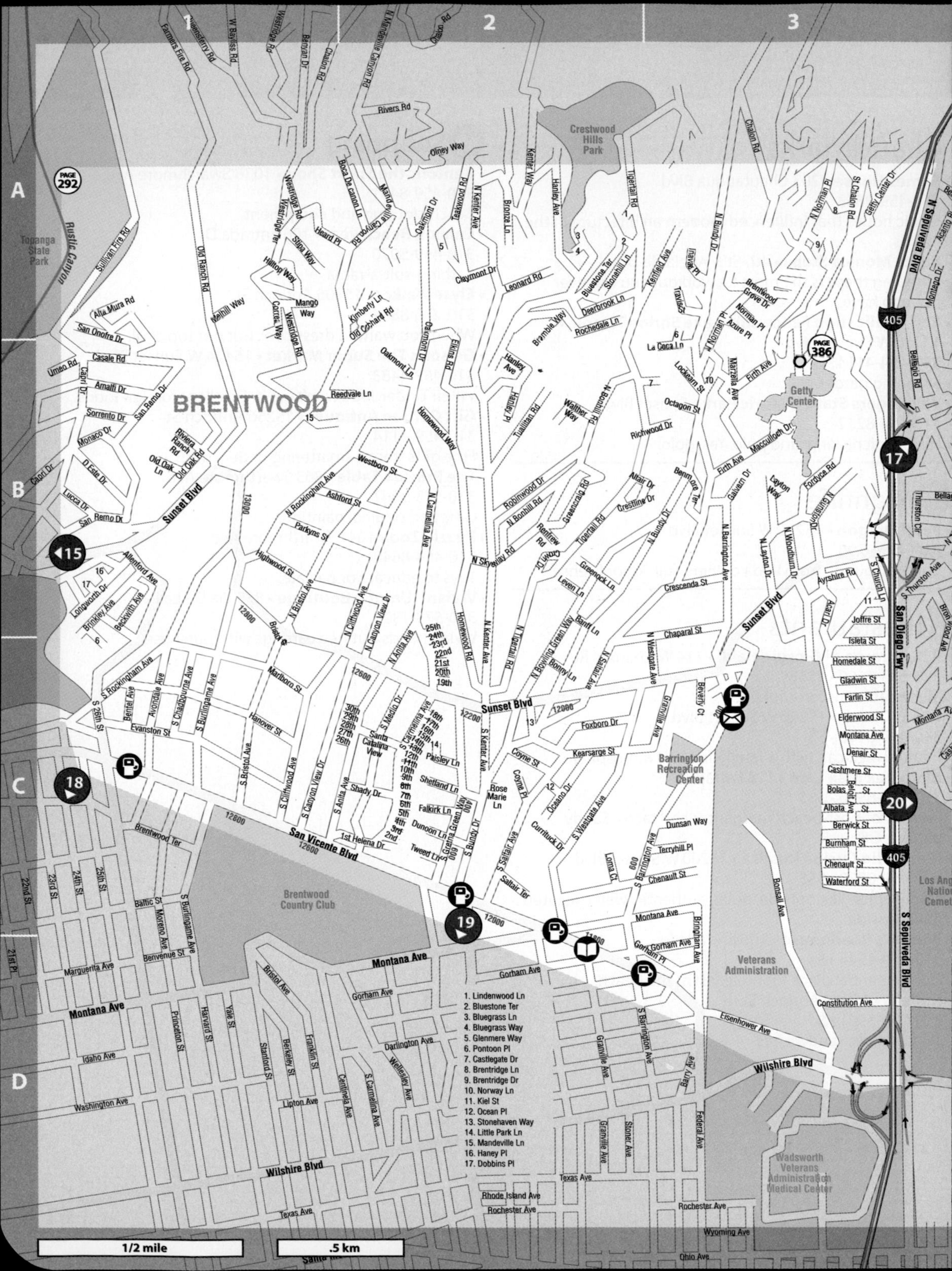

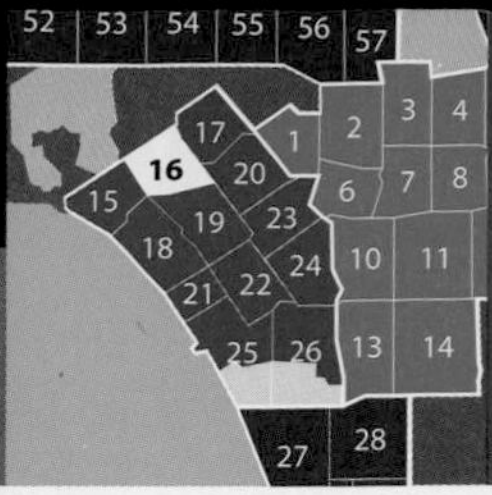

Brentwood is relatively affluent and quite peaceful—some might even go so far as to call it boring. Still, San Vicente Boulevard beckons fans of moderate outdoor activity (plenty of joggers; safe bike path), and hosts the annual Kickin' Cancer 5K Run. Plus, the rent is cheaper than in Santa Monica. The restaurants aren't, though. The Italian joints here are some of LA's most upscale (and priciest). Always carry cash for valet.

Landmarks

- **Getty Center** • 1200 Getty Center Dr
  310-440-7300
  Cool buildings (Meier), great garden (Irwin), fabulous views (G-d).

Restaurants

- **A Votre Sante** • 13018 San Vicente Blvd
  310-451-1813 • $$
  Vegetarian health food.
- **Brentwood Restaurant & Lounge** • 148 S Barrington Ave
  310-476-3511 • $$$$
  California-style comfort food.
- **Chin Chin** • 11740 San Vicente Blvd
  310-826-2525 • $$
  Chinese chain run by non-Chinese.
- **Coral Tree Café** • 11645 San Vicente Blvd
  310-979-8733 • $$
  Yummy lunch among the trophy wives and up-and-comers.
- **Daily Grill** • 11677 San Vicente Blvd
  310-442-0044 • $$$
  Home cooking.
- **Gaucho Grill** • 11754 San Vicente Blvd
  310-447-7898 • $$
  Argentine cuisine with lots of meat.
- **Katsuya** • 11777 San Vicente Blvd
  310-207-8744 • $$$$$
  The Philippe Starck decor is almost as cool as the food.
- **La Scala Presto** • 11740 San Vicente Blvd
  310-826-6100 • $$$
  Classic Italian.
- **Le Pain Quotidien** • 11702 S Barrington Ave
  310-476-0969 • $$
  Classy French sandwich shop.
- **Pizzicotto** • 11758 San Vicente Blvd
  310-442-7188 • $$$
  Pizza and pasta.
- **Reddi Chick** • 225 26th St
  310-393-5238 • $
  Chicken with a cult following.
- **Toscana** • 11633 San Vicente Blvd
  310-820-2448 • $$$$
  Tuscan with great pizzas.
- **Vincenti** • 11930 San Vicente Blvd
  310-207-0127 • $$$$
  Fine Italian food and wine with kitchen view.

Shopping

- **Compartes Chocolatier** • 912 S Barrington Ave
  310-826-3380
  Extremely high-end candy shop.
- **Iliad Bookshop** • 5400 Cahuenga Blvd
  818-509-2665
  One of LA's best used bookstores. Zola, the one-eyed kitty, will greet you.
- **PJ London** • 11661 San Vicente Blvd
  310-826-4649
  Women's fashions, mostly resale.
- **Porta Bella** • 11715 San Vicente Blvd
  310-820-2550
  Antique wood furniture, from armchairs to armoires.
- **Ron Herman** • 11677 San Vicente Blvd
  310-207-0927
  $335 for a bikini? Does it do tricks?
- **Sugar Paper** • 225 26th St
  310-451-7870
  For all your pretty paper and stationary needs
- **SusieCakes** • 11708 San Vicente Blvd
  310-442-2253
  Let us eat cake.
- **Whole Foods Market** • 11737 San Vicente Blvd
  310-826-4433
  Fresh produce and groceries in Brentwood's hippie corner.

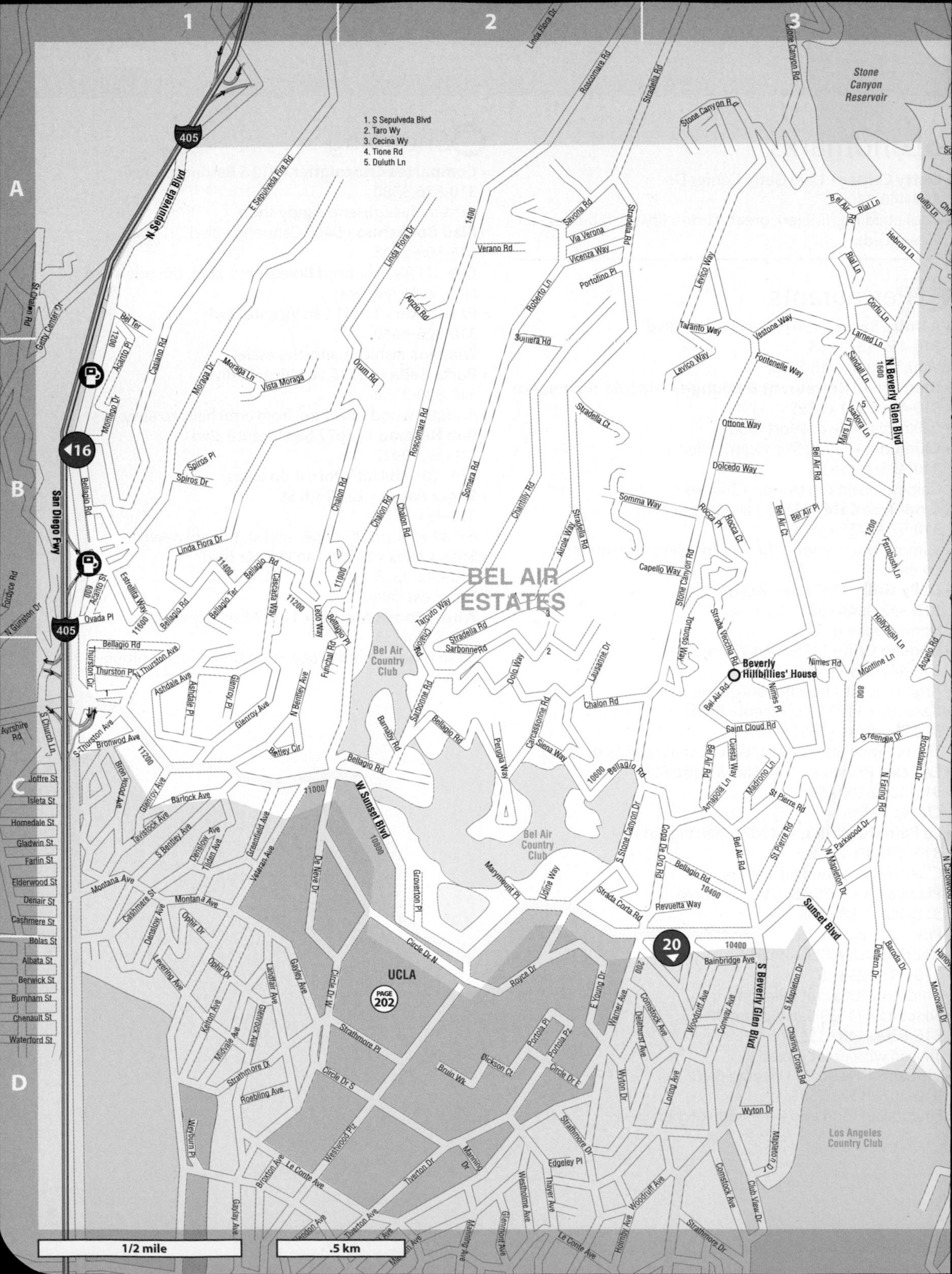
1
2
3
A
B
C
D
1. S Sepulveda Blvd
2. Taro Wy
3. Cecina Wy
4. Tione Rd
5. Duluth Ln
Stone Canyon Reservoir
Stone Canyon Rd
Linda Flora Dr
Roscomare Rd
Stradella Rd
405
N Sepulveda Blvd
E Sepulveda Fire Rd
San Diego Fwy
St Cloud Rd
Getty Center Dr
Bel Ter
Acanto Pl
Casiano Rd
Moraga Dr
Moraga Ln
Vista Moraga
Orum Rd
Anzio Rd
Verano Rd
Savona Rd
Via Verona
Vicenza Way
Portofino Pl
Roberto Ln
Somera Rd
Levico Way
Taranto Way
Vestone Way
Fontenelle Way
Ottone Way
Dolcedo Way
Somma Way
Rocca Pl
Rocca Ct
Capello Way
Stradella Ct
Chantilly Rd
Airole Way
Chalon Rd
Montego Dr
16
Spiros Pl
Spiros Dr
Bellagio Rd
Linda Flora Dr
Estrellita Way
Bellagio Ter
Cascada Way
Ledo Way
Tarcuto Way
Sarbonne Rd
BEL AIR ESTATES
Bel Air Country Club
Funchal Rd
Bellagio Pl
Ovada Pl
Thurston Cir
Thurston Pl
N Thurston Ave
S Thurston Ave
Ashdale Ave
Ashdale Pl
Glenroy Pl
Glenroy Ave
N Bentley Ave
Bentley Cir
Bronwood Ave
Barnaby Rd
Perugia Way
Carcassonne Rd
Siena Way
Lausanne Dr
Dolo Way
Tortuoso Way
Strada Vecchia Rd
Beverly Hillbillies' House
Nimes Rd
Nimes Pl
Bel Air Rd
Bel Air Ct
Bel Air Pl
Saint Cloud Rd
Cuesta Way
Anapola Ln
Madrono Ln
St Pierre Rd
Greendale Dr
Brooklawn Dr
N Faring Rd
Parkwood Dr
N Mapleton Dr
Montline Ln
Angelo Rd
Hollybush Ln
Fernbush Ln
Bel Air Rd
Rial Ln
Quito Ln
Hebron Ln
Corfu Ln
Larned Ln
Sundail Ln
Isadora Ln
Mars Ln
N Beverly Glen Blvd
Fordyce Rd
N Gunston Dr
Ayrshire Rd
S Church Ln
Joffre St
Isleta St
Homedale St
Gladwin St
Farlin St
Elderwood St
Denair St
Cashmere St
Bolas St
Albata St
Berwick St
Burnham St
Chenault St
Waterford St
Barlock Ave
Tavistock Ave
S Bentley Ave
Denslow Ave
Tilden Ave
Greenfield Ave
Veteran Ave
Montana Ave
Cashmere St
Ophir Dr
Levering Ave
Kelton Ave
Midvale Ave
Landfair Ave
Gayley Ave
Glenrock Ave
Strathmore Dr
Roebling Ave
Weyburn Pl
Broxton Ave
Le Conte Ave
Westwood Plz
Tiverton Dr
Manning Dr
Gayley Ave
Hilgard Ave
W Sunset Blvd
De Neve Dr
Groverton Pl
Circle Dr N
Circle Dr W
Circle Dr S
Circle Dr E
UCLA
PAGE 202
Strathmore Pl
Royce Dr
Portola Pl
Portola P2
Dickson Ct
Bruin Wk
E Young Dr
Marymount Pl
Udine Way
Bel Air Country Club
S Stone Canyon Dr
Copa De Oro Rd
Bellagio Rd
Strada Corta Rd
Revuelta Way
20
Bainbridge Ave
Warner Ave
Comstock Ave
Delahurst Ave
Wyton Dr
Loring Ave
Woodruff Ave
Conway Ave
S Beverly Glen Blvd
Sunset Blvd
S Mapleton Dr
Charing Cross Rd
Baroda Dr
Delfern Dr
Los Angeles Country Club
Mapleton Dr
Club View Dr
Comstock Ave
Strathmore Dr
Edgeley Pl
Westholme Ave
Thayer Ave
Woodruff Ave
Holmby Ave
Le Conte Ave
Glenmont Ave
Manning Ave
Hilgard Ave
Tiverton Ave
1/2 mile
.5 km

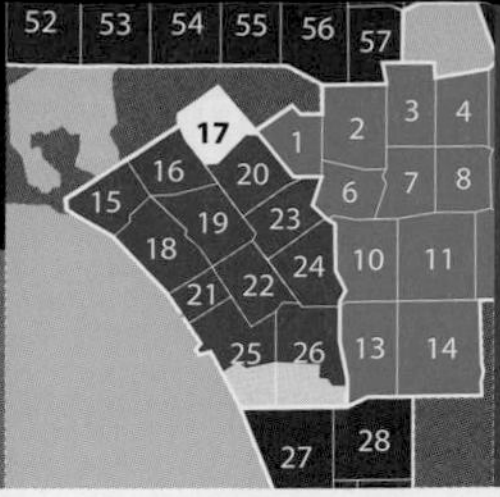

Both of these neighborhoods are almost completely residential. Celebrity fanatics can purchase star maps that chart some of the celebrity homes, or rather, their 15-foot tree-barrier fencing. Roads are confusing and it's easy to get lost in Bel Air, but the homes you can see are so stunning to look at that you may not mind. If you lose your way, just head downhill and eventually you'll (probably) wind up on Sunset Boulevard.

Landmarks

- **Beverly Hillbillies' House** • 700 Bel Air Rd
  Former Clampett stomping ground.

Nightlife

- **Hotel Bel Air Lounge** • 701 Stone Canyon Rd
  310-472-1211
  Where golddiggers and grandpas meet.

Restaurants

- **Bel Air Bar & Grill** • 662 N Sepulveda Blvd
  310-440-5544 • $$$$
  Californian with quick Getty access.

Map 18 • Santa Monica

Santa Monica's beachy creative community gave way long ago to families, young professionals, tourists, and condos. Residents typically avoid **3rd Street Promenade** (the fun is offset by draconian parking regulations, quick-draw meter maids, throngs of confused tourists, and pushy hustlers), preferring to window shop along the boutique- and café-lined Main Street. Montana Avenue hosts a wealth of pricey cafés, pricier boutiques, and severely pricey jewelry stores. The ocean bike path, the picturesque bluffs, and the famous Santa Monica stairs encourage shutting down the laptop and playing outdoors.

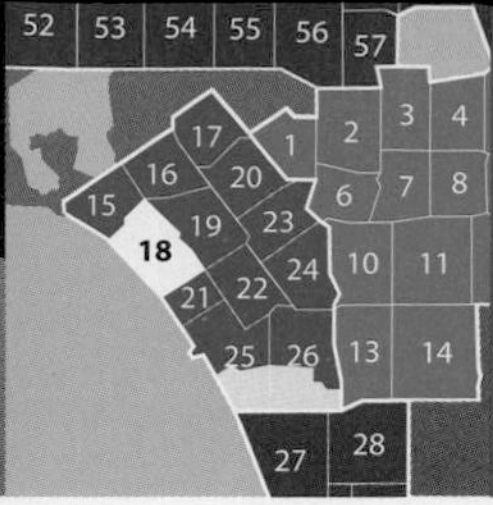

Landmarks

- **3rd Street Promenade** • Broadway & 3rd St
  Day or night, there's always something going on.
- **Heritage Square** • Ocean Park Blvd & Main St
  310-392-8537
  A taste of 19th-century life amidst Starbucks and bagel shops.
- **Santa Monica Civic Auditorium** • 1855 Main St
  310-458-8551
  Bizarre mix of cool rock concerts and antique sales.
- **Santa Monica Pier** • Colorado Ave & Ocean Ave
  310-458-8900
  Tiptoe through the tourists for a ride on the historic carousel.

Nightlife

- **Basement Tavern** • 2640 Main St
  310-396-2469
  This concealed treasure is, by neighborhood standards, practically a dive.
- **Big Dean's Café** • 1615 Ocean Front Walk
  310-393-2666
  Straight off the beach, fried locals.
- **Bodega Wine Bar** • 814 Broadway
  310-394-3504
  Wine by the tumbler.
- **Broadway Ale House** • 129 Broadway
  310-395-6351
  Snob beer without the beer snobs.
- **Cameo Bar** • 1819 Ocean Ave
  310-260-7500
  Chic hotel bar surrounding two swimming pools.
- **Casa del Mar** • 1910 Ocean Way
  310-581-5533
  High-end hotel bar.
- **Circle Bar** • 2926 Main St
  310-450-0508
  Once divey, now trendy.
- **Cock N' Bull** • 2947 Lincoln Blvd
  310-399-9696
  British pub.
- **Copa d'Oro** • 217 Broadway
  310-576-3030
  Pick your fresh fruit and herbs; they'll create a cocktail.
- **The Daily Pint** • 2310 Pico Blvd
  310-450-7631
  The good kind of cramped.
- **Father's Office** • 1018 Montana Ave
  310-736-2224
  Bet your dad didn't have 30 beers on tap.
- **Fig** • 101 Wilshire Blvd
  310-319-3111
  Hotel deluxe, waterfall included.
- **The Gaslite** • 2030 Wilshire Blvd
  310-829-2382
  Karaoke for the tone deaf.
- **Harvelle's** • 1432 4th St
  310-395-1676
  You like your clubs dark and sexy.
- **Loews Santa Monica Beach Hotel** • 1700 Ocean Ave
  866-563-9792
  Swanky.
- **O'Brien's** • 2941 Main St
  310-396-4725
  Neighborhood Irish pub.
- **Rick's Tavern on Main** • 2907 Main St
  310-392-2772
  Nothing fancy, just dive in and drink up.
- **The Room SM** • 1325 Santa Monica Blvd
  310-458-0707
  Westside station of Hollywood spot.
- **Rusty's Surf Ranch** • 256 Santa Monica Pier
  310-393-7437
  Surfboards, margs at sunset.
- **Shutters on the Beach** • 1 Pico Blvd
  310-458-0030
  One of the "beachiest" Santa Monica hotel bars.
- **Viceroy Hotel** • 1819 Ocean Ave
  310-260-7500
  Poolside and lounge, about as swanky as it gets on the Westside.
- **Zanzibar** • 1301 5th St
  310-451-2221
  Grooves spun by KCRW's Garth Trinidad and Jason Bentley.

Restaurants

- **Abode** • 1541 Ocean Ave
  310-394-3463 • $$$$$
  You may have to take out a second mortgage but the gorgeous setting is worth it.
- **Angelato Café** • 301 Arizona Ave
  310-656-9999 • $
  Gelato in every flavor possible
- **Babalu** • 1002 Montana Ave
  310-395-2500 • $$$
  Caribbean—don't skip dessert.

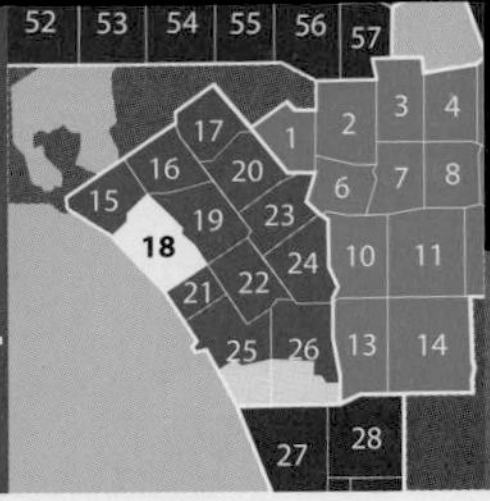

Santa Monica

- **Bay Cities** • 1517 Lincoln Blvd
310-395-8279 • $
Amazing Italian sandwich counter, Italian grocery, and long lines.
- **Border Grill** • 1445 4th St
310-451-1655 • $$$
Mexican restaurant run by popular TV chefs.
- **The Buffalo Club** • 1520 Olympic Blvd
310-450-8600 • $$$$$
Exclusive clubby dining.
- **Café Montana** • 1534 Montana Ave
310-829-3990 • $$$
A neighborhood staple.
- **Cassia** • 1314 7th St
310-393-6699 • $$$
Southeast Asian farm-to-table cuisine.
- **Cha Cha Chicken** • 1906 Ocean Ave
310-581-1684 • $$
Caribbean chicken.
- **Chaya Venice** • 110 Navy St
310-396-1179 • $$$$
Slightly upscale place to meet.
- **Chez Jay** • 1657 Ocean Ave
310-395-1741 • $$$
Californian seafood.
- **Chinois** • 2709 Main St
310-392-9025 • $$$$
Wolfgang Puck does Chinese brilliantly.
- **Dhaba** • 2104 Main St
310-399-9452 • $$
Visit India with a Dhaba Dinner.
- **Earth, Wind & Flour** • 2222 Wilshire Blvd
310-829-7829 • $$
Boston-style pizzas and pastas, whatever that means.
- **Enterprise Fish Company** • 174 Kinney St
310-392-8366 • $$
Where $1.00 oysters make for a very happy hour.
- **Falafel King** • 1315 3rd St Promenade
310-587-2551 • $
One of the cheapest, best meals on the Promenade.
- **Father's Office** • 1018 Montana Ave
310-736-2224 • $$
Burgers so good you'll forget the wait, price, and pretentiousness. Maybe.
- **Finn McCool's** • 2702 Main St
310-452-1734 • $$
Neighborhood comfort food.
- **Fritto Misto** • 601 Colorado Ave
310-458-2829 • $$
Inexpensive California Italian.
- **Fromin's Delicatessen** • 1832 Wilshire Blvd
310-829-5443 • $
Old-school deli and diner.
- **The Galley** • 2442 Main St
310-452-1934 • $$$$
Steak and seafood in marine theme.
- **Hillstone** • 202 Wilshire Blvd
310-576-7558 • $$$
Chain grill that caters to locals.
- **Huckleberry** • 1014 Wilshire Blvd
310-451-2311 • $$
Big menu—but oh, the baked goods.
- **Izzy's Deli** • 1433 Wilshire Blvd
310-394-1131 • $$
Locals, Jews, and obnoxious drunks all enjoy the so-so food at all hours.
- **Jack 'n Jill's** • 510 Santa Monica Blvd
310-656-1501 • $$
Giant omelettes and long wait.
- **Kreation Kafe** • 1023 Montana Ave
310-458-4880 • $$
New owner infuses Mediterranean favorites with organic ingredients.
- **Library Alehouse** • 2911 Main St
310-314-4855 • $$
Beer and classy pub fare.
- **The Lobster** • 1602 Ocean Ave
310-458-9294 • $$$$
Definitely order the lobster.
- **Lula** • 2720 Main St
310-392-5711 • $$
Non-traditional Mexican cuisine with strong margaritas.
- **Ma'Kai** • 101 Broadway
310-434-1511 • $$$
Polynesian by the beach with luaus on the last Sunday of every month.
- **Melisse** • 1104 Wilshire Blvd
310-395-0881 • $$$$
Quiet, upscale, French, many awards.
- **The Misfit** • 225 Santa Monica Blvd
310-656-9800 • $$$
Salted chocolate chip cookies at the end of EVERY. MEAL.
- **Musha** • 424 Wilshire Blvd
310-576-6330 • $$$
Japanese-style tapas.
- **NY&C Pizza** • 1120 Wilshire Blvd
310-393-9099 • $$
Come for the pizza, stay for the resentment.
- **The Ocean Park Omelette Parlor** • 2732 Main St
310-399-7892 • $
Home of well-stuffed, three-egg omelettes.
- **On the Waterfront Café** • 205 Ocean Front Walk
310-392-0322 • $$
Sit outside, drink obscure German beer, and watch LA watch you as it strolls on by.

Santa Monica

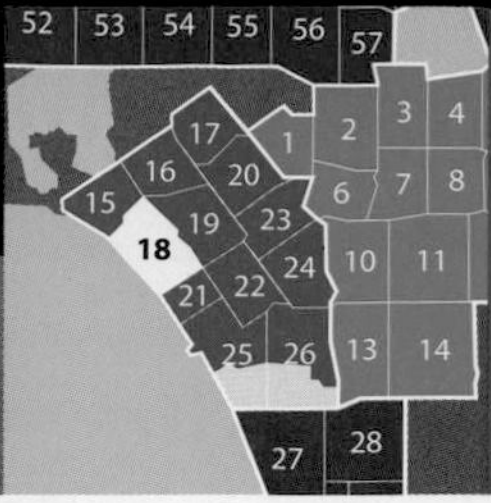

A weekend in Santa Monica should begin at the **Farmers Market** (on Arizona on Saturdays, Main Street on Sundays). Then take a walk along the bluffs or bike ride on the beach path followed by lunch and shopping on Main Street. Next, try the **Library Alehouse** for its personal brews and neighboring **Rick's Tavern** for its burgers. Finally, you can't not check out the **Pier**, unless you're some kind of communist. The Ferris Wheel gives you a view of dolphins on one side and the Valley fires, mudslides, or general frustration on the other, and a perfect make-out spot. And it's your name on a grain of rice, people.

- **One Pico** • 1 Pico Blvd
310-587-1717 • $$$
Fireside dining and a coastal view.
- **Rustic Canyon Wine Bar** • 1119 Wilshire Blvd
310-393-7050 • $$$
Hidden cave of wine.
- **Stella Rossa Pizza Bar** • 2000 Main St
310-396-9250 • $$
Fancy pizzas and strong cocktails.
- **Sugarfish** • 1325 2nd St
310-393-3338 • $$$
You deserve to eat sushi this good.
- **Sushi Roku** • 1401 Ocean Ave
310-458-4771 • $$$
Sushi by the beach.
- **Tar & Roses** • 602 Santa Monica Blvd
310-587-0700 • $$$
Tiny plates of European-influenced food with big bottles of wine.
- **Trastevere** • 1360 3rd St Promenade
310-319-1985 • $$$
Their gnocchi and olive dip rate a trip.
- **Ye Olde King's Head** • 116 Santa Monica Blvd
310-451-1402 • $$
Traditional English fare and beer.

Shopping

- **The Acorn Store** • 1220 5th St
310-451-5845
Unique toy store, handmade dolls and puppets.
- **Anthropologie** • 1402 3rd Street Promenade
310-393-4763
Unique, super-feminine clothes and accessories. Goldmine clearance.
- **Continental Shop** • 1619 Wilshire Blvd
310-453-8655
One stop shopping for everything from AbFab tapes to tea cozies.
- **Diane's Santa Monica** • 620 Wilshire Blvd
310-395-3545
Huge selection of bikinis and beachwear.
- **Fred Segal** • 500 Broadway
310-394-9814
LA institution and celebrity-spotter's paradise.
- **Helen's Cycles** • 2501 Broadway
310-829-1836
Bikes sold by people who know what they're talking about.
- **Holy Guacamole** • 2906 Main St
310-314-4850
Hot sauce heaven.
- **Jill Roberts** • 920 Montana Ave
310-260-1966
Stereotypical Angelenas, both shoppers and staff.
- **Kiehl's** • 1516 Montana Ave
310-255-0055
No more mail-order. NY-fave beauty products.
- **London Sole** • 1331 Montana Ave
310-255-0937
Chic but comfortable flat-soled shoes.
- **Michael Stars** • 1233 Montana Ave
310-260-5558
A variety of one size fit all seasonless tanks and tops.
- **Number One Beauty Supply** • 1426 Montana Ave
310-656-2455
A high-end Montana Ave selection at un-Montana Ave prices.
- **One Life Natural Foods** • 3001 Main St
310-392-4501
Produce, groceries, herbs, everything organic.
- **Palmetto** • 1034 Montana Ave
310-395-6687
Bath supplies, soap, natural beauty products.
- **Paris 1900** • 2703 Main St
310-396-0405
Vintage clothing and Bridal shop w/ gorgeous Art Deco facade.
- **The Pump Station & Nurtury** • 2415 Wilshire Blvd
310-998-1981
Where new moms turn for helpful advice with breastfeeding & baby care.
- **Puzzle Zoo** • 1411 3rd St Promenade
310-393-9201
Toy store caters to the sci-fi geek and child within us all.
- **REI** • 402 Santa Monica Blvd
310-458-4370
Everything you'll need for your camping trips.
- **Santa Monica Farmers Market** • 1299 3rd St
310-458-8712
Overpriced oranges AND an obese man with a monkey asking for your change.
- **Santa Monica Farms** • 2015 Main St
310-396-4069
Organic produce, groceries, juices, sandwiches to go.
- **Starbucks** • 1356 3rd St Promenade
310-458-0266
Knowledgable staff that lets you listen before you buy.
- **Step Shoes** • 1004 Montana Ave
310-899-4409
Luxury and comfort in footware.
- **Wildfiber** • 1453 14th St
310-458-2748
Bright knitting and yarn shop.
- **ZJ Boarding House** • 2619 Main St
310-392-5646
If it's flat and you can ride it, they've got it.

Map 19 • West LA / Santa Monica East

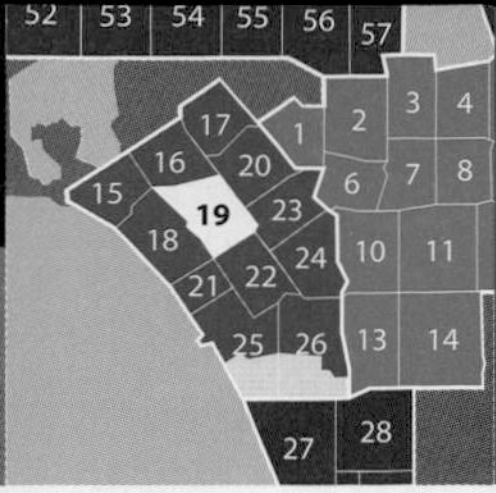

Colloquially "the West Side," this one takes some dedication. The new families, UCLA kids, and other eclectic residents enjoy the beach proximity, world-class window-shopping, and quick freeway access. Living here is swell. If you're driving crosstown, or running errands, pack some books on tape.

Landmarks

- **Bergamot Station** • 2525 Michigan Ave
  310-453-7535
  The best one-stop art experience you can have in LA.
- **Santa Monica Municipal Airport** • 3223 Donald Douglas Loop S
  310-458-8591
  Home to lots of small planes and private jets. And an annual Barneys NY sale.

Nightlife

- **The Arsenal** • 12012 W Pico Blvd
  310-575-5511
  '60s era cool at this quite metro-for-the-Westside bar.
- **Busby's** • 3110 Santa Monica Blvd
  310-828-4567
  Smaller, but as fun as it's mid-Wilshire counterpart.
- **Liquid Kitty** • 11780 W Pico Blvd
  310-473-3707
  Westside lounge with martinis that will make you purr.
- **McCabe's Guitar Shop** • 3101 Pico Blvd
  310-828-4497
  Famed LA haunt for live acoustic music.
- **Mom's** • 12238 Santa Monica Blvd
  310-820-6667
  A pseudo-dive, but it'll do.
- **The Penthouse** • 1111 2nd St
  310-393-8080
  Individual cabana tables for private dining. Bridge and tunnel crowd on weekends.
- **Plan B** • 11637 W Pico Blvd
  310-312-3633
  The Ladies Man would hang at this after 2 am cigar lounge.
- **Sonny McLean's Irish Pub** • 2615 Wilshire Blvd
  310-449-1811
  For homesick Red Sox fans.
- **South** • 3001 Wilshire Blvd
  310-828-9988
  The best sports bar on Westside if the 16 other places are closed.

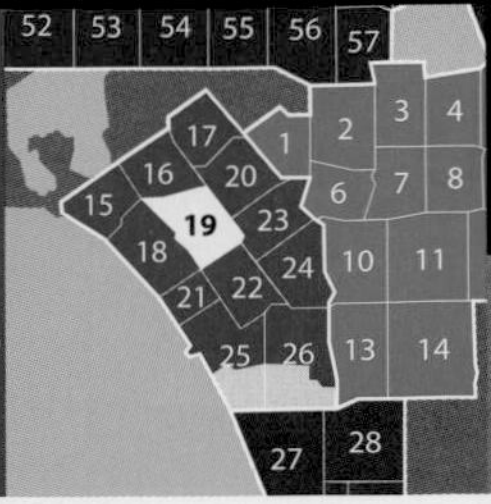

West LA / Santa Monica East

Restaurants

- **Akbar Cuisine of India** • 2627 Wilshire Blvd
  310-586-7469 • $$$
  Creative Indian cooking.
- **Bandera** • 11700 Wilshire Blvd
  310-477-3524 • $$$
  Dimly-lit; yuppy-ish. Reliable New-American cuisine.
- **Benito's Taco Shop** • 11614 Santa Monica Blvd
  310-442-9924 • $
  $3 burritos the size of your Chihuahua.
- **Bombay Café** • 12021 W Pico Blvd
  310-473-3388 • $$$
  Inspired Indian cuisine.
- **The Counter** • 2901 Ocean Park Blvd
  310-399-8383 • $$
  Build your own burger with a zillion choices for toppings.
- **Don Antonio's** • 11755 W Pico Blvd
  310-312-2090 • $$
  Muy autentico.
- **Farmshop** • 225 26th St
  310-566-2400 • $$$
  Family-style dinners and snacks to go.
- **Furaibo** • 2068 Sawtelle Blvd
  310-444-1432 • $$
  Try Japanese dishes you've never heard of at this izakaya.
- **Hide Sushi** • 2040 Sawtelle Blvd
  310-477-7242 • $$$
  Not for the sushi-phobic.
- **Hop Woo** • 11110 W Olympic Blvd
  310-575-3668 • $
  West Side outpost of the highly regarded Chinese chain.
- **Il Forno** • 2901 Ocean Park Blvd
  310-450-1241 • $$$
  Northern Italian cuisine. Great pastas and NYC-style pizzas.
- **Il Grano** • 11359 Santa Monica Blvd
  310-477-7886 • $$$$
  This West LA authentic Italian has been drawing crowds for more than 10 years.
- **Il Moro** • 11400 W Olympic Blvd
  310-575-3530 • $$$$
  Creative Italian specialties.
- **Javan** • 11500 Santa Monica Blvd
  310-207-5555 • $$
  Persian cuisine. Huge portions of tasty charbroiled meats.
- **Josie Restaurant** • 2424 Pico Blvd
  310-581-9888 • $$$$
  Reputable chef. Great interior. New-American cuisine.
- **Kay 'n Dave's** • 262 26th St
  310-260-1355 • $$
  Healthy Mexican with a family-friendly atmosphere.
- **Kiriko Sushi** • 11301 W Olympic Blvd
  310-478-7769 • $$$$$
  Splurge sushi/omakase beyond your wildest tuna roll fantasies.
- **Lares** • 2909 Pico Blvd
  310-829-4550 • $$
  Rich, authentic Mexican meals and potent margaritas.
- **Lazy Daisy Cafe** • 11913 Wilshire Blvd
  310-477-8580 • $$
  Great selection of salads and smoothies.
- **Le Saigon** • 11611 Santa Monica Blvd
  310-312-2929 • $$
  Great Korean food.
- **Lemon Moon** • 12200 W Olympic Blvd
  310-442-9191 • $
  The Santa Monican professional's tasty, economical hour-lunch of choice.
- **Milo and Olive** • 2723 Wilshire Blvd
  310-453-6776 • $$$
  Bread-forward all-day spot featuring wood-fired pizza.
- **Nook Neighborhood Bistro** • 11628 Santa Monica Blvd
  310-207-5160 • $$
  American traditional with European flair.
- **Rae's Restaurant** • 2901 Pico Blvd
  310-828-7937 • $
  Neighborhood hangout-they line up for breakfast!
- **Sasabune** • 11917 Wilshire Blvd
  310-820-3596 • $$
  No California Roll, no menu. Trust the chef.
- **Stefan's at LA Farm** • 3000 Olympic Blvd
  310-449-4000 • $$$
  Absolutely absurd vibe makes the food better than expected.
- **Tlapazola Grill** • 11676 Gateway Blvd
  310-477-1577 • $$$
  Southern Mexican.
- **Tsujita LA** • 2100 Sawtelle Blvd
  310-231-6060 • $$
  Artisan noodle ramen masters.
- **Typhoon** • 3221 Donald Douglas Loop S
  310-390-6565 • $$$
  Eclectic Pan-Asian. Aviation motif. Cool and chic.
- **Valentino** • 3115 Pico Blvd
  310-829-4313 • $$$$
  Classy Italian. Flawless. Dazzling wine list.
- **Vito** • 2807 Ocean Park Blvd
  310-450-4999 • $$$
  Reliable Italian.
- **Yabu** • 11820 W Pico Blvd
  310-473-9757 • $$$
  Hip sushi and noodles.
- **Zabie's** • 3003 Ocean Park Blvd
  310-392-9036 • $
  Neighborhood café. Friendly. Cheap. Good breakfast and lunch.

West LA / Santa Monica East

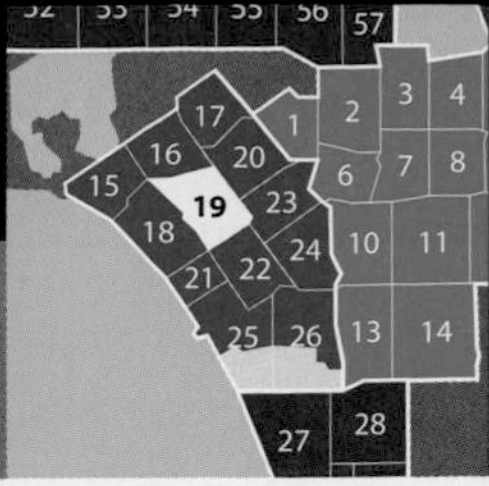

Sawtelle north of Olympic, known as Little Osaka, is an expanse of BBQ, sushi, cozy noodle houses, and cutesy gift shops. Try Japanese dishes you've never heard of, or ones that you have, at **Furaibo**, an excellent izakaya. There's a smidgen of nightlife along Pico and Centinela: **The Arsenal** has time-tested tunes and by-the-book cocktails. The **Royal** and **NuArt** movie theaters show off-beat, foreign, cult, and otherwise hard to find films on the regular.

Shopping

- **Adventure 16** • 11161 W Pico Blvd
  310-473-4574
  Camping supplies that make city slickers want to commune with nature.
- **Any Occasion Balloons** • 12002 W Pico Blvd
  310-473-9963
  Every size balloon, in every shape and color imaginable.
- **Blick Art Materials** • 11531 Santa Monica Blvd
  310-479-1416
  Corporate but comprehensive. Good selection of art magazines.
- **Giant Robot** • 2015 Sawtelle Blvd
  310-478-1819
  Items from Asian pop culture.
- **Graphaids** • 12400 Santa Monica Blvd
  310-820-0445
  They appeal to both serious artists and doodlers.
- **Hiromi Paper Inc.** • 2525 Michigan Ave
  310-998-0098
  Handcrafted paper so gorgeous you won't want to write on it.
- **Hyper Games** • 2130 Sawtelle Blvd
  310-444-1907
  Yes, video game rental stores still exist.
- **McCabe's Guitar Shop** • 3101 Pico Blvd
  310-828-4497
  Geared more toward the fledgling Bob Dylan than Eddie Van Halen.
- **Record Surplus** • 12436 Santa Monica Blvd
  310-979-4577
  No glitz, no pizzazz. For serious music lovers only.
- **Utrecht Arts Supplies** • 11677 Santa Monica Blvd
  310-478-5775
  All manner of stuff for the artsy and the craftsy, and helpful service.

N
1
2
3
A
B
C
D
Playboy Mansion
Los Angeles Country Club
UCLA
PAGE 202
WEST-WOOD
Los Angeles National Cemetery
UCLA Hammer Museum
Westwood Mem. Cemetery
Wadsworth Theater
Federal Building
Westwood Park
Mormon Temple
Westfield Century City
PAGE 236
Roxbury Rec Center
Fox Plaza
Hillcrest Country Club
Rancho Park Golf Course
Cheviot Hills Park
RANCHO PARK
Holmby Park
1. Lomond Ave
2. Norcroft Ave
3. Hillgreen Pl
4. Le Conte Ave
5. Calmar Ct
6. Holman Ave
7. Eastborne Ave
8. Crestview Ct
9. Rochester Ave
W Sunset Blvd
Sunset Blvd
Wilshire Blvd
Santa Monica Blvd
Little Santa Monica Blvd
W Olympic Blvd
W Pico Blvd
Westwood Blvd
Sepulveda Blvd
S Sepulveda Blvd
San Diego Fwy
Santa Monica Fwy
National Blvd
Exposition Blvd
S Beverly Glen Blvd
Avenue Of The Stars
Century Park W
Constellation
Motor Ave
Overland Ave
N Beverly Dr
405
1/2 mile
.5 km

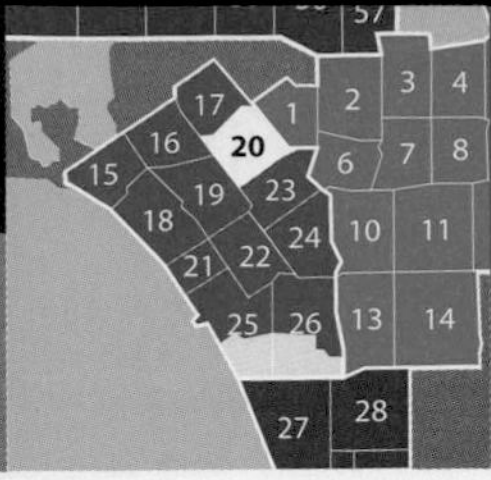

By day, Century City bustles with corporate life. By night, it becomes a ghost town, unless you're at the movie theater at Century City Mall. By contrast, with the exception of the **Westwood Memorial Cemetery** (final resting place for Marilyn Monroe and Natalie Wood), nearby Westwood is always humming with UCLA students, moviegoers, and Bruins fanatics. Consequently, street parking will test your patience and parallel parking abilities. For book enthusiasts, come to the LA Times Festival of Books at UCLA during April.

oLandmarks

- **Federal Building** • Wilshire Blvd & S Sepulveda Blvd
  Picketers of any and all causes seem magnetically drawn to this building.
- **Fox Plaza** • 2121 Avenue of the Stars
  310-282-0047
  Known to locals as "the Die Hard Building." Surely we don't have to explain.
- **Hammer Museum** • 10899 Wilshire Blvd
  310-443-7000
  Cutting-edge art museum with largely contemporary exhibits.
- **Mormon Temple** • 10777 Santa Monica Blvd
  310-474-1549
  Always one of the more festively-lit buildings at Christmastime.
- **Playboy Mansion** • 10236 Charing Cross Rd
  We'd tell you all about it if only Hef would send us an invitation.
- **UCLA** • 405 Hilgard Ave
  310-825-4321
  Picturesque campus, solid academics, and its own blue Pantone color.
- **Wadsworth Theater** • 11000 Wilshire Blvd
  310-479-3003
  They offer free jazz concerts on the first Sunday of every month.
- **Westwood Memorial Cemetery** • 1218 Glendon Ave
  310-272-2484
  Marilyn Monroe and Natalie Wood are among the famous residents.

Nightlife

- **The Cellar** • 1880 Century Park E
  310-277-1584
  Some call it a dive; some call it Century City respite.
- **Habibi Cafe** • 923 Broxton Ave
  310-824-2277
  End your night disgusted and ripped-off at this notorious hookah spot.
- **Westwood Brew Co.** • 1097 Glendon Ave
  310-824-0820
  Microbrewery with comedy upstairs.
- **Whiskey Blue** • 930 Hilgard Ave
  310-443-8232
  Modern, trendy hotel bar.

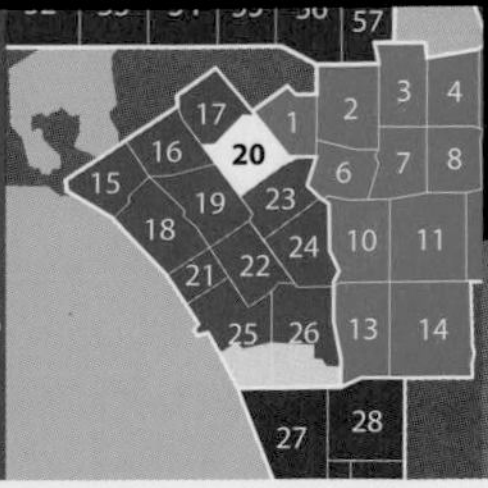

Westwood / Century City

Restaurants

- **800 Degrees** • 10889 Lindbrook Dr
  310-443-1911 • $$
  Made-to-order pizzas, and a burrata bar.
- **Attari Sandwich Shop** • 1388 Westwood Blvd
  310-441-5488 • $
  Persian-style sandwiches, plus kebab plates.
- **The Bigg Chill** • 10850 W Olympic Blvd
  310-475-1070 • $
  Best frozen yogurt in LA!
- **Bread Bar** • 10250 Santa Monica Blvd
  310-277-3770 • $$
  Excellent, fresh-baked breads, with a tasty assortment of sandwiches, soups, and salads.
- **Carvel Ice Cream** • 11037 Santa Monica Blvd
  310-444-0011 • $
  East coast ice cream institution.
- **Chalet Edelweiss** • 8740 S Sepulveda Blvd
  310-645-8740 • $$
  Our version of exotic: meat and potatoes.
- **Clementine** • 1751 Ensley Ave
  310-552-1080 • $$
  True American cuisine with a modern flair.
- **Diddy Riese Cookies** • 926 Broxton Ave
  310-208-0448 • $
  25¢ cookies and ice cream sandwiches.
- **Elysee Bakery & Cafe** • 1099 Gayley Ave
  310-208-6505 • $$
  Decent cafe with bonus points for outside seating.
- **Falafel King** • 1059 Broxton Ave
  310-208-4444 • $
  Fast-food Middle Eastern.
- **Feast from the East** • 1949 Westwood Blvd
  310-475-0400 • $
  Cheap, fast, and tasty.
- **fundamental LA** • 1303 Westwood Blvd
  310-444-7581 • $$
  Farm-to-table, but thoroughly refined.
- **Hoboken** • 2323 Westwood Blvd
  310-474-1109 • $$
  Southern Italian fare with a Jersey flair?
- **In-N-Out Burger** • 922 Gayley Ave
  800-786-1000 • $
  Top California burger joint.
- **Johnnie's NY Pizzeria** • 10251 Santa Monica Blvd
  310-553-1188 • $$
  New York-style pizza.
- **La Bruschetta** • 1621 Westwood Blvd
  310-477-1052 • $$$$
  Classic Italian. Their bruschetta is delicious.
- **Lamonicas** • 1066 Gayley Ave
  310-208-8671 • $
  Excellent thin crust pizza by the slice. Boasts dough imported from NY!
- **Matteo's Restaurant** • 2321 Westwood Blvd
  310-475-4521 • $$$
  Where Sinatra would get pasta in LA.
- **Mr. Noodle** • 936 Broxton Ave
  310-208-7808 • $
  The Baja Fresh of Thai noodles.
- **Napa Valley Grille** • 1100 Glendon Ave
  310-824-3322 • $$$$
  Upscale dining.
- **Ramayani** • 1777 Westwood Blvd
  310-477-3315 • $
  Incredibly slow service for incredibly delicious Indonesian food.
- **Stan's Donuts** • 10948 Weyburn Ave
  310-208-8660 • $
  Try a Reese's Peanut Butter Cup donut.
- **Tommy Taco** • 970 Gayley Ave
  310-824-4114 • $
  "Buck Fifties," great taco stand, even if you're not drunk.

Not a college town but a reasonable facsimile thereof, Westwood's student population feeds on the cheap, undeniably delicious **In N' Out**, **Diddy Riese Cookies** (fresh from the oven), and **Falafel King** (extra baba ganoush, please). For the classic Westwood experience, see a movie here on opening night—people get psyched.

Shopping

- **Bristol Farms** • 1515 Westwood Blvd
  310-481-0100
  Upscale grocery. Newest and biggest of its kind.
- **Cost Plus World Market** • 10860 Santa Monica Blvd
  310-441-5115
  An "everything" superstore.
- **Paris Bakery** • 1448 Westwood Blvd
  310-474-8888
  Great French pastries, breads, and croissants.
- **Writer's Store** • 3510 W Magnolia Blvd
  310-441-5151
  Seminars, books, and computer software for writing.

Map 21 • Venice

Here it is: LA's Coney Island, Woodstock vs. Myrtle Beach, a carnival and an American microcosm, home to billionaires, bombshells, hustlers, and drifters. On the boardwalk, Venice bustles all day (and gets dicey at night). Along Abbot Kinney, Venice is a cozy bohemia, with ample eateries, bars, and boutiques. And with Lincoln Boulevard right there, you don't have to venture far to get that pesky smog check.

oLandmarks

- **Binoculars Building** • 340 Main St
  Frank Gehry's design features a large statue of binoculars marking its entrance.
- **Muscle Beach** • 1817 Ocean Front Walk
  310-578-6131
  Don't forget to oil up first.
- **Venice Boardwalk** • Ocean Front Wk
  A freak show to some, while others thrive on the eclectic crowds. Marvel at the graffiti-bedecked palm trees.
- **Venice Canals** • Pacific Ave & N Venice Blvd
  There used to be more than six, but they were deemed impractical and turned into roads.
- **Venice Pier** • Washington Blvd
  It's been a casualty to weather conditions at least twice.
- **Windward Circle** • Main St & Windward Ave
  A great meeting place for those looking to spend the day at the beach.

Nightlife

- **Baja Cantina** • 311 West Washington Boulevard
  310-821-2252
  Free chips 'n' salsa with your margs.
- **The Brig** • 1515 Abbot Kinney Blvd
  310-399-7537
  For trendy westsiders too lazy to drive to Cahuenga.
- **The Firehouse** • 213 Rose Ave
  310-396-6810
  Neighborhood bar.
- **James' Beach** • 60 N Venice Blvd
  310-823-5396
  Outdoor patio bar with ocean view.
- **The Other Room** • 1201 Abbot Kinney Blvd
  312-396-6230
  Plus/minus thirty bar. Fun ambition minus the Hollywood hustle.
- **Townhouse** • 52 Windward Ave
  310-392-4040
  No longer a dive, not yet a lounge.
- **Venice Whaler** • 10 Washington Blvd
  310-821-8737
  Take out-of-town friends for buckets of beer, sunsets.

Venice

Restaurants

- **Abbot's Pizza** • 1407 Abbot Kinney Blvd
  310-396-7334 • $
  Bagel crust pizza.
- **Axe** • 1009 Abbot Kinney Blvd
  310-664-9787 • $$$$
  Healthfood with a chef's touch, movie star approval, and a long wait.
- **Baby Blues BBQ** • 444 Lincoln Blvd
  310-396-7675 • $$
  Quit whining—LA does have decent BBQ.
- **Baja Cantina** • 311 West Washington Boulevard
  310-821-2252 • $$
  Mexican with seafood specialties and sizeable margaritas.
- **C&O Trattoria** • 31 Washington Blvd
  310-823-9491 • $$
  Cheap Italian.
- **Café 50's** • 838 Lincoln Blvd
  310-399-1955 • $$
  All-American food without pretense.
- **Café Buna** • 3105 Washington Blvd
  310-823-2430 • $$
  Breakfast of champions with excellent coffee.
- **Canal Club** • 2025 Pacific Ave
  310-823-3878 • $$$
  Chinese-Cuban fusion.
- **Casablanca** • 220 Lincoln Blvd
  310-392-5751 • $$$
  Nice evening out, guaranteed.
- **Gjelina** • 1429 Abbot Kinney Blvd
  310-450-1429 • $$$$
  California cuisine with a New York sensibility.
- **Gjusta** • 320 Sunset Ave
  310-314-0320 • $$
  Bakery and deli, sandwich strong.
- **Hama Sushi** • 213 Windward Ave
  310-396-8783 • $$$$
  Hip Japanese.
- **Hinano** • 15 Washington Blvd
  310-822-3902 • $
  Burgers, beer, benches, beach.
- **Joe's** • 1023 Abbot Kinney Blvd
  310-399-5811 • $$$$
  French-Californian unique cuisine, worth the prices.
- **Kifune** • 405 E Washington st
  310-822-1595 • $$
  Try the sushi.
- **La Cabana Restaurant** • 738 Rose Ave
  310-392-7973 • $$
  Very festive atmosphere and diverse meeting place.
- **Rose Café** • 220 Rose Ave
  310-399-0711 • $$
  Trendy eclectic Californian and pleasant brunch in art gallery.
- **The Shack** • 2 Westminster Ave
  323-209-7316 • $
  Beachside Salvadoran snacks.
- **Sunny Spot** • 822 Washington Blvd
  310-448-8884 • $$$
  Roy Choi's take on Caribbean; seafood, peppers, and jerk.
- **The Tasting Kitchen** • 1633 Abbot Kinney Blvd
  310-392-6644 • $$$$
  For special occasions, hipster-style.
- **The Terrace Café** • 7 Washington Blvd
  310-578-1530 • $$
  Convenient lunch spot for rollerbladers.
- **Wabi-Sabi** • 1637 Abbot Kinney Blvd
  310-314-2229 • $$$
  Sushi.

Venice

Venice is an artist colony striving to survive amid the juxtaposition of million-dollar homes and drug houses, walk streets and **canals**. For those with some disposable income, head to funky Abbot Kinney for great shops and restaurants. **Joe's** French-California cuisine is one of the best fusion spots in LA, while wine and tunes go hand-in-hand at **The Other Room**'s exposed-brick wine bar. See also, **The Tasting Kitchen** and **Gjelina.** Venice Beach is okay for surfing, if you can dodge the swarm of dirty needles, but don't confine your voyeurism to **Venice Walk**—Washington Boulevard has more memorable characters.

Shopping

- **A + R Store** • 1121 Abbot Kinney Blvd
  310-392-9128
  Treats for the home from around the globe.
- **Ananda** • 1356 Abbot Kinney Blvd
  310-399-4186
  Unique, affordable, beach Buddha fashion.
- **Burro** • 1409 Abbot Kinney Blvd
  310-450-6288
  Great for gifts. Better for yourself.
- **Fiore Designs** • 1617 Abbot Kinney Blvd
  310-230-5007
  A bridal store that thus far avoids the cheesy.
- **Firefly** • 1405 Abbot Kinney Blvd
  310-450-6288
  Great for gifts. Better for yourself.
- **Green House Smoke Shop** • 1428 Abbot Kinney Blvd
  310-450-6420
  Tools for those high on life.
- **Heist** • 1100 Abbot Kinney Blvd
  310-450-6531
  Decadent beachwear, sexy imperial classics, and well-edited denim.
- **Helen's Cycles** • 2472 Lincoln Blvd
  310-306-7843
  One of the best bike stores in the area.
- **Mollusk Surf Shop** • 1600 Pacific Ave
  310-396-1969
  Respected surfer depot. Fewer familiar logos, more enthusiasm.
- **The Starting Line** • 114 Washington Blvd
  310-827-3035
  If you are a serious walker or runner, this place is for you.
- **Venice Bike & Skates** • 21 Washington Blvd
  310-301-4011
  Rent yourself some boardwalk transport.
- **Waraku** • 1225 Abbot Kinney Blvd
  310-452-5300
  Specializing in custom sneakers and other cool clothes.

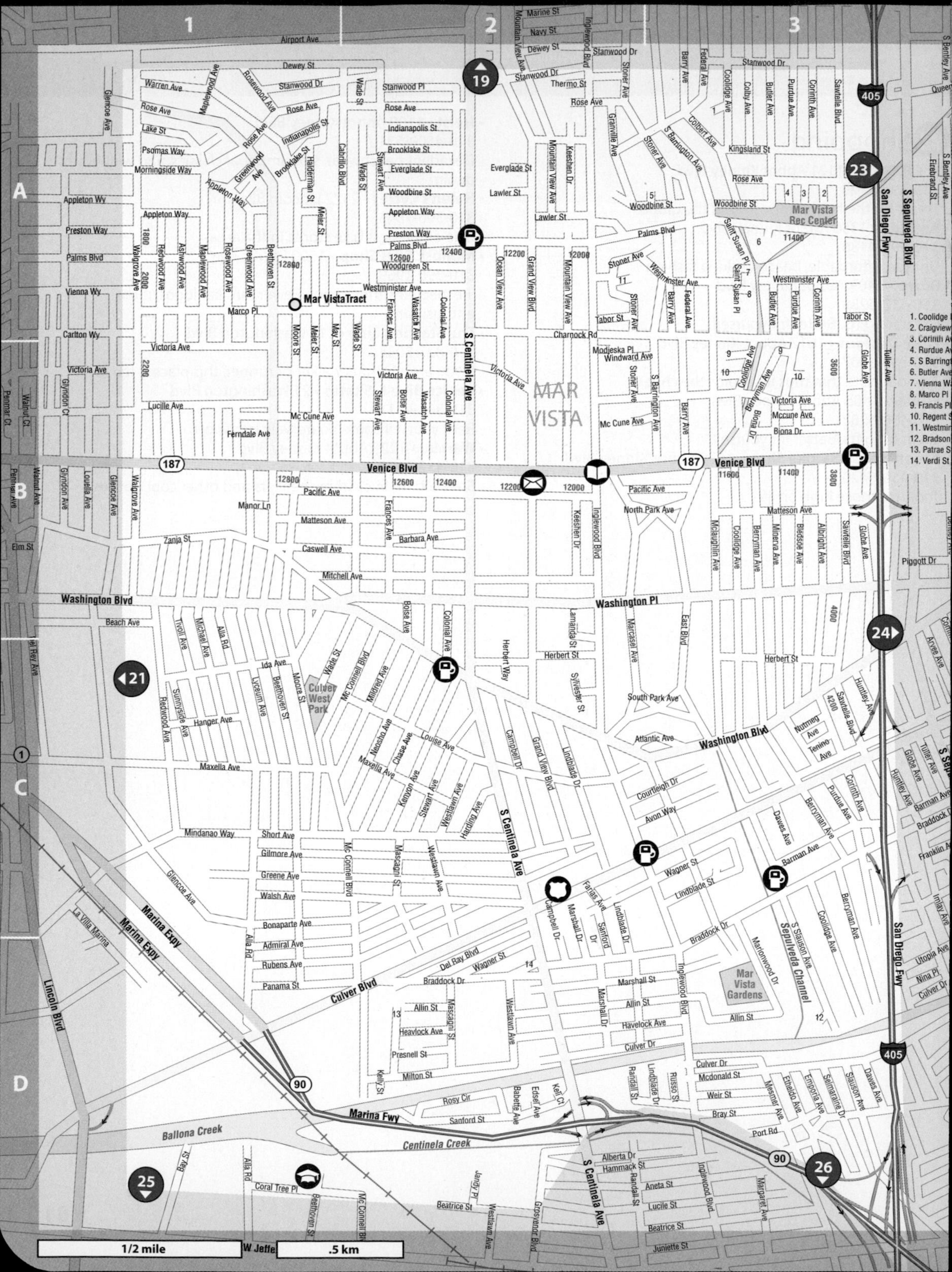
1
2
3
A
B
C
D
19
21
23
24
25
26
Airport Ave
Marine St
Navy St
Dewey St
Stanwood Dr
Stanwood Pl
Thermo St
Rose Ave
Warren Ave
Lake St
Psomas Way
Morningside Way
Indianapolis St
Brooklake St
Everglade St
Woodbine St
Appleton Way
Preston Way
Palms Blvd
Woodgreen St
Westminster Ave
Mar Vista Tract
Marco Pl
Vienna Wy
Carlton Wy
Victoria Ave
Lucille Ave
Mc Cune Ave
Ferndale Ave
Lawler St
Kingsland St
Mar Vista Rec Center
Stoner Ave
Tabor St
Charnock Rd
Modjeska Pl
Windward Ave
Mccune Ave
Biona Dr
MAR VISTA
S Centinela Ave
Venice Blvd
187
Pacific Ave
Manor Ln
Matteson Ave
North Park Ave
Barbara Ave
Zanja St
Caswell Ave
Mitchell Ave
Elm St
Washington Blvd
Washington Pl
Beach Ave
Herbert St
Herbert Way
Ida Ave
Culver West Park
Hanger Ave
South Park Ave
Atlantic Ave
Louise Ave
Maxella Ave
Courtleigh Dr
Avon Way
Mindanao Way
Short Ave
Gilmore Ave
Greene Ave
Walsh Ave
Wagner St
Lindblade St
Barman Ave
Braddock Dr
Bonaparte Ave
Admiral Ave
Rubens Ave
Panama St
Culver Blvd
Del Ray Blvd
Marina Expy
Mar Vista Gardens
Sepulveda Channel
Marshall St
Allin St
Havelock Ave
Heavlock Ave
Presnell St
Culver Dr
Milton St
Mcdonald St
Weir St
Bray St
Port Rd
Rosy Cir
Sanford St
Marina Fwy
90
Ballona Creek
Centinela Creek
Alberta Dr
Hammack St
Aneta St
Lucile St
Beatrice St
Juniette St
Coral Tree Pl
Lincoln Blvd
San Diego Fwy
405
S Sepulveda Blvd
Piggott Dr
Utopia Ave
Nina Pl
Culver Dr
Franklin Av
1. Coolidge
2. Craigview
3. Corinth Av
4. Rurdue Av
5. S Barringt
6. Butler Ave
7. Vienna W
8. Marco Pl
9. Francis Pl
10. Regent S
11. Westmin
12. Bradson
13. Patrae S
14. Verdi St
1/2 mile
.5 km
W Jeffe

In Spanish, it means "view of the sea," although "faint whiff of the sea" is more like it: you won't see the surf, but you'll dig the fresh breezes and cool temperatures. Lodged between blow-dried, pricey Marina Del Rey and Culver City, Mar Vista is still relatively undiscovered—it's easy to get groceries, a bite, and a sip at a reasonable price, without wrangling too much traffic. The Westside, but on a budget.

Landmarks

- **Mar Vista Tract** • Beethoven St & Moore St
  Indulge your retro-modernist fetish.

Nightlife

- **Good Hurt** • 12249 Venice Blvd
  310-390-1076
  Medical-themed beer and wine remedies.

Restaurants

- **A-Frame** • 12565 Washington Blvd
  310-398-7700 • $$
  The Kogi trucks go brick-and-mortar.
- **Asaya Restaurant** • 12740 Culver Blvd
  310-823-8944 • $$
  Local Japanese.
- **Centinela Café** • 4800 S Centinela Ave
  310-391-2585 • $
  Basic Mex/American, cheap.
- **City Tavern** • 9739 Culver Blvd
  310-838-9739 • $$
  Solid eats and crazy good cocktails. Drink the Flyover.
- **The Corner Door** • 12477 W Washington Blvd
  310-313-5810 • $$
  Because you need to dip a cookie in bourbon milk.
- **Empanada's Place** • 3811 Sawtelle Blvd
  310-391-0888 • $
  The name says it all.
- **Maxwell's Café** • 13329 W Washington Blvd
  310-306-7829 • $
  Hearty breakfasts and lunch.
- **Outdoor Grill** • 12630 Washington Pl
  310-636-4747 • $
  Quite literally. Big outdoor flesh grill!
- **Paco's Tacos** • 4141 S Centinela Ave
  310-391-9616 • $
  Cheap Tex-Mex.
- **Pepy's Galley** • 12125 Venice Blvd
  310-390-0577 • $
  Unpretentious bowling alley diner.
- **Ronnie's Diner** • 12740 Culver Blvd
  310-578-9399 • $
  Mom-and-Pop in Marina Del Rey.
- **Sakura Japanese Restaurant** • 4345 S Centinela Ave
  310-822-7790 • $$
  Local sushi. Open for lunch.
- **Santouka** • 3760 S Centinela Ave
  310-391-1101 • $
  Best ramen in LA.
- **Taqueria Sanchez** • 4541 S Centinela Ave
  310-822-8880 • $
  Cheap n' plenty Mexican.
- **Waterloo & City** • 12517 W Washington Blvd
  310-391-4222 • $$$
  Continental classics with California produce (and New World cocktails).

Shopping

- **Los Angeles Wine Co.** • 4935 McConnell Ave
  310-306-9463
  Stemware, gift bags, and wine accessories, too.
- **Mitsuwa Marketplace** • 3760 S Centinela Ave
  310-398-2113
  Everything Japanese. Fast food court.
- **Time Travel Mart** • 12515 Venice Blvd
  310-915-0200
  When you need provisions for the fourth dimension.
- **Vanity Room** • 13217 W Washington Blvd
  310-821-3088
  Anthropologie-like boutique, but affordable.

N
1
2
3
A
B
C
D
Wilshire Blvd
Santa Monica Blvd
Little Santa Monica Blvd
Olympic Blvd
W Pico Blvd
Charleville Blvd
Gregory Way
Whitworth Dr
S Beverly Glen Blvd
Overland Ave
Westwood Blvd
Motor Ave
Manning Ave
Beverwil Dr
Castle Heights Ave
S Robertson Blvd
National Blvd
Exposition Blvd
Santa Monica Fwy
Palms Blvd
S Sepulveda Blvd
San Diego Fwy
Venice Blvd
Washington Blvd
Culver Blvd
Cattaraugus Ave
Museum of Tolerance
20th Century Fox Studios
Rancho Park
Rancho Park Golf Course
Cheviot Hills Park
Hillcrest Country Club
Westside Pavilion
PAGE 248
CHEVIOT HILLS
PALMS
1. Whitworth Dr
2. Castello Pl
3. Dumfries Rd
4. Wicklow Rd
5. Glimerton Ave
6. Kincardine Ave
7. Kilrenney Ave
8. Cresta Pl
9. Monte Mar Pl
10. Duxbury Rd
11. Duxbury Ln
12. Guthrie Ct
13. Castle Heights Pl
14. McConnell Pl
15. Stellbar Pl
16. Robertson Pl
17. Kramerwood Pl
18. Philo St
19. Woodbine St
1/2 mile
.5 km

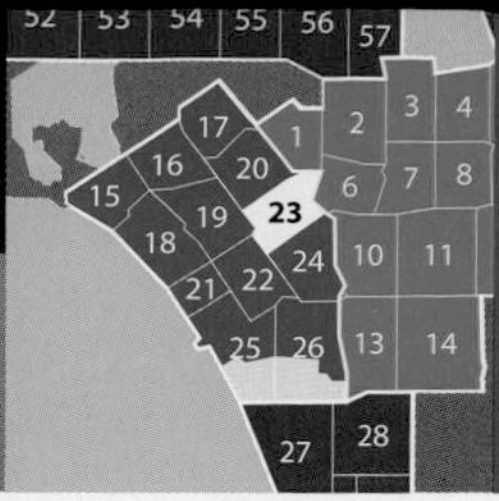

Rancho Park is Beverly Hills without the Chihuahua dyed pink or the U-Haul of baggage. This suburbanesque neighborhood has all the best trappings of small-town America—lovely houses with nice lawns, a walkable downtown area, and plenty of outdoor space for summer evening activity. And it's nestled between Westwood and Culver City, so if you need a little more action, it's not hard to find.

Landmarks

- **20th Century Fox Studios** • 10201 W Pico Blvd
  310-277-2121
  Check out the *Star Wars* mural. It's way cool.
- **Museum of Tolerance** • 9786 W Pico Blvd
  310-553-8403
  A humbling experience that is worth a visit.
- **Rancho Park Golf Course** • 10460 W Pico Blvd
  310-838-7373
  Good municipal golf course, but crowded.
- **Westside Pavilion** • 10800 W Pico Blvd
  310-470-8752
  We defy you to find your car at the end of any shopping expedition.

Nightlife

- **Steingarten** • 10543 W Pico Blvd
  310-441-0441
  Ugly as shit wall art, but decent beer.
- **The Wellesbourne** • 10929 W Pico Blvd
  310-474-0102
  Faux-scholarly turns dance party later on.

Restaurants

- **The Apple Pan** • 10801 W Pico Blvd
  310-475-3585 • $
  Famous hamburger joint.
- **Bourbon Street Shrimp** • 10928 W Pico Blvd
  310-474-0007 • $$
  Cajun and seafood.
- **Factor's Famous Deli** • 9420 W Pico Blvd
  310-278-9175 • $$
  New York diner/deli.
- **Gyu-Kaku** • 10925 W Pico Blvd
  310-234-8641 • $$$
  Japanese-style Korean BBQ.
- **Hop Li** • 10974 W Pico Blvd
  310-441-3708 • $$
  Cantonese cuisine.
- **John O'Groat's** • 10516 W Pico Blvd
  310-204-0692 • $$
  Breakfast hang-out.
- **Junior's** • 2379 Westwood Blvd
  310-475-5771 • $$
  A little bit of Brooklyn in West LA, including charmingly rude servers.
- **La Serenata de Garibaldi** • 10924 W Pico Blvd
  310-441-9667 • $$$
  Mexican with seafood specialties.
- **Label's Table Deli** • 9226 W Pico Blvd
  310-276-0388 • $$
  Friendly and affordable kosher Jewish deli.
- **Marty's Hamburger Stand** • 10558 W Pico Blvd
  310-836-6944 • $
  Old-school burger and hot dog shack.
- **The Milky Way** • 9108 W Pico Blvd
  310-859-0004 • $$$
  Kosher dairy restaurant owned by Steven Spielberg's mom.
- **n/naka** • 3455 S Overland Ave
  310-836-6252 • $$$$$
  Splurge-worthy Japanese kaiseki haute cuisine.
- **Norm's Restaurant** • 11001 W Pico Blvd
  310-479-2978 • $
  Classic diner food. Great sign.
- **Overland Café** • 3601 Overland Ave
  310-559-9999 • $$
  Truly a casual California eatery.
- **Picca** • 9575 W Pico Blvd
  310-277-0133 • $$$$
  A temple to Peruvian food.
- **Sotto** • 9575 W Pico Blvd
  310-277-0210 • $$$
  Pastas and breads and pizzas, side of pork.
- **Sushi Zo** • 9824 National Blvd
  310-842-3977 • $$$$
  Omakase-only and worth a trek, unless you're on a budget.
- **Westside Tavern** • 10850 W Pico Blvd
  310-470-1539 • $$$$
  Far more elegant than the name suggests.
- **Zen Bakery** • 10988 W Pico Blvd
  310-475-6727 • $
  Home of the muffin monk since 1975.

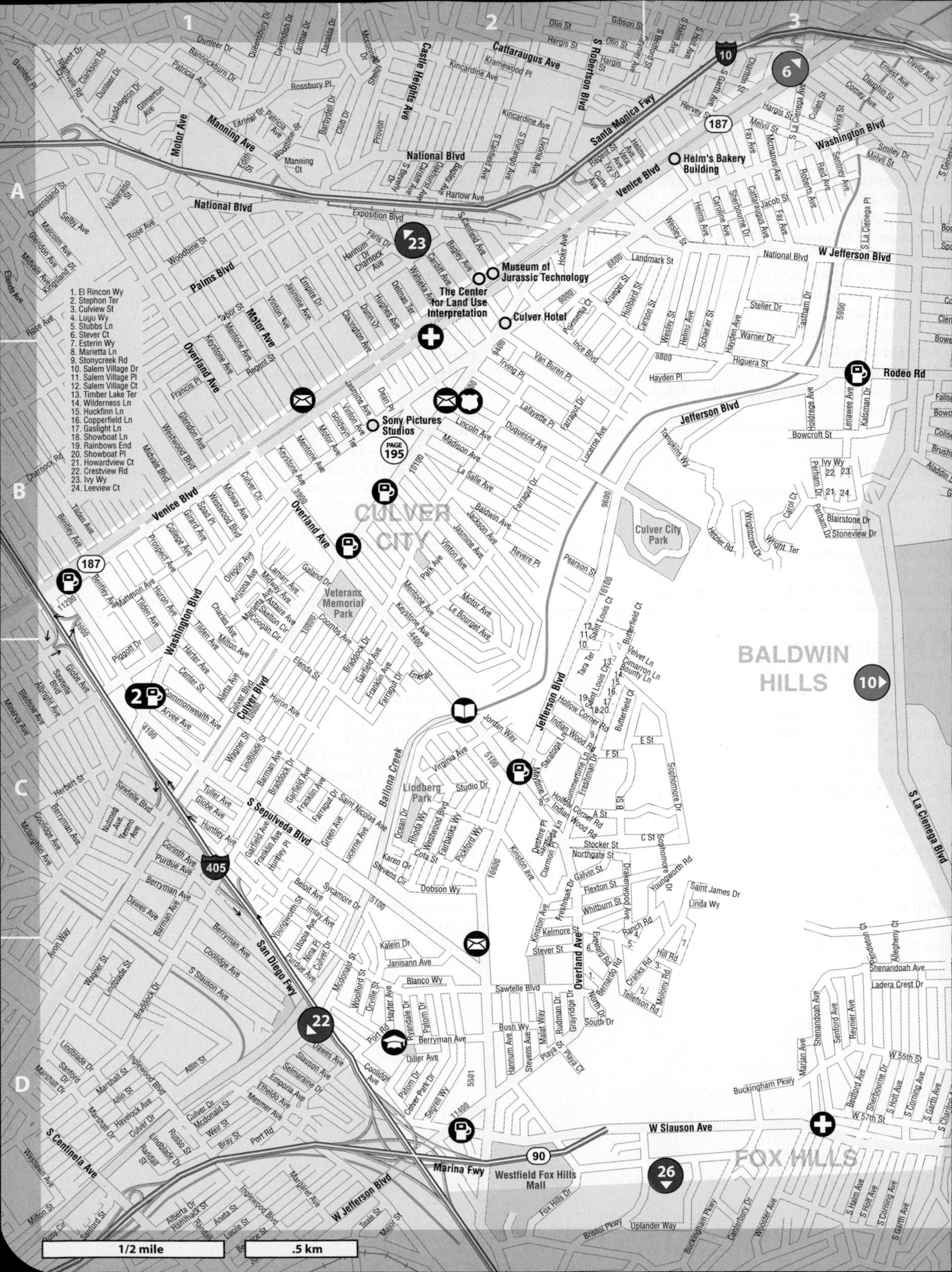
1
2
3
A
B
C
D
1. El Rincon Wy
2. Stephon Ter
3. Culview St
4. Lugo Wy
5. Stubbs Ln
6. Stever Ct
7. Esterin Wy
8. Marietta Ln
9. Stonycreek Rd
10. Salem Village Dr
11. Salem Village Pl
12. Salem Village Ct
13. Timber Lake Ter
14. Wilderness Ln
15. Huckfinn Ln
16. Copperfield Ln
17. Gaslight Ln
18. Showboat Ln
19. Rainbows End
20. Showboat Pl
21. Howardview Ct
22. Crestview Rd
23. Ivy Wy
24. Leeview Ct
CULVER CITY
BALDWIN HILLS
FOX HILLS
Helm's Bakery Building
Museum of Jurassic Technology
The Center for Land Use Interpretation
Culver Hotel
Sony Pictures Studios
PAGE 195
Veterans Memorial Park
Culver City Park
Lindberg Park
Westfield Fox Hills Mall
Santa Monica Fwy
San Diego Fwy
Marina Fwy
Venice Blvd
Washington Blvd
National Blvd
W Jefferson Blvd
Jefferson Blvd
Culver Blvd
Overland Ave
S Sepulveda Blvd
Sawtelle Blvd
W Slauson Ave
Rodeo Rd
S La Cienega Blvd
Ballona Creek
Palms Blvd
Motor Ave
Castle Heights Ave
Manning Ave
S Robertson Blvd
Cattaraugus Ave
Exposition Blvd
S Centinela Ave
10
405
90
187
6
10
22
23
26
1/2 mile
.5 km

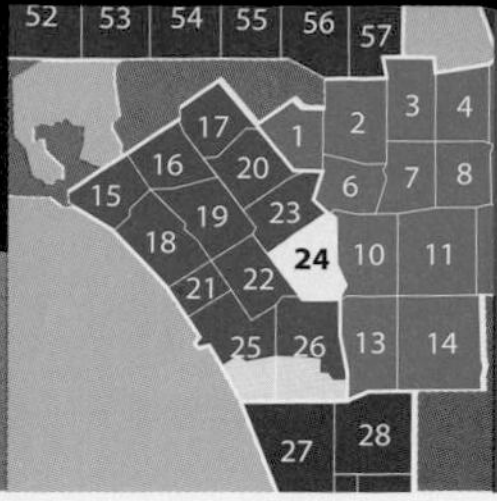

Culver City was once regarded as the New Jersey of Los Angeles, but call it "the armpit" no more. Not only have people realized the charm behind this once-maligned corner of the city but they're coming here to play, too. Today there are tons of great places to eat and hang out at along Washington and Culver Boulevards. And the addition of the **Kirk Douglas Theatre**, the restoration of the **Culver Hotel**, and the **Helms Bakery Building**, now full of elegant furniture for sale, have all added touches of class to the area.

Landmarks

- **The Center for Land Use Interpretation** • 9331 Venice Blvd
  310-839-5722
  Sublime presentation of humanity's impact on the face of America.
- **Culver Hotel** • 9400 Culver Blvd
  310-558-9400
  Home to many a munchkin during the shooting of *The Wizard of Oz*.
- **Helms Bakery** • 8758 Venice Blvd
  310-204-1865
  They used to make bread, now they sell furniture.
- **Museum of Jurassic Technology** • 9341 Venice Blvd
  310-836-6131
  The coolest. Check out Mary Davis's horn.
- **Sony Pictures Studios** • 10202 Washington Blvd
  310-244-6926
  Before Sony and Spider-Man, it was MGM and the Munchkins.

Nightlife

- **Backstage** • 10400 Culver Blvd
  310-839-3892
  Karaoke joint across from the Sony lot.
- **Blind Barber** • 10797 Washington Blvd
  310-841-6679
  Doesn't deserve the name "speakeasy," but it'll do in a pinch.
- **The Cinema Bar** • 3967 Sepulveda Blvd
  310-390-1328
  World's smallest honkytonk.
- **Cozy Inn** • 11155 Washington Pl
  310-838-3826
  Culver City dive-ish spot with good dancing.
- **Dear John's** • 11208 Culver Blvd
  310-397-0276
  Old-school piano bar.
- **Father's Office** • 3229 Helms Ave
  310-736-2224
  One of LA's original great-beer spots.
- **The Jazz Bakery** • 9820 Washington Blvd
  310-271-9039
  Live theatre-style jazz and yes, dessert.
- **Oldfields** • 10899 Venice Blvd
  310-842-8066
  Speakeasy-vibe and mighty fine cocktails.

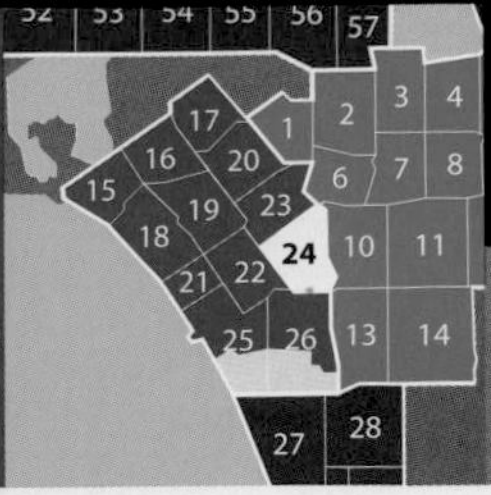

Culver City

Restaurants

- **Bamboo** • 10835 Venice Blvd
  310-287-0668 • $$$
  Caribbean.
- **Café Brasil** • 10831 Venice Blvd
  310-837-8957 • $$
  The fresh-squeezed juices are amazing!
- **Café Surfas** • 8777 Washington Blvd
  310-558-1458 • $
  Sandwiches made by food experts.
- **Conservatory for Coffee, Tea & Cocoa** • 10117 Washington Blvd
  310-558-0436 • $
  They roast their own and serve it up graciously.
- **The Coolhaus Shop** • 8588 Washington Blvd
  310-424-5559 • $
  The ice cream sandwich goes upscale.
- **Ford's Filling Station** • 9531 Culver Blvd
  310-202-1470 • $$$$
  Hip "gastropub" headed by Harrison Ford's chef son, Ben Ford.
- **George Petrelli's Famous Steakhouse** • 5615 S Sepulveda Blvd
  310-397-1438 • $$$
  Meat and potato lovers' paradise.
- **Honey's Kettle Fried Chicken** • 9537 Culver Blvd
  310-202-5453 • $$
  Tasty fried chicken, mouth-watering biscuits.
- **In-N-Out Burger** • 9245 W Venice Blvd
  800-786-1000 • $
  Top California burger joint.
- **India Sweets and Spices** • 9409 Venice Blvd
  310-837-5286 • $
  Cheap, filling veggie Indian fare.
- **Jasmine** • 4135 Sepulveda Blvd
  310-313-3767 • $
  Like Indian, but not. And halal.
- **Johnnie's Pastrami** • 4017 Sepulveda Blvd
  310-397-6654 • $
  The best dang dip in town. Great signage.
- **L'Epicerie Market** • 9900 Culver Blvd
  310-815-1600 • $$
  Casual dining, grocery-shopping, and Frenchness.
- **La Dijonaise** • 8703 Washington Blvd
  310-287-2770 • $$
  Typical Parisian entrees without the stuffiness or high prices. Divine desserts.
- **Lukshon** • 3239 Helms Ave
  310-202-6808 • $$$$
  Southeast Asian fine dining; eclectic menus, good cocktails.
- **Natalee Thai** • 10101 Venice Blvd
  310-202-7003 • $$
  Popular Pad Thai and curries.
- **S&W Country Diner** • 9748 Washington Blvd
  310-204-5136 • $
  Yee-haw! Breakfast's on.
- **Tito's Tacos** • 11222 Washington Pl
  310-391-5780 • $
  Cheap taco stand.
- **Versailles** • 10319 Venice Blvd
  310-558-3168 • $
  The LA institution's garlicy Cuban grub will stay with you.

Culver City

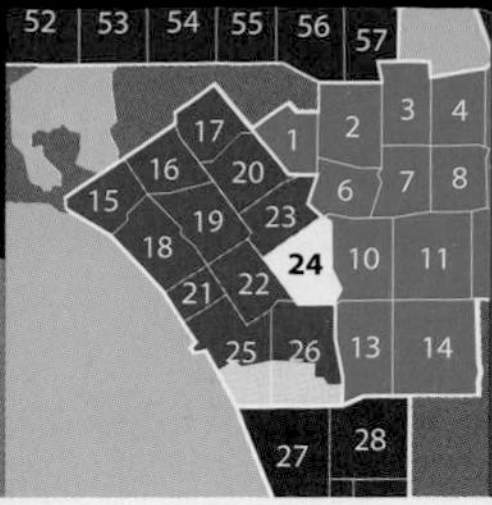

Culver City contains some of LA's more popular home-grown fast food joints (**Tito's Tacos**, **Johnnie's Pastrami**) and **The Jazz Bakery** still spins tunes you might barely remember, but of late this mini-city is perhaps better known for its grown-up restaurants. Try anything in the **Helms Bakery** complex, from dressed-up burgers to Asian fusion, or visit **La Dijonaise** for French without the stuffiness or prices. Meanwhile, **BottleRock** is a date-friendly wine bar.

Shopping

- **Attire** • 5879 Washington Blvd
  310-287-2333
  Discount women's clothing from major brands.
- **Comic Bug** • 4267 Overland Ave
  310-204-3240
  Comic books.
- **H.D. Buttercup** • 3225 Helms Ave
  310-558-8900
  Interior-design mecca in Helms Bakery building.
- **Surfas** • 8777 Washington Blvd
  310-559-4770
  They'll design your kitchen and stock it, too.

Map 25 • Marina del Rey / Westchester West

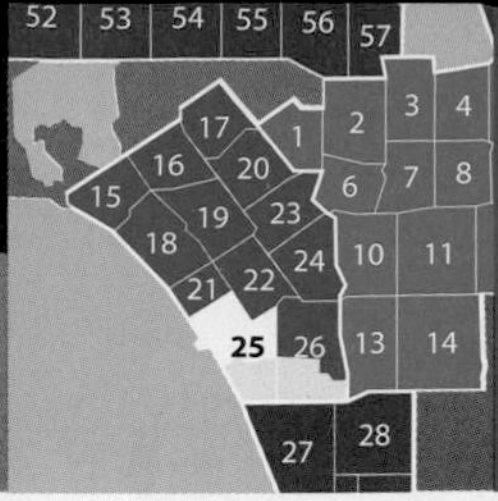

The mid-rise condos and taut-canvas feel of Marina del Rey's smartly dense marina area are perfect for Three's Company-style aging swingers who never quite got over the '80s. This is the largest man-made harbor in the world, and is full of every type of water vessel imaginable, from paddleboats to 200-foot yachts. Here the real estate ranges from charming to hideous, but always expensive.

oLandmarks

- **Ballona Wetlands** • Lincoln Blvd & W Jefferson Blvd
  Restored wetlands. View flora and fauna from walkway.
- **Fisherman's Village** • 13755 Fiji Way
  310-823-5411
  Quaint shopping and dining are geared to resemble a New England fishing town.
- **Marina City Club** • 4333 Admiralty Way
  310-822-0611
  Massive condo complex that has even turned up on shows like *Melrose Place*.

Nightlife

- **Brennan's** • 4089 Lincoln Blvd
  310-821-6622
  Irish pub with turtle racing.
- **Mo's Place** • 203 Culver Blvd
  310-822-6422
  Refer to Simpsons bartender. Add in dancing bartenders, violent patrons.
- **Prince O' Whales** • 335 Culver Blvd
  310-823-9826
  Low-key; divey not trendy.
- **Tompkins Square Bar and Grill** • 8522 Lincoln Blvd
  310-670-1212
  Love child of a dive and a sports bar. Good happy hour.

Restaurants

- **Alejo's** • 8343 Lincoln Blvd
  310-670-6677 • $$
  Classic cheap Italian.
- **Café Del Rey** • 4451 Admiralty Way
  310-823-6395 • $$$$
  Eclectic seafood.
- **Caffe Pinguini** • 6935 Pacific Ave
  310-306-0117 • $$$
  Italian on the beach.
- **Hacienda Del Rey** • 8347 Lincoln Blvd
  310-670-8588 • $$
  No-frills cheap Mexican, in a good way.
- **jer-ne** • 4375 Admiralty Way
  323-574-4333 • $$$$$
  The Ritz Carlton's restaurant; amazing views.
- **Kanpai Japanese Sushi Bar and Grill** • 8325 Lincoln Blvd
  310-338-7223 • $$$
  Great sushi in a trendy, modern atmosphere.
- **Mendocino Farms** • 4724 Admiralty Way
  310-822-2300 • $$
  Potentially the best sandwiches in town.
- **The Shack** • 185 Culver Blvd
  310-823-6222 • $$
  Cheap burgers and more.
- **Shanghai Red's** • 13813 Fiji Way
  310-823-4522 • $$$
  Lovely Victorian-style restaurant with incredible brunch.
- **Tandoor-A-India** • 8406 Pershing Dr
  310-822-1435 • $$
  Cozy dining. Order the mango lassi.
- **Tony P's Dockside Grill** • 4445 Admiralty Way
  310-823-4534 • $$
  Kick-back tavern with a nice breeze.
- **The Warehouse** • 4499 Admiralty Way
  310-823-5451 • $$$
  Romantic enough to ask someone to marry you.

Shopping

- **Celebrity Extensions** • 8328 Lincoln Blvd
  310-338-9300
  Designer duds mixed with indie clothing.
- **Panini Coffee & Café** • 4325 Glencoe Ave
  310-823-4446
  Delicious sandwiches and friendly service!

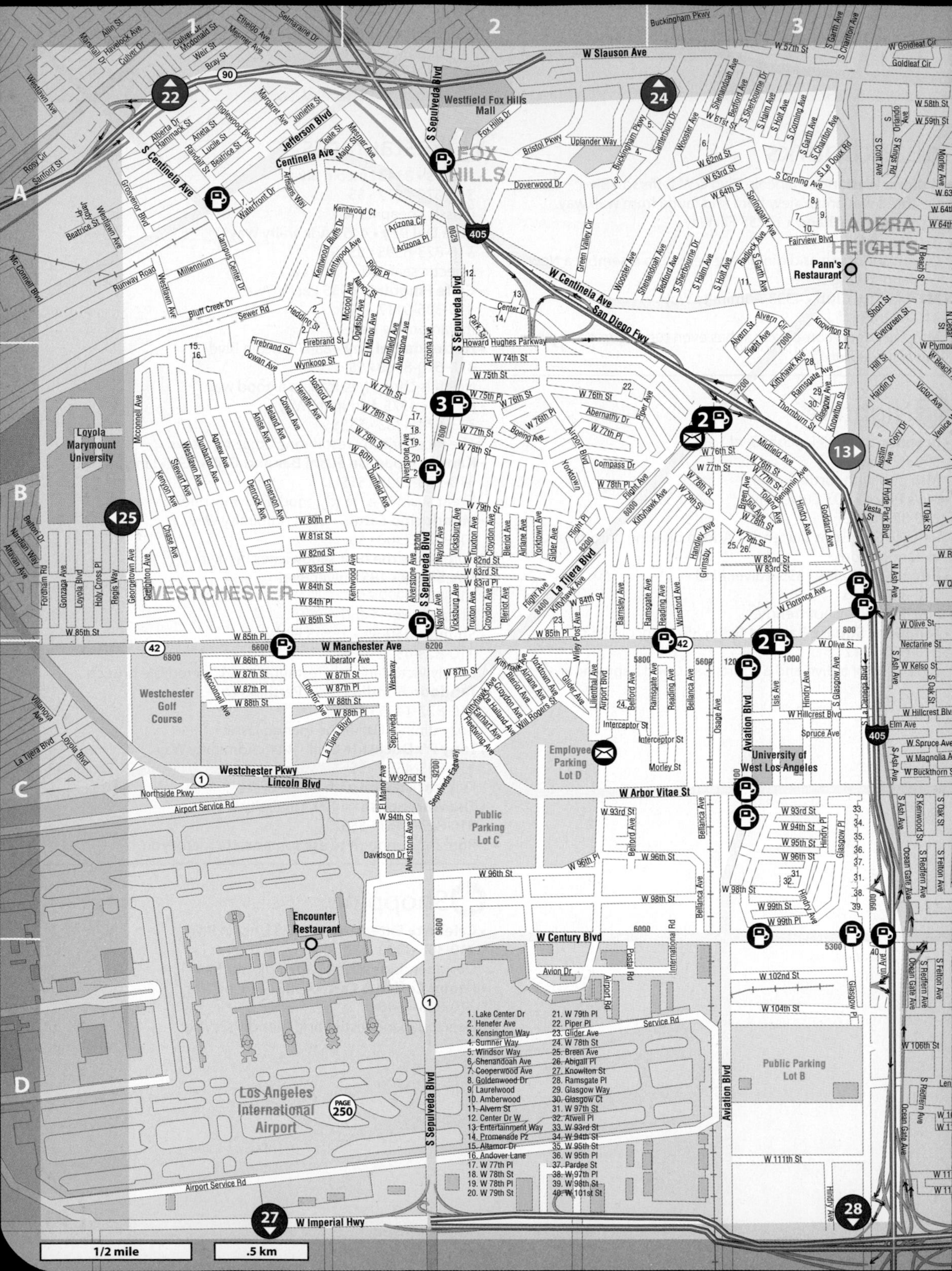
1
2
3
A
B
C
D
22
24
13
25
27
28
Westfield Fox Hills Mall
FOX HILLS
LADERA HEIGHTS
Pann's Restaurant
Loyola Marymount University
WESTCHESTER
Westchester Golf Course
Employee Parking Lot D
University of West Los Angeles
Public Parking Lot C
Encounter Restaurant
Public Parking Lot B
Los Angeles International Airport
PAGE 250
W Slauson Ave
S Sepulveda Blvd
Jefferson Blvd
Centinela Ave
S Centinela Ave
W Centinela Ave
San Diego Fwy
Howard Hughes Parkway
La Tijera Blvd
W Manchester Ave
Westchester Pkwy
Lincoln Blvd
Airport Service Rd
W Arbor Vitae St
W Century Blvd
Aviation Blvd
W Imperial Hwy
Service Rd
W Florence Ave
1/2 mile
.5 km
1. Lake Center Dr
2. Henefer Ave
3. Kensington Way
4. Sumner Way
5. Windsor Way
6. Shenandoah Ave
7. Cooperwood Ave
8. Goldenwood Dr
9. Laurelwood
10. Amberwood
11. Alvern St
12. Center Dr W
13. Entertainment Way
14. Promenade Pz
15. Altamor Dr
16. Andover Lane
17. W 77th Pl
18. W 78th St
19. W 78th Pl
20. W 79th St
21. W 79th Pl
22. Piper Pl
23. Glider Ave
24. W 78th St
25. Breen Ave
26. Abigail Pl
27. Knowlton St
28. Ramsgate Pl
29. Glasgow Way
30. Glasgow Ct
31. W 97th St
32. Atwell Pl
33. W 93rd St
34. W 94th St
35. W 95th St
36. W 95th Pl
37. Pardee St
38. W 97th Pl
39. W 98th St
40. W 101st St

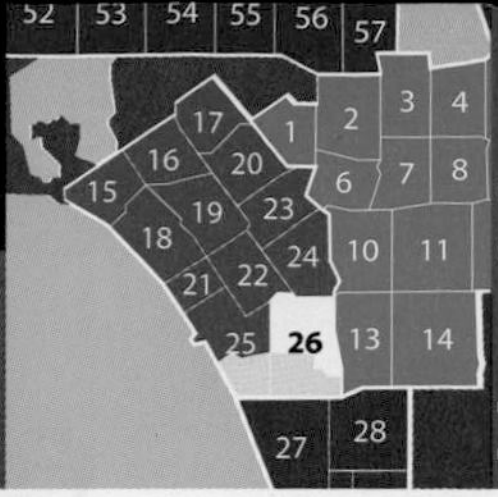

If you're coming through Fox Hills or Ladera Heights, you probably either live in the neighborhood or you're making your way out to LAX. For those of you with golf clubs and a day off, or a long flight delay, come out to the putting green at the **Westchester Golf Course**. Or if you need new sneakers, the selection at Westfield Fox Hills Mall is more than enough to keep you busy for a while.

Landmarks

- **Encounter Restaurant** • 209 World Way
  310-215-5151
  Spaceship architecture from '60s with a 360-degree view.
- **Pann's Restaurant** • 6710 La Tijera Blvd
  323-776-3770
  Mid-century modern diner designed by Armet & Davis.

Restaurants

- **Buggy Whip** • 7420 La Tijera Blvd
  310-645-7131 • $$$$$
  Go for the piano bar more than the food.
- **Encounter Restaurant** • 209 World Way
  310-215-5151 • $$$
  Pre-flight futuristic meals.
- **In-N-Out Burger** • 9149 S Sepulveda Blvd
  800-786-1000 • $
  Top California burger joint.
- **Paco's Tacos** • 6212 W Manchester Ave
  310-645-8692 • $
  Inexpensive Tex-Mex.
- **Panera Bread** • 8647 S Sepulveda Blvd
  310-641-9200 • $
  Excellent soup, coffee, sandwiches, and pastries.

Shopping

- **Westfield Culver City** • 6000 Sepulveda Blvd
  310-390-5073
  Middle-of-the-road fashion needs off the I-405.

Map 27 • El Segundo / Manhattan Beach

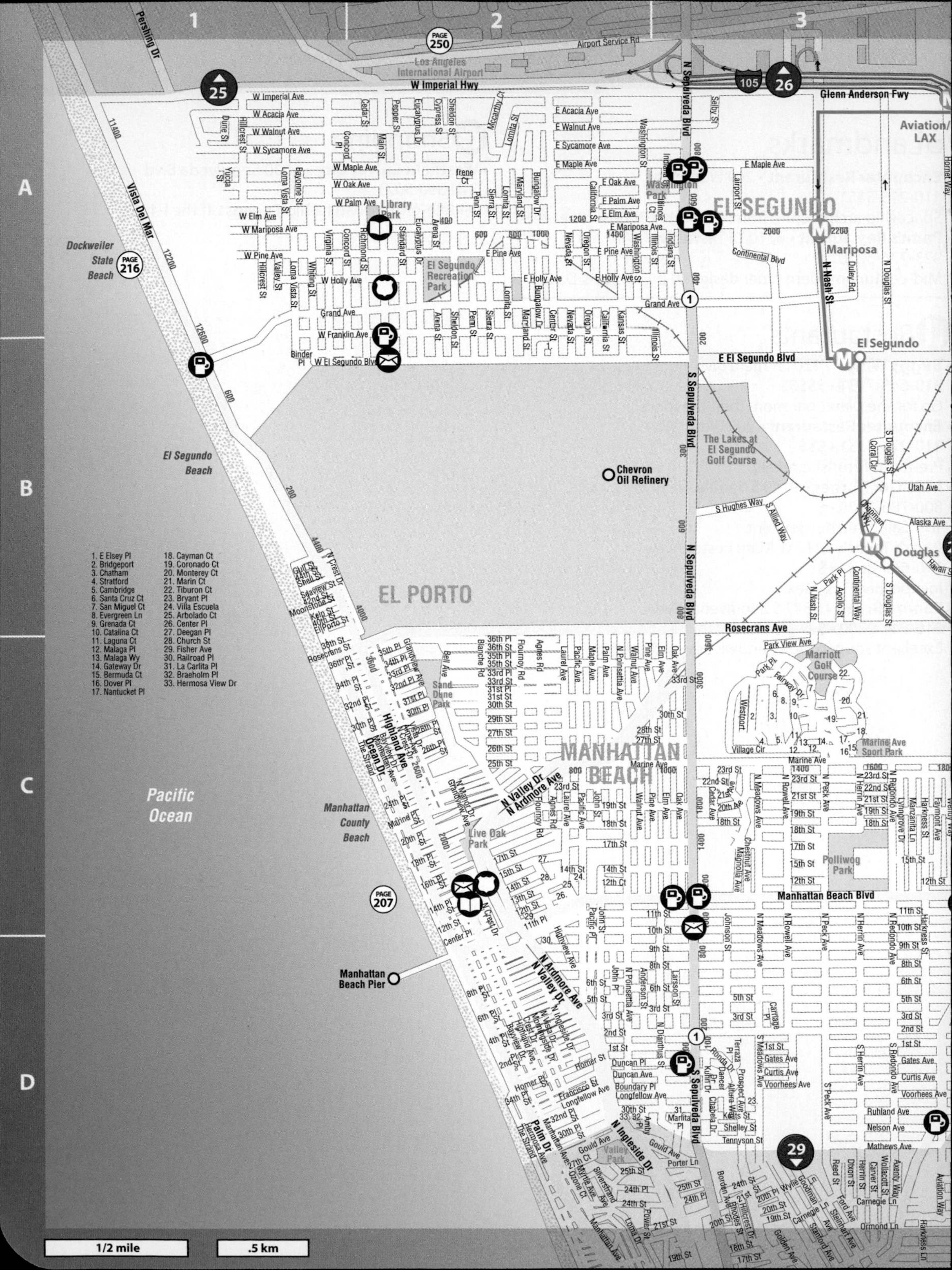

The mutation continues while Marvel Studios is making movies down the street. This area now includes its own mini-Hollywood; *CSI: Miami* and other shows film at Raleigh Studios. Planes from LAX rip the sky, and the 405's congestion encroaches, heightening the odd juxtaposition of Main Street coziness and increasingly obvious pollution. Generally, LA natives seem to prefer Manhattan to any other beach, smog and chemtrails notwithstanding—it's an international volleyball and wave-catching mecca, and the place where the Beach Boys first saw people surfing.

oLandmarks

- **Chevron Oil Refinery** • Rosecrans Ave & Sepulveda Blvd
  It ain't pretty, but it's definitely noticeable.
- **Manhattan Beach Pier** • West of Manhattan Beach Blvd
  Don't miss the Roundhouse Marine Studies Lab and Aquarium at the end of the pier!

Nightlife

- **2nd Half** • 516 N Sepulveda Blvd
  310-372-4343
  Uber sports junkies bar with lots o' games.
- **Baja Sharkeez** • 3600 Highland Ave
  310-545-8811
  Post-college hangout with good grub.
- **Ercoles** • 1101 Manhattan Ave
  310-372-1997
  Ultimate late-night meet-up spot; laid back meat market.
- **Hennessey's Tavern** • 313 Manhattan Beach Blvd
  310-546-4813
  Typical Irish pub; nuff said.
- **OB's Pub and Grill** • 3610 N Highland Ave
  310-546-1542
  Taco Tuesdays, beer, and TVs galore. Plus peanuts, to chuck at your buddies.
- **Pancho's** • 3615 Highland Ave
  310-545-6670
  Great house band on weekends and killer margs.
- **Pockets Sports Bar** • 516 N Sepulveda Blvd
  310-372-4343
  Uber sports junkies bar with lots o' games.
- **Purple Orchid** • 221 Richmond St
  310-322-5829
  Come for the Tikis, stay for the stiff drinks.
- **Rock and Brews** • 143 Main St
  310-615-9890
  Gene Simmons-owned bar featuring huge patio.
- **Shark's Cove** • 309 Manhattan Beach Blvd
  310-545-2683
  Sports bar with nightly specials.
- **Shellback Tavern** • 116 Manhattan Beach Blvd
  310-376-7857
  Roll off the beach to this South Bay staple with good stiff drinks.
- **Side Door** • 900 Manhattan Ave
  310-372-1084
  South Bay's attempt at a Hollywood lounge.
- **Summer's Sports Bar** • 3770 N Highland Ave
  310-545-9333
  Lots of TVs, two pool tables, not much else.
- **The Tavern on Main** • 123 Main St
  310-322-3645
  Big beer steins and above average bar food. Definitely a local spot.

Map 27

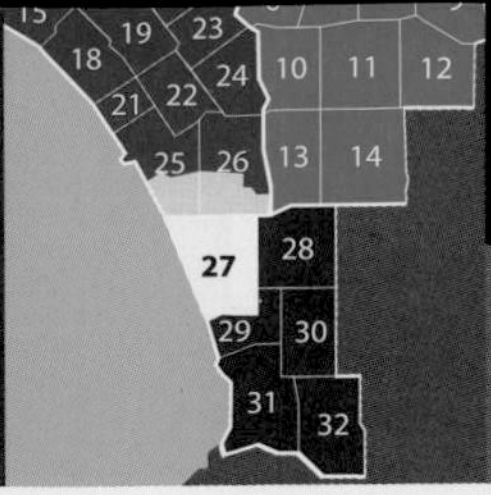

El Segundo / Manhattan Beach

Restaurants

- **Blue Butterfly Coffee Co.** • 351 Main St
  310-640-7687 • $
  Coffee house cafe.
- **Brew Co.** • 124 Manhattan Beach Blvd
  310-798-2744 • $$
  Burgers and home brewed beer.
- **Café Pierre** • 317 Manhattan Beach Blvd
  310-545-5252 • $$
  Fine dining with an eclectic menu.
- **Cozymel's** • 2171 Rosecrans Ave
  310-606-5464 • $$
  Tex-Mex.
- **El Tarasco** • 316 Rosecrans Ave
  310-545-4241 • $
  Open late; good Mexican food a block from the beach.
- **Fishing With Dynamite** • 1148 Manhattan Ave
  310-893-6299 • $$$$
  Cozy, seasonal, eclectic seafood; raw bar and rotating menu.
- **Fonz's** • 1017 Manhattan Ave
  310-376-1536 • $$$
  Steak and seafood. Good for group dinners.
- **Fusion Sushi** • 1150 N Morningside Dr
  310-802-1160 • $$
  Innovative without sacrificing taste.
- **The Habit Burger Grill** • 311 N Sepulveda Blvd
  310-524-9016 • $
  Simple menu, quality food. Crowded especially at lunch.
- **Houston's** • 1550 Rosecrans Ave
  310-643-7211 • $$$
  Casual, upscale American favorites.
- **The Hummus Factory** • 204 E Grand Ave
  310-322-1000 • $
  Super friendly staff makes the mediocre food more enjoyable.
- **Il Fornaio** • 1800 Rosecrans Ave
  310-725-9555 • $$$
  Tuscan chain.
- **Katsu!** • 302 Rosecrans Ave
  310-546-3761 • $$
  Happy Hour = 99 cent beer + $2.50 hand rolls. Awesome.
- **The Kettle** • 1138 Highland Ave
  310-545-8511 • $$
  24 hours, a block from the Manhattan Pier, good brunch.
- **La Sosta Enoteca** • 3713 Highland Ave
  310-796-1200 • $$$
  An Italian gem with charming waiters.
- **Le Pain Quotidien** • 451 Manhattan Beach Blvd
  310-546-6411 • $$
  Tasty and healthy salads, sandwiches, and desserts.
- **The Local Yolk** • 3414 Highland Ave
  310-546-4407 • $
  Get breakfast here after you drop Aunt Mira off at the airport.
- **Mama D's** • 1125 Manhattan Ave
  310-546-1492 • $$$
  Old school Italian with large portions. Complimentary garlic knots are delicious but lethal.
- **Mangiamo** • 128 Manhattan Beach Blvd
  310-318-3434 • $$$$
  Light Northern Italian with romantic wine grotto.
- **MB Post** • 1142 Manhattan Ave
  310-545-5405 • $$$
  Inimitable burgers, swaggering sauce, and laid-back Manhattan Beach attitude.
- **Mucho Ultima Mexicana** • 903 Manhattan Ave
  310-374-4422 • $$$$$
  Upscale Cal-Mexican with good margaritas.
- **North End Caffé** • 3421 Highland Ave
  310-546-4782 • $
  Sandwiches, salads, and fries with four dipping sauces.
- **OB's Pub and Grill** • 3610 N Highland Ave
  310-546-1542 • $$
  Taco Tuesdays, beer, and TVs galore. Plus peanuts, to chuck at your buddies.
- **The Original Rinaldi's** • 323 Main St
  310-647-2860 • $
  Comes highly recommended…and rightfully so.
- **Petros** • 451 Manhattan Beach Blvd
  310-545-4100 • $$$$$
  Styling' Greek food in hip setting. Don't miss the limoncello shots.
- **Rock'n Fish** • 120 Manhattan Beach Blvd
  310-379-9900 • $$
  Always packed. Lunch and dinner from the sea.
- **Second City Bistro** • 223 Richmond St
  310-322-6085 • $$$
  Food is creative American. Don't miss the free wine tastings on Mondays.
- **Simmzy's** • 229 Manhattan Beach Blvd
  310-546-1201 • $$
  Open air and great food for the beer connoisseur.
- **Sloopy's** • 3416 Highland Ave
  310-545-1373 • $
  Go for the burgers and patio seating.
- **Snax Burgers** • 202 E Imperial Ave
  310-640-9766 • $
  Burgers and Mexican? Yes, please.
- **The Spot** • 110 2nd St
  310-376-2355 • $$
  Vegetarian specialties.
- **SusieCakes** • 3500 N Sepulveda Blvd
  310-303-3780 • $$$
  Cakes, cupcakes, and cookies made from scratch…(try the German Chocolate!)
- **Uncle Bill's Pancake House** • 1305 Highland Ave
  310-545-5177 • $$
  Breakfast by the beach.
- **Veggie Grill** • 720 S Allied Way
  310-535-0025 • $
  Where the vegetarians go to eat "meat". Surprisingly delish and meat-like.
- **Versailles** • 1000 N Sepulveda Blvd
  310-937-6829 • $$
  The LA institution's garlicy Cuban grub will stay with you.

El Segundo / Manhattan Beach

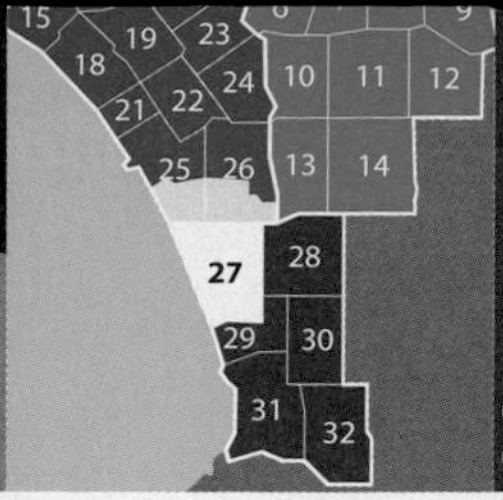

Map 27

This mostly residential community boasts a more laid-back, mature nightlife scene than its scrappier neighbor Hermosa Beach. There's an abundance of eccentric shops and cafes. **Café Pierre**, a French bistro, has been a local fixture since '77. The area near the main pier of Manhattan County Beach draws the biggest crowds, and stays lively at night after the beachcombers, volleyball players, and metal detector dudes clear out. Savvy locals love the nearby El Porto Beach for its quiet(er) shores and massive waves.

Shopping

- **Bacchus Wine Made Simple** • 1000 Manhattan Ave
310-372-2021
The best neighborhood wine store with a huge variety of gourmet food.
- **Diane's Beach Fever** • 1125 Manhattan Beach Blvd
310-546-9868
Huge selection of bikinis and beachwear.
- **Diane's Beachwear** • 125 Manhattan Beach Blvd
310-546-5869
Huge selection of bikinis and beachwear.
- **Dolly Rocker** • 212 Manhattan Beach Blvd
310-374-3396
Rock star clothes and accessories.
- **East Coast Bagel** • 3014 N Sepulveda Blvd
310-546-0089
Big selection of bagels and bagel accoutrements.
- **Fry's Electronics** • 3600 N Sepulveda Blvd
310-364-3797
Polynesian-themed electronic superstore.
- **Growing Wild** • 1201 Highland Ave
310-545-4432
Great floral creations.
- **Katwalk** • 312 Manhattan Beach Blvd
310-543-4500
Brilliant designer knockoffs at low prices
- **Lucky Brand** • 1113 Manhattan Ave
310-798-8000
You can't help but get lucky here.
- **Magpie** • 1141 Highland Ave
310-546-5132
Classy, conversation-starting home décor.
- **Mandarine** • 329 Manhattan Beach Blvd
310-546-1545
Trendy clothing that's well made and at low prices. Be sure to always check out the sale rack.
- **Michael Stars** • 1114 Manhattan Ave
310-376-8700
A variety of one size fit all seasonless tanks and tops.
- **Skechers** • 1121 Manhattan Ave
310-318-3116
Funky sneakers and sandals at corporate headquarters' shop.
- **Tabula Rasa Essentials** • 919 Manhattan Ave
310-318-3385
Greatest bath and body store ever. Ideal for girly-girl presents.
- **True Religion Brand Jeans** • 451 Manhattan Beach Blvd
310-406-3882
Uber trendy and expensive jeans that only look good on a few.

N
1
2
3
A
B
C
D
LAX
PAGE 250
DEL AIRE
Aviation/ LAX
26
13
14
27
29
30
105
405
Hawthorne
Crenshaw
Redondo Beach
HAWTHORNE
LAWNDALE
EL CAMINO VILLAGE
Los Angeles Air Force Base
Del Aire County Park
Eucalyptus Park
Hawthorne Municipal Airport
Hawthorne Memorial Park
Jim Thorpe Park
Jane Adams Park
Budger County Park
The Beach Boys Monument
Glenn Anderson Fwy
San Diego Fwy
W Imperial Hwy
W El Segundo Blvd
W Rosecrans Ave
Manhattan Beach Blvd
Marine Ave
Space Park Blvd
Santa Fe Ave
Aviation Blvd
Inglewood Ave
Hawthorne Blvd
Prairie Ave
S Crenshaw Blvd
Broadway
Northrop Ave
Lennox Blvd
Dominguez Creek
W Redondo Beach Blvd
W 106th St
W 107th St
W 108th St
W 109th St
W 110th St
W 111th St
W 112th St
W 113th St
W 115th St
W 116th St
W 117th St
W 118th St
W 119th St
W 120th St
W 126th St
W 129th St
W 130th St
W 132nd St
W 135th St
W 145th St
W 147th St
W 149th St
W 152nd St
W 153rd St
W 154th St
W 156th St
W 159th St
W 160th St
W 161st St
W 162nd St
W 163rd St
W 164th St
W 165th St
1/2 mile
.5 km

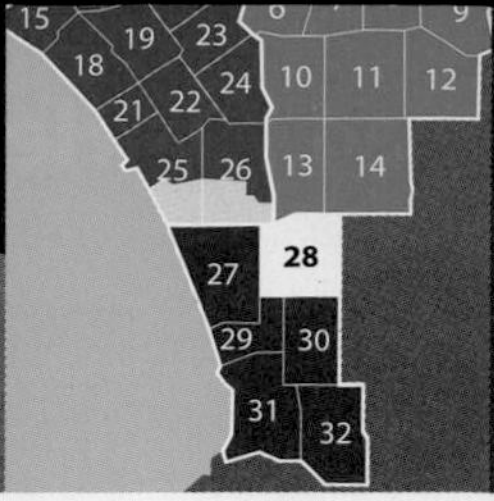

Covering six square miles and ensconced by the 105, 110, and 405 freeways, Hawthorne, named after author Nathaniel, calls itself "the hub of the South Bay." Hawthorne is headquarters for Northrop Grumman and borders LAX, so the aviation and aerospace industries are kind of a big deal here—it's also known as "the cradle of aviation." Hawthorne's own municipal airport is aptly known as Jack Northrop Field.

oLandmarks

- **The Beach Boys Monument** • 3701 W 119th St
  A brick monument where the Wilson house used to stand.

Restaurants

- **B & R's Old Fashion Burgers** • 3512 W Rosecrans Ave
  310-679-4774 • $
  Huge, delicious, world-famous burgers!
- **Daphne's Greek Café** • 2700 Marine Ave
  310-676-9165 • $
  Excellent Baklava!
- **El Pollo Inka** • 15400 Hawthorne Blvd
  310-676-6665 • $$
  Chicken fit for Virococha.
- **In-N-Out Burger** • 3801 Inglewood Ave
  800-786-1000 • $
  Top California burger joint.
- **Piggie's** • 4601 W Rosecrans Ave
  310-679-6326 • $
  Older style Greek coffee shop.

Map 29 • Hermosa Beach / Redondo Beach North

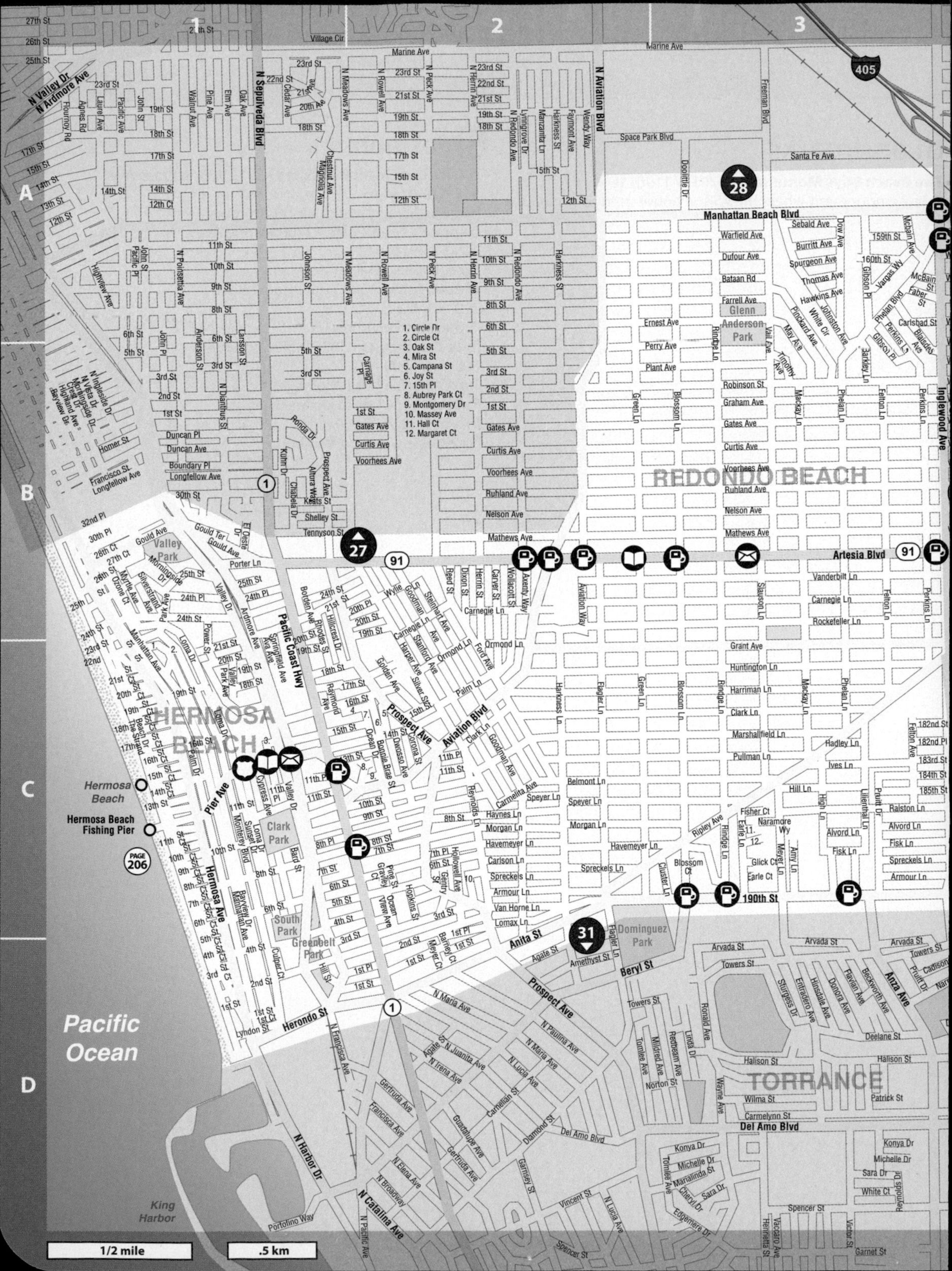

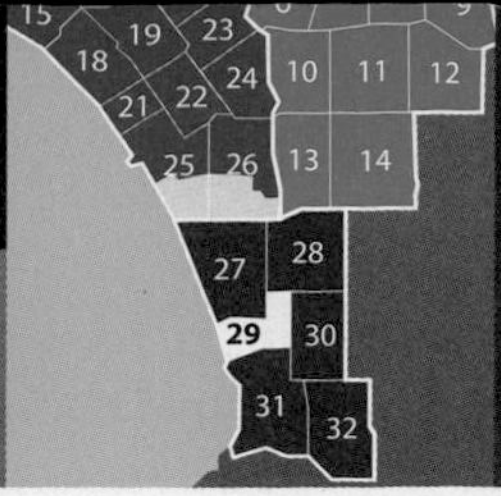

Part quaint beach town, part post-college town, Hermosa Beach incubated Black Flag, the Descendents, and The Beach Boys. An unusual combination of homey and hoppin', you'll know you're there when you begin to notice the street signs, which are brown with an almost antique typeface. Hermosa is anything but outdated, however. Whether you want to stroll through an art gallery with a latte, blade on the Strand, or catch the sunset with a margarita during happy hour, you'll find somewhere to do it near the cross streets of Pier and Hermosa Avenues. Make sure to stop by the statue of Tim Kelly surfing that's right on the pier.

oLandmarks

- **Hermosa Beach •**
  Laid back, surf-centric; Spanish for "beautiful."
- **Hermosa Beach Fishing Pier •** Pier Ave
  Just bring your pole. There are bait and tackle shops right on the pier.

Nightlife

- **Abigaile •** 1301 Manhattan Ave
  310-798-8227
  A one-time Stone brewer brews here now.
- **Café Boogaloo •** 1238 Hermosa Ave
  310-308-4326
  New Orleans café with live music. Attracts 30+ crowd.
- **Comedy & Magic Club •** 1018 Hermosa Ave
  310-372-1193
  Off-Hollywood club with an all-star lineup.
- **Dolphin Bar •** 1995 Artesia Blvd
  310-318-3339
  South Bay's only gay bar; cheap drinks and fun regulars.
- **Fat Face Fenner's Fishack •** 53 Pier Ave
  310-379-5550
  A local hangout: more bar, less nightclub.
- **Hennessey's Tavern •** 8 Pier Ave
  310-372-5759
  Californian favorites.
- **Hermosa Beach Yacht Club •** 66 Hermosa Ave
  310-376-6767
  No ships are pulling in this port. Local dive with schooners of beer.
- **The Lighthouse Café •** 30 Pier Ave
  310-376-9833
  Jazz by the beach.
- **Patrick Molloys •** 50 Pier Ave
  310-798-9762
  Good brews on tap inside and a shorter line outside.
- **Poop Deck •** 1272 The Strand
  310-376-3223
  Guy paradise with lots of games. Pool, cheap beer, and back patio.
- **Saint Rocke •** 142 Pacific Coast Hwy
  310-372-0035
  Variety of live music. Becomes a piano bar on Tuesday nights.
- **Underground Pub & Grill •** 1334 Hermosa Ave
  310-318-3818
  English themed sports pub with darts and pool. Attracts the ex-pats.

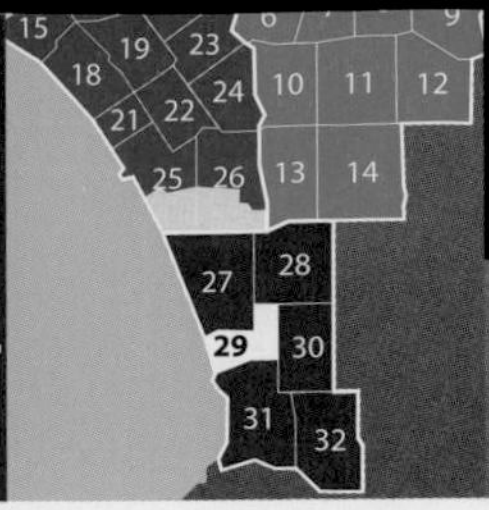

Hermosa Beach / Redondo Beach North

Restaurants

- **The Bottle Inn** • 26 22nd St
  310-376-9595 • $$$
  Campy old school Italian restaurant with phenemonal wine list.
- **Buona Vita** • 439 Pier Ave
  310-379-7626 • $$
  Best Italian in town. BYO vino.
- **Créme de la Crepe** • 424 Pier Ave
  310-937-2822 • $$
  Savory or sweet. How do you say "yum" in French?
- **El Burrito Jr** • 919 Pacific Coast Hwy
  310-316-5058 • $
  Always a line outside this amazingly authentic Mexican food stand.
- **El Gringo** • 2620 Hermosa Ave
  310-376-1381 • $
  Cheap Mexican. Enjoy 2 for 1 tacos on Tuesday and sit on the open air roof.
- **Fritto Misto** • 316 Pier Ave
  310-318-6098 • $$
  Create your own pasta combo or choose a house special.
- **Good Stuff Restaurant** • 1286 The Strand
  310-374-2334 • $$
  Fabulous people watching on the Strand. Oh, and they have good healthy food, too.
- **Havana Mania** • 3615 Inglewood Ave
  310-725-9075 • $$
  Cuban cuisine at its finest!
- **Hennessey's Tavern** • 8 Pier Ave
  310-372-5759 • $$
  Californian favorites.
- **La Sosta Enoteca** • 2700 Manhattan Ave
  310-318-1556 • $$$
  An Italian gem with charming waiters.
- **Martha's 22nd Street Grill** • 25 22nd St
  310-376-7786 • $$
  American fusion.
- **The Med** • 73 Pier Ave
  310-318-2666 • $$
  Try tapas on the patio.
- **Paisanos** • 1132 Hermosa Ave
  310-376-9883 • $
  Pizza straight from New York.
- **Pedone's Pizza** • 1332 Hermosa Ave
  310-376-0949 • $
  One of the few places at the beach where you can get NY-style pizza.
- **Phuket Thai** • 901 N Pacific Coast Hwy
  310-374-9598 • $$
  Try to say the name out loud without giggling! Tasty Thai in pretty setting.

Hermosa Beach / Redondo Beach North

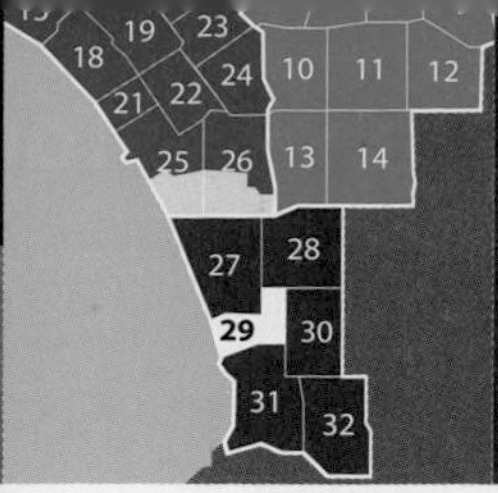

f you're under 25 or over 30 and experiencing a midlife crisis, Pier Avenue is the place to go for a night out. Go arly or spend the evening standing in queue on the pier. The dress code includes bleached hair, flip-flops, and heap shades. **Patrick Molloy's** represents all that's typical of the Hermosa scene (practice saying "dude," "like," nd "that's so random" like you mean it).

Shopping

Aardvarks • 2621 Artesia Blvd
310-370-6500
Vintage clothes and great costumes all year round.

Stars Antique Market • 526 Pier Ave
310-318-2800
Grandma's barn in a beach town.

• **Yak & Yeti** • 1124 Hermosa Ave
310-372-4315
Best Tibetan shop for Buddha statues or singing bowls.

• **Yari** • 327 Pier Ave
310-937-9800
Trendy, affordable clothing that doesn't fall apart.

Map 30 • Torrance North

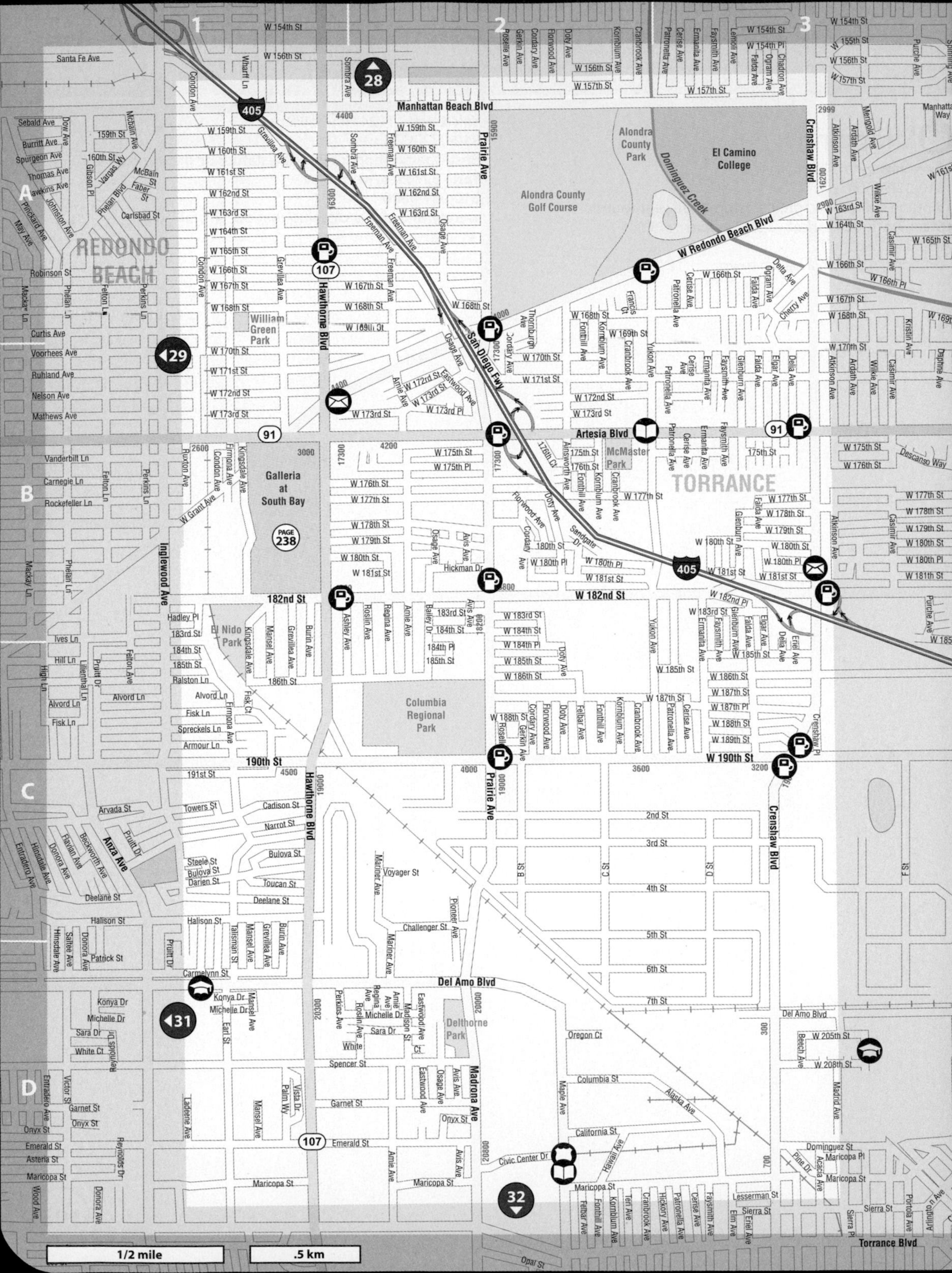

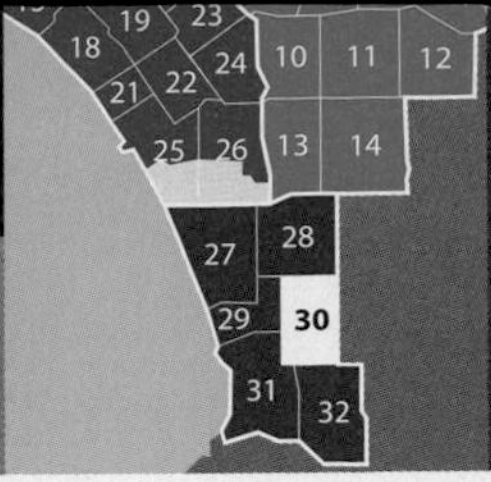

Torrance is still conspicuously suburban, with its tract homes and big-box retail outlets, but it, too, is feeling the residential push from the west. If you're looking for a mall-style chain retailer, you'll likely find it in the **South Bay Galleria**. El Camino isn't just a bitchin' ride, it's also a local community college that's worth a gander for recent North High grads or those wishing to rejoin the educational world.

Restaurants

- **Flossie's** • 3566 Redondo Beach Blvd
  310-352-4037 • $
  The fried chicken is legendary.
- **Pitalicious** • 20527 S Western Ave
  310-328-7482 • $
  Amazing cucumber dip; popular with the local working crowd.

Shopping

- **Pleasure Island** • 18426 Hawthorne Blvd
  310-793-9477
  All the sexy stuff you'll ever need.
- **South Bay Galleria** • 1815 Hawthorne Blvd
  310-371-7546
  Galleria means mall in California speak.

Map 31 • Redondo Beach

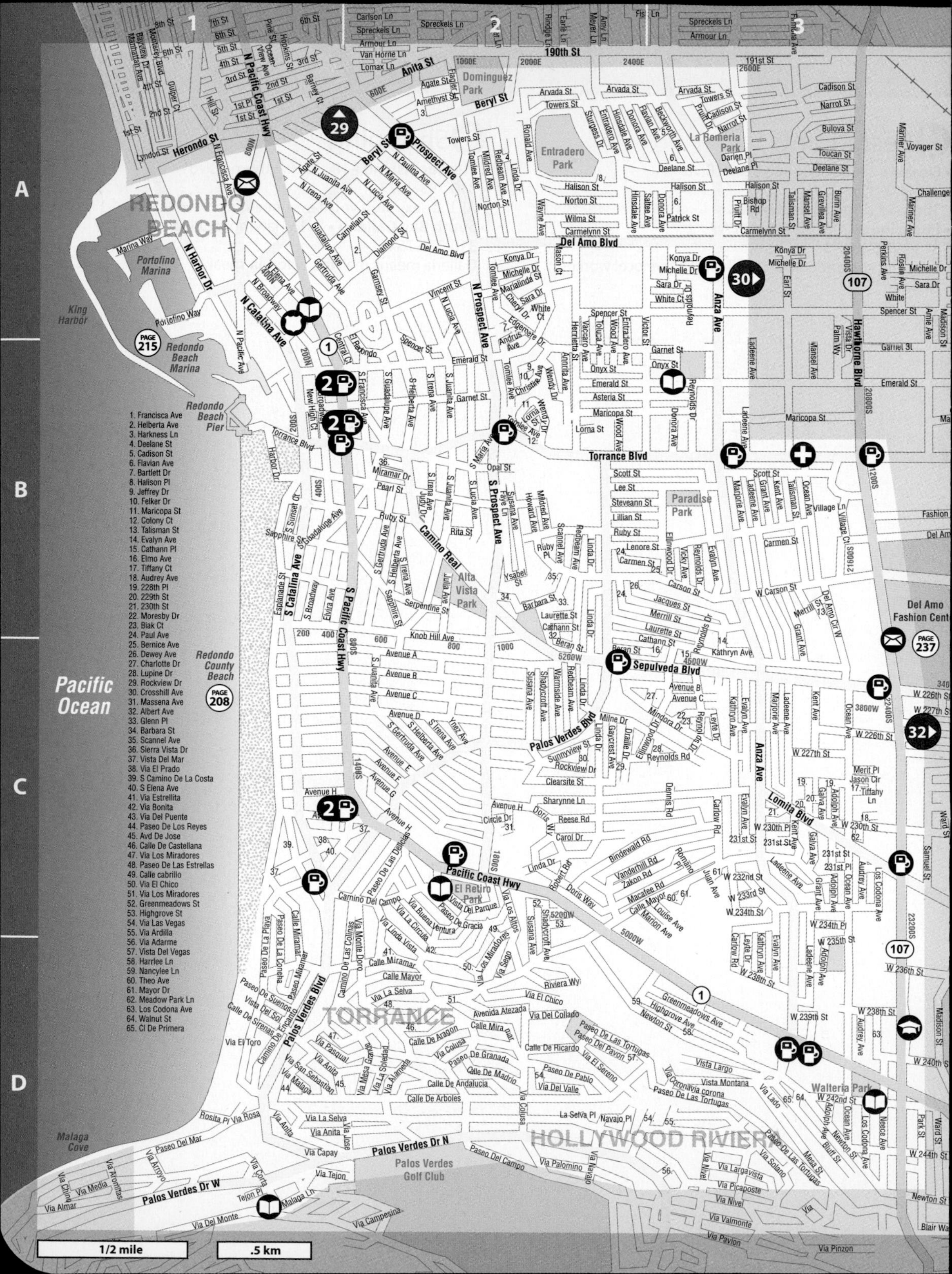

Sun, surf, and a beautiful beach are the hallmarks of Redondo Beach. The largest beach city is also the most suburban. Not that there aren't hotspots, but Redondo lacks a concentrated nightlife scene. That also means that the beaches are less crowded and parking is more plentiful.

Nightlife

- **Hudson House** • 514 N Pacific Coast Hwy
310-798-9183
Specialty throwback cocktails and a great beer selection.
- **Naja's Place** • 154 International Boardwalk
310-376-9951
Humongous selection of beer on tap; don't miss weekend house hair band.
- **Old Tony's** • 210 Fishermans Wharf
310-374-1442
Old School Vegas meets the beach with campy live music.
- **The Portofino Hotel & Marina** • 260 Portofino Way
310-379-8481
Jazz nights. On the water, great view, solid wine list.

Restaurants

- **Bluewater Grill** • 665 N Harbor Dr
310-318-3474 • $$$
Fresh fish and seafood specialties.
- **The Bull Pen** • 314 Avenue I
310-375-7797 • $$
Good old-school steak joint.
- **Captain Kidd's** • 209 N Harbor Dr
310-372-7703 • $$
Seafood dinners run from $7.99 to $22.00 for a whole lobster!
- **Catalina Coffee Company** • 126 N Catalina Ave
310-318-2499 • $
Homier than Starbucks. Breakfast, sandwiches, and, of course, coffee.
- **Charlie's** • 601 N Pacific Coast Hwy
310-374-8581 • $$
Neighborhood gem with real east coast Italian food at low prices.
- **Chez Melange** • 1611 S Catalina Ave
310-540-1222 • $$$$
Foodies from all over LA flock to the eclectic, continental menu.
- **Eat At Joe's** • 400 N Pacific Coast Hwy
310-376-9570 • $$
Classic diner fare, bring your appetite. Beer and wine available.
- **El Torito Grill** • 21321 Hawthorne Blvd
310-543-1896 • $$
Good food, great margaritas, free tortillas you can't stop eating.
- **Gina Lee's Bistro** • 211 Palos Verdes Blvd
310-375-4462 • $$
Neighborhoody Cal-Asian bistro food.
- **The Green Temple** • 1700 S Catalina Ave
310-944-4525 • $
Eat away the toxins at this organic, holistic garden spot.
- **Hennessey's Tavern** • 1712 S Catalina Ave
310-540-8443 • $
Bar food at its finest, a great place to watch the game and drink hearty.
- **HT Grill** • 1701 S Catalina Ave
310-791-4849 • $$
Innovative, eclectic bistro food at reasonable prices.
- **Japonica** • 1304 S Pacific Coast Hwy
310-316-9477 • $$$
Fresh designer sushi and private booths.
- **Kincaid's** • 500 Fishermans Wharf
310-318-6080 • $$$
A room with an ocean view…and great seafood.
- **Lucille's Smokehouse BBQ** • 21420 Hawthorne Blvd
310-370-7427 • $$
Southern cooking in Southern CA. Big portions, big menu.
- **The Original Pancake House** • 1756 S Pacific Coast Hwy
310-543-9875 • $
Line up with the weekend breakfast crowd.
- **Pedone Pizza** • 1819 S Catalina Ave
310-373-6397 • $
Just follow the heavenly smell to NY-style pizza.
- **Redondo Beach Brewing Co.** • 1814 S Catalina Ave
310-316-8477 • $$
Basic brews and burgers.
- **Riviera Mexican Grill** • 1615 S Pacific Coast Hwy
310-540-2501 • $$
Casual; yummy quesadillas.
- **Splash Bistro** • 300 N Harbor Dr
310-798-5348 • $$$
Mediterrean bistro.
- **W's China Bistro** • 1410 S Pacific Coast Hwy
310-792-1600 • $$
Non-greasy, non-tacky Chinese. Really.
- **Yogurtland** • 21213 Hawthorne Blvd
310-543-0391 • $
Self-serve yogurt that's affordable and low in calories.
- **Zazou** • 1810 S Catalina Ave
310-540-4884 • $$$$
Mediterranian-Italian fusion.

Shopping

- **Cookin Stuff** • 2722 Sepulveda Blvd
310-371-2220
Possibly the largest selection of cooking supplies for the layperson in all of LA County.
- **Cost Plus World Market** • 22929 Hawthorne Blvd
310-378-8331
An "everything" superstore.
- **Dive 'N Surf** • 504 N Broadway
310-372-8423
Surf shop catering to girlz.
- **Lindberg Nutrition** • 3804 Sepulveda Blvd
310-378-9490
A mecca for bodybuilders and others wishing to "keep in the pink."

Map 32 • Torrance South

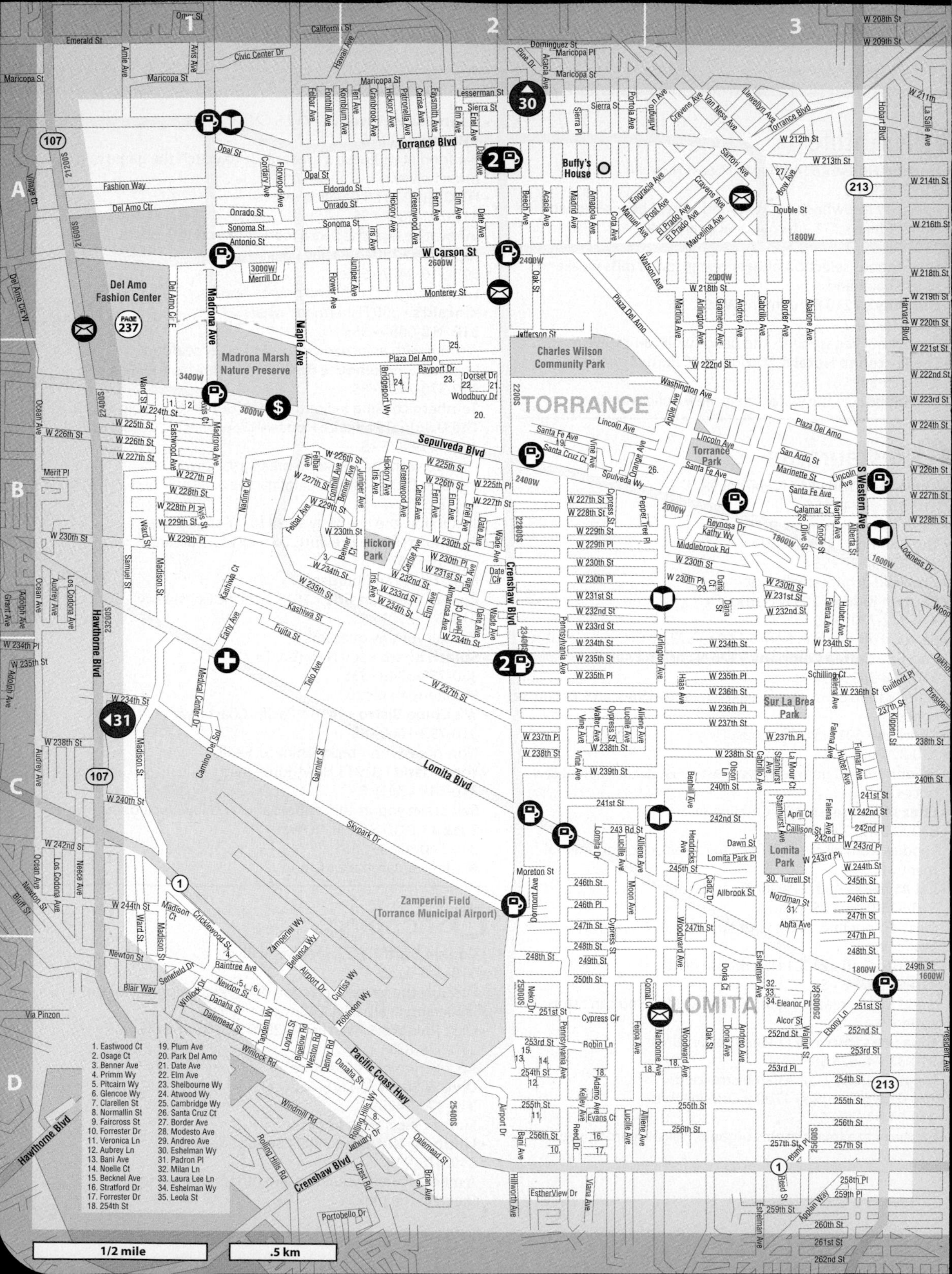

Del Amo Fashion Center is one of the nation's biggest malls, and it's a serious presence. Down the street, the Madrona March Nature Preserve, one of the few remaining urban wetlands, is well maintained by the local nature society. Across the marsh is **King's Hawaiian** which has the best French toast in town. And the family-owned **Torrance Bakery** makes mean sandwiches and gorgeous wedding cakes, as well as a panorama of pastries.

Landmarks

- **Buffy's House** • 1313 Cota Dr
  Is that? Yes, that's actually Buffy the Vampire Slayer's house.

Nightlife

- **1321 Downtown Taproom Bistro** • 1321 Sartori Ave
  310-618-1321
  Hip, cute decor and a wide selection of craft beers.
- **The Crest** • 1625 Cabrillo Ave
  310-320-9347
  Pool tables and a million TVs to watch any game.
- **Keegan's Pub** • 1434 Marcelina Ave
  310-328-3750
  Recently renovated with a great patio.

Restaurants

- **Angara Indian Restaurant** • 2170 Torrance Blvd
  310-320-9090 • $$
  Lots of curry variety.
- **By Brazil** • 1615 Cabrillo Ave
  310-787-7520 • $$
  Great grilled meats, and they always have the soccer game.
- **Depot** • 1250 Cabrillo Ave
  310-787-7501 • $$$$
  Broad range of chef Michael Shafer's culinary creations.
- **Eat at Rudy's** • 1340 Post Ave
  310-533-0752 • $
  Cute half-diner, half-cafe indoor/outdoor breakfast spot.
- **Get Shaved** • 1790 Carson St
  310-293-2523 • $
  Crowds love nothing better than shaved ice on a hot day.
- **In-N-Out Burger** • 24445 Crenshaw Blvd
  800-786-1000 • $
  Top California burger joint.
- **King's Hawaiian** • 2808 W Sepulveda Blvd
  310-530-0050 • $$
  Famous for sweet rolls which they use for French toast.
- **Lazy Dog Cafe** • 3525 W Carson St
  310-921-6080 • $$
  Everything from fish 'n' chips to wok dishes & hand crafted drafts to boot.
- **Red Car Brewery and Restaurant** • 1266 Sartori Ave
  310-782-0222 • $$
  A beer-soaked seed of hope in Old Torrance.
- **Santouka** • 21515 S Western Ave
  310-212-1101 • $
  Hands down LA's best ramen at this mall food court.
- **Snax** • 4535 Sepulveda Blvd
  310-316-6631 • $$
  Burgers and Mexican? Yes please.
- **Yogurtland** • 24631 Crenshaw Blvd
  310-534-9572 • $
  Self-serve yogurt, cheap dessert with fewer calories.

Shopping

- **Mitsuwa Marketplace** • 21515 S Western Ave
  310-782-0335
  Japanese snacks and knick-knacks.
- **Road Runner Sports** • 25359 Crenshaw Blvd
  310-326-8530
  Not cheap but worth the money. These guys know their stuff.
- **South Bay Brewing Supply Co.** • 1311 Post Ave
  310-328-2133
  Everything you need to make your own beer. Even classes!
- **Torrance Bakery** • 1341 El Prado Ave
  310-320-2722
  Family-owned bakery plus wedding cakes.

EAGLE ROCK
HIGHLAND PARK
MOUNT WASHINGTON
Occidental College
Eagle Rock Community Cultural Center
Eagle Rock Rec Center
Judson Studios
Highland Park
Southwest Museum
Ventura Fwy
Glendale Fwy
Pasadena Fwy
Colorado Blvd
York Blvd
Eagle Rock Blvd
N Figueroa St
N Avenue 54
Verdugo Rd
134
123
110
2
51
34
36
38
1/2 mile
.5 km
1. El Canto Dr
2. Kerwin Dr
3. Janet Pl
4. Castle Crest Dr
5. Rodin Pl
6. Zaca Pl
7. Prismo Dr
8. Dicturn St
9. Banbury Pl
10. Lytelle Pl
11. York Hill Pl
12. College View Pl
13. Westdale Ave
14. Eagle View Cir
15. Montiflora Ave
16. Linda RosaAve
17. Algoma Ave
18. Glen Aylsa Ave
19. Tenshaw Pl
20. Frackelton Pl
21. Rockview Ter
22. Upton Pl
23. Upton Ct
24. Eagle Vista Dr
25. Hillmont Ave
26. Cedaredge Ct
27. Hillmont Ave
28. Highcrest Ave
29. Maison Ave
30. Genevieve Ave
31. Kipling Ave
32. Colorado Al
33. Glengarry Rd
34. Melrose Al
35. Melrose Ave
36. Cherry Dr
37. Shelby Pl
38. Minden Pl
39. Juniper Dr
40. Cheviotdale Pl
41. Cheviotdale Dr
42. Evergreen Dr
43. Pleasant Wy
44. Pine Grove Ave
45. Poppy Peak Dr
46. Strickland Ave
47. Burwood Ter
48. Cheviotdale Pl
49. Jacqueline Pl
50. Rosswood Ter
51. Highgrove Ter
52. Palm View Dr
53. Adelaide Pl
54. Planada Ave
55. Crescent St
56. Ruby St
57. Salonica St
58. Garvanza Ave
59. Weaver Ln
60.Aldama St
61. Myosotis St
62. Albans St
63. La Prada Ter
64. Highgate Ave
65. Eaton Ter
66. Dogwood Pl
67. Onarga Ave
68. Farrington Ln
69. Crestwood Wy
70. Crestwood Ter
71. Annan Ter
72. Manantonga Ter
73. Betty Pl
74. Rice St
75. High St
76. Beconia Ave
77. Brevis St
78. Silverwood Ln
79. Loleta Pl
80. Loleta Ave
81. Oak Grove Pl
82. Silver Oak Ter
83. Ellita Pl
84. Gracita Pl
85. Longfellow St
86. Roselawn Pl
87. Leslie Wy
88. S Ave 59
89. Hayes Ave
90. Shults St
91. S Ave 61
92. S Ave 63
93. S Ave 83
94. Arroyo Glen St
95. S Ave 64
96. La Riba Wy
97. Roble Ave
98. S Ave 66
99. Stowe ter
100. Livermore Ter
101. Mount Angelus Dr
102. La Follette Dr
103. Wayland St
104. Lamont Dr
105. Garrison Dr

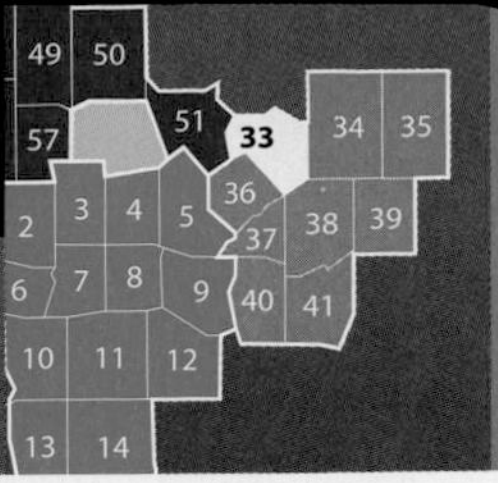

With its mix of recent nesters, creative-class types, and long-time residents, Eagle Rock is holding onto its quirky blue-collar spirit even as it gets a facelift. The gentrification of this northeast LA neighborhood stalled during the Great Recession, but there are signs it is picking up again, especially in nearby Highland Park. You can watch the change unfold on York Boulevard, where galleries and high-end coffee shops are popping up between the dive bars and taco trucks.

oLandmarks

- **Center for the Arts Eagle Rock** • 2225 Colorado Blvd
  323-226-1617
  Classes, performances, and exhibitions for the local community.
- **The Judson Studios** • 200 S Ave 66
  323-255-0131
  Stained glass like you've never seen before.

Nightlife

- **All Star Lanes** • 4459 Eagle Rock Blvd
  323-254-2579
  Bowling? Ha! Locals flock for cheap drinks and wild karaoke.
- **The Eagle Rock Lounge** • 1954 Colorado Blvd
  323-257-2245
  Impressive beer selection accompanies food from the bistro next door.
- **Johnny's Bar** • 5006 York Blvd
  323-982-0775
  Mellow atmosphere, acclaimed juke.
- **La Cuevita** • 5922 N Figueroa St
  323-255-6871
  Quality tequila and mezcal that won't break the bank.
- **Mr. T's Bowl** • 5621 N Figueroa St
  323-256-7561
  Dive bar + live bands.
- **The York** • 5018 York Blvd
  323-255-9675
  Upscale pub food and craft beer.

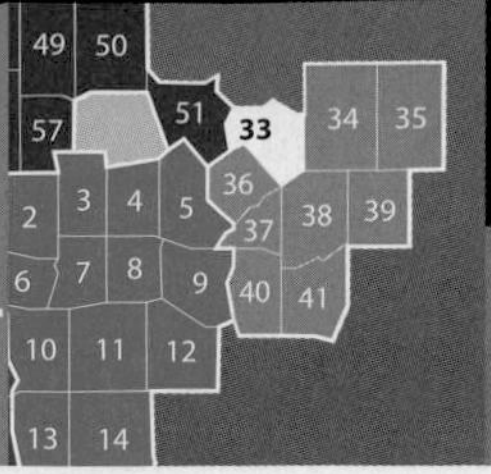

Eagle Rock / Highland Park

Restaurants

- **Auntie Em's Kitchen** • 4616 Eagle Rock Blvd
  323-255-0800 • $
  Home-made, unique goodness.
- **Ba** • 5100 York Blvd
  323-739-6243 • $$$
  Fine French cuisine in an intimate setting.
- **Blue Hen Vietnamese Kitchen** • 1743 Colorado Blvd
  323-982-9900 • $$
  Family recipes with an organic update.
- **The Bucket** • 4541 Eagle Rock Blvd
  323-257-5654 • $
  Servin' old-school burgers since 1935.
- **CaCao Mexicatessen** • 1576 Colorado Blvd
  323-478-2791 • $$
  Mexican, sure, but a little different than what we're used to.
- **Café Beaujolais** • 1712 Colorado Blvd
  323-255-5111 • $$
  Delicious French romanticism, but for dinner only.
- **The Capri** • 4604 Eagle Rock Blvd
  323-257-3225 • $
  Twin Italian bros serve up a warm neighborhood spot.
- **Casa Bianca** • 1650 Colorado Blvd
  323-256-9617 • $$
  Legendary pizza with atmosphere to spare.
- **Cinnamon** • 5511 N Figueroa St
  323-982-9480 • $$
  Don't miss the vegan pies.
- **Classic Thai Restaurant** • 1708 Colorado Blvd
  323-478-0530 • $
  Bustling Thai with a home-y feel.
- **The Coffee Table** • 1958 Colorado Blvd
  323-255-2200 • $
  Spacious and satisfying bistro, bearable even on Sundays.
- **Colombo's** • 1833 Colorado Blvd
  323-254-9138 • $$
  Incredible Continental cuisine at reasonable prices.
- **Dave's Chillin-n-Grillin** • 2152 Colorado Blvd
  323-490-0988 • $
  Dave serves fresh sandwiches, shakes, and more.
- **Eagle Rock Italian Bakery & Deli** • 1726 Colorado Blvd
  323-255-8224 • $
  Famous rum cake and amazing deli sandwiches.
- **El Arco Iris** • 5684 York Blvd
  323-254-3402 • $
  Mexican.
- **El Pavo Bakery** • 5815 N Figueroa St
  323-257-5050 • $
  Champurado purists unite.
- **Fatty's** • 1627 Colorado Blvd
  323-254-8804 • $
  Vegetarian pace-setter. Eat a "Fat Elvis" for breakfast.
- **Fusion Burgers** • 5933 York Blvd
  323-257-8705 • $$
  Upscale burger joint brings the trend to the east side.
- **The Highland Cafe** • 5010 York Blvd
  323-259-1000 • $
  Refurbished café offers breakfast, lunch and quality coffee.
- **Huarache Azteca** • 5225 York Blvd
  323-478-9572 • $
  The best tacos, huaraches, tortas, and sopes in town.
- **La Fuente** • 2256 Colorado Blvd
  323-258-4303 • $$
  Gigantic margaritas wash down satisfyingly greasy Mexican food.
- **Maximiliano** • 5930 York Blvd
  323-739-6125 • $$
  Updated Italian classics served alongside craft brews and small-batch wines.
- **Metro Balderas** • 5305 N Figueroa St
  323-478-8383 • $
  Visit on the weekend to sample eight kinds of carnitas.
- **Mia Sushi** • 4741 Eagle Rock Blvd
  323-256-2562 • $$$
  Cool sushi comes to the east side.
- **Oasis Ice Cream** • 5526 Monte Vista St
  323-259-1507 • $
  Homemade yogurt and ice cream in many imaginative flavors.
- **The Oinkster** • 2005 Colorado Blvd
  323-255-6465 • $
  Pastrami and Belgian frites.
- **Original Tommy's** • 1717 Colorado Blvd
  323-982-1746 • $
  The chain's legendary chili burgers offer gassy goodness.
- **Pete's Blue Chip** • 1701 Colorado Blvd
  323-478-9022 • $
  Greasy burgers and everything else.
- **Señor Fish** • 4803 Eagle Rock Blvd
  323-257-7167 • $
  Amazing fish tacos and other hot stuff.
- **Sicha Siam** • 4403 Eagle Rock Blvd
  323-344-8285 • $$
  Thai.
- **Spitz** • 2506 Colorado Blvd
  323-257-5600 • $
  Do the "doner": a gyro in a toasted panini.
- **Tacos El Pique** • 5300 York Blvd
  $
  Good selection of Mexican sodas to wash down your tacos.
- **The York** • 5018 York Blvd
  323-255-9675 • $$
  Upscale pub food and craft beer.

Eagle Rock / Highland Park

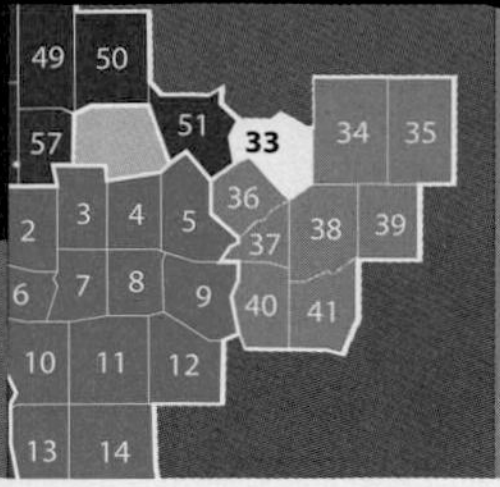

Eagle Rock has long been a foodie's paradise, offering up impeccable pizzas from **Casa Bianca**, upscale vegetarian fare at **Fatty's**, and fast food done right at **The Oinkster**. Highland Park is quickly catching up with its more established sibling, with gastropub staple **The York** anchoring a restaurant renaissance. Enjoy fine French cuisine at **Ba** or head east for **Maximiliano**'s clever take on Italian—but don't forget about neighborhood classics like **Huarache Azteca** and its satisfying Mexican antojitos.

Shopping

- **Cactus Gallery & Gifts** • 3001 Eagle Rock Blvd
  323-801-8669
  South American art with a gallery space.
- **Colorado Wine Company** • 2305 Colorado Blvd
  323-478-1985
  Helpful owners and numerous tastings keep you *Sideways*.
- **Galco's Soda Pop Stop** • 5702 York Blvd
  323-255-7115
  Who knew there were so many different brands of root beer?
- **Mi Vida** • 5159 York Blvd
  323-257-0103
  Mexican crafts with an urban twist.
- **Michaels** • 1155 Colorado Blvd
  626-431-2850
  Pipe cleaners, felt, and puff paints galore!
- **Owl Talk** • 5060 Eagle Rock Blvd
  323-258-2465
  Secondhand and new clothes.
- **Read Books** • 4972 Eagle Rock Blvd
  323-259-9068
  Pronounced "red" (used) or "reed" (read a book, dummy)—your choice.
- **Seafood City** • 2700 Colorado Blvd
  323-543-2660
  This underpriced Filipino grocer could be your lifestyle.
- **Stained Glass Supplies** • 2104 Colorado Blvd
  323-254-4361
  Classes, supplies and other shiny things.
- **Urchin** • 5006 York Blvd
  323-259-9059
  Affordable vintage fashions for men and women.

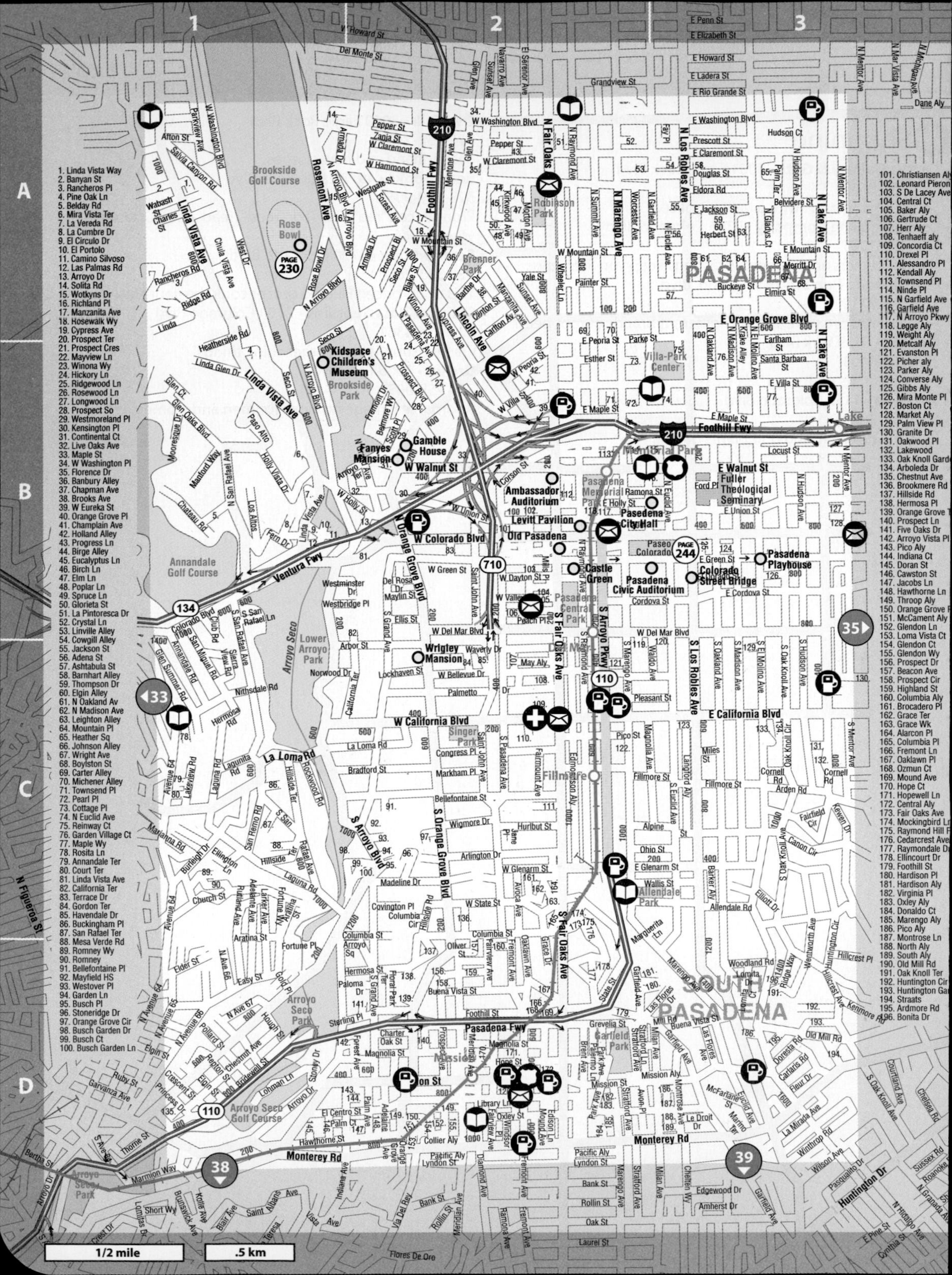
1. Linda Vista Way
2. Banyan St
3. Rancheros Pl
4. Pine Oak Ln
5. Belday Rd
6. Mira Vista Ter
7. La Vereda Rd
8. La Cumbre Dr
9. El Circulo Dr
10. El Portolo
11. Camino Silvoso
12. Las Palmas Rd
13. Arroyo Dr
14. Sofita Rd
15. Wotkyns Dr
16. Richland Pl
17. Manzanita Ave
18. Hosewalk Wy
19. Cypress Ave
20. Prospect Ter
21. Prospect Cres
22. Mayview Ln
23. Winona Wy
24. Hickory Ln
25. Ridgewood Ln
26. Rosewood Ln
27. Longwood Ln
28. Prospect So
29. Westmoreland Pl
30. Kensington Pl
31. Continental Ct
32. Live Oaks Ave
33. Maple St
34. W Washington Pl
35. Florence Dr
36. Banbury Alley
37. Chapman Ave
38. Brooks Ave
39. W Eureka St
40. Orange Grove Pl
41. Champlain Ave
42. Holland Alley
43. Progress Ln
44. Birge Alley
45. Eucalyptus Ln
46. Birch Ln
47. Elm Ln
48. Poplar Ln
49. Spruce Ln
50. Glorieta St
51. La Pintoresca Dr
52. Crystal Ln
53. Linville Alley
54. Cowgill Alley
55. Jackson St
56. Adena St
57. Ashtabula St
58. Barnhart Alley
59. Thompson Dr
60. Elgin Alley
61. N Oakland Av
62. N Madison Ave
63. Leighton Alley
64. Mountain Pl
65. Heather Sq
66. Johnson Alley
67. Wright Ave
68. Boylston St
69. Carter Alley
70. Michener Alley
71. Townsend Pl
72. Pearl Pl
73. Cottage Pl
74. N Euclid Ave
75. Reinway Ct
76. Garden Village Ct
77. Maple Wy
78. Rosita Ln
79. Annandale Ter
80. Court Ter
81. Linda Vista Ave
82. California Ter
83. Terrace Dr
84. Gordon Ter
85. Havendale Dr
86. Buckingham Pl
87. San Rafael Ter
88. Mesa Verde Rd
89. Romney Wy
90. Romney
91. Bellefontaine Pl
92. Mayfield HS
93. Westover Pl
94. Garden Ln
95. Busch Pl
96. Stoneridge Dr
97. Orange Grove Cir
98. Busch Garden Dr
99. Busch Ct
100. Busch Garden Ln
101. Christiansen Aly
102. Leonard Pieron
103. S De Lacey Ave
104. Central Ct
105. Baker Aly
106. Gertrude Ct
107. Herr Aly
108. Tenhaeff aly
109. Concordia Ct
110. Drexel Pl
111. Alessandro Pl
112. Kendall Aly
113. Townsend Pl
114. Ninde Pl
115. N Garfield Ave
116. Garfield Ave
117. N Arroyo Pkwy
118. Legge Aly
119. Weight Aly
120. Metcalf Aly
121. Evanston Pl
122. Picher aly
123. Parker Aly
124. Converse Aly
125. Gibbs Aly
126. Mira Monte Pl
127. Boston Ct
128. Market Aly
129. Palm View Pl
130. Granite Dr
131. Oakwood Pl
132. Lakewood
133. Oak Knoll Garde
134. Arboleda Dr
135. Chestnut Ave
136. Brookmere Rd
137. Hillside Rd
138. Hermosa Pl
139. Orange Grove T
140. Prospect Ln
141. Five Oaks Dr
142. Arroyo Vista Pl
143. Pico Aly
144. Indiana Ct
145. Doran St
146. Cawston St
147. Jacobs Ln
148. Hawthorne Ln
149. Throop Aly
150. Orange Grove P
151. McCament Aly
152. Glendon Ln
153. Loma Vista Ct
154. Glendon Ct
155. Glendon Wy
156. Prospect Dr
157. Beacon Ave
158. Prospect Cir
159. Highland St
160. Columbia Pl
161. Brocadero Pl
162. Grace Ter
163. Grace Wk
164. Alarcon Pl
165. Columbia Pl
166. Fremont Ln
167. Oaklawn Pl
168. Ozmun Ct
169. Mound Ave
170. Hope Ct
171. Hopewell Ln
172. Central Aly
173. Fair Oaks Ave
174. Mockingbird Ln
175. Raymond Hill R
176. Cedarcrest Ave
177. Raymondale Dr
178. Ellincourt Dr
179. Foothill St
180. Hardison Pl
181. Hardison Aly
182. Virginia Pl
183. Oxley Aly
184. Donaldo Ct
185. Marengo Aly
186. Pico Aly
187. Montrose Ln
188. North Aly
189. South Aly
190. Old Mill Rd
191. Oak Knoll Ter
192. Huntington Cir
193. Huntington Gar
194. Straats
195. Ardmore Rd
196. Bonita Dr
PASADENA
SOUTH PASADENA
Foothill Fwy
Ventura Fwy
Pasadena Fwy
Rose Bowl
Brookside Golf Course
Annandale Golf Course
Arroyo Seco Golf Course
Kidspace Children's Museum
Gamble House
Fanyes Mansion
Wrigley Mansion
Ambassador Auditorium
Levitt Pavilion
Old Pasadena
Pasedena City Hall
Castle Green
Pasadena Civic Auditorium
Pasadena Playhouse
Colorado Street Bridge
Fuller Theological Seminary
Memorial Park
Villa-Park Center
Brookside Park
Lower Arroyo Park
Arroyo Seco Park
Singer Park
Allendale Park
Garfield Park
1/2 mile
.5 km

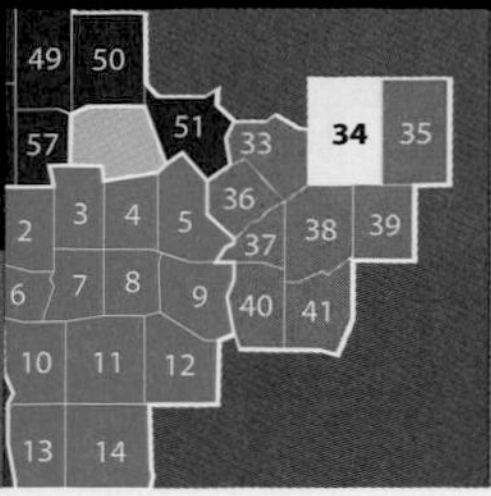

With the aggressive development of Old Town and the Paseo, it may seem like Pasadena is nothing more than an outdoor mall. But its history as LA's artsy half-sibling shines through if you look beyond Colorado Boulevard. Check out the **Norton Simon Museum**'s small but eclectic art collection, enjoy an outdoor concert at the restored **Levitt Pavilion**, or hike the **Arroyo Seco** to see a different side of LA's neighbor to the northeast.

Landmarks

- **The Ambassador Auditorium** • 131 S St John Ave
  626-354-6407
  Operated by the Worldwide Church of God.
- **Castle Green** • 99 S Raymond Ave
  626-385-7774
  This Moorish Colonial marvel may be a has-been, but it's a beautiful one.
- **Colorado Street Bridge** • Colorado Blvd & Orange Grove Blvd
  626-795-9311
  This stunning Beaux-Arts bridge is a romantic ode to Pasadena's majestic past.
- **Fenyes Mansion** • 470 W Walnut St
  626-577-1660
  Beaux-Arts oppulence at its best, the mansion's museum and gardens are open to the public for tours.
- **The Gamble House** • 4 Westmoreland Pl
  626-793-3334
  Pasadena's Craftsman style at its best.
- **Kidspace Children's Museum** • 480 N Arroyo Blvd
  626-449-9144
  Way cool kid-geared activities and exhibits.
- **Levitt Pavilion** • 166 N Raymond Ave
  626-683-3230
  This historic band shell hosts outdoor concerts all summer long.
- **Old Pasadena** • W Colorado Blvd & S Fair Oaks Ave
  626-356-9725
  A fine example of urban regentrification at work.
- **Pasadena City Hall** • 100 N Garfield Ave
  626-744-4000
  A lovely building with even lovelier gardens.
- **The Pasadena Civic** • 300 E Green St
  626-449-7360
  Home to both the Pasadena Symphony and the People's Choice Awards.
- **The Pasadena Playhouse** • 39 S El Molino Ave
  626-356-7529
  Back in the day, the Playhouse's now-defunct acting school turned out many a movie star.
- **Rose Bowl Stadium** • 991 Rosemont Ave
  626-577-3100
  UCLA football, Galaxy soccer games, and the infamous monthy swap meet.
- **Wrigley Mansion** • 391 S Orange Grove Blvd
  626-449-7673
  This Italian Renaissance mansion built by chewing gum magnate now serves as HQ for the Tournament of Roses.

Nightlife

- **The 35er** • 12 E Colorado Blvd
  626-356-9315
  Neighborhood bar.
- **Bodega Wine Bar** • 260 E Colorado Blvd
  626-793-4300
  Ideal for chilled wines on warm nights.
- **The Ice House** • 24 N Mentor Ave
  626-577-1894
  Stand-up comedy, improv, booze.
- **Jake's** • 38 W Colorado Blvd
  626-568-1602
  Pool hall and bar.
- **Lucky Baldwins Pub** • 17 S Raymond Ave
  626-795-0652
  Expat Brits, imported ales, high tea.
- **POP Champagne & Dessert Bar** • 33 E Union St
  626-795-1295
  Sweets + bubbly = classy, classy date spot.
- **Yard House** • 330 E Colorado Blvd
  626-577-9273
  More than 200 beers on tap.

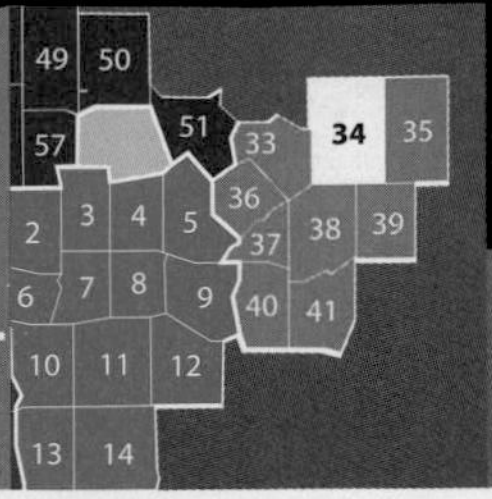

Pasadena

Restaurants

- **Akbar Cuisine of India** • 44 N Fair Oaks Ave
  626-577-9916 • $$$
  Creative Indian cooking.
- **All India Cafe** • 39 S Fair Oaks Ave
  626-440-0309 • $$
  Delicious dosas, curries, and regional specialties from all over India
- **Arroyo Chop House** • 536 S Arroyo Pkwy
  626-577-7463 • $$$$
  Take your father here for steaks.
- **Bar Celona** • 46 E Colorado Blvd
  626-405-1000 • $$
  Tapas by the plate and hipsters by the glass.
- **Bistro 45** • 45 S Mentor Ave
  626-795-4278 • $$$$
  High-end gourmet food and wine.
- **Café Bizou** • 91 N Raymond Ave
  626-792-9923 • $$$
  BYOB French bistro.
- **Café Santorini** • 64 W Union St
  626-564-4200 • $$$
  Mediterranean magic on the rooftop terrace.
- **Celestino** • 141 S Lake Ave
  626-795-4006 • $$$$
  Italian.
- **Euro Pane Bakery** • 950 E Colorado Blvd
  626-577-1828 • $
  Sophisticated pastries for subtle palates.
- **Fair Oaks Pharmacy and Soda Fountain** • 1526 Mission St
  626-799-1414 • $
  Enjoy an old fashioned sundae while picking up your prescription
- **Father Nature's Lavash Wraps** • 17 N De Lacey Ave
  626-568-9811 • $
  Father sure knows his lavashes (thin leavened flatbread).
- **Firefly Bistro** • 1009 El Centro St
  626-441-2443 • $$
  Seasonal charm, tent style.
- **Green Street Restaurant** • 146 Shoppers Ln
  626-577-7170 • $$
  A Pasadena staple.
- **Hey That's Amore** • 27 E Holly St
  626-844-8716 • $
  Italian subs with names like the Heavy Hitter, Taxi Driver, and Soprano.
- **Houston's** • 320 S Arroyo Pkwy
  626-577-6001 • $$$
  Chain with a little something for everyone.
- **Intelligentsia Coffee** • 55 E Colorado Blvd
  626-578-1270 • $$
  Acclaimed coffee snobs tackle beer, wine, and café classics.
- **Julienne** • 2651 Mission St
  626-441-2299 • $$$
  Charming sidewalk bistro that is trés délicieux.
- **La Luna Negra** • 44 W Green St
  626-844-4331 $$
  Vibrant, colorful Spanish tapas bar.
- **Magnolia House** • 492 S Lake Ave
  626-584-1126 • $$
  Chic and sexy with a tantalizingly creative menu.
- **Maison Akira** • 713 E Green St
  626-796-9501 • $$$$
  Light, French-Japanese cooking.
- **Marston's** • 151 E Walnut St
  626-796-2459 • $$
  Awesome breakfasts and traditional American dinners.
- **Mi Piace** • 25 E Colorado Blvd
  626-795-3131 • $$$
  Italian chain with outdoor tables.
- **Noodle World** • 24 W Colorado Blvd
  626-585-5885 • $
  Big portions. We're talking LARGE.
- **Parkway Grill** • 510 S Arroyo Pkwy
  626-795-1001 • $$$$
  Pasadena's perennial upscale favorite; live music in the bar.
- **Pie 'N Burger** • 913 E California Blvd
  626-795-1123 • $
  Juicy burgers, homey pies.
- **Ración** • 119 W Green St
  626-396-3090 • $$$
  Aggressively authentic pintxos and wine from Spain's Basque Country.
- **The Raymond** • 1250 S Fair Oaks Ave
  626-441-3136 • $$$$
  Romantic, special occasion dining.
- **Roscoe's House of Chicken and Waffles** • 830 N Lake Ave
  323-466-7453 • $$
  Cheap Southern chain.
- **Shiro** • 1505 Mission St
  626-799-4774 • $$$$
  Low-key interior, sublime fusion cuisine.
- **The Slaw Dogs** • 720 N Lake Ave
  626-808-9777 • $
  Delectable hot dogs and sausages piled high with innovative toppings.

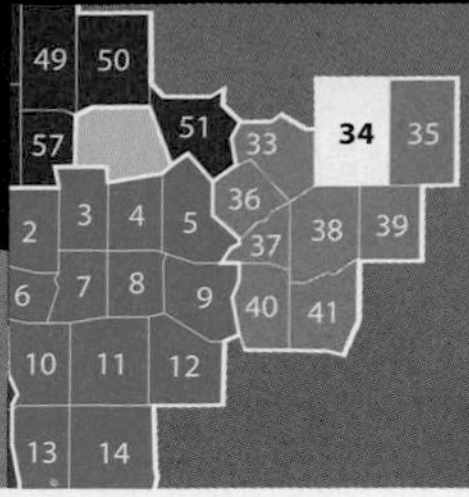

All that development is good for something—the shopping in Pasadena can't be beat. While Old Town is chock-a-block with chain stores, don't overlook enduring mom-and-pop spots like **Canterbury Records** and **Vroman's Bookstore**. Those looking to score unique clothing, furniture, and antiques on a budget should prepare to approach bargain shopping nirvana every second Sunday of the month at the famous **Rose Bowl Flea Market**.

- **Sorriso** • 46 E Colorado Blvd
  626-405-1000 • $$
  Surprise! There's a good, non-chain restaurant on Old Town Pasadena's main drag.
- **Tonny's** • 843 E Orange Grove Blvd
  626-797-0866 • $$
  24-hour Mexican grub.
- **Tutti Gelati** • 62 W Union St
  626-440-9800 • $
  A hidden paradiso for sweet treats.
- **Vertical Wine Bistro** • 70 N Raymond Ave
  626-795-3999 • $$$$
  A variety of wine flights. Don't miss the mini-grilled sandwiches.
- **Yahaira's Café** • 698 E Colorado Blvd
  626-844-3254 • $$
  Mexicali fusion food.

Shopping

- **Abuelita's Knitting and Needlepoint** • 696 E Colorado Blvd
  626-799-0355
  Cozy craft store offering luxurious yarns and needlepoint supplies.
- **Angels School Supply** • 600 E Colorado Blvd
  626-584-0855
  Back to school isn't so bad after all.
- **Blick Art Materials** • 44 S Raymond Ave
  626-795-4985
  Art supplies for everyone from the career artist to the scrapbook hobbyist.
- **Canterbury Records** • 805 E Colorado Blvd
  626-792-7184
  New and used, plus DVD and video. Great jazz, blues, and classical.
- **Carroll & Co.** • 425 N Canon Dr
  310-273-7060
  Classic men's clothier.
- **Elisa B.** • 12 Douglas Alley
  626-792-4746
  Contemporary clothing for women.
- **Jacob Maarse Florists** • 655 E Green St
  626-449-0246
  Fabulous floral arrangements.
- **Julienne Fine Foods** • 2649 Mission St
  626-441-2299
  Carry home some gourmet goodies or order Le Pique-Nique for your next Hollywood Bowl foray.
- **Lather** • 17 E Colorado Blvd
  626-396-9636
  Modern apothecary products that smell good and feel good.
- **Lula Mae** • 100 N Fair Oaks Ave
  626-304-9996
  Dream a little (weird) dream.
- **Lush** • 24 E Colorado Blvd
  626-792-0901
  Super-fresh beauty and bath products.
- **Messarian Oriental Rugs** • 493 E Colorado Blvd
  626-792-9858
  Beautiful rugs from the Near and Middle East.
- **Mignon Chocolate Boutique** • 6 E Holly St
  626-796-7100
  Build your box of favorites!
- **Nicole's Gourmet Imports** • 921 Meridian Ave
  626-403-5751
  French cheese rocks. And stinks.
- **Old Focals** • 45 W Green St
  626-793-7073
  Vintage and custom glasses frames to keep you looking retro-chic.
- **Pasadena Antique Center & Annex** • 444 S Fair Oaks Ave
  626-449-7706
  Dozens of dealers under one roof.
- **Rose Bowl Flea Market** • 1001 Rose Bowl Dr
  323-560-7469
  Food, drink, gadgets and antiques; yours for the haggling.
- **Rose Tree Cottage** • 801 S Pasadena Ave
  626-793-3337
  English tea room and gift shop.
- **Run with Us** • 235 N Lake Ave
  626-568-3331
  For those who still have knees enough to run.
- **Stats Floral** • 120 S Raymond Ave
  626-795-9308
  Every imaginable supply and bauble for your décor, floral, crafting projects.
- **Target** • 777 E Colorado Blvd
  626-584-1606
  Perfect-sized, not too big, two story, very manageable.
- **Three Dog Bakery** • 36 W Colorado Blvd
  626-440-0443
  Fancy biscuits you'd be proud to offer man's best friend.
- **Vroman's Bookstore** • 695 E Colorado Blvd
  626-449-5320
  Indie, eclectic, charming and famous for its children's department.

Map 35 • Pasadena East / San Marino

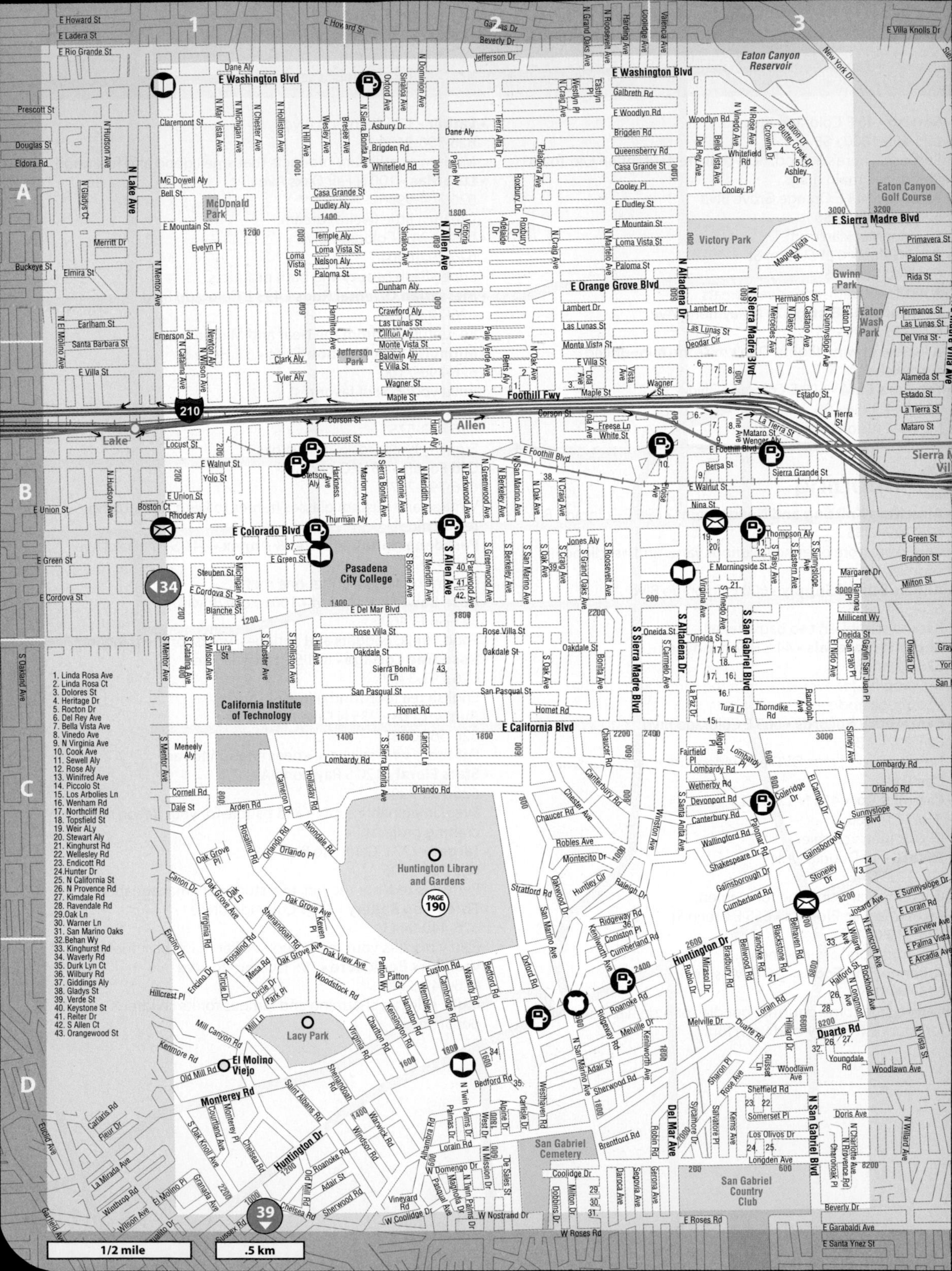

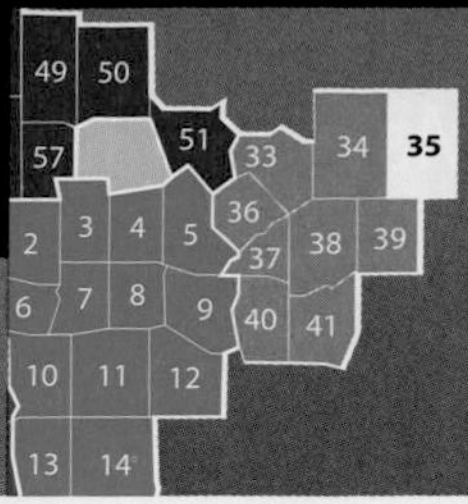

As you venture east past Lake Avenue along Colorado, the cute shops and restaurants segue into drab auto repair shops, dingy motels, and the attendant detritus. But head south and you'll find not only some of the smartest people in southern California (thanks to the presence of Caltech), but also some of the richest. The homes around Pasadena City College make for a fancy Sunday drive.

oLandmarks

- **The Huntington** • 1151 Oxford Rd
  626-405-2100
  The perfect place to take relatives from out-of-town.
- **Lacy Park** • 1485 Virginia Rd
  626-300-0790
  Second only to the Huntington, Lacy Park is 30 acres of gorgeous greenery.
- **The Old Mill - El Molino Viejo** • 1120 Old Mill Rd
  626-449-5458
  Southern California's first water-powered gristmill. Who needs Disney's California Adventure?

Restaurants

- **Café Verde** • 961 E Green St
  626-356-9811 • $$
  Tiny and tasty BYOB spot.
- **In-N-Out Burger** • 2114 E Foothill Blvd
  800-786-1000 • $
  Top California burger joint.
- **Noodle World** • 932 Huntington Dr
  626-300-1010 • $
  Big portions. We're talking LARGE.
- **Rose Garden Tea Room & Cafe** • 1151 Oxford Rd
  626-683-8131 • $$
  The Huntington Library's famous tea room runs rather pricey, but is a definite don't miss.
- **Yoshida** • 2026 Huntington Dr
  626-281-9292 • $$$
  San Marino's only place for raw fish and dim sum.

N
1
2
3
A
B
C
D
Forest Lawn Memorial Park (Glendale)
Glassell Park & Rec Center
Glassell Park
GLASSELL PARK
MOUNT WASHINGTON
CYPRESS PARK
Bicentennial Park
Mount Washington Hotel/ Self-Realization
Southwest Museum
The Lummis Home
Ernest E Debs Regional Park
Elysian Park
Heritage Square/ Arroyo
Lincoln Heights/ Cypress Park
PAGE 245
Glendale Fwy
Golden State Fwy
Pasadena Fwy
Los Angeles River
Eagle Rock Blvd
York Blvd
N Figueroa St
N San Fernando Rd
Division St
Stadium Way
Academy Rd
1. Charters Ave
2. W Ave 44
3. Verdugo Vista Ter
4. Division Pl
5. Cleland Pl
6. Holyoke Dr
7. Isabel Cir
8. Knob Dr
9. Kemper St
10. Kemper Ct
11. Tacuba St
12. Beauvais Ave
13. Clermont St
14. Shanley Ave
15. N Ave 49
16. N Ave 48
17. Sonata Ln
18. Montezuma Ct
19. Pasadena Ave Ter
20. Theresa St
21. Shelburn Ct
22. Andalusia Ave
23. Vista Gloriosa Dr
24. American Pl
25. Glenalbyn Pl
26. Beech St
27. Seymour St
28. Gay St
1/2 mile
.5 km

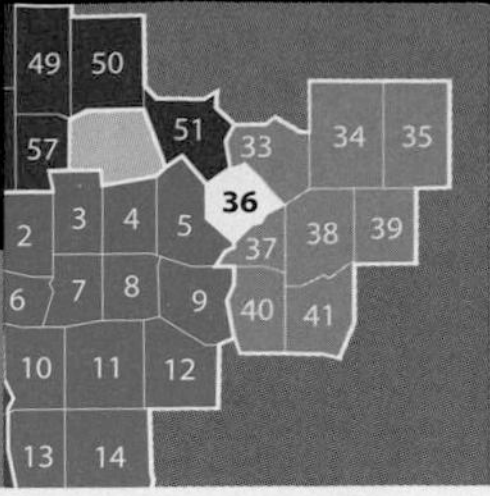

Recently, Mt. Washington has become an asylum for artists, aspiring scene-jockeys, and other fashionable folk content hovering near the bottom of the economic totem pole. It's still got plenty of gangs, graffiti, and property crime, but the rents are manageable and aren't likely to shoot up anytime soon. The hilly areas have better views and a more low-key lifestyle than downtown and the surrounding areas.

oLandmarks

- **The Lummis Home** • 200 E Ave 43
  323-222-0546
  An original home conceived by an original man.
- **Self-Realization Fellowship** • 3880 San Rafael Ave
  323-225-2471
  Beautiful gardens, open to the public.

Nightlife

- **Footsie's** • 2640 N Figueroa St
  323-221-6900
  Simply brilliant and hopefully the home of all future NFT release parties.
- **Verdugo** • 3408 Verdugo Rd
  323-257-3408
  Secluded. Atmospheric. Potent mixers. Formidable beer selection.

Restaurants

- **Chico's** • 100 N Ave 50
  323-254-2445 • $
  Mexican seafood.
- **La Abeja** • 3700 N Figueroa St
  323-221-0474 • $
  Mexican.

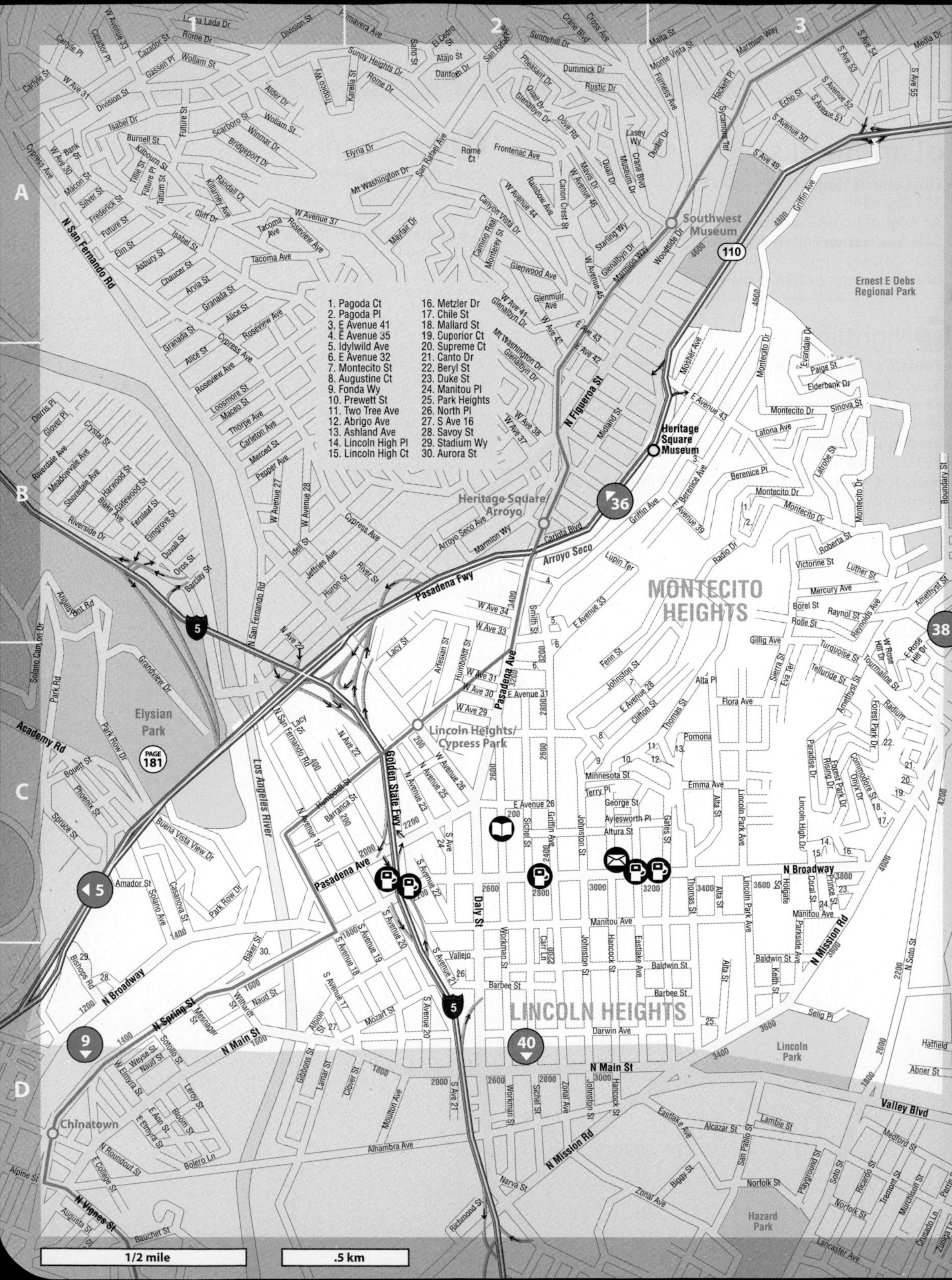
N
1
2
3
A
B
C
D
1. Pagoda Ct
2. Pagoda Pl
3. E Avenue 41
4. E Avenue 35
5. Idylwild Ave
6. E Avenue 32
7. Montecito St
8. Augustine Ct
9. Fonda Wy
10. Prewett St
11. Two Tree Ave
12. Abrigo Ave
13. Ashland Ave
14. Lincoln High Pl
15. Lincoln High Ct
16. Metzler Dr
17. Chile St
18. Mallard St
19. Cuporior Ct
20. Supreme Ct
21. Canto Dr
22. Beryl St
23. Duke St
24. Manitou Pl
25. Park Heights
26. North Pl
27. S Ave 16
28. Savoy St
29. Stadium Wy
30. Aurora St
Southwest Museum
Ernest E Debs Regional Park
Heritage Square Museum
Heritage Square/ Arroyo
MONTECITO HEIGHTS
Lincoln Heights/ Cypress Park
Elysian Park
PAGE 181
LINCOLN HEIGHTS
Lincoln Park
Hazard Park
Chinatown
Los Angeles River
Pasadena Fwy
Golden State Fwy
Arroyo Seco
N Figueroa St
N San Fernando Rd
Pasadena Ave
N Broadway
N Main St
N Spring St
N Mission Rd
Valley Blvd
Alhambra Ave
N Vignes St
110
5
36
38
40
9
1/2 mile
.5 km

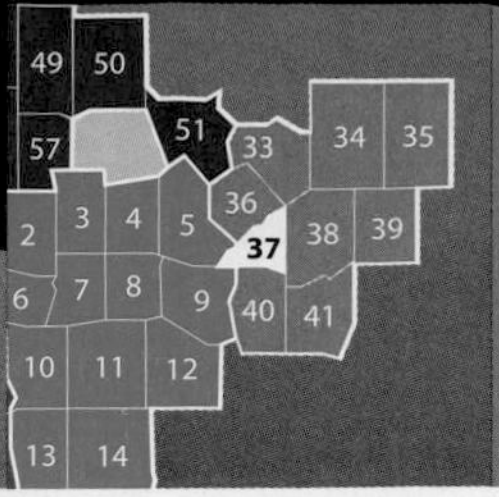

Just east of the river, Lincoln Heights, established in 1910, was once noted for its fauna population: alongside ostrich and alligator farms, it featured a private zoo for animals used in silent films. Now a vibrant Mexican enclave, but it's full of fantastic restaurants, walkable streets, and a unique nightlife -- if you know where to look.

Landmarks

- **Heritage Square Museum** • 3800 Homer St
  323-225-2700
  A cluster of buildings that have been saved from demolition through relocation to Heritage Square.

Nightlife

- **The Airliner** • 2419 N Broadway
  323-221-0771
  Cheap drinks, and the four fundamentals of hip hop, including graffiti.
- **Le Blanc** • 2834 N Broadway
  323-222-5705
  Brood and/or watch soccer.
- **Marcelino's Cafe** • 2119 N Broadway
  323-221-5444
  Neighborhood vino oasis. Keep it more secret than we did.

Restaurants

- **Carnitas Michoacan** • 1901 N Broadway
  323-225-2729 • $
  Perfect for satisfying your late-night nacho craving.
- **Cemitas Poblanas Elvirita** • 3010 E 1st St
  323-881-0428 • $
  Puebla's unique sandwich comes to California.
- **El Huarachito** • 3010 N Broadway
  323-223-0476 • $
  Classic Mexican breakfasts done right.

Shopping

- **Society of St. Vincent de Paul Thrift Store** •
  210 N Avenue 21
  323-224-6280
  Cult thrift store. Undersifted enough to tender serious rewards.

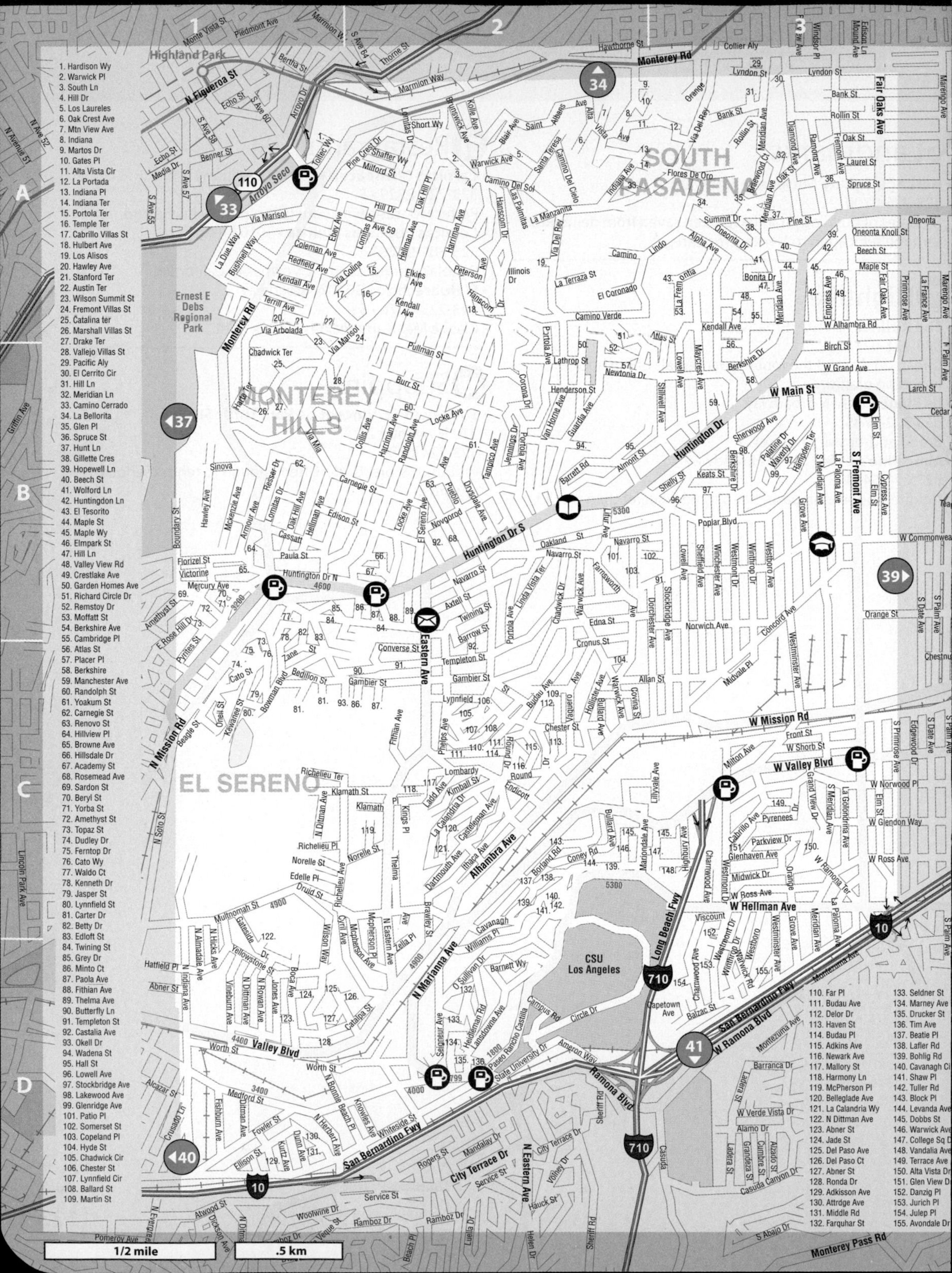

Highland Park
South Pasadena
Monterey Hills
El Sereno
Ernest E Debs Regional Park
CSU Los Angeles
1. Hardison Wy
2. Warwick Pl
3. South Ln
4. Hill Dr
5. Los Laureles
6. Oak Crest Ave
7. Mtn View Ave
8. Indiana
9. Martos Dr
10. Gates Pl
11. Alta Vista Cir
12. La Portada
13. Indiana Pl
14. Indiana Ter
15. Portola Ter
16. Temple Ter
17. Cabrillo Villas St
18. Hulbert Ave
19. Los Alisos
20. Hawley Ave
21. Stanford Ter
22. Austin Ter
23. Wilson Summit St
24. Fremont Villas St
25. Catalina ter
26. Marshall Villas St
27. Drake Ter
28. Vallejo Villas St
29. Pacific Aly
30. El Cerrito Cir
31. Hill Ln
32. Meridian Ln
33. Camino Cerrado
34. La Bellorita
35. Glen Pl
36. Spruce St
37. Hunt Ln
38. Gillette Cres
39. Hopewell Ln
40. Beech St
41. Wolford Ln
42. Huntingdon Ln
43. El Tesorito
44. Maple St
45. Maple Wy
46. Elmpark St
47. Hill Ln
48. Valley View Rd
49. Crestlake Ave
50. Garden Homes Ave
51. Richard Circle Dr
52. Remstoy Dr
53. Moffatt St
54. Berkshire Ave
55. Cambridge Pl
56. Atlas St
57. Placer Pl
58. Berkshire
59. Manchester Ave
60. Randolph St
61. Yoakum St
62. Carnegie St
63. Renovo St
64. Hillview Pl
65. Browne Ave
66. Hillsdale Dr
67. Academy St
68. Rosemead Ave
69. Sardon St
70. Beryl St
71. Yorba St
72. Amethyst St
73. Topaz St
74. Dudley Dr
75. Ferntop Dr
76. Cato Wy
77. Waldo Ct
78. Kenneth Dr
79. Jasper St
80. Lynnfield St
81. Carter Dr
82. Betty Dr
83. Edloft St
84. Twining St
85. Grey Dr
86. Minto Ct
87. Paola Ave
88. Fithian Ave
89. Thelma Ave
90. Butterfly Ln
91. Templeton St
92. Castalia Ave
93. Okell Dr
94. Wadena St
95. Hall St
96. Lowell Ave
97. Stockbridge Ave
98. Lakewood Ave
99. Glenridge Ave
101. Patio Pl
102. Somerset St
103. Copeland Pl
104. Hyde St
105. Chadwick Cir
106. Chester St
107. Lynnfield Cir
108. Ballard St
109. Martin St
110. Far Pl
111. Budau Ave
112. Delor Dr
113. Haven St
114. Budau Pl
115. Adkins Ave
116. Newark Ave
117. Mallory St
118. Harmony Ln
119. McPherson Pl
120. Belleglade Ave
121. La Calandria Wy
122. N Dittman Ave
123. Abner St
124. Jade St
125. Del Paso Ave
126. Del Paso Ct
127. Abner St
128. Ronda Dr
129. Adkisson Ave
130. Attrdge Ave
131. Middle Rd
132. Farquhar St
133. Seldner St
134. Marney Ave
135. Drucker St
136. Tim Ave
137. Beatie Pl
138. Lafler Rd
139. Bohlig Rd
140. Cavanagh Cl
141. Shaw Pl
142. Tuller Rd
143. Block Pl
144. Levanda Ave
145. Dobbs St
146. Warwick Ave
147. College Sq D
148. Vandalia Ave
149. Terrace Ave
150. Alta Vista Dr
151. Glen View D
152. Danzig Pl
153. Jurich Pl
154. Julep Pl
155. Avondale Dr
1/2 mile
.5 km

You won't mistake El Sereno for the Hollywood Hills, but it's got ample corazón and a deep sense of comunidad. Ringed by snow-capped mountains and minutes from downtown and Pasadena, it's a quiet little gem of a neighborhood. The eclectic mix of small businesses and family restaurants make it a good place to explore while you get your auto fixed. In Spanish, the name means "serene," "night air," or "night watchman"—take your pick.

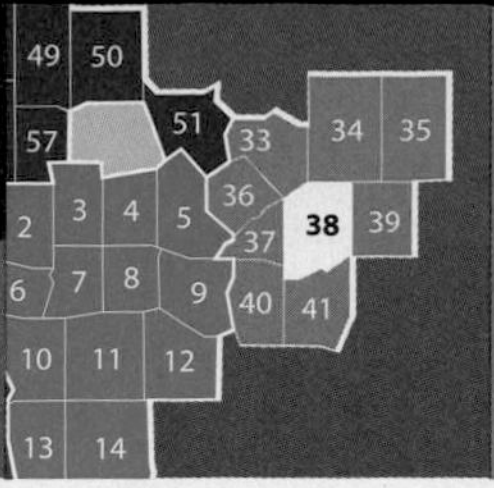

Restaurants

- **Bamboo House** • 2718 W Valley Blvd
  626-458-8888 • $
  Popular and authentic Chinese.
- **Granny's Donuts** • 1681 N Eastern Ave
  323-266-6918 • $
  No granny. Just killer donuts.
- **Hecho en Mexico** • 4976 S Huntington Dr
  323-226-0010 • $$
  Family restaurant. Authentic food.
- **La Parilla Mexicana** • 2938 W Valley Blvd
  626-289-2412 • $
  Family Mexican.
- **Mariscos El Kora De Nayarit** • 4863 Huntington Dr N
  323-223-3322 • $
  Seafood Nayarit style. Healthy.
- **Tamale Man** • 3320 N Eastern Ave
  323-221-5954 • $
  From sweet to savory, this man knows tamales. Hence the name.

Shopping

- **Kohl's** • 1201 S Fremont Ave
  626-289-7250
  Latest addition to Alhambra shopping scene.

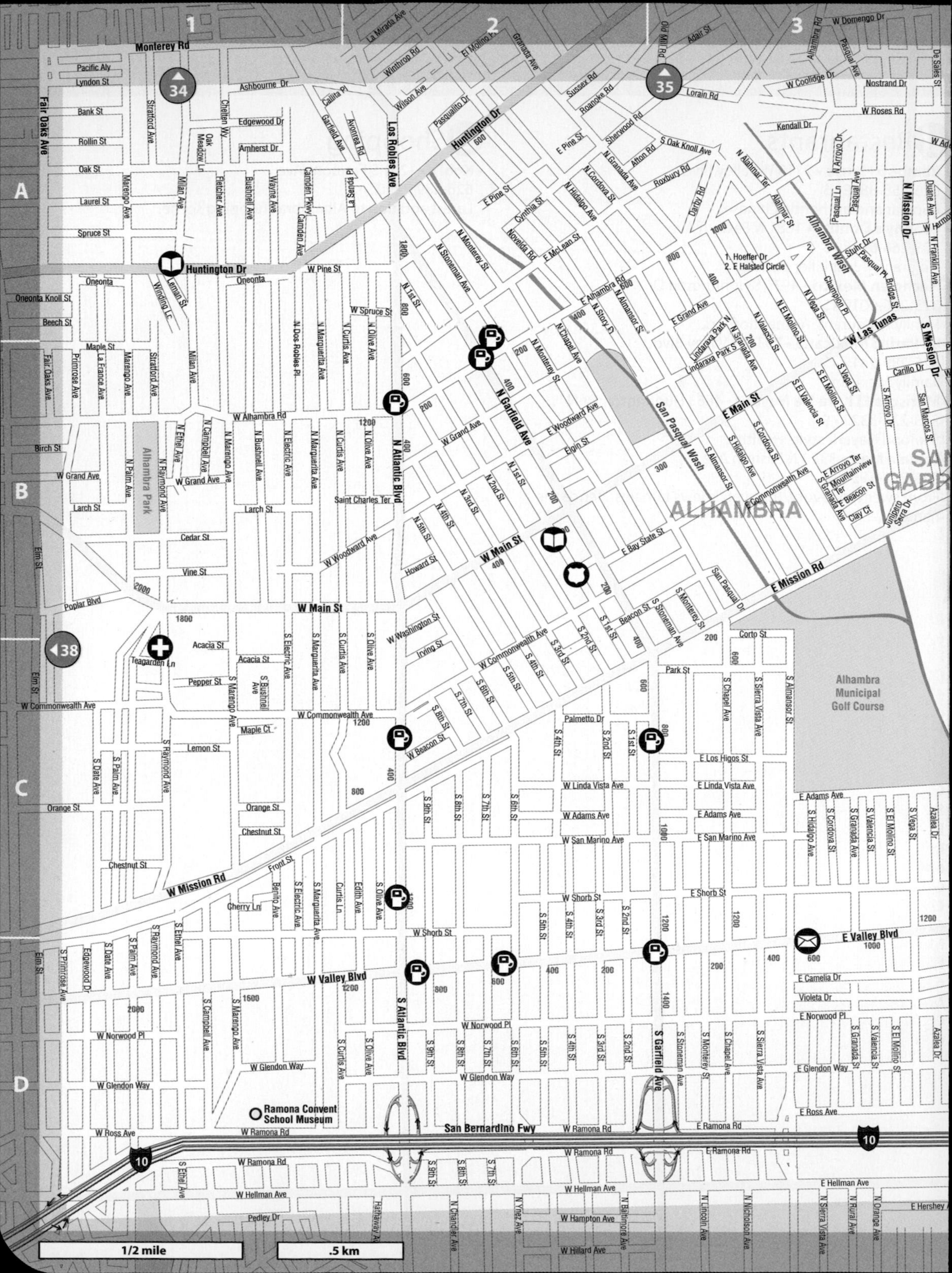
N
1
2
3
A
B
C
D
34
35
38
10
Monterey Rd
Pacific Aly
Lyndon St
Bank St
Rollin St
Oak St
Laurel St
Spruce St
Fair Oaks Ave
Ashbourne Dr
Edgewood Dr
Amherst Dr
Stratford Ave
Chelten Wy
Oak Meadow Ln
Marengo Ave
Milan Ave
Fletcher Ave
Bushnell Ave
Wayne Ave
Camden Pkwy
Camden Ave
Garfield Ave
Avonrea Rd
Callita Pl
Wilson Ave
Winthrop Rd
La Mirada Ave
El Molino Pl
Granada Ave
Pasqualito Dr
Los Robles Ave
Huntington Dr
Old Mill Rd
Adair St
Sussex Rd
Roanoke Rd
Lorain Rd
Sherwood Rd
E Pine St
Afton Rd
S Oak Knoll Ave
Roxbury Rd
N Alhambra Ter
Alhambra Rd
W Domengo Dr
Pasqual Ave
W Coolidge Dr
Nostrand Dr
W Roses Rd
Kendall Dr
De Sales St
N Arroyo Dr
Pasqual Ln
N Mission Dr
Duane Ave
N Franklin Ave
Alhambra Wash
Stuhr Dr
Pasqual Pl
Bridge St
Champion Pl
W Las Tunas
S Mission Dr
Carillo Dr
S Arroyo Dr
San Marinos St
1. Hoeffer Dr
2. E Halsted Circle
Darby Rd
N Granada Ave
N Cordova St
N Hidalgo Ave
Cynthia St
Novelda Rd
E McLean St
N Monterey St
N Stoneman Ave
N 1st St
E Alhambra Rd
N Story Ct
N Almansor St
E Grand Ave
Lindaraxa Park N
Lindaraxa Park S
N Valencia St
N El Molino St
N Vega St
N Chapel Ave
Huntington Dr
Oneonta
Oneonta Knoll St
Beech St
W Pine St
Leman St
Winding Ln
W Spruce St
N Dos Robles Pl
N Marguerita Ave
N Curtis Ave
N Olive Ave
Maple St
La France Ave
Primrose Ave
W Alhambra Rd
Birch St
N Ethel Ave
N Campbell Ave
N Marengo Ave
N Bushnell Ave
N Electric Ave
N Marguerita Ave
N Curtis Ave
N Olive Ave
N Atlantic Blvd
W Grand Ave
N Palm Ave
N Raymond Ave
Alhambra Park
Larch St
Saint Charles Ter
Cedar St
Vine St
Poplar Blvd
W Main St
Acacia St
Teagarden Ln
Pepper St
W Commonwealth Ave
N Garfield Ave
E Woodward Ave
Elgin St
San Pasqual Wash
E Main St
S Valencia St
S El Molino St
S Vega St
S Almansor St
S Hidalgo Ave
S Cordova St
E Commonwealth Ave
E Arroyo Ter
Mountainview Ter
E Beacon St
S Granada Ave
Clay Ct
Junipero Serra Dr
ALHAMBRA
SAN GABR
W Woodward Ave
N 5th St
N 4th St
N 3rd St
N 2nd St
N 1st St
Howard St
W Main St
E Bay State St
E Mission Rd
San Pasqual Dr
S Monterey St
S Stoneman Ave
Beacon St
S 1st St
S 2nd St
S 3rd St
S 4th St
S 5th St
S 6th St
S 7th St
S 8th St
W Washington St
Irving St
W Commonwealth Ave
Corto St
Park St
S Chapel Ave
S Sierra Vista Ave
S Almansor St
Alhambra Municipal Golf Course
S Electric Ave
S Marguerita Ave
S Curtis Ave
S Olive Ave
S Marengo Ave
S Bushnell Ave
Maple Ct
Lemon St
S Date Ave
S Palm Ave
S Raymond Ave
W Beacon St
Palmetto Dr
S 4th St
S 2nd St
S 1st St
E Los Higos St
W Linda Vista Ave
E Linda Vista Ave
W Adams Ave
E Adams Ave
W San Marino Ave
E San Marino Ave
Orange St
Chestnut St
W Mission Rd
Front St
Benito Ave
Curtis Ln
Edith Ave
Cherry Ln
S 9th St
S 8th St
S 7th St
S 6th St
S Hidalgo Ave
S Cordova St
S Granada Ave
S Valencia St
S El Molino St
S Vega St
Azalea Dr
W Shorb St
E Shorb St
S 5th St
S 3rd St
E Valley Blvd
W Valley Blvd
S Atlantic Blvd
S Ethel Ave
S Primrose Ave
Edgewood Dr
Elm St
E Camelia Dr
Violeta Dr
E Norwood Pl
W Norwood Pl
S Campbell Ave
S Garfield Ave
S Stoneman Ave
S Monterey St
E Glendon Way
W Glendon Way
Ramona Convent School Museum
E Ross Ave
W Ross Ave
San Bernardino Fwy
W Ramona Rd
E Ramona Rd
W Hellman Ave
E Hellman Ave
Pedley Dr
Hathaway Ave
N Chandler Ave
N Ynez Ave
W Hampton Ave
N Baltimore Ave
N Lincoln Ave
N Nicholson Ave
N Sierra Vista Ave
N Rural Ave
N Orange Ave
E Hershey
W Hillard Ave
1/2 mile
.5 km

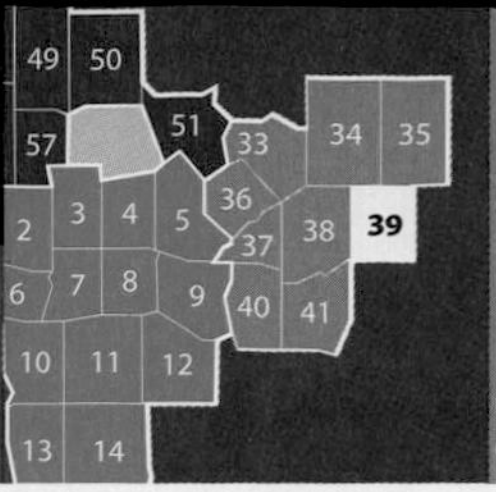

This independent city bills itself as "the Gateway to the San Gabriel Valley," but it's too modest. t's quickly becoming a destination for connoisseurs of Chinese food and medicine and for city evacuees looking for cozy homes, tree-lined streets, and some of the last affordable housing in the rea. It's a quick hop from Pasadena, the financial district, and the mountains. It's also that rarity in SoCal: a walking town.

oLandmarks

Ramona Convent Secondary School • 1701 W Ramona Rd
626-282-4151
Some of the campus buildings have been here since the 19th century.

Nightlife

Azul • 129 W Main St
626-282-6320
Dance and drink your blues away.

The Granada • 17 S 1st St
626-227-2572
Offers lessons and three dance floors to practice on.

Havana House • 133 W Main St
626-576-0547
Dress-code-enforced cigar lounge.

Jay-Dee Café • 1843 W Main St
626-281-6887
Great dive bar.

Restaurants

Angelo's Italian Restaurant • 1540 W Valley Blvd
626-282-0153 • $$
Pizza worth the wait.

Charlie's Trio Café • 47 W Main St
626-284-4943 • $$
Good, solid Italian.

Crane Sushi • 17 W Main St
626-458-0388 • $$
Half-price sushi.

Crazy Sushi • 201 E Bay State St
866-567-1332 • $$
Rock 'n' Roll sushi.

Diner on Main • 201 W Main St
626-281-3488 • $
Great food. Nostalgic setting. The Real Deal.

El Ranchero Restaurant • 511 S Garfield Ave
626-300-9320 • $
Mexican flavors in a friendly neighborhood setting.

Fosselman's Ice Cream • 1824 W Main St
626-282-6533 • $
Made on the premises since 1926.

Green Papaya • 1800 W Valley Blvd
626-282-1291 • $
Healthy and innovative Thai.

• **The Hat** • 1 W Valley Blvd
626-282-0140 • $
Best burgers for miles.

• **Indo Kitchen** • 5 N 4th St
626-282-1676 • $$
Padang-style cooking.

• **Mission 261** • 261 S Mission Dr
626-588-1666 • $
Chinese fare from dim sum to dinner served in mission-style former city hall.

• **Noodle World** • 700 W Valley Blvd
626-293-8800 • $
Every conceivable kind of noodle.

• **Perfectly Sweet** • 126 W Main St
626-282-9400 • $
Decadent and deadly desserts.

• **Pho 79** • 29 S Garfield Ave
626-289-0239 • $
Go for the noodle soup and dessert drinks.

• **Phoenix Dessert** • 220 E Valley Blvd
626-299-1918 • $$
Limited menu for fast snacks and desserts.

• **Rick's Drive In & Out** • 132 W Main St
626-576-8519 • $
Fast food at its best.

• **Sam Woo Barbeque** • 514 W Valley Blvd
626-281-0038 • $
Chinese fast food.

• **Señor Fish** • 115 W Main St
626-299-7550 • $$
Eat Mexican seafood with Caltech students.

• **Thai Purple** • 27 N Garfield Ave
626-300-9083 • $
Small, unassuming, super-convenient for movie theaters.

• **Twohey's** • 1224 N Atlantic Blvd
626-284-7387 • $
Old-style coffee shop.

• **Wahib's Middle East** • 910 E Main St
626-281-1006 • $$
Very traditional Middle Eastern cooking.

Shopping

• **Ross** • 201 E Main St
626-281-8453
Popular discount stop for housewares, clothes, and shoes.

• **Webster's Hallmark** • 147 W Alhambra Rd
626-577-0162
Huge selection of cards and doodads.

Map 40 • Boyle Heights

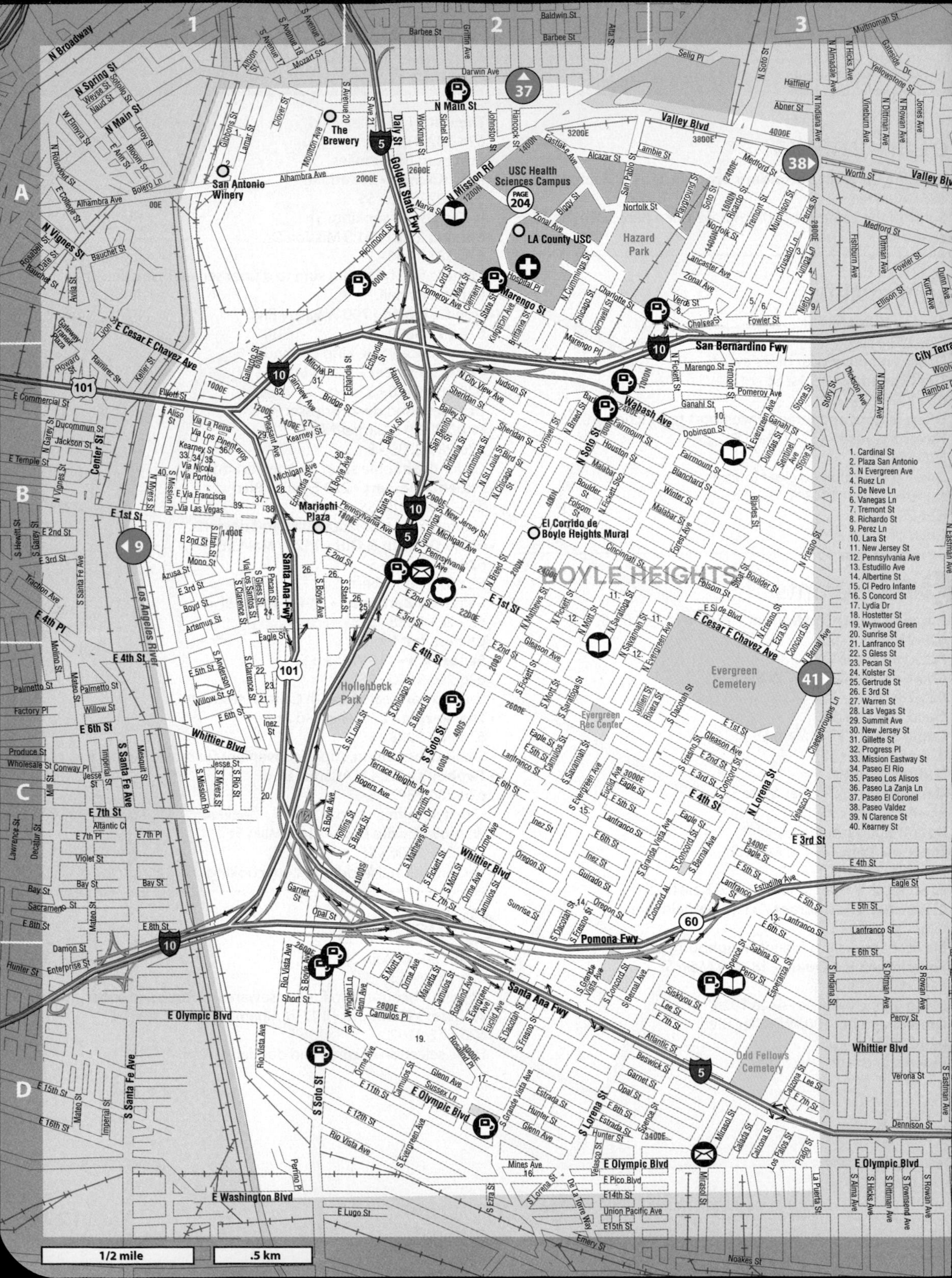

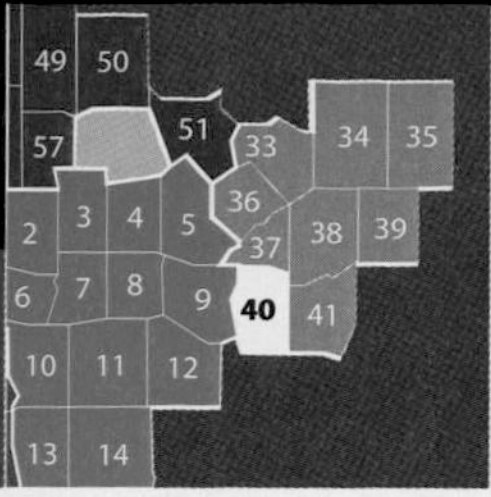

Situated just east of the LA River, Boyle Heights is a neighborhood rich with history. Explore the neighborhood's past as a Jewish enclave at the restored **Breed Street Shul**, or celebrate its distinctly Latino present by buying a song or two from the bands at **Mariachi Plaza**. Hollenbeck Park is a great place to relax, but keep an eye out for the ghosts said to live nearby at the abandoned Linda Vista Hospital.

Landmarks

- **Barbara's at the Brewery** • 620 Moulton Ave
  323-221-9204
  Former Pabst Blue Ribbon brewery turned artists' studios.
- **El Corrido de Boyle Heights Mural** •
  2336 E Cesar E Chavez Ave
  Public art at its most colorful.
- **LA County USC Medical Center** • 1200 N State St
  213-240-7926
  The facade may look familiar to viewers of *General Hospital.*
- **Mariachi Plaza** • 1804 E 1st St
  Need a mariachi? Look no further!
- **San Antonio Winery** • 737 Lamar St
  323-223-1401
  Last remaining winery along LA river basin; killer tasting room.

Nightlife

- **Barbara's at the Brewery** • 620 Moulton Ave
  323-221-9204
  Rub elbows with artists in old Pabst brewery.
- **Eastside Luv** • 1835 E 1st St
  323-262-7442
  Burlesque shows + mad atmosphere = $10 cover.

Restaurants

- **Barbara's at the Brewery** • 620 Moulton Ave
  323-221-9204 • $$
  Bar food and drinks for the art crowd.
- **Ciro's** • 705 N Evergreen Ave
  323-269-5104 • $
  Family fave for flautas.
- **El Tepeyac Cafe** • 812 N Evergreen Ave
  323-268-1960 • $$
  Famous hole-in-the-wall Mexican.
- **King Taco** • 2400 E Cesar E Chavez Ave
  323-264-3940 • $
  The benevolent ruler of Mexican fast food.
- **La Parrilla** • 2126 E Cesar E Chavez Ave
  323-262-3434 • $$
  Better than average Mexican chain.
- **La Serenata de Garibaldi** • 1842 E 1st St
  323-265-2887 • $$$
  Creative Mexican seafood.

Shopping

- **Skeletons in the Closet** • 1104 N Mission Rd
  323-343-0760
  County Coroner's gift shop stocks chalk outline beach towels and post-its.

1. Dodds Circle
2. Dodds Ave
3. Dundas St
4. N Rowan Ave
5. Schick Ave
6. Meisner St
7. Pomeroy St
8. Lott Ave
9. N Herbert Ave
10. Knowles Ave
11. Norman Pl
12. N Connell Pl
13. Sampson Pl
14. N Bonnie Beach Pl
15. E Almanza Ln
16. Buelah Circle
17. Miller Ave
18. Gifford Ave
19. Purcell Dr
20. Rogers St
21. Hayes St
22. Tarzon St
23. Shorey Pl
24. N Steele Ave
25. Centre Plaza
26. Lafler Dr
27. Wybro Wy
28. Rosilyn Dr
29. Milbrun Dr
30. N Cordon Dr
31. Lotta Dr
32. Machado Ave
33. Comly
34. Rollins Dr
35. Loren St
36. Watland Ave
37. Mesa Way
38. Durango Dr
39. Westminster Ave
40. Orange Grove Ave
41. Sierra Alta Wy
42. W Bonita Ter
43. W Elevado Ter
44. Campo St
45. Feliz
46. W Arboles St
47. W Colina Ter
48. W Casitas St
49. Aurora Ter
50. Ridgecrest Wy
51. North Ridge Pl
52. Star Ridge Dr
53. Ridgecrest Ct
54. Lightview St
55. Sunnyhill Dr
56. Stonewell St
57. Stone Gate St
58. Pebbleton St
59. Pebble Vale St
60. Pebble Hurst St
61. Rock View St
62. Rock Haven St
63. N Carmelita Ave
64. Gifford Ave
65. N Mariana Ave
66. Capistrano Way
67. N Nevada Ave
68. N Bonnie Beach Pl
69. S Indiana St
70. S Alma Ave
71. S Hicks Ave
72. S Rowan Ave
73. S Eastman Ave
74. S Gage Ave
75. S Herbert Ave
76. Dickerson Ave
77. Gleason St
78. Zaring St
79. Carmelita Ave
80. Nassau Ave
81. S Record Ave
82. Gleason St
83. S Fetterly Ave
84. Colonia de las Rosas
85. Colonia de los Cedros
86. Colonia de las Magnolias
87. Colonia de las Palmas
88. Sherbrook Ave
89. Schoolside Ave
CSU Los Angeles
City Terrace
Jose Luis Gonzalez Library Mural
Mural: The Kennedy Saga II 1973
City Park
Obregon Park
Monterey Park Golf Course
Monterey Park
Belvedere Park
New Calvary Cemetery
Salazar Park
East Los Angeles
San Bernardino Fwy
Long Beach Fwy
Pomona Fwy
Santa Ana Fwy
1/2 mile
.5 km

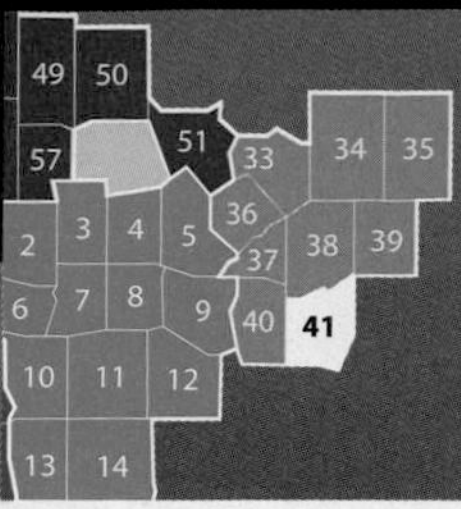

When Los Angeles was still called "el Pueblo de Nuestra Señora la Reina de los Ángeles," East LA was a hub of Mexican culture. And it still is. A perusal of the streets reveals a panoramic homage to the motherland. Home-style eateries, stunning murals, and singular shops are infused with el espíritu de la raza. If you're new to Los Angeles, there's no place like East LA to get a sense of our city's deep Mexican roots.

Landmarks

- **Jose Luis Gonzalez Library Mural** • 4025 City Terrace Dr
  A whole lot of badass aesthetics at once.
- **Mural: The Kennedy Saga II 1973** • 1126 N Hazard Ave
  Located inside the City Terrace Park social hall.

Restaurants

- **East LA Pizza Company** • 5616 E Beverly Blvd
  323-838-9110 • $
  This Eastside legend heaps on the toppings like woah.
- **Juanito's Tamales** • 4214 Floral Dr
  323-268-2365 • $
  Tender tamales by the dozen.
- **Tamales Lilianas** • 4629 E Cesar E Chavez Ave
  323-780-0989 • $
  The most famous tamales in LA.
- **Tamayo** • 5300 E Olympic Blvd
  323-260-4700 • $$
  Mexican.

N
1
2
3
A
B
C
D
CHATSWORTH
Ronald Reagan Frwy
118
27
43
45
De Soto Reservoir
Stoney Point Park
Chatsworth Park North
Chatsworth Park South
Oakwood Memorial Park Cemetery
Mason Park
Monteria Lake
Winnetka Park
h Reservoir
Santa Susanna Pass Rd
San Fernando Mission Blvd
Topanga Canyon Blvd
Canoga Ave
De Soto Ave
Winnetka Ave
Valley Circle Blvd
Devonshire St
Lassen St
Plummer St
Nordhoff St
Roscoe Blvd
Chatsworth St
Germain St
Tulsa St
Bermuda St
Kingsbury St
Stanwell St
San Jose St
Hiawatha St
Blackhawk St
Tuba St
Lemarsh St
Romar St
Mayall St
Merridy St
Vintage St
Septo St
Marilla St
Superior St
Itasca St
Gledhill St
Prairie St
Knapp St
Dearborn St
Osborne St
Gresham St
Parthenia St
Bryant St
Michale St
Malden St
Chase St
Rodax St
Eccles St
Mandell St
Community St
Schoenborn St
Lanark St
Baltar St
Cantara St
Burton St
Celtic St
Rinaldi St
Nashville St
Oakwood Memorial Park Cemetery
Baden Ave
Mason Ave
Independence Ave
Owensmouth Ave
Remmet Ave
Deering Ave
Eton Ave
Irondale Ave
Cozycroft Ave
Sunnybrae Ave
Fullbright Ave
Keokuk Ave
Laramie Ave
Comanche Ave
Quakertown Ave
Variel Ave
Jordan Ave
Hanna Ave
Nevada Ave
Farralone Ave
Glade Ave
Mason Ave
1/2 mile
.5 km

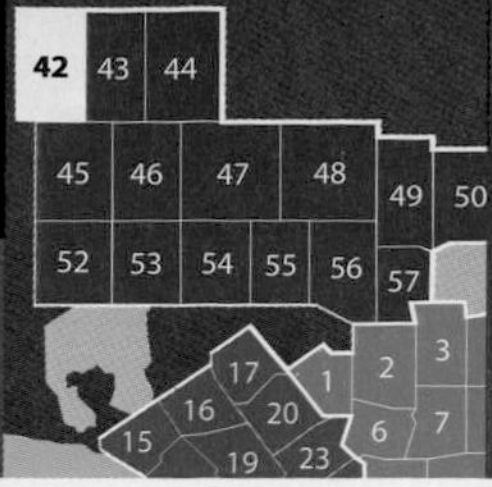

Well removed from LA proper, Chatsworth is its own entity. As late as the 1980s, it was quite rural; it was home to Roy Rogers and Dale Evans, and the setting for countless western flicks, classic and otherwise. But it's kept up with the times: Charles Manson and his homicidal minions camped at Spahn Ranch, and Chatsworth is now the world's epicenter of porn. Look for spray-tans and implants at the local **Ralph's.**

Landmarks

- **Oakwood Memorial Park Cemetery** • 22601 Lassen St
  818-341-1198
  The final resting place of dance legends Fred Astaire and Ginger Rogers.

Restaurants

- **Omino Sushi** • 20959 Devonshire St
  818-709-8822 • $$
  Live scallops and very recently live sushi deep in the Valley.

Shopping

- **Catherine's Cake Decorating & Candy Supplies** •
  21534 Devonshire St
  818-407-0653
  Cake, cookie, and candy decorating supplies & classes.

Map 43 • Granada Hills / Northridge

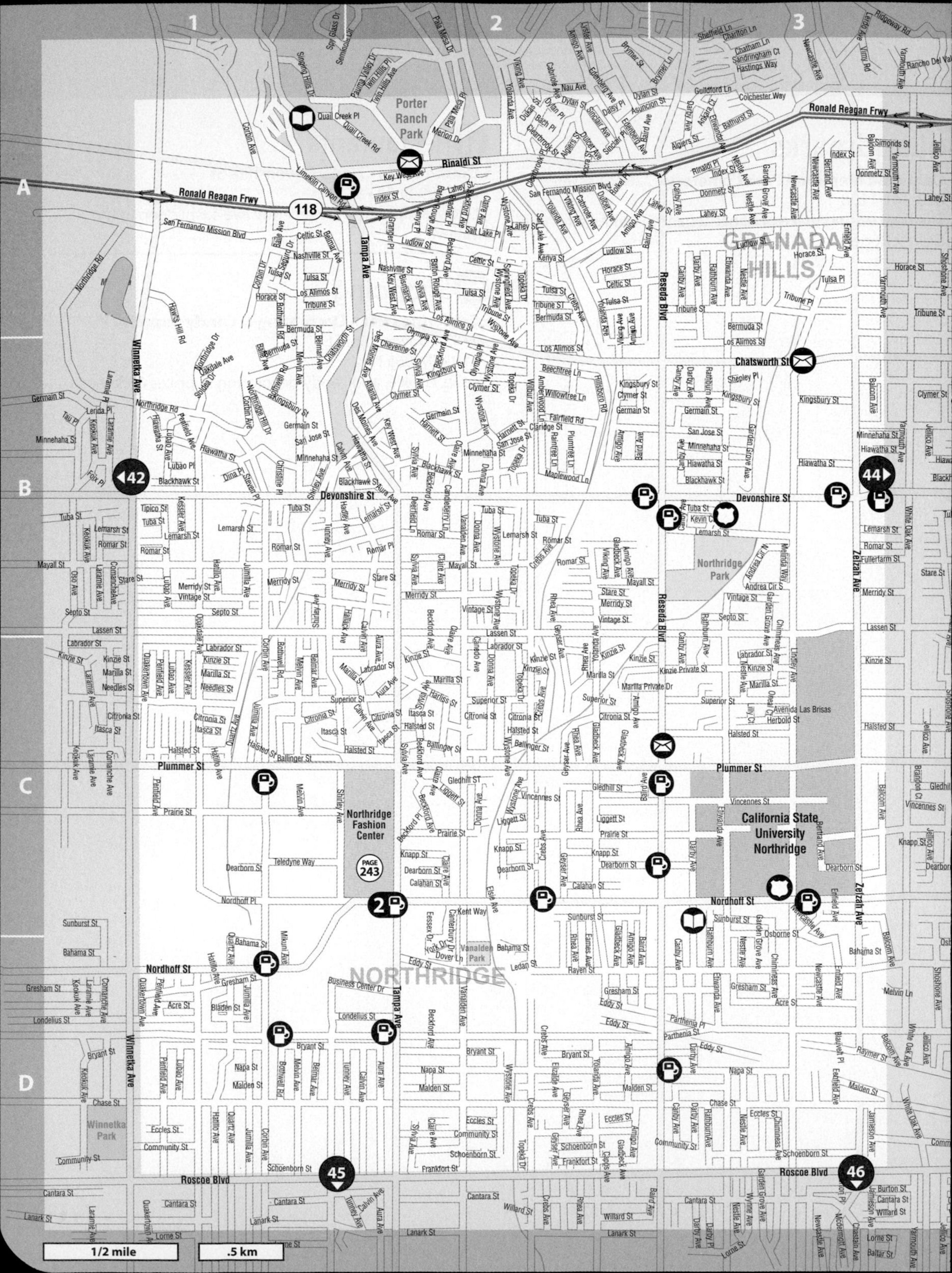

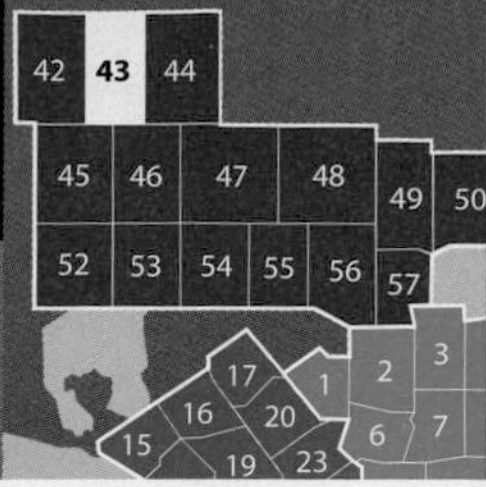

Once, Granada Hills spelled wide-open spaces, endless citrus groves, and everything classically outhern Californian. More recently, developers took over, building strip malls, chain restaurants, nd modernist condo-boxes faster than you can order a double tall latte. Suburbia aside, make sure ou don't neglect the incredible views, which, if it's not summer, stretch to the Pacific.

Restaurants

Brent's Delicatessen • 19565 Parthenia St
818-886-5679 • $
Once you go black pastrami, you'll never go back.

Claim Jumper Restaurant • 9429 Tampa Ave
818-718-2882 • $$$
A beef-eater's paradise; the night the giant potato ate the patrons; includes a full bar.

• **El Torito** • 8855 Tampa Ave
818-349-1607 • $$
The Mexican-styled dishes are delicious and the atmosphere is fun.

• **Maria's Italian Kitchen** • 9161 Reseda Blvd
818-341-5114 • $$
This restaurant's motto, "Your Neighborhood Italian Restaurant," is a perfect fit.

• **Orange Grove Bistro** • 18111 Nordhoff St
818-677-2076 • $$
California cuisine, sandwiches, Sunday brunch.

Map 44 • Mission Hills / North Hills

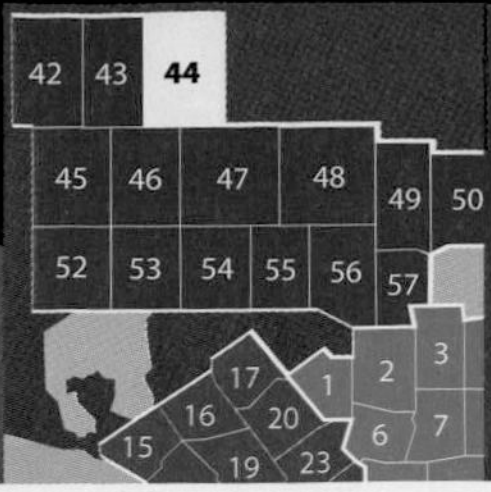

The San Fernando Valley's first oil well was dug right here in 1916, in what had been fertile farm and orchard land. Though most of the homes in Mission Hills and North Hills were built in the '50s, if you look hard you can find a few adobes that have been standing since those early days of well drilling and ranching.

oLandmarks

- **Greer House** • 9200 Haskell Ave
  Frank Lloyd Wright Jr. crawled out from under his father's shadow and built a house.
- **Sepulveda Unitarian Universalist Society Building** •
  9550 Haskell Ave
  818-894-9251
  A church shaped like an onion—only in LA.

Restaurants

- **In-N-Out Burger** • 9858 Balboa Blvd
  800-786-1000 • $
  Top California burger joint.

Map 45 • Canoga Park / Woodland Hills

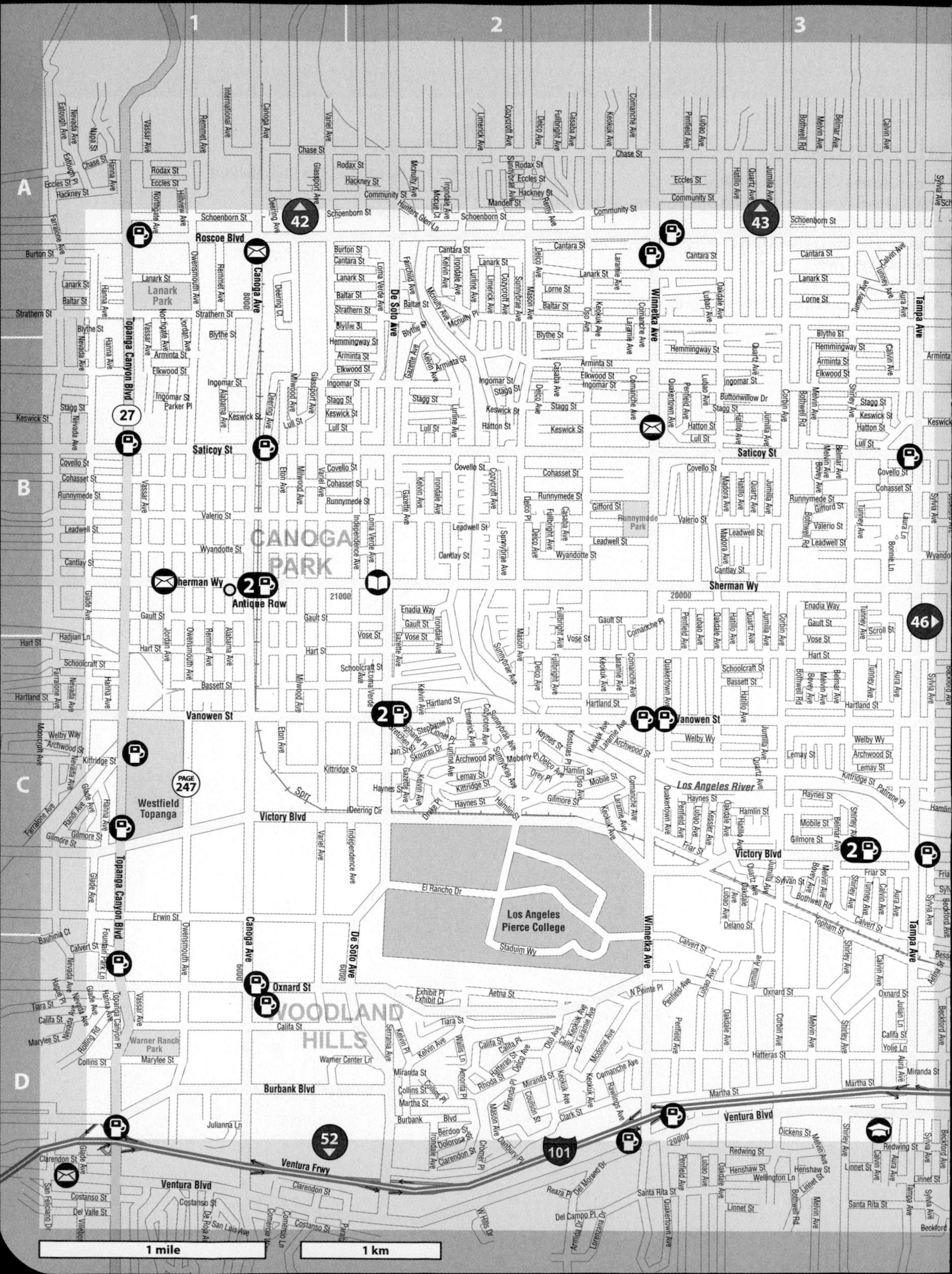

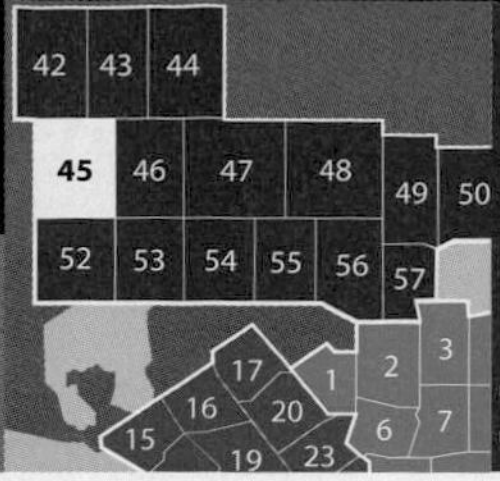

Canoga Park is home to Warner Center, a small city of office buildings, chain stores, restaurants, and big corporations. But only a stone's throw away sits Pierce College, a community college whose emphasis on sustainable agriculture shows: the college boasts a working farm, a veterinary science program, and a green philosophy that includes solar power and drought-resistant plants—adding rustic charm to what would otherwise be a wasteland of pre-fab business parks.

Landmarks

- **Antique Row** • Sherman Way
  It is what it is.

Nightlife

- **Corbin Bowl** • 19616 Ventura Blvd
  818-996-2695
  Ain't no Lucky Strike; serious bowlers abound.

Restaurants

- **Bistro Ka** • 6600 Topanga Canyon Blvd
  818-340-1300 • $$$
  Classic Japanese with a California twist.
- **Follow Your Heart** • 21825 Sherman Way
  818-348-3240 • $$
  Vegetarian cuisine.
- **In-N-Out Burger** • 19920 Ventura Blvd
  800-786-1000 • $
  Top California burger joint.
- **Roy's Restaurant** • 6363 Topanga Canyon Blvd
  818-888-4801 • $$$
  The dreams of Don Ho come alive.

Shopping

- **Babyland** • 7134 Topanga Canyon Blvd
  818-704-7848
  Bargain kids' stuff.
- **Green Thumb Nursery** • 21812 Sherman Way
  818-340-6400
  Mega-nursery.
- **Kake Kreations** • 21851 Sherman Way
  818-346-7621
  All your baking needs.
- **Westfield Promenade** • 6600 Topanga Canyon Blvd
  818-594-8732
  Dining, movies, and shops.
- **Westfield Topanga** • 6600 Topanga Canyon Blvd
  818-594-8732
  Behemoth mall.

N
1
2
3
A
B
C
D
43
44
45
47
53
Roscoe Blvd
Saticoy St
Sherman Wy
Vanowen St
Victory Blvd
Burbank Blvd
Ventura Fwy
Ventura Blvd
Reseda Blvd
White Oak Ave
Balboa Blvd
Tampa Ave
Vanalden Ave
Hayvenhurst Ave
RESEDA
Van Nuys Airport
Jesse Owens Park
Louise Park
Reseda Park and Recreation Center
Lake Balboa Park
Lake Balboa
Balboa Sports Center
Balboa Golf Course
Encino Golf Course
Los Angeles River
101
1. Cantara St
2. Willard St
3. Lanark St
4. Lorne St
5. Baltar St
6. Arminta St
7. Hemmingway St
8. Elkwood St
9. Driscoll Ave
10. Ostrom Ave
11. Wish Ave
12. Nestle Ave
13. Wynne Ave
14. Garden Grove Ave
15. Chimineas Ave
16. Wyandotte St
17. Canby Ave
18. Bianca Ave
19. Lasaine Ave
20. Jellico Ave
21. Lasaine Ave
22. Delano St
23. Lyptus Ct
24. Newcastle Ave
25. Bertrand Ave
26. Enfield Ave
27. Alonzo Ave
28. Jamieson Ave
29. Balcom Ave
30. Yarmouth Ave
31. Emelita St
32. Hatteras St
33. Bromley St
34. Andasol Ave
35. Mclennan Ave
36. Killion St
37. Albers St
38. Forbes Ave
39. Aldea Ave
40. Ostrom Ave
1 mile
1 km

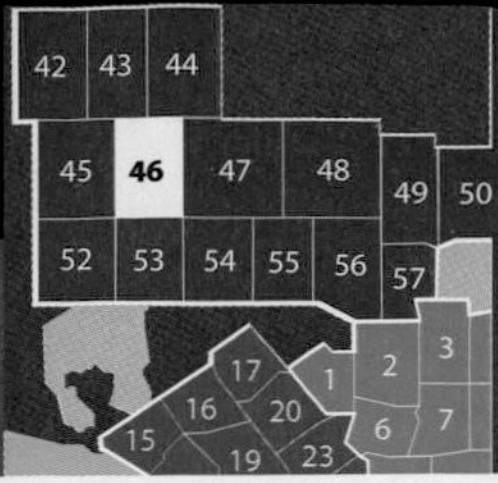

Reseda is more blue collar than upmarket neighbors Encino and Tarzana, but it alone has been immortalized in a Tom Petty song, "Free Fallin'." It has been mostly forgotten that the epicenter of the 1994 Northridge earthquake was located in Reseda at Wilbur Avenue and Saticoy Street, not in its namesake town, Northridge. Too bad the geologists didn't figure that out until a week after the quake, by which time the media had already churned out graphics and segments—accuracy be damned.

Restaurants

- **Lum-Ka-Naad** • 8910 Reseda Blvd
  818-882-3028 • $$
  Authentic and Americanized Thai. Menu is ginormous.
- **Melody's Mexican Kitchen** • 6747 Reseda Blvd
  818-609-9062 • $$
  Great Mexican in a casual, artsy atmosphere.

Shopping

- **Hobby People** • 5541 Balboa Blvd
  818-995-1162
  For crafters and hobbyists.

Map 47 • Van Nuys

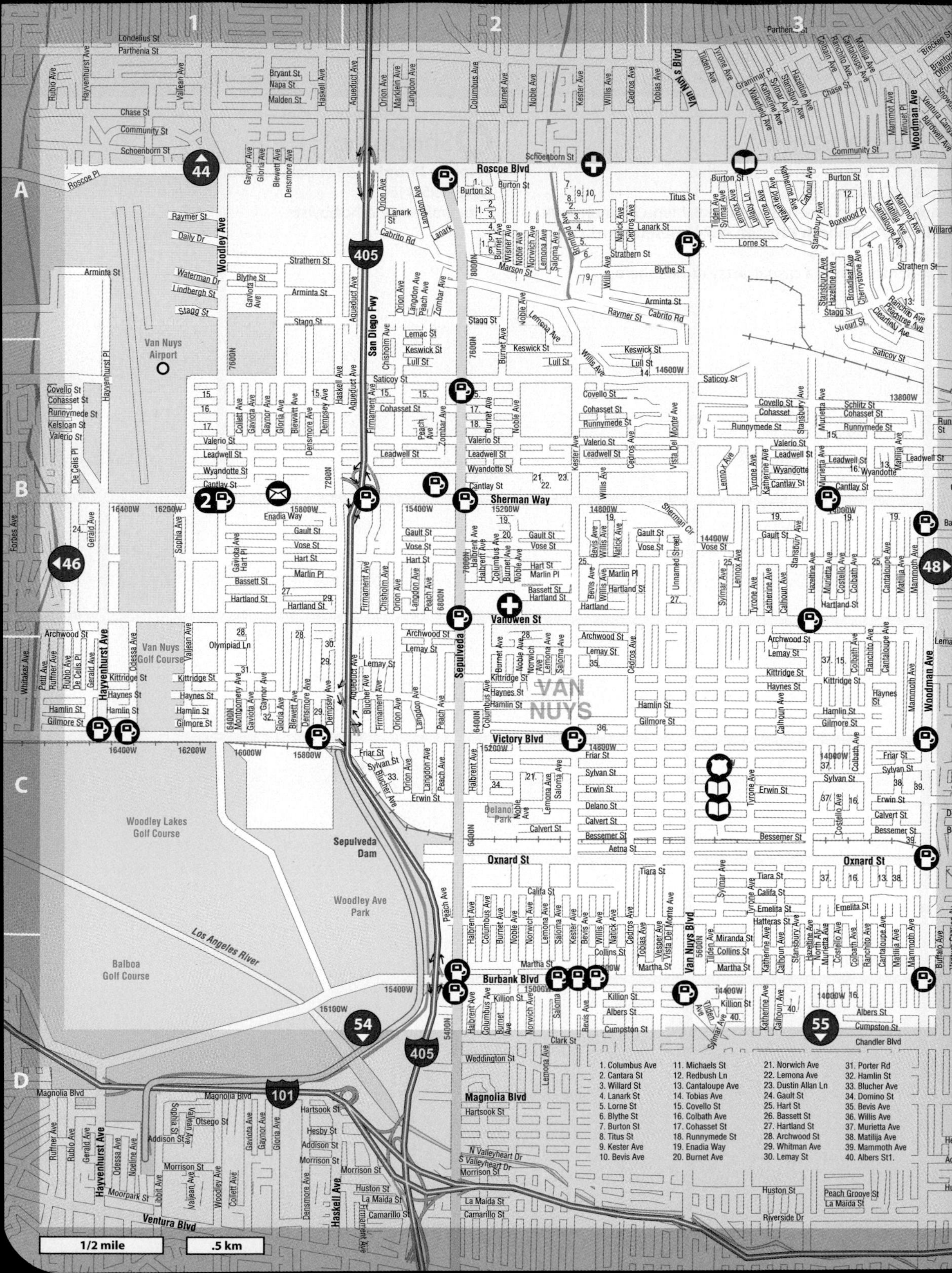

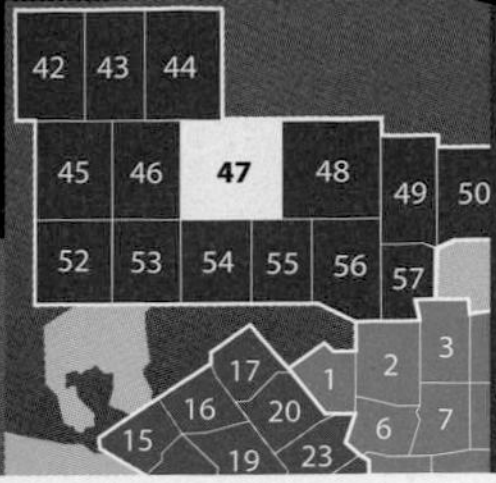

It's easy to miss freeway-encased Van Nuys, which most of LA knows mainly through their commute through it. That's because a lot of it isn't there anymore. The closing of the GM plant in 1992 caused a massive flight out of Van Nuys, and middle class sections that remained successfully petitioned to be reclassified into other neighborhoods. When you are cruising through Van Nuys north or south, always take Kester over Van Nuys and Sepulveda.

Landmarks

- **Van Nuys Airport** • 16461 Sherman Way
  818-442-6500
  The world's busiest general aviation airport.

Nightlife

- **Robin Hood British Pub** • 13640 Burbank Blvd
  818-994-6045
  Beer and bangers.

Restaurants

- **Bill & Hiroko's Burgers** • 14742 Oxnard St
  818-785-4086 • $
  Veteran burgermeisters.
- **Dr. Hogly Wogly's Tyler Texas BBQ** •
  8136 Sepulveda Blvd
  818-780-6701 • $$
  Texas BBQ.
- **In-N-Out Burger** • 7930 Van Nuys Blvd
  800-786-1000 • $
  Top California burger joint.
- **Kinnara Thai** • 15355 Sherman Way
  818-988-7788 • $$$
  Stylish, upscale Asian.
- **Pho 999** • 6411 Sepulveda Blvd
  818-782-1999 • $
  Pho good.
- **Sam Woo BBQ** • 6450 Sepulveda Blvd
  818-988-6813 • $
  Peking duck to go or stay, Chinatown-style.
- **Zankou Chicken** • 5658 Sepulveda Blvd
  818-781-0615 • $
  Palm-licking, Beck-serenaded chicken.

Shopping

- **Big Kid Collectables** • 14109 Burbank Blvd
  818-785-9208
  Maybe the coolest store in LA.
- **Chefs' Toys** •
  6178 Sepulveda Blvd
  818-782-4460
  Serious cookware.
- **Educative Toys & Supplies** • 6416 Van Nuys Blvd
  818-782-5580
  School-supply heaven.
- **Robin Hood British Pub** • 13640 Burbank Blvd
  818-994-6045
  Jolly 'ol' goods from the UK.

North Hollywood
Valley Glen
Los Angeles Valley College
Valley Plaza Park
Victory Vineland Park
Sun Valley Park Rec Center
North Hollywood Park and Recreation Center
Erwin Park
Hollywood Fwy
Roscoe Blvd
Sherman Wy
Vanowen St
Victory Blvd
Oxnard St
Burbank Blvd
Magnolia Blvd
Laurel Canyon Blvd
Lankershim Blvd
Coldwater Canyon Ave
Woodman Ave
Vineland Ave
San Fernando Rd
47
49
55
56
170
5
1/2 mile
.5 km
1. Stagg St
2. Wixom St
3. Keswick St
4. Wortser Ave
5. Morse Ave
6. Goodland Ct
7. Goodland Ave
8. Goosfold Ave
9. Bonfield Ave
10. Daha Pl
11. Armita St
12. Elkwood St
13. Divan Pl
14. Solvang St
15. Covello St
16. Todd Ct
17. Milldale Ct
18. Doran Pl
19. Jolene Ct
20. Eloise Ave
21. Morse Ave
22. Mary Ellen Ave
23. Ortley Pl

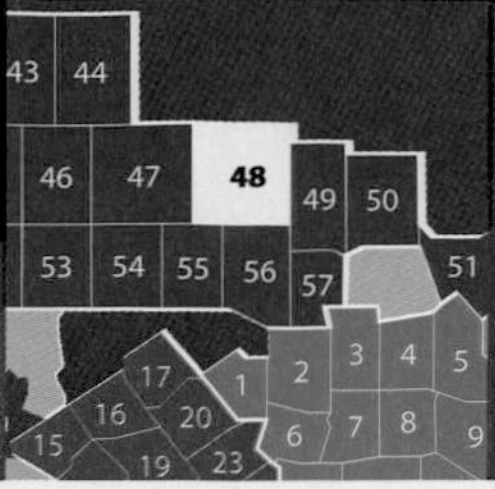

North Hollywood has the least "Valley/suburban" feel of any neighborhood north of The Hills, and that divide between NoHo and the rest of the SFV continues to widen. NoHo sports a burgeoning, urban-feeling array of shops, vintage clothing stores, theaters, and a growing, walkable Arts District. NoHo's Metro Red and Orange Line hubs keep it well connected, satisfying the increasing number of Valley dwellers who dare brave the city without a car.

Nightlife

- **Blue Zebra** • 6872 Farmdale Ave
  818-765-7739
  Strip joint. Big names; big prosthetics.
- **The Federal Bar** • 5303 Lankershim Blvd
  818-980-2555
  Speakeasy-themed hotspot. Refuge of the endangered Valley Hipster.
- **Tonga Hut** • 12808 Victory Blvd
  818-769-0708
  Charming dive's been dishing Mai Tais and cheap beer since 1958.

Restaurants

- **The Federal Bar** • 5303 Lankershim Blvd
  818-980-2555 • $$
  Go for the mac-n-cheese.
- **In-N-Out Burger** • 5864 Lankershim Blvd
  800-786-1000 • $
  Top California burger joint.
- **Krua Thai** • 13130 Sherman Way
  818-759-7998 • $
  Authentic, spicy Thai open till the wee hours.
- **MP's Soul Food Eatery** • 5643 Lankershim Blvd
  818-506-2930 • $$
  Southern specialties.
- **Que Rico Tacos** • 12940 Victory Blvd
  818-985-8014 • $
  Nothing beats carne asada from a taco truck at 3 am.

Shopping

- **99 Cents Only Store** • 12711 Sherman Way
  818-764-9991
  Plus tax!
- **Baklava Factory** • 12909 Sherman Way
  818-764-1011
  Baklava and more.
- **Big Lots** • 13005 Sherman Way
  818-982-1687
  Monster close-out store. Always something surprising and marked way, way down.
- **Kmart** • 13007 Sherman Way
  818-764-0250
  Welcome, shoppers…
- **Scandinavian Designs** • 12240 Sherman Way
  818-765-0401
  Cool furnishings for home and office.

N
1
2
3
A
B
C
D
1. Glenhill Ave
2. Glencrest Dr
3. Via Pavia
4. Via Nola
5. Via Udine
6. Via Siena
7. Via Genova
8. Via Catalina
9. Via Zibello
10. Via Sorrento
11. Via Napoli
12. Scott Rd
13. Scott Wy
14. Via Rimini
15. Via Bernard
16. Via Milano
17. Rosa Maria
18. Via Ronaldo
19. Via Foggia
20. Via Tivoli
21. Wyandotte St
22. N Valley St
23. Jannetta Ave
24. Kittridge St
25. W Chestnut St
26. Riverton Ave
SUN VALLEY
NORTH HOLLYWOOD
Woodbury University
Burbank Airport
PAGE 252
Pierce Valhalla Cemetery
Pacific Park
Gross Park
Burbank Empire Center
PAGE 234
Victory Vineland Park
Portal of the Folded Wings Shrine to Aviation
Ralph Foy Park
Vickroy Park
Valley Park
Griffith Manor Park
Whitnall Park
Warner Ranch
The Burbank Studios
PAGE 195
San Fernando Blvd
Golden State Fwy
N Glenoaks Blvd
N Hollywood Wy
W Vanowen St
W Empire Ave
W Victory Blvd
W Burbank Blvd
W Magnolia Blvd
W Olive Ave
W Verdugo Ave
W Alameda Ave
Ventura Fwy
Riverside Dr
Lankershim Blvd
Vineland Ave
Burbank Blvd
Cahuenga Blvd
N Buena Vista St
N Victory Pl
Scott Rd
Sherman Way
Moorpark St
Forest Lawn
W Riverside
S Buena Vista
5
134
48
50
56
57
2
1/2 mile
.5 km

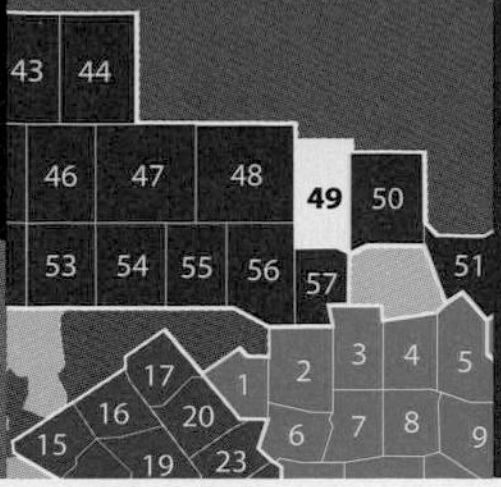

Burbank sports an exceedingly low crime rate and an affordability (free parking everywhere!) that makes it a big draw for families—and consequently the chains families patronize. It's also the best way to fly into the LA metro area—through the wonderfully sleepy Bob Hope Airport. To the west of Warner Brothers lot, Magnolia Boulevard is an up-and-coming destination strip, featuring vintage shops, kitschy stores, and a few hip bars full of young "Industry" types.

Landmarks

- **The Burbank Studios** • 3000 W Alameda Ave
  Former NBC Studios; "Beautiful Downtown Burbank" was here.
- **Portal of the Folded Wings Shrine to Aviation** • 10621 Victory Blvd
  This Spanish/Mission revival-style monument shows up in the occasional TV show and movie.
- **Warner Ranch** • W Verdugo Ave & Pass Ave
  818-954-6000
  That NY fountain where TV's *Friends* dance in the opening credits? Right here on the ranch.

Nightlife

- **Champs Sports Pub** • 4103 W Burbank Blvd
  818-840-9493
  Old school sports pub, in both upkeep and M.O.
- **Dimples** • 3413 W Olive Ave
  818-842-2336
  Claims to be the "first karaoke club in America."
- **Flappers** • 102 E Magnolia Blvd
  818-845-9721
  Traditional comedy club with actually decent food.
- **Library Lounge** • 322 N Pass Ave
  818-842-8887
  Graciela's swanky-yet-cozy hotel bar with killer martinis.
- **No Bar** • 10622 Magnolia Blvd
  818-753-0545
  Plush, darkly fabulous interior belies the seedy exterior.
- **Sardo's** • 259 N Pass Ave
  818-846-8127
  Great karaoke.
- **The Snug** • 4108 W Magnolia Blvd
  818-557-0018
  Laid back neighborhood bar in the heart of the Valley.
- **Tinhorn Flats Saloon and Grill** • 2623 W Magnolia Blvd
  818-567-2470
  Classic neighborhood joint dressed up like a Wild West saloon.

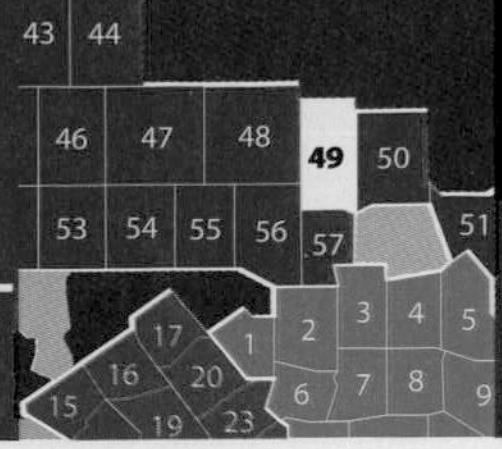

Burbank

Restaurants

- **Buchanan Arms** • 2013 W Burbank Blvd
818-845-0692 • $$
Sample British eats seated 'neath a portrait of the Queen.
- **Chili John's** • 2018 W Burbank Blvd
818-846-3611 • $
Best chili this side of the Mississippi.
- **Coral Café** • 3321 W Burbank Blvd
818-566-9725 • $
Burbank landmark serves breakfast 24/7, along with wholesome American favorites.
- **Full O' Life** • 2515 W Magnolia Blvd
818-845-7411 • $
Health food store/restaurant.
- **Kuru-Kuru Sushi** • 521 N Hollywood Way
818-848-3355 • $$
Generous portions of high quality, reasonably priced sushi in a friendly atmosphere.
- **Le Petit Chateau** • 4615 Lankershim Blvd
818-769-1812 • $$$
Romantic little French bistro.
- **Mucho Mas** • 10405 Burbank Blvd
818-980-0300 • $
Mexican standards on the patio or in a cozy cavern.
- **Poquito Mas** • 10651 Magnolia Blvd
818-994-8226 • $
Cheap, fresh Mexican chain.
- **Porto's Bakery & Café** • 3614 W Magnolia Blvd
818-846-9100 • $
Yummy Cuban sandwiches and an amazing array of baked goods.
- **Tallyrand** • 1700 W Olive Ave
818-846-9904 • $
Greasy spoon institution with all the fixins.
- **Taste Chicago** • 603 N Hollywood Way
818-563-2800 • $
Sweet Home Chicago comfort food.
- **Tony's Bella Vista** • 3116 W Magnolia Blvd
818-848-3389 • $
Italian standards in a friendly, straw-covered-Chianti-bottle setting.
- **Urban Eats** • 3501 W Magnolia Blvd
818-848-1106 • $
Fresh, healthy…good.

Burbank

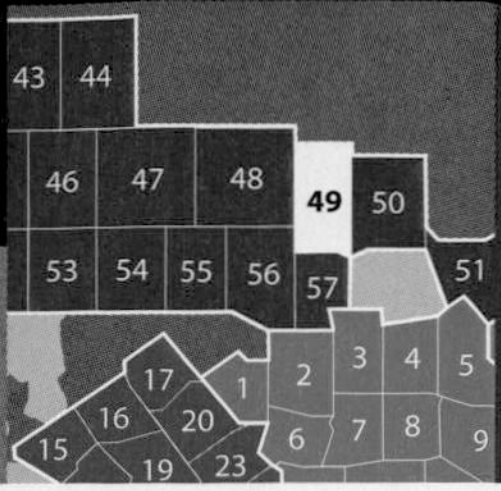

Thanks to its easy access to the 5, 101, and 134, Burbank is a favorite of commuters who don't want to pay city prices. If your car does have something weird go wrong with it, Victory Boulevard sports a Murderer's Row of quality specialty mechanics. Speaking of cars, it's not unusual to see Jay Leno zipping up Hollywood Way, probably coming from or going to the classic car show at Bob's Big Boy.

Shopping

- **Atomic Records** • 3812 W Magnolia Blvd
  818-848-7090
  Used records. An eclectic inventory at reasonable prices.
- **Dark Delicacies** • 3512 W Magnolia Blvd
  818-556-6660
  Everything for your D&D/goth/horror/fantasy friend (we all have one).
- **Fry's Electronics** • 2311 N Hollywood Way
  818-526-8100
  Huge electronics store with a B-movie, spaceship-themed exterior.
- **It's a Wrap** • 3315 W Magnolia Blvd
  818-567-7366
  Clothes previously worn by your favorite TV stars.
- **Monte Carlo Deli & Pinocchio Restaurant** •
  3103 Magnolia Blvd
  818-845-3516
  Authentic Italian market.
- **Otto's Hungarian Import Store & Deli** •
  2320 W Clark Ave
  818-845-0433
  All manner of Hungarian delicacies and deliciousness.
- **Playclothes** • 3100 W Magnolia Blvd
  818-557-8447
  Vintage retailer that does the wardrobe for *Mad Men*.
- **Rocket Fizz** • 3524 W Magnolia Blvd
  818-846-7632
  Indie sodas and candies galore.
- **Swift** • 3216 W Magnolia Blvd
  818-558-1289
  Vintage goodies.
- **The Train Shack** • 1030 N Hollywood Way
  818-842-3330
  Fun model train store.
- **Western Bagel** • 513 N Hollywood Way
  818-567-0413
  Local favorite.

Map 50 • Burbank East / Glendale West

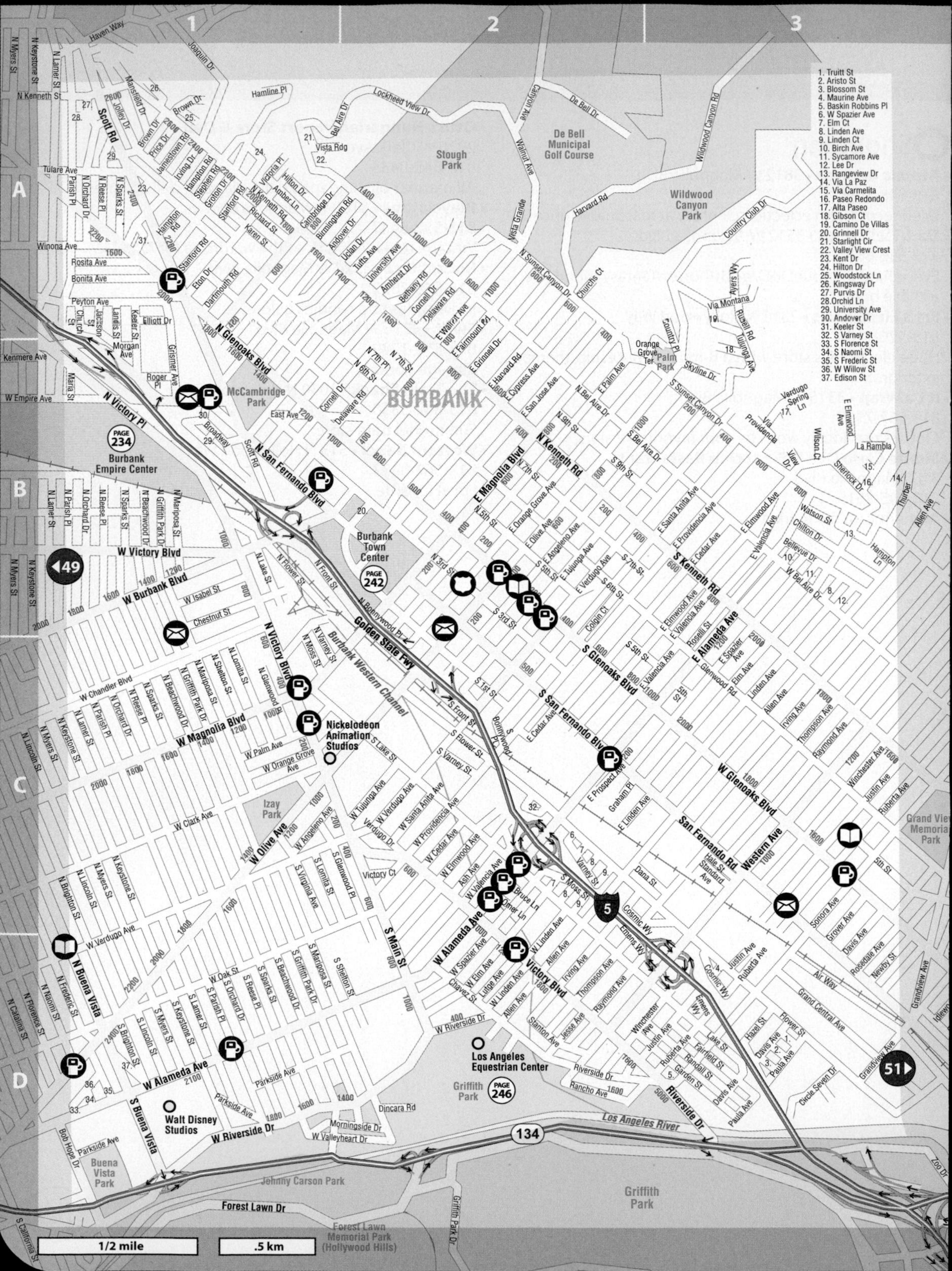

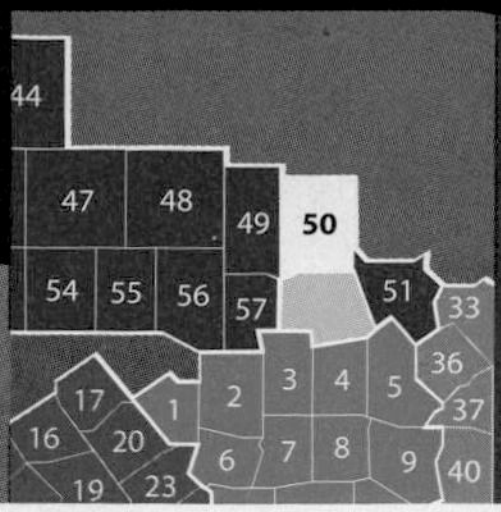

Though Hollywood is known the world over as home of the entertainment industry, it's actually this unassuming section of Burbank that is. And considering it's the unheralded king of the American entertainment industry, it's refreshingly quiet and laid-back. On the east edge of Burbank, LA horse owners stable their stallions in the Equestrian District. And Chandler Boulevard provides a nice walking path popular with Valley hikers.

oLandmarks

- **Los Angeles Equestrian Center** • 480 Riverside Dr
  818-840-9063
  Polo, dressage, and the Los Angeles Gay Rodeo.
- **Nickelodeon Animation Studios** • 231 W Olive Ave
  818-736-3000
  Look out for the slime!
- **Walt Disney Studios** • 500 S Buena Vista St
  818-560-1000
  The quirkiest architecture of all of the major motion picture studios.

Nightlife

- **The Blue Room** • 916 S San Fernando Blvd
  323-849-2779
  Somewhat upscale neighborhood bar.
- **Corner Bar** • 924 S San Fernando Blvd
  818-845-1861
  Your standard cheap dive, complete with karaoke and trivia.
- **Tony's Darts Away** • 1710 Magnolia Blvd
  818-253-1710
  Megapopular pub stocked entirely with esoteric Cali beers.

Restaurants

- **Adana** • 6918 San Fernando Blvd
  818-843-6237 • $$
  Highly regarded Middle Eastern with Armenian bent.
- **Doughnut Hut** • 2025 W Magnolia Blvd
  818-840-8718 • $
  Good donuts, great sign.
- **Gordon Biersch** • 145 S San Fernando Blvd
  818-569-5240 • $$$
  Basic American brewpub.
- **Gourmet 88** • 230 N San Fernando Blvd
  818-848-8688 • $$
  No fuss, no muss…just good Chinese.
- **Granville** • 121 N San Fernando Blvd
  818-848-4726 • $$
  Yummy organic food in a casual setting.
- **Harry's Family Restaurant** • 920 N San Fernando Blvd
  818-842-8755 • $
  American diner fare; open 24/7.
- **In-N-Out Burger** • 761 N 1st St
  800-786-1000 • $
  Top California burger joint.
- **Knight Restaurant** • 138 N San Fernando Blvd
  818-845-4516 • $$
  Savory Greek and Mediterranean dishes.
- **Mambo's** • 1701 Victory Blvd
  818-545-8613 • $$
  Little place packs powerful authentic Cuban punch.
- **Market City Caffé** • 164 E Palm Ave
  818-840-7036 • $$
  Inexpensive Italian chain.
- **North End Pizzeria** • 212 E Orange Grove Ave
  818-557-8325 • $$
  Best pizza in Burbank + delivery = success.
- **Picanha Churrascaria** • 269 E Palm Ave
  818-972-2100 • $$
  Tasty Brazilian all-you-can-eat meat-on-a-stick.
- **Poquito Mas** • 2635 W Olive Ave
  818-563-2252 • $
  Cheap, fresh, Mexican chain.
- **Ribs USA** • 2711 W Olive Ave
  818-841-8872 • $$
  Cheap casual BBQ.
- **Tony's Darts Away** • 1710 Magnolia Blvd
  818-253-1710 • $$
  Deliciously quirky bar eats like vegan brats and disco fries.
- **Viva Cantina** • 900 W Riverside Dr
  818-845-2425 • $$
  Mexican restaurant/lounge.

Shopping

- **7 Days Food Store** • 1700 Victory Blvd
  818-551-0300
  Where McLovin buys his booze.
- **Arte de Mexico** • 1000 Chestnut St
  818-753-4559
  Furniture and crafts with a Mexican flair.
- **Firing Line Indoor Shooting Range** • 1060 N Lake St
  818-954-9810
  Access your inner sniper at these 50-foot ranges.
- **Pickwick Gardens Conference Center** • 1001 Riverside Dr
  818-845-5300
  Bowling alley, ice rink, often hosts antique or art fairs.
- **rA Organic Spa** • 119 N San Fernando Blvd
  818-848-4772
  A classy and eco-conscious spa in the Valley. No joke.
- **Unique Vintage** • 2013 W Magnolia Blvd
  818-848-1540
  New clothes in vintage styles.
- **Valley Dealer Exchange** • 6530 San Fernando Rd
  818-638-8130
  One of the most painless used car-buying experiences you will ever have.

Map 51 • Glendale South

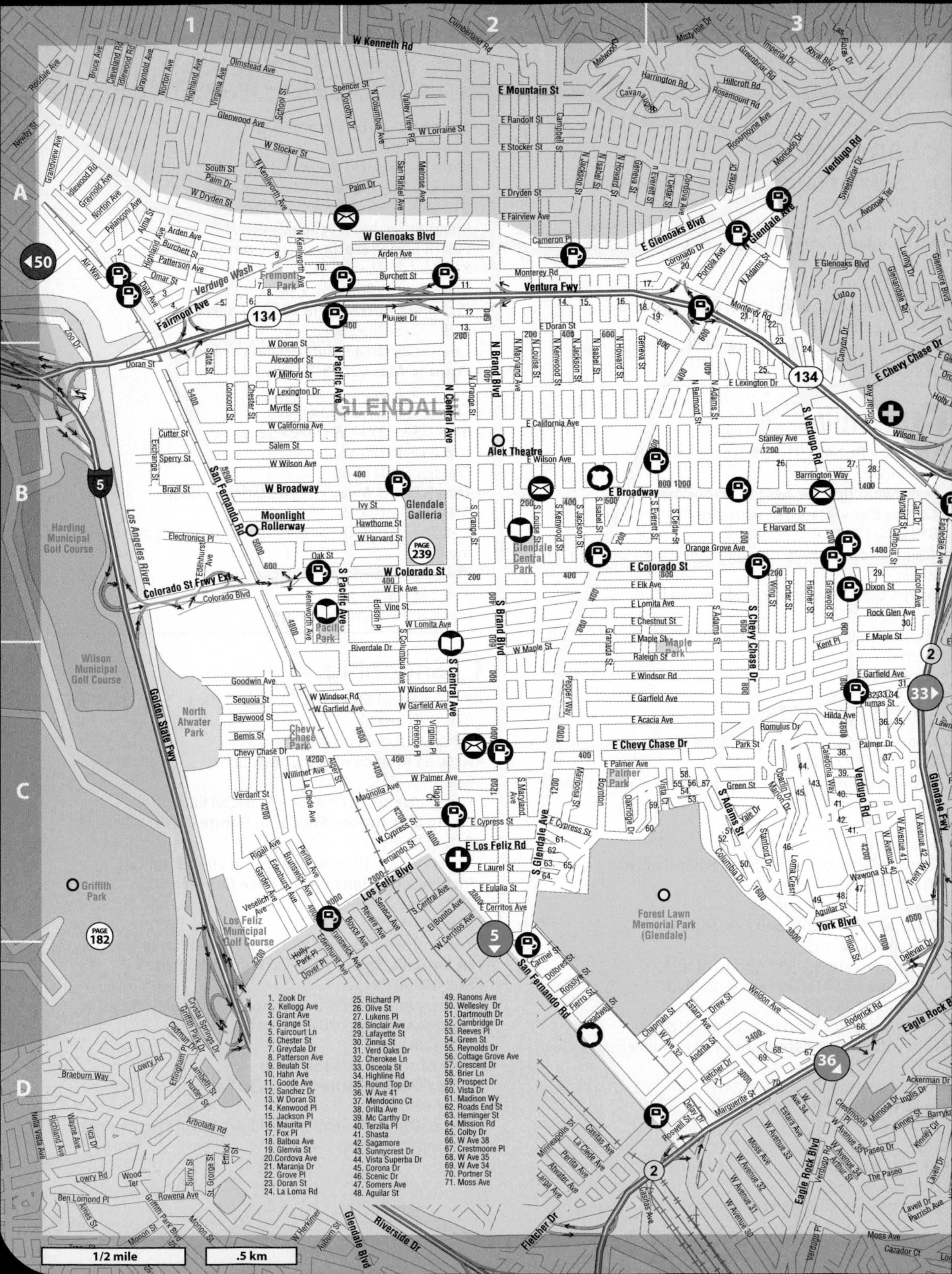

Glendale has grown up. Statistically, it's one of the safest cities in the state, if not the nation. Thanks to one of the largest Armenian populations in the world, you can score legit kebabs and baklava along Colorado Boulevard, or just about anywhere you look. Between the **Alex Theatre**, the **Glendale Galleria**, and **Americana on Brand**, it's the all-American, ridiculously overcrowded weekend family getaway. And, at **Foxy's Restaurant** and the diver bar **Big Fish**, it flaunts peaceful, limitless diversity.

oLandmarks

- **Alex Theatre** • 216 N Brand Blvd
  818-243-2539
  Former Vaudeville house opened in 1925.
- **Forest Lawn Memorial Park** • 1712 S Glendale Ave
  800-204-3131
  The Disneyland of LA cemeteries.
- **Griffith Park** • 4730 Crystal Springs Dr
  323-913-4688
  Ride the carousel.
- **Moonlight Rollerway** • 5110 San Fernando Rd
  818-241-3630
  Time stands still at Glendale's premier roller-boogie spot.

Nightlife

- **Big Fish** • 5230 San Fernando Rd
  818-244-6442
  The gold-medal dive.
- **Dave's** • 708 E Broadway
  818-956-9123
  Hard-swilling dive dominated by regulars. Famous Friday-night karaoke.
- **Eagle Rock Brewery** • 3056 Roswell St
  323-257-7866
  LA proper's first microbrewery. Woop!
- **Far Niente** • 204 N Brand Blvd
  818-242-3835
  More polished than an actual dive.
- **Golden Road Brewing** • 5410 San Fernando Rd
  213-542-6039
  Great local brewery with large, chill brewpub and taproom. Lawn games!
- **Jax Bar and Grill** • 339 N Brand Blvd
  818-500-1604
  Jazz club.
- **Left Coast Wine Bar** • 117 E Harvard St
  818-507-7011
  European sports and good—if arguably costly—wine. All Democrats should be so lucky.

Restaurants

- **Carousel** • 304 N Brand Blvd
  818-246-7775 • $$$
  Delicious Armenian food, BYO liquor.
- **Damon's Steakhouse** • 317 N Brand Blvd
  818-507-1510 • $$$
  Lots of red meat and cheesy tropical drinks.
- **Eat Well** • 1013 S Brand Blvd
  818-243-5928 • $
  Comfort food, great breakfasts.
- **Elena's Greek Armenian Cuisine** • 1000 S Glendale Ave
  818-241-5730 • $$
  A small, fattening Greek date spot.
- **Favorite Place** • 115 W Wilson Ave
  818-507-7409 • $$
  True to its name for many charmed by the owner. Try the rosewater lemonade.
- **Foxy's Restaurant** • 206 W Colorado St
  818-246-0244 • $$
  Toast your own bread at the table!
- **Ichiban** • 120 S Brand Blvd
  818-242-9966 • $$
  Affordable, fresh sushi.
- **Kabab Way** • 919 S Glendale Ave
  818-242-3150 • $
  Tasty Armenian kebab joint. Ask for the garlic sauce.
- **Max's** • 313 W Broadway
  818-637-7751 • $
  Famous Filipino fried chicken.
- **Porto's Bakery & Café** • 315 N Brand Blvd
  818-956-5996 • $
  To-die-for Cuban pastries and cakes.
- **Raffi's Place** • 211 E Broadway
  818-240-7411 • $
  Meat on a stick.
- **Scarantino's Italian Inn** • 1524 E Colorado St
  818-247-9777 • $
  Cozy, friendly pizza/pasta joint.
- **Zankou Chicken** • 1415 E Colorado St
  818-244-2237 • $
  Cheap Armenian chain.

Shopping

- **The Americana at Brand** • 300 S Brand Blvd
  818-637-8982
  Consumer extravaganza.
- **Cost Plus World Market** • 223 N Glendale Ave
  818-241-2112
  An "everything" superstore.
- **The Costume Shoppe** • 746 W Doran St
  818-244-1161
  Amazing costume rental house.
- **Glendale Galleria** • 100 W Broadway
  818-246-6737
  Praise be to an American original: the typical suburban mall.
- **Luigi's** • 5630 San Fernando Rd
  818-246-7579
  Fountains, tiles, heavy stuff to sit out in the garden.
- **Mignon Chocolate & Coffee Lounge** •
  315 N Verdugo Rd
  818-549-9600
  Start the day with coffee and dessert.

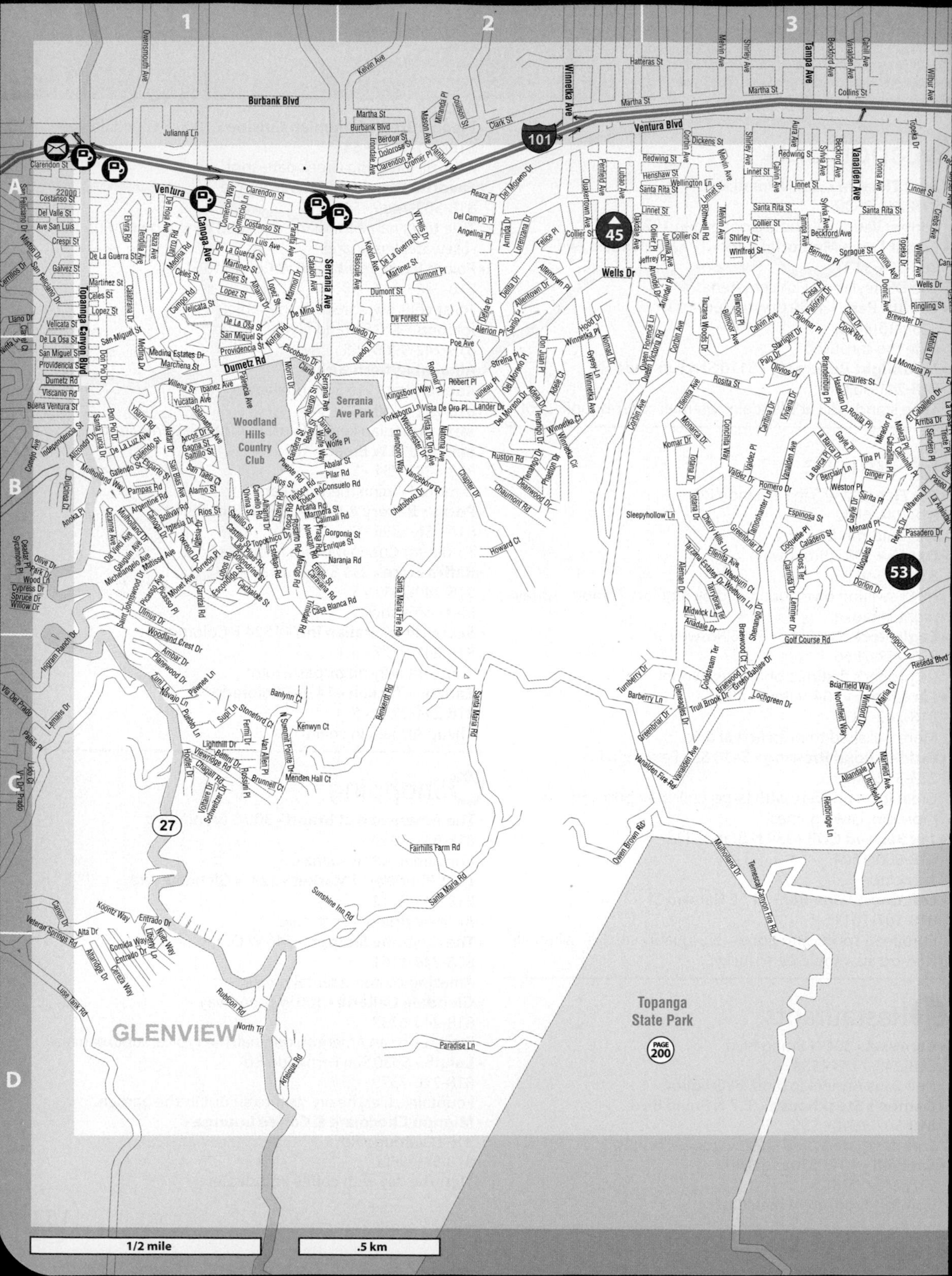
1
2
3
A
B
C
D
Burbank Blvd
Ventura Blvd
Ventura
101
Clarendon St
Topanga Canyon Blvd
Canoga Ave
Serrania Ave
Dumetz Rd
Winnetka Ave
Tampa Ave
Vanalden Ave
Wells Dr
Corbin Ave
Reseda Blvd
Mulholland Dr
Mulholland Way
Woodland Hills Country Club
Serrania Ave Park
Topanga State Park
GLENVIEW
45
53
27
PAGE 200
Santa Maria Rd
Santa Maria Fire Rd
Vanalden Fire Rd
Temescal Canyon Fire Rd
Owen Brown Rd
Sleepyhollow Ln
Golf Course Rd
Fairhills Farm Rd
Sunshine Inn Rd
Rubicon Rd
North Trl
Paradise Ln
Arteique Rd
Veteran Springs Rd
Luise Tank Rd
Kelvin Ave
Hatteras St
Martha St
Collins St
Clark St
Owensmouth Ave
Julianna Ln
Costanso St
Del Valle St
Ave San Luis
Crespi St
Galvez St
Velicata St
San Miguel St
Providencia St
Buena Ventura St
Independencia St
Ingram Ranch Dr
Woodland Crest Dr
Benkeradt Rd
Chalk Point
1/2 mile
.5 km

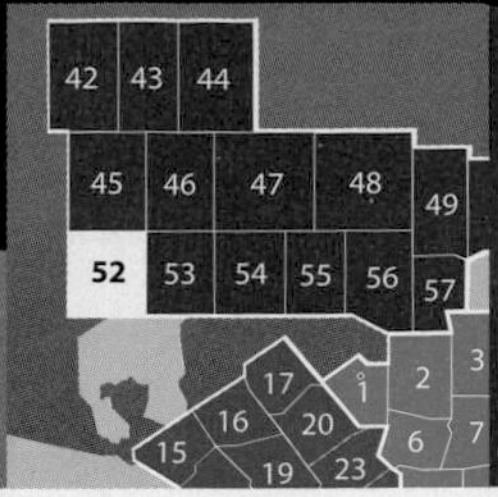

As in most Valley suburbs, Ventura Boulevard serves as a dividing line for the "Haves" and the "Have Mores." Homes north of the boulevard are largely condos and rental apartments, while larger, more expensive single-family homes are found to the south. Woodland Hills and Tarzana are home to almost any chain restaurant or store one could ever need, with most found on either Topanga Canyon Boulevard or Canoga Avenue, north of Ventura.

Restaurants

- **Cricca's Italian Deli** • 4876 Topanga Canyon Blvd
  818-340-0515 • $
  Massive meaty sandwiches.
- **Pat's Topanga Grill** • 1861 N Topanga Canyon Blvd
  310-455-0533 • $
  Laid-back service and pleasant surroundings.

Shopping

- **Crazy Inkjets** • 4867 Topanga Canyon Blvd
  818-346-5538
  Discount toner, inkjets, etc.

Map 53 • Encino

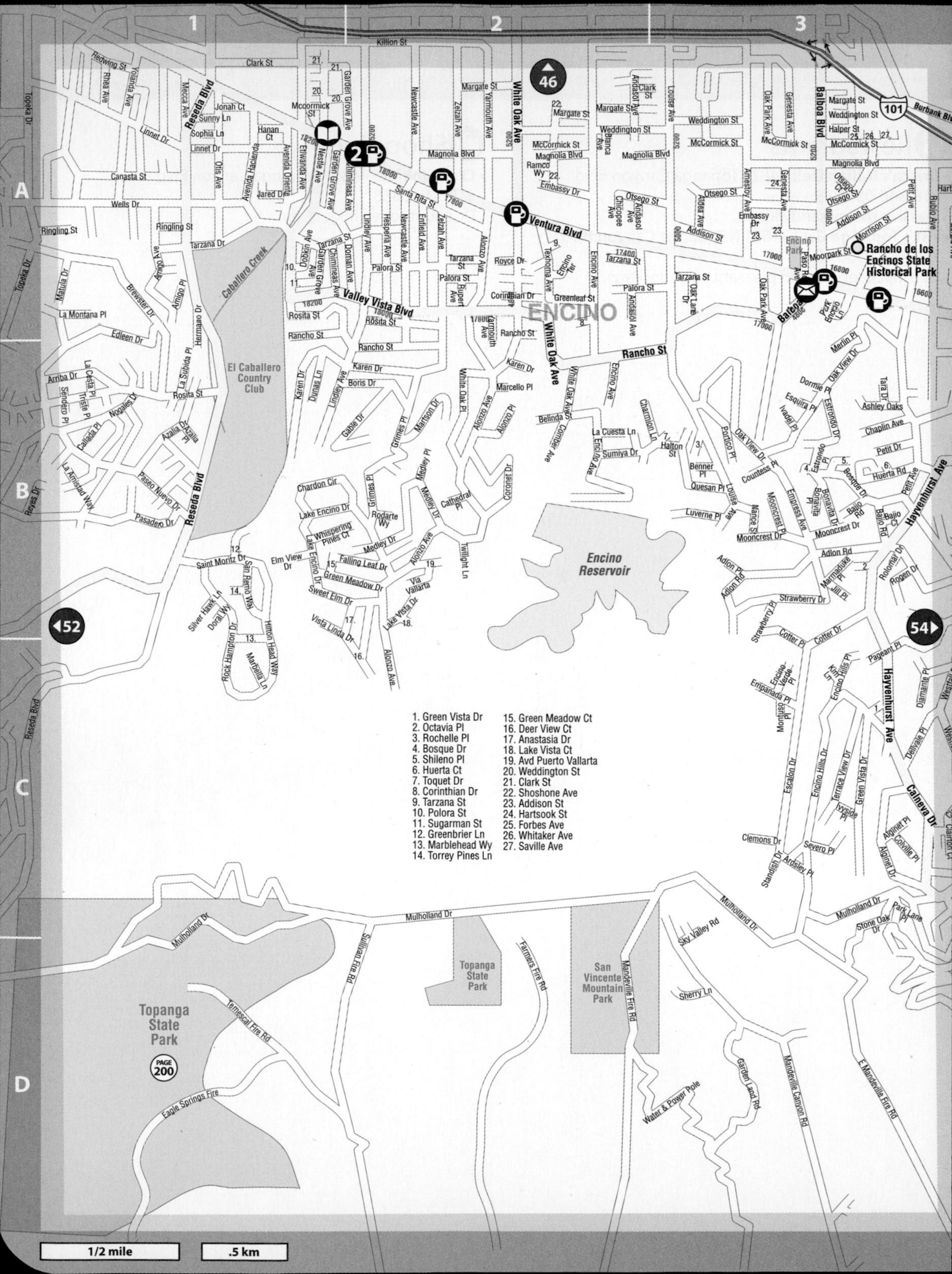

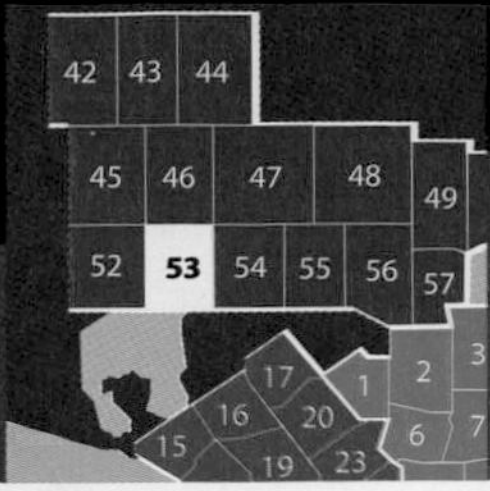

Encino's location, convenient to both the 405 and the 101 freeways, makes it one of LA's most desirable suburbs. It's about as "Valley" as the Valley gets, having been immortalized in Frank Zappa's "Valley Girl," *The Karate Kid*, *Fast Times at Ridgemont High*, *Encino Man*, and—just as important, culturally—*Match Game* with Gene Rayburn and Brett Somers. Whatever.

Landmarks

- **Rancho de los Encinos State Historic Park** • 16756 Moorpark St
  818-784-4849
  The rancho was damaged in the Northridge quake, but the park is still open.

Nightlife

- **Vino Tapas & Wine Room** • 18046 Ventura Blvd
  818-343-2525
  Tapas, live music and a popular wine-centric happy hour.

Restaurants

- **Baklava Factory** • 17540 Ventura Blvd
  818-981-3800 • $
  European and Eastern pastries.
- **Buca di Beppo** • 17500 Ventura Blvd
  818-995-3288 • $$
  Lively, traditional Italian chain, dinner only.
- **Cafe Carolina** • 17934 Ventura Blvd
  818-881-8600 • $$
  Italian with emphasis on vegan and veggie options.
- **California Wok** • 16656 Ventura Blvd
  818-386-0561 • $$
  Healthy Chinese food.
- **Jerry's Famous Deli** • 16650 Ventura Blvd
  818-906-1800 • $$
  Everything from pizza to salads, Mexican to Jewish food.
- **Johnny Rockets** • 16901 Ventura Blvd
  818-981-5900 • $$
  '50s-style family diner.
- **More Than Waffles** • 17200 Ventura Blvd
  818-789-5937 • $
  They don't lie: Belgian waffles and more.
- **Mulberry Street Pizzeria** • 17040 Ventura Blvd
  818-906-8881 • $$
  Thin-crust NY-style pizza.
- **The Stand** • 17000 Ventura Blvd
  818-788-2700 • $
  Best hot dog in LA.
- **Versailles** • 17410 Ventura Blvd
  818-906-0756 • $$
  The LA institution's garlicy Cuban grub will stay with you.
- **Vino Tapas & Wine Room** • 18046 Ventura Blvd
  818-343-2525 • $$
  Tapas, live music and a popular wine-centric happy hour.
- **Vittorio's Italian Cucina** • 17644 Ventura Blvd
  818-986-9074 • $$
  Pasta, chicken, seafood.

Shopping

- **Antik Shop** • 4909 Genesta Ave
  818-990-5990
  Funky antiques.
- **Hansen's Cakes** • 18432 Ventura Blvd
  818-708-1208
  Cakes for all occasions.
- **Herbalogics** • 17514 Ventura Blvd
  818-990-9990
  Get acupuncture and troll the herb store.
- **Mitzvahland** • 16733 Ventura Blvd
  818-705-7700
  All things Judaica.
- **Sneaker Warehouse** • 16736 Ventura Blvd
  818-995-8999
  Shoes galore!

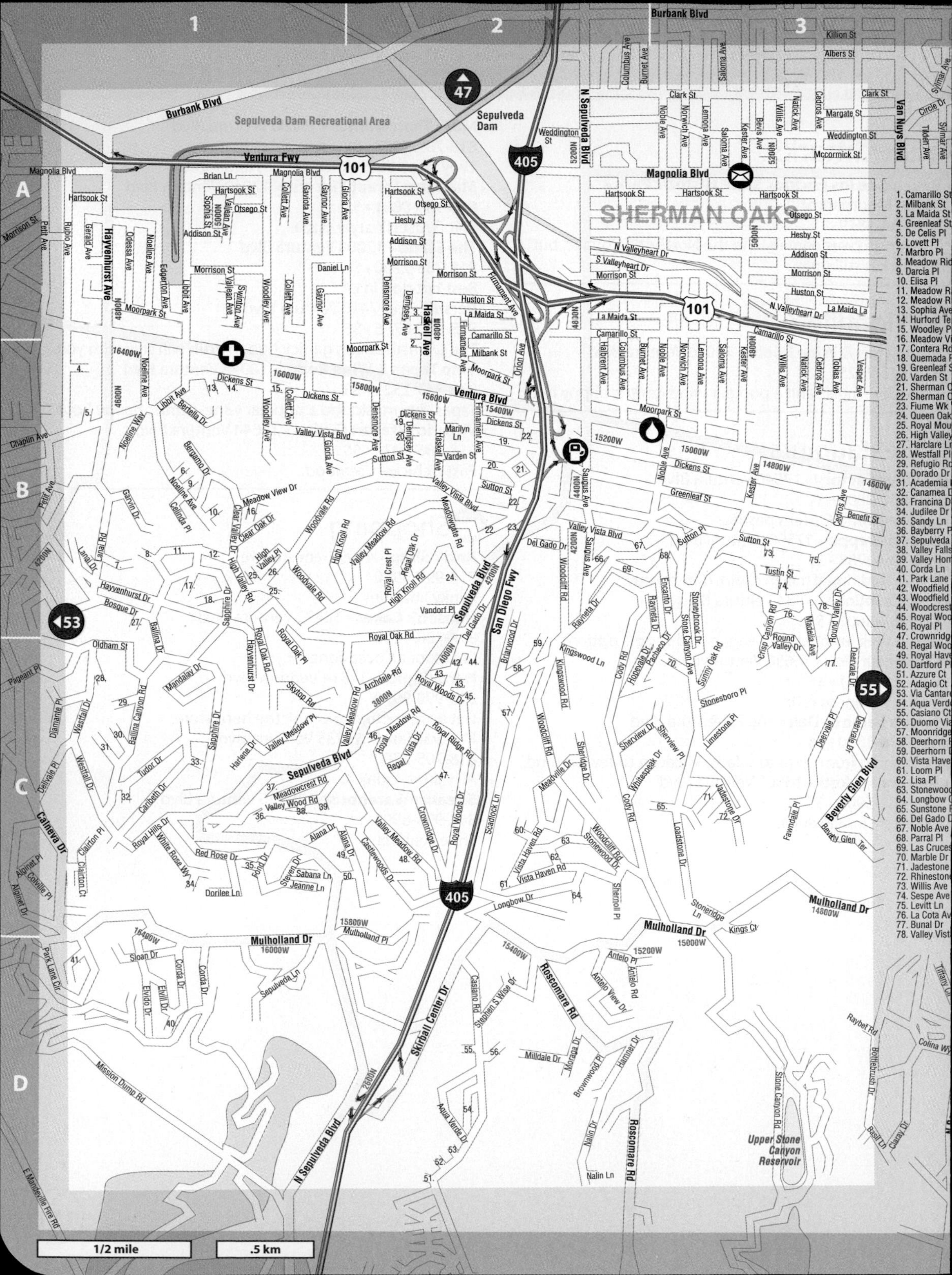
N
1
2
3
A
B
C
D
47
53
55
405
101
Burbank Blvd
Sepulveda Dam Recreational Area
Sepulveda Dam
Ventura Fwy
Magnolia Blvd
SHERMAN OAKS
N Sepulveda Blvd
San Diego Fwy
Sepulveda Blvd
Ventura Blvd
Moorpark St
Dickens St
Mulholland Dr
Skirball Center Dr
Roscomare Rd
Beverly Glen Blvd
Van Nuys Blvd
Valley Vista Blvd
Mission Dump Rd
E Mandeville Fire Rd
Stone Canyon Rd
Upper Stone Canyon Reservoir
1/2 mile
.5 km
1. Camarillo St
2. Milbank St
3. La Maida St
4. Greenleaf St
5. De Celis Pl
6. Lovett Pl
7. Marbro Pl
8. Meadow Rid
9. Darcia Pl
10. Elisa Pl
11. Meadow R
12. Meadow R
13. Sophia Ave
14. Hurford Te
15. Woodley P
16. Meadow Vi
17. Contera Rd
18. Quemada
19. Greenleaf S
20. Varden St
21. Sherman O
22. Sherman O
23. Fiume Wk
24. Queen Oak
25. Royal Mou
26. High Valley
27. Harclare Ln
28. Westfall Pl
29. Refugio Rd
30. Dorado Dr
31. Academia
32. Canamea D
33. Francina D
34. Jubilee Dr
35. Sandy Ln
36. Bayberry P
37. Sepulveda
38. Valley Falls
39. Valley Hom
40. Corda Ln
41. Park Lane
42. Woodfield
43. Woodfield
44. Woodcrest
45. Royal Woo
46. Royal Pl
47. Crownridg
48. Regal Woo
49. Royal Have
50. Dartford Pl
51. Azzure Ct
52. Adagio Ct
53. Via Cantar
54. Aqua Verde
55. Casiano Ct
56. Duomo Via
57. Moonridge
58. Deerhorn
59. Deerhorn D
60. Vista Have
61. Loom Pl
62. Lisa Pl
63. Stonewood
64. Longbow D
65. Sunstone
66. Del Gado D
67. Noble Ave
68. Parral Pl
69. Las Cruces
70. Marble Dr
71. Jadestone
72. Rhinestone
73. Willis Ave
74. Sespe Ave
75. Levitt Ln
76. La Cota Av
77. Bunal Dr
78. Valley Vist

herman Oaks is home to the most congested freeway interchange in the nation—the intersection f the 405 and 101 freeways. Local surface streets have been unable to provide relief because of a engthy Caltrans project intended to improve the connections and on-ramps. We remain dubious.)ur advice: avoid the whole ugly mess. Get on the 405 at either Burbank Boulevard or Valley Vista, nd avoid the 101 altogether during anything approximating a rush hour.

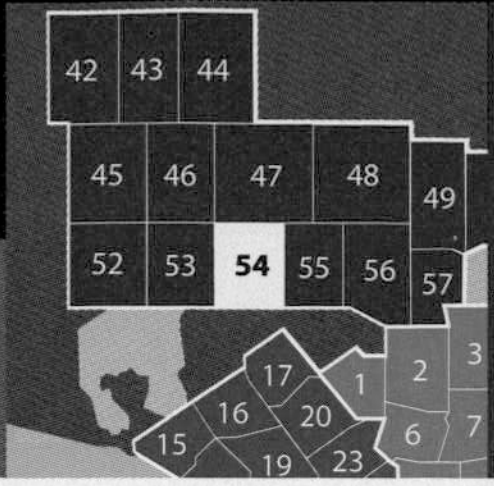

Nightlife

Blue Dog Beer Tavern • 4524 Saugus Ave
818-990-2583
Lotsa CA craft beers.

Restaurants

Blue Dog Beer Tavern • 4524 Saugus Ave
818-990-2583 • $$
Get the Chi Chi burger then call the doctor.

California Chicken Café • 15601 Ventura Blvd
818-789-8056 • $
Cheap and fresh chicken in every way on every day.

Delmonico's Steak & Lobster House •
16358 Ventura Blvd
818-986-0777 • $$$$$
Upscale seafood.

Katsu-Ya • 16542 Ventura Blvd
818-788-2396 • $$$
Yummy raw fish.

Marmalade Café • 14910 Ventura Blvd
818-905-8872 • $$
Salads and other CA cuisine.

Mel's Drive-In • 14846 Ventura Blvd
818-990-6357 • $
Upscale diner chain.

Midori Sushi • 13905 Ventura Blvd
818-789-1188 • $$$
Pig out on the surprisingly good AYCE sushi.

Panzanella • 14928 Ventura Blvd
818-784-4400 • $$$$$
Higher-end Italian.

Shopping

- **Buffalo Exchange** • 14621 Ventura Blvd
  818-783-3420
  Revolving door of used clothing. Buy, sell, trade.
- **Cost Plus World Market** • 15201 Ventura Blvd
  818-205-9620
  An "everything" superstore.
- **Culver City Home Brewing Supply** •
  4358 Sepulveda Blvd
  310-397-3453
  Literally everything you need to brew beer.
- **Drum Connection** • 4846 Libbit Ave
  818-788-5550
  Percussion!
- **Karen's Toys** • 16101 Ventura Blvd
  818-906-2212
  Independent toy store.
- **The Massage Place** • 16350 Ventura Blvd
  818-986-9333
  Sounds creepy, but isn't. Won't kill the wallet.
- **Party City** • 14735 Ventura Blvd
  818-981-0099
  Discount party supplies.
- **Samy's Camera** • 4411 Sepulveda Blvd
  310-450-4551
  The only place to go to for cameras in LA.
- **Sherman Oaks Galleria** • 15301 Ventura Blvd
  818-382-4100
  Take refuge from the Valley and shop like you're in LA.

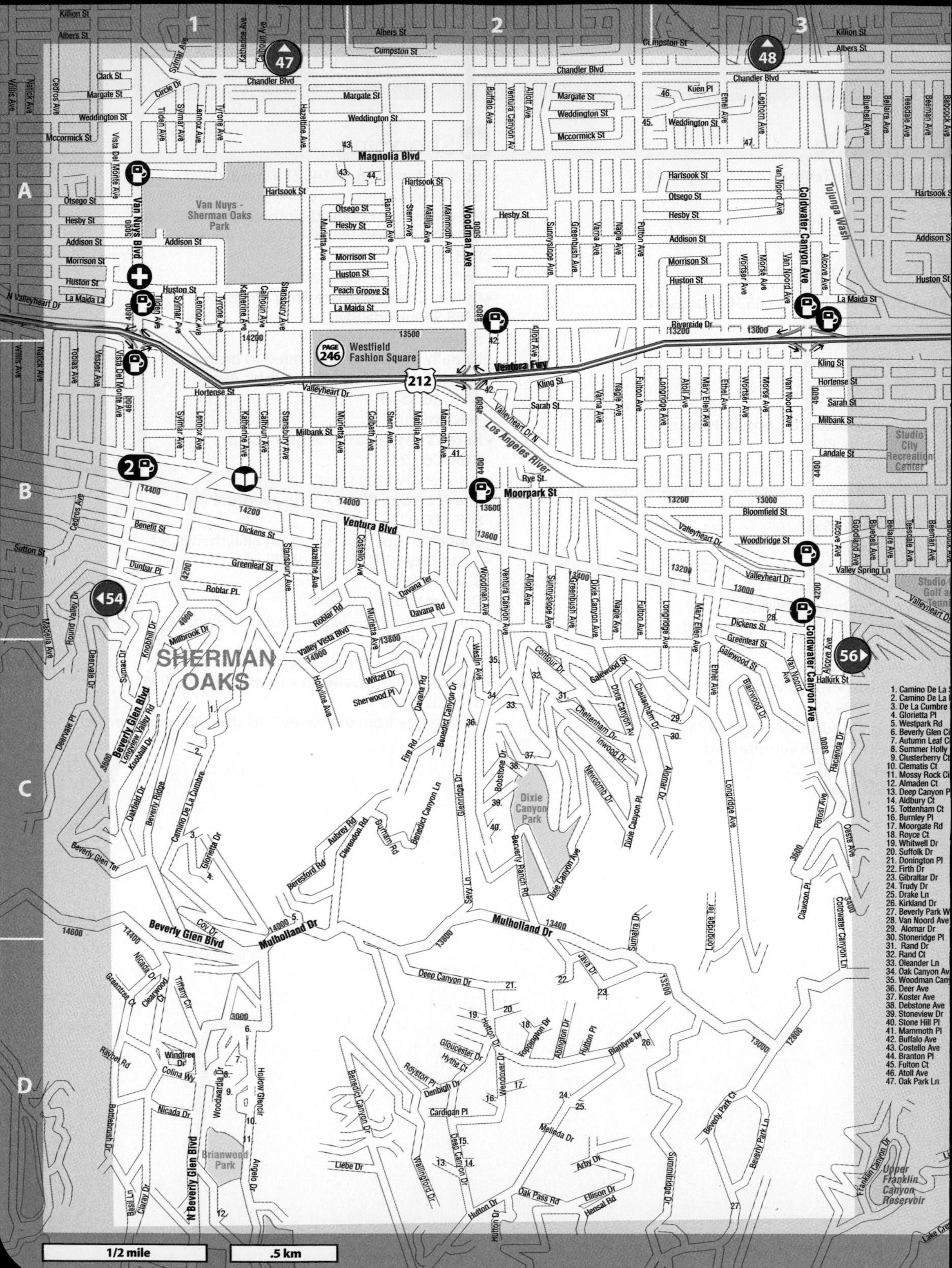
N
1
2
3
A
B
C
D
47
48
54
56
PAGE 246
Westfield Fashion Square
Van Nuys - Sherman Oaks Park
Studio City Recreation Center
Dixie Canyon Park
Brianwood Park
Upper Franklin Canyon Reservoir
SHERMAN OAKS
Ventura Fwy
212
Ventura Blvd
Moorpark St
Magnolia Blvd
Chandler Blvd
Van Nuys Blvd
Woodman Ave
Coldwater Canyon Ave
Mulholland Dr
Beverly Glen Blvd
N Beverly Glen Blvd
Los Angeles River
Tujunga Wash
Valleyheart Dr
Riverside Dr
Killion St
Albers St
Cumpston St
Margate St
Weddington St
Mccormick St
Hartsook St
Otsego St
Hesby St
Addison St
Morrison St
Huston St
Peach Groove St
La Maida St
Hortense St
Kling St
Sarah St
Milbank St
Landale St
Rye St
Bloomfield St
Woodbridge St
Benefit St
Dickens St
Greenleaf St
Dunbar Pl
Roblar Pl
Valley Spring Ln
Halkirk St
1. Camino De La S
2. Camino De La I
3. De La Cumbre
4. Glorietta Pl
5. Westpark Rd
6. Beverly Glen Ci
7. Autumn Leaf C
8. Summer Holly
9. Clusterberry Ct
10. Clematis Ct
11. Mossy Rock Ci
12. Almaden Ct
13. Deep Canyon P
14. Aldbury Ct
15. Tottenham Ct
16. Burnley Pl
17. Moorgate Rd
18. Royce Ct
19. Whitwell Dr
20. Suffolk Dr
21. Donington Pl
22. Firth Dr
23. Gibraltar Dr
24. Trudy Dr
25. Drake Ln
26. Kirkland Dr
27. Beverly Park W
28. Van Noord Ave
29. Alomar Dr
30. Stoneridge Pl
31. Rand Dr
32. Rand Ct
33. Oleander Ln
34. Oak Canyon Av
35. Woodman Can
36. Deer Ave
37. Koster Ave
38. Debstone Ave
39. Stoneview Dr
40. Stone Hill Pl
41. Mammoth Pl
42. Buffalo Ave
43. Costello Ave
44. Branton Pl
45. Fulton Ct
46. Atoll Ave
47. Oak Park Ln
1/2 mile
.5 km

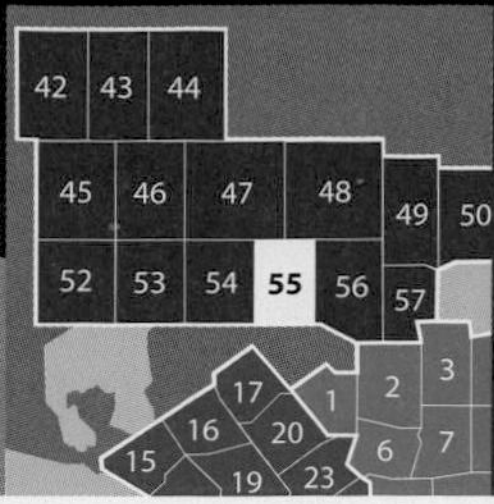

If Studio City is the Valley's answer to West Hollywood, then Sherman Oaks is its Beverly Hills. Mini-mansions are everywhere, while mega-mansions are found south of Ventura Boulevard in areas like the Longridge Estates. The area features a high-end mall, good public and private schools, and easy access to the Westside via Coldwater Canyon or Beverly Glen. Rush hour traffic can be a drag, but both roads provide pleasant drives that make you realize things could be a lot worse.

Nightlife

- **Coda** • 5248 Van Nuys Blvd
  818-273-1371
  NYC-style lounge w/ dress code, so not really.

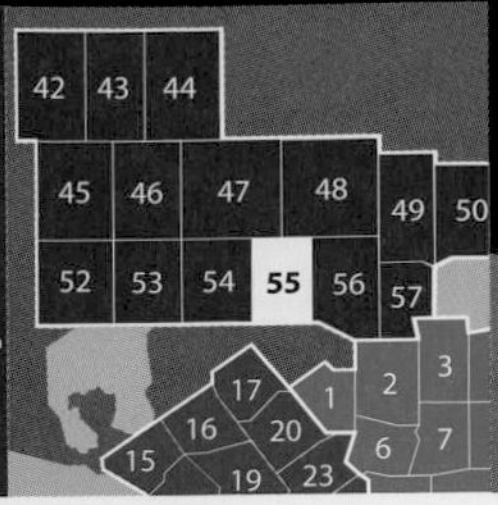

Sherman Oaks East

Restaurants

- **Antonio's Pizzeria** • 13619 Ventura Blvd
818-788-1106 • $$
Tasty. So old-school they still take Diners Club.
- **Bistro Garden at Coldwater** • 12950 Ventura Blvd
818-501-0202 • $$$$
Longtime Studio City favorite. Take your parents!
- **Boneyard Bistro** • 13539 Ventura Blvd
818-906-7427 • $$
Fancy BBQ joint.
- **Café Bizou** • 14016 Ventura Blvd
818-788-3536 • $$$
Popular French bistro.
- **Carnival Restaurant** • 4356 Woodman Ave
818-784-3469 • $$
Lebanese Food.
- **Casa Vega** • 13301 Ventura Blvd
818-788-4868 • $$
Very popular restaurant and bar. Good food, even better margaritas.
- **The Great Greek** • 13362 Ventura Blvd
818-905-5250 • $$$
Lively, fun Greek.
- **Gyu-Kaku** • 14457 Ventura Blvd
818-501-5400 • $$
Korean BBQ via Japan.
- **Hanami Sushi** • 4454 Van Nuys Blvd
818-986-7060 • $$
Fresh sushi, hot sake.
- **Hugo's** • 12851 Riverside Dr
818-761-8985 • $$
Neighborhood restaurant and tea house, good food.
- **Hugo's Tacos** • 4749 Coldwater Canyon Ave
818-762-7771 • $
Yes, there is such a thing as gourmet tacos.
- **Il Tiramisu** • 13705 Ventura Blvd
818-986-2640 • $$$
Who says you need to leave LA for good Italian?
- **In-N-Out Burger** • 4444 Van Nuys Blvd
800-786-1000 • $
Top California burger joint.
- **Iroha** • 12953 Ventura Blvd
818-990-9559 • $$$$
Great sushi and ambience.
- **Jinky's** • 14120 Ventura Blvd
818-981-2250 • $$
Neighborhood diner known for breakfast.
- **La Fogata Mexican Restaurant** • 5142 Van Nuys Blvd
818-501-9065 • $
Cheap food in a cozy cafe atmosphere.
- **Le Chine Wok** • 2958 Beverly Glen Cir
310-475-1146 • $$
Fancy Chinese.
- **Le Petit Restaurant** • 13360 Ventura Blvd
818-501-7999 • $$$$
Busy French bistro.
- **Maria's Italian Kitchen** • 13353 Ventura Blvd
818-906-0783 • $$
Casual family Italian.
- **Marrakesh** • 13003 Ventura Blvd
818-788-6354 • $$
Studio City Morroccan.
- **Mistral** • 13422 Ventura Blvd
818-981-6650 • $$$$
French bistro with cozy atmosphere.
- **Mulholland Grill** • 2932 Beverly Glen Cir
310-470-6223 • $$$
Neighborhood Northern Italian.
- **Rive Gauche** • 14106 Ventura Blvd
818-990-3573 • $$$$
French bistro with courtyard setting.
- **Senor Fred** • 13730 Ventura Blvd
818-789-3200 • $$$
Upscale CA Mexican, NFT pick!
- **Stanley's** • 13817 Ventura Blvd
818-986-4623 • $$
Excellent salads, casual neighborhood restaurant and bar
- **Tony's Mexican Grill** • 12910 Magnolia Blvd
818-769-5754 • $$
Home cookin' in a strip mall.

Sherman Oaks East

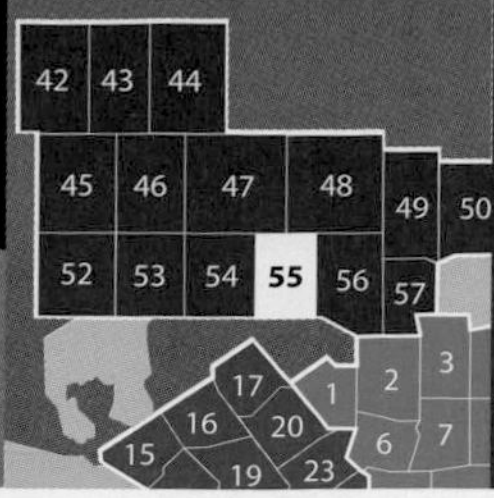

Map 55

Dining in Sherman Oaks has never been better. **Senor Fred** has killer margaritas and delicious food to boot. **Gyu-Kaku** is Japan's sublime take on Korean barbecue, while **Boneyard Bistro** represents an American take on grilling.

Shopping

- **Aunt Teek's Consignment House** • 14080 Ventura Blvd
  818-784-3341
  Antique furniture and collectables on consignment.
- **Baxter Northup Music** • 14534 Ventura Blvd
  818-788-7510
  Great selection of sheet music. Also instrument sales.
- **Bloomingdale's** • 14060 Riverside Dr
  818-325-2200
  Quieter than the Century City location. Especially good shoes, kids, and women's departments.
- **Juvenile Shop** • 13356 Ventura Blvd
  818-986-6214
  A civilized alternative to Babies"R"Us.
- **Light Bulbs Unlimited** • 14446 Ventura Blvd
  818-501-3492
  Every bulb under the sun.
- **Mark's Garden** • 13838 Ventura Blvd
  818-906-1718
  Florist.
- **Natas Pastries** • 13317 Ventura Blvd
  818-788-8050
  Portuguese baked goods.
- **Pink Cheeks** • 14562 Ventura Blvd
  818-906-8225
  Spa claiming to have invented the famous "playboy" bikini wax.
- **Pure Aesthetics Pure Wellness** • 2980 N Beverly Glen Cir
  310-470-6362
  Well-known day spa frequented by ladies who lunch, as well as celebrities.
- **Runnergy** • 14082 Ventura Blvd
  818-905-0020
  Athletic shoes sold by athletic, knowledgeable staff.
- **Sportie LA** • 14510 Ventura Blvd
  818-990-7575
  Sneakers galore.
- **Storyopolis** • 16740 Ventura Blvd
  818-990-7600
  You can get lost in here for hours amidst the Dr. Seuss and Maurice Sendak books.

N
Valley Village
Studio City
North Hollywood
North Hollywood Park
El Portal Theatre
Television Hall of Fame
Studio City Rec Center
Studio City Golf and Tennis
CBS Radford Studios
PAGE 195
Brady Bunch House
Woodbridge Park
North Weddington Park
Wilacre Park
Coldwater Canyon Park
Laurel Canyon Park
Upper Franklin Reservoir
Los Angeles River
Ventura Fwy
Hollywood Fwy
Tujunga Wash
Ventura Blvd
Laurel Canyon Blvd
Coldwater Canyon Ave
Mulholland Dr
Magnolia Blvd
Moorpark St
Burbank Blvd
Chandler Blvd
101
134
170
48
49
55
57
2
1. Alta Mesa Pl
2. Moonridge Ter
3. Hidden Valley Pl
4. Eden Pl
5. Briarcrest Ln
6. Calle Juela Dr
7. Leander Pl
8. Skywin Wy
9. Robin Hood Ln
10. Burroughs Rd
11. Charl Ln
12. Green View Dr
13. Mar Lu Dr
14. Eastwood Rd
15. Byron Pl
16. Coreyell Pl
17. Oakwilde Ln
18. Vado Pl
19. Horseshoe Canyon Rd
20. E Horseshoe Canyon Rd
21. Hermits Glen
22. McKim Ct
23. Laurelmont Pl
24. Vulcan Dr
25. N Laurel Canyon Pl
26. Cornett Dr
27. Okean Ter
28. Okean Pl
29. Paulcrest Dr
30. Dominion Wy
31. Thames Pl
32. Thames St
33. Woodstock Dr
34. Streamview Ln
35. Dona Lola Pl
36. Dona Rosa Dr
37. Mountcastle Rd
38. Wrightview Pl
39. Wrightwood Ct
40. Terry View Dr
41. Willowcrest Pl
42. Hendley Dr
43. Tropical Dr
44. Farley Ct
45. Hazelbrook Rd
46. Canton Ln
47. Roberts View Pl
48. Viewcrest Ct
49. Viewcrest Ln
50. Carpenter Ct
51. Pastel Pl
52. Blue Canyon Dr
53. Big Oak Dr
54. Berry Ct
55. Sunshine Ct
56. Ridgemoor Dr
57. Decente Ct
58. Woodhill Canyon Pl
59. Mound View Pl
60. Shady Oak Rd
61. Boughton Pl
62. Laurel Grove Ave
63. Vanetta Pl
64. Tolenas Dr
65. Fryman Pl
66. Oakdell Ln
67. Duque Dr
68. Lockridge Rd
69. Lockridge Estate Rd
70. Brookdale Ln
71. Dona Raquel Pl
72. Dona Cecilia Dr
73. Dona Christina Pl
74. Dona Conchita Pl
75. Dona Elena Pl
76. Dona Pepita Pl
1/2 mile
.5 km

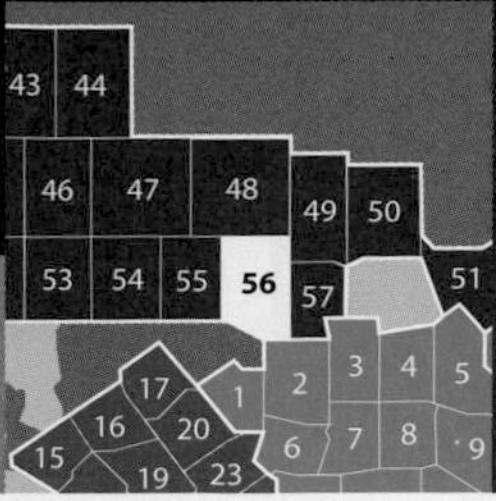

/alley Village is still cheap, comfortable, and kid-friendly. Studio City still sounds cool enough to ustify bringing dates to the Valley. But no one, whether resident, cartographer, or postal worker, claims to understand the borders. But, if you find yourself settling here (which is easy), you'll want to know about the **Studio City Farmers Market**, where produce-scavenging locals and harried parents intermingle each Sunday for the face-painting, animal-petting, moon-bouncing kiddie fare.

oLandmarks

- **Academy of Television Arts & Sciences •** 5220 Lankershim Blvd
  818-754-2800
  An in-your-dreams-sized Emmy perched atop a fountain marks the spot.
- **Brady Bunch House** • 11222 Dilling St
  You too can pretend to be part of America's favorite blended family.
- **CBS Radford Studios** • 4024 Radford Ave
  818-655-5000
  Seinfeld's NY sensibilities were actually found here, in the heart of the Valley.
- **El Portal Theatre** • 5269 Lankershim Blvd
  818-508-0281
  Former Vaudeville/Silent Movie house now anchors the NoHo Arts District.

Nightlife

- **The Brickyard Pub** • 11130 Magnolia Blvd
  818-505-0460
  BIG beer bar with lotsa pool tables.
- **Firefly** • 11720 Ventura Blvd
  818-762-1833
  Bookshelves paint the scene at this signless valley draw.
- **The Fox & Hounds** • 11100 Ventura Blvd
  818-763-7837
  English pub.
- **Foxfire Room** • 12516 Magnolia Blvd
  818-766-1344
  Unchanged since the '70s, a fun local dive bar.
- **Idle Hour** • 4824 Vineland Ave
  818-980-5604
  Ignore the dumb exterior and accept that it's NoHo good.
- **Kulak's Woodshed** • 5230 Laurel Canyon Blvd
  818-766-9913
  Much-loved folk music venue/scene. Popular Monday-night open mic.
- **Maeve's Residuals** • 11042 Ventura Blvd
  818-761-8301
  Low-key entertainment industry hangout.
- **Tiki No** • 4657 Lankershim Blvd
  818-766-0116
  Trendy Tiki dive with DJs.

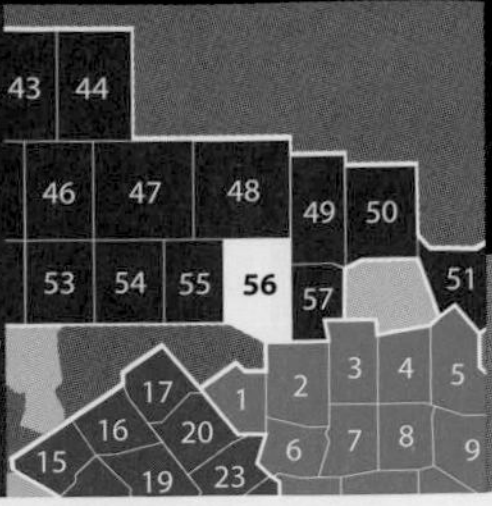

Studio City / Valley Village

Restaurants

- **Art's Deli** • 12224 Ventura Blvd
  818-762-1221 • $$
  New York-style deli.
- **Asanebo** • 11941 Ventura Blvd
  818-760-3348 • $$$
  Fantastic sashimi + retro setting = 1985 flashback.
- **Caioti Pizza Café** • 4346 Tujunga Ave
  818-761-3588 • $$
  Trendy, creative Italian.
- **Carney's** • 12601 Ventura Blvd
  818-761-8300 • $
  Fast-food institution.
- **Crown Burger** • 5072 Lankershim Blvd
  818-980-3709 • $
  Strange combo of burgers, teriyaki bowls, and leche liquada.
- **Daichan** • 11288 Ventura Blvd
  818-980-8450 • $$
  Japanese "soul food."
- **Du-par's** • 12036 Ventura Blvd
  818-766-4437 • $$
  Cheap breakfast joint.
- **EAT** • 11108 Magnolia Blvd
  818-760-4787 • $
  Try the steak salad.
- **Eclectic Wine Bar & Grille** • 5156 Lankershim Blvd
  818-760-2233 • $$
  California cuisine and art.
- **Ernie's** • 4410 Lankershim Blvd
  818-985-4654 • $
  Legendary, old-school Mexican eats and drinks, for 50+ years.
- **Firefly** • 11720 Ventura Blvd
  818-762-1833 • $$$$
  Gourmet French bistro with a cozy, clubby atmosphere.
- **Four 'N 20** • 4723 Laurel Canyon Blvd
  818-761-5128 • $$
  Old-school restaurant with homemade pie.
- **The Gadarene Swine** • 11266 Ventura Blvd
  818-508-5500 • $$$$
  High-end vegan cuisine.
- **Good Earth Restaurant** • 12345 Ventura Blvd
  818-506-7400 • $
  Healthy meals served against a backdrop of soothing fountains.
- **Great India Café** • 12321 Ventura Blvd
  818-761-8140 • $$
  People either hate or love their chicken tikka masala.
- **Henry's Tacos** • 4389 Tujunga Ave
  818-769-0343 • $
  Deluxe ground beef tacos.
- **JINYA** • 11239 Ventura Blvd
  818-980-3977 • $$
  Unpretentious noodle shop dishes out fantastic tonkotsu ramen.
- **Katsu-Ya** • 11680 Ventura Blvd
  818-985-6976 • $$$$
  Great Sushi; gets crowded on weekends. Try the baked crab roll in soy paper.
- **La Loggia** • 11814 Ventura Blvd
  818-985-9222 • $$$$
  Homestyle Italian.
- **Lala's Argentine Grill** • 11935 Ventura Blvd
  818-623-4477 • $$$
  Empanadas, chorizo, steak, and more. Trendy casual.
- **Laurel Tavern** • 11938 Ventura Blvd
  818-506-0777 • $$
  Beer/burger joint popular with the neighborhood "industry" folk.
- **Mantee** • 10962 Ventura Blvd
  818-761-6565 • $$$
  So you think you know Armenian food.
- **Matsuda** • 11837 Ventura Blvd
  818-760-3917 • $$$
  Yet another decent mini-mall sushi experience.
- **Menchie's Frozen Yogurt** • 4849 Laurel Canyon Blvd
  818-985-9150 • $
  Pay by the pound.
- **Mexicali Cocina Cantina** • 12161 Ventura Blvd
  818-985-1744 • $$
  Lively California-Mexican.
- **Out Take Bistro** • 11929 Ventura Blvd
  818-760-1111 • $$$
  Interesting fusion cuisine.
- **Panera Bread** • 12131 Ventura Blvd
  818-762-2226 • $
  Freshly baked bread and tasty sandwiches; laptop-friendly.
- **Pitfire Artisan Pizza** • 5211 Lankershim Blvd
  818-980-2949 • $$
  Trendy, crowded California-style pizza establishment. Great patio.

Studio City / Valley Village

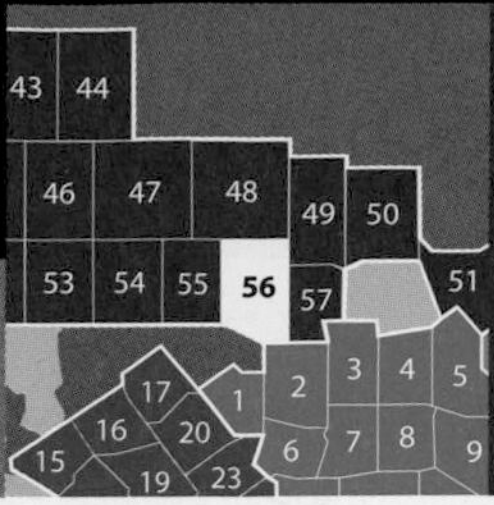

While the mutual hostility continues between the Valley and the balance of LA, Studio City quietly distinguishes itself as a cultural magnet on the other side of the hill. Branching off from the Ventura Boulevard smorgasbord, it presents a host of trendy, glad-I-didn't-drive-to-Hollywood restaurants (**Firefly**, **Spark**, etc.), shops, and neighborhood secrets.

- **Salomi** • 5225 Lankershim Blvd
  818-506-0130 • $$
  Vegetarian-Indian cuisine with heat that's not for wimps.
- **Sattdown Jamaican Grill** • 11320 Ventura Blvd
  818-766-3696 • $$
  Tasty island classics like meat pies, jerk chicken and oxtail.
- **Spark Woodfire Grill** • 11801 Ventura Blvd
  818-623-8883 • $$$
  Come for the meat, stay for the mojitos.
- **Sushi Dan** • 11056 Ventura Blvd
  818-985-2254 • $$
  Excellent sushi on a budget. Fun atmosphere.
- **Suzanne's Country Deli** • 11273 Ventura Blvd
  818-762-9494 • $
  Great salads and sandwiches. Bright and cheery.
- **Teru Sushi** • 11940 Ventura Blvd
  818-763-6201 • $$$$
  Basic—but delicious—sushi.
- **Tokyo Delve's Sushi Bar** • 5239 Lankershim Blvd
  818-766-3868 • $$$$
  Sushi.
- **Vegan Plate** • 11943 Ventura Blvd
  818-506-9015 • $
  Vegan food at mouthwatering prices. Spicy mint leaves a must!
- **Vitello's** • 4349 Tujunga Ave
  818-769-0905 • $$
  Robert Blake's favorite Italian.

Shopping

- **Almost Christmas Prop Shoppe** • 5057 Lankershim Blvd
  818-285-9627
  Holiday decorations specializing in film sets.
- **Artisan Cheese Gallery** • 12023 Ventura Blvd
  818-505-0207
  THE place for cheese.
- **Bedfellows** • 12250 Ventura Blvd
  818-985-0500
  Clocks, pillows, and bedside tables make wonderful bedfellows.
- **Crossroads Trading Co.** • 12300 Ventura Blvd
  818-761-6200
  Upscale resale.
- **Dari** • 12184 Ventura Blvd
  818-762-3274
  One of the Valley's outposts for trendy women's clothes.
- **Flask Fine Wines & Spirits** • 12194 Ventura Blvd
  818-761-5373
  Newly renovated as a haven for fine wines.
- **Hoity Toity** • 4381 Tujunga Ave
  818-766-2503
  Upscale women's clothing boutique.
- **Kit Kraft** • 12109 Ventura Pl
  818-509-9739
  Art supplies, model kits, and more.
- **La Knitterie Parisienne** • 12642 Ventura Blvd
  818-766-1515
  The best knitting store around.
- **M Frederic** • 12124 Ventura Blvd
  818-985-4404
  Retail haven for the young and trendy.
- **Marie et Cie** • 11704 Riverside Dr
  818-508-5049
  Coffee, home furnishings, and gifts all in one.
- **Maxwell Dog** • 12336 Ventura Blvd
  818-505-8411
  For the pampered pet.
- **Tennis Ace** • 12544 Ventura Blvd
  818-762-8751
  Everything tennis! Clothes, shoes, balls, etc.
- **Verona** • 4350 Tujunga Ave
  818-508-6377
  Shoe boutique. Handbags, too.
- **Village Gourmet** • 4357 Tujunga Ave
  818-487-3807
  Great gifts for the foodie in your life.
- **Village Market** • 11653 Moorpark St
  818-761-4848
  Old style, family-owned local market. Good deli.
- **Voila Boutique** • 12500 Magnolia Blvd
  818-766-9449
  Nice knock-offs to get you through each season.
- **Wasteland** • 12144 Ventura Blvd
  818-980-8800
  Hipster skinny jeans and vintage plaid trading depot.

Map 57 • Universal City / Toluca Lake

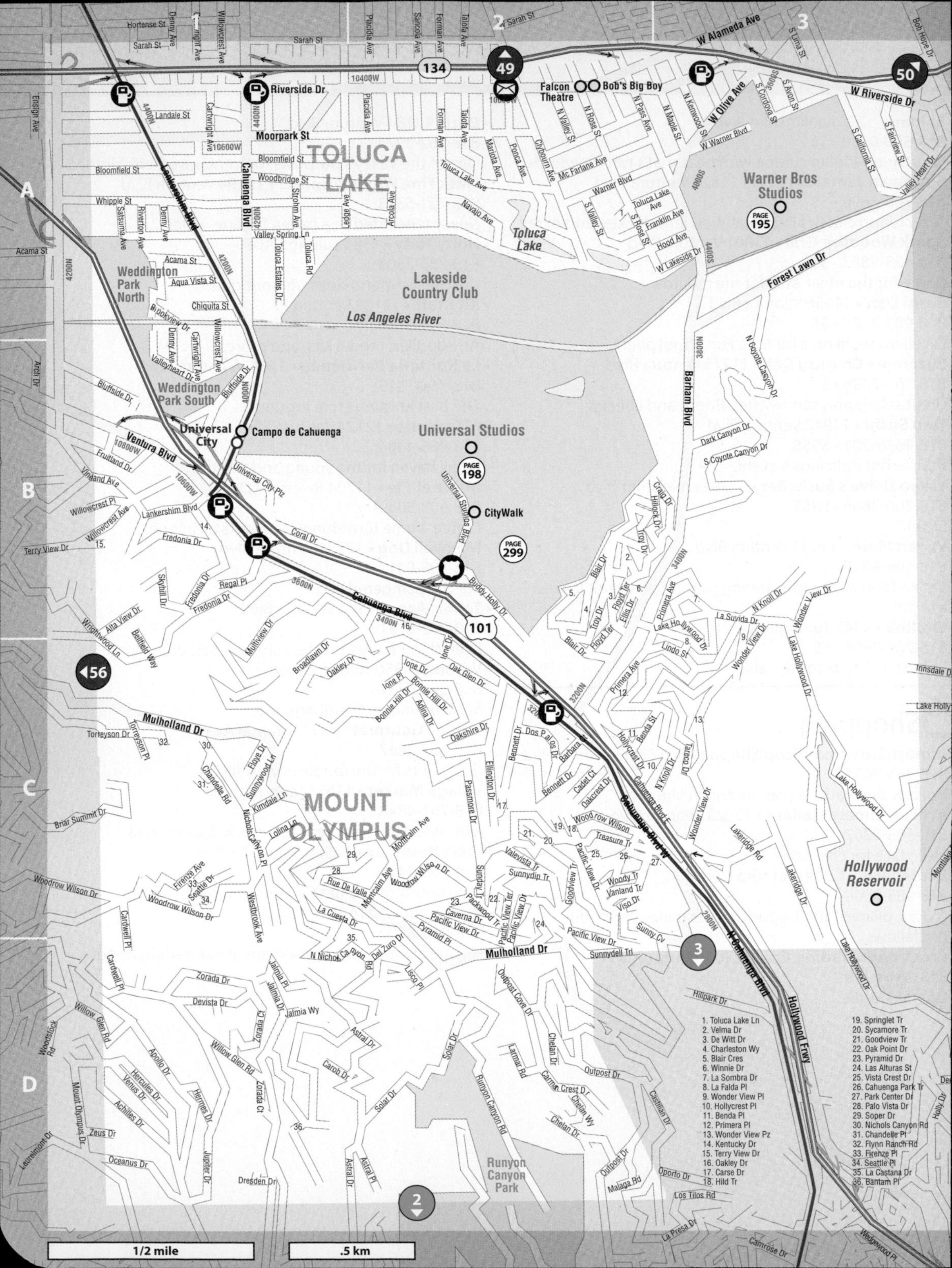

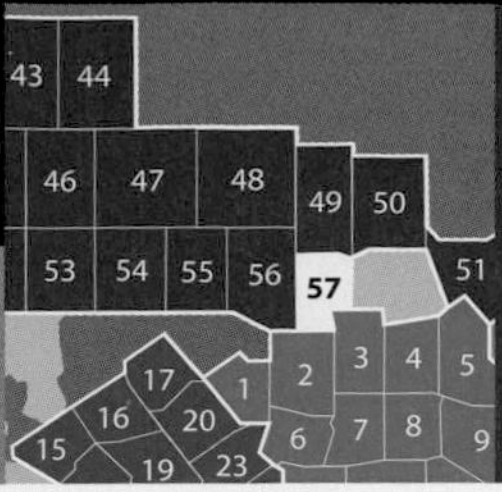

Though it's hard to exactly pinpoint Toluca Lake's exact borders, you'll know it when things turn quietly posh. This churchmouse-quiet community that sits at the base of the Hills provides easy access to **NBC Universal**, and the plethora of shows that tape there. Riverside boasts a nice collection of yuppie-ish shops and restaurants. Just south of Toluca Lake, Universal City contains the megapopular, postmodern behemoth known as **Universal CityWalk**. You have been warned.

Landmarks

- **Bob's Big Boy** • 4211 Riverside Dr
  818-843-9334
  The original Bob's Big Boy, as if the giant "Big Boy" out front didn't tip you off.
- **Campo de Cahuenga** • 3919 Lankershim Blvd
  818-762-3998
  This historic park is not regularly open to the public.
- **CityWalk** • 100 Universal City Plaza
  818-622-4455
  Entering City Walk is like walking through the glitzy gates of mega-franchise hell.
- **Falcon Theatre** • 4252 W Riverside Dr
  818-955-8101
  High-profile Valley theatre.
- **Lake Hollywood Reservoir** • Lake Hollywood Dr
  323-463-0830
  Jog or stroll around lovely "Lake Hollywood."
- **Universal Studios** • 100 Universal Center Dr
  818-777-1000
  New Yorkers scoff at the Studio's diminutive "tower."
- **Warner Brothers Studios** • 3400 W Riverside Dr
  877-492-8687
  The studio's water tower serves as a beacon for much of downtown Burbank.

Nightlife

- **The Baked Potato** • 3787 Cahuenga Blvd
  818-980-1615
  Low-key jazz with your choice of fancy baked potatoes.
- **CiaoCristina!** • 4201 W Olive Ave
  818-563-2426
  Neighborhood Italian joint with a gelato bar and a bar-bar.
- **Smoke House** • 4420 W Lakeside Dr
  818-845-3731
  Charming lounge music and stiff old man drinks.
- **Timmy Nolan's** • 10111 Riverside Dr
  818-985-3359
  Irish pub.

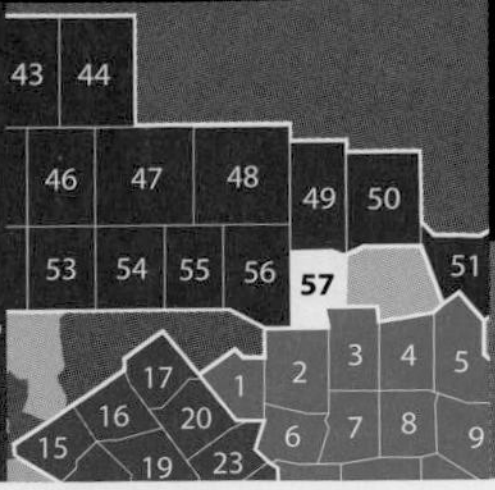

Universal City / Toluca Lake

Restaurants

- **Buca di Beppo** • 1000 Universal Studios Blvd
  818-509-9463 • $$
  Lively traditional Italian chain, dinner only.
- **Ca' del Sole** • 4100 Cahuenga Blvd
  818-985-4669 • $$$$
  Italian with garden tables.
- **California Canteen** • 3311 Cahuenga Blvd
  323-876 1702 • $$
  French.
- **CiaoCristina!** • 4201 W Olive Ave
  818-563-2426 • $$
  Neighborhood Italian joint with a gelato bar and a bar-bar.
- **Don Cuco** • 3911 W Riverside Dr
  818-842-1123 • $$
  Cheap prices, strong margaritas, kitschy Mexican ambience.
- **Honey Baked Ham** • 10106 Riverside Dr
  818-766-3958 • $
  Ham lovers unite!
- **Miceli's** • 3655 Cahuenga Blvd W
  323-851-3344 • $$
  Lively, fun Italian known for its singing waiters.
- **Mo's** • 4301 Riverside Dr
  818-845-3009 • $$
  Hamburger haven.
- **Paty's** • 10001 Riverside Dr
  818-761-0041 • $$
  American classics.
- **Priscilla's** • 4150 W Riverside Dr
  818-843-5707 • $
  Good variety of coffees and pastries in a cozy setting.
- **Prosecco** • 10144 Riverside Dr
  818-505-0930 • $$$
  Northern Italian.
- **Smoke House** • 4420 W Lakeside Dr
  818-845-3731 • $$$
  Beloved dinosaur steakhouse.
- **Wolfgang Puck Bistro** • 1000 Universal Studios Blvd
  818-985-9653 • $$
  Casual California chic.
- **Zach's Café** • 10820 Ventura Blvd
  818-762-4225 • $$
  Satisfying Italian, with one of the city's best courtyards.

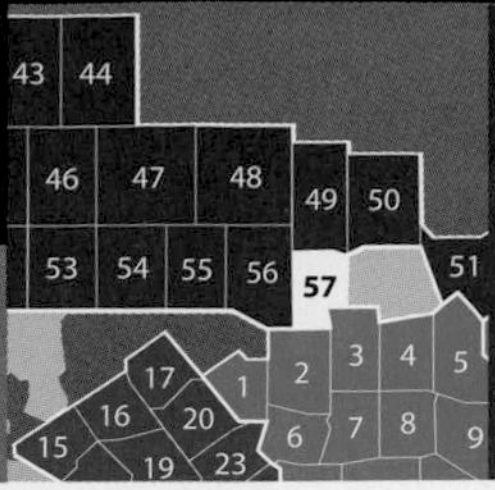

Though the neon assault and outrageous prices ($14 for parking? I thought we were in the Valley) are certainly a turn-off, there is something strangely alluring about **CityWalk**'s faux urban bonanza. The bars, restaurants, movies and shows are constantly packed with throngs of humanity. It's become a must-do for tourists, so if you like to get your gawk on and engage in a little people-watching, this is the place to do it.

Shopping

- **Cinema Secrets Beauty Supply** • 4400 W Riverside Dr
  818-846-0579
  Fabulous selection, including film makeup.
- **Pergolina** • 10139 Riverside Dr
  818-508-7708
  Gifts and items for home.
- **Sit 'N Stitch** • 10154 Riverside Dr
  818-760-9330
  Get yo' stitch on.

Peck Park
Leland Park
110
47
N Front St
W Summerland Ave
N Western Ave
Miraleste Dr
N Gaffey St
N Pacific Ave
N Harbor Blvd
ART Walk
San Pedro
Farmer's Market
San Pedro
Peninsula
Hospital
S Weymouth Ave
S Gaffey St
W 9th St
Friendship Park
Averill Park
Ports O' Call
San Pedro
High School
S Pacific Ave
S Crescent Ave
W 19th St
Palos
Verdes
Shores
W 25th St
W 22nd St
W 25th St
S Western Ave
Fort MacArthur
Lower Reservation
PAGE
214
Cabrillo Marina
W Paseo Del Mar
Los Angeles
Harbor
Angels Gate
Cultural Center
Angels Gate Park
Point Fermin Park
Cabrillo Beach
Cabrillo Beach
Bathhouse
Point Fermin
Lighthouse
Shepard St
Pacific Ocean
W Macarthur St
W Macarthur Ave
W Upland Ave
W Crestwood Ave
W Elberon Ave
W Amar St
W Ofarrell St
W Sepulveda St
W Santa Cruz St
W 1st St
W 2nd St
W 3rd St
W 4th St
W 5th St
W 6th St
W 7th St
W 8th St
W 10th St
W 11th St
W 12th St
W 13th St
W 14th St
W 15th St
W 16th St
W 17th St
W 18th St
W 20th St
W 21st St
W 22nd St
W 23rd St
W 24th St
W 26th St
W 27th St
W Hamilton Ave
W 29th St
W 30th St
W 31st Ct
W 32nd St
W 33rd St
W 34th St
W 35th St
W 36th St
W 37th St
W 38th St
W 39th St
W 40th St
Bonita St
W Oliver St
Sampson Way
Nagoya Wy
Berth
Outer St
S Adams St
Watchorn Wk
Whalers Wk
Shoshonean Rd
Officers Rd
Via Cabrillo Marina
Barbour Ct
Bluff Pl
S Beacon St
Friendship Park Dr
Titan Dr
Atlas Dr
Onizuka Cir
Adams Cir
White Pl
Grissom Dr
Kay Florentino Dr
Royal Palms Dr
Leavenworth Dr
Meade Rd
Osgood Farley Rd
Ord Rd
Barlow Saxton
Baywater Ave
Leary Merriam Dr

General Information

San Pedro Chamber of Commerce:
www.sanpedrochamber.com

Overview

On the southern side of the Palos Verdes Peninsula lies a fiercely proud community that's worth a visit. The port city of San Pedro (pronounced "PEE-dro") relies heavily on boat traffic, with freighters and barges from points all over the world drifting in and out, creating an industrial feel. Despite that, San Pedro is a delightful place for a day-trip—the city maintains a sense of history and small-town vibe, and you'd swear you were in some New England fishing town. Live out your deepest SoCal transit fantasies: Ride in one of the city's "Big Red Cars," restored railcars that run 12 pm to 9:30 pm Friday through Sunday and pay a mere buck for fare. San Pedro also boasts sweet hidden delights, from the Mediterranean-style Cabrillo Beach Bathhouse (3800 Stephen M White Dr, 310-548-7554) built in 1932, to the charming seaside village Ports O' Call (Berths 75-79 on the waterfront), to the enriching Angels Gate Cultural Center (3601 S Gaffey St, 310-519-0936; www.angelsgateart.org or @AngelsGateArt) and the Victorian Point Fermin Lighthouse and Park (807 Paseo Del Mar; www.pfls.org). Visit the Korean Fellowship Bell (and definitely hang with the sick seals while in the park: www.marinemammalcare.org), see the grunion run at night on Cabrillo Beach (the Cabrillo Marine Aquarium has a schedule at www.cabrillomarineaquarium.org), or find placid tide pools beneath the cliffs. And do not miss the Sunken City, a neighborhood that fell over the cliffs due to seismic shifting. (Walk south from Point Fermin Lighthouse and hop the wall.)

As befits a seafaring town, some of the country's foremost tattoo parlors can be found in San Pedro (to start, try Ink Divine Tattoo, 305 W 7th St, or So Cal Tattoo, 339 W 6th St). It also boasts the Warner Grand Theatre (478 W 6th St, 310-548-7672; www.warnergrand.org or @GrandAnnex), an opulent Art Deco venue built in 1931 that is rich in both history and culture. Visit Green Hills Memorial Park (27501 Western Ave; www.greenhillsmemorial.com) to see the graves of Charles Bukowski and The Minutemen's D Boon. But what defines and distinguishes San Pedro most is the monthly ART Walk. On the first Thursday of every month, art galleries, retail shops, restaurants, and street vendors celebrate creativity by staying open late and offering discounts and specials. Live entertainment accompanies the action throughout the historic downtown Arts District, located between 4th and 8th Streets and Pacific Avenue and Centre Street. Visit www.1stthursday.com for an extensive list of participating establishments.

San Pedro is also a bridge away from Long Beach via Terminal Island (St. Vincent Thomas Bridge), and has ferries to Catalina Island for fantastic day trips.

How to Get There

From Downtown LA, take the Harbor Freeway south (110 S) to Gaffey Street, then head south to San Pedro.

Landmarks

Angels Gate Cultural Center • 3601 S Gaffey St
Art Walk • S Pacific Ave & W 4th St
Cabrillo Beach Boosters • 3800 Stephen M White Dr
Cat Beach at White's Point • 1799 W Paseo del Mar
Catalina Express Terminal •
N Harbor Blvd & Swinford St
Point Fermin Lighthouse • 807 W Paseo del Mar
Ports O' Call • 1100 Nagoya Way
San Pedro Farmers' Market • W 6th St & S Mesa St

Nightlife

Godmother's Saloon • 302 W 7th St
Off the Vine • 491 6th St

Restaurants

- **Beach City Grill** • 376 W 6th St
- **Bonello's New York Pizza** • 832 S Gaffey St
- **BUNZ Gourmet Burgers** • 655 W 7th St
- **Jasmine Hana** • 114 N Gaffey St
- **Michael's Tuscany Room** • 470 W 7th St
- **Mishi's Strudel Bakery & Cafe** • 309 W 7th St
- **Nam's Red Door** • 2253 S Pacific Ave
- **Omelette and Waffle Shop** • 1103 S Gaffey St
- **Pacific Diner** • 3821 S Pacific Ave
- **Ports O' Call** • Berth 76
- **Raffaello Ristorante** • 400 S Pacific Ave
- **Rex's Café** • 2136 S Pacific Ave
- **Think Café** • 302 W 5th St
- **The Whale and Ale** • 327 W 7th St

Shopping

- **Badfish Clothing Company** • 337 W 6th St
- **Behind the Scenes Costumes** • 285 W 6th St
- **Drop In Gifts** • 385 W 6th St
- **The Grand Emporium** • 323 W 7th St
- **Office Depot** • 810 N Western Ave
- **Pacific Wilderness** • 1719 S Pacific Ave

General Information

City of Malibu Phone: 310-456-2489
City of Malibu Website: www.ci.malibu.ca.us
Weather/Surf Reports: www.surfline.com/surf-report/malibu-southern-california_4209

Overview

When outsiders fantasize about Southern California, it's not the smog-filled sky of downtown LA that runs through their minds. It's the sandy beaches and sunny skies of Malibu and its 21-mile coastline—the city that inspired a coconutty rum and perhaps the most famous Barbie doll ever. It's the place where Baywatch lifeguards roam and the rich and famous come to play.

The area's first settlers were the Chumash Indians. The names of some of their villages are still a part of local culture—Ojai, Mugu, and Zuma, to name just a few. But Malibu's current residents are a very different tribe indeed. For instance, The Colony, a gated community, is home to a wide array of celebrities, business-folk, and anyone else that can spare the $7 million-plus that it takes to buy a parcel of beachfront land.

Depending upon weather and other acts of God (like the fires and mudslides that frequently strike this beautiful stretch of coastline), Malibu is about a 45-minute trip from downtown LA, or approximately 35 miles. The best thing about Malibu is definitely its isolation. You feel as though you've left LA and gone somewhere else. The worst thing about Malibu is...its isolation. You feel as though you've left LA and gone somewhere else. Somewhere very far away.

The Beaches

Beaches are the main attraction in Malibu, and you have a number from which to choose. Keep in mind that dogs are not allowed on any public beach—though Angelenos are not known for following rules—and parking is a big challenge. Though many stretches of Malibu beach may seem privately owned due to their inaccessibility, you have every right to frolic on any acre of sand. There are three options: 1) Pay whatever the day's going rate is at parking lots conveniently located at each Malibu beach. 2) Find street parking in Malibu's residential areas—which then requires hiking down to the beach, often with the added challenge of crossing the PCH (Malibu's answer to the video game *Frogger*). 3) Get all of the planets to align just so, allowing you to score that perfect parking spot on the beach side of the PCH, right outside the entrance to your chosen beach. We grudgingly admit that option #1 may be your best bet.

Many of Malibu's private beaches are accessible to the public via causeways or public gates. Some of Malibu's more popular public beaches are:

- **Topanga State Beach** • Located along the PCH at Topanga Canyon Boulevard. Popular for surfing. Call 310-457-9701 for the northern surf report. Good luck finding parking.
- **Malibu Lagoon State Beach** • Located just west of the Malibu Pier. Features a bird sanctuary as well as the Malibu Lagoon Museum.
- **Malibu Surfrider Beach** • Home of the Malibu Pier, located along the 23000 block of the PCH. This is one of the most famous surfing beaches in the world.
- **Dan Blocker Beach** • Named for the actor who played "Hoss" on the TV series *Bonanza*. He was one of the original owners of this stretch of beach, along with his co-stars, Lorne Greene and Michael Landon, who donated it to the state after Blocker's death. This beach is on the PCH between Puerco Canyon and Corral Canyon.
- **Point Dume State Beach** • This state-owned beach is accessed from Westward Beach Road. One of the area's most beautiful beaches, it features nearby hiking trails, reefs for scuba diving, and tide pools.
- **Zuma Beach** • This very popular beach is located on the PCH, just west of Heathercliff Drive. It's expansive, is home to a number of volleyball courts, and tends to be very crowded in the summer.
- **Robert H. Meyer Memorial State Beach** • This is actually a grouping of three small beaches—El Pescador, La Piedra, and El Matador. They are located about 10 miles west of Malibu proper. Lots of rocky cliffs, sand dunes, and picturesque sunsets.
- **Nicholas Canyon Beach** • Located at 33850 Pacific Coast Highway. Lots of room for lying out in the sun or tossing a Frisbee.

The Adamson House

Located at Malibu Lagoon State Beach, the Adamson House was the home of Merritt Huntley Adamson and his wife Rhoda Rindge Adamson, whose family, the Rindges, once owned the Malibu Spanish Land Grant (as the area was originally known). The house features liberal use of the ceramic tile manufactured by the then-famous Malibu Potteries. The Adamson House and the adjacent

Malibu Lagoon Museum are open Wednesday through Saturday from 11 am to 3 pm, while the grounds are open daily from 8 am until sunset. Admission to the adjoining Malibu Lagoon Museum is free while tours of the Adamson House cost $7 for adults, $2 for children aged 6–16 years, and nothing for children 5 years and under. (Cash only, thanks.) The property is also available for weddings and other special events, though weekend wedding season requires a year-and-a-half wait, so be prepared for a long engagement. 310-456-8432; www.adamsonhouse.org.

Malibu Creek State Park

What is now a 7,000-acre state park once belonged to motion picture studio Twentieth Century Fox, which used the park as a double for Korea in the TV series *M*A*S*H*. The park is home to some 30 miles of hiking and riding trails, as well as a campground featuring sixty campsites, with barbecues, showers, and bathroom facilities. Campsites can be booked online. The park's entrance is located along Las Virgenes/Malibu Canyon Road, just south of Mulholland Highway. 818-880-0367; www.parks.ca.gov/.

Pepperdine University

It's hard to imagine getting any studying done on a campus just a few hundred yards from the ocean, but Pepperdine students manage to pull it off (well…sometimes; we guess the curfew helps). Visible from PCH with its enormous thin cross stretching toward the heavens that created Malibu, Pepperdine sprawls across some of the greenest acreage in the land. The campus may be best known as the location for the 1970s TV spectacular *The Battle of the Network Stars*, but Pepperdine is represented by 15 NCAA Division I athletic teams in sports ranging from men's water polo to women's golf. The university's Center for the Arts hosts an eclectic slate of events including piano recitals, modern dance, and children's theater. 24255 Pacific Coast Hwy, 310-506-4000; www.pepperdine.edu.

Where to Eat

Malibu relies upon the PCH as its Main Street and most of the town's dining establishments are located along either side. Dining experiences in Malibu tend to be one extreme or the other—either ultra-casual or ultra-pricey. Here are some restaurants that we recommend at both ends of the spectrum:

- **Coogies**, Malibu Colony Plaza, 23755 Malibu Rd, 310-317-1444. Upscale diner fare. This unpretentious restaurant is healthier than the typical diner and is a great bet for breakfast by the beach.
- **Neptune's Net**, 42505 PCH, 310-457-3095. Seafood. Though it's almost at the Ventura county line, this place is worth the drive. Very "beachy," Neptune's Net serves up a variety of seafood either steamed or fried.
- **Duke's Malibu**, 21150 PCH, 310-317-0777. California-Hawaiian. Lots of seafood dishes served amidst a fun, surfer theme dedicated to famed surfer Duke Paoa Kahanamoku. Avoid the Sunday brunch—the bar menu is always better—and try to snag a table at the barefoot bar.
- **Marmalade Café**, 3894 Cross Creek Rd, 310-317-4242. California-style sandwiches and salads. If you want a nice lunch in a nice setting, this is the place to go. Their food also travels well as take-out, and they have a great catering business too.
- **Taverna Tony**, Malibu Country Mart, 23410 Civic Center Wy, 310-317-9667. Greek. Delicious food in a fun, festive setting with live music.
- **Geoffrey's**, 27400 PCH, 310-457-1519. California-eclectic. Pronounced "Joffrey's," this restaurant serves delicious food that merits the snooty attitude you may occasionally encounter here. This is one of the most beautiful and romantic restaurants in LA.
- **Reel Inn**, 18661 PCH, 310 – 456-8221. An old Malibu holdover, the Reel Inn has been a reliable and casual seafood outpost for decades. Fresh snapper, shrimp, and calamari are on the picnic table menu, with requisite cold beer in abundance.
- **Moonshadows**, 20356 PCH, 310-456-3010. The fancy-ish restaurant's food hardly compares to its ocean views, but it's not terrible. The highlight is the outdoor patio with cabanas and futons. A giant spotlight shines on the ocean like moonlight, hence the establishment's name.

How to Get There

With few exceptions, it's difficult to go anywhere in Malibu without encountering the Pacific Coast Highway for at least some of the trip. From the southern half of LA, the easiest option is to take the 10 Freeway to the PCH and head north. On summer weekends, the PCH becomes a virtual parking lot, but at least you can enjoy the smell and view of the ocean.

From the Valley and points north, your best bet is to hop on the 101 Freeway and head north toward Ventura. Exit at Las Virgenes and follow the signs for Las Virgenes Road/Malibu Canyon; then take Malibu Canyon Road to the PCH. If you're planning on going even farther north into Malibu, you can also exit the 101 at Kanan Road, which becomes Kanan Dume Road and terminates at the PCH.

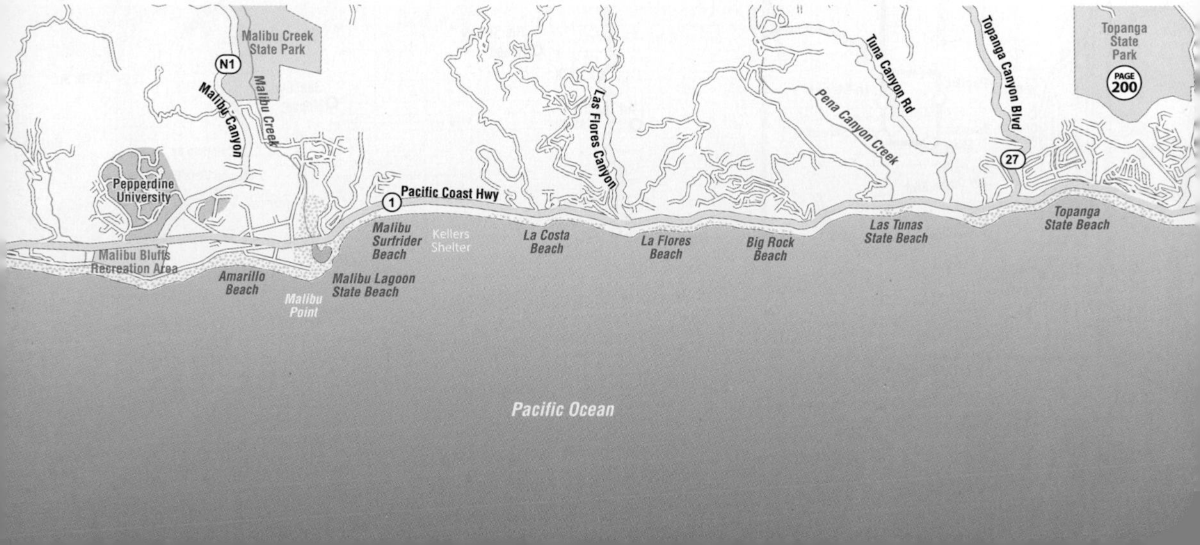

Del Amo
E Del Amo Blvd
Forest Lawn Memorial Park Long Beach
Del Amo Blvd
Del Amo Blvd
S Santa Fe Ave
N Long Beach Blvd
Scherer Park
Cherry Ave
Paramount Blvd
N Lakewood Blvd
N Bellflower Blvd
Cherry Avenue Park
All Souls Cemetery
LAKEWOOD
Virginia Country Club
Atlantic Ave
Lakewood Country Club
19
E Carson St
Long Beach City College Liberal Arts Campus
E Carson St
Heartwell Park
LONG BEACH
405
LONG BEACH
710
Wardlow
W Wardlow Rd
Long Beach Airport
E Donald Douglas Dr
Skylinks Golf Course
E Wardlow Rd
PAGE 254
W Spring St
Veterans Memorial Park
E Spring St
E Spring St
SIGNAL HILL
W Willow St
Willow
W Willow St
405
E Willow St
Santa Fe Ave
Los Angeles River
Magnolia Ave
N Long Beach Blvd
Atlantic Ave
Cherry Ave
Redondo Ave
19
Stearns Champions Park
E Los Coyotes Diagonal
N Bellflower Blvd
Martin Luther King Jr Park
Long Beach City College Pacific Coast Campus
Chittick Field Park
1
Pacific Coast Highway
E Pacific Coast Hwy
Outer Traffic Circle
E Atherton St
Whaley Park
PAGE 178
710
Alexander House
Matlock House
California State University Long Beach
W Anaheim St
Anaheim
E Anaheim St
E Pacific Coast Hwy
W 9th St
Pacific Ave
Alamitos Ave
LONG BEACH
The Skinny House
Recreation Park
1
E 7th St
E 7th St
W 6th St
Pacific
5th Street
Seashell House
Pico Ave
N Harbor Scenic Dr
Cesar Chavez Park
Transit Mall
1st Street
Art Theater
E 4th St
Park Ave
E Colorado St
Bixby Villa Golf Cour
Lincoln Park
Marine Vista Park
W Ocean Blvd
W Ocean Blvd
E Broadway
Long Beach Museum of Art
E Ocean Blvd
Bluff Park
S Harbor Scenic Dr
Queens Hwy
E Shoreline Dr
Island Grissom
E Livingston Dr
PAGE 213
Shoreline Aquatic Park
Marina Green Park
Long Beach Marina
E 2nd St
Long Beach Middle Harbor
Queensway Bay
Queensway Dr
Queens Hwy
Queens Hwy
Queen Mary Seaport
Island White
Windsor Wy
Long Beach Harbor
Alamitos Bay

General Information

City of Long Beach:
www.longbeach.gov or @LongBeachCity

Long Beach Convention and Visitors Bureau:
www.visitlongbeach.com or @VisitLB

Overview

The birthplace of the silent film industry, Snoop Dogg, and Sublime, Long Beach holds the distinction of being one of the most ethnically diverse cities in the United States. The first silent movie studio—Balboa Studios—was located here, and today numerous television shows and feature films continue to be shot in the area. These days, perhaps the city's biggest claim to fame is the Port of Long Beach, the second busiest port in the United States and one of the largest in the world. Despite the great earthquake of 1933 destroying many buildings, Long Beach has managed to successfully retain much of its charm, as evidenced in the Art Deco architecture along Ocean Boulevard. A massive downtown revitalization aimed at attracting a young, artsy crowd with new lofts, cafes, and theaters has also helped to develop the city.

The city is divided into pocket neighborhoods, each as different as the next. Belmont Shore is the quintessential beach community, with narrow streets and open-minded residents. Belmont Heights and Bluff Park are where the former residents of Belmont Shore go once they have kids and want a yard. North Long Beach is a residential working-class neighborhood near the 405 Freeway. Bixby Knolls is suburbia near the beach, with the usual lineup of ranch homes and minivans. Shoreline Village is a tourist's paradise, with shops and restaurants on the north end of the 11-mile beach.

How to Get There

Although it sits only 21 miles from Downtown Los Angeles, the roads to Long Beach are often congested and fraught with delays. Find your way to the 405 or the 5 and head south, taking either freeway to the 710 S. The 10 also intersects with the 710 east of Downtown LA, so that's a viable option as well.

You can also take the Metro Blue Line to downtown Long Beach from either the 7th Street/Metro Center stop or the Pico Boulevard stop (near the Los Angeles Convention Center) for a round-trip fare of $3.50. The train makes several stops in Long Beach, including one at the Transit Mall on 1st Street, between Pine and Pacific. 800-COMMUTE; www.mta.net or @metrolosangeles.

Once you've arrived, Long Beach Transit (562-591-2301, www.lbtransit.com or @lbtransit) offers several services, such as the Pine Avenue Link and the Passport, that shuttle visitors all over town from the Queen Mary to Pine Avenue and Belmont Shore. Fares are reasonable at $1.25, $65 for a monthly pass, with discounted rates for seniors, disabled riders, and children. In the warmer months, another transportation alternative is the AquaBus. This 40-foot-long water taxi costs just $1 and will ferry you to a number of Long Beach's coastal attractions. There are stops at the Aquarium, the Queen Mary, Catalina Landing, Shoreline Village, Pine Avenue Circle at Dock 7, and the Hotel Maya. The AquaLink water taxi is another option for nautical travel, but while it's faster and bigger than the AquaBus, this boat costs $5 to ride and only makes stops at Alamitos Bay Landing, the Queen Mary, the Aquarium, and Belmont Pier. 800-481-3470; www.lbtransit.com/Services/ Aqualink.aspx.

oLandmarks

- **Adelaide A. Tichenor House** • 852 E Ocean Blvd
- **Alexander House** • 5281 E El Roble St
- **Aquarium of the Pacific** • 100 Aquarium Way
- **Art Theater** • 2025 E 4th St
- **California State University at Long Beach** • 1250 N Bellflower Blvd
- **Catalina Landing** • 320 Golden Shore
- **Edison Theater** • 213 E Broadway
- **Long Beach Convention & Visitor's Bureau** • 301 E Ocean Blvd
- **Long Beach Museum of Art** • 2300 E Ocean Blvd
- **Matlock House** • 1560 Ramillo Ave
- **Museum of Latin-American Art** • 628 Alamitos Ave
- **The Pike at Rainbow Harbor** • S Pine Ave & W Shoreline Dr
- **The Queen Mary** • 1126 Queens Hwy
- **Seashell House** • 4325 E 6th St
- **Shoreline Village** • 419 Shoreline Village Dr
- **The Skinny House** • 708 Gladys Ave
- **Villa Riviera** • 800 E Ocean Blvd

W 5th St
W Cowles St
W 14th St
E 14th St
E 15th St
E New York St
E 14th St
W Anaheim St
Anaheim
E Anaheim St
W 12th St
Moro Pl
Regal Wy
E 12th St
E Atlas Wy
E Lily Wy
E 11th St
W 11th St
St Mary's Medical Center
W 10th St
E 10th St
Emerald Pl
W Nardo Wy
E Nardo Wy
W 9th St
E 9th St
W Cypress Wy
E Cypress Wy
W 8th St
E 8th St
Ruby Pl
W La Reina Wy
E La Reina Wy
York Rite Masonic Temple
Drake Park
N Loma Vista Dr
W Chester Pl
Corvo Ct
W 7th St
E 7th St
Cobre Wy
W 6th St
5th Street
Museum of Latin-American Art
Cereza Wy
W 5th St
E 5th St
Pacific
W Melrose Wy
Long Beach Plaza
W 4th St
E 4th St
Roble Wy
W 3rd St
E 3rd St
Maple Wy
Edison Theatre
W Broadway
E Broadway
E Alta Wy
1st Street
E 1st St
Cesar E Chavez Park
World Trade Center Long Beach Convention & Visitors Bureau
Lincoln Park
Transit Mall
W Ocean Blvd
E Ocean Blvd
W Windsor Pl
E Medio St
Villa Riviera
Adelaide A Tichenor House
W Seaside Wy
E Seaside Wy
W Shoreline Dr
E Shoreline Dr
Ocean Shore St
Long Beach Convention & Entertainment Center
Catalina Landing
Bay St
The Pike at Rainbow Harbor
Aquarium of the Pacific
Aquarium Wy
Rainbow Lagoon Park
Marina Green Park
Shoreline Village
Shoreline Village Dr
Shoreline Park
Queensway Bridge
Queensway Bay
Queensway Dr
Long Beach Marina
Island Grissom
PAGE 213
Magnolia Ave
Pacific Ave
Pine Ave
S Pine Ave
Long Beach Blvd
Atlantic Ave
Alamitos Ave
Locust Ave
Cedar Ave
Chestnut Ave
Daisy Ave
San Francisco Ave
Golden Ave
Maine Ave
De Forest Ave
N Harbor Scenic Dr
Pico Ave
S Pico Ave
Pier F Ave
710

Nightlife

- **49rs Tavern** • 5660 E Pacific Coast Hwy
- **Belmont Brewing Co.** • 25 39th Pl
- **The Blind Donkey** • 149 Linden Ave
- **Congregation Ale House** • 201 E Broadway Ave
- **District Wine** • 144 Linden Ave
- **Murphy's Pub** • 4918 E 2nd St
- **Portfolio Coffeehouse** • 2300 E 4th St
- **Rock Bottom Brewery** • 1 Pine Ave
- **The Sky Room** • 40 S Locust Ave

Restaurants

- **555 East** • 555 E Ocean Blvd
- **Alegria** • 115 Pine Ave
- **Angelo's Italian Deli** • 190 La Verne Ave
- **The Breakfast Bar** • 70 Atlantic Ave
- **Chen's Chinese Restaurant** • 2131 E Broadway
- **Chuck's Coffee Shop** • 4120 E Ocean Blvd
- **Enriques** • 6210 E Pacific Coast Hwy
- **Gladstone's** • 330 S Pine Ave
- **King's Fish House** • 100 W Broadway
- **L'Opera** • 101 Pine Ave
- **La Traviata** • 301 N Cedar Ave
- **Long Beach Café** • 615 E Ocean Blvd
- **Michael's Pizzeria** • 5616 E 2nd St
- **Ocean Market Grill** • 6332 E 2nd St
- **Open Sesame** • 5215 E 2nd St
- **Park Pantry** • 2104 E Broadway
- **Parkers' Lighthouse** • 435 Shoreline Village Dr
- **Phnom Penh Noodle Restaurant** • 1644 Cherry Ave
- **Pier 76 Fish Grill** • 95 Pine Ave
- **Sushi Kinoya** • 5521 E Stearns St
- **Sweet Dixie Kitchen** • 401 E 3rd St
- **Utopia** • 445 E 1st St
- **Yard House** • 401 Shoreline Village Dr

Shopping

- **Buffalo Exchange** • 4608 E 2nd St
- **City Place** • 151 E 5th St
- **ELEV8** • 132 Linden Ave
- **Fingerprints Music** • 420 E 4th St
- **Le Bijou Boutique** • 455 E Ocean Blvd
- **Lil Devils Boutique** • 2218 E 4th St
- **Long Beach Antique Market** • 4901 E Conant St
- **The Long Beach Depot for Creative ReUse** • 320 Elm Ave
- **Make Collectives** • 430 E 1st St
- **Olives Gourmet Grocer** • 3510 E Broadway
- **The Pike at Rainbow Harbor** • 95 S Pine Ave
- **Songbird** • 2240 E 4th St
- **Vintage Emporium** • 3423 Orange Ave

Attractions

Catalina

The Catalina Express ferry service currently monopolizes the seaways in the 22 mile stretch between mainland California and Catalina Island. The boats leave Long Beach for Catalina from a variety of ports and on a variety of schedules depending on the season; the best thing to do is check times and locations directly with the Catalina Express by calling 800-481-3470 or going online at www.catalinaexpress.com. Tickets cost $74.50 for a roundtrip, or you can go for free on your birthday. Take sunscreen, a beach towel, and Dramamine—the ride is often a rough one. Reservations are recommended.

You can also opt for a quicker route (15 minutes) via the Island Express Helicopter Service for $250 round trip per person (but if it's the off season, you might be able to snag a discounted rate). For just a little bit more, Island Express offers daily packages at $280 per person that include flight, taxi, and two Santa Catalina Island Company Discovery tours. 800-AVALON; www.islandexpress.com or at @islandexpress1.

Whether by air or by sea, once you land you can take advantage of all the leisure activities the island has to offer, from renting a golf cart to snorkeling and parasailing—all with that kitschy ski resort town feel...minus the skiing.

There's camping available on both sides of the island: Avalon has restaurants within walking distance or a trolley shuttle ride away, while sites at Two Harbors come with fewer tourists, but also less running water, for the more rugged camper. www.catalina.com or @catalinadotcom.

Queen Mary

Once a vessel that ferried WWII troops, movie stars, and heads of state across the Atlantic Ocean, the *Queen Mary* has since retired and is now a floating hotel and museum available for weddings, bar mitzvahs, and rubber stamp conventions—for real. In all seriousness, the ship is awesome in scope and historical significance. The *Queen Mary* offers something for the tourist in you—from brunch and hotel stays to ghost tours and comedy shows. A popular filming location, the liner boasts cameos in *Arrested Development* and *Pearl Harbor*, reminding us that Hollywood is just a hop, skip, and a freeway away. 562-435-3511; www.queenmary.com or @TheQueenMary. Check the site for special offers, particularly off season.

Ticket prices vary depending on what package you want; there are a variety of options including historical tours and special exhibits, but tickets start at $25 for adults and $14 for kids.

Directions: The *Queen Mary* is located at 1126 Queens Highway, at the south end of the 710 Freeway.

Aquarium of the Pacific
The Aquarium of the Pacific opened with much fanfare—and a massive PR campaign—in 1998. Don't expect to see Atlantic salmon or Maine lobsters here—this aquarium lives up to its name by focusing solely on the Pacific Ocean's three regions: Southern California/Baja, the Tropical Pacific, and the Northern Pacific, emphasizing interactive education over entertainment. 562-590-3100; www.aquariumofpacific.org or @AquariumPacific.

Admission: Prices start at $28.95 for grown folks, $14.95 for kids, and $25.95 for seniors. (Online booking sometimes entails a discounted fare.) Additional options include a Behind-the-Scenes tour and an Ocean Experience tour for a few extra bucks. The aquarium is open every day from 9 am until 6 pm. It's closed on Christmas and for the entire weekend of the Grand Prix of Long Beach, which is usually in April.

Directions: Take the 405 S to the 710 S, and follow the signs to Downtown Long Beach and the Aquarium. The Aquarium is located at 100 Aquarium Way, off Shoreline Drive. Parking is available at a municipal lot located just a few feet from the Aquarium. The cost is $8 if you scan your parking ticket at the Aquarium or pre-pay at a ticket window.

Long Beach Convention & Entertainment Center
Located at 300 East Ocean Boulevard, this complex is home to an eclectic assortment of events. The Terrace Theater hosts a variety of plays and musical performances, the Convention Center includes a large ballroom that serves as the site for many a senior prom, and of course, there are conferences, expos, and competitions galore. 562-436-3636; www.longbeachcc.com or @LBConventionCtr.

Directions: Take the 405 S to the 710 S and head for the Downtown exits. The 710 turns into Shoreline Drive. Follow this to Linden and turn into the parking lot.

Shoreline Village
Designed to look like an old-fashioned fishing village, Shoreline Village is a collection of shops, restaurants, and amusements that might best be described as "quaint." Don't get us wrong—there's great stuff here (cough cough Skee-ball). The area also caters to more athletic pursuits such as rollerblading, bike riding, and sailing, as well as offering a number of great restaurants and tasty snack shops. 562-435-2668; www.shorelinevillage.com or @ShorelineVillag.

Directions: Take the 710 S and follow signs for the Aquarium. Continue past the Aquarium and Pine Avenue, and turn right onto Shoreline Village Drive. Make sure to get your parking validated.

Hours: Shoreline Village is open seven days a week from 10 am until 9 pm, closing an hour later during the summer months.

The Pike at Rainbow Harbor
Today's Pike at Rainbow Harbor is in many ways reminiscent of the celebrated Pike of yore. Over 100 years ago, the Pike was one of the most famous beachside amusement parks on the west coast with rides, a pier, movie houses, shops, and cafes. The new Pike at Rainbow Harbor includes modern-day incarnations of commercialized fun, including dining options such as Bubba Gump Shrimp Co. and Smoothie King, a 14-screen multiplex, and an antique carousel. The Pike, covering 18 acres of downtown waterfront, is located smack-dab between the Convention Center and the Aquarium. www.thepikeatlongbeach.com.

Directions: Take the 405 S to the 710 S and head for the Downtown exits. The 710 turns into Shoreline Drive. Park anywhere between Pine and Chestnut Avenues, or in Shoreline Village, and then walk a few steps north. There's limited free parking with validation, but beware of the sizable lost-ticket fee.

Toyota Grand Prix
For one weekend every April, Long Beach turns into Daytona Beach and the sound of revving car engines echoes throughout the usually subdued downtown area. The real draw of the Grand Prix is the Pro/Celebrity Race, where the likes of Patrick Dempsey, William Shatner, Martina Navratilova, and Frankie Muniz get fast and furious with the best of the pros. Tickets are available online at www.gplb.com, or by calling 888-82-SPEED.

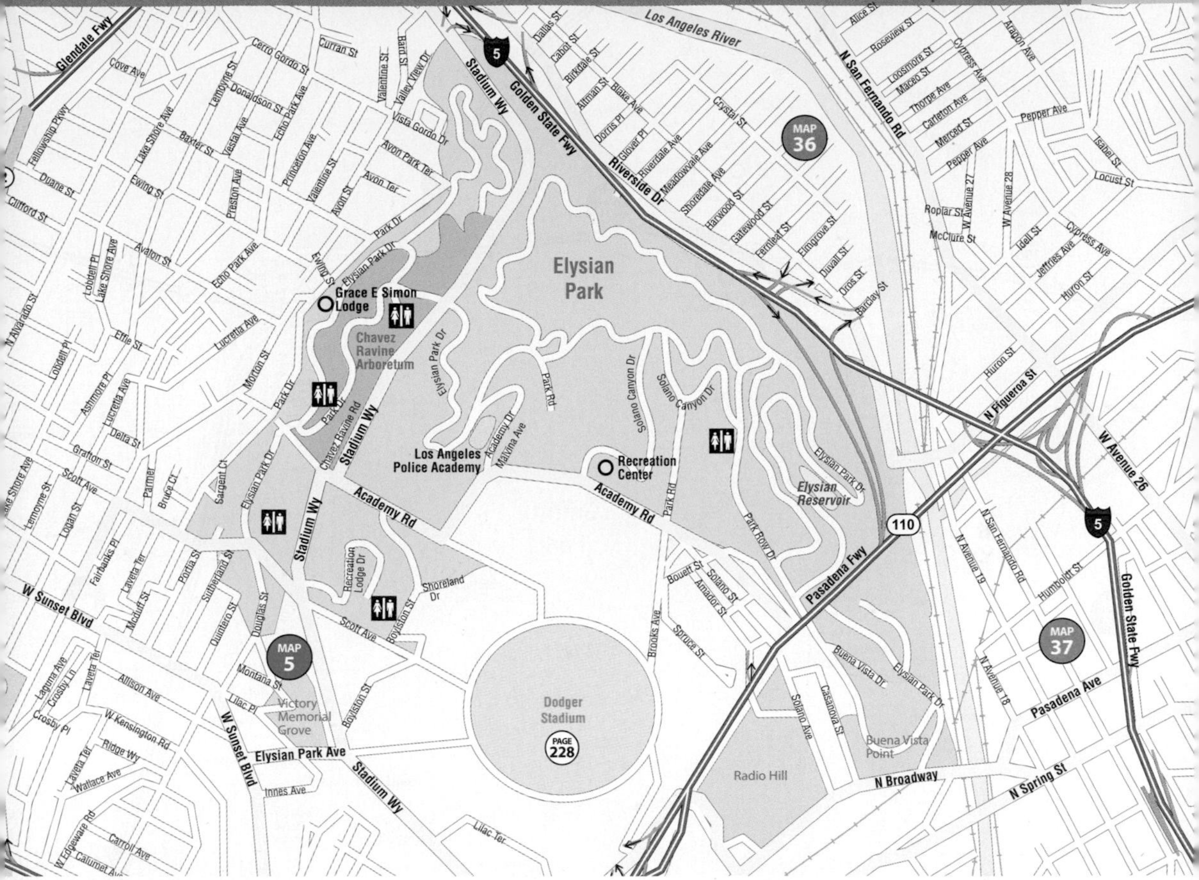

General Information

NFT Maps: 5, 36 & 37
Address: 835 Academy Rd
Los Angeles, CA 90012
Phone: 213-485-5054
Website: www.laparks.org/dos/parks/facility/elysianPk.htm

Overview

When Los Angeles was founded in 1781, more than 600 acres of parkland was set aside for public use. That allotted land, today known as Elysian Park, is the oldest and second-largest park in the LA area. The majority of the park, crisscrossed with hiking trails, has been maintained in its original state since it opened. In 1965, the "Citizens Committee to Save Elysian Park" formed to organize public support to preserve the parkland as public open space. Over 40 years later, the park has seen no redevelopment, but the committee continues to "arouse public and official awareness of the value of saving the last of these Pueblo lands set aside two centuries ago." (The park actually includes the last large piece of Pueblo land granted to the city by Carlos III, King of Spain, in 1781.) Despite the fact that the park is also home to the Los Angeles Police Academy headquarters (and their shooting range), one can still get away from it all and enjoy a relaxing respite from the city. But don't wander too far while alone. Even with the high occupancy of officers-in-training, the more isolated sections of the park are just that—and not always the safest, especially when it gets dark. Use the buddy system—in daylight—and aside from the fault line running underneath the park, you should be fine.

Practicalities

The central picnic area on Stadium Way has several barbecue pits, a small human-made lake, and a children's play area. The Recreation Center has basketball and volleyball courts. A café at the Police Academy is open to the public on weekdays from 6 am until 3 pm. The annual Chinatown Firecracker 10K Run passes through the park every February.

Admission to the park and arboretum is free. Elysian Park is located next to Dodger Stadium and the Police Academy and can be reached from the 5 or 110 Freeways (exit Stadium Way). The Chavez Ravine Arboretum is on the west side of Stadium Way near the Grace E. Simon Lodge.

FYI: If you're headed to a game at Dodger Stadium, park near Elysian Park (on Douglas Street or Stadium Way), then cut along the park and up to the stadium. Nature and a parking alternative—you gotta love it.

Chavez Ravine Arboretum

In 1893, the Los Angeles Horticultural Society established the arboretum and extensive botanical gardens in Elysian Park. The Chavez Ravine Arboretum was declared "City Historical-Cultural Monument Number 48" in 1967, and today Los Angeles Beautiful sponsors the arboretum. Many of the trees are the oldest and largest of their kind in California—some even in the United States—and there are over 1,000 tree species from around the world that can be grown in the arboretum's moderate climate. The Los Angeles Beautiful Arbor Day is held annually at the Chavez Ravine Arboretum. 213-485-5054; www.laparks.com/dos/horticulture/chavez.htm.

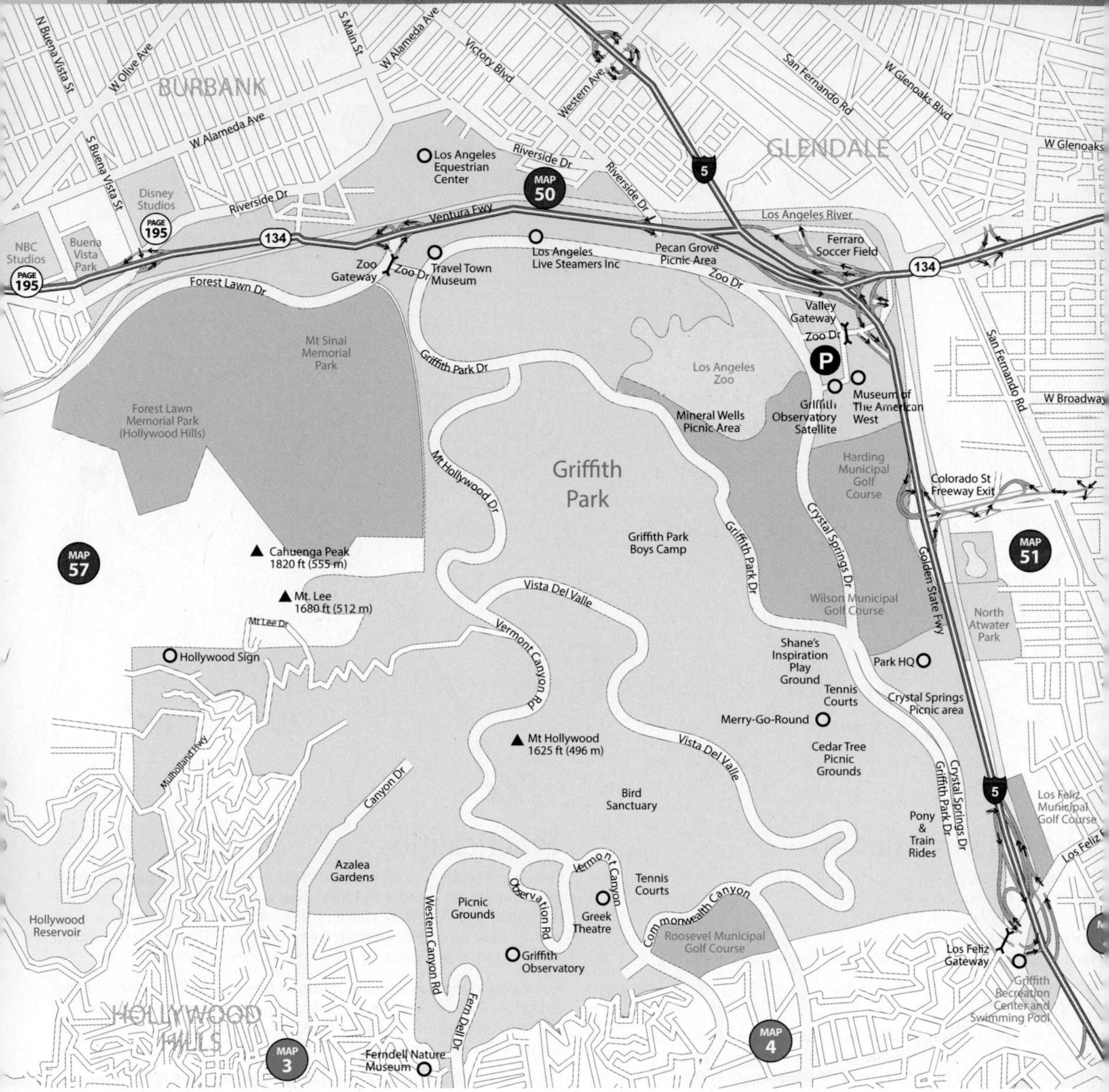

General Information

NFT Maps:	3, 4, 5, 50, 51 & 57
Address:	4730 Crystal Springs Dr Los Angeles, CA 90027
Phone:	323-913-4688
Website:	www.laparks.org/dos/parks/facility/griffithPk.htm
Hours:	6 am–10 pm, daily (bridle trails, hiking paths, and mountain roads close at sunset)

Overview

It's one of LA's great tragedies that we Angelenos do not make better or more frequent use of Griffith Park. It's the largest municipal park in the United States, far larger than New York's Central Park, yet not nearly as convenient. Sure, it's easily accessible from both the 5 and the 134 freeways, but Griffith Park is still a hike (pun intended) from the Westside, a slow crawl from the West Valley, and might as well be a world away from the South Bay. Most park-goers come to Griffith Park for its museums and attractions (the Zoo, the Greek Theatre, etc.), but these are just the beginning of the wide variety of activities the park has to offer.

Unfortunately, brush fires hit Griffith Park hard in 2007. Dante's View and Captain's Roost, both scenic respites for weary hikers, were both destroyed, and the bird sanctuary suffered heavy damage as well. Hydromulching has spurred regrowth, but burned areas will remain closed until further notice, and barbecues and fires of any kind are now prohibited as well (but locals don't seem to know that). And if it's not the fire, it's the rain—flooding is easier in the convalescence.

For updated information about repair status, openings, and closings, check www.lagriffithpark.org before making your trip to the park. And watch out for rattlesnakes!

Practicalities

Located northwest of downtown LA, Griffith Park is easily reached from either I-5 or the 134. From I-5, get off at Los Feliz Boulevard, Griffith Park (direct entry), or Zoo Drive. From 134 eastbound, take either the Forest Lawn Drive or Victory Boulevard exits. From 134 westbound, take Zoo Drive or Forest Lawn Drive. Speed at your own risk: the 25 mph speed limit on all park roads is strictly enforced.

Activities

Located within the park are facilities for golf (Harding, Los Feliz, Roosevelt, and Wilson Municipal golf courses); swimming (the Plunge Pool is open in summer months); hiking; jogging; horseback riding; tennis (Griffith-Riverside Pay, Vermont Pay, and the free Griffith Park Drive Courts); soccer (John Ferraro Athletic Fields at the northeast corner of the park); and camping and picnicking at one of the five main picnic areas.

Several playgrounds are located throughout the park, usually near picnic areas. The newest among them, Shane's Inspiration, is a "boundless playground" designed to allow children with disabilities to play alongside their able-bodied peers. Bicycles, including tandems, can be rented from Crystal Springs Bike and Skate Rental, located in a shack behind the Crystal Springs Ranger Station.

Young park-goers also enjoy the pony and train rides located near the Los Feliz Boulevard entrance to the park. The Griffith Park Southern Railroad takes riders on a one-mile-plus ride over a meadow, through an old Western town, and past a Native American village. The hours of operation are 10 am to 4:30 pm on weekdays, and the train runs until 5 pm on Saturdays and Sundays. Tickets cost $2 for adults and $1.50 for kids ages 1–13. The pony rides come in three speeds—slow, slower, and barely breathing—but neither the kids nor the horses ever seem to mind. There is also a surprisingly peppy merry-go-round located between the Zoo and the Los Feliz entrance to the park that's always worth a spin. The Fern Dell "hike" is an easy walk for a parent with a stroller or even a more mobile small child. This nature walk is located at the Fern Dell Drive entrance and features waterfalls, tunnels, and a picnic area for snacking.

From Thanksgiving until New Year's, Griffith Park hosts the annual LADWP Holiday Light Festival from 5 pm until 10 pm nightly. Music plays over twinkling light displays intended both to dazzle and to celebrate the history of LA. However, because the program is free, you might argue that there are finer light shows to be seen at some of the nearby mansions of Toluca Lake and Los Feliz. But a wiser, more polite person would argue that this is the LADWP's gift to the City of Los Angeles and we should appreciate it for the kind holiday gesture that it is. And, of course, for its considerable kitsch value. The light show really does draw the crowds, so you might consider parking at the zoo and going through the mile-long display on foot.

Griffith Park Museums

Griffith Observatory

2800 E Observatory Rd, 323-664-1181; www.griffithobservatory.org

After closing its doors and shutting down its telescopes in January 2002 for a much-needed renovation, the observatory reopened in 2007, just in time for its 71st anniversary. At first glance, you might not even notice many of the multi-million-dollar improvements, since so much care went into retaining the observatory's Art Deco style, and because a majority of the expansion is hidden beneath the front lawn. But the Hall of Science is bigger, there's a 200-seat presentation theater (called the Leonard Nimoy Event Horizon Theater, for all the Trekkies in the house), classrooms, conference rooms, an expanded book store, and just about anything else a stargazer could hope to find. Admission is free if you're a pedestrian or cyclist, but the Observatory now follows a Getty-like system that forces visitors to reserve parking and shuttle services in advance. Parking is available at Hollywood & Highland or the Observatory Satellite (near the zoo), and a shuttle reservation is $8 for adults, $4 for children. Visit the above website to reserve your spot.

The Autry National Center

4700 Western Heritage Wy, 323-667-2000; theautry.org

Part museum of history, part art gallery, the Autry is devoted to the stories, the people, the cultures, and the events that have shaped the legacy of the region. Learn about Spanish explorers, discover how the genre of the western evolved through radio, movies, and television, and see paintings by Remington and Russell. Grab a bite at the museum's Autry Café (open for breakfast and lunch). Hours: Tues-Fri, 10 am–4 pm; Sat-Sun, 11 am-5pm. Admission costs $10 for adults, $6 for students and seniors, $4 for children ages 3–12. The museum is free for kids under 3 and is free for all on the second Tuesday of every month.

Greek Theatre

2700 N Vermont Canyon Rd, 323-665-5857; www.greektheatrela.com

Built with funds left to the city by affluent psycho Griffith J. Griffith, LA's outdoor theater has been hosting live music under the stars since 1930. In recent years, the 6,100-seat venue has hosted Sir Paul McCartney, The White Stripes, Tina Turner, Elton John, and the Russian National Ballet, just to name a few. At the ripe old age of 75, the theater recently underwent a multi-million-dollar facelift that has improved the acoustics and comfort of the outdoor arena. Tickets to performances can be purchased in person at the box office, or through Ticketmaster.

Los Angeles Zoo

5333 Zoo Dr, 323-644-4200; www.lazoo.org

The Los Angeles Zoo is located in Griffith Park at the junction of the Ventura (134) and Golden State (5) Freeways. The most popular attractions are the Red Ape Rain Forest, the Treetops Terrace, and the newly renovated Sea Lion Cliffs. The zoo is open daily from 10 am until 5 pm (except on Christmas Day). Note that the zoo puts animals in for the night an hour before closing time. Admission costs $13, $10 for seniors over 62, and $8 for children 2-12. Children under two and parking are both free. Annual memberships are a smart move for families with children. Packages start at $45.

Travel Town Museum

5200 Zoo Dr, 323-662-5874; www.traveltown.org

Travel Town Museum is an outdoor museum that spotlights the railroad heritage of the western US. The collection includes locomotives, freight cars, passenger cars, and a couple of cabooses, as well as a miniature train ride for kids (one of three in the park). Hours: Mon–Fri: 10 am–4 pm; Sat–Sun: 10 am–5 pm. Admission and parking are free, and a ride on the miniature train costs just $2.50.

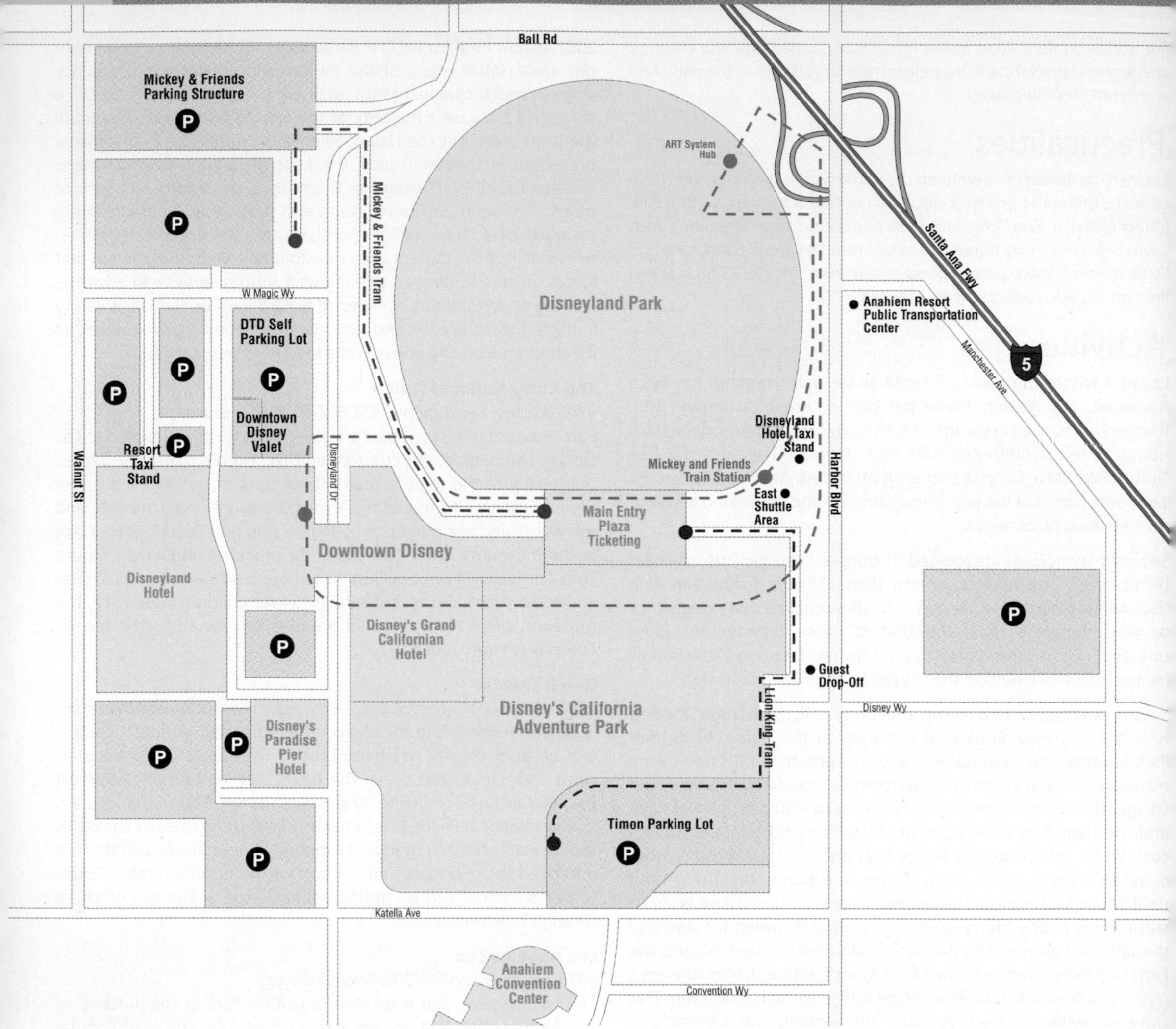

General Information

Address:	1313 S Harbor Blvd Anaheim, CA 92803-3232
Disneyland Info (recorded):	714-781-4565
Disneyland Info (operator):	714-781-7290
Disneyland Travel Packages:	714-520-5060
Disneyland Resort Hotels:	714-956-6425
Disneyland Ticketing:	714-781-4400
Website:	disneyland.disney.go.com

Overview

Sure, you can walk around all day with a chip on your shoulder blaming "The Happiest Place on Earth" for sucking your pocketbook dry at every turn. And, yes, the crowds can be a total pain. But there's something so pleasantly surreal about a visit to the Magic Kingdom. The staff is almost militant about being kind; there's usually some childhood memory running through your head, whether you like it or not; and the second there's a chill in the air—*whammo*!—the hot chocolate carts arrive at your service. It's like…magic!

Disneyland recently souped up and promoted its after-sundown "Nighttastic!" fare, including the rightly famous fireworks displays, California Adventure's Electrical Parade, and Fantasmic!, a rococo night show in which Mickey Mouse (whose pan-Disneyland ubiquity makes him almost a religious figure) uses magic to battle the eye-catching forces of darkness. There's still plenty to do during the day, natch. If there's even a smidgen of the Force within you, take your inner Jedi to Tomorrowland Terrace to enroll in the Jedi Training Academy, where adolescent boys' heads implode as they defend the galaxy against a living, breathing Darth Vader. For updates on construction, parades and promotions, www.mouseplanet.com is invaluable.

If you're heading to Disneyland with a group of adults, cruise in during the evening (at least during the summer, when the park is open late) or ditch work for shorter lines and more breathing room. For popular rides, always look for the Fastpass kiosks near the ride entrances. These allow you to take a ticket and return at an appointed time to join the less congested Fastpass queue.

The Downtown Disney district, just outside the park's gates, is a loose collection of shops and restaurants, most of which appeal to kids ranging from youngster (Build-A-Bear, Lego) to tween (Club Libby Lu) to Jeff Spicoli (Quiksilver). The restaurants generally offer wider menus and better food than you'll find inside the park, though with few exceptions (Jamba Juice, Wetzel's Pretzels), they won't necessarily save you any money. The World of Disney store is conveniently located next to the parking-lot trams, guaranteeing that you give Disney the last dollar in your wallet before returning to your car at the end of the day.

The California Adventure Park has never quite lived up to the Disney standard. Annual passport holders may park-hop, and can thus experience rides like the Twilight Zone Tower of Terror (which is really quite frightening) and the Soarin' Over California motion ride. Take a little girl to the Princess Celebration (lunch or dinner) at Ariel's Grotto and you will be a rock star, at least until you tell them it's time to leave the park and go home. A Bug's Land, scattered with oversized food, will make you glad you're not on acid. California Adventure has been revamped to look more like the Los Angeles of the 1920s, when Disney arrived.

Hours of Operation

The park's hours change depending on the season. During the summer months, school vacations, and holidays, Disneyland is usually open from 9 am until 9 pm, and California Adventure Park is open from 10 am until 7 pm. In the off-season, Disneyland is open from 10 am until 8 pm, and California Adventure Park is open from 10 am until 6 pm. Call the park, or check their website, for more accurate times before heading down. The website is also useful for finding out what rides may be closed for maintenance on any given day. (After all, there's nothing more disappointing than having your Pirates of the Caribbean dreams squashed due to renovations.) The website also lists daily, weekly, and monthly special entertainment events.

Entrance Fees

There are not many places you'll visit where the child admission fee cuts off at 9 years of age—but Disneyland is one of them. One-day, one-park tickets for Disneyland or California Adventure are now $96 for adults, $90 for children. The two-day Park Hopper is $217 for adults and $204 for children. You can sign up online for free admission on your birthday. Disney sometimes posts special deals on their website, so make sure you check it before you buy tickets—it also saves time waiting in the entrance line. Disneyland typically offers reduced rates to Southern California residents for Park Hopper tickets and annual passports, so if you plan on visiting the park twice or more during the year, this may be a wise investment.

Lockers

For tourists on the move, or for visitors who inexplicably brought along valuables to the park, there are lockers located outside the main entrances to Disneyland and California Adventure. Locker rentals cost between $7 and $15 per day.

Package Check

If you purchase more mouse ears than you can carry while inside the park, you may leave your packages at the Newsstand (Main Entrance), Star Trader (Tomorrowland), or Pioneer Mercantile (Frontierland) and pick them up on your way out.

Kennels

Traveling with your pooch can create problems, and orchestrating a trip to Disneyland is no exception to this rule. Hotels in the Disneyland Resort do not allow pets, but if you're passing through and plan on staying elsewhere overnight, indoor day kennel facilities, located to the right of the Main Entrance of Disneyland, are available for $20 a day.

How to Get There—Driving

Traveling southbound on I-5 (Golden State/Santa Ana Freeway), exit at Disneyland Drive and turn left (south). Follow the signs to the Mickey & Friends Parking Structure. If you're traveling northbound on I-5 (Santa Ana Freeway), exit on Katella Avenue and turn left (west). Proceed across Katella Avenue and merge onto Disney Way (on the left). Follow the signs to the most convenient parking area. The same goes for if you're traveling eastbound or westbound on the 22 (Garden Grove Freeway).

Parking

Once in the Mickey & Friends parking lot, head to the escalators, which take you directly to the Mickey & Friends Loading Zone. Trams collect visitors and drop them off at the Mickey & Friends Tram Station, located within walking distance of both theme parks. Parking costs $17 a day for cars, $22 for oversized vehicles, and $27 for buses.

How to Get There—Mass Transit

All of the LA area airports provide shuttle services to the Disneyland Resort. Bus 460 goes somewhere near the park, but we recommend driving a car or taking a shuttle if you can.

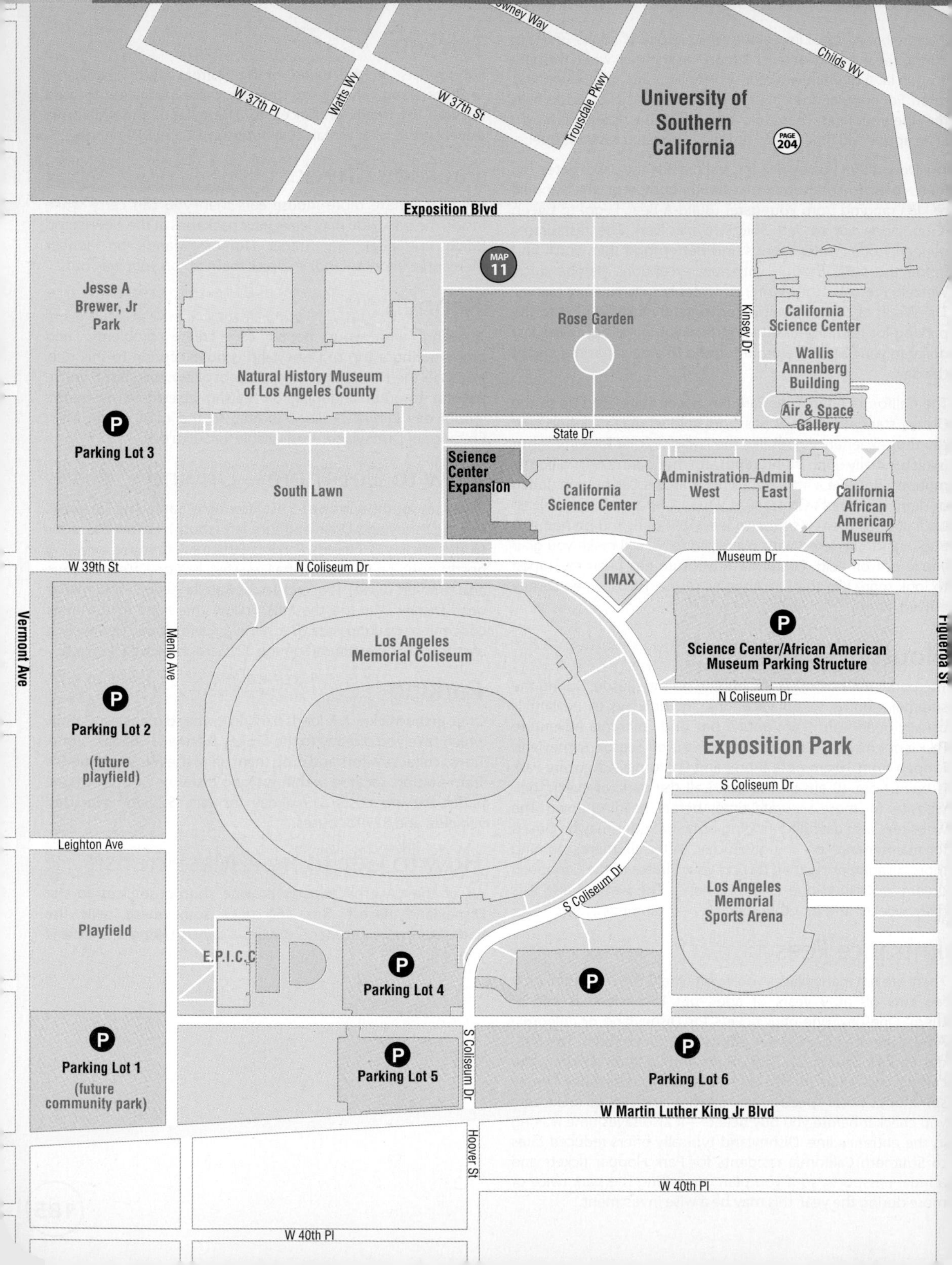
Downey Way
Childs Wy
W 37th Pl
Watts Wy
W 37th St
Trousdale Pkwy
University of Southern California
PAGE 204
Exposition Blvd
MAP 11
Jesse A Brewer, Jr Park
Natural History Museum of Los Angeles County
Rose Garden
Kinsey Dr
California Science Center
Wallis Annenberg Building
Air & Space Gallery
State Dr
Parking Lot 3
South Lawn
Science Center Expansion
California Science Center
Administration West
Admin East
California African American Museum
W 39th St
N Coliseum Dr
Museum Dr
IMAX
Vermont Ave
Menlo Ave
Los Angeles Memorial Coliseum
Science Center/African American Museum Parking Structure
Figueroa St
N Coliseum Dr
Parking Lot 2
(future playfield)
Exposition Park
S Coliseum Dr
Leighton Ave
S Coliseum Dr
Los Angeles Memorial Sports Arena
Playfield
E.P.I.C.C
Parking Lot 4
Parking Lot 1
(future community park)
Parking Lot 5
S Coliseum Dr
Parking Lot 6
W Martin Luther King Jr Blvd
Hoover St
W 40th Pl
W 40th Pl

Overview

NFT Map: 11

Exposition Park is bounded by Figueroa Street to the east, Martin Luther King Jr. Boulevard to the south, Menlo Avenue to the west, and Exposition Boulevard to the north. The grounds face the University of Southern California's (USC) campus, tying the two into a blend of extensive education and learning. Originally called Agricultural Park, the area was developed in 1876 as a showground for agricultural and horticultural fairs. In June 1923, the Los Angeles Memorial Coliseum, named in honor of those who died in World War I, was completed. The stadium was enlarged for the 1932 Olympics and also hosted the 1984 Olympics. Today Exposition Park houses the Natural History Museum, IMAX Theater, Rose Garden, California Science Center, California African American Museum, LA Memorial Coliseum, and the indoor Los Angeles Memorial Sports Arena.

Los Angeles Memorial Coliseum & Los Angeles Memorial Sports Arena

The history of the Coliseum/Sports Arena complex spans eight decades. It is the only arena in the world to play host to two Olympiads (10th and 23rd), two Super Bowls (1st and 7th), and one World Series (1959). In the past, the complex has played host to the Rams, the Dodgers, and the Lakers, and was the expansion home of the San Diego Chargers and the Kings. Today, the Coliseum is home to USC's juggernaut Trojan football team (call 213-740-GOSC for tickets) and various other special events. Autumn is particularly vibrant during home games–if you're trying to visit the park then, traffic and parking will be double nightmares. Check the website (www.lacoliseum.com) for event details. The main box office switchboard is open from 10 am to 6 pm and can be reached at 213-747-7111.

Rose Garden

The 7.5-acre Rose Garden was completed in 1928, and there were 15,793 roses in full bloom for the opening. Today the sunken garden contains more than 20,000 rose bushes representing 190-plus varieties. It's the perfect place for an afternoon stroll and a nearby retreat when the screaming at the Coliseum during USC football season starts to become a headache. In Southern California, roses bloom from March to November. The garden is open daily, free to the public, and located within Exposition Park at 701 State Drive (213-765-0114). While beautiful during the day, it's awfully sketchy at night—like much of its neighborhood.

Natural History Museum of LA County

The Natural History Museum houses many California-specific exhibits not found at other natural museums. Its Marine Hall highlights Californian ocean life, and its California history section shows a chronological progression since the 1500s. The museum is located at 900 Exposition Boulevard in Exposition Park, across from USC between Vermont Avenue and Figueroa Street. Parking is available off Menlo Avenue. The fee for parking will run between $8 and $10, depending on events in the Exposition Park area. The museum is open 9:30 am to 5 pm daily. Adults can expect to pay $12 for entry, seniors, students, and youth (13-17) are $9, kids 3–12 are $5, and ages 2 and under are free. If you schedule your visit on the first Tuesday of the month, it won't cost you a cent! Although the museum is open during USC football games, we highly recommend that you avoid the Exposition Park area at all costs on those days unless you're attending the game. 213-763-DINO; www.nhm.org.

California Science Center & IMAX

You can't miss the giant jet airplane sitting out front. The Science Center is open daily from 10 am until 5 pm, and admission to Science Center exhibition halls is free. The IMAX is open daily; admission is $8.25 for adults, $6 for seniors, and $5 for children (without the member discount). Check the website (www.californiasciencecenter.org) or call 213-744-7400 for show information. Parking is $10 for cars and "yellow" school buses and $25 for charter buses and oversized vehicles (cash only). The entrance to the visitor parking lot is on Figueroa at 39th Street.

California African American Museum

The California African American Museum researches, collects, preserves, and interprets the art, history, and culture of African Americans, with emphasis on California and the western United States. The museum is open Tuesdays through Saturdays, from 10 am until 5 pm. Admission is free. 213-744-7432; www.caamuseum.org.

How to Get There—Driving

From the north, take 101 S to 110 S, exit at Martin Luther King Jr. Boulevard W, and enter on Hoover Street. From the south, take 405 N to 110 N, exit at Martin Luther King Jr. Boulevard W, and enter on Hoover Street. From the west, take 10 E to the 110 S and follow the above directions. From the east, take 10 W to 110 S and follow the above directions.

Parking

There are parking spaces located at various places within the park. Parking rates and availability will vary for special events. Four-hour and two-hour metered parking is available on Figueroa Street and Jefferson Boulevard. There are a number of lots on the streets surrounding the park, and the usual weekday rate is $3. Rates vary when special events are in progress, and the average cost of parking in a lot is $10. You can also park at any of the USC lots for $7 a day, except on game days and special events where parking may not be available to non-Trojans, in which case the price of a parking spot escalates and locals rent out their driveways and yards for a considerable bargain.

How to Get There—Mass Transit

If you're taking public transport, take the Metro Rail Expo Line to Expo Park/USC.

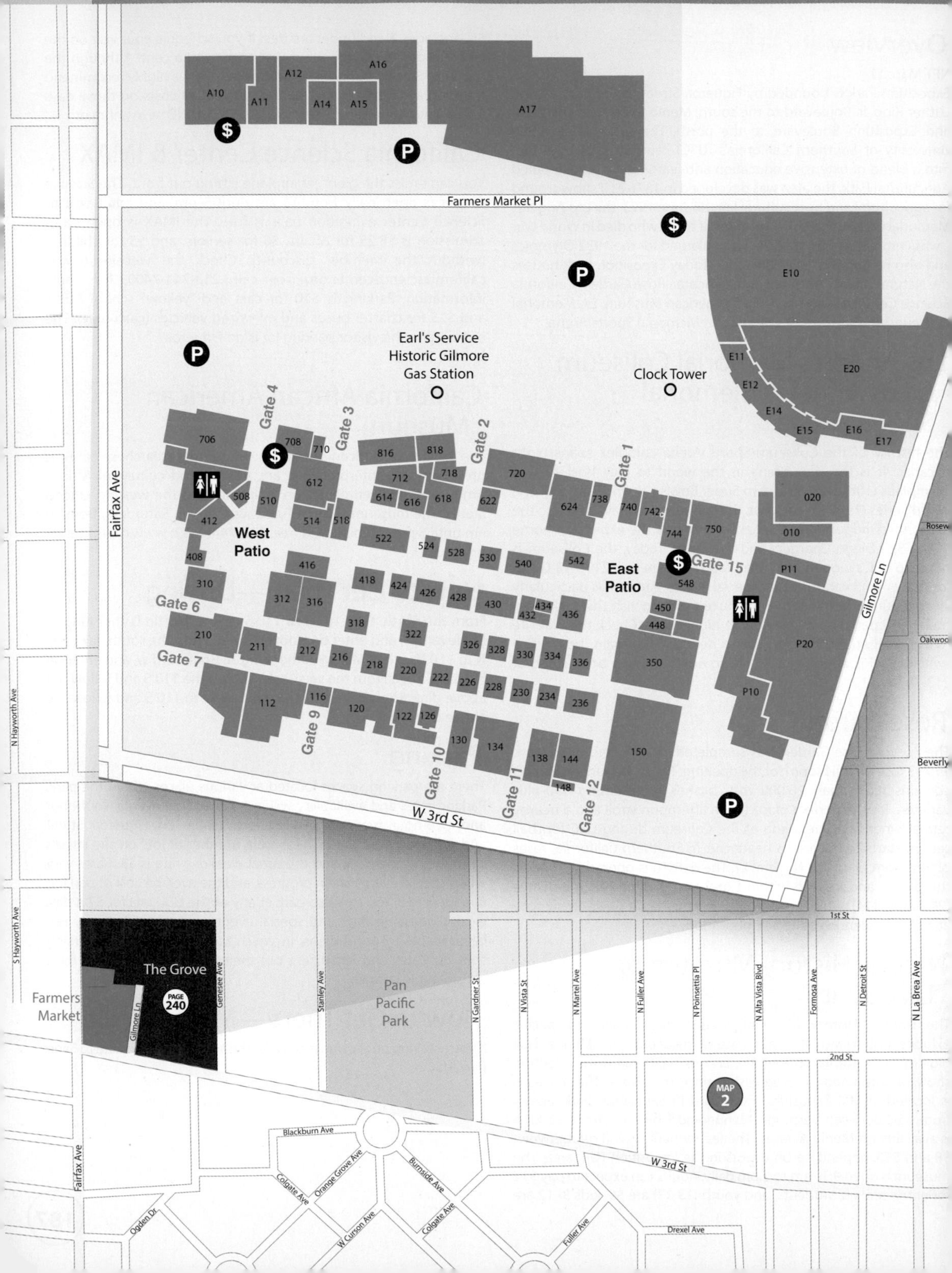
A10
A11
A12
A14
A15
A16
A17
Farmers Market Pl
E10
E11
E12
E14
E15
E16
E17
E20
Earl's Service
Historic Gilmore
Gas Station
Clock Tower
Gate 1
Gate 2
Gate 3
Gate 4
Gate 6
Gate 7
Gate 9
Gate 10
Gate 11
Gate 12
Gate 15
West
Patio
East
Patio
706
708
710
816
818
712
718
720
612
614
616
618
622
624
738
740
742
744
750
020
010
508
510
412
514
518
522
524
528
530
540
542
548
408
416
310
418
424
426
428
430
434
432
436
450
448
312
316
318
322
210
211
212
216
218
220
222
226
228
230
234
236
326
328
330
334
336
350
112
116
120
122
126
130
134
138
144
148
150
P11
P20
P10
Fairfax Ave
Gilmore Ln
W 3rd St
Rosew
Oakwo
Beverly
N Hayworth Ave
S Hayworth Ave
1st St
2nd St
The Grove
PAGE
240
Farmers
Market
Gilmore Ln
Genesee Ave
Stanley Ave
Pan
Pacific
Park
N Gardner St
N Vista St
N Martel Ave
N Fuller Ave
N Poinsettia Pl
N Alta Vista Blvd
Formosa Ave
N Detroit St
N La Brea Ave
MAP
2
Blackburn Ave
W 3rd St
Fairfax Ave
Colgate Ave
Orange Grove Ave
Burnside Ave
Ogden Dr
W Curson Ave
Colgate Ave
Fuller Ave
Drexel Ave

General Information

NFT Map: 2
Address: 6333 W 3rd St
Los Angeles, CA 90036
Phone: 323-933-9211
Website: www.farmersmarketla.com
Hours: Mon–Fri: 9 am–9 pm; Sat: 9 am–8 pm; Sun: 10 am–7 pm (merchant hours may vary)

Overview

The Farmers Market opened in the 1930s as a humble dirt lot where farmers parked their trucks and sold their produce right off their tailgates. Over the years, it's slowly morphed into an occasional motley crew of souvenir shops and food stalls. And even though it was scaled back a few years ago to make way for the fancy, schmancy Grove shopping mall, it's still one of the best melting-pot LA experiences around. Old timers are eating the same Sunday brunch they've been looking forward to for years; there's always a young, semi-recognizable Hollywood type from TV's latest teen drama or cash-cow horror to point and gawk at; and hipsters are drawn to it for the kitsch, good grub, seasonal festivals, and, during the right time of year, live music. Patrons can keep abreast of updates and soirées via the Farmers Market Bugle, available at the market or online. Plus, when you're with a group of friends that can't decide on what to eat, this place is a godsend.

Where to Shop

There are two kinds of shops at the Farmers Market—the kinds that sell food and the kinds that don't. It's hard to go wrong with any of the food-sellers. Mr. Marcel Gourmet Market has an extensive selection of imported cheese, and you can watch the whole candy-making process at Littlejohn's English Toffee House. Magee's House of Nuts has been in operation at the Farmers Market since it began and will open your eyes to a world of nut butters that goes far beyond peanuts. The Fruit Company always offers a wide variety of fruits that are consistently fresher and more reasonably priced than any local supermarket.

The Farmers Market's other businesses are a bit more eclectic and can be somewhat hit-or-miss. By Candlelight has an impressive selection of candles and Light My Fire sells bottled hot sauce that ranges from mild to downright combustible. There are also many shops that cater to the tourist crowd and sell cheap, Hollywood-themed souvenirs. If you're hoping to do some serious shopping of the mainstream variety, hop on the trolley (or take a short walk) and head over to The Grove.

Where to Eat

There may be no better place for breakfast in all of LA than Kokomo Café, one of the Farmers Market's few sit-down dining establishments. This casual café serves up an eclectic breakfast and lunch menu and, best of all, their egg dishes come with coffeecake. Even with its new fancy remodel, Du-par's has an old-school feel that tourists and locals can't resist. Then, there's always the food court. If you can handle the wait, the French Crepe Company serves 'em up sweet and savory. The Gumbo Pot dishes the tastiest Gumbo YaYa this side of the Mississippi and is tucked away in a courtyard corner with a bar to help wash down the spicy stuff. And no matter how much you've gorged, you must try at least one of Bob's Coffee and Doughnuts' doughy delights—they're considered by many to have the best donuts in town. Some of the finest Mexican dishes west of Alvarado are found at ¡Lotería! Grill. For a more elegant Farmers Market experience, check out the wine bar at Mr. Marcel Pain Vin et Fromage. In other words, it's pretty much impossible to go wrong here.

How to Get There—Driving

To drive to the Farmers Market from almost anywhere south of the Valley or north of LAX, your best bet is to take surface streets. The Grove's opening has made 3rd Street slower going than it used to be, and Beverly Boulevard isn't much better. Take whichever east-west thoroughfare you choose until you hit Fairfax Avenue, and head north. You can't miss the Farmers Market at the corner of 3rd and Fairfax. If you're coming from the Westside or South Bay, you might hop on the 10 Freeway, exit at Fairfax, and head north. Valley residents can hop on the 101 and exit at Highland. Take Highland to 3rd Street and turn right. Continue on 3rd until you reach Fairfax, and the Farmers Market will be on your right.

Parking

Before the opening of The Grove, parking at the Farmers Market was a challenge, but at least it was free. To discourage mall patrons from hogging the smallish parking lot, however, the Farmers Market now charges for parking. With validation, you get two hours of free parking and the third hour is $4. If you find that the lot more resembles a war zone, street parking may be your best bet.

A10. Gilmore Bank, 549-2100*
A11. Farmers Market Postal Center, 933-2322
A12. Chipotle, 857-0608
A14. Unique Tan, 933-2826
A15. Elements Spa & Salon, 933-0212
A16. Beauty Collection Apothecary, 930-0300
A17. The Children's Place, 939-1813
CT1. Tashen, 933-9211
E10. Cost Plus World Market, 935-5530
E11. Coffee Bean and Tea Leaf, 857-0461
E12. Francesca's Collection, 935-2474
E16. Zara, 935-5041
E17. Marmalade Café, 954-0088
P10. Sur La Table, 954-9190
P11. Designer Details, 931-9632
D10. Bath & Body Works, 965-1724
112. Starbucks, 965-9594
116, 818. Lottery Booth, 934-0318
122. Singapore's Banana Leaf, 933-4627
126,130. Pinkberry, 933-9211
138. Tusquellas Seafoods, 938-1919
150. Mr. Marcel Gourmet Market, 935-9451
210. Du-par's Restaurant, 933-8446
211. Du-par's Pie Shop, 933-8446
212. T (Tea Shop), 930-0076
216. Farmers Market Poultry, 936-8158
218. Magee's House of Nuts, 938-4127
220. Sticker Planet, 939-6933
222. Tbilisi & Yerevan Bakery, 930-2355
226. Puritan Poultry, 938-0312
230. Light My Fire, 930-2484
236, 144. Mr. Marcel Pain Vin et Fromage, 939-7792
310. Deano's Gourmet Pizza, 935-6373
312. The Gumbo Pot, 933-0358
316. Thee's Continental Pastries, 937-1968
318. The French Crepe Company, 934-3113
322. ¡Lotería! Grill, 930-2211
326. 326 Beer & Wine, 549-2156
328. Treasures of the Pacific, 936-9208
330. Breadworks, 936-0785
334. The Village, 936-9340
336. Moishe's Restaurant, 936-4998
350. Huntington Meats & Sausages, 938-5383
408. E.B.'s Beer & Wine, 549-2157
412. Charlie's Coffee Shop, 933-0616
416. Gill's Old Fashioned Ice Cream, 936-7986
424. The Salad Bar, 933-3204
426. By Candlelight, 549-0458
430. Gift & Gadget Nook, 933-1898
432. Littlejohn's English Toffee House, 936-5379
434. Sushi a Go Go, 930-7874
436. Tusquellas Fish & Oyster Bar, 939-2078
448. Patsy D'Amore's Pizza, 938-4938
450. Bob's Coffee and Doughnuts, 933-8929
508. Peking Kitchen, 936-1949
510. La Korea, 936-3930
514. Marconda's Meats, 938-5131
522, 418. The Magic Nut & Candy Company, 938-1555
524. Essence of Nature, 931-9593
528. Gadget Nook Gourmet, 933-1898
530. Country Bakery, 937-1968
540. Phil's Deli & Grill, 936-3704
542. Coffee Corner, 938-0278
548. Bennett's Ice Cream, 939-6786
612, 518. Farm Boy, 936-6363
614. Lustre, 933-6449
616. Farmers Market Variety Store, 933-1086
618. Pampas Grill, 931-1928
622. The Refresher, 939-6786
624. Magee's Kitchen, 938-4127
706. Johnny Rockets, 937-2093
708. Market Optometrix, 936-5140
710. Three Dog Bakery, 935-7512
712. Farmers Market Shoe Repair/Shine, 939-5622
718. Sporte Fashion, 932-6454
720. Kip's Toyland, 939-8334
738. Weiss Jewelry, 934-1623
740. Bryan's Pit Barbecue, 931-2869
742. Market Grill, 934-0424
744. China Depot, 937-6868
750. Ulysses Voyage Greek Restaurant, 939-9728
816. Farm Fresh Produce, 931-3773
818. Farmers Market Newsstand, 934-0318

**All area codes 323 unless noted*

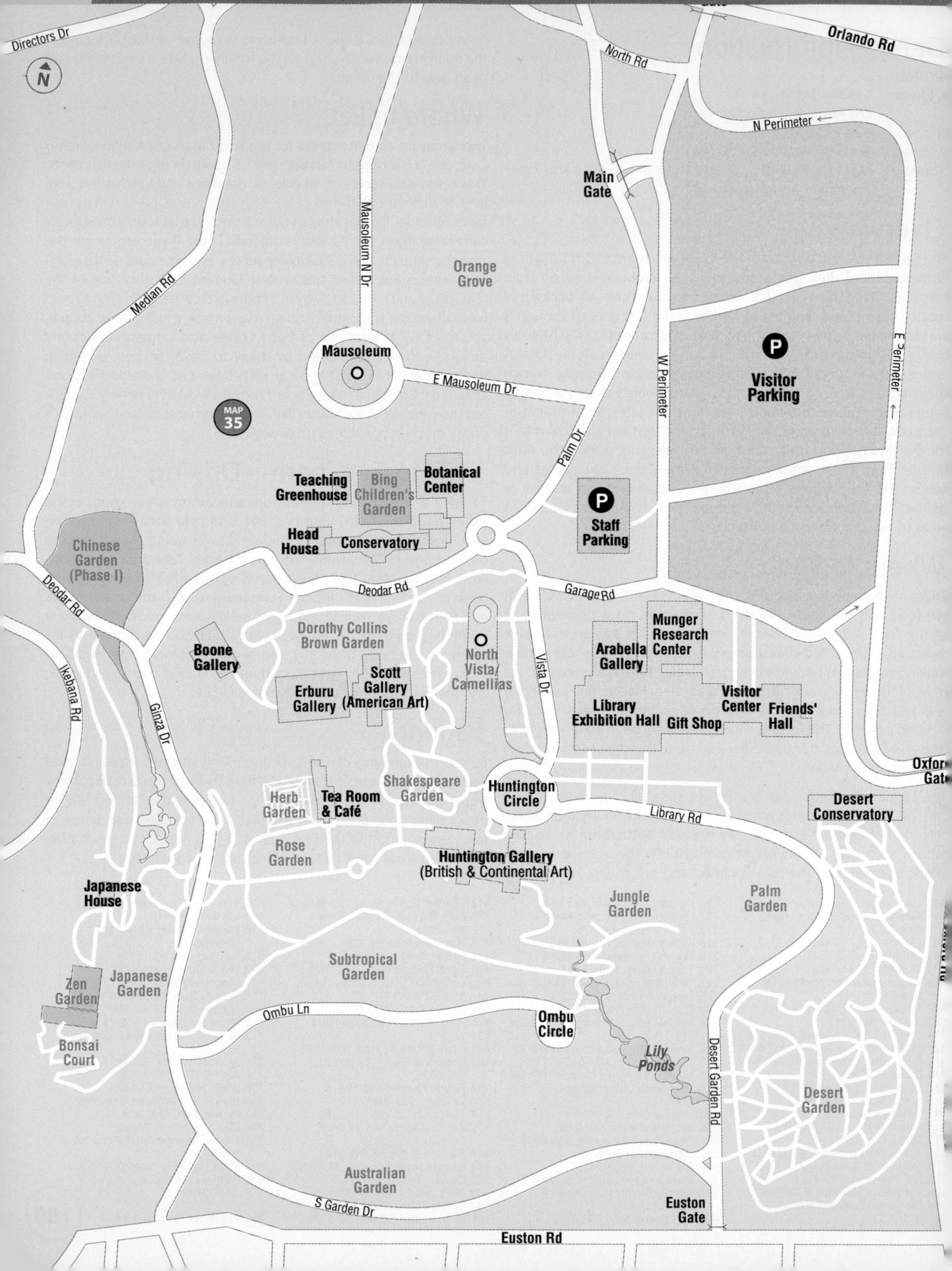
Directors Dr
N
Orlando Rd
North Rd
N Perimeter
Main Gate
Mausoleum N Dr
Median Rd
Orange Grove
Mausoleum
E Mausoleum Dr
W Perimeter
Visitor Parking
E Perimeter
MAP 35
Palm Dr
Teaching Greenhouse
Bing Children's Garden
Botanical Center
Staff Parking
Head House
Conservatory
Chinese Garden (Phase I)
Deodar Rd
Garage Rd
Dorothy Collins Brown Garden
North Vista/ Camellias
Munger Research Center
Arabella Gallery
Boone Gallery
Scott Gallery (American Art)
Erburu Gallery
Vista Dr
Library Exhibition Hall
Gift Shop
Visitor Center
Friends' Hall
Ikebana Rd
Ginza Dr
Shakespeare Garden
Huntington Circle
Herb Garden
Tea Room & Café
Library Rd
Oxford Gate
Desert Conservatory
Rose Garden
Huntington Gallery (British & Continental Art)
Japanese House
Jungle Garden
Palm Garden
Subtropical Garden
Japanese Garden
Zen Garden
Ombu Ln
Ombu Circle
Bonsai Court
Lily Ponds
Desert Garden Rd
Desert Garden
Australian Garden
S Garden Dr
Euston Gate
Euston Rd

General Information

NFT Map: 35
Address: 1151 Oxford Rd
San Marino, CA 91108
Phone: 626-405-2100
Website: www.huntington.org
Hours: Mon, Wed, Thurs, Fri: 12 pm–4:30 pm;
Sat–Sun: 10:30 am–4:30 pm
Closed Tuesdays
Admission: adults $20 on weekdays and $23 on weekends, seniors $15, students $12, youth (ages 5–11) $8;
Free first Thursday of each month, and always free for members and children under five.

Overview

Part library, part research center, part art gallery, part botanical garden, the Huntington's diverse collection of art and flora is a retreat for researchers or families simply looking to get away from it all. The 150 acres of gardens, covered with 14,000 varieties of plants, has the look of a picturesque college campus on steroids, with plenty of room to stretch out, run around with the kids, or simply doze off in the sun. The best way to see the gardens is by joining up with a free group tour—otherwise you risk missing out on the Desert Garden's menacing cacti or the lush canopy of the Jungle Garden. Kids go crazy over the Children's Garden, where you'll see groups of them running through and squealing over the fog grotto and the prism tunnel, while tired parents rest their weary feet. For a Zen experience, stroll the winding path in the Japanese Garden past the bonsai trees and rock garden and through the bamboo grove. Well-informed docents are permanently stationed in the herb and rose gardens to answer any horticulture questions. After a lot of conspicuous construction, Liu Fang Yaun (literally "the garden of flowing fragrance"), the largest classical Chinese garden outside China, is now open for tranquil enchantment.

Art Collections

The majestic Huntington is best-known for its collection of British and French art from the 18th and 19th centuries. Highlights include Thomas Gainsborough's celebrated *The Blue Boy* and Sir Thomas Lawrence's *Pinkie*. The Virginia Steele Scott Gallery showcases the works of American painters from the 1730s to the 1930s. This intimate gallery is the perfect place to contemplate masterworks by Sargent, Bellows, and Hopper. In the Library building, the Arabella Huntington Memorial Collection contains 18th-century French furniture, sculpture, and Renaissance paintings.

The Library

The library includes some of the world's most famous rare books—including a Gutenberg Bible and a world-class edition of Shakespeare's complete works. These pieces are on display for the general public, but only professional researchers can gain access to the library's entire collection, which specializes in 15th-century European books, maritime and scientific history, and Renaissance cartography, among other things. Yeah…we knew we'd scare you back out into the gardens.

Dining & Shopping

Treat your favorite aunt to afternoon tea in the Rose Garden Tea Room for an all-you-can-eat buffet of scones, tea sandwiches, and petit fours. Reservations are required (626-683-8131). For a more casual snack or sandwich, try the adjoining café (although it'll cost you about as much as lunch at the Tea Room). If you're harboring romantic (or thrifty) fantasies of picnicking in the gardens, we will crush them for you right now: the Huntington has a strict "no picnics" policy.

The Huntington's spacious gift shop stocks coffee-table books and scholarly titles relating to its varied collections—it's the perfect place to score Mother's Day presents.

How to Get There—Driving

The Huntington is adjacent to Pasadena in the city of San Marino, about 12 miles northeast of downtown Los Angeles. The Huntington has two entrance gates: one on Oxford Road and one at Allen Avenue, just south of California Boulevard.

From the Harbor or Pasadena Freeways (110): Take the 110 N towards Pasadena where it turns into Arroyo Parkway. Turn right on California Boulevard and continue for about three miles. At Allen Avenue, turn right and proceed two blocks to the Huntington's gates.

Foothill Freeway (210): Traveling westbound on the 210, exit at the Allen Avenue off-ramp in Pasadena. Turn left and drive south for two miles to the Huntington's gates. Traveling eastbound on the 210, exit at Hill Avenue and drive alongside the freeway for about three blocks. Turn right at Allen Avenue and head south for two miles to the Huntington's gates.

Santa Monica Monica Freeway (10): Take the 10 E to the 110 N and follow the above directions for the 110.

From San Bernardino Freeway (10): Exit at San Gabriel Boulevard and go north for three miles. Turn left on Huntington Drive and continue for one mile, then make a right on Monterey Road. Bear right onto Oxford Road and continue to the Huntington's gates.

How to Get There—Mass Transit

The Metro Gold Line (Allen Avenue stop) and a few MTA bus routes (the 79 and the 379) stop between one to 1.5 miles from the Huntington. For the most updated routes visit www.mta.net or www.foothilltransit.org.

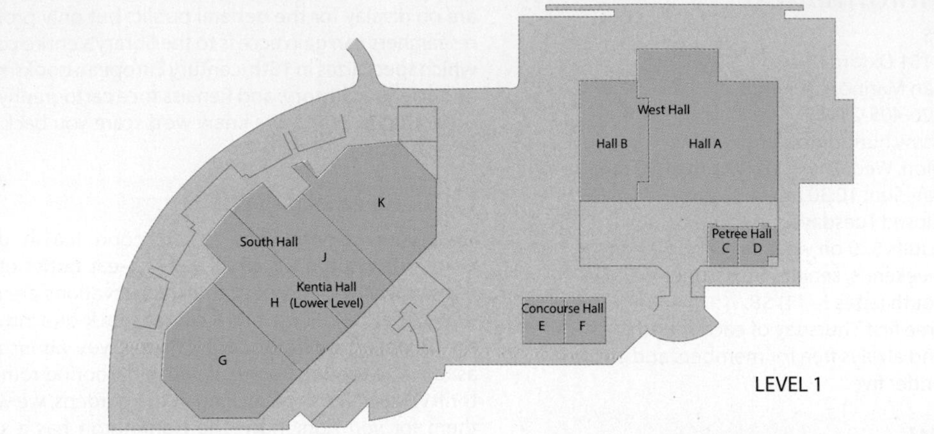
West Hall
Hall B
Hall A
Petree Hall
C
D
Concourse Hall
E
F
K
South Hall
J
Kentia Hall
H (Lower Level)
G
LEVEL 1

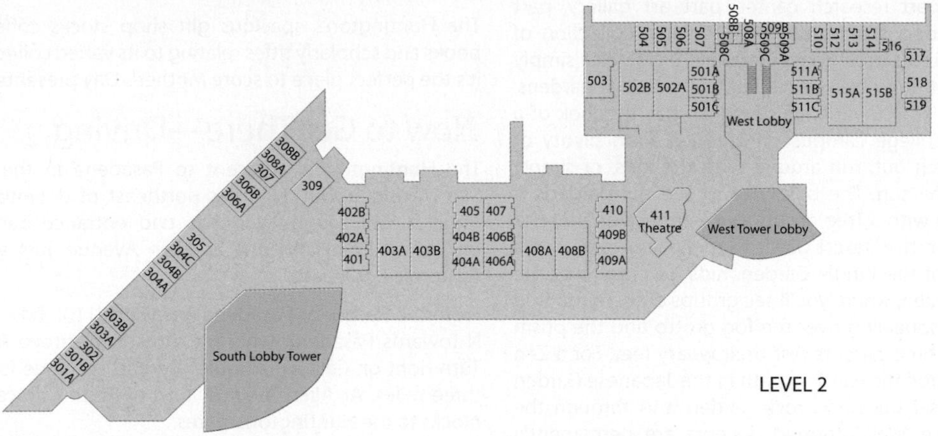
504
505
506
507
508B
508A
508C
509B
509C
509A
510
512
513
514
516
517
518
519
503
502B
502A
501A
501B
501C
511A
511B
511C
515A
515B
West Lobby
410
409B
409A
411
Theatre
West Tower Lobby
402B
402A
401
403A
403B
405
407
404B
406B
404A
406A
408A
408B
309
308B
308A
307
306B
306A
305
304C
304B
304A
303B
303A
302
301B
301A
South Lobby Tower
LEVEL 2

W 7th St
W 8th St
W 8th Pl
Corydon Dr
W 10th Pl
Connecticut St
W 11th St
S Bonnie Brae St
S Westlake Ave
Valencia St
Sunbury St
Georgia St
Francisco St
Cottage Pl
Cherry St
S Bixel St
Ottawa Ct
110
Alvarado Ter
Powers Pl
W Pico Blvd
W 12th St
W 12th Pl
Albany St
Blaine St
W 10th Pl
S Flower St
S Hope St
W Olympic Blvd
W 9th St
Federal Reserve
Magnolia Ave
Arapahoe St
Courtland St
Malvern Ave
S Burlington Ave
W 14th St
MAP 8
LA Convention Center
STAPLES Center
PAGE 231
S Grand Ave
S Olive St
Midway Pl
Blackstone Ct
S Broadway
Hill St
S Hoover St
Constance St
S Union Ave
Toberman St
Venice Blvd
Bond St
Cherry St
S Hall Dr
W 12th Dr
Gilbert Lindsay Dr
W 11th St
S Pembroke Ln
MAP 9
W 17th St
W 18th St
W 15th St
Oak St
Convention Ctr Dr
Pico
W 12th St
Wright St
Figueroa Dr
S Figueroa St
W Pico Blvd
Transamerica Center
E 11th St
Magnolia Ave
Wilmot St
Arapahoe St
W Washington Blvd
15th Dr
Lebanon St
S Flower St
S Pembroke Ln
S Hope St
Catesby Ln
Cameron Ln
Margo St
S Olive St
Midway Ln
W 14th Pl
E 12th St
10

General Information

ꟷFT Maps:	8 & 9
ꟷddress:	1201 S Figueroa St Los Angeles, CA 90015
ꟷhone:	213-741-1151
ꟷebsite:	www.lacclink.com

Overview

'es, it's ugly and, yes, the parking is outrageously overpriced, but ooner or later you'll probably find yourself wandering through he large, airy halls with a glazed look in your eyes. And you'll ›robably drop a bundle on some home improvement gewgaw, :ar, cruise, or brand-new personality. (They sometimes rent out heir meeting rooms for EST-like marathon weekends.) Recent hows have included the 50th Annual LA Boat Show, Wizard Vorld, and Erotica LA. For years the LACC was home to the E3 :lectronic Entertainment Expo, but E3 has since undergone estructuring that will diffuse the rabidly popular annual trade how. Not to worry—the calendar of events never goes slack: :ue Baby Celebration LA, Star Wars Celebration VII, and the Vomen of Destiny and Purpose Conference!

'he Convention Center is impossible to miss from the street, ınd its glass-and-girder exterior is clearly visible from both he 10 and 110 Freeways. That doesn't mean you can actually jet to it, but it will appear comfortingly close as you pass a ›leasant hour cruising through the downtown one-way street ystem. The building's design allows for a maximum amount ıf natural light to flood the lobbies and concourses, in stark :ontrast to the windowless exhibit halls and meeting rooms, vhere it's easy to lose track of time—especially if you keep 'our eyes on the floor; thanks to an art installation in the '90s, map of the world flanks the floor of the main lobby, while constellation map blankets the floor of the upstairs lobby. 'he Convention Center has three major exhibit halls, West Hall, outh Hall, and Kentia Hall (located beneath South Hall), as vell as fifty-four meeting rooms. It's possible to book anything rom a small, intimate gathering for less than twenty people to large-scale event for over 20,000. The really big exhibitions, ke the Auto Show, tend to be held in either the South or West Halls—sometimes even both.

How to Get There—Driving

ocated just a stone's throw from STAPLES Center at the ıtersection of the Santa Monica Freeway (10) and the Harbor Freeway (110), the Los Angeles Convention Center is theoretically) easily accessible from any part of LA. The simplest ıption is to exit the 110 at Pico Boulevard and head north. But if ou're coming from the West Side or Central Los Angeles area, 'ou may be better off skipping the freeways altogether and ısing either Olympic or Pico Boulevards to get downtown. The :onvention Center's cross street is Figueroa Street.

Parking

There are five parking structures available to patrons of the Convention Center that all charge $12 per day. Parking for the West Hall is located just north of Pico Boulevard. Make a right turn at the intersection of Cherry Street and 12th Street into the parking garage. To park near the South Hall, look for Convention Center Drive just off Venice Boulevard on the center's south side.

How to Get There—Mass Transit

Mass transit. Great concept. The Metro Blue Line stops on Pico Boulevard for both the Convention Center and STAPLES Center. This is a convenient alternative from the Valley, as well as the South Bay.

Buses 30, 31, 81, 381, 439, 442, 444, 445, 446, 447, 460, LX422, LX423, LX448, and LX419 also stop near the Convention Center.

Where to Eat

Pack a lunch. If you must eat-in, the Galaxy Café located in the lobby of the West Building is probably the center's nicest. (Bear in mind this is a relative recommendation. You don't go to the Convention Center to eat. You go to buy cars, Jacuzzis, or all-inclusive package deals. Consider, then, that you're actually dining at your local car dealership or travel agent.) It offers the option of outdoor seating and boasts a full bar (should you be at the Center against your will and need a power hour), though it's only open for breakfast and lunch. Inside the South Building is the more casual Compass Café, which offers a variety of sandwiches, salads, and beverages. Do not, under any circumstances, patronize the concession stands inside both the West and South exhibit halls. We're talking airport prices and sad-looking food. If it's all too depressing, you can always head for Gordon Biersch, a full bar famous for its microbrews.

Better to get some fresh air and take a stroll to some of the local landmarks surrounding the center. Here are some nearby eateries that are worth a visit:

- **Philippe's the Original,**
  1001 N Alameda St, 213-628-3781.
  Fabulous deli. They supposedly invented the French Dip sandwich. Would you even think of ordering anything else?
- **Original Pantry Café,**
  877 S Figueroa St, 213-972-9279.
  American/comfort food. The restaurant never closes. It's a LA landmark, known for heaping helpings of American classics cooked from scratch.
- **Langer's,**
  704 S Alvarado St, 213-483-8050.
  Deli menu. Their pastrami sandwich is legendary.
- **Pacific Dining Car,**
  1310 W Sixth St, 213-483-6000.
  Steaks and chops. This meat-and-potatoes restaurant is a LA institution that leaves the engine running 24 hours.

General Information

Address: 26101 Magic Mountain Pkwy
Valencia, CA 91355
Phone: 661-255-4100 or 818-367-5965
Website: www.sixflags.com/magicmountain
Hours: Open year-round. Hours are generally 10 am–10 pm, but vary daily. See website for specific hours and dates.
Entry: $64.99 adult fare, $39.99 for kids under 48" free for kids 2 and under for Magic Mountain; $37.99 adult fare, $29.99 for kids under 48", free for kids 2 and under for Hurricane Harbor

Overview

The more viable option for those who prefer thrill rides to the G-rated fairy fare over in Anaheim. Though Six Flags, who acquired Magic Mountain in 1979, toyed with selling the park in 2006, a recent Q1 announcement showed that the Mountain would prevail. With the debut of the flying coaster Tatsu in 2006, Magic Mountain officially set the record (beating out Cedar Point in Ohio) for most roller coasters at a theme park with a whopping 17 rides; however, Cedar Point has since regained the title and, for the time being, locked it up. Meanwhile, recent additions include Terminator: Salvation and a kiddie land devoted to Thomas the Tank Engine. So maybe the mighty Mountain has to forfeit its title—for now—but it unequivocally holds the record for the highest concentration of obnoxious preteens in any given place. The motley equation of hormones, sunburn, and skewed centers of gravity combine to effect a navigational free-for-all. Be prepared to swim upstream, and if you're bringing small children, consider leashes.

Tickets

Reduced rates are available for advance purchase through the website and via promotions throughout the season. You can also look for discounted deals at Ralphs supermarkets, as well as on specially marked cans of Coke. For those who live within 300 miles of the park, Season Passes are undoubtedly the best deal—a one-time cost of $69.99 will buy you a year's worth of long lines and overpriced, greasy food. Individual tickets and season passes can be purchased online at www.sixflagsticketing.com.

For the Kiddies

Bugs Bunny World offers easy-going rides and games for kids 48 inches and under, while Bugs, Yosemite Sam, et al. amble around for photo ops. Goliath Jr., the choo-choo train version of the popular full-sized Goliath, offers mini-thrills for tykes and tired-but-not-to-be-outdone parents alike.

Thrill Rides

The longstanding rival competition with Cedar Point ir Sandusky, Ohio, has upped the ante for Magic Mountain which now houses 17 coasters and boasts 11 worlc records. The jewel of the park is X, a "four-dimensional thrill ride that loops and twists riders strapped tc 360-degree rotating chairs—it's the only ride in the parl worth the sometimes three-hour wait (what's a wait really, to those inured to Southern California freeways?) Park-goers can count on the same long lines at Déjà V and Tatsu, Magic Mountain's newest "flying" rollercoaste Goliath and Scream, both solid steel coasters, are alway worth checking out if the wait at the other three become unbearable.

Hurricane Harbor Water Park

With the exception of a six-story blue-and-yellow funne slide known as Tornado, Hurricane Harbor typically offer the same water slides and kiddie pools as most wate parks. Expect speed slides, wave pools, and a "scenic inner-tube river.

Insider Tips

To avoid the extremely long lines and young crowds, w suggest you visit on a weekday during the school yea The theme park is also sprawled across a mountain (henc the oh-so-creative name), so expect to give your thigh a solid workout while climbing up and down the park' hills. Comfortable shoes are an absolute necessity, as i sneaking in your own bottled water—unless you don' mind dropping $15 on a day's worth of H_20.

Make a Night of It

Where to stay in or near Valencia:

- **Country Side Inn,** 14955 Roxford St, Sylmar, 866-427-3219
- **Holiday Inn Express,** 27513 Wayne Mills Pl, Valencia, 661-284-2101
- **Rodeway Inn,** 31558 Castaic Rd, Castaic, 661-295-1100
- **Hilton Garden Inn,** 27710 The Old Road, Valencia, 661-254-8800
- **Best Western Valencia,** 27413 Wayne Mills Pl, Valencia, 661-255-0555

How to Get There

Take I-5 north to the Magic Mountain Parkway exit. 200 brought a plan to widen the Magic Mountain Parkwa and the erection of a new retaining wall, which mean an ongoing detour is in place for the northbound I- off-ramp. But with a little magic you'll get there just fine Parking costs $15 per day.

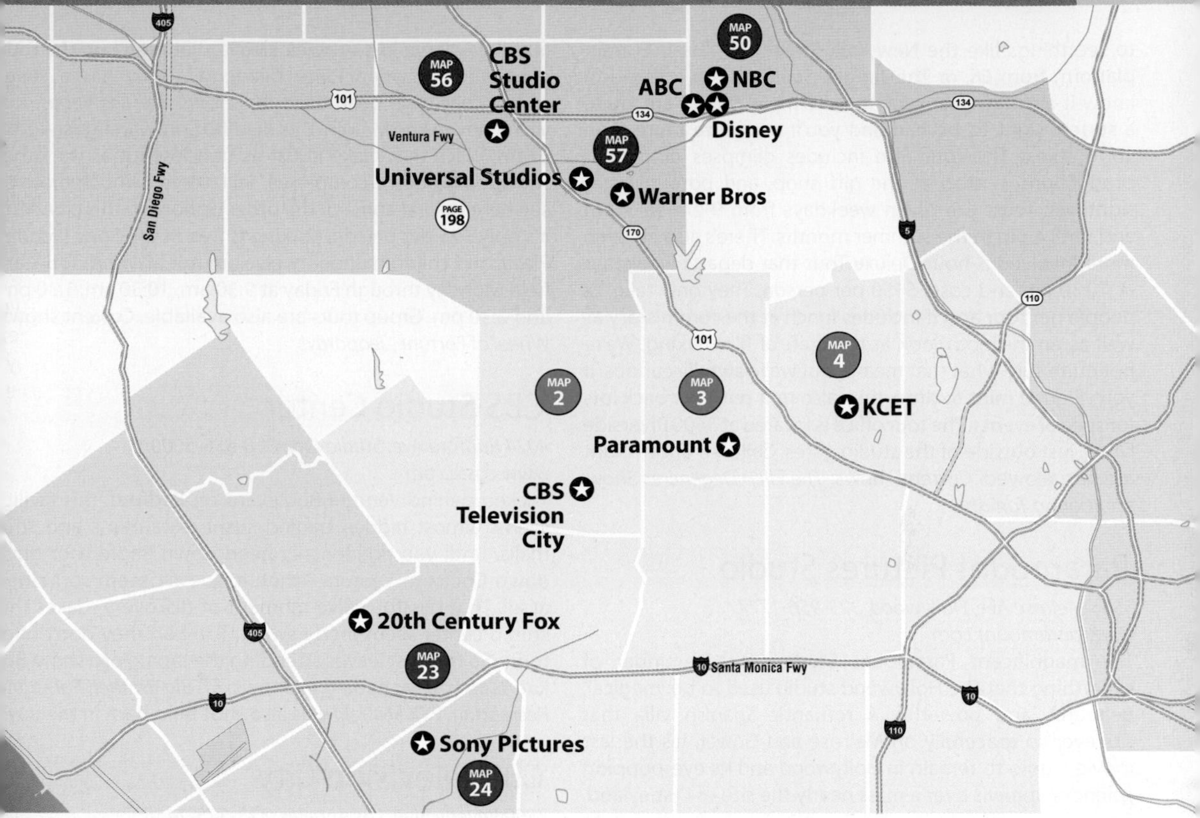

Overview

)epending upon whom you ask, LA is many things: a ashion capital of the US, the modern purveyor of the raw ood diet, or the center of the real estate universe. But with he past century of its history and the most current Census ureau report at hand, we're pretty sure it's safe to say that A is the mecca of the film and television industries. In the ity that coined the word "tourism," those industries are rimed to cart and prod you through the mazes of their tudios; but don't be fooled, as all Tinsel Town tours are not reated equal.

e you resident, tourist, or the next Martin Scorsese, nowing what you're in for could save you hours of ustration. The studios aren't what they used to be, as nyone who survived the strike with payroll intact can tell ou. The studios are sliding ever more toward operating as iant service providers to production companies. Post – /11, the days when Steven Spielberg stole away from his our at Universal and faked employment there until he was fficially hired are long gone. Many tours were cancelled or ave changed since then, and security is tighter at some tudios than it is at LAX. So expect to bring photo ID to all ours and make reservations. But there is still some good tuff out there and plenty of tourist-y fun to be had. Just eep your ears to the ground: changes are afoot. The WB and UPN have joined forces to form the CW (CBS Warner Bros.) in Burbank (much to the chagrin of UPN employees who were accustomed to staying on the proper side of the hill). CBS is looking to move its operations over to the Valley completely, making it a regular bastion of network television and film production. So take our suggestions below and keep alert. LA's entertainment industry redefines itself more frequently than the Madonna of yesteryear.

Warner Bros. Studio

4000 Warner Blvd, Burbank, 818-977-8687; vipstudiotour.warnerbros.com

The Warner Bros. Studios tour is the créme de la créme of studio tours. The Warner Bros. lots in Burbank are like a miniature Disneyland. The buildings look like decorative castles with towering posters of the popular shows taped at the studio, and its renowned WB emblem looms over the gates of its main building. When the average person pictures a California studio with row upon row of cream-colored square buildings lined with crisscrossing little roads and palm trees, this is it. On their 2 1/4-hour VIP Tour (this is the basic tour, but for $52 per person, you'd better be a VIP), you'll be driven about the 100-acre facility on a small tram to see things like the New York Street, the raised El train platform from *ER*, or The Jungle. Scoff though a skeptical know-it-all may, many of these simple things are quite a surreal sight to be had and you'll recognize more than you'd think. The tour also includes glimpses of current productions, a stop at the gift shop, and potential star sightings. Tours are given weekdays from 9 am to 3 pm and until 4 pm in the summer months. There's also an even more involved 5-hour Deluxe Tour that departs weekdays at 10:30 am and costs $150 per person. They only take 12 people per tour and it includes lunch at the commissary as well as an in-depth look at the craft of filmmaking. We're not quite sure what that means, but we're awfully curious. If you've got a mint to drop, they also rent out their back lots for special events. The tour office is located at 3400 Riverside Drive, just outside of the studio gates. Children under eight are not allowed. Current shows: *The Ellen Degeneres Show*, and *Conan Tonight*.

Paramount Pictures Studio

5555 Melrose Ave, Hollywood, 323-956-1777; www.paramount.com

The magnificent Paramount Studios is a reminder of everything that the Hollywood studio used to be: magical, beautiful, and powerful. A romantic Spanish villa that sits ever so gracefully off Melrose and Gower, it's the last movie studio to remain in Hollywood and its eye-popping splendor sprawls over a mass nearly the size of Disneyland. From the main gate immortalized in *Sunset Boulevard*, to the iconic Paramount water tower, the studio is as classic as old Hollywood itself. The Paramount Studio's walking tour has been reinstated after a post-9/11 hiatus and, for the film enthusiast, just the chance to walk in the same steps as Gary Cooper, Claudette Colbert, and Audrey Hepburn is enough in itself, as is the chance to have lunch at the studio's famous Commissary. But sadly, the studio tour is a letdown, owing largely to an uninspired itinerary and guides that seem passively interested at best in the studio's rich history. For the $35 ticket price, the tour should definitely allow you to see more than just soundstage exteriors. Our advice? Save your money (and your feet) and take in a TV show taping where you're guaranteed to see the inside of a soundstage—not to mention a famous face or two. Current shows: *Girlfriends, Dr. Phil, Judge Judy*.

Sony Pictures Studios

10202 W Washington Blvd, Culver City, 323-520-TOUR; www.sonypicturesstudios.com

The design and main gate of Sony Pictures Studios are a little too clean and corporate, and their Main Street really does feel like a facade. It's all very Disney-esque, and not in a good way. Though this is the old MGM studio where *The Wizard of Oz* was shot, Sony seems more interested in billing it as the home of *Men in Black* and *Spiderman*. They also have some lots up their sleeve that aren't on the tou over where Hayden Place deadends. Sony has a serie of lots that have been used for shows like *Las Vegas*, bu you'd never know from the distribution-warehouse-look of the place that make it just as nondescript as the othe surrounding office complexes. Still, there is much more t see here than at some of the other options in this city. Alsc it's only $25 per person, parking is free in the Sony Picture Plaza, and children under twelve are not allowed. Tours ar held Monday through Friday at 9:30 am, 10:30 am, 1:30 pm and 2:30 pm. Group tours are also available. Current shows *Wheel of Fortune, Jeopardy!*

CBS Studio Center

4024 Radford Ave, Studio City, 818-655-5000; www.cbssc.com

Tucked behind Ventura Boulevard on Radford, this facilit seems almost hidden behind sushi restaurants and stri malls, until you accidentally head down Radford or driv down Colfax to Ventura—then it doesn't seem so hidde at all. That blissful, naive moment of discovery makes thi studio center seem pretty sweet. Too bad they don't offe tours. So that just leaves attending the taping of a show. Bu kudos to you for finding it! Shows: *ET, Big Brother, Parks an Recreation*. FYI: *Seinfeld* was also shot here back in the day.

CBS Television City

7800 Beverly Blvd, Los Angeles, 323-575-2458; www.cbs.com

Not to be confused with CBS Studio Center, Television Cit films such gems as *The Price is Right* and *The Late Late Show* If you want to see a taping and you don't care which shov it is, you can walk up to the studio's ticket office (near th corner of Beverly & Fairfax) and pick up tickets. If you'r after tickets for a specific show, you'll need to call 323 575-2458 (live) or 323-575-2449 (*The Price is Right* recorde hotline) in advance.

NBC Studios

3000 W Alameda Ave (at Bob Hope Dr), Burbank, 818-840-3537; www.nbc.com

NBC is the only television studio in LA to offer tours. Fror the outside it looks like a bland corporate office buildin and it's not exactly in a lively section of Burbank. To top tha off, it's only a 70-minute walking tour and—sorry to spo the surprise–it's basically just a visit to *The Tonight Shov* set. However, entry can be gained for the bargain pric of $7.50 for adults, $6.75 for seniors, $4 for children age 5–12, and free for kids under 5. They do take you deep int the belly of NBC (even if it's just a lot of viewing-from-afa and standing-behind-the-velvet-rope kind of deal). Mayb empty sets, display cases, and seeing Jay Leno's parkin space is your thing – meaning you weren't a Conan fan.

ot, you can always just go to see a taping of *The Tonight how*, and lining up for free tickets to shows with a live tudio audience might even be more fun. If you do plan on eeing *The Tonight Show*, tickets are available in person the ay of taping or in advance by mail. We suggest you phone head for availability if you plan on lining up, otherwise you night just get a good view of the corporate building with o glimpse at Leno's parking space to soften the blow.

ABC TV

300 Riverside Dr, Burbank, 818-460-7477; www.abc.com
he ABC TV Studios have been recently relocated to the isney Studio lot in Burbank. The studios still do not offer ublic tours, but tickets to some shows can be obtained. or more information, visit the network's website to find out vhich ticket agents provide free tickets to shows such as *merica's Funniest Home Videos* and *Dancing with the Stars*.

Disney Studios

00 S Buena Vista St, Burbank, 818-560-1000; www.disney.com
there's one thing Disney can do better than anyone else, s set up a great photo op. And that's pretty much all you an do at the Walt Disney Studios: take a picture of the laborate stone and glass building and the 160-foot stone tatues of the Seven Dwarfs seemingly holding up the ont of its roof. The studio is closed to the public, which eally is a pity because it's a Disney fan's dream. You can vander through the hugely impressive prop warehouse vhere a good deal of the stuff is quite recognizable (like Madonna's *Evita* portrait), you can ogle at an original Multiplane camera on display (the pioneering technology nat made *Snow White and the Seven Dwarfs* possible), there re trailers belonging to people like, say, Jennifer Garner, nd the studio also hosts a lovely miniature museum with verything from Mary Poppins' iconic blue dress to vintage Mickey memorabilia and an impressive art archive. The ack lot's manicured lanes and lawns are typical, formulaic isney: homogenous and sterile, but it's a formula we're all uckers for, admit it. The studio would make for a killer tour nd also make a lot of fans happy—but you'll just have to nake do with snapping a picture at the main gate.

KCET Studio

401 W Sunset Blvd, Hollywood, 323-953-5238; www.kcet.org
CET, the local public television (PBS) station Channel 3, is a historic studio where classics like *The Jazz Singer* ere filmed. Sadly, they have temporarily suspended free alking tours for security reasons.

Universal Studios

100 Universal City Plz, Universal City, 800-UNIVERSAL; www.universalstudios.com
If this studio tour feels like a theme park ride, that's because it is. Universal Studios is really more like 60% theme park, 40% studio, and the theme park features are certainly more famous. The studio itself is part of the Universal City experience, which includes the CityWalk, a mini Las Vegas of restaurants, shops, stores, and a movie theater. As you ride their tram tour, you'll suffer the onslaught of *Jaws* and *King Kong*. There are several rides and shows within the park for favorite spectacle blockbusters like *Back to the Future*, *Jurassic Park*, *Terminator*, and *War of the Worlds*. There are TV shows taped here as well, and film production is always in full swing, but the theme park experience—standing in the extremely long lines after the $61 ticket price—can become somewhat trying. Nevertheless, Universal Studios remains a tour favorite—you just can't get attacked by a shark and a giant ape on the same day anywhere else. If you do decide to take this wild ride, try visiting their website before you go as they often have special reduced rate offers and deals that allow free entry for the rest of the year with the purchase of a full price ticket.

20th Century Fox

10201 W Pico Blvd, Century City; www.fox.com
You can see this studio by heading south down Avenue of the Stars (though this is a misnomer of a street, really), and it'll be on your right just before Pico. Much of what used to be this studio's back lots were sold off to make room for the Century City shopping centers. The facilities that have remained or relocated continue to shoot movies and television. Most of these television shows do not require live audiences, but you can get tickets for the few shows, like *Reba*, by contacting Audiences Unlimited (see below).

Audiences Unlimited

Audiences Unlimited is an agency that distributes free tickets to the tapings of television shows. Call 818-753-3470, visit www.tvtickets.com, or get tickets through the mail (include an SASE) by writing to Audiences Unlimited, 100 Universal City Plz, Bldg 153, Universal City, CA 91608. Be sure to specify the name of the show, date, and number of people in your party. However, we suggest visiting the website or calling the company directly. The tickets are free, so they don't exactly have trouble handing them out.

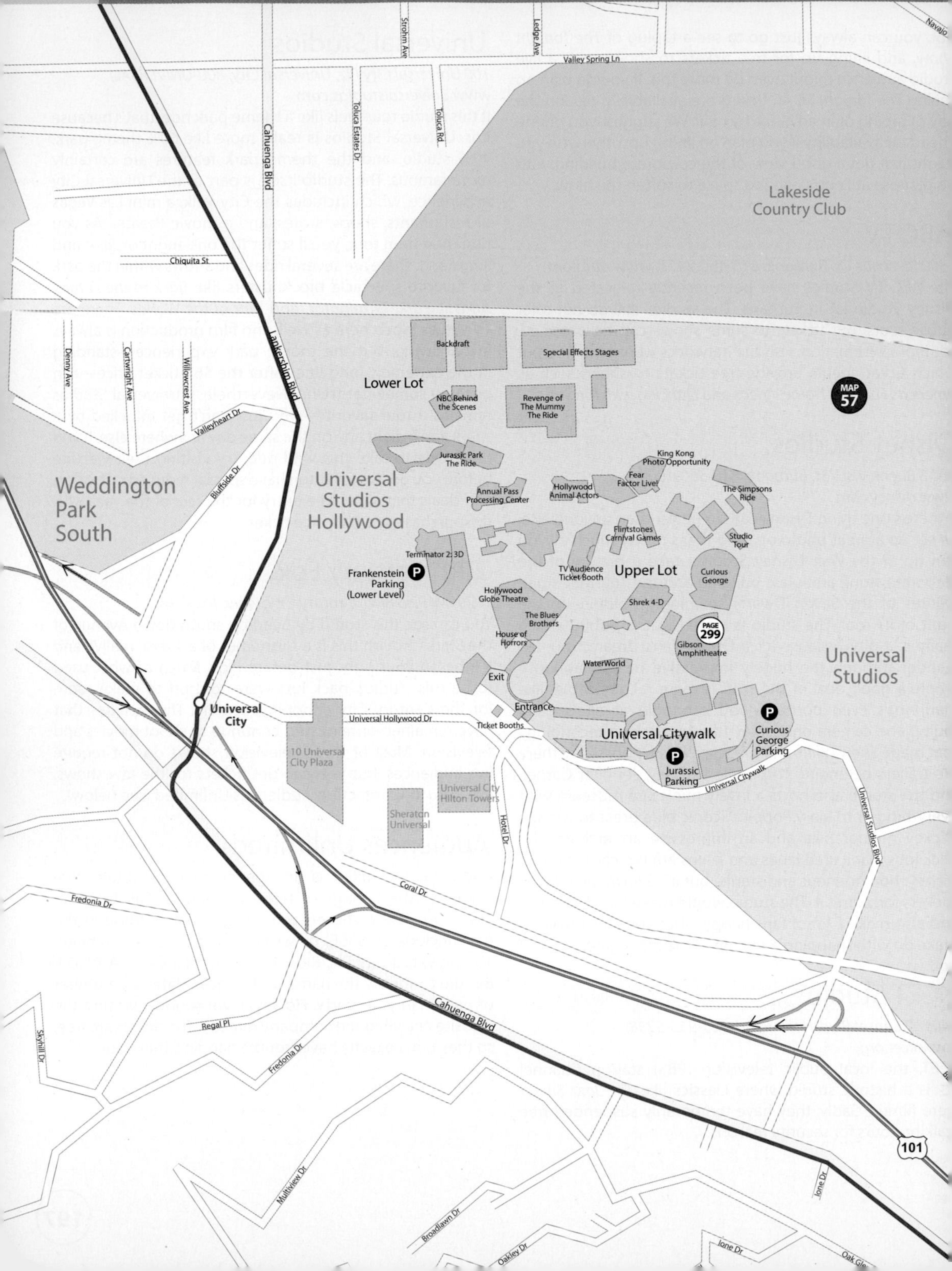
Navajo
Strohm Ave
Ledge Ave
Valley Spring Ln
Toluca Estates Dr
Toluca Rd
Cahuenga Blvd
Lakeside Country Club
Chiquita St
Lankershim Blvd
Denny Ave
Cartwright Ave
Willowcrest Ave
Valleyheart Dr
Backdraft
Special Effects Stages
Lower Lot
NBC Behind the Scenes
Revenge of The Mummy The Ride
MAP 57
Bluffside Dr
Weddington Park South
Jurassic Park The Ride
King Kong Photo Opportunity
Universal Studios Hollywood
Annual Pass Processing Center
Hollywood Animal Actors
Fear Factor Live!
The Simpsons Ride
Flintstones Carnival Games
Studio Tour
Terminator 2: 3D
Frankenstein Parking (Lower Level)
TV Audience Ticket Booth
Upper Lot
Curious George
Hollywood Globe Theatre
Shrek 4-D
The Blues Brothers
House of Horrors
PAGE 299
Gibson Amphitheatre
Universal Studios
WaterWorld
Exit
Entrance
Universal City
Universal Hollywood Dr
Ticket Booths
Universal Citywalk
Curious George Parking
10 Universal City Plaza
Jurassic Parking
Universal Citywalk
Universal City Hilton Towers
Sheraton Universal
Hotel Dr
Universal Studios Blvd
Fredonia Dr
Coral Dr
Cahuenga Blvd
Regal Pl
Skyhill Dr
Fredonia Dr
101
Multiview Dr
Ione Dr
Broadlawn Dr
Oakley Dr
Ione Dr
Oak Gle

General Information

IFT Map:	57
ddress:	100 Universal City Plaza Universal City, CA 91608
ark Information:	800-UNIVERSAL
pecial Events:	818-622-3036
ost & Found:	818-622-3522
iroup Sales:	800-959-9688 x2
Vebsite:	www.universalstudioshollywood.com

Overview

you live in Hollywood, you've probably a) seen a movie being lmed during your daily commute, b) been to a show taping, c) vorked as an extra, or d) all of the above. Universal Studios, with s hissing animatronic Jaws and silly stunt shows, doesn't offer nuch of an escape from your daily grind.

lowever, if you've got out-of-town guests, send them to niversal immediately; it rivals Disneyland with its interactive ttractions for both kids (*Shrek 4-D*) and adults (the new *Fear actor Live*). Aunt Mary will flip when she sees *Desperate lousewives'* Wisteria Lane and Uncle Jerry can channel his nner Tom Cruise while viewing the actual set of *War of the Vorlds*. The park is much more manageable than the Happiest lace on Earth, and rides, like *Revenge of the Mummy*, are lways improving. Plus, now that the much-hyped *Simpsons* de is completed, you can expect a correlative increase in andemonium.

ust outside the theme park gates, CityWalk truly embraces ne concept of Hollywood hype. Garish storefronts beckon ou into knick-knack shops and the restaurant roster reads like condensed sampling of LA's most popular eateries: Saddle anch Chop House, Wolfgang Puck Café, and Daily Grill all have ocations here. Even locals come out to appreciate movies at ne 19-screen CityWalk Cinemas, (call 818-508-0711 for movie mes), music at B.B. King's Blues Club, and seasonal treats like a vintertime outdoor skating rink. The new VIP Party Pass gives ou access to all CityWalk clubs with a couple of free drinks and ride on Saddle Ranch's mechanical bull thrown in. (You'll pay or it the morning after.)

Hours of Operation

niversal Studios is open all year (except Thanksgiving and hristmas), but operating hours are subject to change without otice, so call the park or check the website before you plan our visit. Typically the park is open from 9 am until 9 pm on veekends during peak times, and 9 am until 8 pm during busy veekdays. During the slower months, it's open from 10 am until pm. But again, check before you go.

Entrance Fees

ne-day tickets cost $80 for adults and $72 for those under 48 nches tall. Children 2 and under—regardless of height—are ee. Book tickets online using Universal's Print@Home option avoid the lines. If money is no object, consider purchasing ne Front of Line Pass for $139-$159, which allows you to cut to the front of the line for rides and snag the best seats in the house for any performance.

Check the website for packages and deals like the Southern California CityPass which allows you to visit multiple parks in SoCal at a flat rate. Promotions are abundant during high season and vary wildly, so be sure to check everything from the supermarket to your empty Coke can for special coupons.

Lockers

Cash – and credit card–operated rental lockers are located just inside the park at varying costs depending on size. And since they're inside the park, you can keep adding junk as the day goes by.

Package Delivery

If you buy merchandise within the park and you don't feel like schlepping it around, there's a handy delivery service that will have your parcels waiting for you as you leave. The pickup point is located near the exit at Universal Film Co.

Kennels

If you can't bear to leave your pet at home or if you're passing through on a longer journey, Universal provides a complimentary kennel service for park guests. Go to the Guest Services window at the entrance to the park, and your pet will be escorted to the facilities by one of the guest service representatives.

How to Get There—Driving

Universal Studios Hollywood is located between Hollywood and the San Fernando Valley, just off the 101 Hollywood/ Ventura Freeway. Exit at Universal Center Drive or Lankershim Boulevard and follow the signs to the parking areas.

Parking

Preferred Parking ($20) is located in the Rocky & Bullwinkle Lot and is one of the closest parking lots to the theme park. If you would prefer to park your car yourself, general parking is located in the Curious George Garage, Jurassic Parking Garage, and the Frankenstein and Woody Woodpecker Lots. All are within walking distance to any Universal destination and cost $11 for the day. If you simply must save your cash for that Jurassic Park T-shirt, park at the bottom of the hill and take the free tram to the park.

How to Get There—Mass Transit

Universal Studios is the only Southern Californian theme park accessible by subway. Take the Metro Red Line to Universal City. MTA Buses 96, 150, 152, 156, 163, 166, 240, and 750 also run to Universal City Station. Shuttles, airport, and charter services are available to and from Universal Studios Hollywood with SuperShuttle. A free tram will take you to the top of the hill upon arrival. 800-258-3826; www.supershuttle.com.

Mulholland Dr
Mulholland Dr (unpaved)
MAP 52
MAP 53
MAP 15
Encino Reservoir
Reseda Blvd
Caballero Canyon Trail
Department of Water & Power (No Public Access)
Bent Arrow Trail
Mulholland Dr (unpaved)
San Vincente Mountain
27
Topanga Canyon Blvd
Garapito Canyon Trail
Cheney Fire Rd
Fire Rd 30
Eagle Springs
Hub Junction (2,000 ft)
Musch Meadows
Musch Trail
Camping
Eagle Junction
Eagle Springs Fire Rd
Topanga State Park
Temescal Ridge Trail
Sullivan Ridge Fire Rd
Sullivan Canyon Fire Rd
Old Topanga Canyon Rd
Dead Horse Trail
Entrada Rd
Trippet Ranch
Santa Ynez Canyon Trail
Waterfall
Rogers Rd Trail
Topanga
Canyon Fire Rd
Temescal Ridge Trail
Michael Ln
Lone Oak
Rustic Canyon Trail
Chastain Pkwy
East Topanga Fire Rd
Santa Ynez Reservoir
Palisades Highlands
Skull Rock
Waterfall
Non-Maintained Trail
East Topanga Fire Rd
Bienveneda Trail
Temescal Canyon Trail
Palisades Dr
Temescal Ridge Trail
Bienveneda Ave
Parker Mesa Overlook (1,525 ft)
Will Rogers State Historical Park
Los Liones Trail
Los Liones Dr
Sunset Blvd
Temescal Canyon Rd
Sunset Blvd
Pacific Coast Hwy
Topanga State Beach
Pacific Coast Hwy
1
Santa Monica Bay

General Information

NFT Maps:	15, 16, 52 & 53
Address:	20825 Entrada Rd Topanga, CA 90290
Phone:	310-455-2465
California State Parks Website:	www.parks.ca.gov

Overview

Depending on which translation you accept, *topanga* means "the place above," or "the place where the mountains meet the sea," *or* "the place of green water" (and we just thought it meant "really big"). Located entirely within Los Angeles's city limits (although you wouldn't know it by visiting), Topanga State Park's 11,000 acres make it the largest wilderness located within the boundaries of a major city *in the entire world*. It feels more like New Mexico than Los Angeles. It also has its own community complete with homes, local artists, churches, restaurants, and a historical society—secluded far away from the LA bustle.

Bottom line—it's beautiful. It's *the* place to hit the trails (they've got over 36 miles worth of those) enjoy some nature (take two antihistamines and check out the spring blooms), or bring a book and read trailside. Topanga offers breathtaking views of the ocean and plenty of fresh air—which you'll need once you actually get out of your car and witness just what Mother Nature has in store for you.

Practicalities

The park is open daily from 8 am until dusk. Entry into the park is free, but parking costs $4 per vehicle. Depending on where you hit the trails, street parking is close and free. From Pacific Coast Highway (1), travel north on Topanga Canyon Boulevard, past the post office at the center of the village, then turn right onto Entrada Road. Keep to the left until you reach the park's main parking lot (about one mile). From the Ventura Freeway (101), exit at Topanga Canyon Boulevard, drive south over the crest of the mountains and proceed three miles to Entrada Road and turn left. Follow the above directions from here.

Activities

Topanga is ideal for uninterrupted walking, running, cycling, and horseback riding (although horse rentals are not available at the park). Mountain bikers are supposedly restricted to the fire roads, but they often fly down the pedestrian-only paths anyway. Dogs are not allowed on back-country trails, partly due to the free-roamin' mountain lions. There are many marked trails for hikers, most of which can be accessed from Trippet Ranch (off Entrada Road), a former "gentleman's ranch" used as a weekend escape from the city back in the day. In addition to the Park Office, Trippet Ranch provides parking facilities, picnic areas, and a great little Visitor's Center that offers guided walking tours on Sunday mornings. If it's relaxation, not activity, that you're after, you might want to try the self-guided nature trail (the trail map costs a quarter and is available at the parking lot) or join one of the Sunday guided walks with experts well-versed in the flora and fauna of the area. Call the park for more information about walk schedules.

Topanga's restaurants are worth visiting. Writers, poets, and city people looking to escape bring their laptops, books, and blankets to spend a day by the giant fireplace at **Froggy's Fish Market & Restaurant** (1105 N Topanga Canyon Blvd). In tune with its surroundings, Froggy's serves healthier items on its menu as well as burgers and quesadillas. **Inn of the Seventh Ray** (128 Old Topanga Canyon Rd) is a wildly romantic restaurant with vegan and vegetarian options, but the restaurant's mouth-melting rack of lamb would make anyone eat meat again.

Another visual highlight of the park is the blooming flowers that attract thousands of avid gardeners and photographers each year. For information on the different varieties of flowers that grow in the park, call 818-768-3533.

Hiking Trails

Many of the park's trails can be accessed from Trippet Ranch. The Eagle Springs loop begins at the Eagle Junction, just under two miles from Trippet. A climb up the northern section of the loop will afford you a nice panoramic view of the park. At the eastern end of the Eagle Springs loop, you'll come to the Hub Junction, from where you can take the Temescal Ridge Trail south or the fire road north, or simply circle back and complete the Eagle Springs loop to Trippet Ranch.

To reach the unpaved Mullholland Drive, hike north from Hub Junction, and follow the fire road for two miles through chaparral. Heading south on the Temescal Ridge Trail leads you high above the canyons to gorgeous views of sycamore and oak riparian forests below.

Another option from Trippet Ranch is to walk east to the Topanga Fire Road and then north for a short distance to the Santa Ynez Trail. As you descend into the Santa Ynez Canyon, look out for the crumbly sandstone formations with pockets where moisture collects—there are tiny cliff gardens in these areas. Near the bottom of the trail is a short 0.8-mile trail leading to a lovely waterfall (assuming there's been any rainfall, that is) that's definitely worth a look.

Shorter hikes can be taken from other parking lots in Topanga State Park. From the Los Liones Drive parking lot, you can complete a 1.7-mile loop hike on the Los Liones Trail. For a longer hike, take the East Topanga Fire Road to the Parker Mesa Overlook for stunning views of the canyon. The Overlook can also be accessed from Paseo Miramar. From PCH, take Sunset Blvd north and a left onto Paseo Miramar to the top, then park on the street. The nearly 90-degree climb makes for a great workout with incredible ocean views.

If you park in the first lot on Entrada Road (if you hit Trippet Ranch, you've gone too far), you can take the 1.1-mile Dead Horse Trail to Trippet Ranch.

To access the Caballero Canyon Trail or the Bent Arrow Trail, take Reseda Boulevard into the Caballero Canyon Park lot and head out from there.

Camping

Camping facilities are available on a first-come, first-served basis. Your best bet is to follow the Musch Trail to the Musch Trail Campground, but we recommend contacting the park directly for more information before heading out.

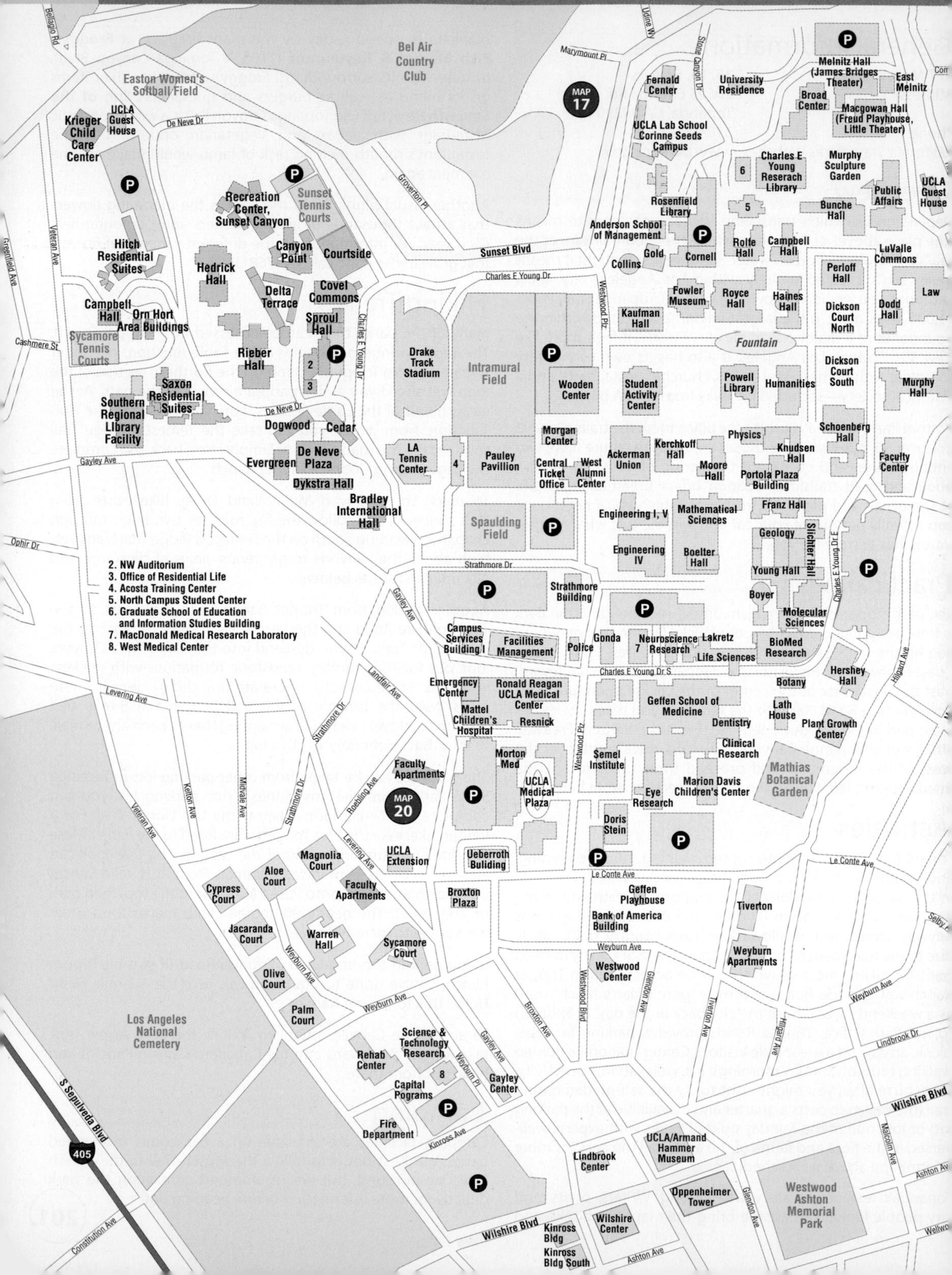
Bellagio Rd
Bel Air Country Club
Udine Wy
Marymount Pl
Stone Canyon Dr
Easton Women's Softball Field
MAP 17
Fernald Center
University Residence
Melnitz Hall (James Bridges Theater)
East Melnitz
Broad Center
Macgowan Hall (Freud Playhouse, Little Theater)
Krieger Child Care Center
UCLA Guest House
De Neve Dr
UCLA Lab School Corinne Seeds Campus
Charles E Young Research Library
Murphy Sculpture Garden
6
UCLA Guest House
Groverton Pl
Public Affairs
Recreation Center, Sunset Canyon
Sunset Tennis Courts
Rosenfield Library
5
Bunche Hall
Anderson School of Management
Hitch Residential Suites
Canyon Point
Courtside
Sunset Blvd
Rolfe Hall
Campbell Hall
LuValle Commons
Greenfield Ave
Veteran Ave
Hedrick Hall
Gold
Cornell
Collins
Charles E Young Dr
Perloff Hall
Law
Delta Terrace
Covel Commons
Westwood Plz
Fowler Museum
Royce Hall
Haines Hall
Dickson Court North
Dodd Hall
Campbell Hall
Orn Hort Area Buildings
Sproul Hall
Kaufman Hall
Cashmere St
Sycamore Tennis Courts
Charles E Young Dr
Drake Track Stadium
Fountain
Rieber Hall
2
Intramural Field
Dickson Court South
3
Powell Library
Humanities
Murphy Hall
Saxon Residential Suites
Wooden Center
Student Activity Center
Southern Regional Library Facility
De Neve Dr
Dogwood
Cedar
Morgan Center
Schoenberg Hall
Physics
Kerchkoff Hall
De Neve Plaza
Knudsen Hall
Faculty Center
Evergreen
LA Tennis Center
4
Pauley Pavillion
Ackerman Union
Central Ticket Office
West Alumni Center
Moore Hall
Portola Plaza Building
Gayley Ave
Dykstra Hall
Bradley International Hall
Franz Hall
Mathematical Sciences
Spaulding Field
Engineering I, V
Geology
Ophir Dr
Slichter Hall
Engineering IV
Boelter Hall
Charles E Young Dr E
Young Hall
Strathmore Dr
2. NW Auditorium
3. Office of Residential Life
4. Acosta Training Center
5. North Campus Student Center
6. Graduate School of Education and Information Studies Building
7. MacDonald Medical Research Laboratory
8. West Medical Center
Strathmore Building
Boyer
Gayley Ave
Molecular Sciences
Campus Services Building I
Facilities Management
Police
Gonda
Neuroscience Research
7
Lakretz
BioMed Research
Life Sciences
Hilgard Ave
Landfair Ave
Charles E Young Dr S
Hershey Hall
Emergency Center
Ronald Reagan UCLA Medical Center
Botany
Levering Ave
Geffen School of Medicine
Lath House
Mattel Children's Hospital
Resnick
Dentistry
Plant Growth Center
Strathmore Dr
Westwood Plz
Clinical Research
Morton Med
Semel Institute
Mathias Botanical Garden
Faculty Apartments
UCLA Medical Plaza
Marion Davis Children's Center
Roebling Ave
MAP 20
Eye Research
Kelton Ave
Midvale Ave
Strathmore Dr
Veteran Ave
Doris Stein
Magnolia Court
Levering Ave
UCLA Extension
Ueberroth Building
Le Conte Ave
Le Conte Ave
Aloe Court
Cypress Court
Faculty Apartments
Broxton Plaza
Geffen Playhouse
Tiverton
Bank of America Building
Selby Ave
Jacaranda Court
Warren Hall
Sycamore Court
Weyburn Ave
Westwood Center
Weyburn Apartments
Weyburn Ave
Olive Court
Westwood Blvd
Glendon Ave
Weyburn Ave
Broxton Ave
Tiverton Ave
Hilgard Ave
Weyburn Ave
Palm Court
Los Angeles National Cemetery
Science & Technology Research
Gayley Ave
Lindbrook Dr
Rehab Center
8
Weyburn Pl
Gayley Center
S Sepulveda Blvd
Capital Programs
Wilshire Blvd
Fire Department
Kinross Ave
UCLA/Armand Hammer Museum
Malcolm Ave
405
Lindbrook Center
Ashton Ave
Westwood Ashton Memorial Park
Oppenheimer Tower
Glendon Ave
Wilshire Blvd
Kinross Bldg
Wilshire Center
Constitution Ave
Kinross Bldg South
Ashton Ave
Wellworth Ave

General Information

NFT Maps: 17 & 20
Address: 405 Hilgard Ave
Los Angeles, CA 90095
Phone: 310-825-4321
Website: www.ucla.edu

Overview

Located on a picturesque campus in Westwood, UCLA is a behemoth public research university that offers 127 undergraduate degree programs and 200 graduate degree programs. Its faculty of Nobel prize laureates, MacArthur grant winners, and National Medal of Science winners has earned UCLA an international reputation for academic excellence. The school has also consistently produced champion sports teams and athletes since it was founded in 1919.

UCLA's Extension Program is extremely popular and offers continuing education for adults in topics ranging from architecture to screenwriting to wine tasting. The courses, offered quarterly, are popular among locals debating career changes, as well as those merely interested in bettering themselves.

Tuition

Tuition estimates for the 2013-14 academic year: $23-32K for California residents, $46-52K for non-residents.

Facilities

The UCLA campus is like a small city – indeed, during the 1984 Olympics, parts of the campus comprised the Olympic Village. UCLA has its own police department and fire marshal, and a range of services including shops, restaurants, post offices, and banks. Eleven parking and information booths located across the campus will aid visitors in their confusion about where to park. UCLA's circular drive loops around the entire campus and is easy to navigate. If you're just popping in, metered parking is available for 25¢ per eight minutes (go heavy on the quarters) or $8 for the entire day. Student parking (granted quarterly through application) is assigned on a need-based point system, which takes into consideration class standing, employment/academic obligations, and commuter distance. An evening van service, which stops every fifteen minutes and traverses the campus starting at Ackerman Union, is available during Fall, Winter, and Spring quarters.

Culture on Campus

UCLA also provides the community with a variety of cultural programs. The university is affiliated with the Geffen Playhouse in Westwood (10886 Le Conte Ave, 310-208-5454), which has been the LA stop for Broadway plays such as *The Weir* and *Wit*. On campus, UCLA LIVE! at Royce Hall (cap.ucla.edu, 310-825-2101) has hosted a wide variety of music, literary, and dance programs, from the Los Angeles Philharmonic to jazz legend Alice Coltrane to French actress Isabelle Huppert. The Fowler Museum of Cultural History holds an impressive collection of art from Africa, Asia, and the Pacific (fowler.ucla.edu, 310-825-4361). The Hammer Museum hosts cutting-edge readings, screenings, and music and art celebrations throughout the year (www.hammer.ucla.edu, 310-443-7000). The annual student talent show, *Spring Sing*, doubles as a convocation for recipients of the George and Ira Gershwin Award, which honors music industry magnates (James Taylor and Burt Bacharach are recent awardees). And each April, UCLA is home to the *Los Angeles Times's* Festival of Books—the literary event of the year.

Sports

You don't need to be affiliated with the university to appreciate the talents of UCLA's athletes, though you'll want to curb any lurking support of the cross-town Trojans. UCLA's top-ten nationally ranked teams include men's water polo, women's soccer, women's volleyball, and men's basketball. For up-to-date information, scores, and schedules, check out the official athletics website at uclabruins.cstv.com. Ticket prices for football and men's basketball games depend on the event. All other sporting events cost $4 with a student ID and $6 without. For tickets, call 310-825-2101.

Department Contact Information

College of Letters & Science	310-825-9009
Graduate Admissions	310-825-7290
Undergraduate Admissions	310-825-3101
Anderson School of Management	310-825-7982
Graduate School of Education and Information Studies	310-825-8326
UCLA Extension (UNEX)	310-826-9971 or 818-784-7006
School of the Arts & Architecture	310-206-6465
The Henry Samueli School of Engineering & Applied Science	310-825-8162
School of Dentistry	310-825-2337
School of Law	310-207-4736
School of Medicine	310-825-6373
School of Nursing	310-825-7181
School of Public Health	310-825-6381
School of Public Affairs	310-206-7568
School of Theater, Film and TV	310-825-5761

General Information

NFT Maps:	11,12 & 40
Mailing Address:	University Park Campus University of Southern California Los Angeles, CA 90089
Location:	University Park, b/w Figueroa St, Exposition Park, Vermont Ave & Jefferson Blvd
Phone:	213-740-2311
Website:	www.usc.edu

Overview

The University of Southern California opened its doors with 53 students in 1880, when the city of Los Angeles was still in its frontier, beta version. Four years later, three of the original 53—one woman, two men—became the first class to graduate from the private school. Enrollment has since jumped to more than 33,000, and the school now straddles two main campuses.

The University Park Campus, home to USC's College of Letters, Arts & Sciences and 15 professional schools, is located three miles south of downtown Los Angeles. Seven miles from the University Par Campus, the 50-acre Health Sciences Campus houses the medica and pharmaceutical schools, as well as programs in occupationa therapy, physical therapy, and nursing. A shuttle bus runs betwee the two campuses approximately every hour throughout the week

USC's film school boasts an impressive pedigree. Its foundin faculty included Douglas Fairbanks and D. W. Griffith, and it ha churned out equally famous alumni, including George Luca and Robert Zemeckis. USC rejected filmmaker Steven Spielberg' application (oops!); he has since sucked up his pride and now sit on the USC Board of Trustees. At least one USC alumnus has bee nominated for an Academy Award every year since 1973. Talk abou hegemony.

Tuition

For the 2013-14 academic year, annual undergraduate tuition an fees will, based on 12-18 units for two semesters, total in excess c $45K. Add in room, board, books, supplies, transportation, and th rest, and your education will approach $62K per year.

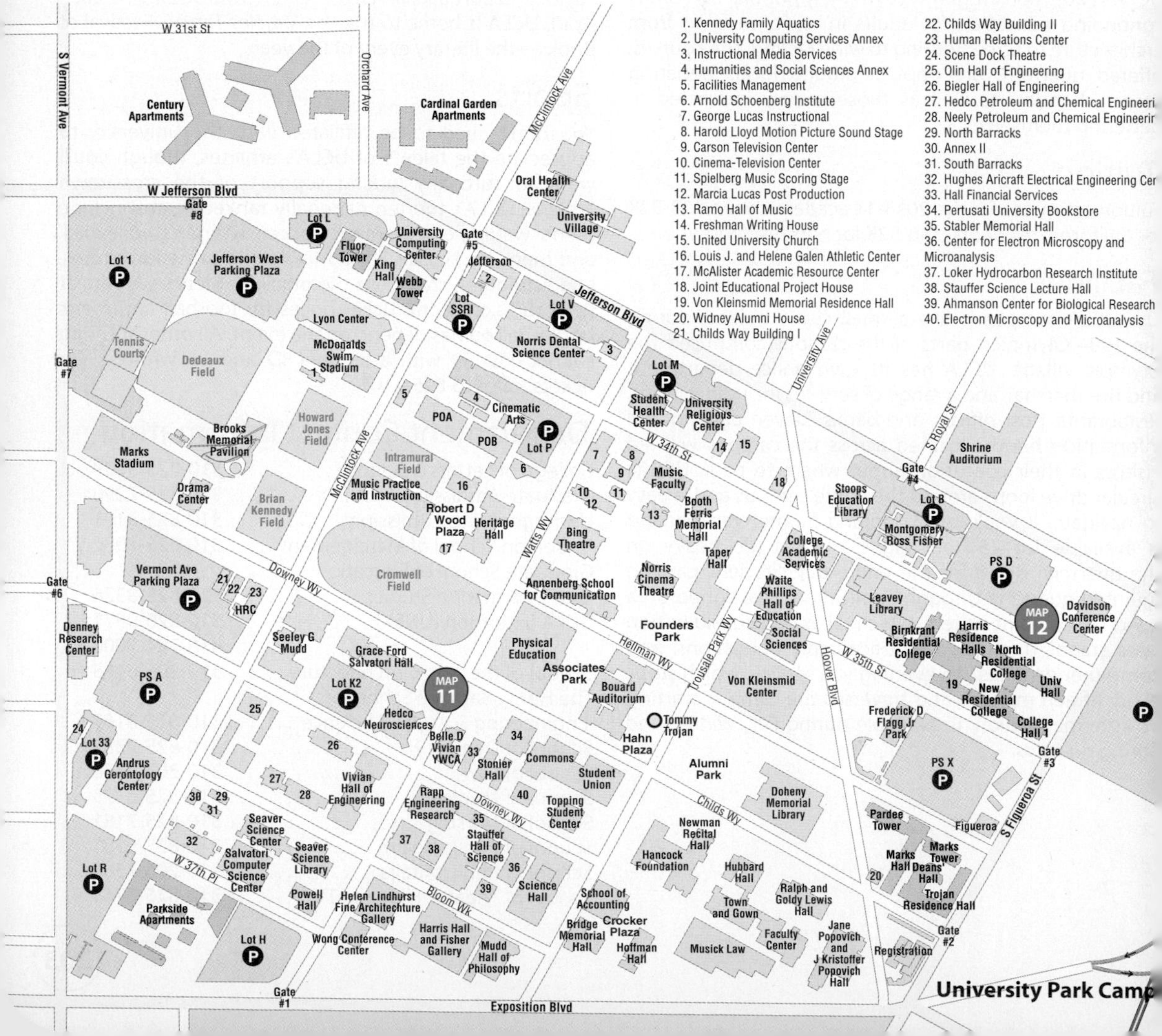

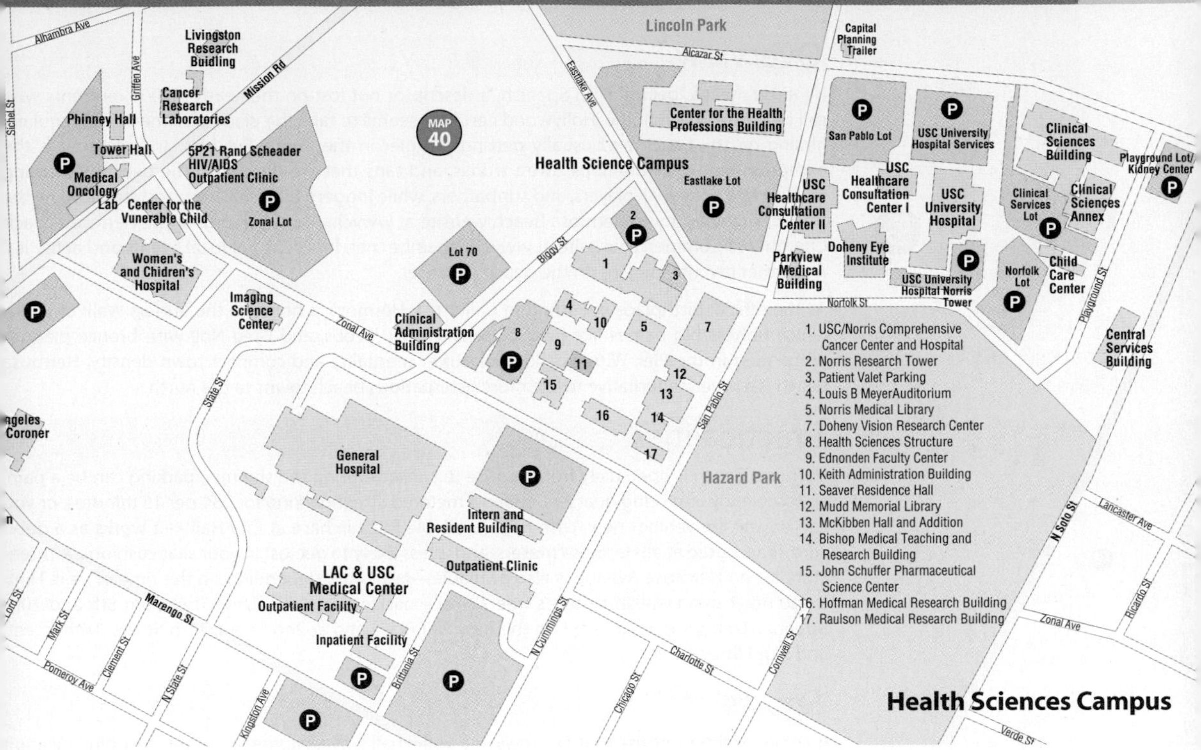

Parking

Parking on campus costs $7. There are also a smattering of one-hour metered parking spaces available, and a couple of lots inside campus offer two-hour parking for $4. Four-hour and two-hour metered parking is available on Figueroa Street and Jefferson Boulevard. $3 – to $5-a-day lots are available Monday through Friday across the street from the campus on Figueroa Street (next to the Sizzler restaurant) and on Jefferson Boulevard (next to the Shrine Auditorium). Parking rates for these lots may vary for special events. Daily rates for parking are $5 in the Parking Center and $8 in all other structures/lots; hourly parking spots are also up for grabs right in front of the Vermont Avenue Parking Plaza (aka PSA).

Culture on Campus

USC hosts a plethora of academic and arts events, from concerts and theater performances to exhibits and public lectures. Many events are inexpensive (if not free) and can be found on the USC website at www.usc.edu/calendar. Throughout the academic year, USC's prestigious Thornton School of Music, USC Fisher Gallery, and the KUSC classical radio station are among the many campus cultural institutions that stage full schedules of arts-related events. For a schedule of performances by the Thornton's symphony, chamber orchestra, wind ensemble, and choir, check out www.usc.edu/music. The USC orchestra also performs regularly at Disney Hall, home of the LA Philharmonic. (Frank Gehry, the architect of the famous performance hall, was a USC man himself!)

Sports

USC's top-ten nationally ranked teams include men's water polo, women's water polo, women's swimming, and women's golf. The USC Trojan football team was the back-to-back 2003 and 2004 National Championship winner and played for the 2005 National Championship, but to the cheer of a particular Westwood rival, lost to the Texas Longhorns at the Pasadena Rose Bowl, despite having two Heisman trophy winners—Reggie Bush and Matt Leinart—on board. For up-to-date information, scores, and schedules, check out the official athletics website at www.usctrojans.com. For tickets, call 213-740-4672.

Department Contact Information

Admissions	213-740-1111
College of Letters, Arts & Sciences	213-740-2531
Leventhal School of Accounting	213-740-4838
School of Architecture	213-740-2723
Marshall School of Business	213-740-6422
School of Cinematic Arts	213-740-2804
Annenberg School for Communication	213-740-6180
School of Dentistry	213-740-2800
Rossier School of Education	213-740-0224
Viterbi School of Engineering	213-740-4530
School of Fine Arts	213-740-2787
Leonard Davis School of Gerontology	213-740-6060
Occupational Science and Occupational Therapy	323-442-2850
Department of Biokinesiology and Physical Therapy	332-442-2900
The Law School	213-740-7331
Keck School of Medicine	323-442-1900
Thornton School of Music	213-740-6935
School of Pharmacy	323-442-1369
School of Policy, Planning & Development	213-740-6842
School of Social Work	213-740-2711
School of Theatre	213-821-2744

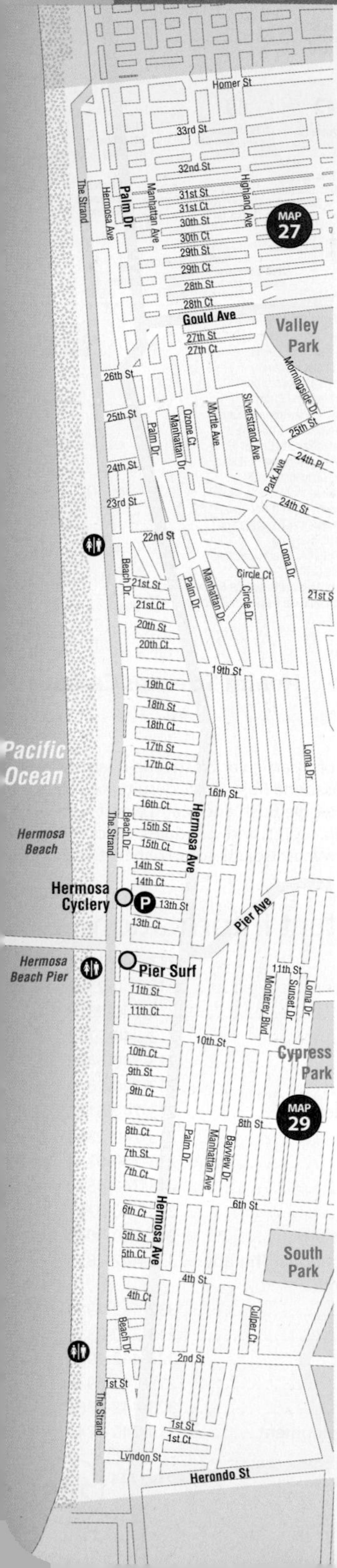

Overview

Hermosa means "beautiful" in Spanish, a descriptor not lost on the nearly 20,000 residents who call Hermosa Beach home. Hollywood certainly seems to take the place at name-value, regularly filming on the beach and usually getting the pier in the frame. But glitz and glamour is the exception here—it's flip-flops, swim trunks, and tans that are the norm. The beach is teeming with surfers, volleyball players, and sunbathers, while joggers, bikers, skaters, and strollers line the Strand. Visit the City of Hermosa Beach website at www.hermosabch.org, or the Hermosa Beach Chamber of Commerce website at www.hbchamber.net, for listings of local events and activities. A summer favorite: movies on the beach at sunset.

As the official birthplace of surfing in California, Hermosa is home to the Surfers Walk of Fame, which honors big names like Bing Copeland, Hap Jacobs, and Greg Noll with bronze plaques embedded in the Pier. With its laid-back surfer mentality and compact town density, Hermosa Beach is a breezy alternative to the more ostentatious beach towns to the north.

Practicalities

Hermosa Beach is open daily from sunrise to sunset. During the summer, parking can be a pain, so come early and bring quarters. There is metered street parking for 25¢ per 15 minutes, or you can try the convenient new "cash key" (available for purchase at City Hall)—it works as a debit card, is accepted at all Hermosa meters, and is less likely to get lost in your seat cushions. A three-story lot on Hermosa Avenue is also available—rates vary depending on the time of year. Hint: if you don't mind walking, there's free 12-hour parking on Valley Drive (between 8th and 10th Streets). Restrooms are located on the new Pier Plaza and at 2nd Street, 11th Street, 14th Street, and 22nd Street.

Sports

It comes as little surprise that TV crews and volleyball players agree to use this beautiful location as a site for nationally televised AVP Volleyball Tournaments. Hermosa's other favorite pastime is honored every year when the International Surf Festival comes to neighboring Manhattan Beach (www.surffestival.org). The three-day event, held annually in August, features an amateur volleyball tournament complete with costumes and lots of libations as well as land activities like a two-mile beach run and a sand castle design contest, along with traditional surf and lifeguard competitions.

Surfing and volleyball lessons are always available right on the beach, as are rental boogie boards, surfboards, or skates. Pier Surf (21 Pier Ave, 310-372-2012), located just up from the Hermosa Beach Pier, rents surfboards for $12 an hour ($35 a day) and boogie boards for $6 an hour ($20 a day) with varying security deposits.

Hermosa Cyclery (20 13th St, 310-374-7816) provides a good selection of rental bikes, boogie boards, skates, umbrellas, and chairs at affordable prices; rates start at $7 an hour ($21 a day) for bikes and $6 an hour ($18 a day) for rollerblades. Check the Hermosa Cyclery website at www.hermosacyclery.com for a complete list of rental offers.

Hermosa Pier

The century-old Hermosa Pier recently got a much-needed renovation. Among the improvements: fresh pylons, resurfacing, more lights, and a new three-story lifeguard station. The pier continues to serve as the epicenter and backdrop for most of the city's main events, including Fiesta Hermosa, a biannual arts and crafts festival.

Shopping

While Roxy and Quiksilver reign supreme in this surf-driven community, there are plenty of diverse shopping opportunities within walking distance of the beach along Pier Avenue, Hermosa Avenue, Artesia Boulevard, and the Pacific Coast Highway. The streets are lined with clothing and jewelry boutiques, Sunglass Huts, antiques showrooms, and quaint general stores featuring beach themed merchandise. If you're after fresh produce or flowers, the Farmers Market, located on Valley Drive (between 8th and 10th Streets), is open every Friday from noon until 4 pm, rain or shine.

Overview

Manhattan Beach is like Beverly Hills' younger, hotter sister. The houses, people and clothes surpass anything you'd see in the 90210. Multi-million dollar homes line the well-tended shorefront of the public beaches here. There's no shortage of hip boutiques or places to eat in this beach community. Park your car and spend the afternoon walking down Manhattan Beach Boulevard and Manhattan Avenue for shops galore. Choose from on-the-run dining like a tasty beef pastrami sandwich from Papa Jake's or splurge on trendy Greek food at Petros Restaurant. But the beach here is really where its at—soak in the marvelous rays and miles of sand as you head out for volleyball, surfing, boogie boarding, body surfing, swimming, diving, and fishing.

For information about activities and events in the area, check out the City of Manhattan Beach website at www.ci.manhattan-beach.ca.us, or the Chamber of Commerce website www.manhattanbeachchamber.com.

Practicalities

Manhattan Beach is open daily from sunrise until midnight. There are six metered parking lots and three free lots within walking distance of the beach. If you want good parking, though, you'd better get there early, as the conveniently located lots fill up fast. An underground parking facility, located at 1220 Morningside Drive, has 260 long-term meter spots and 200 short-term meter spots. If you're looking to park your Beamer convertible for beach time and you're short on cash, arrive early at Lot 3 off Valley Drive; the lot has 51 free spaces. Metered street parking is available, but one quarter buys you a measly 15 minutes. Note: during December, the city offers free three-hour parking at some meters as a little holiday gift to the diehard beach lovers.

Restrooms

Clean restrooms and showers are located at the end of the pier as well as at 8th Street, Manhattan Beach Boulevard, Marine Street, and 40th Street.

Sports

Surfers, boogie boarders, and body surfers all find decent breaks at Manhattan Beach, especially in El Porto (North Manhattan Beach). Everyone's happy to share the waves, but you gotta know your place: surfers go to the south of the pier, boogie boarders to the north, and everyone rides the waves in fear of infringing upon the posted swimming areas and enraging the lifeguards. For the land-loving folk, the bike path on the Strand separates the wheels from the pedestrians. There are plenty of volleyball nets (usually occupied by very tanned and toned athletes). The kiddies can enjoy the swing sets scattered along the beach.

Manhattan Pier

The pier at Manhattan Beach is a basic, no frills place, but it's worth a trip to see. Spend some contemplative time taking in the ocean and waves or fish off the pier. If you take a walk to the end, you'll reach the Roundhouse Marine Lab & Aquarium, an oceanographic teaching station. It's a small two-story building with a sampling of marine-life tanks and a touch pool. It is open to the public from 3 pm until sunset during the week and from 10 am until sunset on the weekends. Entry is free, although a $2 per person ($5 per family) donation is suggested (310-379-8117; www.roundhouseaquarium.org). Metered parking is available for $1 per hour. There are telescopes that offer terrific views of Palos Verdes and Catalina to the left and the northern beaches to the right. If you're lucky, you may even spot a dolphin or two.

Shopping

The streets within walking distance of downtown Manhattan Beach are treasure troves of eclectic shops and boutiques. Start at the intersection of Manhattan Beach Boulevard and Manhattan Avenue and walk a few blocks any direction and you'll find a great variety. The Manhattan Village Mall on Sepulveda Boulevard carries a mix of shops like Sephora, Macy's, and Pottery Barn and is just a short drive away.

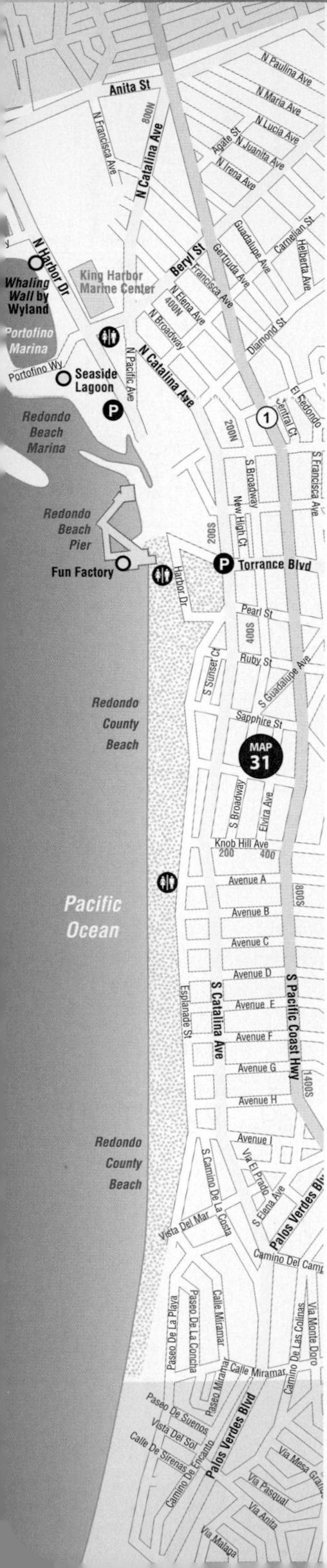

Overview

The Redondo Beach Harbor Enterprise occupies over 150 acres of land and water area, including the beach, parks, pier, boardwalk, and arcade. Redondo Beach may be a historic beach town, but it offers the most modern of amusements, from scuba diving to sport fishing. Because of the vast array of recreational activities it offers, Redondo Beach tends to be the most family-friendly of the South Bay beaches (which means the college kids head north to Hermosa, but you'll still find a share of shell-wearing surfer dudes). Famed environmental artist Wyland was so inspired by the natural beauty and sea life here that he created *"Whaling Wall 31"* in 1991—a spectacular mural that welcomes visitors on North Harbor Drive at Marina Way. From the beach, you get a beautiful view of the Palos Verdes Peninsula, and if you wait around until dusk, you'll be rewarded with a Southern Californian sunset that's so perfect, it might make you sick. For an up-to-date calendar of events visit www.redondo.org.

Practicalities

Like most of the other South Bay beaches, Redondo is open daily during daylight hours. (You can still walk along the beach after sunset, but swimming is forbidden.) Between the pier parking structure (corner of Pacific Coast Hwy and Torrance Blvd) and the plaza parking structure (N Harbor Dr at Pacific Ave), you should have no trouble finding parking. Lots are open daily 11 am–7 pm, and charge $5 per day on weekdays and $7 per day on weekends during summer months. If you come during winter, you'll find that many things, including parking, are discounted. If you shop along the pier, be sure to validate your parking ticket. Metered street parking is also available, just make sure to keep it fed. Well-marked restrooms are located throughout the pier (and there's even one on the beach for bathers).

Sports

In addition to the usual beach activities of swimming, skating, and surfing, boating has gained quite a following in Redondo Beach. Whether you're launching your own or riding as a guest on an excursion boat, the Redondo Pier is a good departure point. The double-decked Voyager will take you on a 20-minute cruise of King's Harbor and the marinas. The *Voyager* is a good family activity, but the daredevils might prefer the *Ocean Racer* speedboat for a one-of-a-kind thrill ride. Avid anglers head out into the South Bay's waters for sport fishing opportunities, and cyclists speed to Redondo as a point of origin for LA County's 26-mile bike path that winds up the Pacific coast to Malibu.

Redondo Pier

The pier, boardwalk, and arcade together provide many dining options. The horseshoe-shaped pier holds a couple of upscale restaurants, but for less formal, fresh-from-the-ocean fare, head to any one of the great fish markets in the area (after all, Redondo Beach is known as the "seafood capital" of Southern California, and when in Rome…). Nestled next to the pier, the boardwalk is also stacked with restaurants, bars, and mostly tacky souvenir stores. Located under the pier, the Fun Factory is open seven days a week and features over 300 arcade and prize-redemption games, as well as a Tilt-A-Whirl and kiddie rides. Hours: Mon–Thurs 10am–10pm; Fri–Sat:10am–midnight; Sun 10 am–10 pm. For more pier info, check out www.redondopier.com, or call 310-318-0631.

Seaside Lagoon

The Seaside Lagoon (200 Portofino Wy) is a saltwater lagoon, heated by a steam-generating plant surrounded by man-made sunbathing beaches, beach volleyball courts, and a snack bar. The shallow lagoon is perfect for families—bring a picnic and spend the afternoon swimming under a lifeguard's watch. From 190th Street, go west toward the beach until the street ends, then turn left onto Harbor Drive, and proceed for about one mile. Parking is available at the Redondo Beach Marina and can be validated at the Lagoon. Admission costs $6.00 for adults and $5.00 for children ages 2-17. Hours: 10 am–5:45 pm, daily during the summer months. For more information, call 310-318-0681.

Shopping

When your interest in the shops along the pier and boardwalk begins to flag, check out Riviera Village. In South Redondo, between the Pacific Coast Highway and Catalina Avenue, south of Avenue 1, you'll find a bevy of unique boutiques, galleries, cafés, and restaurants.

Overview

Santa Monica Beach is the jewel in the crown of Los Angeles beaches. An offshore breakwater assures a gentle surf—good enough for neighborhood boogie boarders, novice surfers, and even the occasional pro in the everlasting search for that perfect wave. (For even better beginner waves, go to Manhattan Beach.) Aside from die-hard beach bums, Santa Monicans tend to stay away from the pier unless they're entertaining visitors. In 1909, the pier opened to an excited public and was a boom town of entertainment until the 1940s, when it experienced a bit of a mid-life crisis. The beloved structure was slated to be torn down after years of deterioration, but local residents rallied, and it was rebuilt in 1988. Film crews, photographers, and sun bunnies came flooding back, and today the place is buzzing with activity once again. Check out the Twilight Dance Series concerts on Thursday nights during the summer, featuring popular performers from a wide variety of musical genres. For more information, visit www.santamonicapier.org, www.santamonica.com, or call 310-319-6263.

Amusement Park

Located right on the Santa Monica Pier, Pacific Park Amusement Center is home to the nine-story Ferris Wheel, with a terrific view of the coastline and the city. Take a moonlit ride over the ocean on a summer night. The famous 1920s vintage carousel was featured in the Paul Newman/ Robert Redford movie *The Sting* and still costs just 25 cents for kids and 50 cents for adults. Other amusements include a fairly slow and uneventful rollercoaster, skeeball, air hockey, pinball, and video games. 310-260-8744; www.pacpark.com.

Camera Obscura

1450 Ocean Ave, 310-458-8644. Hours: Mon–Fri: 9 am–3 pm; Sat-Sun: 11am–3 pm;

Camera Obscura is another popular attraction. Entering the dark room on a sunny day, you can see images from the outside cast onto a table by a long-focus camera lens. The Camera Obscura—essentially a camera the size of a building—is in the Santa Monica Senior Recreation Center. Admission is free, just leave your driver's license at the Rec Center's office in exchange for the key. It may not be as exciting as the nearby ferris wheel, or as portable as your sleek, little digital camera, but it's definitely worth popping in.

Santa Monica Pier Aquarium

1600 Ocean Front Walk; 310-393-6149; www.healthebay.org/smpa.

Hours: Sat–Sun: 12:30pm–5 pm; Tues–Fri: 2 pm–5 pm

At the hands-on marine science aquarium, located underneath the carousel, exhibits focus on local sealife. Sea stars, crabs, snails, and sea urchins populate the touch tanks, but the shark tanks are strictly for eyes only. Suggested donation for admission is $5, but if you have no shame, you can pay as little as $2. Children under 12 enter free with an adult.

Practicalities

The parking lot on the north of the pier at 1550 PCH costs $5 weekdays and $7 weekends during the off-season, and $7 weekdays and $8 weekends during the summer months. There is metered parking along Ocean Avenue north and south of the pier. The visitor information stand is located on the corner of Ocean Avenue and Santa Monica Boulevard. You'll also find some rather grungy restrooms underneath and near the end of the pier.

Shopping

The best shopping in the area is two blocks east of Ocean Avenue along the Third Street Promenade. This three-block pedestrian mall is lined with restaurants, bars, movie theaters, and retail stores including everything from bookstores to swimwear shops. Venture a little south of the pier towards Main Street for more unique boutiques and restaurants. Le Sanctuaire is a fancy culinary boutique frequented by the professionals (2710 Main St, 310-581-8999); Splash Bath & Body sells scented soaps that you can smell a block away (2823 Main St, 310-581-4200); Blonde is the ultimate beach apparel boutique in a kitschy and fun setting (2430 Main St., 310-396-9113); and ZJ Boarding House supplies everything surf and snowboard-related (2619 Main St, 888-799-5646). Also check out Montana Avenue for more specialty shops and restaurants. Sample the best burger in LA at Father's Office (1018 Montana Avenue, 310-393-2337); and don't miss the biannual Montana Avenue sidewalk sale held in early December and mid May every year.

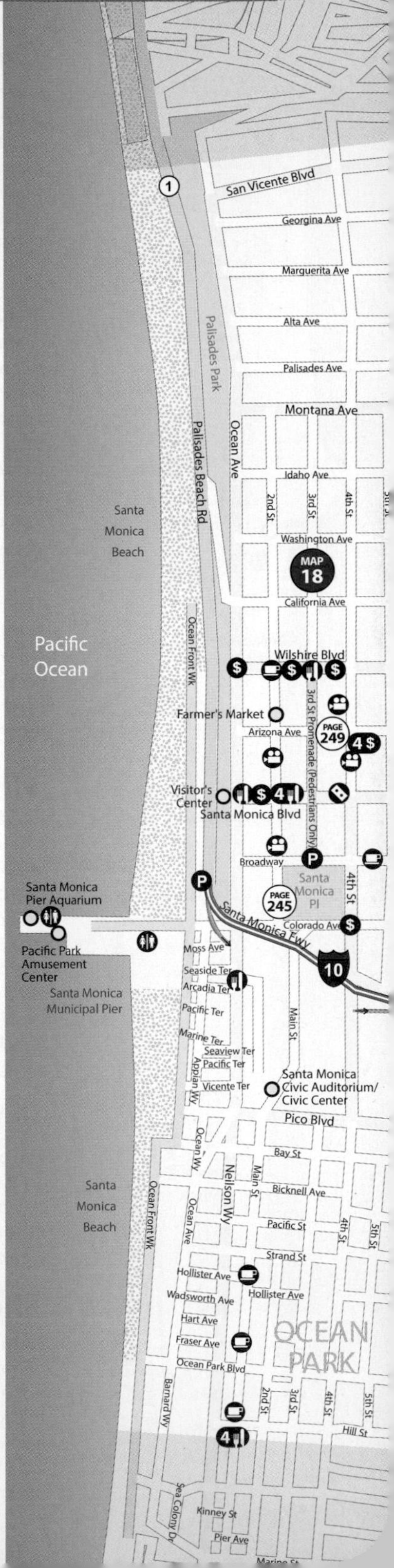

Overview

Freaks, hippies, artists, and bohemians have been attracted to this stretch of oceanfront nuttiness since, well, the beginning. It was at Venice Beach that Jim Morrison and Ray Manzarek—old UCLA buddies—ran into each other in 1965 and decided to form The Doors. Venice Beach is also the famous backdrop of the 1970s roller-disco movie *Xanadu*, and the beach was home to legendary skateboarding crew the Z-Boys (as in, the guys in *Lords of Dogtown*). Nearby Venice High School, a Hollywood location favorite, substituted for Rydell High in *Grease* and was the set of Britney Spears's "Baby One More Time" video.

While some of the shops have acquired better paint jobs since Morrison's day, the funky attitude of the neighborhood still exists despite the influx of luxury lofts and the martini-and-Manolos crowd. The beach boardwalk is the place to rock your bathing suit and flip flops, people-watch people watching you, and maybe pick up a steal (sometimes literally) from a wide-variety of non-commercial vendors. It's a chill, youth-friendly carnival melting pot replete with performance artists, psychics, bodybuilders, hand-in-hand couples, and people showing off their puppies. Step out to the beach to play volleyball, sunbathe, or perhaps brave the questionably clean LA bay for a surf or a swim. For hippies and people who don't mind them, the weekend sunset drum circles are a place to dance, play music, and celebrate the cosmic wonder of the end of another day in LA.

Practicalities

The beach area is closed nightly from 10 pm until 5 am. The main parking lot is located where North Venice intersects with Ocean Front Walk and is open 7 am to 8 pm weekdays ($5) and closes at 9 pm weekends ($6.50). Parking costs $3 before 9 am, but it goes up to $10 and up on summer weekends and holidays. If you're lucky and persistent, you might find free parking on the side streets. The area surrounding Venice Beach can get a bit seedy at night, so we don't recommend walking around alone after dark⊠unless that's your thing.

Sports

Considering its sunny seaside location, it comes as no surprise that Venice Beach is a hot spot for surfers, skaters, cyclists, and ballers. One of Venice Beach's main sporting attractions is world-famous Muscle Beach, which attracts an international set of weightlifters and spectators. For just five bucks, you can buy a day pass and pump iron with the best of them from 10 am to 6 pm, artificial enhancement not included (Venice Beach Recreation Center, 1800 Ocean Front Walk, 310-399-2775). The Recreation Center is also renowned for its high-level pick-up basketball and has popular paddle tennis and handball courts. Additionally, there is a roller rink, skate park, legal graffiti area, punching bag hookups, rings, parallel bars, and a climbing rope—in short, a monkey's paradise. Street vendors along the boardwalk rent out bikes and skates. The Redondo Beach bike path, which runs parallel to Venice Beach, is a perfect place to try out your rented wheels.

Venice Pier

The pier is open daily from 5 am to 10 pm, and the parking lot is located at Washington Boulevard & Ocean Front Walk. A popular spot for anglers, the pier is looking more sturdy than ever after recent renovations. Despite the abundance of locals fishing, be wary. In these parts the "catch of the day" may come with a mandatory tetanus shot. Parking costs $5 weekdays and $6.50 weekends. Restrooms are available on the pier, not off of it.

Shopping

From cheap t-shirts and sunglasses, 'tobacco' pipes and tattoos, to fancy surfboards and negotiable jewelry, Venice Beach offers quite a range of shopping opportunities in a unique bohemian environment. Also, some kid will try to sell you his hip hop CD, and another guy will tell you a joke for a quarter. In addition to the shops and vendors along the boardwalk, one can also venture a few blocks inland to Abbot Kinney Boulevard (just east of Main St & Brooks Ave) for a beachtown stretch of art galleries and hipster shops. Every May over 60 area art galleries open up their studios to the public for the annual Venice Art Walk (www.venicefamilyclinic.org).

Overview

In 1978, idyllic Zuma Beach was the setting for an eponymous made-for-TV movie starring Suzanne Somers (also featuring Rosanna Arquette and Delta Burke). The premise involved an aging rocker who moved to the beach to try and "get away from it all," but who instead became wrapped up in the lives of beach-going teens. Though today old rockers opt to escape behind the high walls of their private beachfront compounds, the clean waters and mile-long stretch of broad, sandy beach still attract Malibu High students and a laid-back, local crowd of surfers, families, young beach bums, and sun-worshipers.

Getting to Zuma means taking a beautifully scenic drive along the Pacific Coast Highway—speaking of rock star compounds, you'll drive by Cher's on the way up. The beach is a 30-minute drive north from Santa Monica on a good day, so avoid the nightmarish weekend traffic on the PCH (especially in the summer) and get an early start.

Practicalities

The parking lot is open from 7 am to 7 pm daily and costs $4.75 to park in the winter, $6 in the summer. The lot has more than 2,000 spaces, but there's also plenty of free parking along the west side of the PCH. Be forewarned that a temperamental marine layer may not burn off until the early afternoon, if at all on some days, and the beach is often windy, so check the weather first and don't forget a cover-up. You may also want to pack some snacks before you head out, though there's a fast food stand near the volleyball courts and a small market across the highway. Get an early start if heading up to Malibu to avoid traffic and claim a good parking and beach spot.

Restrooms

Your typical beach-level of cleanliness should be expected in these restrooms, which also have showers and child-sized toilet stalls with walls so low you can peer over to your neighbor.

Sports

The wide, flat stretch of sand between lifeguard towers 6 and 7 features volleyball courts. The waves in this area can be strong enough for body surfing as well as board surfing. In other areas, visitors are allowed to fish and dive, though hopefully not in the same spot. For the kids, there's a swing set.

Surfing Beaches

Zuma's water is divided for surfers and swimmers, so one doesn't crash into the other. Malibu's coast is covered with more than 20 beaches and secret surfing spots. For experienced surfers, body surfers, and body boarders, a couple of good surfing beaches to the north of Zuma include Leo Carrillo and Nicholas Canyon Beach. The latter, known locally as Zero Beach, offers picnic tables, shore fishing, and plenty of parking. To the south, test the waters around Point Dume, or head straight for Surfrider, one of the most famous surfing beaches in the world. Located at the Malibu Pier, this surf spot's no secret, so if everyone's dropping in on your waves during summer months, you may have to hightail it or settle for volleyball. Check the LA County Coastal Monitoring Network for current weather and surf conditions (www.watchthewater.org/beach.cfm?bid=19).

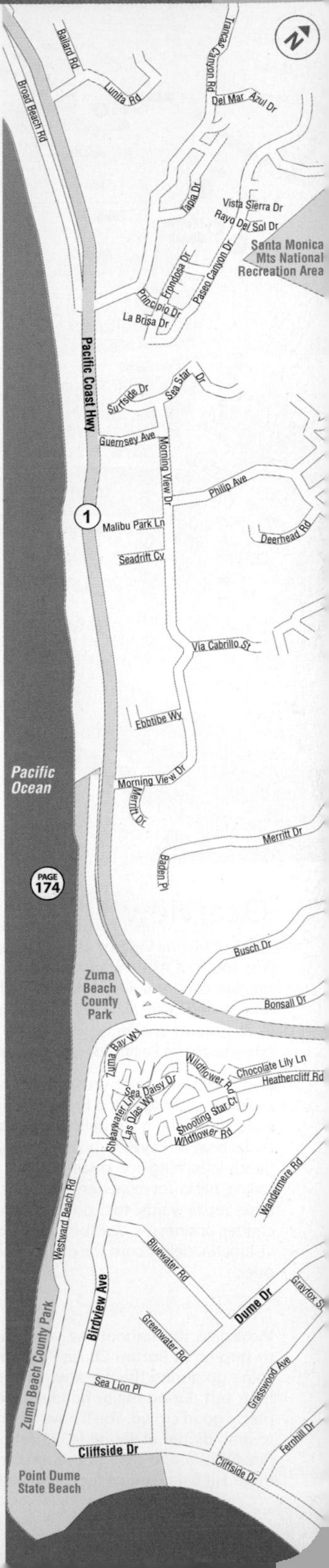

Overview

Think of Marina Del Rey as Venice Beach's more conservative step-sibling. Just south of its flamboyant relative, Marina Del Rey is a cross between upscale condominium living at its finest and commercialized areas for tourists and locals alike. This man-made marina (one of the world's largest) is capable of sheltering over 5,000 sea-faring vessels and stands as a gateway to the Pacific for recreational and commercial vehicles.

If you're looking to go out into the water in a boat, you can find it all here: charter a yacht, go for a brunch or dinner cruise, or spend the day whale watching. If you don't mind breaking out into a little sweat, get your own pedal boat or kayak to explore the waters. Amenities for boaters include beach-launching for small boats, a launch ramp for trailered boats, a sailing basin for boats and windsurfers, dry dock storage, a Sea Scout base, repair yards, fuel dock, pump-out stations, boat brokerages, and charter businesses. Visit beaches.lacounty.gov/wps/portal/dbh or www.visitmarinadelrey.com for more information on what the marina has to offer.

Most days throughout the year you'll find the weather warm enough to stop off at Burton Chace Park for a picnic. If you want to save a few coins, go during the week when you can park for free. It's usually quiet here, but during major holidays like the Fourth of July, you can find a pretty good crowd. You'll have to drop some extra bills, but it's worth it to grab dinner at Jer-ne (4375 Admiralty Wy, 310-823-1700) inside The Ritz-Carlton and take in the amazing view of the marina while you're there. Hit Baja Cantina for cheap and tasty grub and some great scoping and socializing on the patio (311 Washington Blvd. 310-821-2252). Fisherman's Village is a bit like hanging out at another spot tailor-made for tourists, but come see the live music and check out the breathtaking water view. You'll find kayaks, jet skis, ice cream, smoothies, free live concerts on the weekends, and, if you're here in early December, the annual Holiday Boat Parade.

Harbor Info

The entrance to the marina is situated between two jetties (north and south) that sit inside the breakwater that runs parallel to the shore. The north and south ends of the breakwater and the ends of both jetties are marked with lights that can be distinguished by their color and length between flashes: North Breakwater Light, 1 WHITE flash every six seconds; South Breakwater Light, 2 RED flashes every six seconds; North Jetty Light, 3 WHITE flashes every five seconds; South Jetty Light, 4 RED flashes every four seconds. Impress your date!

Practicalities

Located in the Santa Monica Bay 15 miles southwest of downtown LA, Marina Del Rey can be easily accessed from the 405 and the 90 freeways. Daily parking rates vary in the 15 lots surrounding the marina; however the lowest one can expect to pay is $5 for cars, and $7 for cars with boats in tow. Limited free parking is also available on Dock 52. If you plan on parking overnight, you will need to make arrangements with the harbormaster/sheriff's department beforehand (310-823-7762). There are also 18 metered boat washdown spaces, which cost 50 cents for three minutes (requires quarters). Restrooms are located at Fisherman's Village, near Mother's Beach, and next to the launch ramp.

Launch Ramp & Fuel Dock

Small, hand-carried vessels such as kayaks and tin boats are easily launched at the public beach in Basin D, also known as Mother's Beach because of the absence of surf, making it an ideal swimming beach for children. For larger vessels, there is a public launch ramp at the head of the first finger at Mindanao Way on the east side of the channel. The eight-lane ramp can get very busy, especially on the weekends and during summer months, so be prepared to wait. The fee is $7, and includes one launch, recovery, and 24-hour parking for your car. The fuel dock is located on the west side of the channel just inside the bend.

Guest Slips

The Los Angeles County Department of Beaches and Harbors offers boat slips to guests near Burton Chace Park. There is a free 4-hour tie-up dock between the H and G basins on the east side of the main channel, and overnight docking (for up to 7 days within a 30 day period) can be arranged at the Community Building in the park at a cost of 50 cents per foot per night. To obtain an overnight slip, you will need to produce your registration papers and identification. Overnight facilities include electricity, water, showers, and restrooms. If you are a yacht club member, try contacting the yacht clubs in the area to see if they offer reciprocal guest slips.

Harbor Patrol & Anchorage

The Harbor Patrol is run by the Los Angeles County Sheriff's Department and located on the east side of the main channel. They are on call 24 hours a day and can be reached on Channel 16, with 12 as the working channel (310-823-7762). During storms or other emergencies, anchoring is permitted in the north end of the entrance channel.

No Boat?

If you don't have your own water craft, several commercial boating companies leave from Dock 52 and provide all of the gear you will need for a great day of fishing, including rods, reels, and bait. If pier fishing is more your style, head down Fiji Way to Fisherman's Village and throw a line in from the docks.

Overview

The south-facing bay and nearby offshore breakwaters make Long Beach Marina one of the calmest and most popular boat mooring spots in Southern California. It ranks low on the snob-scale, too, making it a much better bet than its sister to the north, Marina Del Rey. The protected enclave and the idyllic boating conditions make sailing the number-one recreational activity in Long Beach, home of the Congressional Cup, Transpac, and the Olympic trial races. The 3,800-slip marina is run by the City of Long Beach and includes Alamitos Bay Marina (562-570-3215), Long Beach Shoreline Marina (562-570-4950), and Rainbow Harbor/Rainbow Marina (562-570-8636).

Practicalities

Daily parking is available near the marina. Boaters who wish to park in the launch parking lot for more than 24 hours need to visit the Alamitos Bay office and pay for a parking pass in advance.

Launch Ramps & Fuel Docks

Five separate launch ramps serve the Long Beach Marina population. The Granada Launch Ramp (Granada Ave and Ocean Blvd) and the Claremont Launch Ramp (Claremont and Ocean Blvds) are sand launches exclusively for small sailing vessels. Water skiers and larger vessels looking to get in the water need look no further than Marine Stadium (Appian Wy between 2nd and Colorado Aves). Boats in the stadium must be under 20 feet long, have a reverse gear, and travel counter-clockwise within the stadium. Davies Ramp, across from Marine Stadium, is the only launch open 24 hours a day. And last but not least, the South Shore Launch Ramp is a small boat launch ramp near the Queen Mary on Queensway Drive. All launch ramps cost $10 and are open year-round, usually from 8 am until dusk. For more information, call 562-570-8636.

Long Beach has two fuel docks—one in Downtown Shoreline Marina (562-436-4430) and one in Alamitos Bay (562-594-0888). The Alamitos fuel dock stocks propane, snacks, beer, ice, and frozen bait, along with gas and diesel fuels. The smaller Downtown Marine fuel dock features gas, CNG, and limited sundries. Both docks accept credit cards or cash. Fuel dock hours (May 31–Labor Day): Mon–Fri: 8 am–5 pm; Sat–Sun: 7 am–6 pm.

Guest Slips

Guest moorings can be rented year-round for 60¢ per foot per night. While it's always best to call ahead, it's only on holiday weekends that reservations are required (with 3,000 slips for rent, you can usually find a spot at short notice on weeknights).

Patrols

The Harbor Patrol looks after the water, while the Marine Patrol guards the land. All Lifeguard/Harbor Patrol boats are run by trained, professional lifeguards and are also equipped for emergencies such as fire, capsized boats, or pump-outs. If you need your boat towed, the Harbor Patrol/Rescue Boats will always oblige, but if it's not an emergency, they'll charge you for the towing.

No Boat?

If you're on a budget but you still want a piece of the action, check out the Belmont Pier at Ocean Boulevard and 39th Place, which offers free public fishing. No license is required as long as you stay on the pier (562-434-1542). If you decide to fish from the beach or the jetties, you'll need a salt-water fishing license. If you get tired of the salt and sand, you might opt for the Belmont Plaza Olympic Pool (4000 Olympic Plaza Dr, 562-570-1805), or grab a pint and a bite at the Belmont Brewing Company (25 39th Pl, 562-433-3891) on the pier. There are often events held along the shoreline that people enjoy from their boats, such as the Long Beach Jazz Festival. Unfortunately, there's no swimming allowed at the marina.

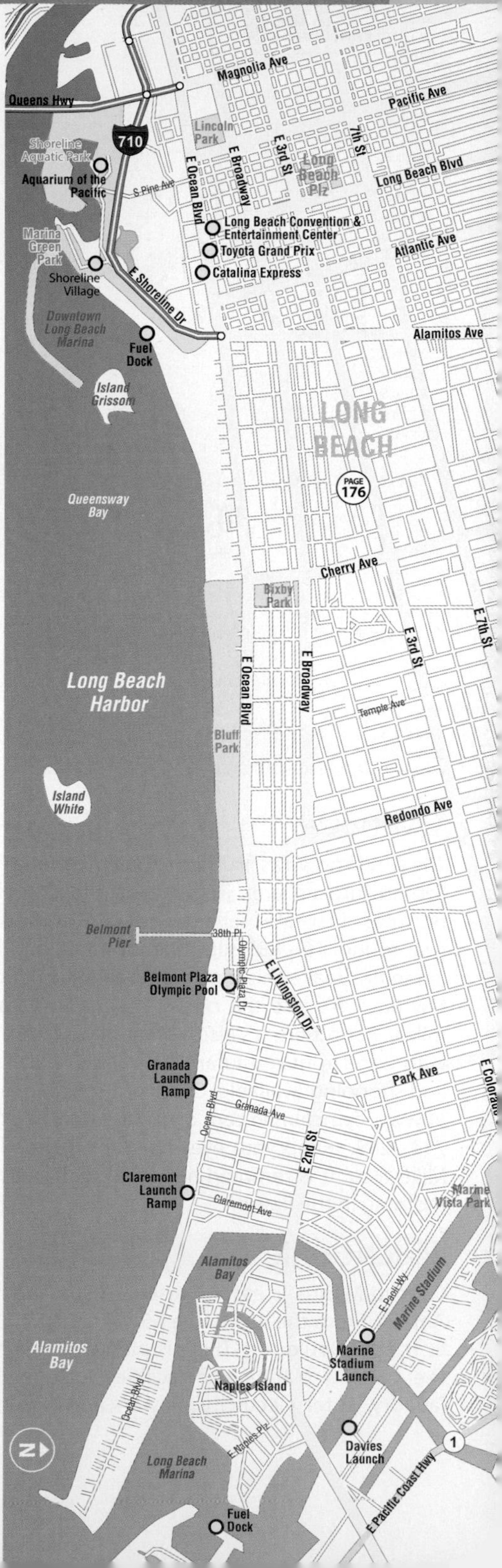

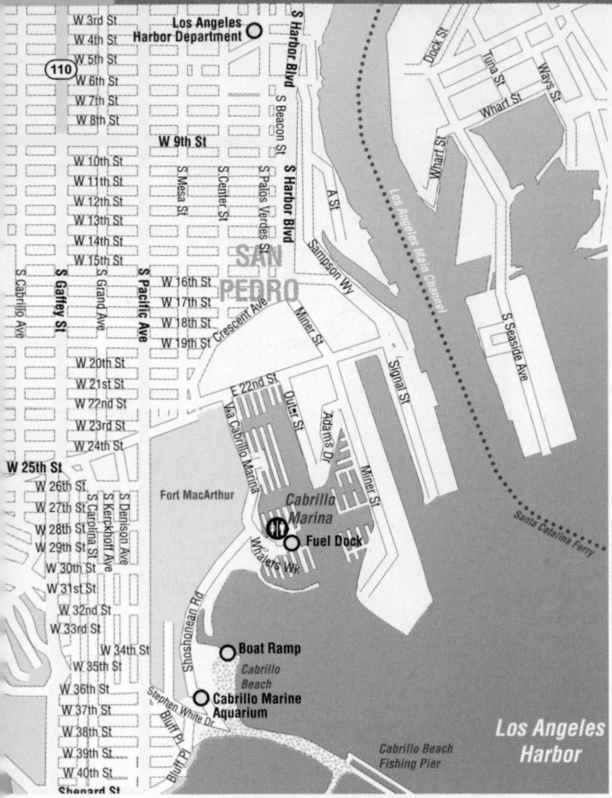

Launch Ramp & Fuel Dock

Run by the LA County Department of Recreation and Parks, the boat ramp is open 24 hours a day and has nearby space for trailer parking and boat washing, as well as restroom facilities. You will find fuel at the Cabrillo Marine Fuel Dock, which is located at Berth 31, 210 Whalers Walk.

Harbor Info

The breakwater entrance to the western end of San Pedro Bay is marked by the Los Angeles Harbor Lighthouse (33°42.5′N-118°15.0′ W), also known as Angel's Gate. This marina has a lot of traffic, including huge ships and other commercial vehicles, so boat owners should study their charts in order to navigate the waters appropriately.

Guest Slips

Guest end-ties are available for overnight docking for boats up to 55 feet long for up to three days. Four mooring buoys are offered in the inner harbor for vessels up to 40 feet long, and in the outer harbor 14 mooring buoys are available for boats up to 50 feet long. However, overnight mooring is not permitted.

Harbor Patrol

The Port Warden and staff of the Los Angeles Harbor Department monitor the harbor. They are located at 425 S Palos Verdes Street, San Pedro.

No Boat?

Fishing is permitted from the Cabrillo Pier. During grunion season, the silvery fish emerge twice a month, like clockwork, to lay their eggs under a full or new moon. During part of the season, it is legal to catch these fish—but only by hand! If you want to participate you will need to take a flashlight. If you don't fancy getting wet, it's almost as much fun to watch—especially the people who try to lure them in by singing Barry White songs. The Cabrillo Marine Aquarium (3720 Stephen M. White Dr), a delightful way to spend a few hours with the kids, is nearby and free (with a suggested donation of $5 for adults and $1 for children and seniors). Visit www.cabrillomarineaquarium.org or call 310-548-7562 for more information. The 22nd Street Landing houses fishing and diving boats that can be taken out for half, 3/4, or full-day excursions of diving and deep-sea fishing. Whale-watching tours are also available. The beach and bathhouse are also enjoyable playgrounds.

Overview

The wind known as "Hurricane Gulch" coming from Point Fermin into an area just outside the Cabrillo Marina provides first-rate sailing and windsurfing weather year-round. The 885 slips, friendly staff, and abundant amenities make this a pleasant marina to dock in for a few days. It's also the closest marina to Catalina (19.4 miles). For others, it's also a great place to run and bike, with waterfront restaurants for a quiet lunch or dinner and shopping available. Check out the marina's website at www.cymcabrillo.com or call the dockmaster at 310-732-2252. Keep your eyes open for Pedro's legendary Mike Watt; it is rumored he kayaks with pelicans every morning in the harbor.

Practicalities

Cabrillo Marina is easy to reach—just a shout from LA Airport. From the 405 or the I-5, take the 110 S and exit at Harbor Boulevard. There is plenty of free parking at the Cabrillo Marina and facilities include restrooms, laundry, water, electricity, showers, and lockers.

Overview

Redondo Beach sits south of the communities of Manhattan Beach and Hermosa Beach, part of the South Bay beach communities. A home to families who make a comfortable living for themselves, Redondo Beach is a land by the sea with all the elements of fun in the sun, but less of the flash and pretense. It has four marinas—King Harbor, Port Royal, Portofino, and Redondo Beach—and over 1,400 boat slips. The marinas host seasonal activities, such as whale-watching in January, the annual Super Bowl Sunday 10K Run in February (with a beer garden at the finish line), and the Bayou Bash and Crawfish Boil, complete with music straight from New Orleans, in May. For those of you who just can't get enough seafood and fanfare, head out here in the fall for the annual Redondo Beach Lobster Festival for live music, wacky seafood paraphernalia, carnival games, and, of course, more lobster than you'd care to eat. Between sailing, kayaking, and enjoying a seafood dinner by the water, let's just say there are worse things in life than having to spend a week at Redondo Beach.

Practicalities

The marina provides several double-spaced parking spots for vehicles with boat trailers. If you're hoping for a space during the summer months, you better head out early—the place gets mobbed. Expect to pay between $3 and $7 per day for parking, depending on the season and location.

Boat Hoist & Fuel Docks

Unlike most other marinas, the Redondo Beach Marina has a boat hoist instead of a launch ramp. Skilled hoist operators launch boats mechanically via slings using two five-ton hoists, which can lift boats up to 10,000 pounds and 30 feet long. Round-trip hoist fees are $8 for a hand-launch size boat, $18 for personal watercraft, $30 for boats 18-24 feet long, and $40 for boats over 25 feet long. Reservations are not needed. Locals with proof of boat registration can obtain boat hoist coupons from City Hall for $7.50. If you're launching a boat by hand, you'll want to go behind Seaside Lagoon, via the Redondo Beach Marina parking lot, or by Portofino Way.

Fuel docks are located at the commercial basin and across from the Harbor Patrol office.

Boat Hoist Regular Hours: Mon–Fri: 7 am–5 pm; Sat–Sun: 6 am–6 pm. Extended summer hours—6 am–6 pm on weekdays and 6 am–8 pm on weekends—begin Memorial Day weekend. For more information, visit www.rbmarina.com.

…Two If by Sea

If you're coming in from the water, use the lighted buoy to the SSW of the exterior jetty to guide you into the marina. The entrance is at the south end of the harbor, between two lighted jetties.

Guest Slips

King Harbor Marina (208 Yacht Club Wy, 310-376-6926) and the Redondo Beach Yacht Club both offer guest boat slips and docking accommodations. Boat slips come fully equipped with storage lockers, cable TV and phone hook-ups, laundry facilities, and plenty of parking.

Harbor Patrol

The Harbor Patrol office is located at the west end of Marina Way, adjacent to Moonstone Park. If you need them call 310-318-0632.

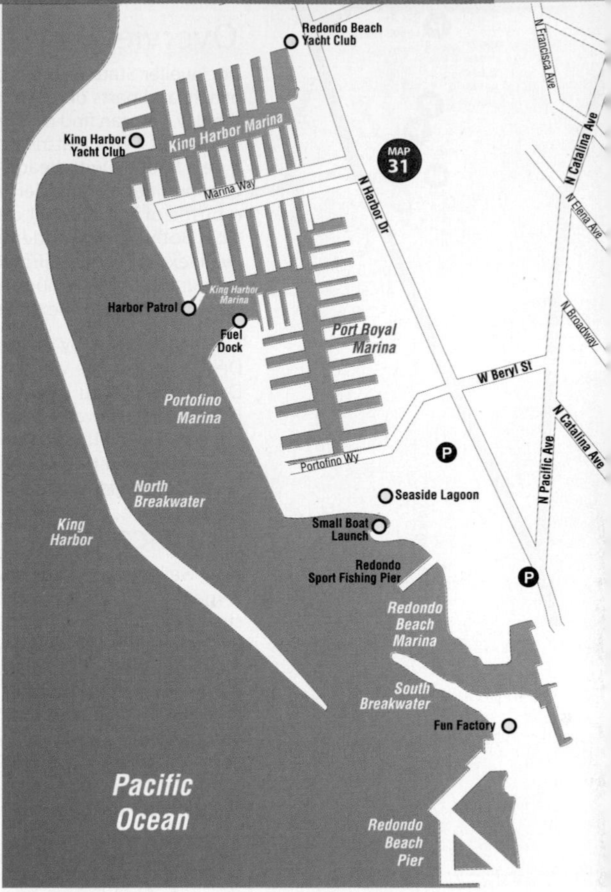

No Boat?

No worries! You can hire fishing rods, tackle, bait, and a salt water fishing license right on the Redondo Sport Fishing Pier. If you prefer being out on the water, fishing trips range from $32 ($27 kids) for a half-day to $650 for a ten-person charter boat for the day. For something a little racier, try sailing classes (310-937-3180) or a high-speed tour of the coast on the *Ocean Racer* (310-374-3481).

Restrooms

Restrooms are located in and around the harbor, on the Pier, and along the beach areas.

Redondo Beach Pier

The Redondo Beach Pier has a host of dining spots, a few bars, *many* touristy shops, and an arcade. If nothing else, you'll get a semi decent meal and find some places to pass the time. You can park at the Pier Parking Structure (100 W Torrance Blvd) south of the Boardwalk or the Plaza Parking Structure (180 N Harbor Dr) north of the Boardwalk. There's metered parking as well in the area. For seafood, try Oceanside Seafood (100-F Fishermans Wharf) and then make a stop at the Pier Bakery (100-M Fishermans Wharf) for fresh churros. Then you can browse through places like the Sunshine Kite Company and Shark Attack to round out your pier experience.

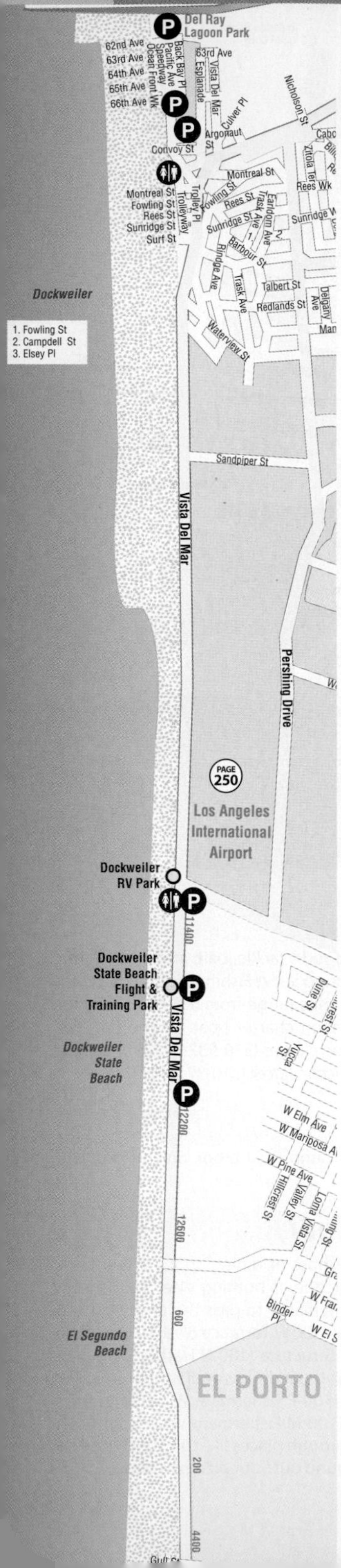

Overview

Dockweiler State Beach is hardly the jewel of the California coast – it's more like LA's dive-bar beach, and parts of it can be dicey at night. However, if you stay close to the entrance during the day, you can find quiet area to get some rays. At night Dockweiler's most obvious feature is the fire pits, which attract dancers, fire-twirlers and other Burning Man types; at 10 pm sharp, it gets flooded with beach cops, and all flame must be extinguished. This beach is part of the communities of Playa del Rey and El Segundo—two areas away from the freeways and hustle-n-bustle of the city that can almost make you forget you're in LA with their neighborhood-y vibe. Both mostly residential, Playa Del Rey and El Segundo are quiet seaside communities (well, except for the airplanes overhead) with a sprinkling of shops and a fair share of local restaurants. If you're hungry and want to bring a snack to the sand, try Beach Pizza in Playa Del Rey for a relatively inexpensive meal.

The beach starts by Ballona Creek, where you can set your sights on the yachts of Marina Del Rey across the way, and the beach ends three miles south at El Segundo. At this end of Dockweiler, if you catch a whiff of something awful, it's probably coming from the nearby Hyperion Wastewater Treatment Plant. The ocean breeze will help temper the smell a bit, but once in a while there's not much you can do about the stench. The Los Angeles Department of Beaches and Harbors has a website with some pretty basic information about Dockweiler. Visit http://beaches.co.la.ca.us/BandH/Beaches/Dockweiler.htm if you feel like taking a look.

Practicalities

Dockweiler is open daily from 7 am until 10 pm. On most days, especially when the weather is mediocre, you can find parking pretty easily in one of the lots along the beach or on the street. Playa Del Rey has one lot with a fee (a quarter for every fifteen minutes) at the end of Pacific Avenue and one free lot further south on Pacific Avenue. There's also a free lot by the playground off of Esplanade Street. El Segundo has two lots with fees on Vista Del Mar with entrances near the Imperial Highway. Lifeguard towers are manned on both sides of the beach, and this is also one of the few beaches in the LA area (Cabrillo Beach is the other one) where you can have a bonfire. Go to the area near El Segundo if you want to sit next to a fire pit. If you're hungry and can't bear to leave the seaside, stop off at the RC Grill, a concession stand located just north of Imperial Highway. On occasion, a hot dog vendor parks his cart in Playa Del Rey near the parking lot at the end of Pacific Avenue.

Restrooms

One set of public restrooms is located on the Playa Del Rey side of the beach and one set of restrooms is located at the El Segundo area. They are generally kept pretty clean, but as with all public restrooms, sometimes you have to lower your expectations juuust a bit.

Sports

You won't find a ton of amenities for sports out here, but you can expect to get a good game of volleyball going, and folks do occasionally surf or boogie board as well. The bike path tends to have light traffic passing through this part of the beach. When the sun's out, you'll find roller bladers and bikers making their way from Santa Monica to Manhattan Beach and back. There's also a hang gliding facility called the Dockweiler State Beach Flight Training Park that is perfect for beginners since the bluff isn't too steep and you have a nice patch of sand to cushion your landing. Windsports runs the program and offers a beginning lesson for $120. You can call 818-367-2430 for more information. The closest parking lot is located off Vista Del Mar just south of Imperial Highway. Expect to pay $2 from 6 am to 9 am, $5 from 9 am to 5 pm, and $2 from 5 pm to closing. The lot directly off of West Imperial Highway has a flat fee of $5 per day.

Dockweiler RV Park

One big draw to Dockweiler for out-of-towners is the RV Park. The unique thing about this place is that it's right on the beach. You'll find everything you need here, including hot showers, picnic tables, barbecue pits, RV spaces with hook-ups, dump stations, and a laundromat. Depending on the season and which space you get, expect to pay $24–32 per day to park your recreational vehicle. For an extra fee of two dollars per day, you can bring your pet, too. Make your reservations far in advance since this is a popular spot—you can reserve up to three months ahead of time by calling the office at 800-950-7275, Monday through Friday from 8 am–4 pm. Drive to 12001 Vista Del Mar and enter the park off of West Imperial Highway.

If you find yourself in the area for a summer swim at midnight, go to Main and Imperial in El Segundo for a late-night snack. There are a few 24 hour doughnut shops that cater to the late-night airport workers.

City of LA Tennis Courts

The city of Los Angeles runs two types of public tennis courts: Open Play courts, like the excellent ones at the **Mar Vista Recreation Center (Map 22)**, which are free and available on a first-come, first-served basis, and Reservation/Pay Tennis, like the **Cheviot Hills Recreation Center (Map 23)** courts, where hourly fees apply per court and reservations are required. Courts cost $5 per hour weekdays from 7 am until 4 pm, and $8 per hour all other times—$10 per hour/per court if you're booking tournaments. You must have a reservation card to reserve a court, and be aware they'll charge you $3 per "incident" if you don't show. Call 323-644-3536 to purchase a reservation card, which runs $15 for residents and $30 for nonresidents and is good for one year. To reserve a court, call 213-625-1010 and follow the verbal prompts or call 323-644-3536. Hours vary depending on facility and date. Consult www.laparks.org/dos/sports/tennis/paytennis.htm or call Los Angeles Parks and Recreation at 323-586-6543 or 213-738-2965.

Facility	*Address*	*Phone*	*Type of Court*	*No. of Courts*	*Map*
West Hollywood Park	647 N San Vicente Blvd	323-848-6534	Open Play/ Free	2	2
Peck Park Community Center	560 N Western Ave	310-548-7580	Open Play / Free		4
Vermont Canyon	2715 Vermont Cyn	326-664-3521	Reservation / Pay	12, Unlit	4
Echo Park Rec	1632 Bellevue Ave	213-250-3578	Open Play / Free		5
Elysian Park Therapeutic	929 Academy Dr	323-226-1402	Open Play / Free		5
Riverside	3401 Riverside Dr	323-661-5318	Reservation / Pay	12	5
Queen Anne Rec Center	1240 West Blvd	323-857-1180	Open Play / Free		7
Lafayette Community Center	625 S Lafayette Pk Pl	213-384-0562	Open Play / Free		8
Shatto Rec Center	3191 W 4th St	213-386-8877	Open Play / Free		8
Daniels Field Sports Center	845 W 12th St	310-548-7728	Open Play / Free		9
Arthur Ashe Center	5001 Rodeo Rd	323-290-3141	Open Play / Free		10
Jim Gilliam Rec Center	4000 S La Brea Ave	323-291-5928	Open Play / Free		10
Loren Miller Rec Center	2717 Halldale Ave	323-734-1302	Open Play / Free		11
Van Ness Rec Center	5720 2nd Ave	323-296-1559	Open Play / Free		11
Ross Snyder Rec Center	1501 E 41st St	323-298-3629	Open Play / Free		12
South Park	345 E 51st St	213-847-6746	Open Play / Free		12
Ladera Park	6027 Ladera Park Ave	310-217-8361	LA County Tennis Courts		13
Algin Sutton Rec Center	8800 S Hoover St	323-753-5808	Open Play / Free		14
Jackie Tatum/Harvard Rec Center	1535 W 62nd St	323-778-2579	Open Play / Free		14
Jesse Owens Park	9651 S Western Ave	323-241-6704	LA County Tennis Courts		14
St Andrews Rec Center	8701 S St Andrews Pl	213-485-1751	Open Play / Free		14
Pacific Palisades	851 Alma Real Dr	310-454-1412	Reservation / Pay	8	15
Rustic Canyon Rec Center	601 Latimer Rd	310-454-5734	Open Play / Free		15
Barrington Rec Center	333 S Barrington Ave	310-476-4866	Open Play / Free		16
Stoner Rec Center	1835 Stoner Ave	310-479-7200	Open Play / Free		19
Westwood	1350 Sepulveda Blvd	310-473-3610	Reservation / Pay	8	19
Oakwood Rec Center	767 California St	310-452-7479	Open Play / Free		21
Penmar Rec Center	1341 Lake St	310-396-8735	Open Play / Free		21
Glen Alla Park	4601 Alla Rd	310-396-1615	Open Play / Free		22
Mar Vista Rec Center	11430 Woodbine St	310-398-5982	Open Play / Free		22
Cheviot Hills	2551 Motor Ave	310-837-5186	Reservation / Pay	14	23
Westchester	7000 W Manchester Ave	310-670-7473	Reservation / Pay	8	26
Eagle Rock Rec Center	1100 Eagle Vista Dr	323-257-6948	Open Play / Free	Unlit	33
Yosemite Rec Center	1840 Yosemite Dr	323-257-1644	Open Play / Free		33
Glassell Park Rec Center	3650 Verdugo Rd	323-257-1863	Open Play / Free		36
Sycamore Grove Park	4702 N Figueroa St	323-225-0370	Open Play / Free		36
Montecito Heights Rec Center	4545 Homer St	213-485-5148	Open Play / Free		37
Arroyo Seco Park	5568 Via Marisol St	323-255-0370	Open Play / Free		38
El Sereno Rec Center	4721 Klamath Pl	323-225-3517	Open Play / Free		38
Aliso Pico Rec Center	370 S Clarence St	323-264-5261	Open Play / Free		40
Hazard Rec Center	2230 Norfolk St	213-485-6839	Open Play / Free		40
Hollenbeck Rec Center	415 S St Louis St	323-261-0113	Open Play / Free		40
Lincoln Park Rec Center	3501 Valley Blvd	213-847-1726	Open Play / Free		40
Belvedere Park	4914 E Cesar E Chavez Ave	323-260-2342	LA County Tennis Courts		41
City Terrace Park	1126 N Hazard Ave	323-260-2371	LA County Tennis Courts		41
Ruben F Salazar Park	3863 Whittier Blvd	323-260-2330	LA County Tennis Courts		41
Balboa	5651 Balboa Blvd	818-995-6570	Reservation / Pay	16	46
Reseda Rec Center	18411 Victory Blvd	818-881-3882	Open Play / Free		46
Van Nuys Rec Center	14301 Vanowen St	818-756-8400	Open Play / Free		47
Valley Plaza Rec Center	12240 Archwood St	818-765-5885	Open Play / Free		48
Victory-Vineland Rec Center	11112 Victory Blvd	818-985-9516	Open Play / Free		48
Studio City Rec Center	12621 Rye St	818-769-4415	Open Play / Free		51
Encino Park	16953 Ventura Blvd	818-995-1690	Open Play / Free		53
Van Nuys/Sherman Oaks	14201 Huston St	818-756-8223	Reservation / Pay	8	55
North Hollywood Rec Center	5301 Tujunga Ave	818-763-7651	Open Play / Free		56

Van Nuys Airport
Sepulveda Dam Recreation Area
Burbank Airport
PAGE 252
Angeles National Fore
Switzer Falls
Eaton Canyon Falls
To Char Sturteva
MAP 56
Universal Studios
PAGE 198
Mt Lee
Griffith Park
PAGE 182
Ferndell/ Mt Hollywood
Dante's View
Wilacre Park
Runyon Canyon Park
MAP 2
Topanga State Park
PAGE 200
Mandeville Canyon
UCLA
PAGE 181
Elysian Park
Dodger Stadium
Will Rogers State Park
MAP 15
Temescal Canyon
To Malibu
Will Rogers State Beach
Santa Monica Municipal Airport
MAP 10
Kenneth Hahn State Recreation Area
Santa Monica Beach
PAGE 209
To Point Dume State Beach
To Malibu Creek State Park
PAGE 216
Dockweiler State Beach
LAX
PAGE 250
Manhattan Beach
PAGE 207
Redondo Beach
PAGE 208
Torrence Municipal Airport
PAGE 254
Long Beach Airport
Pacific Ocean

Overview

A week of bumper-to-bumper commuting will no doubt leave you desperate to escape the concrete jungle of LA. Angelenos enjoy a surprising number of great local hikes year-round, thanks to the city's average temperature of 70 degrees. And they do—if only to show off their designer sneaks or brag about an Orlando Bloom dog-walking sighting. Whether it's a casual jaunt through Runyon Canyon or an epic mountain trek in the Angeles National Forest, you're sure to find a hike that fits your ability and fitness level—just try to ignore the traffic on the drive to the trailhead.

Afoot and Afield in Los Angeles County by Jerry Schad (Wilderness Press) is an excellent resource, covering a total of 192 hikes accompanied by detailed maps. If you want to test out new terrain and make new friends, the Sierra Club organizes hikes throughout the city that range in difficulty and cater to a variety of special interests (angeles2.sierraclub.org). Below you'll find a handful of hikes that come with our highest endorsement. Happy trails!

West Hollywood

Runyon Canyon Park

This is the perfect early-morning or after-work hike, as it's less than two miles and can be completed in an less than an hour. If the main path isn't enough of a workout for you, veer left just after the gates near the Vista entrance for a more challenging uphill climb. Runyon Canyon's no-leash western trail makes it a favorite for pooch owners, and the dog park at the base means an abundance of four-legged hikers. You might also see a downward dog or two at one of the free yoga classes that take place Monday through Thursday inside the park. Enter Runyon from either Fuller Street or Vista Street just north of Franklin Avenue, or try the northern trail options by entering from Mulholland Drive. Parking is available on neighboring streets, but check the signs for restrictions. runyoncanyon-losangeles.com , 323-666-5046.

Griffith Park

Ferndell/Mt Hollywood

The relatively flat terrain of Ferndell makes it a popular choice for family hikes, and the rich plant life means that the area is almost always bathed in shade. If you decide to keep going past the shade lines, the hike up Mt. Hollywood turns steep and uncovered, though the end reward for the uphill workout is a fantastic view of the LA Basin (and the air-conditioned Observatory). Enter Griffith Park from Los Feliz Boulevard by turning left at Ferndell Drive. Enter at the beginning of the trail in Ferndell at the bottom entrance to Griffith Park, or cut your hike in half by entering at the north end of the Griffith Observatory parking lot at the Charlie Turner trailhead. The top of Mt. Hollywood is the reward, and—on a clear day—offers stunning views of the Pacific Ocean and the great urban sprawl.

Mount Lee (a.k.a. the Hollywood Sign)

While some actors toil for years to climb to the top of Hollywood, this trail will only take you a couple hours. Drive up Beachwood Canyon to Hollyridge Drive. Hollyridge Trail will take you up to the summit of Mount Lee, where you can look down on the letters of the 450-foot-long Hollywood sign and enjoy 360-degree views of the LA basin and the San Fernando Valley. Enjoy it while it lasts—success in Hollywood is fleeting, and so are the smog-free views. The round trip is approximately three miles. Parking is free. And watch out for rattlesnakes!

Baldwin Hills

Kenneth Hahn State Recreation Area

Located at 4100 South La Cienega Boulevard, Kenneth Hahn State Recreation Area features more than seven miles of trails for hiking from the Bowl Loop (just 0.8 miles) to the 2.6-mile Ridge Trail.

Pacific Palisades

Will Rogers State Park

The most popular walk in this park, located just north of Sunset Boulevard, is to the idyllic Inspiration Point. The hike is easy—almost too easy—and can be completed in one hour, round-trip. The view to Catalina on a clear day is lovely and makes for a nice change of pace. For a tougher challenge, go for the Backbone Trail, leading into the Santa Monica mountains up to Point Mugu. The trails at Will Rogers are open to hikers, mountain bikers, and horseback riders.

Temescal Canyon

Head north at the intersection of Sunset Boulevard and Temescal Canyon Road and park at Temescal Gateway Park. Once inside, you have two options—Canyon trail or Ridge trail. Be sure to follow the trail markers for the appropriately named Skull Rock, this hike's must-see. At approximately four miles round-trip, this hike is moderately difficult and takes about 2.5 hours.

Brentwood

Mandeville Canyon

The hike, which can be completed in less than two hours, begins with challenging, hilly terrain, but levels off after a bit. From Sunset Boulevard, go north on Mandeville Canyon Road until you reach Garden Land Road and find street parking. A fire road takes you to the Nike Missile Site, which has been turned into a park with restrooms and drink machines.

Pasadena/San Gabriel Valley

Chantry Flat/Sturtevant Falls

These waterfalls in Angeles National Forest are breathtaking, close to LA, and just a three-mile hike up a mountain—i.e. totally within reach. The hike to the falls passes private cabins nestled in the woods that look like something out of a fairy tale. Take the 210 to Santa Anita Avenue and head north. Follow the road up the mountain and use the parking lot at Chantry Flat. The whole trip can be completed in 90 minutes.

Eaton Canyon Falls

The Eaton Canyon Falls hike also leads to a waterfall, and it's especially friendly to dogs (on leashes) and kids because of its relatively flat terrain. The trail crosses over a creek several times during the 2-mile round trip, so you may get wet—dress accordingly and watch your footing. Exit the 210 at Altadena and travel north to the Eaton Canyon Natural Area (just past New York Drive).

Switzer Falls

This is not a difficult hike (roughly 4.5 miles round-trip, depending on how far afield you venture), but hopping over rock bridges and fallen logs while wading in the clear, cool waters takes some maneuvering. At the intersection with Bear Canyon, you can travel up the canyon for awesome views before doubling back. The sound of rushing waterfalls will stay with you long after you've returned to civilization. From the 210 Freeway in La Canada, follow 2 N (Angeles Crest Hwy) for ten miles into the Angeles National Forest. Stop at the Visitor Center at the intersection of Angeles Crest and Angeles Forest Highways to pick up your $5 day pass and map. Then continue on Angeles Crest for about a quarter mile to the Switzer Picnic Area, driving down to the parking lot near the stream. Stop for a sandwich or throw a burger on one of the grills before your trek toward Switzer Falls.

Studio City

Wilacre Park

This short and intense hike (2.7 hilly miles) can be finished in about an hour and is another great walk to save for the end of the day (especially in the hot summer months) or to do with a canine friend (only if leashed, unfortunately). Park ($1) in the gravel lot at the corner of Laurel Canyon Boulevard and Fryman Road and travel up the Dearing Mountain Trail. You'll emerge from the canyon in the midst of a residential neighborhood, on Iredell Lane. Follow this street back out to Fryman Road and turn left to return to the parking lot.

Malibu

Malibu Creek State Park

This 10,000-acre park offers horseback riding, camping, fishing, swimming, and, picturesque hiking trails. The trail will take you on a moderately challenging 3.5-mile hike along gurgling creeks, past swimming holes, and to the spot where *M*A*S*H* was filmed. When you reach the fork in the road, hang a left toward the Visitor Center and follow signs to Rock Pool, a swimming hole popular with families and the site of the *Planet of the Apes* climbing rock. Retrace your steps back to the fork and turn left (away from the Visitor Center) to continue on the wildflower-studded Crags Road trail. When you cross the creek, turn left to explore the marshy Century Lake, or turn right to hike to the *M*A*S*H* site—both make good turn-around points and, on the downhill trek back to the parking lot, you can enjoy the craggy mountain vistas, fragrant lavender fields, and chirping wildlife. Summers are hot and dusty, so visit the park after rainfall or in springtime to experience the scenery at its best. From the 101 Freeway, exit at Las Virgenes Road and follow the signs to Malibu Canyon. The entrance to the park is clearly marked just after Mulholland Highway. One bummer when you arrive—there's an $12 day-use fee. Our recommendation: park in the second lot and start at the Crags Road trail that runs past the bathrooms to avoid having to use the port-o-lets.

Point Dume State Beach

At 4 miles round trip, this trail is less of a hike and more of a sightseeing trip. While you may not break a sweat, the spectacular cliffside scenery and the semi-isolated beach at the end of the trail makes for a magical day in the great outdoors. From the 101 Freeway, exit at Kanan Road, follow it south for 12 miles, and then make a right on PCH. Turn left on Westward Beach Road and try to find parking before you hit the pay lot. If you can't score a free spot, at least you can drive to the trailhead, located at the far end of the parking lot. The viewing platform is a great place to take a break and to enjoy a marvelous view of the Santa Monica Bay, north Malibu coast, Santa Monica Mountains and, if you're lucky, Catalina Island. Dolphins almost always bob in the waves below, and watch for California gray whales between December and March. On the other side of the bluff, descend a stairway to Paradise Cove, a haven for tide-pool gazers and topless sunbathers. Follow the coast for about a mile to the pier, where you can enjoy a mid-hike meal at the Paradise Cove Beach Café. Check the tide tables before setting out or this hike may become a swim.

Los Angeles is famously dotted with blue swimming pools. Even for the unfortunate few without their own private pools, local municipal pools are abundant. The City of Los Angeles operates 59 pools: 47 seasonal (outdoor) pools and 12 year-round (8 indoor, 4 outdoor) pools. Individual cities and towns within Los Angeles County also run their own public pools, open to both residents and non-residents (with a discounted fee for residents). The best one by far is the **Santa Monica Swim Center (Map 18)**, located at Santa Monica College, featuring two nicely heated outdoor pools and diving area, with "Dive-in" movies on weekends.

The Aquatics Division of the City's Department of Recreation & Parks maintains all of the pool facilities, with the seasonal pools open during the summer from the third Saturday in June though Labor Day. Adults (ages 18 through 64) are required to pay a $2.50 admission charge—or just $2.00 if they can show an LA County library card. Children and seniors swim for free. It's a good deal, but now only six days a week—beginning September 10, 2012 LA Recreation and Parks pools will be closed on Mondays.

The department also offers Learn to Swim classes for various ages and swimming abilities. The beginning toddler class for children aged 4 to 7 requires that parents participate with their child in the water. Students then progress to Level 1, which involves face-submerging and blowing bubbles, all the way up to Level 7, in which they will learn to complete 500 yards of continuous swimming using various strokes, conduct an in-water rescue, and perform a springboard dive in tuck and pike positions. Most pools also offer team sports, like inner-tube water polo, synchronized swimming, and lifeguard training. Visit your local pool for more information regarding classes and teams.

For public safety, there is an extensive published list of pool rules. Our favorite is "No snapping towels." For a complete list of pool rules and everything Aquatics Division–related, visit www.laparks.com/dos/aquatic/aquatic.htm. Check with the local Recreation & Parks department about municipalities in individual cities and towns.

Pools	Address	Phone	Map
Pan Pacific Pool	141 S Gardner St	323-975-4524	2
West Hollywood Pool	647 N San Vicente Blvd	323-848-6538	2
Hollywood Pool	1122 Cole Ave	323-957-4501	3
Echo Lake Pool	1419 Colton	213-481-2640	5
Echo Shallow Pool	1632 Bellevue Ave	213-580-3733	5
Griffith Park Pool	3401 Riverside Dr	323-644-6878	5
Laces Pool	5931 W 18th St	323-933-8345	6
EG Roberts Indoor Pool	4526 W Pico Blvd	323-936-8483	7
MacArthur Park Lake	653 S Alvarado St	213-368-4160	8
Celes King III Indoor Pool	5001 Rodeo Dr	213-847-3406	10
John C Argue Swim Stadium	3980 S Menlo Ave	213-763-0129	11
Van Ness Pool	5720 2nd Ave	323-290-3134	11
Central Pool	1357 E 22nd St	213-765-0565	12
Ross Snyder Pool	1501 E 41st St	213-847-3430	12
South Park Pool	345 E 51st St	323-846-5366	12
Algin Sutton Pool	8800 S Hoover St	323-789-2826	14
Rustic Canyon Pool	601 Latimer Rd	310-230-0137	15
Santa Monica Swim Center	2225 16th St	310-458-8700	18
Stoner Park Pool	1835 Stoner Ave	310-575-8286	19
Mar Vista Pool	11655 Palms Blvd	310-390-2016	22
Venice High School Indoor Pool	2490 Walgrove Ave	310-575-8260	22
Cheviot Hills Pool	2693 Motor Ave	310-202-2844	23
Westchester Pool	9100 Lincoln Blvd	310-478-7019	25
Westwood Indoor Pool	1350 S Sepulveda Blvd	310-478-7019	32
Highland Park Pool	6150 Piedmont Ave	323-257-5924	33
Yosemite Pool	1840 Yosemite Dr	323-226-1668	33
Robinson Park	1081 N Fair Oaks Ave	626-585-2025	34
Glassell Park Pool	3704 Verdugo Rd	323-226-1670	36
Downey Pool	1775 N Spring St	323-227-5025	37
Richard Alatorre Indoor Pool	4721 Klamath St	323-276-3042	38
Costello Pool	3121 E Olympic Blvd	323-526-3073	40
Lincoln Park Pool	3501 Valley Blvd	213-847-3382	40
Pecan Pool	120 S Gless St	323-526-3042	40
Roosevelt Pool	456 S Mathews St	213-485-7391	40
Lanark Pool	21817 Strathern St	818-887-1745	42
Granada Hills Pool	16730 Chatsworth St	818-360-7107	44
Cleveland High Indoor Pool	8120 Vanalden Ave	818-756-9798	46
Lake Balboa	6300 Balboa Blvd	818-756-9743	46
Reseda Pool	18411 Victory Blvd	818-756-9361	46
Valley Plaza Swimming Pool	6715 Laurelgrove Ave	818-756-9362	48
Van Nuys Sherman Oaks Pool	14201 Huston St	818-783-6721	55
North Hollywood Pool	5301 Tujunga Ave	818-755-7654	56

Just like the city itself, Los Angeles's golf courses are diverse. They range wildly in difficulty and lawn manicure, as well as in views (sweeping ocean vistas in Palos Verdes, power plants and overhead airplanes in El Segundo). Many courses are more expensive on Fridays than other weekdays, so if you're teeing off at the end of the workweek it won't hurt to check. Also, some courses offer discounts for residents— but if you are one you probably already know that. This warm-weather city offers golf daily all year-round, especially considering the novices who forget their manners about playing through. On weekends, the best tee times are at the crack of dawn to avoid waiting. The city operates a total of 13 courses, including seven 18-hole championship courses, five 9-hole courses, and one 18-hole pony course. Call ahead for conditions, particularly after heavy rainfall. The County operates 16 courses as well (three 9-hole, 13 regulation 18-hole). In summer, bear in mind the weather, as temperatures can easily pass 100 degrees in the Valley. In addition, individual cities and hotels have 3-par courses available to the public. Some public courses will require a city permit; check with the club when booking a tee time. We like the one at the **Marriott Hotel in Manhattan Beach (Map 27).** There's no real dress code (sneakers are permitted), but some people like to hide their handicap behind a smart pair of pants and polo shirt.

Golf Courses	Address	Phone	Fee	Par	Map
Roosevelt Golf Course	2650 N Vermont Ave	323-665-2011	$14.50 weekdays, $19.00 weekends	Par 33	4
Los Feliz Golf Course	3207 Los Feliz Blvd	323-663-7758	$5.50 weekdays, $7.00 weekends	Par 27	5
Maggie Hathaway Golf Course	9637 S Western Ave	323-755-6285	$5.75 weekdays, $7.50 weekends (18 hole)	Par 27	14
Armand Hammer	601 Club View Dr	310-276-1604		Par 3	20
Penmar Golf Course	1233 Rose Ave	310-396-6228	$14.50 weekdays, $17 weekends	Par 33	21
Rancho Park	10460 W Pico Blvd	310-838-7373	$23 weekdays, $28 weekends (9-hole); $38 weekdays, $48 weekends (18-hole)	Par 71	23
Westchester Golf Course	6900 W Manchester Ave	310-649-9173	$23 weekdays, $29 weekends	Par 53	26
Manhattan Beach Marriott	1400 Park View Ave	310-546-7511	$12 weekdays, $14 weekends	Par 27	27
Alondra Park Golf Course	16400 S Prairie Ave	310-217-9919	$26 weekdays, $35 weekends	Par 72	28
Arroyo Seco Golf Course	1055 Lohman Ln	323-255-1506	$14 weekdays, $15 weekends	Par 3	34
Brookside Golf Course	1133 Rosemont Ave	626-585-3594	$38 weekdays, $60 weekends	Par 70	34
Alhambra Golf Course	630 S Almansor St	626-570-5059	$19 weekdays, $20 weekends (9-hole) $27 weekday/ $34 weekend (18-hole)	Par 70	39
Balboa/Encino Golf Course	16821 Burbank Blvd	818-995-1170	$15 weekdays, $19 weekends (9-hole); $30 weekdays, $40 weekends (18-hole)	Par 72	42
Van Nuys Golf Course	6550 Odessa Ave	818-785-8871	$11 weekdays, $13 weekends	Par 30; also an 18-hole Par 3	47
Woodley Lakes Golf Course	6331 Woodley Ave	818-780-6886	$15 weekdays, $17 weekends (9-hole); $22.50 weekdays, $28.50 weekends (18-hole)	Par 72	47
De Bell Municipal Golf Course	1500 E Walnut Ave	818-845-0022	$31 weekdays, $38 weekends	Par 71	50
Altadena Golf Course	1456 E Mendocino St, Altadena	626-797-3821	$15.75 weekdays, $19.50 weekends	Par 36	n/a
Diamond Bar Golf Course	22751 Golden Springs Dr, Diamond Bar	909-861-8282	$25 weekdays, $33 weekends	Par 72	n/a
Eaton Canyon Golf Course	1150 Sierra Madre Villa Ave, Pasadena	626-794-6773	$15.75 weekdays, $19.50 weekends	Par 35	n/a
El Cariso Golf Course	13100 Eldridge Ave, Sylmar	818-367-8742	$22 weekdays, $29 weekends	Par 62	n/a
Knollwood Golf Course	12040 Balboa Blvd, Granada Hills	818-363-8161	$23 weekdays; $31 weekends	Par 72	n/a
La Mirada Golf Course	15501 Alicante Rd, La Mirada	562-943-7123	$26 weekdays, $35 weekends	Par 70	n/a
Lakewood Golf Course	3101 Carson St, Lakewood	562-429-9711	$34 weekdays, $40 weekends	Par 72	n/a
Los Amigos Golf Course	7295 Quill Dr, Downey	562-869-0302	$23.50 weekdays, $31.50 weekends	Par 70	n/a
Los Verdes Golf Course	7000 W Los Verdes Dr, Rancho Palos Verdes	310-377-7370	$23 weekdays, $30 weekends	Par 71	n/a
Mountain Meadows	1875 Fairplex Dr, Pomona	909-629-1166	$25 weekdays, $33 weekends	Par 72	n/a
Santa Anita Golf Course	405 S Santa Anita Ave, Arcadia	626-447-2331	$26 weekdays, $35 weekends	Par 71	n/a
Victoria Golf Course	340 E 192nd St, Carson	310-323-6981	$26 weekdays,$35 weekends	Par 72	n/a
Wilson Golf Course	4730 Crystal Springs Dr, Los Angeles	323-663-2555	$23 weekdays, $28 weekends (9-hole), $38 weekdays, $48 weekends (18-hole)	Par 71	n/a

Driving Ranges	*Address*	*Phone*	*Fee*	*Map*
Westchester Golf Course	6900 W Manchester Ave	310-649-9166	$3/5/$8 buckets	26
Alondra Park Golf Course	16400 S Prairie Ave	310-217-9919	$4.50/$9 buckets	28
Arroyo Seco Golf Course	1055 Lohman Ln	323-255-1506	$3/6/$8 buckets	34
Alhambra Golf Course	630 S Almansor St	626-570-5059	$3/$5/$7 buckets	39
Woodley Lakes Golf Course	6331 Woodley Ave	818-787-8163	$3/$5/$8 buckets	47
Altadena Golf Course	1456 E Mendocino St, Altadena	626-797-3821	$3 (33 balls)	n/a
Diamond Bar Golf Course	22751 Golden Springs Dr, Diamond Bar	909-861-8282	$3.50/$5.50/$7	n/a
Eaton Canyon Golf Course	1150 Sierra Madre Villa Ave, Pasadena	626-794-6773	$3.25/$6.50/$9	n/a
El Cariso Golf Course	13100 Eldridge Ave, Sylmar	818-367-8742	$4/$7/$9 buckets	n/a
Knollwood Golf Course	12040 Balboa Blvd, Granada Hills	818-363-8161	$6/$10 buckets	n/a
La Mirada Golf Course	15501 Alicante Rd, La Mirada	562-943-7123	$10 buckets	n/a
Lakewood Golf Course	3101 Carson St, Lakewood	562-429-9711	$6/$10 buckets	n/a
Los Amigos Golf Course	7295 Quill Dr, Downey	562-869-0302	$4.50/$7/$9.50 buckets	n/a
Mountain Meadows	1875 Fairplex Dr, Pomona	909-629-1166	$6/$10/$20 reuseable cards	n/a
Santa Anita Golf Course	405 S Santa Anita Ave, Arcadia	626-447-2331	$5/$7/$8.50 buckets	n/a
Victoria Golf Course	340 E 192nd St, Carson	310-323-6981	$3/$5/$8 buckets	n/a

Pool halls in LA are usually one extreme or the other: dirty dives with questionable restrooms or swanky clubs where you'll pay $6 for an Amstel Light. If you're looking for a scruffy good time, grab a table and some homemade carne asada tacos at **Highland Park Billiards (map 33)**. If more of a scene is what you're after, check out the upwardly mobile after-work crowd at **Q's Billiard Club (Map 19)**.

Billiards

Billiards	*Address*	*Phone*	*Fees*	*Map*
Koray Billiard	401 S Vermont Ave	213-386-0402	$12/hr	8
Oriental Pool Room	2528 W Olympic Blvd	213-380-1310	$12/hr	8
Young Billiards	132 S Vermont Ave	213-387-9691	$12/hr	8
Young Dong Billiards	555 S Western Ave, Ste 202	213-368-0479	$12/hr	8
Sportsman's Family Billiards & Restaurant	3617 Crenshaw Blvd	323-733-9615	$9/hr	10
House of Billiards	1901 Wilshire Blvd	310-828-2120	$14/hr	18
Q's Billiard Club	11835 Wilshire Blvd	310-477-7550	$14/hr	19
Mr. Lucky's Billiards	21020 Hawthorne Blvd	310-793-6948	$12/hr	31
Highland Park Billiards	5043 York Blvd	323-258-4427	$8/hr	33
Jerry's Family Billards II	1312 N Lake Ave	626-791-5114	$12.50/hr	34
Broadway Social Center Pool Hall	2205 N Broadway	323-221-4924	$6/hr	37
Plush Pocket	16950 Parthenia St	818-893-1380	$10/hr	44
Canoga Billiard Parlor	22025 Sherman Wy	818-348-8798	$7.50/hr	45
Lucky 8 Ball Billiard	13325 Victory Blvd	818-786-9202	$8/hr	48
Fantasia Billiards	131 N San Fernando Blvd	818-848-6718	$12/hr	50
Charles Billiard	224 N Brand Blvd	818-547-4859	$14.75/hr	51

Boxing

Train to be the next Oscar De La Hoya—onscreen or in the ring. If you like a bit of history with your blood, sweat, and tears, visit the Broadway Boxing Gym.

Gym	Address	Phone	Map
Hollywood Boxing Gym	1551 N La Brea Ave	323-845-1420	2
Wild Card Gym	1123 Vine St	323-461-4170	3
Broadway Boxing Gym	10730 S Broadway	323-755-9016	14

Just as Hollywood can take anything sincere and turn it into kitsch, Los Angeles has a way of taking true-blue Americana and making it seem forced and co-opted. So it is with the pastime of bowling. Luckily, for each too-hip alley in the city, there is another Suds and Rock place around the corner. **Lucky Strike Lanes (Map 3)** is as Hollywood as it gets. Located behind a velvet rope in the heart of tourist-driven Hollywood and Highland, you'll find more model/actor-types than league-nighters. After 7pm it becomes 21 and over and good luck getting a lane.

For a more true-to-its-roots experience, check out **AMF**'s **(Map 18)** lanes on Pico in Santa Monica. The rentals are fairly priced, the attached diner is as down-home as you'll find on the Westside, and the bar serves bowling pin shaped long-necks. Just make sure to call ahead to avoid a league night. On the Eastside, **Shatto 39 Lanes (Map 8)** is not to be missed. The many lanes are populated by diehards, hipsters, teens, and families. There's a decent arcade, a full bar, and snackbar with the greasiest, cheapest tater tots in town.

To give yourself the pre-teen birthday party you never had, check out **Pickwick Bowling (Map 50)** in Burbank. A veritable wonderland of activity, this complex includes an arcade, ice rink, and pro shop. Fridays and Saturdays at Pickwick bring on the fog, blacklights, and pop music, making for good group fun.

Bowling Alleys	Address	Phone	Map	
Lucky Strike Lanes	6801 Hollywood Blvd	323-467-7776	3	Weekdays $4.95–6.95 / game; Weekends $5.95–6.95; $3.95 for shoes
Shatto 39 Lanes	3255 W 4th St	213-385-9475	8	Weekdays $3–4.50 / game; Weekends $5.50 / game; $2.50 for shoes
Bowlmor Santa Monica	234 Pico Blvd	310-399-7731	18	$4.50–$6 / game; $4.50 for shoes
AMF El Dorado Lanes	8731 Lincoln Blvd	310-670-0688	25	$4.50–$6 / game; $4.50 for shoes
Gable House Bowl	22501 Hawthorne Blvd	310-378-2265	31	Weekdays $3.75–$5.00; Weekends $2–$5; $4.50 for shoes
AMF Bowl-O-Drome	21915 S Western Ave	310-328-3700	32	$4.50–$6 after 6pm; $4.50 for shoes
All Star Lanes	4459 Eagle Rock Blvd	323-254-2579	33	Weekdays $2.50–$3.50, Weekends $3.50, $2 for shoes
Palos Verdes Bowl	24600 Crenshaw Blvd	310-326-5120	36	Weekdays $3; Weekends $4.50, $3 for shoes
Golden Mile Bowling	1400 E Valley Blvd	626-289-5168	39	Weekdays $2.25/game; Weekends $2.25–$4.50/game, $2–3.75 for shoes
Brunswick Matador Bowl	9118 Balboa Blvd	818-892-8677	44	Weekdays $3.49–$5.49 / game; Weekends $5.49 per game; $2 for shoes
Canoga Park Bowl	20122 Vanowen St	818-340-5190	45	Weekdays $4–$5 / game, $15 / hour; Weekends $5 / game, $30 / hour; $3.25 for shoes
Corbin Bowl	19616 Ventura Blvd	818-996-2695	45	Weekdays $3.50–$4.50 / game, $16–$25 /hour; Weekends, $5.50 / game, $35/hour; $3.50 for shoes
Pickwick Gardens Conference Center	1001 Riverside Dr	818-845-5300	50	Weekdays $3–$4 / game; Weekends $3.75–$5; $3 for shoes
Jewel City Bowl	135 S Glendale Ave	818-243-1188	51	Weekdays $3.50–$5.50 per game, $21–$34 per hour; Weekends $5.50 per game, $21–$34 per hour; $3 for shoes
Pinz Bowling Center	12655 Ventura Blvd	818-769-7600	56	Weekdays $4–$6 / game; Weekends $6–$9 / game; $4 for shoes
Jillian's	1000 Universal Studios Blvd	818-985-8234	57	$4–$5.50 / game; $3.50 for shoes
AMF Woodlake Lanes	23130 Ventura Blvd, Woodland Hills	818-225-7181	n/a	$4.50–$6 / game; $4.50 for shoes

Options for yoga devotees in Los Angeles are as varied as it gets, ranging from basic classes that can be taken at most larger gyms to advanced sessions in smaller studios, after which many newbies throw up (Bikram yoga, you know who you are). Most offer single tickets so you don't have to buy a group of tickets until you know exactly where you'd like to find your inner OM.

Yoga	*Address*	*Phone*	*Website*	*Map*
BKS Lyengar Yoga	8233 W 3rd St	323-653-0357	www.iyila.org	2
City Yoga	1067 N Fairfax Ave	323-654-2125	www.cityyoga.com	2
Dancing Shiva Yoga and Ayurveda	7466 Beverly Blvd	323-934-8332	www.dancingshiva.com	2
Earth's Power Yoga	7901 Melrose Ave	323-655-9642	www.earthspoweryoga.com	2
Liberation Yoga	124 S La Brea Ave	323-964-5222	www.liberationyoga.com	2
Tar Pit Yoga	636 S Burnside Ave	323-934-5171	www.tarpityoga.com	2
Swerve Fitness	8250 W 3rd St	323-782-0741	www.swervestudio.com	2
Golden Bridge Yoga	1357 North Highland	323-936-4172	www.goldenbridgeyoga.com	3
Karuna Yoga	4436 1/2 Camero	323-665-6242	www.karunayoga.net	4
Yoga Vibe	1717 Hillhurst Ave	323-953-8449	www. yogavibela.com	4
Ashtanga Yoga	2815 Sunset Blvd, 2nd Fl	213-483-0400	www.ashtangayogala.org	5
Bikram Yoga Silverlake	3223 Glendale Blvd	323-668-2500	www.bikramyogasilverlake.com	5
Silverlake Yoga	2810 1/2 Glendale Blvd	323-953-0496	www.silverlakeyoga.com	5
Yoga East	2815 W Sunset Blvd	213-483-0400	www.yogaeast.us	5
Bikram Yoga College of India	11500 W. Olympic	310-854-5800	www.bikramyoga.com	6
The Blessings Center	1310 Carmona Ave	323-930-2803	www.gurutej.com/blessingscenter.html	6
Yoga West	1535 S Robertson Blvd	310-552-4647	www.yogawestla.com	6
YogaWorks	230 1/2 N Larchmont Blvd	323-464-1276	www.yogaworks.com	7
Yoga Circle Downtown	400 S Main St	213-620-1040	www.yogacircledowntown.com	9
Crenshaw Yoga and Dance	5426 Crenshaw Blvd	323-294-7148	www.crenshawyogaanddance.com	11
Center for Yoga	15327 W Sunset Blvd	310-454-7000	www.yogaworks.com	15
Maha Yoga	13050 San Vicente Blvd	310-889-0047	www.mahayoga.com	16
Center for Yoga	1426 Montana Ave	310-393-5150	www.yogaworks.com	18
Center for Yoga	2215 Main St	310-664-6470	www.yogaworks.com	18
Exhale Center for Sacred Movement	245 Main St	310-450-7676	www.exhalespa.com	18
Exhale Mind and Body Spa	1422 2nd St	310-899-6222	www.exhalespa.com	18
Santa Monica Yoga	1640 Ocean Park Blvd	310-396-4040	www.santamonicayoga.com	18
Center for Yoga	1256 Westwood Blvd	310-234-1200	www.yogaworks.com	20
YAS Kimberely Fowler's	1101 Abbot Kinney Blvd	310-396-6993	www.go2yas.com	21
Sivananda Yoga Vendanta Center	13325 Beach Ave	310-822-9642	www.sivananda.org/la	22
Goda Yoga	9711 W Washington Blvd	310-287-1255	www.godayoga.com	24
Creative Chakra Downtown	3401 Pacific Ave	310-287-1255	www.creativechakra.com	25
The Awareness Center	2801 E Foothill Blvd	626-796-1567	www.insightyoga.com	34
Yoga House	11 W State St	626-403-3961	www.yogahouse.com	34
Progressive Power Yoga	21800 Burbank Blvd	800-545-9642	www.progressivepoweryoga.com	45
Yoga Blend	1921 W Magnolia Blvd	818-598-8400	www.yogablend.com	50
The Absolute Yoga and Pilates Studio	20855 Ventura Blvd	818-226-0695	www.theabsoluteyoga.com	52
The Yoga Loft	21228 Ventura Blvd	818-710-9057	www.yogaloftla.com	52
Yoga House	11 W State St	626-403-3961	www.yogahouse.com	57

Overview

From the old geezer skating on the Venice Boardwalk to the loose-limbed ingénue posing on her yoga mat, Angelenos love their exercise. All the fun options, not to mention the year-round sunshine, make it easy to join the city's tanned and toned without becoming a gym drone.

Play in the Park

The Los Angeles Department of Recreation and Parks oversees over 175 parks, including 59 swimming pools, ten lakes, 13 golf courses, 59 tennis courts, eight skateboarding parks, nine dog parks, as well as numerous basketball, volleyball, and handball courts and baseball, softball, and soccer fields. Archery ranges are also available, as are beautiful, well maintained hiking trails. A variety of sports leagues and camps are offered for both children and adults and pick-up games of sports such as basketball and soccer are also popular. Visit www.laparks.org or call 888-LA-PARKS for more information.

Some of the cities within the Los Angeles metropolitan area maintain their own park and recreation departments including Santa Monica, Beverly Hills, West Hollywood, Burbank, Glendale, and Pasadena. Information about park and recreational opportunities in these cities can be found at: www.smgov.net or 310-458-8411 for Santa Monica, www.beverlyhills.org or 310-285-2536 for Beverly Hills, weho.org or 323-848-6400 for West Hollywood, www.burbankca.gov or (818) 238-5330 for Burbank, www.ci.glendale.ca.us or 818-548-2000 for Glendale, and www.ci.pasadena.ca.us or 626-744-4000 for Pasadena.

Table Tennis

If you own your own paddle and watch the tournaments on ESPN, stop by the Westside Table Tennis Center (www.alphatabletennis.com) for tips from the pros.

Table Tennis Center	Address	Phone	Map
Westside Table Tennis Center	11755 Exposition Blvd	626-584-6377	19
Pasadena Table Tennis Club	85 E Holly St	626-584-6377	34

Horseback Riding

If you are more equine-inclined, check out one of the many companies offering guided trail rides and riding lessons. Looking for a novel way to spend a Friday night? Try one of the Sunset Ranch dinner rides through Griffith Park, which include a stop for margaritas at a restaurant with hitching posts.

Stable	Address	Phone	Map
Sunset Ranch Hollywood Stables	3400 N Beachwood Dr	323-469-5450	3
Griffith Park Horse Rental	480 Riverside Dr	818-840-8401	50
Traditional Equitation School	480 Riverside Dr	818-569-3666	50
Escape on Horseback	2623 Old Topanga Canyon Rd	818-591-2032	p200

Roller Skating

Here's your chance to dig those hot pants and leg warmers out of the far reaches of your closet. For the ultimate dance party on wheels, take to the streets of Santa Monica, Hollywood, or Downtown with the Friday Night Skate crew. Visit www.fridaynightskate.org for details.

Rinks & Lessons	Address	Phone	Map
Moonlight Rollerway Roller Skating Rink	5110 San Fernando Rd	818-241-3630	5
World on Wheels	4645 ½ Venice Blvd	323-933-5170	9
California Skate School	multiple locations, www.skateschool.com	888-880-ROLL	n/a

Paintball & Other Forms of Combat Play

For information about local activities check out www.paintball-players.org or perhaps www.streetwars.net if this controversial urban stalking game is your thing.

Dodgeball

The Los Angeles Dodgeball Society offers a fun take on that sport you missed out on when you ditched 7th grade PE to go smoke cigarettes behind the dumpster. Two leagues are offered—Staypuft Marshmallow, fun and co-ed, played with "no-sting" balls; and Charles Bronson for the more Death Wish types. League and open gym play are at various times throughout the year, and at different locations. Costs are low but vary. Checkout dodgeball4ever.com for more details.

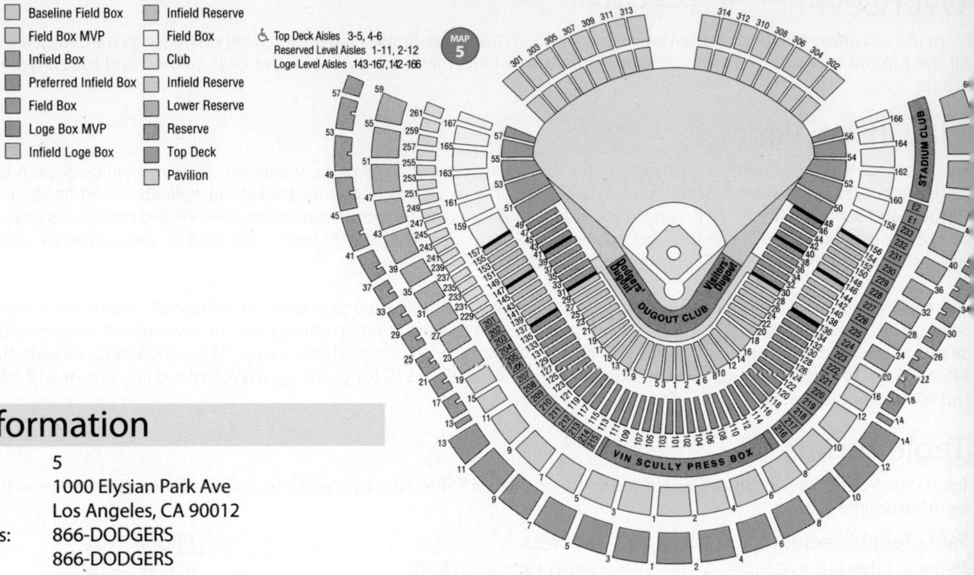

General Information

NFT Map:	5
Address:	1000 Elysian Park Ave Los Angeles, CA 90012
Information & Tickets:	866-DODGERS
Lost & Found:	866-DODGERS
Blue Crew Fan Club:	323-224-1315
Website:	losangeles.dodgers.mlb.com

Overview

Now that LA has reignited its love affair with the Dodgers (Los Angeles Angels of who?), games are a must go-to for fun sun burnt weekends and breezy evenings—and not just for Dodger Dogs and ice cream bars. With Don Mattingly managing, and emerging superstars Matt Kemp and Clayton Kershaw, visiting Chavez Ravine is again a sporting event, not just a day at Disneyland North.

If you're lucky, or lucky enough to be rich, score Dugout Club seats where you'll enjoy an open buffet and might bump into Larry David or any number of Hollywood regulars. If you are sensitive to folklore, avoid the Top Deck because of its alleged "gang element."

Win or lose, on game days just about the only sure bet is popping into the classic local dive bar, the Short Stop (1455 Sunset Blvd), for drink specials and plenty of folks in blue.

How to Get There—Driving

From the 101, exit at Alvarado, head north, then turn right on Sunset. Go approximately one mile and turn left on Elysian Park Avenue. You will run into Dodger Stadium. From the 110, take the Dodger Stadium exit and follow signs. From the 5 S, exit at Stadium Way, turn left, and follow the signs to Dodger Stadium. From the 5 N, exit at Stadium Way and turn left on Riverside Drive. Turn left onto Stadium Way and follow the signs.

Whenever possible, use surface roads. Sunset Boulevard will take you to Elysian Park Avenue. Beverly Boulevard is often less congested—and more direct—than Sunset Boulevard. Take Beverly to Alvarado, then follow directions above from the 101

Parking

To make things more exciting for motorists, the Dodgers have instituted something called "Controlled Zone Parking", basically meaning that where you park will be determined by which parking gate you enter. This means that if you want to park near right field, you have to drive around until you find the corresponding gate. It's supposed to be easier…we'll see about that. Prices have gone up as well—general parking for cars and motorcycles is $10 and parking for large vehicles, including buses, motor homes, limousines, and other oversized vehicles costs $35. If you're feeling cheap (and with the price of Dodger Dogs, nobody blames you) you can usually find free parking reasonably close by on a residential street in Echo Park, and huff it up the hill from there.

How to Get There—Mass Transit

Getting to Dodger Stadium via mass transit once included a three-quarter-mile walk up an incredibly steep hill, but if you're a car-less fan, there is another option: the Roundtripper Station to Stadium Shuttle. Take the Metro to the Chinatown Gold Line Station or to Berth 6 of Union Station and hop on the shuttle. At Dodger Stadium you'll be dropped off in Lot 13, which is a short walk to Lot 5 and the entrance to all levels of the stadium. Buses leave Union Station every 15 minutes from 5:40 pm to 8 pm, and Chinatown every half-hour. Return service, leaving from Lot 13, begins at the top of the 8th inning and the last bus leaves 60 minutes after the last out or 11 pm, whichever comes first. Free to Dodger ticket holders (or $1.50 each way) at the station before boarding and Metro passes are not accepted. Unfortunately, the shuttle service is not available for all games, so call 866-DODGERS to check schedules.

If you take a cab to the game and you plan to depart from the stadium by cab, a taxi service is available in Lot 3 on the western side of the stadium or at the Union 76 Service Station near Lot 37 beyond the center field wall.

How to Get Tickets

You can order Dodgers tickets by phone, through the box office at Dodger Stadium (Monday through Saturday, 9 am to 5 pm and during all Dodger home games), and online through the Dodgers website. Also, be sure to Google ticket resellers for great bargains on sites like stubhub.com.

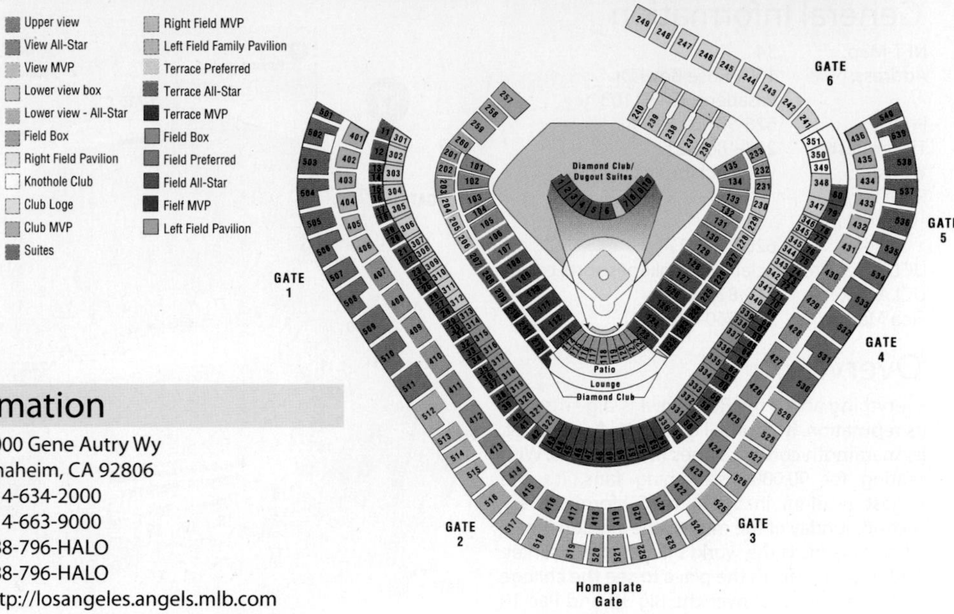

General Information

‹ddress:	2000 Gene Autry Wy Anaheim, CA 92806
›ox Office:	714-634-2000
icketmaster:	714-663-9000
iroup Tickets:	888-796-HALO
ost & Found:	888-796-HALO
Vebsite:	http://losangeles.angels.mlb.com

Overview

‹ consistently competitive club, coupled with an aggressive narketing campaign has made the Angels a worthy regional rival o the storied Dodgers. Those who find some rugged elements f Dodgers Stadium less "charming" and more "annoying," will ppreciate Angels Stadium. Better organized, easier access, and heaper parking makes it the Orange County of SoCal baseball tadiums. But even with a few LA defectors in their fanbase, it's till the team of skinny-jeaned Santa Ana Chipsters (Chicano ipsters) and Suburban driving soccer moms.

you can stomach rally monkeys and fireworks at home-runs, hen you'll have a lovely day in Anaheim. The stadium comes vith all of the amenities that a modern-day baseball fan could vant: three full-service restaurants, family-oriented seating, n interactive game area for the kids, and, of course, Vlad the mpaler. It's almost more amusement park than stadium. But if hat's what it takes to get a new generation out to the old ball ame, who can really complain?

How to Get There—Driving

rom downtown, take 605 S to the CA-91/Artesia Freeway east. ake the I-5/Santa Ana Freeway exit on the right towards Santa ına. Merge onto I-5 S and take the exit on the right towards naheim Boulevard/Haster Street/Katella Avenue. Turn left nto West Freedman Way, turn right onto South Anaheim oulevard, and turn left onto East Katella Avenue.

Parking

he parking lot opens two-and-a-half hours prior to the start f the scheduled first pitch and, since there are only three ntrances to the Angel Stadium parking lot (via Douglass oad, State College Boulevard, and Orangewood Avenue), ve suggest you get there early. Parking staff will direct you towards vacancies. Day-of-game parking is $10 and oversized vehicles (greater than 20 feet in length) are $20.

The bus parking lot is located by the Orangewood Avenue entrance. Season ticket holders with parking coupons can use the Express Entry Lane on Orangewood Avenue.

How to Get There—Mass Transit

If you can get yourself to Union Station (Metro Red Line), you can catch the Amtrak Pacific Surfliner bound for San Diego, which stops not too far from the stadium at Anaheim Station. A one-way fare will set you back $14 and the Orange County Transportation Authority has a bus service to the ballpark. Call 800-636-RIDE for more information on bus schedules.

But unless you're watching a pitchers' duel or a complete blowout, the train may not be an option for most night games. The last train back to LA leaves Anaheim just after 10 pm, making an overnight stay in beautiful downtown Anaheim a definite possibility.

Patrons who require a taxi service from Angel Stadium can swing by the Guest Relations Center and ask a concierge to call them a cab.

How to Get Tickets

You can purchase tickets in person at the box office, which is open Monday through Saturday, as well as on Sunday game days, from 9 am to 5:30 pm, or by phoning the box office at 714-634-2000. Online tickets can be purchased through Ticketmaster at www.ticketmaster.com, or look for great seats for cheap on eBay where many locals put up their season tickets for sale.

General Information

NFT Map:	34
Address:	1001 Rose Bowl Dr Pasadena, CA 91103
Phone:	626-577-3100
Ticketmaster:	213-480-3232
Website:	www.uclabruins.com
Rose Parade Grandstand Tickets:	626-795-4171
UCLA website:	uclabruins.collegesports.com
UCLA tickets:	310-825-2101
Flea Market:	323-560-7469

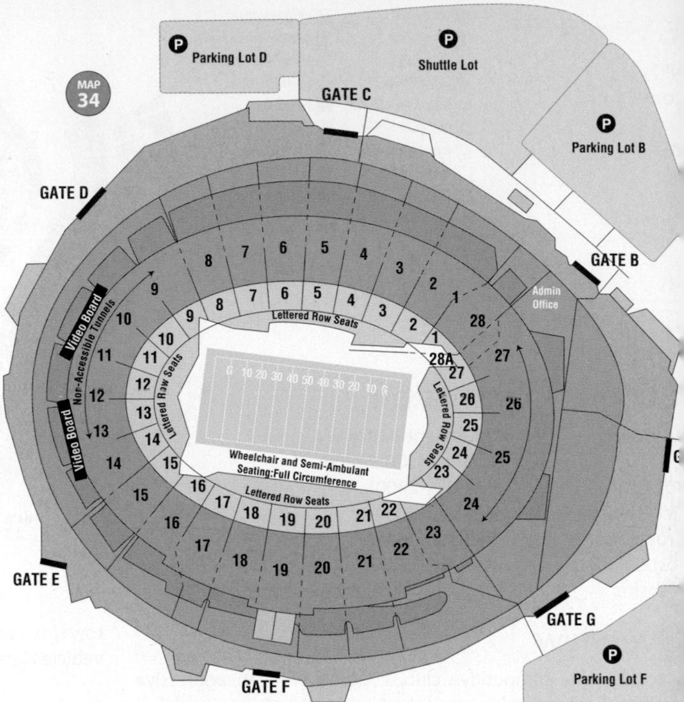

Overview

Everything about the Rose Bowl is big—its size, its reputation, its football games, its flea market, its mammoth concert stages fit for a Bono. With seating for 90,000+ screaming fans, it's the largest stadium in Southern California. Every second Sunday of the month, the stadium hosts what it claims is the world's largest flea market. And once a year, it's the place to see the college kids lose their cool over the Big 10 and Pac 10 champs. The Rose Bowl is home to the UCLA Bruins football team and has hosted five NFL Super Bowl Games, the 1984 Olympic soccer matches, the 1994 Men's World Cup Soccer, and the 1999 Women's World Cup Soccer. It doesn't get much bigger than that.

While the stadium hosts world-class events, there's nothing particularly exceptional about the super-sized structure, except maybe its size. The stadium is moderately accessible by car, and the surrounding area of Pasadena offers good walking and shopping opportunities, with a choice of restaurants and sports bars where you can celebrate your team's victory—or drown out a nasty defeat.

Flea Market

On the second Sunday of each month, the flea market takes over the entire Rose Bowl complex. Inside the gates, you'll find a slapdash array of new merchandise, antique collectibles, vintage clothing, and goodness knows what else. All of which is just a precursor to what you'll find in the parking lots: the world's most overwhelming garage sale (come with patience, if not cash to burn). Entry into the flea market costs $8 after 9 am. If you want first dibs on the goods, you can gain early entry: admission costs $10 from 8 am to 9 am; $15 from 7 am to 8 am; and $20 from 5 am to 7 am. Serious shoppers arrive at dawn, and few go home empty-handed.

How to Get There—Driving

There is one major consideration you need to take into account when driving to the Rose Bowl—AVOID the 110 Pasadena Freeway at all costs! The best approach to the stadium is the Pasadena 210 Freeway. Take the Mountain/Seco/Arroyo Boulevard/Windsor exit and follow signs to the stadium. If you approach on the 134, exit at Linda Vista and follow signs.

A less congested alternative if you're coming from the west is t take 134 to 2 North then take 210 East to Pasadena and exit a Mountain/Seco/Arroyo Boulevard/Windsor.

Parking

Parking for UCLA games costs $10 for cars, $20 for motor homes limousines, and is free of charge for buses. On Rose Bowl da parking costs $25 for cars and $100 for motor homes. For th Rose Parade, paid parking is available on a first-come, first-serve basis at various lots and parking structures near the parad route, including locations at Boston Court/Mentor, Union/I Molino, Euclid/Union, Raymond/Union, 40 North Mentor/Lak 465 East Union near Los Robles, 44 South Madison near Gree 462 East Green near Los Robles, and Colorado/Los Robles.

How to Get There—Mass Transit

No city buses or trains stop near the stadium, but on Rose Bov game day the MTA provides regular bus service from locatior throughout the county. Call 800-266-6883 for departur locations. A shuttle is available on UCLA game days from Ol Pasadena to the Stadium. The shuttle picks up fans at th Parsons Technology Building (100 W Walnut Ave). Parking cos $9, and the shuttle is free. Service begins four hours prior to th game and continues for one hour after the game.

How to Get Tickets

Tickets to the Rose Bowl, Rose Parade, and UCLA games can b purchased online through Ticketmaster.

General Information

FT Map: 9
ocation: 1111 S Figueroa St
Los Angeles, CA 90015
Vebsite: www.staplescenter.com
ox Office: 213-742-7340
arking: 213-742-7275
A Sparks (WNBA): www.wnba.com/sparks; 213-929-1300
A Lakers (NBA): www.nba.com/lakers; 310-426-6000
A Clippers (NBA): www.nba.com/clippers; 888-895-8662
A Kings (NHL): kings.nhl.com; 213-742-7100

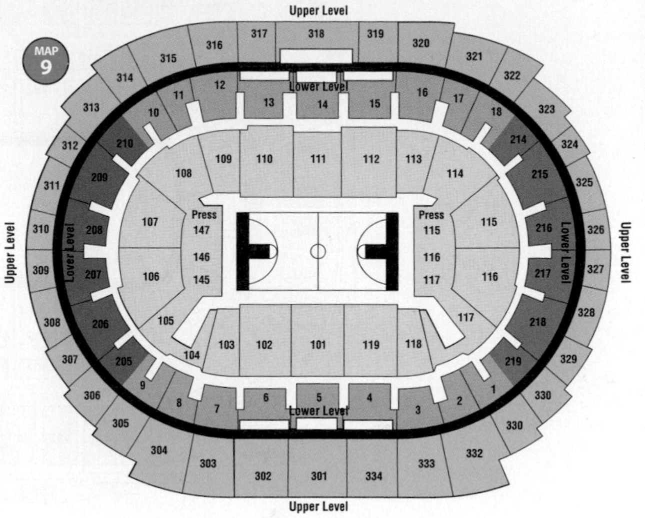

Overview

'en Master Phil has decamped and the dynasty ppears to have ended, but Lakers tickets remain he hottest (and costliest) game in town. Love 'em r love to hate 'em, the purple and gold call this ehemoth home and share it with the Clippers not just LA's Washington Generals, the Clippers are lisproportionally popular with our writers and crew, ossibly because of cheap tix, probably because they're ctually winning now) and the NHL's 2012 Stanley Cup vinning Kings.

uilt in 1999, it's not only a sports mecca but it's also big nough to handle, say, the 2000 Democratic National Convention and Jay-Z's last tour. In stadium years, the TAPLES Center is no spring chicken, but the place still eems modern and is more than capable of handling the 9,000+ fans who flood its gates for the 230+ sports and ntertainment events held annually. With concession tands at every turn, and the Fox Sports Sky Box's rowdy ub open before and after the games, food and booze vill never be more than a couple of steps away (but, like ll stadium concession stands, they jack up the prices just ecause they can and the food is mediocre at best).

Add the brand new LA Live center surrounding STAPLES nd you find a glut of excuses to visit the area even in the ff-seasons. The Nokia Theater brings brand name acts nd between various restaurants, bars, a movie theater, nd Lucky Strike Lanes bowling alley, the days of the lowntown yawn are over. North of Staples, you'll find a evitalized downtown with impressive nightlife options or a post-game drink. Even parking isn't all that bad, given lowntown's cramped layout. And that's a major victory for ny Angeleno right from the get-go.

How to Get There—Driving

'he STAPLES Center is located in downtown Los Angeles, ear the intersection of Routes 10 (Santa Monica) and 110 Harbor). The best advice we can offer is to get off of the reeway as soon as possible and make your way to Olympic Boulevard. If you're coming from the north, take I-5 S (or 101 S) to 110 S (Harbor Freeway/Los Angeles). Exit at Olympic Boulevard and turn left onto 11th Street. Continue past Cherry Street and Georgian Street and the STAPLES Center is on the right. From the south, take the 110 N and exit at Adams Boulevard. Turn left onto Figueroa Street, then make another left at 11th Street.

Parking

Parking at the STAPLES Center is just about as easy as getting your hands on playoff tickets. Lot 7 opens at 8 am for guests visiting the box office, Fox Sports Sky Box, or Team LA store. Lots 1 and C open 2.5 hours before the start of an event. The remaining lots open 90 minutes before an event. The lots at STAPLES Center are overpriced (up to $30), and many are available only to VIPs and season ticket holders. If you're willing to arrive a little early for an event and walk a few blocks, there is a fair amount of cheaper parking available at various lots. Keep in mind that loading zones downtown are free to park in after six p.m. Though we'd prefer not everyone knew this.

How to Get There—Mass Transit

The Metro Blue Line to Pico will land you just a block from the stadium. Buses 27, 28, 30, 31, 33, 81, 333, 434, 439, 442, 444, 445, 446, and 447 all stop in the vicinity.

How to Get Tickets

Tickets for Sparks, Lakers, Clippers, and Kings games can all be purchased online through Ticketmaster at www.ticketmaster.com or through the individual websites and phone numbers listed above.

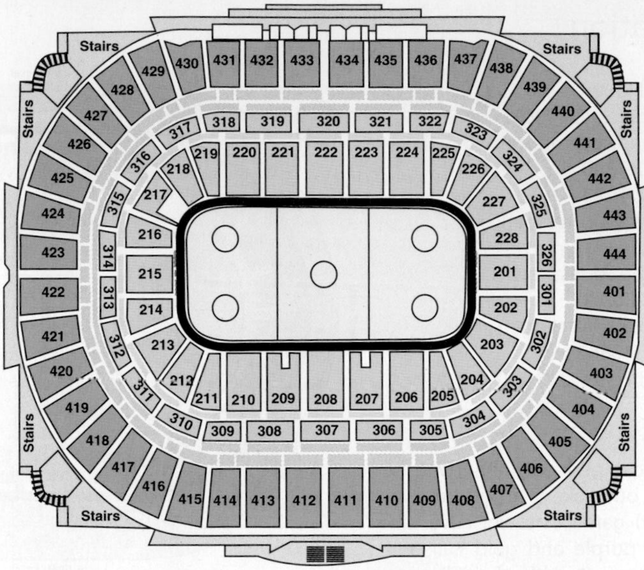

General Information

Location:	2695 East Katella Ave Anaheim, CA 92806
Admin Phone:	714-704-2400
Box Office Phone:	714-704-2500
Group Sales:	714-704-2420
Website:	www.hondacenter.com
Mighty Ducks Website (NHL):	ducks.nhl.com

Overview

Ever since the Ducks have proven themselves hockey contenders, the drive down to the OC to catch some action on the ice is almost worth it. Sure, it kind of blows getting there, especially if there's an event at Angels Stadium on that same night (they're right across the freeway from one another, guaranteeing road rage-inducing traffic congestion), but once inside, you'll discover that Anaheim's answer to the STAPLES Center is a snappy, efficient facility. (A facility that until recently had a much snappier name—Arrowhead Pond.) Whether you're one of the 17,000+ fans who flock to see the latest UFC bout, or even the occasional Tina Turner concert, you'll appreciate the friendly staff, the easy flow of people traffic, and the edible offerings that will find you before you find them. It's almost enough to clear up that road rage. Almost.

How to Get There—Driving

From Los Angeles, take 405 S to 22 E to 57 N. Exit on Katella Avenue and turn right, then turn left on Douglas Street. If you're approaching on I-5 S, exit on Katella Avenue and turn left, then go left on Douglas Street. From I-10, head east to 57 S and exit on Katella Avenue and turn left, then turn left on Douglas Street.

Parking

General parking is $20 for most events, $15 for Ducks games and other sporting events (like UFC); $25 for preferred $25 limos, and $30 RVs and buses (unlimited drop-off and pick-up for an event).

How to Get There—Mass Transit

The Orange County Transit Authority provides transport to Honda Center. Check www.octa.net for schedules or phone 714-560-6272. In addition to OCTA, Amtrak's station is located within walking distance of the arena, in the parking lot at Angel Stadium. But Amtrak riders beware—the last train back to LA from Anaheim leaves shortly after 10 pm, so unless you're camping out or leaving early, you might want to make other arrangements for getting home after evening events.

How to Get Tickets

Tickets can be purchased in person at the box office or at Ticketmaster outlets, by calling your local Ticketmaster, or online at www.ticketmaster.com. The box office is open Monday through Friday, 10 am until 6 pm, and Saturday 10 am until 4 pm. Purchase same-day tickets on Sundays—the box office opens three hours before the scheduled event and sells tickets only to that day's event. A "wristband lottery" for any remaining tickets to popular events takes place the morning of the event and line-ups begin at 7 am. But even if you're first in line and receive a wristband, obtaining a ticket is no guarantee. Fifteen minutes before tickets go on sale, one wristband number is drawn randomly and it becomes the starting number for ticket sales.

General Information

Address:	18400 Avalon Blvd Carson, CA 90746
General Information:	310-630-2000
Stadium Website:	www.homedepotcenter.com
LA Galaxy Website:	www.lagalaxy.com
LA Galaxy Tickets:	877-342-5299
Chivas USA Website:	www.cdchivasusa.com
Chivas USA Tickets:	877-244-8271
Group Sales:	877-234-8425
Ticketmaster:	213-480-3232
Parking:	310-630-2060

Overview

The Home Depot Center is a jack of all trades: home of the LA Galaxy and Chivas USA soccer teams, the official training site of the US Track & Field team as well as USA cycling, the US Soccer Federation, and the US Tennis Association. Not to mention it's one heck of a rockin' concert venue.

The Home Depot Center is definitely up to the task of becoming a world-renowned sporting venue with its 27,000 seat capacity soccer stadium, 8,000-seat tennis venue, a track-and-field stadium, a boxing ring, a 3,000-square-foot weight room, 30 tennis courts, nine soccer training fields, and a three-mile jogging trail. And speaking of attractions, The Home Depot Center has the best bathroom and food stand layouts around: they reside in a wideopen perimeter that is above not only the action on the field, but a majority of the seating, so the occasional trip to the bathroom or to go buy a margarita means that you'll miss none of the action. And let's not forget the parking: there's so much parking, you might just decide to stick around and enroll at Cal State Dominguez Hills, the university campus where HDC is housed.

How to Get There—Driving

A lack of signs makes the Home Depot Center a little difficult to find. Leave time in your travel plans for getting lost.

Approaching on 110 S, exit on 190th Street and make a left. 190th Street becomes Victoria Street. Continue past Avalon Boulevard. For reserved parking, use Gates C or D on your right. For general unreserved parking, head farther along and use Gates E or F on your right. From 110 N, take the Del Amo Boulevard exit and make a left on Figueroa Street. Make a right on Del Amo Boulevard and a left on Avalon Boulevard. For reserved parking, continue past University Drive and use Gate B on your right. For general unreserved parking, make a right on University Drive and use Gate I on your left.

From the 405 S, exit on Vermont. At the bottom of the ramp, make a left on 190th Street, which becomes Victoria Street. Follow directions for 110 S. From 405 N, exit on Avalon Boulevard, and make a right. Follow directions for 110 N.

Parking

Parking rates are different for each event. For a Galaxy or Chivas regular season game, parking costs between $10 and $15 per vehicle preferred is $30, valet is $40. For Galaxy playoffs or other special events, such as concerts, parking costs between $15 and $20 per vehicle. The lot generally opens two hours before game time, but tailgating is prohibited (whatever).

How to Get There—Mass Transit

Take the Metro Blue Line to the Artesia Station. Transfer to Metro Bus 130 and take it to Victoria Street and Avalon Boulevard.

How to Get Tickets

Tickets for all events can be purchased at the box office (Avalon and 184th St), through any Ticketmaster retail location, or online at www.ticketmaster.com. The box office is open Monday through Friday from 10 am–6 pm, as well as three hours before game time on event days.

General Information

NFT Map:	49 & 50
Address:	1727 N Victory Pl Burbank, CA 91502

Shopping

The Burbank Empire Center is for serious shoppers. There is no leisurely window-shopping, no frivolous detours to mall staples like Claire's Accessories or Brookstone, no movie theater. The Empire Center is all about the essentials—life's most basic necessities, from super-sized televisions at Best Buy to supersized packs of legal pads at Staples to super-sized bags of Cheetos at Target. The center is home only to big-box retailers and national chains, and it expertly straddles the line between high end (The Great Indoors) and discount (Marshalls) with an emphasis on stores geared toward folks in the mood for nesting (Lowe's Home Improvement, Linens 'n Things, and the aforementioned Great Indoors). The absence of diversions makes the Burbank Empire Center an ideal place for holiday shopping—the roomy parking lot is easily navigated and there is a store that suits everyone on your list, from athlete (Sportmart) to crafter (Michaels) to toy-addicted kid (Target). And this utilitarian shopping center features an equally utilitarian hotel, the Marriott Courtyard, should your Empire experience prove to be too exhausting to make the drive home. There is the new Ulta Beauty Store It's a larger Sephora that has high-end and lower-end products. You can get any makeup product, and they have a beauty salon.

Food

Fuel up for a grueling day of paint-matching and window-treatment ordering at Hometown Buffet or Outback Steakhouse. Or perhaps even the Krispy Kreme. The Great Indoors has a Starbucks inside the store when shopping for shower curtains wears you down. A freestanding Starbucks located in a cluster of restaurants bordering Empire Drive features extra room for the laptop-wagging set. Options for a mid-shopping respite run from the lighter fare of Jamba Juice, Subway, Sbarro, Wendy's and Panda Express, to the more substantial Outback Steakhouse, Olive Garden and Hometown Buffet (where the line begins forming about 10:30 a.m. and wraps around the building by noon, so plan accordingly).

Drawbacks

True to its name, the place is empire-sized. The Great Indoors and Lowe's are at opposite ends of the mall which can be inconvenient for those on intensive home-improvement missions. The long walk can be especially rough on hot summer days when the heat is shimmering off the parking lot. The Burbank Empire Center is also adjacent to a very busy, very big Costco, which means the intersection of Burbank Boulevard, Victory Place, and Victory Boulevard can tie itself into quite a knot. The good news is that there are long left-turn arrows to ease you through.

How to Get There

From the 5 in either direction, exit at Burbank Boulevard. Head west on Burbank Boulevard to Victory Place and turn right. The Empire Center is about a mile down on your left. Just look for the signs shaped like airplanes and stores the size of airplane hangars. The Great Indoors is at the southern end of the mall; Target and Lowe's are at the northern end. In case you can't smell your way to them, the donuts are to be found on the east side of the mall where the stand-alone stores are located. The bus lines that stop at the mall are BurbankBus Empire Route and Downtown Route stop at Empire Center as well as Metro Bus 94, 165, and Metro Rapid 794.

General Information

NFT Map: 2
Address: 8500 Beverly Blvd
Los Angeles, CA 90048
Phone: 310-854-0070
Website: www.beverlycenter.com

Shopping

Like a well-dressed phoenix rising from the ashes, the Beverly Center opened in 1982 to replace Kiddyland, a modest amusement park featuring a ferris wheel and pony rides. With its highly recognizable exterior escalators and plethora of bored housewives carrying pint-sized pets, this shopping stronghold is but an evolved version of Kiddyland. Despite the younger, scrappier Grove opening in 2002 and soaking up much of its limelight, the Beverly Center forges on and continues to be one of LA's premier shopping destinations. When it was announced that H&M was coming to town, shopping centers lobbied for the honors the way most cities lobby to host the Olympics. The Beverly Center is now home to one of the still-rare LA locations of the famous discount retailer. Who needs gold medals when you can buy babydoll dresses for $19.99?

Today's Beverly Center is something of a study in contrasts. Stores such as D&G, Louis Vuitton, Diesel, Dior, A/X Armani Exchange, Ben Sherman, and a brightly lit Bloomingdale's cater to 21st-century America's love affair with labels; but there's a distinct middle-of-the-road factor at the Beverly Center, embodied by the presence (persistence?) of GNC, Macy's, Brookstone, Sunglass Hut, and the rest of the chain gang. The scales may have been tipped on the luxe side with the closing of that staple of malls from coast to coast, the Gap. Shops like Forever 21, Claire's, and Steve Madden and eateries like the Grand Lux Café remind us all that the survival of the mall as a species depends on its ability to attract teenage girls and out-of-towners.

Food

There are a few higher-end chains like The Capital Grille and Obika Mozzarella Bar where those who like uniformity in dining can lay down some serious cash. The eighth floor Food Court features all of the usual suspects (Auntie Anne's, Sbarro's, Panda Express, Starbucks, and the like). Patio seating is plentiful, non-smoking, and features an almost panoramic eastern view of the city. Street-level options include mall mainstays like CPK, PF Chang's and Chipotle Mexican Grill.

Drawbacks

This is a fairly popular mall in a busy part of town; it's bordered by another mall (the Beverly Connection) and a huge medical center (Cedars-Sinai). That's why it's a good idea to enter from the San Vicente (westernmost and least congested) side of the building. Although traffic flows

well inside the mall, traffic in the parking lot does not. Stay cool—the good stuff's waiting upstairs. Don't be too intimidated by its size, because although it has eight levels, in classic LA style, five are parking. If it's women's clothes you're after, be advised that the Beverly Center best serves those under the age of 30 and smaller than a size 10. Strangely there is no mall access to Bed, Bath and Beyond or the Macy's Men's Department—enter from the street or the valet parking area.

How to Get There—Driving

From the 10 in either direction, exit at La Cienega Boulevard. Head north on La Cienega for approximately 2.25 miles, and you'll see the behemoth just ahead on your left. Cross 3rd Street and turn left into the mall at the next signal. From the 101 in either direction, exit Highland Boulevard and head south on Highland for approximately two miles until you hit Beverly Boulevard. Turn right onto Beverly, and head west about two miles to La Cienega Boulevard. Make a left onto La Cienega Boulevard, and an immediate right into the mall. The bus lines to Beverly Center are LADOT DASH Fairfax, Metro Bus 14, 16/316, 30/330, 105, 218, Metro Rapid 705, and West Hollywood CityLine.

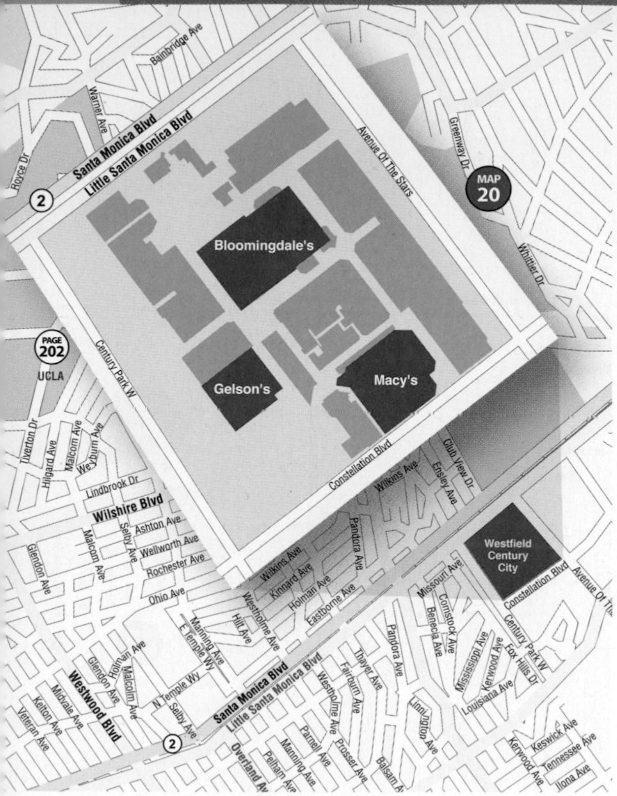

General Information

NFT Map:	20
Address:	10250 Santa Monica Blvd Los Angeles, CA 90067
Phone:	310-277-3898
Website:	www.westfield.com/centurycity

Shopping

What was once a neighborhood shopping center (albeit an outsize one—everything in this part of town is huge) is now a big, shiny temple of consumerism that people actually make a point of driving to from other, distant parts of town. Locals go too, for groceries from Gelson's. Westfield is a big corporation, and they decided to make this outpost pretty high end, the Macy's anchor nothwithstanding; other shops include Tiffany, Louis Vuitton, and Brooks Brothers, and Bloomingdale's for those in search of the department store experience. For the big spender in training, H&M, Hollister, and True Religion fit the bill. Though most of the stores are big chains, the occasional local purveyor shows up, too. The non-clothing stores speak to a certain aesthetic, too: one salon is dedicated to shaving beards, another to shaping brows.

If your idea of relaxation doesn't include hair removal, check out the 15-screen movie theatre, where the seats are designed to feel like easy chairs and some screening allow cocktails. The crowd mirrors the mall outside, with plenty of privileged teeny boppers and latter-day ladies who lunch, but it's still quieter than among the crowds outside.

Food

As with the shops, the restaurants here are pretty high end, for a mall. Sure, there's a Panda Express, a pizza joint, a Wetzel's Pretzels: typical stuff scattered throughout the premises. Those are perfectly fine for a quick bite with no surprises and the end of an arduous day of shopping. For a more civilized meal, check out Breadbar, a bakery and bistro with real, actual gourmet cred. You might get lucky and go when they have a visiting chef in the kitchen. If size matters, Gulfstream and RockSugar take the "huge, calorie-laden platter" restaurant concept up a notch or two.

Drawbacks

There are two key points to remember about the horrific parking situation here: one, if driving into the mall via the official main entrance, you might get confused and think this is a valet-only situation. It's not. Two, remember to pre-pay before you leave. The first three hours of self-parking are free; after that the garage gets pretty pricey. The movie theater, Pink Taco, Gulfstream, and RockSugar validate, but that'll just bring the price down, it doesn't cover it entirely. And don't be afraid to walk a bit, the whole parking situation calms down farther away from the mall entrances.

How to Get There

From the 405 in either direction, exit Santa Monica Boulevard and head east past Sepulveda. Make a slight jog right onto Little Santa Monica Boulevard, and follow it approximately one-and-a-half miles to the mall. The entrance is on your right just past Century Park. From Olympic Boulevard in either direction, head north on Avenue of the Stars to Constellation. Turn left on Constellation and look for the parking entrance 150 yards down on your right.

General Information

NFT Map: 32
Address: 525 Carson Street
Torrance, CA 90503
Phone: 310-542-8525
Website: www.simon.com/mall/del-amo-fashion-center

Shopping

First, the Del Amo Fashion Center is massive. It is a huge sprawling building that has 3,000,000 sq ft of prime retail shopping space. It was first built in 1971 and for a while in the 1980s was the largest mall in America, before Mall of America was built. Over the years large sections of the mall have been added piece by piece which has led to the mall twisting and turning like a maze. It's easy to get lost in this mall, and don't forget where you park your car, otherwise you'll have to trek all the way back to the other end. What it lacks in design it makes up in spades in sheer volume of stores. There are ten jewelry stores, over a dozen shoe stores and five optometric businesses. This doesn't even count the chain stores, restaurants and stores that can only be found in Del Amo Mall. A word of warning, a section of the mall stretches over Carson Street and the only way to cross from the Sears side to the newer side of the mall is to go to the second floor of the middle Macy's (there are two). Once there you'll have to walk through that second floor to get to the other stores.

The most recent mall addition is an outdoor section. It has all the newest stores, Anthropologie, Forever 21, H&M along with the new restaurants like Ra Sushi, P.F. Changs, and the Lazy Dog Café. Wild Buffalo Wings is a local sports haunt, they get all the games and pay for the fights. If you're looking to watch a sport they'll have it on their massive TV screens. AMC Del Amo 18 boasts 18 screens and has all the newest movies in 3D. The self-serve booths are your best bet to miss the line, but watch out Fridays and Saturdays, most of the local high school population likes to hang out there.

Food

The food court is centrally located and features Mexican, Mediterranean, and Pacific Rim cuisines in addition to fast-food offerings like Chick-fil-A and Hot Dog on a Stick. The area is clean, brightly lit, and well attended. To break up a long expedition, consider going outside the mall. Black Angus (3405 W Carson St, 310-370-1523) and Lucille's Smokehouse BBQ (21420 Hawthorne Blvd, 310-370-7427), both adjacent to the mall, offer a chance to protein-load on pretty decent fare in relatively quiet surroundings.

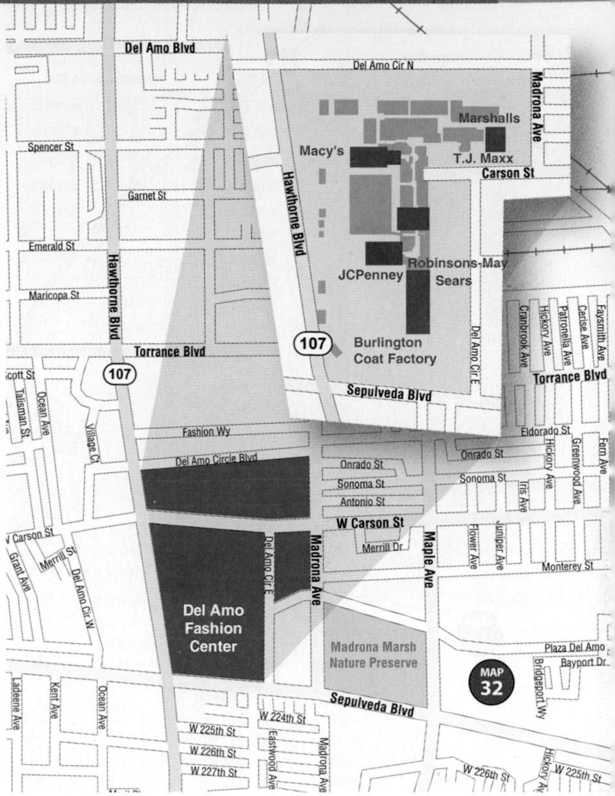

Drawbacks

The upside to the Del Amo Mall (lots of stores) is also its downfall (lots of stores). Besides the fact that you need your own GPS tracker to find where you're going, you need to hike on a mini expedition trek to get there. Del Amo is best approached with very comfortable shoes, an open mind, and an extra cup of coffee—from Starbucks. Shoppers seeking a smaller venue should consider the Galleria at South Bay as an alternate venue.

How to Get There

From the 405 S, exit Redondo Beach, head south on Prairie Avenue, and take Prairie approximately three miles. Turn right on Carson to enter the parking lot. From the 405 N, exit Artesia Boulevard and head west on Artesia to Prairie Avenue. Make a left at Prairie and continue on Prairie approximately three miles. Turn right on Carson to enter the parking lot. From the 110 in either direction, exit Carson and proceed west three miles on Carson to the Del Amo Fashion Center. All of the Torrance Buses stop at or near Del Amo mall as well as Metro Bus 344 and Beach Cities Transit 104.

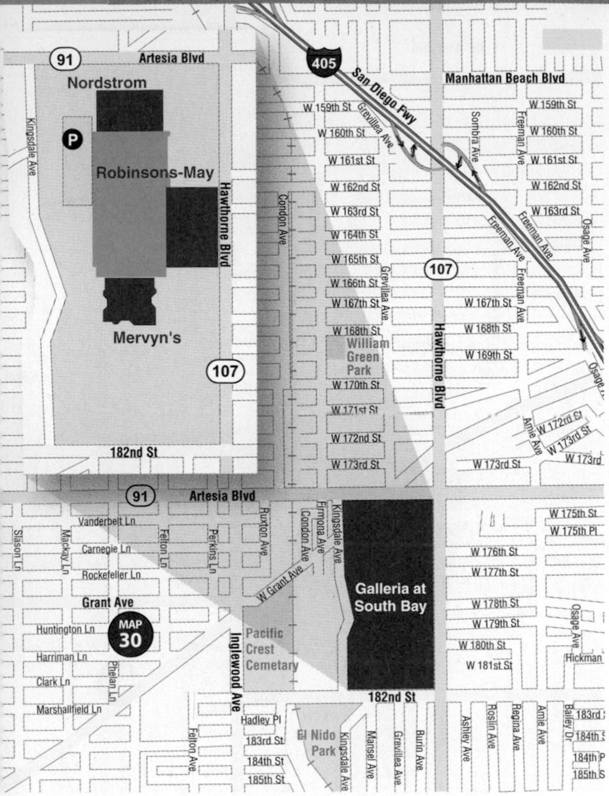

General Information

NFT Map:	30
Address:	1815 Hawthorne Blvd Redondo Beach, CA 90278
Phone:	310-371-7546
Website:	www.southbaygalleria.com

Shopping

All the malls bearing the name "Galleria" base their design (in theory at least) on the Galleria Vittorio Emmanuele in Milan, a four-story shopping center with a glass arcade roof that floods the space with natural light. Well, it's not Milan or even close, but you can see the glass structure effect at the South Bay Galleria. You are much better off heading a few miles north to Century City for much more enjoyable shopping, dining, and movie-going experience. Department stores include Macy's and Nordstrom, and have poorer selections when compared to their other Southern California locations. The mall has three stories of standard mall fare including Gap, Abercrombie & Fitch, and Bebe. In the past few years they've been trying to update not the mall, but it's surroundings. The two story Target is one of the better Targets in the area and comes with lots of parking. Between the mall and the Ralph's grocery store they bulldozed the run down theatre and put in a new shopping center. It has a Nordstrom Rack, an Ulta, a Sprouts Farmer's Market (which has the best produce prices in town) as well as best liquor store ever Total Wine. Imagine a liquor store as big as a grocery store with rock bottom prices.

Food

The Galleria's food court, however, is excellent compared to much of the competition. Take the express escalator from the main floor and grab a table overlooking the fountain in center court. There's a nice range of food options from Great Khan's Mongolian BBQ to Stone Oven Grill. The area is clean and well tended. If you want to eat your meal in a quieter, less ricochet-prone setting, try California Pizza Kitchen (CPK) or Red Robin downstairs. For all you Internet surfers, bring your laptops—the food court has free WiFi.

Drawbacks

As with practically everywhere, weekend parking is a big hassle and not worth it. It's five dollars to valet. (Valets are near CPK on the east side and adjacent to Nordstrom on the west.) Hot tip: check with the guest services booth just inside the Galleria, as they often have free valet passes stashed behind the counter.

How to Get There

From the 405 S, exit Hawthorne Boulevard and head south one mile. The mall entrance will be on your right.

From the 405 N, exit Redondo Boulevard and head west on Artesia approximately three-quarters of a mile to Hawthorne and make a left. The mall will be on your right. The bus lines to the Galleria are Beach Cities Transit 102, Gardena 3, Lawndale Beat Express Route, Lawndale Beat Residential Route, Metro Bus 40, 130, 210, 211, 344, Metro Rapid 710, 740, Municipal Area Express 2, and finally Torrance 2, and 8.

General Information

NFT Map: 51
Address: 100 West Broadway, Suite 700
Glendale, California 91210
Phone: 818-246-6737
Website: www.glendalegalleria.com

Shopping

In the giant game of mall Tetris, Glendale Galleria is the "L": not only because of its shape, but also because it's simultaneously the most annoying and rewarding piece of the puzzle. It's the mall that locals love to hate—for all of its faults, you simply can't find a more comprehensive or utilitarian shopping experience. The mall is anchored by the usual stalwarts: Macy's, JCPenney, Target, and Nordstrom. Coach, Swarovski, and the Apple store represent the high end at this otherwise middle-class temple of mass consumerism. You'll find typical mall fare like Hot Topic and Foot Locker mixed in with boutique-type stores. The Galleria has an impressive selection of dedicated children's stores including Janie & Jack, Naartjie, and the ubiquitous Gap Kids. Forever 21 and Charlotte Russe are the standard go-to for trendy Valley girls while their mothers can stock up on chi-chi cosmetics at Sephora, MAC, and Aveda. A motley crew of kiosks finishes off the retail landscape, peddling everything from "miracle" face creams to rhinestone-encrusted belt buckles.

Food

The Galleria's main food court is on the second level, but you can often smell it from the third. The smoke from Massis International Grill is mainly responsible—the popular kabob shop serves up steak, lamb chops, and Cornish game hen along with a selection of Armenian and American beers. You'll find everything you'd expect in a food court, including Panda Express, Cinnabon, La Salsa, and Hot Dog on a Stick. The third level has its own selection of fast-food restaurants.

Drawbacks

If malls aren't your thing, the Galleria probably won't change your mind: on a bad day, it can be a long, echoing chamber of crying babies and shrieking teenagers. The place is also short on elevators and escalators, meaning you may end up walking the length of a football field just to change floors. On the weekends, you run the risk of being swept up in the herds of stroller-pushers, young lovers, and junior high cliques that roam the mall's narrow corridors. Of course—to some hard-core shoppers—this is all just part of the fun.

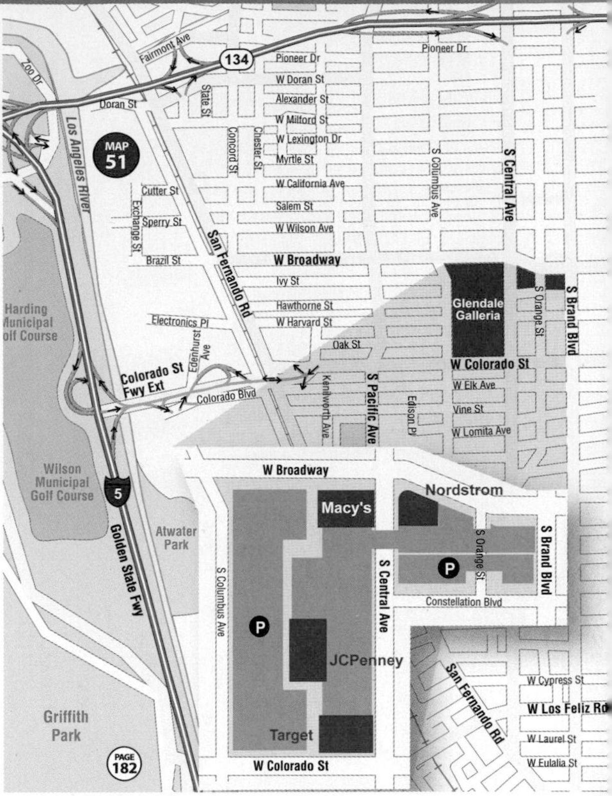

How to Get There

From the 5 in either direction, exit Colorado and take Colorado east about a mile and a half. The entrance to the mall parking lot is at a light on the left a hundred or so yards before you get to the intersection at Central. From the 134 in either direction, exit Central/Brand Boulevard and head south on Brand about a mile and a half. Turn right on Broadway, and head west an eighth of a mile. The entrance to the mall parking lot is at a light on the left about a hundred or so yards after Central. Look for the "Galleria" sign. For Nordstrom's valet service, enter the smaller parking lot on the east side of Central, just south of Broadway. The Buses to Glendale Galleria are Glendale Beeline 1/2, 3, 4, 5, 6, 11, Metro Bus 92, 180, 181, 183, 210, 603, and Metro Rapid 780.

General Information

NFT Map:	2
Address:	189 The Grove Dr Los Angeles, CA 90036
Phone:	323-900-8080
Website:	www.thegrovela.com

Shopping

Like Vegas, to which it has aptly been compared, the Grove polarizes Angelenos. There are those who hate it with a passion, resent the way it has commercialized the ancient, historic Farmers Market, and believe it has congested the streets of the Fairfax District beyond repair. Then there are the Grove supporters, open-minded, adaptable and happy consumers who can't help but smile when the dancing waters of the fountain break into yet another choreographed routine to the sound of Donna Summer's "Last Dance." Yes, the Grove is sterile. Yes, the Grove is pre-fab. But like the character of Melanie in *Gone With the Wind*, it's just so darned nice that we're able to table our cynicism for the length of a shopping trip and sing the mall's praises.

The Grove is fairly restrained, with just one anchor store—Nordstrom—and a small one at that. The emphasis here is on high-end specialty stores. NikeWomen carries fitness wear for gym goddesses. This family-friendly mall houses the area's only Pottery Barn Kids and recently opened American Girl Place, home to a series of overpriced, over-accessorized dolls, a theater, and a cafe. The usual suspects—the Gap and its brethren—are well represented, but the Grove also houses the unexpected: LA's first Barneys New York CO-OP, Amadeus Aveda Spa & Salon, and what might be the mall's most beautifully designed retail store, Anthropologie. If none of these stores fit your style, there's always Barnes & Noble. They've got something in everyone's size. Keep your eye out for celebs, this is one mall in LA they'll actually go to. Plus, they film *Extra* here, if you're lucky you can be in the audience.

Food

We've got good news and bad news. The bad news is that there is no food court—only full-service restaurants, so lunch or dinner at the Grove is going to cost you. The Farm of Beverly Hills offers American comfort food, while the Wood Ranch BBQ & Grill is a carnivore's paradise. The good news is you can head for the adjacent Farmers Market and enjoy its less expensive, eclectic, and far-superior food stalls. The Gumbo Pot features the best muffuletta this side of N'awlins, ¡Loteria! Grill offers some of the finest Mexican specialties west of Alvarado, and there's no better place for breakfast than Kokomo. Also worth checking out are the handful of specialty kiosks, like Haägen-Dazs and Surf City Squeeze.

Drawbacks

The lack of cheap places to eat can be a drag, and traffic and parking are always a problem. Third Street gets congested, and the traffic light at Beverly Boulevard and The Grove Drive is so poorly timed that two cars are lucky to advance on a green light. Entering from Fairfax Avenue is your best bet.

How to Get There

From the 10 in either direction, exit at Fairfax and head north approximately three miles. Go through the intersection at Third and Fairfax and turn right at Farmers Market Way. Drive past the Farmers Market and enter The Grove's parking structure. From the 101 in either direction, exit at Highland and head south toward Franklin Avenue. Turn right onto Franklin, and continue until you hit La Brea Avenue. Make a left turn and continue south on La Brea to Third Street. Turn right onto Third Street, and continue until you reach The Grove Drive. Make a right turn into the mall. Parking at The Grove is free for the first hour, and $3 per hour for the second and third hours. Valet parking is also available near each of the main entrances of The Grove's parking structure and costs $8 for the first two hours and $2 for each block of 30 minutes thereafter. While parking can get pricy here, most shops validate with purchase. And here's a trick, Nordstrom has validation machines. You don't even have to buy anything and you'll get a couple of hours of parking free. The bus lines that stop at The Grove are LADOT DASH Fairfax, Metro Bus 14, 16/316, 217 and 218.

General Information

NFT Map: 3
Address: 6801 Hollywood Blvd
Hollywood, CA 90028
Phone: 323-817-0200
Website: www.hollywoodandhighland.com

Shopping

Hollywood & Highland opened in late 2001 to much fanfare. Like the Strip in Las Vegas and the "new" Times Square, it's exceptionally clean, well lit, and family friendly. The center is most famous for its state-of-the-art Kodak Theater, which hosts the Academy Awards each year (right across from the Roosevelt Hotel, where the first Academy Awards was held in 1929). Yes, you heard correctly, the Oscars are held at a shopping mall! It's also home to Lucky Strike, a very glossy bowling alley serving a whole lotta top shelf liquor. The complex provides a safe haven from panhandlers and impersonators of Spiderman and Charlie Chaplin on the Boulevard out front.

But let's be honest here: Hollywood & Highland is a gajillion-dollar complex built for the amusement of tourists who come to shop, take pictures of each other, and take pictures of each other shopping. Hollywood & Highland makes little effort to cater to the local set, which is why you won't find many locals here. At this point you have no doubt flipped to the front of this book to confirm that the title is "Not For Tourists." Understandable. We include it here, because eventually we all must entertain our paler friends from the eastern parts of the country who show up to visit in February for what seems to be the express purpose of telling us that California has neither weather nor seasons. But we digress.

Yeah, they've got a Hot Topic and an interactive candy megastore, SWEET!, but this mall tries to provide a little something else: a calendar of events like the wine & jazz summer series keeps the culture alive. Besides, the convenience of the Metro, along with shuttle services to the Pantages Theatre, Hollywood Bowl, and Griffith Observatory makes H&H an unavoidable convenience. Even Spiderman has to get home after a long day.

Food

Two high-profile brands raise the meaning of mall food to an unprecedented level: CPK for pizza and Johnny Rockets for burgers. Cho Oishi and Chado Tea Room are reliable choices for a lunch date. Green Earth Café serves up speciality coffees and iced blended drinks. The cream puffs at Beard Papa's will have you asking, "Krispy Kreme who?" The clever (and discreet) visitor might venture up to the Loews Hollywood Hotel rooftop pool for a spectacular view and a cool drink. On the elevator ride up be sure to practice your straight face when you tell the guards that you "totally didn't see the 'For Hotel Guests Only' sign."

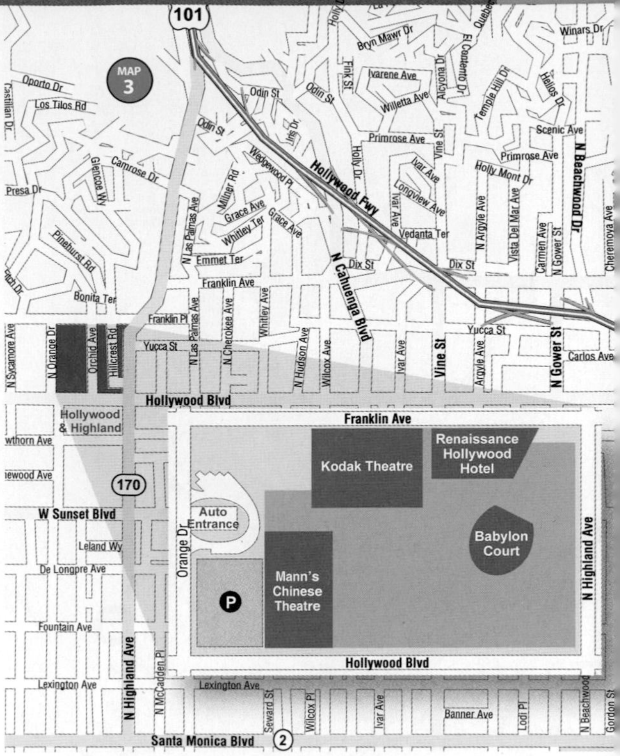

Drawbacks

The drawbacks of Hollywood & Highland are pretty much the same as those of the Strip or the "new" Times Square: it's crowded, air-brushed, fabricated out of whole cloth, and devoid of organic materials—but that's why you moved here, right? Then there's the mind-boggling traffic in the area around the complex. The streets surrounding the place get distressingly backed up on weekends. Also, the entrance to the never-crowded Mann Chinese 6 Theaters (not to be confused with the Grauman's legendary Chinese Theater next-door) is not well marked. Parking at Hollywood & Highland costs $2 for up to four hours with validation. For an additional five bucks, you can splurge on valet.

How to Get There

If you're using mass transit, take LADOT DASH Hollywood, Metro Bus 156, 212/312, 217, 222, 656, Metro Rapid 780 or the Red Line to the Hollywood & Highland station. From the 101 S, exit at Highland Avenue/Hollywood Bowl and merge onto Cahuenga Boulevard. Cahuenga becomes North Highland Avenue. Stay on Highland until Hollywood Boulevard. From the 101 N, exit at Highland Avenue/Hollywood Bowl and keep right at the fork in the ramp. Merge onto Odin Street, and turn left onto Highland Avenue. From 405 in either direction, exit onto Santa Monica Boulevard. Head east on Santa Monica Boulevard through Beverly Hills, West Hollywood, and into Hollywood. Turn left on Highland. The bus lines that stop at Hollywood and Highland are LADOT DASH Hollywood, Metro Bus 156, 212/312, 217, 222, 656, and Metro Rapid 780.

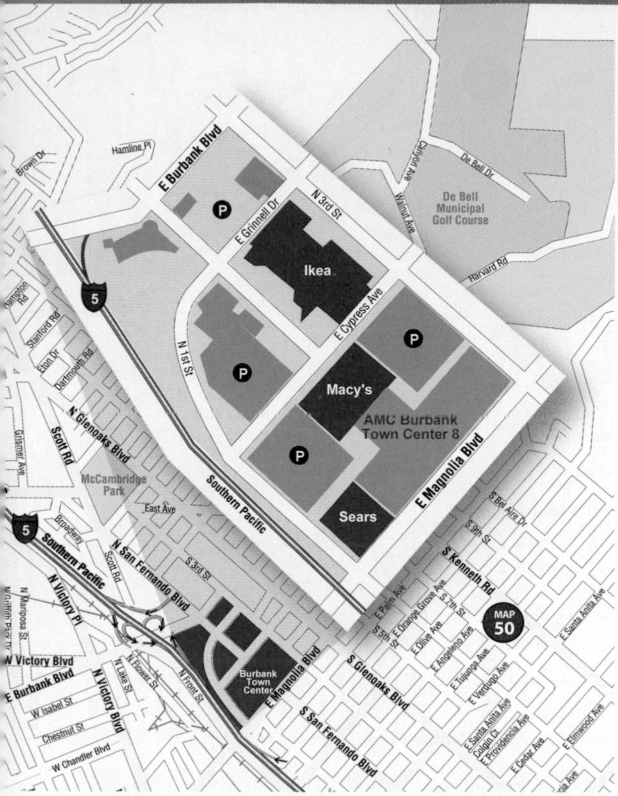

General Information

NFT Map:	50
Address:	201 E Magnolia Blvd Burbank, CA 91501
Phone:	818-566-8556
Website:	www.burbanktowncenter.com

Shopping

At some point in the early stages of their assimilation into LA, all new arrivals pass through the portals of IKEA, thus making Burbank Town Center the Ellis Island of Los Angeles. To see this area only for its prefab Swedish furnishings would be to miss the point entirely. It also has a full-service, mid-range mall (with an oversized chessboard on the first level centercourt), a boatload of movie theaters, and access to a rapidly developing stretch of San Fernando Boulevard where shoppers can browse movie scripts and used books, migrate toward the peculiar glow emanating from Urban Outfitters, and shoot a game of pool in between all the shopping, eating, and movie-going.

The Burbank Town Center mall itself provides the moderately priced fare you'd expect from anchors such as Macy's and Sears. Sport Chalet is fun and well stocked, while the newly minted Bed, Bath & Beyond delivers its reliable supply of home furnishings and gadgetry. Women's clothing outlets (Georgiou, Lane Bryant, Express, and the like) outnumber men's (Corsine, Express Men, etc.) by nearly five to one, while kid magnets like KB Toys proliferate like bunnies at Easter. The chocolate-minded can get their fix at See's Candies. Outside the mall, Barnes & Noble is always good for pre- or post-movie browsing.

Food

On the Magnolia Boulevard side of the mall's upper level, you'll find all of the standard Food Court fare, while Johnny Rockets, PF Chang's, and Pomodoro Cucina Italiana offer sit-down respites from mall madness. Just outside, along the strollable San Fernando Boulevard you'll find Market City Caffe (164 E Palm Ave, at San Fernando), specializing in Italian antipasti and inspired martinis; Romano's Macaroni Grill (102 E Magnolia Blvd) serving more Italian standards; Knight Restaurant (138 N San Fernando Blvd), offering savory Mediterranean treats; and Picanha Churrascaria (269 E Palm Ave), trotting out abundant quantities of Brazilian meat-on-a-stick fare. Hurried shoppers can also hit the drive-thru at In-N-Out Burger (761 N 1st St) just outside the mall's 1st Street exit, or pause to admire the view over their meal at Hooters (600 N. 1st St).

Drawbacks

Three AMC Theaters with a total of 30 screens are clustered around Burbank Town Center, including one in the Burbank Town Center. Double-check your movie location before you go, or you'll surely miss the previews in a desperate dash between theaters. Parking gets complicated on weekends. Your best bet is to park in the East Garage on 3rd between San Jose and Magnolia.

How to Get There

From I-5 in either direction, exit at Burbank Boulevard and head east on Burbank to N 3rd Street. Turn right on 3rd and go four blocks. The East Parking Garage is on your right, the block after IKEA. The Buses that stop at Burbank Town center are Metro Bus 94, 154, 164, 165, 292, and Metro Rapid 794. There is also a metrolink stop right near the mall, it's the Downtown Burbank Station.

General Information

NFT Map: 43
Address: 9301 Tampa Ave
Northridge, CA 91324
Phone: 818-701-7051
Website: www.northridgefashioncenter.com

Shopping

Although there's ample spending opportunity at Northridge Fashion Center, nothing did as much financial damage to it as 1994's earthquake. Since the quake, Northridge has been renovated twice to become the extravagant structure of retail magnificence you see today, with 200 stores, ten restaurants and a charming outdoor pedestrian area. Cost Plus offers more exotic home décor ideas than you can shake a rain stick at, while conventionalists can rely on department store standards like Sears, JC Penney, and Macy's. With all that Northridge has to offer—including an Apple store and a ten-screen cinema—it's a shame that it's tucked just far enough out of the way that you'd never think to go there. However, if you're already headed to Sears for a fridge or new tires, or if you're fairly deep in the West San Fernando Valley, there's no reason not to go check it out.

Food

The NFC food court is clean, well lit, and offers outdoor seating. You can choose between a variety of cuisines at restaurants like La Salsa, Sansei, and Surf City Squeeze. The line for Donatello's Pizza is always long, but it moves surprisingly fast. Sit-down restaurants in the complex include Red Robin (hamburgers) and Yard House. For a break (weather permitting), sit outside on the patio at Wood Ranch BBQ for good food and better people watching.

Drawbacks

Whether you're coming from the 101 or the 118, the drive along Tampa can be slow. The parking lot fills up quickly, too, so in summer you may be in for a long, 100+ degree walk to and from the mall. There is a beautiful Gelson's supermarket nearby—far enough away from the main mall to require moving your car, but close enough to make you feel guilty for doing so.

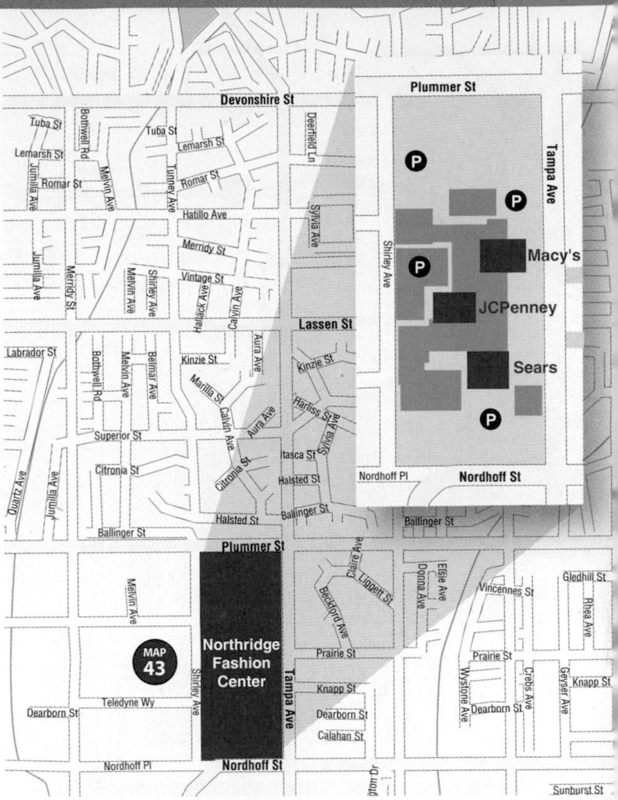

How to Get There

From the 101 in either direction, exit at Tampa Boulevard and head north on Tampa approximately four miles to Plummer. The mall entrance is on the left. From the 118 in either direction, exit at Tampa Boulevard and head south on Tampa approximately four miles to Plummer. The mall entrance is on the right. The bus lines that stop at NFC are AVTA 787,LADOT DASH Northridge, Metro Bus 166/364, 167, 242.

General Information

NFT Map:	34
Address:	280 E Colorado Blvd Pasadena, CA 91101
Phone:	626-795-9100
Website:	www.paseocoloradopasadena.com

Shopping

If Carrie Bradshaw lived in LA (as if!) this is where she'd pick up her Manolo Blahniks. Paseo Colorado is a self-consciously upscale outdoor mall with the usual yadda yadda stores. Fashionistas beat a path to DSW Shoe Warehouse for super-affordable designer shoes and drop by the venerable Loehmann's for discount chi-chi threads. Looking a little like Walt Disney's vision of a shopping mall (minus the life-size cartoon characters), Paseo Colorado boasts cutesy Mexican architecture and inviting open spaces that encourage strolling and exploration. Once inside the mall it's easy to forget you're just yards away from the busiest thoroughfare in Pasadena. Paseo Colorado proudly bills itself as an urban village; and it's true, you literally could live here—if you won the lottery—as light and airy apartment towers form the perimeter of the mall. Pick up your furnishings from the Bombay Company and Brookstone. Grocery shop at the world's most expensive supermarket—Gelson's—and meet your neighbors for a $5 happy hour martini or work your way through the "world's largest selection of draft beer" at the Yard House. If your jaw doesn't drop at the idea of single digit cocktail prices, you're not quite a local.

If you must move with the herd, know that Paseo Colorado is also home to Macy's, Tommy Bahama, and Ann Taylor Loft as well as a variety of smaller, more distinctive stores such as J. Jill. At the end of a hard day's consumerism, fold yourself into a seat in front of one of the Pacific Paseo Theater's 14 screens.

Food

There isn't one centrally located food court, thank God, but there are a variety of places to eat on the second floor. Sit-down restaurants include Island's (huge burgers and frou-frou drinks with umbrellas in them) and PF Chang's China Bistro. Tokyo Wako has its fans if you're in the mood for sushi. During the day you can get takeout from Gelson's excellent deli and hot food sections...but aside from the aforementioned cheap drinks, Paseo Colorado isn't really a fine wining or dining location. Better to make the short hop to Old Town Pasadena for an eclectic array of really fine ethnic restaurants and street life.

Drawbacks

Avoid the permanently full underground garage at all costs. Your endless gas-guzzling loops will easily take on the qualities of a Twilight Zone episode. There's plenty of street parking and it's safe. There isn't one contiguous second floor, so be sure and check the shopping directory before you head upstairs to your restaurant of choice.

How to Get There

From the 134 in either direction, exit at Marengo Avenue and head south on Marengo for a half-mile until you hit Colorado Boulevard. Parking is available in the structure on the right, just past Colorado.

From the 110 N, exit Fair Oaks Boulevard and head north on Fair Oaks to Colorado Boulevard. Turn right and head approximately a half-mile to Marengo Avenue. Turn right at Marengo Avenue to enter parking. There is also parking on the Green Street side of the Paseo. Don't forget to validate your parking ticket! There is a metro rail station near by, Memorial Park Station. The buses that stop at or near Paseo Colorado are Amtrak Thruway 19, Foothill Transit 187, 690, LADOT Commuter Express 549, Metro Bus 180, 181, 256, 267, 686, 687, Metro Rapid 780, and Pasadena ARTS 10 and 40.

General Information

NFT Map: 18
Address: 395 Santa Monica Pl
Santa Monica, CA 90401
Phone: 310-260-8333
Website: www.santamonicaplace.com

Shopping

Santa Monica Place is a perfectly average mall in a spectacular location. Adjacent to the 3rd Street Promenade, the mall, designed by Frank Gehry in 1980, is barely a quarter-mile from the beach. The location, combined with the usual line-up of unremarkable store offerings, make it hard to justify a visit. There are simply better places in the neighborhood to be. Better places, of course, unless it's raining. The typical mall shops serve the local Santa Monica community well for last-minute gifts and clothing necessities. Unless you know that what you're looking for is in one of the stores (Victoria's Secret, Brookstone, etc.), your best bet is to stroll around and take the mall on its own terms. Recently, Macy's was replaced by Bloomingdale's, which is now the only department store left, since acquisitions closed down Robinsons-May. Santa Monica Place caters to the young, so take your teenaged niece to Wet Seal and Forever 21. If you've arrived at the beach unprepared, you can buy bathing suits at one of the sporting goods stores and then find some new shades at Sun Shade or Sunglass Hut. (Both have good sales, making it worth at least a drive-by.)

Nearly wiped out in a gloriously stupid 2004 decision to go condo, subject to regular shakeups in ownership and management, and closed for years pending renovations, Santa Monica Place is now reopened for business and rainy-day wandering.

Food

The food court is bustling and cacophonous. Hot Dog on a Stick and Charlie Burgers will put you in a good-time mood if you're one of the lucky ones to snag a table, but more likely you'll have to place those orders "to go." Take them outside to eat on the Promenade, where the weather's better, anyway.

Drawbacks

This particular area of Santa Monica gets particularly congested on the weekends. Pedestrians, some on roller blades or skateboards, will wear out your patience. Once inside the mall, the clientele consists mostly of teens and tourists. Parking is killer here; plan on paying at least $10 a day. You won't find free parking anywhere.

How to Get There

From 10 W, head north on Lincoln Boulevard for a quarter-mile until you hit Colorado Avenue. Head west on Colorado Avenue and enter the parking lot from that side.

From PCH heading east, exit at Ocean Avenue. Turn left on Ocean and then right on Colorado Avenue. The bus lines that stop near Santa Monica Place are Mini Blue Downtown, Big Blue Bus 1, 2, 3, Rapid 3, 4, 5, 7, Rapid 7, 8, 9, Rapid 10, Metro Bus 4 (Night), Metro Bus 20 (Owl), Metro Bus 33 (Owl), Metro Express 534, Metro Rapid 704, 720, 733, and the intra-California Shuttle Bus.

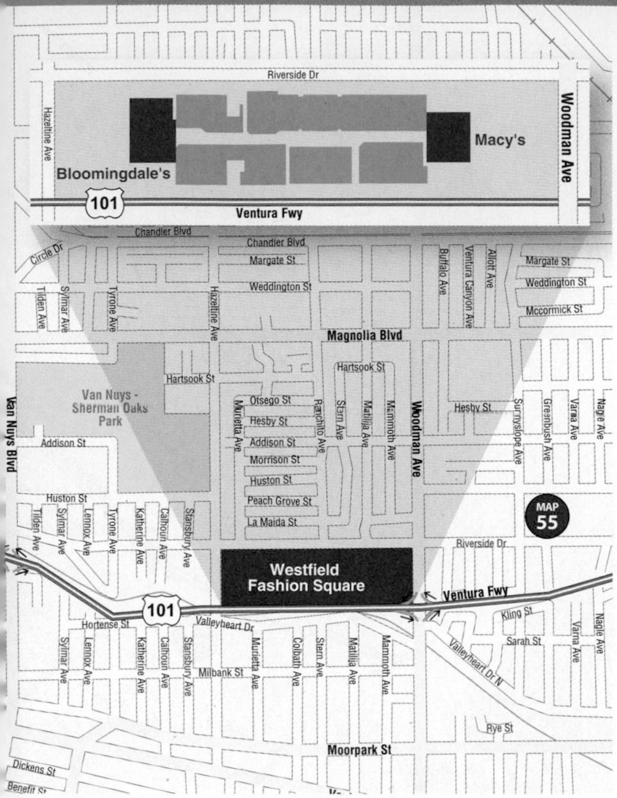

General Information

NFT Map:	55
Address:	14006 Riverside Dr Sherman Oaks, CA 91423
Phone:	818-783-0550
Website:	www.westfield.com/fashionsquare

Shopping

When fun-loving couples in their twenties evolve into responsible parents in their thirties, they move to the Valley. Indicative of this shift, while the Westfield Century City unveils a spanking new multiplex, the Westfield Fashion Square in Sherman Oaks is the recipient of a new kiddie playground and a passel of children's clothing stores (Naartjie, Janie & Jack, babystyle). The mood at the Fashion Square is cool, but not hip. Upscale, but not ostentatious. Entertaining, but not necessarily fun. The Fashion Square caters to the locals who have moved to Sherman Oaks because it is clean, tasteful and safe. Similar qualities may be found in the home furnishings dealers at the Fashion Square, a group which includes Pottery Barn, Williams Sonoma, and Z Gallerie.

Clothing choices are an equally predictable mix of Abercrombie & Fitch, the Gap, Banana Republic, and Victoria's Secret. The Square is not without its high-end perks—the Bloomingdale's shines and Teavana shows that there's a world of tea that goes way beyond Earl Grey. Expectant mothers are treated like queens with two apparel stores (babystyle, A Pea In the Pod) and a group of dedicated parking spots located close to the mall entrance reserved just for them. Those few Valley denizens without kids in tow can hold on to their freedom, shopping solo at the Apple store or pampering themselves at the Aspect Beauty health club and spa, which could only be further from the playground if it had been placed outside the mall on the other side of Riverside Drive.

Food

The choices in the Garden Café Food Court seem so limited that the most appealing lunch selection often seems to be an Ice Blended from the Coffee Bean & Tea Leaf and a Cinnabon, extra icing please. Chain restaurants rule, from healthy(-ish) chains like California Crisp or La Salsa to those that are decidedly not healthy at all (Carl's Jr., Sbarro). Downstairs options are more appealing. Barney's is a Westside institution that now offers burgers, sandwiches, and salads, and the California Pizza Kitchen ASAP offers a faster-food version of its usual dine-in menu. For your convenience and snacking pleasure, gumball machines are strewn throughout the mall, filled with assorted candy and chocolate treats.

Drawbacks

The long line of cars waiting to turn into the mall can frequently serve as a deterrent for shoppers, sending them off to stand-alone alternatives in nearby Studio City or Encino. Also, the absence of a supermarket, a movie theater, and a decent sit-down restaurant prevents the Fashion Square from being a destination in its own right.

How to Get There

From the 101 in either direction, exit Woodman. Head north on Woodman one block, and go left onto Riverside. The parking lot can be accessed on both the Riverside and the Hazeltine sides of the mall, though Bloomingdale's shoppers will want to enter on Hazeltine. The bus lines that stop at Fashion Square are LADOT DASH Van Nuys/Studio City, Metro Bus 155 and 158.

General Information

NFT Map: 45
Address: 6600 Topanga Canyon Blvd.
Canoga Park, CA 91303
Phone: 818-594-8732
Website: www.westfield.com/topanga/

Shopping

For any Valley resident who has ever gone behind the Orange curtain to Costa Mesa and lamented, "Where is our South Coast Plaza?" we have an answer. It's in Canoga Park and it's called Westfield Topanga. Before the Northridge Quake did some serious damage, Topanga Plaza (as it was then known) was a run of the mill neighborhood mall. But out of the rubble has emerged a lesson in civic planning, a utopia, if you will, of how retail—and society—should be.

The brilliance of the Topanga mall is in how it manages to be the big tent that draws everyone in. The planner who thought to include a two-story Target along with a newly renovated Nordstrom deserves a Nobel Prize for malls. Low end, high end…it's all covered. The major apparel chains are all represented, along with an occasional higher-end surprise (Benetton and Hanna Andersson). Male shoppers have established a beachhead in the upper level "Canyon" with the one-two punch of the Apple Store and the spa-like Art of Shaving.

Food

The mall's egalitarian qualities extend to the food available to its guests. Westfield eschews the term "food court" for the far more posh "dining terrace." Choices there are a little more focused on Asian meals, from the sushi at Seiki-Shi Sushi to the Korean BBQ and kimchee at Sorabol, but it's all definitely fast food. If you've got the time (and the cash) spend a little more and have breakfast, lunch, or dinner at The Farm of Beverly Hills, an export from Beverly Hills and The Grove.

Drawbacks

In a bizarre attempt at world domination, the folks at Westfield now own both the former Topanga Plaza and a complex they call The Promenade just down the street (6100 Topanga Plaza). The good news is that together they are home to just about any retailer you might ever want to visit. The bad news is that there's no easy way to get to the Promenade from the Westfield Topanga and vice versa — you can walk about five blocks, or drive and repark (an unbearable thought on a weekend evening). It's rumored that Westfield will one day connect the two malls by bridge or walkway or—we hope you're sitting down for this—build a new mall to unite the two squabbling ones that we have.

How To Get There

Take the 101 to Topanga Canyon Blvd and head north. Westfield Topanga will be the second mall on your right (the first being the Westfield Promenade), at Victory. The bus lines that stop at Westfield Topanga are AVTA 787, Metro Bus 150, 161, 164, 165, 245, 645, Metro Rapid 750, Santa Clarita Transit 791, 796, and VISTA Hwy 101/Conejo Connection Route.

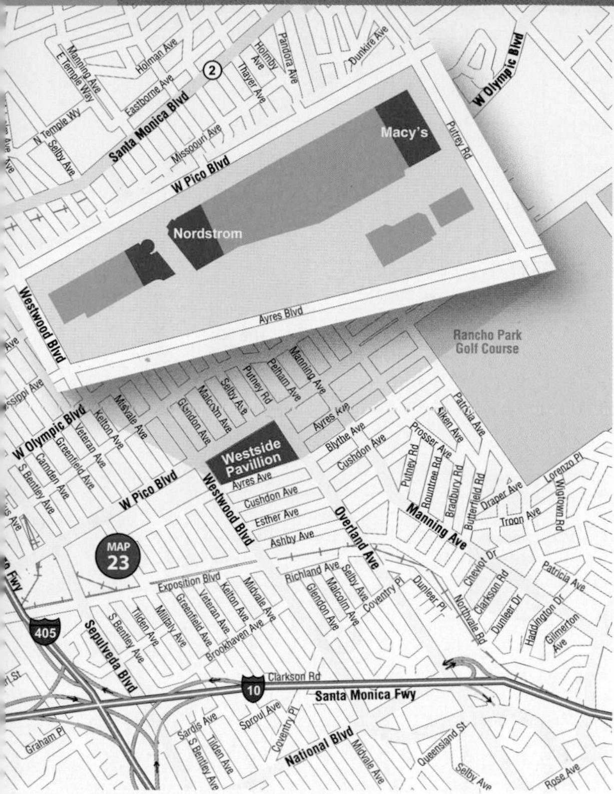

General Information

NFT Map:	23
Address:	10800 W Pico Blvd Los Angeles, CA 90064
Phone:	310-470-8752
Website:	www.westsidepavilion.com

Shopping

The Westside Pavilion is a rarity. A no-attitude shopping location with all the usual suspects in terms of stores and resources, but with solid ties to the local community. This may not sound exciting, but this mall has hotspots for everyone, including a dance studio, post office, and hairstylist. There are more kid's stores than you can hit in an afternoon: Gymboree, E.B. Games, Disney Store, and Three Cheeky Monkeys, to name a few. You can park the teens at Pop Star or Claire's Accessories. Dad will probably park himself at Sisley's Italian Kitchen wine bar while Mom is giving the plastic an airing at BCBG.

The mall is a long narrow space anchored by Nordstrom's and Macy's. Despite being home to over 160 stores it never feels crowded. The original space has an end-to-end skylight which gives a plein air feel even in winter. The newer annex is reached by way of a covered walkway across Westwood Boulevard. Periodically W.P. hosts wine and food samplings and honors local schools. There's even a monthly Kid's Club for the little brats that presents mimes jugglers and puppet shows. On the upper level there's the ubiquitous food court and a couple of cozy movie theaters that actually show films you don't mind paying to see including exclusive indie presentations not found anyplace else in the city. All in all a great, well-balanced mall.

Food

Not much to write home about. Basically, if you can fry it, put it on a stick, or smother it with cheese, you'll find a counter devoted to it in the food court. If you want real food, try Sisley's Italian Kitchen on the street level. Also surprisingly good is the Nordstrom Café, located inside the store on the top level. The best food, however, is just outside the mall: the Apple Pan (10801 W Pico Blvd) is a Los Angeles institution. The small shack serves affordable old-school hickory burgers in a lunch-counter setting. Be prepared to wait. Down the street on Pico is Louisa's Trattoria and the venerable (but pricey) Junior's Deli is just around the corner on Westwood Boulevard. It's been there for 50 years and some of the waitresses look as if they haven't missed a day. God bless 'em.

Drawbacks

Do not attempt to navigate the parking lot without medication and a pocketful of breadcrumbs. Hands down the worst, most confusing parking lot in the greater Los Angeles area. Take the express ramp directly to the top level. Or better yet, splurge on the best valet bargain in town—$3, no waiting. Enter next to Nordstrom. If you start thinking about trying your luck outside the structure, don't. There's minimal street parking and, since it's so close to both the 405 and 10 freeways, making your way around the surrounding streets (especially the biggies like Pico and Westwood) can be a slow-moving pain.

How to Get There

From the Valley, take 405 S and exit at the Pico/Olympic off ramp. Make a left to reach Pico Boulevard, and then another left. Continue east on Pico. Westside Pavilion extends from Westwood Boulevard to Overland Avenue. From the South Bay and Orange County, take 405 N, exit at National Boulevard and turn right. Make a left at Westwood Boulevard and travel north until you reach Pico Boulevard. From downtown LA, take 10 W and exit at Overland Avenue. Take a right on Overland Avenue heading north to Pico Boulevard. Westside Pavilion extends west from Overland Avenue to Westwood Boulevard. From Santa Monica, take 10 E and exit at National/Overland. Turn right on National and another right on Overland Avenue. Head north on Overland Avenue to Pico Boulevard. The bus lines that stop at Westside Pavillion are Big Blue Bus VA Commuter, Big Blue Bus 4, 7, Rapid 7, 8, 12, Super 12, 13, Culver City Bus 3, LADOT Commuter Express 431.

General information

NFT Map: 18

Address: Wilshire Blvd & 3rd St
Santa Monica, CA 90403

Website: www.downtownsm.com

Shopping

Third Street Promenade is a tourist magnet with a force greater than gravity. The street is closed off to traffic from Wilshire to Colorado, providing wide-open walking space. Its outdoor shopping and alfresco dining options theoretically make it a pleasant place to spend an afternoon or evening, but its weekend crowds of high schoolers, out-of-towners, and visitors from the Inland Empire can make it a little less than charming to navigate. However, the Farmers Market on Wednesday and Saturday mornings lives up to its renowned reputation (Arizona & 3rd St). The usual mall suspects—Gap, J. Crew, Urban Outfitters, Pottery Barn, Victoria's Secret—flank the Promenade, intermixed with small boutiques selling cutesy, perhaps dubiously priced clothes. The selection of stores clustered in one walkable area does make it easy for someone on a mission to quickly find exactly what he or she is looking to buy, and on the way one might even spot a celebrity browsing the magazines at the giant newsstand in the middle of the Promenade that features newspapers and magazines from all over the world. Additionally, three movie theaters span the Promenade and are a popular place to watch big premieres.

Food

Third Street Promenade offers up a range of eateries from McDonald's and Johnny Rocket's to more upscale Italian and Greek cuisines. Monsoon (1212 3rd Street Promenade) has a daily happy hour, along with sushi and potsticker deals, and a view of the tango entertainment on the street. Yankee Doodle's (1410 3rd Street Promenade) features 39 screens for sports watching over burgers and beer, and has several pool tables on two levels (also a good place to get quarters for parking meters). Gaucho Grill's Santa Monica location (1251 3rd Street Promenade) has a quiet, intimate dining room away from the outside hubbub. Though Broadway Deli (1457 3rd Street Promenade) is only an attempt to be a New York deli on the left coast, the food isn't so bad. Of course, dining weekday nights on the Promenade makes for a more soothing evening than on the weekends.

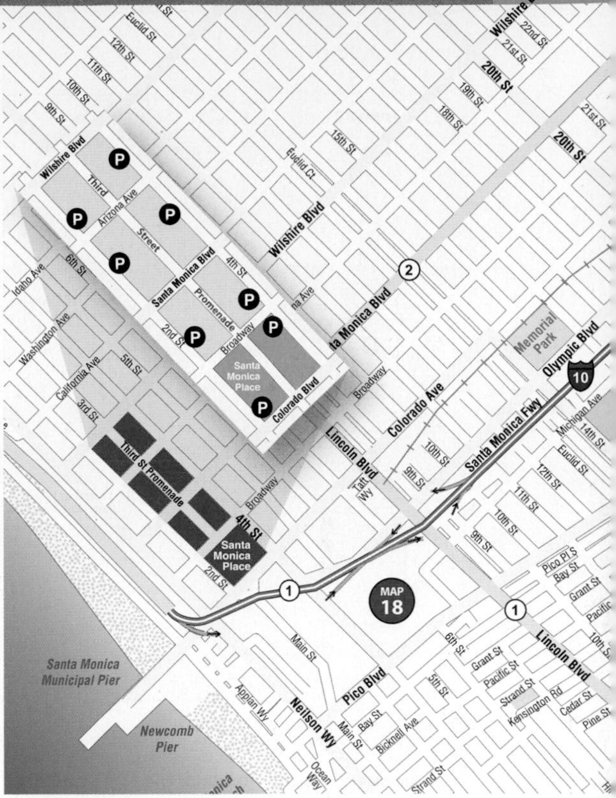

Drawbacks

Parking can be a challenge on the weekends, and if you park on the street, rest assured that the meter maids stand to watch the second your meter expires. Street performers often cause a clog up of pedestrian traffic as people stop to watch the man who juggles bowls or listen to the mini-Elvis crooning the King's songs a foot from the ground. But if you can snag an outdoor dining table, the people-watching is endless.

How to Get There

From I-10 W, take the 5th Street exit going north. From PCH heading east, exit at Ocean Avenue. Turn left on Ocean and right on Colorado Avenue. Parking is available at a number of structures on 2nd and 4th Streets, and along Broadway and Colorado (free for the first two hours during the day). The Buses that stop at 3rd st are Mini Blue Downtown, Big Blue bus 1, 2, 3, Rapid 3, 4,7, Rapid 7, 8, 9, Rapid 10, Metro Bus 20 (Owl) Metro Bus 33 (Owl), Metro Express 534 Metro Rapid 704, Metro Rapid 720, Metro Rapid 733.

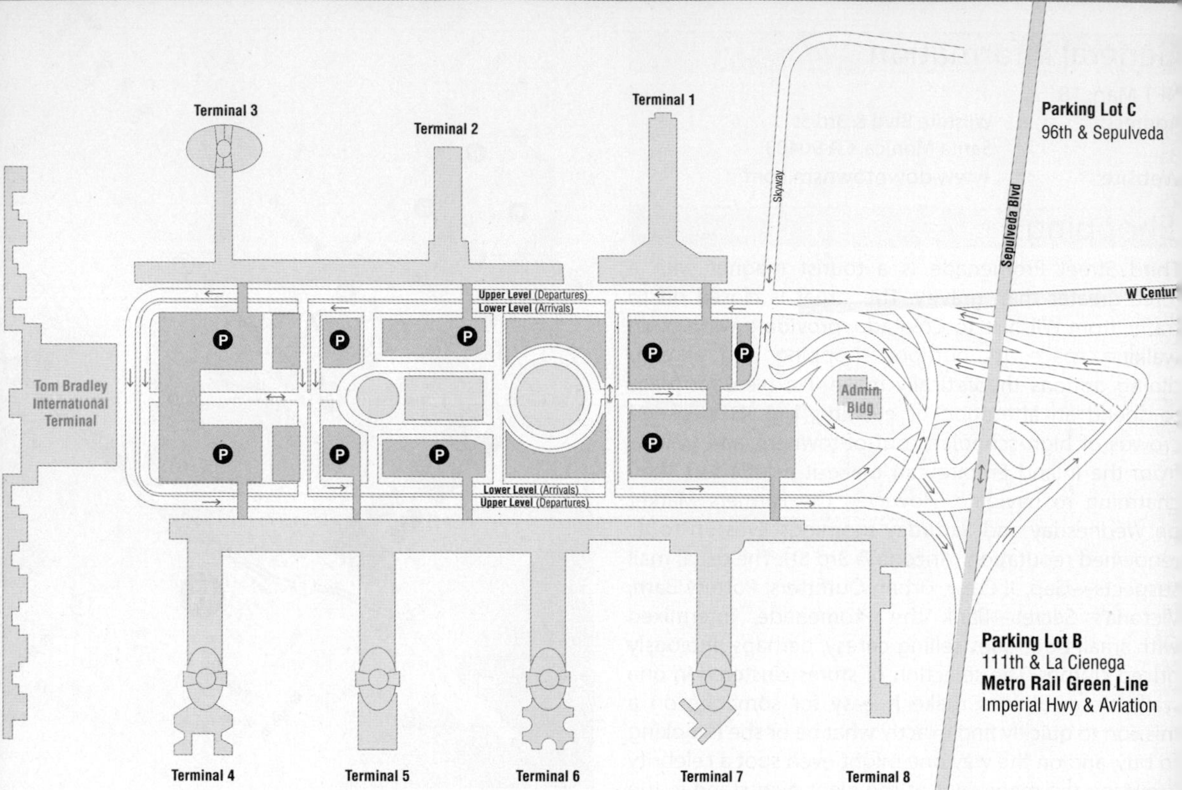

Airline	*Terminal*
Aer Lingus	TBIT
Aero California	TBIT
Aeroflot	TBIT
Aeromexico	2
Air Canada	2
Air China	2
Air France	2
Air Jamaica	5
Air New Zealand	2
Air Pacific	TBIT
Air Tahiti Nui	TBIT
AirTran Airways	3
Alaska Airlines	3, TBIT
Allegiant	6
All Nippon Airways (ANA)	TBIT
American Airlines	3, 4, 5
American Eagle	4
Asiana Airlines	TBIT
Avianca Airlines	2
British Airways	TBIT
Cathay Pacific Airways	TBIT
Champion Air	TBIT

Airline	*Terminal*
China Airlines	TBIT
China Eastern	TBIT
China Southern Airlines	TBIT
Continental Airlines	6
Copa Airlines	6, TBIT
Corsair	TBIT
Delta Air Lines	5
El Al Israel	TBIT
EVA Air	TBIT
Frontier Airlines	5
Hawaiian Airlines	2
Horizon Air	3
Japan Airlines	TBIT
JetBlue	3
KLM Airlines	2
Korean Air	TBIT
LACSA Costa Rica	TBIT
LAN Chile	TBIT
LTU International Airways	TBIT
Lufthansa	TBIT
Malaysia Airlines	TBIT
Mexicana Airlines	TBIT

Airline	*Terminal*
Miami Air	2
Midwest Express Airlines	3
Philippine Airlines	TBIT
Qantas	TBIT
Singapore Airlines	TBIT
Southwest Airlines	1
Spirit Airlines	6
Swiss Air Lines	TBIT
TACA Int'l Airlines	TBIT
Thai Airways	TBIT
Transmeridian	5
United Air Lines	6, 7
United Express	6, 7
US Airways	1
Varig Brazilian Airlines	TBIT
Virgin Atlantic Airways	2
World Airways	2

** TBIT = Tom Bradley International Termina*

General Information

Address:	1 World Way Los Angeles, CA 90045
Phone:	310-646-5252
Baggage Storage:	310-646-0222
Lost & Found:	424-646-5678
TSA Lost & Found	310-242-9073 (for things left/confiscated at security)
Police:	310-646-7911
First Aid:	310-215-6000
Customs information:	310-215-2415
Los Angeles MTA:	800-266-6883
Website:	www.lawa.org

Overview

Los Angeles International Airport is one of the busiest airports in the world. Driving here is like braving a whirlpool with all its frustrating eddies, but as long as you start out correctly (take the upper ramp for departures, the lower one for arrivals) you'll be just fine. You can't get lost, because it's a big circle. Yes, a circle filled with honking traffic, overzealous parking cops, TV news trucks during the holidays, and a hustler or two looking to take advantage of lost tourists, but a circle nonetheless.

Give yourself plenty of time to get through the check-in and security lines, especially during Thanksgiving and Christmas when the lines at Terminal 1 will wrap around the check-in area, out the door and all the way to Terminal 2. Good thing it's warm in Los Angeles during December. Always check in online if you can. Once you're through all of the hassle, each terminal offers a variety of places to grab a bite, pick up a magazine, or pep up with a coffee (Starbucks, of course). If you want to avoid eating airline food, try the Wolfgang Puck Café or the Gordon Biersch Brewery. Since security is so tight, your choices are limited to whatever is in your airline's terminal.

How to Get There—Driving

The most direct route to LAX is unfortunately not the fastest. The San Diego Freeway (405) to the Century Freeway (105) leads right into the airport, but the 405 is almost always congested. The 105 has accommodating carpool lanes—which can be tantalizing when you're sitting in gridlock—but it's a mousetrap; the cops are primed to apprehend the fast and furiously late for their flights. The 110 to the 105 is another option, but if it's the 110 or the 405, you might as well flip a coin. As cab drivers know, surface roads are the preferable way to access LAX whenever possible. From the northern beach cities (Santa Monica, etc.), take Lincoln Boulevard south until it joins Sepulveda Boulevard. This will lead you right to LAX, but be prepared to make a sudden right turn into the airport. From the South Bay, Sepulveda is also the preferred route, but this time the airport will be on your left. The quickest route to LAX from Central LA is La Cienega Boulevard. South of Rodeo, La Cienega becomes a mini-freeway that rarely becomes congested except during rush hour. Take La Cienega to Century Boulevard, then turn right towards the airport.

How to Get There—Mass Transit

Unless you're right off the FlyAway (more about that later), don't. Though many buses will take you to LAX, the trip may last longer than your actual flight. Sure, you're getting a lot of bang out of your $1.50–$3 fare, but this is the way to go only if you have time for a "leisurely" ride to the airport, or if you're trying to log some field work for your anthro degree. City buses deposit passengers at the LAX Transit Center, where a free shuttle travels to each of the airport's terminals. Another free shuttle connects LAX to the Metro Green Line Aviation Station, where LA's Light Rail system ferries travelers to outlying areas like Redondo Beach (to the south) and Norwalk (to the east).

How to Get There—Really

If you're at all clever, convince a friend to drive you. If that's not an option, car services and taxis are truly the best way to go. That is, unless you live near one of the pick-up points for LAX's FlyAway service: Van Nuys, Union Station in downtown LA, or Westwood Village near the UCLA campus—in which case, it's a deal, even though they jacked up the one-way fare to $8. Take advantage of the remote luggage checking (for domestic flights only) at the Van Nuys and Westwood locations, and glide into LAX with only your carry-on. For particulars, visit www. lawa. org/welcomeLAX.aspx and click on Ground Transportation.

Parking

Now that LAX has removed the metered parking, there are three parking options. The Central Terminal Area (CTA) has nearly 8,000 spots in eight parking structure. Rates range from $3 for the first hour to a maximum of $30 for a 24 hour period. Economy Parking Lot C at Sepulveda Boulevard and 96th Street is better for long-term parking and rates range from $4 for the first hour to $12 for a 24 hours. Be sure to allow an extra half-hour in your schedule for dealing with the parking lot shuttle bus. Adjacent to Economy Parking Lot C is the Cell Phone Waiting Lot where drivers can wait up to two hours for free until the arriving passengers they plan to meet let them know they are ready.

Car Rental

Advantage	310-671-0503
Alamo	888-826-6893
Avis	800-331-1212
Budget	310-642-4500
Dollar	800-800-4000
Enterprise	310-649-5400
Fox	800-225-4369
Hertz	310-568-3400
National	800-462-5266
Payless	310-342-5392
Thrifty	877-283-0898

Hotels

Best Western Airpark • 640 W Manchester Blvd • 800-233-8060
Comfort Inn • 850 N Sepulveda Blvd • 310-318-1020
Days Inn • 901 W Manchester Blvd • 310-649-0800
Hilton Garden Inn • 2100 E Mariposa Ave • 310-726-0100
Marriott Hotel • 5855 W Century Blvd • 310-641-5700
Motel 6 • 5101 W Century Blvd • 310-419-1234
Sheraton Gateway • 6101 W Century Blvd • 310-642-1111
Travelodge • 5547 W Century Blvd • 310-649-4000

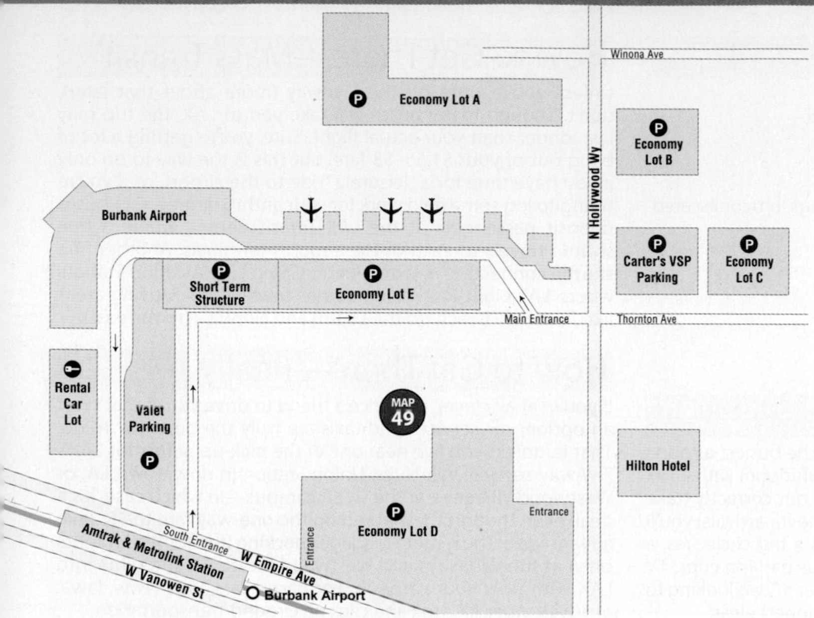

General Information

NFT Map:	49
Address:	2627 N Hollywood Wy Burbank, CA 91505
Phone:	818-840-8840
Parking Information:	818-565-1308
Website:	www.burbankairport.com

Overview

Burbank (BUR)—also known as the Bob Hope Airport (if you build it, LA will name it after an old celebrity)—is a small, low-key alternative to LAX, and a must if you live east of La Brea, or in the San Gabriel or San Fernando Valley. The parking is cheaper (especially in the nearby discount lots), the lines are shorter, and travelers coming through here are simply happier. From groups of partiers hopping a quick Southwest jaunt to Vegas to the smiling folks boarding JetBlue for NYC's JFK, Burbank is as stress-free as flying gets. Sure, the addition of JetBlue and Delta cross-country service has busied up the place and put some stress on the parking situation, but that's just a bit of turbulence during an otherwise smooth trip.

How to Get There—Driving

The airport is just off the 5, so if you're approaching from the north or south, take the 5 and exit at Hollywood Way. Take Hollywood Way south and find the airport entrance on your right.

If you're coming from the west, take the 101 S to the 134 E and use the Hollywood Way exit. Travel north on Hollywood Way until you hit the airport on your left.

From the East, you can make your way to either the 134 W or I-5N and follow the above directions.

From most parts of the Valley, it's preferable to take surface streets to Burbank Airport. Burbank or Victory Boulevards provide a fairly direct route to the airport from the western end of the Valley. From all other directions, it's best to choose your favorite non-freeway route to Hollywood Way and take that straight into the airport.

How to Get There—Mass Transit

Similar to the rail systems in Europe and Japan, Metrolink and Amtrak trains both go right to the airport—well, almost. The terminals are just a short walk or free shuttle bus away.

The Burbank Airport station is on the Ventura County (yellow) Metrolink Line and, depending on where you're coming from, during peak hours it will cost between $4.75 to $5.00 one-way (same zone) and $11.75-$12.00 (if you're starting from the very end of the Orange County Line). Off-peak you can expect to pay between $3.50 and $8.75. Trains link up Monday–Friday only. 800-371-LINK; www.metrolinktrains.com.

Amtrak's Pacific Surfliner Train (which runs from San Diego to Paso Robles) makes a stop at the Burbank Airport Rail Station as does their Motor Coach Service to the San Joaquin trains in Bakersfield. 800-USA-RAIL www.amtrak.com.

MTA buses are slower but cheaper. Numbers 94, 163, 165, and 394 all make stops at Burbank Airport. 800-COMMUTE www.mta.net.

Parking

Short-term parking is located in the four-story garage across the entry road from the terminal. It can be pricey if you stick around for more than an hour or two: $5 for the first hour, $13 for the second, and up to a $31 daily maximum. There's economy parking in lots A, B, C, and E and rates range from $3 for the first hour to $10-$23 for 24 hours, depending on the lot. A number of companies also offer covered long-term parking in locations adjacent to the airport. Got more money than time? Valet parking is $23 per day and located a scant 30 yards from the terminal.

Airlines

Alaska Airlines
Delta Air Lines
jetBlue Airways
Seaport Airlines
Southwest Airlines
United Air Lines
US Airways

Car Rental

On-Site:	
Alamo	800-327-9633
Avis	800-331-1212
Hertz	800-654-3131
National	800-227-7368
Off-Site:	
Advantage	800-777-5500
All-Rite	818-972-2490
Budget	800-527-0700
Discovery	800-641-4141
Enterprise	818-558-7336
Rent4Less	800-993-5377

Hotels

- **Anabelle Hotel** • 2011 W Olive Ave • 818-845-7800
- **Marriott** • 2500 N Hollywood Wy • 818-843-6000
- **Universal City Hilton & Towers** • 555 Universal Hollywood Dr • 818-506-2500
- **Ramada Inn** • 2900 N San Fernando Blvd • 818-843-5955
- **Safari Inn** • 1911 W Olive Ave • 818-845-8586
- **Sheraton** • 333 Universal Hollywood Dr • 818-980-1212
- **Travelodge** • 1112 N Hollywood Wy • 818-845-2408

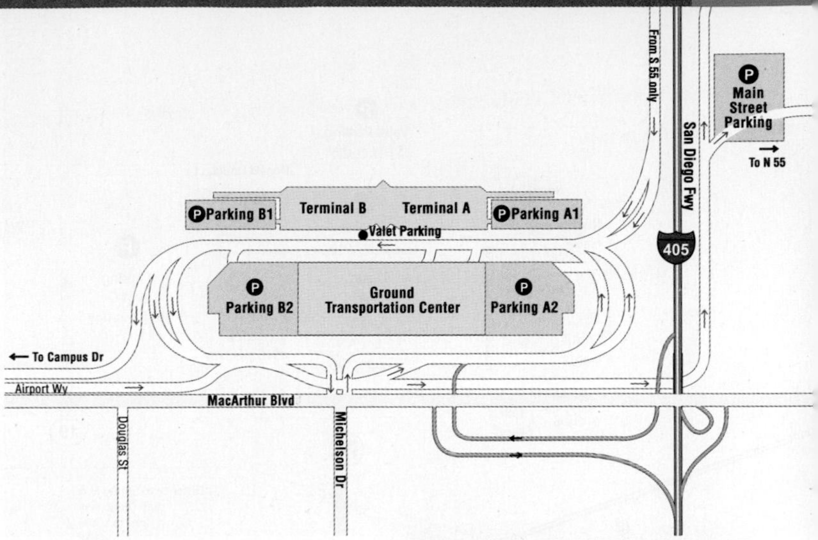

General Information

ıddress:	18601 Airport Wy Santa Ana, CA 92707
'hone:	949-252-5200
ost & Found:	949-252-5000
/ebsite:	www.ocair.com

Overview

hough most of us typically associate John Vayne with dusty Hollywood westerns ather than aviation, Orange County has een fit to name its only commercial irport after the leather-chapped actor, longtime OC resident. They've even rected an impressive nine-foot bronze tatue out front honoring the Duke in mid-wagger, complete with cowboy hat and purs. Located well behind the "Orange :urtain," John Wayne Airport (SNA) is uite a trek from LA (approximately fifty niles), but airlines can sometimes make he commute worth your while with lower ares. Aesthetically, the airport makes a olid effort, featuring rotating art exhibits lisplayed on the departure level at each nd of the terminal. Probably the best thing ve can say about John Wayne Airport is hat it isn't LAX.

How to Get There—Driving

)riving yourself or tapping that indebted uddy is definitely your best means of ransportation to the airport. Sadly, most aths from LA County to John Wayne ıirport at some point lead to the 405 reeway—one of LA's more congested outes. The 405 will bring you closest to ohn Wayne, which lies just a short distance rom the MacArthur Boulevard exit (CA-73). rom downtown or the eastern part of Los ıngeles, however, there is another option. ake the Santa Ana Freeway (5 S) to the :osta Mesa Freeway (55 S), exiting at the amp marked "I-405 S to San Diego/John Vayne Airport," and follow the signs from here.

How to Get There—Mass Transit

rom LA? You've got to be kidding. If you're ead-set on taking this course, you'd better ave a LOT of free time. Several hours, in act, as there are no direct bus routes that onnect Los Angeles County with John Vayne Airport. However, for only $2.25 the ITA can get you as far as Disneyland on he 460. After the over-two-hour bus ride rom downtown LA, get out and kill some ime with a few rides on Space Mountain, then board Bus 43 heading south toward Costa Mesa, and take this to the corner of Harbor and MacArthur Boulevards. Are we there yet? Hardly. THEN transfer to Bus 76 heading east toward Newport Beach, which will take you right by the airport. All in all, you sure saved a bundle going the thrifty route for a grand total of $4.75, but not if you missed your flight.

How to Get There—Ground Transportation

A taxi ride from Los Angeles to John Wayne Airport starts at about $80. Some companies to consider are LA Yellow Cab, (877-733-3305) and the Beverly Hills Cab Company (310-273-6611). Leaving the airport, the John Wayne Airport Yellow Cab Service (800-535-2211) is the only company authorized to pick up fares. They'll charge around $90 from the airport to downtown. Compared to those prices, SuperShuttle (800-258-3826) is a veritable bargain at $65 from downtown LA to John Wayne.

Parking

Terminal parking lots (A1, A2, B1, B2, and C) charge $2 per hour with a $20 maximum per day. The Main Street long-term lot is also $2 per hour but only $14 per day with a courtesy shuttle to the terminal available every 15 minutes. Selected parking spaces are available in Lots A1, B2, and C for a two-hour maximum, and are ideal for dropping people off and picking up, but you still have to fork over $2. If you're really a high roller—or, say, on your way to Vegas—valet your car at $30 per day.

Airlines

	Terminal
Airtran Airways	C
Alaska Airlines	A
American Airlines	A
Delta Air Lines / Delta Connection	A
Frontier Airlines	C
Interjet	B
Southwest Airlines	C
United Air Lines	B
US Airways/US Airways Express	B
WestJet Airlines	A

Car Rental

On-Site:	
Alamo	800-327-9633
Avis	800-230-4898
Budget	800-527-0700
Enterprise	800-736-8222
Hertz	800-654-3131
National	800-227-7368
Thrifty	800-847-4389
Off-Site:	
Advantage	800-777-5500
AM-PM	800-220-4310
Beverly Hills	800-479-5996
Fox/Payless	800-225-4369
Go Rent-A-Van	800-464-8267
OC Car & Truck	800-349-6061
Rent4Less	866-945-7368
Stop-Then-Go	888-704-7867
United Auto	866-878-6483

Hotels

Best Western • 2700 Hotel Terrace Dr • 714-432-8888

Embassy Suites • 1325 E Dyer Rd • 714-241-3800

Holiday Inn • 2726 S Grand Ave • 714-481-6300

Quality Suites • 2701 Hotel Terrace Dr • 714-957-9200

Travelodge • 1400 SE Bristol St • 714-557-8700

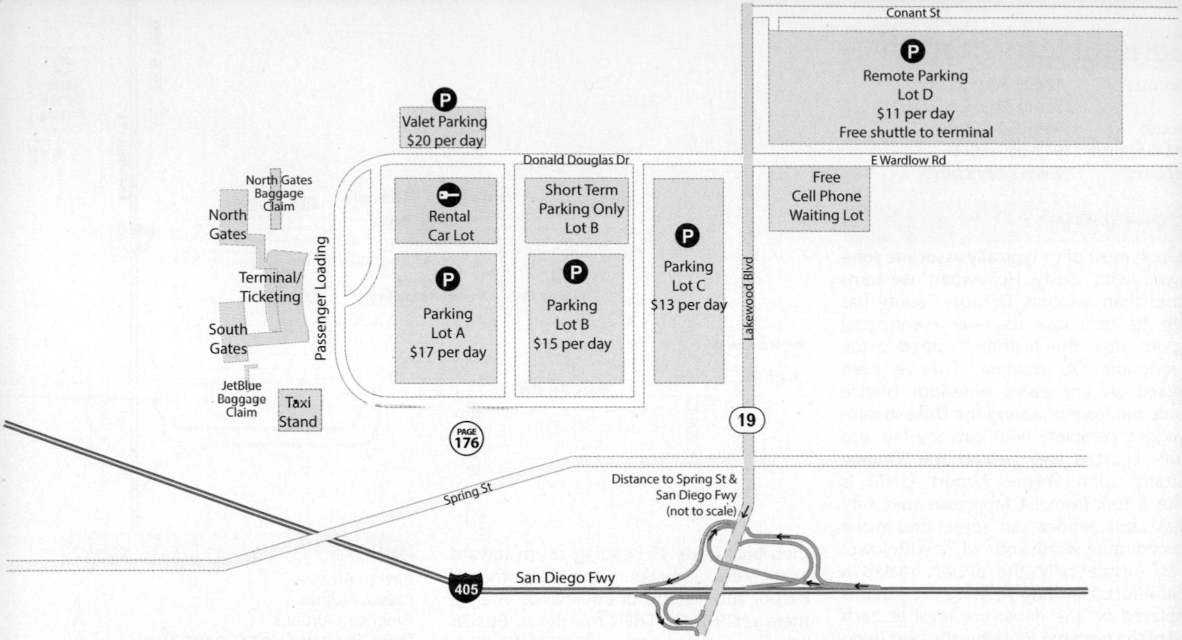

General Information

Address: 4100 Donald Douglas Dr, Long Beach, CA 90808
Phone: 562-570-2619
Website: www.lgb.org

Overview

What the Long Beach Airport (LGB) lacks in amenities, it makes up for with efficiency. The television show *Wings* comes to mind when popping into the quaint terminal (yes, that's *one* terminal) with its Art Deco style and historical aviation pictures. With a handful of carriers, some of which aren't represented at LAX, checking in is a snap. Retrieving your luggage is even easier. Flying into LGB sure beats the sensory overload of walking out into LAX's smog-ridden, traffic-choked arrivals area.

The best way to get there is to take a shuttle service. Let some other sucker brave the 405 while you read, nap, or crank the iPod. You might want to go on a full stomach, since dining options are traditionally limited, and one can't live off those JetBlue terra chips. (Some have tried.) LGB is currently undergoing expansion, so a friendly, more modern dynamic may be forthcoming.

How to Get There—Driving

Long Beach Airport can be reached easily from just about anywhere in the Los Angeles basin. From the 405, take the Lakewood Boulevard exit northbound. Proceed past Spring Street and turn left on the next stop light, which is Donald Douglas Drive. From the 91, take the Lakewood Boulevard exit and proceed southbound approximately four miles. Make a right at Donald Douglas Drive into the main airport entrance.

How to Get There—Mass Transit

For $1.25 the Long Beach Transit Bus Route 111 runs from Broadwa to South Street via Lakewood Boulevard and makes a stop right a the airport (www.lbtransit.com; 562-591-2301). You can take th Blue Line train from downtown LA to the Transit Mall station i Long Beach to connect with the Route 111 bus (www.metro.net).

Taking a taxi, the best bet is a Long Beach Yellow Cab (562-435 6111). Alternatively, a number of van and limousine services ar available including Advantage Ground Transportation (800-752 5211), SuperShuttle (800-BLUE-VAN), Airport Express Limousin (866-800-0700), and Diva Limousine (800-427-DIVA).

Parking

The first twenty minutes in all lots is free. Each hour after that wi clock up $2. The maximum daily rate in the long-term parking lot is $19 in Lot A and $17 in Lot B. Try the "Park & Walk" lot at the mai airport entrance on the corner of Donald Douglas Drive and Lakewoo Boulevard. The rate declines as you get farther from the airport, s decide how far you want to walk versus how much you want to spen ($12 versus $9 per day). If you've got a lot of time, try the $6 per da remote off-site lot at Lakewood Boulevard and Conant Street with free shuttle to the airport. Valet parking is $24 per day with a free ca wash thrown in. Short-term parking has a two-hour limit.

Hotels

Holiday Inn • 2640 N Lakewood Blvd • 562-597-4401
Marriott • 4700 Airport Plaza Dr • 562-425-5210
Residence Inn by Marriott • 4111 E Willow St • 562-595-0909

Airlines

US Airways (North Gates)
Delta Air Lines (North Gates)
Alaska Airlines (North Gates)
JetBlue Airways (South Gates)

Car Rental

Avis	800-331-1212
Budget	800-221-1203
Enterprise	800-736-8222
Hertz	800-654-3131
National	800-227-7368

Airline	Phone	LAX	John Wayne	Burbank	Long Beach
Aer Lingus	800-474-7424	■			
Aeroflot	888-340-6400	■			
Aeromexico	800-237-6639	■			
Air Canada	888-247-2262	■			
Air China	800-882-8122	■			
Air France	800-237-2747	■			
Air Jamaica	800-523-5585	■			
Air New Zealand	800-262-1234	■			
Air Pacific	800-227-4446	■			
Air Tahiti Nui	877-824-4846	■			
AirTran Airways	1-800-247- 8726				
Alaska Airlines	800-426-0333	■	■	■	
All Nippon Airways (ANA)	800-235-9262	■			
Aloha Airlines	800-367-5250		■		
Allegiant	1-702 505 8888				
American Airlines	800-433-7300	■	■	■	
American Eagle	800-433-7300	■	■		
Asiana Airlines	800-227-4262	■			
Avianca Airlines	1-800-284-2622	■			
British Airways	800-247-9297	■			
Cathay Pacific Airways	800-233-2742	■			
China Airlines	800-227-5118	■			
China Eastern	626-583-1500	■			
China Southern Airlines	888-338-8988	■			
Copa Airlines (Panama)	800-359-2672	■			
Delta Air Lines	800-221-1212	■	■	■	■
Delta Connection	888-750-3284		■		
El Al Israel	800-352-5747	■			
EVA Air	800-695-1188	■			
Express Jet	888-958-9538				■
Frontier Airlines	800-432-1359	■	■		
Hawaiian Airlines	800-367-5320	■			
Horizon Air	800-547-9308	■			
Japan Airlines	800-525-3663	■			
JetBlue Airways	800-538-2583			■	■
KLM Airlines	800-225-2525	■			
Korean Air	800-438-5000	■			
LACSA Costa Rica	800-225-2272	■			
LAN Chile	866-435-9526	■			
LTU International Airways	866-266-5588	■			
Lufthansa	800-645-3880	■			
Malaysia Airlines	800-552-9264	■			
Mesa Airlines	800-637-2247		■		
Midwest Express Airlines	800-452-2022	■			
Philippine Airlines	800-435-9725	■			
Qantas	800-227-4500	■			
Singapore Airlines	800-742-3333	■			
Southwest Airlines	800-435-9792	■	■	■	
Spirit Airlines	800-772-7117	■			
Swiss Airlines	877-359-7947	■			
TACA International Airlines	800-535-8780	■			
Thai Airways	800-426-5204	■			
United Air Lines	800-241-6522	■	■	■	
United Express	800-241-6522	■	■		
US Airways	800-428-4322	■	■	■	■
Varig Brazilian Airlines	800-468-2744	■			
Virgin Atlantic Airways	800-862-8621	■			
Volaris	1-800-988-3527				
West Jet	1-888-937-8538				

Union Station

Union Station is located at 800 N Alameda Street between the Santa Ana Freeway (US 101) and Cesar E. Chavez Avenue. Built in 1939, it's widely considered the last great train station built in the States, at least by Art Deco snobs. Its architecture alone renders it a stunning piece of Los Angeles history. With distinct Art Deco, Spanish Colonial, and postmodern influences, it's impressive enough to merit a visit even if you're not looking to jump on a train. The scenic waiting room's ceiling stands 52 feet above its marble floors, and large, distinctive archways at each end give way to peaceful courtyards. Have you ever been in a train station that offered both the daily edition of the local paper *and* repose in a beautiful garden? Exactly. The station services three rail networks—the local Metro Rail Red, Purple, and Gold Lines, Amtrak (including the Pacific Sunliner and Coast Starlight Lines), and Southern California's Metrolink. Union Station is also home to the elegant Traxx Restaurant—a good spot to go if your boss is paying.

Amtrak

800-872-7245; www.amtrak.com

Amtrak, i.e., what passes for a reliable national rail network in this country, runs five major lines into LA's Union Station. The Pacific Surfliner (formerly the San Diegan) runs between San Diego, LA, and Santa Barbara, and on to San Luis Obispo and Paso Robles. You're not guaranteed to arrive on time, but at least you'll have beautiful ocean views to enjoy if you're delayed. A one-way trip from San Diego to LA will set you back about $36 and will (hopefully) get you there in under three hours. Traveling the length of the line costs around $46. Since the Desert Wind line closed down, Amtrak no longer offers transportation to Las Vegas via train, but it does provide a bus service, which takes between five and six hours and costs $110 round trip.

Shuttle service to Bakersfield connects the Pacific Surfliner with the San Joaquin trains, which run from Bakersfield through Fresno to Oakland. The Coast Starlight runs the length of the coast from LA through Oakland, and up to Eugene-Springfield and Seattle. The LA-to-Oakland fare costs between $58 and $70 one-way (buying round-trip is no less expensive than buying two one-way tickets), and if you're traveling all the way to Seattle, you'll be paying about $146. If you're heading east, the Sunset Limited line will be your train of choice. It runs from LA through Tucson, Phoenix, San Antonio, Houston, New Orleans, Jacksonville, and Orlando. The Texas Eagle has a similar first leg and covers Los Angeles, Tucson, San Antonio, Dallas, Little Rock, St. Louis, and Chicago. The Southwest Chief goes from LA to Albuquerque to Kansas City to Chicago. Check the Amtrak website or call to check schedules on the days you wish to travel.

Metrolink

800-371-5465; www.metrolinktrains.com

Not to be confused with the MTA's Metro Rail, Metrolink is an above-ground rail network that serves Southern California, including Los Angeles County, Ventura County, San Bernardino County, Orange County, Riverside County, and San Diego County. The lines run as far south as Oceanside in San Diego County, and as far north as Montalvo in Ventura County and Lancaster in LA County. Fares are calculated according to the number of zones traversed. A one-way fare costs between $4.50 and $11.75 during peak times, and it is always cheaper to purchase a round-trip ticket ($7.25 peak, one zone) at the beginning of your journey rather than two one-way fares. Buying a round trip fare is always cheaper than a one-way ticket (which range from $5.00 to $14.50). If you're going to be riding the rails between 7 PM on Friday and 11:59 PM Sunday, your best bet is definitely the $10 Weekend pass, which allows unlimited systemwide travel. Monthly passes are also available at varying rates. When in doubt, check the online fare calculator.

Metro Rail

800-266-6883; www.metro.net

The Metro Rail network is really, at its best, a confusion of contradictions, debate, and public necessity. It's an expanding public transportation network in a city that is notorious for its lack of just that; it's a contentious subway system in a city with a Mediterranean climate and over 200 earthquake fault lines; but it's also one of the few things trying to shake things up in a city where the freeways have been allowed to run wild. Locked in a battle of ambivalence, a begged-for expansion has been delayed by NIMBYs and car-lovers who consider public transit irrelevant. Luckily, Mayor Villaraigosa (a former president of the MTA) has been taking steps toward an extended Orange Line and the long-awaited "Subway to the Sea" and has made slow but sure progress towards said sea. The Expo Line from just south of USC to Culver City is up and running and is (tentatively) slated to go all the way to downtown Santa Monica by 2015. And, now that we know how it feels to pay four bucks for a gallon of gas, one has to wonder: Should I neglect my precious car and help save the environment in a potential death trap? Consider that riders on San Francisco's BART trundling beneath the Bay felt not a twitch during the 1989 temblor that rocked the area. Perhaps we're lying awake at 3 a.m. worrying about the wrong things.

The bus system is expanding in shaky bursts. With the new Orange Line in the Valley, one rarely wants to risk driving along Chandler. Granted, the street is all decked out with rather nice bus stops and the new eye-catching bus design is working hard to remind us that the bus isn't just for the blind and the homeless anymore. This new line even has its own transit lane, separate from the regular flow of traffic. But when the line opened, there was accident upon accident between buses and confused Angelenos. The new traffic guidelines and signs at the intersections really are hard to miss, but apparently LA drivers are doing their best. So be careful—of the bus and your fellow drivers.

With the Red, Blue, Gold, and Green Lines, the Rail system will carry you from the Valley to Hollywood to Downtown, over to Pasedena, and down to Redondo Beach. (When riding toward North Hollywood or Wilshire/Western, make sure you know where your particular train is going—it can be confusing.) With stops at Union Station, Hollywood and Highland, the STAPLES Center, Universal City, and the Wiltern, one does feel the temptation to jump out of the car and onto the Metro Rail band wagon. The only real drawback is the limited hours, particularly obvious on weekend nights, when clubbing by rail would be possible, if only it didn't stop running at midnight.

As far as ticketing goes, the Metro Rail works on the honor system. And by honor system, we mean the occasional threat of a ticket. While this may be hard to grasp for someone coming from a city with a reliable, untrusting transportation system, that's just how it's done here in the City of Angels. But you've been forewarned: Police check tickets onboard trains at random and unpredictable intervals, and if you fail to produce a valid ticket, you'll receive a fine a whole lot higher than the fare. Beware of eating or drinking on board as well—what seems like a minor infraction carries a major fine. Metro Rail sells a Monthly Metro Pass for $75 on their website.

Bicycles are happily allowed on the Metro Rail and buses. On the rail, they are not allowed on weekdays 6:30 am to 8:30 am and 4:30 pm to 6:30 pm. There are no restrictions during weekends and on holidays. Bicycle racks are available on a first-come, first-served basis, free of charge. Lockers may be rented for $75 for one year by calling 213-922-2660. Buses can accommodate two bikes per bus on their racks. The Orange Line provides a bikeway alongside its own transitway, as well as bike racks and bicycle parking at all of its stations.

Chatsworth
Nordhoff
Roscoe
Sherman Way
De Soto
Pierce College
Tampa
Reseda
Balboa
Woodley
Sepulveda
Van Nuys
Woodman
Valley College
Laurel Canyon
North Hollywood
Universal City
Hollywood/Highland
Hollywood/Vine
Hollywood/Western
Vermont/Sunset
Vermont/Santa Monica
Vermont/Beverly
Wilshire/Western
Wilshire/Normandie
Wilshire/Vermont
Westlake/MacArthur Park
7th Street/Metro Center
Civic Center
Pershing Square
Union Station
Little Tokyo
Chinatown
Lincoln/Cypress
Heritage Square
Southwest Museum
Highland Park
Mission
Fillmore
Del Mar
Memorial Park
Lake
Allen
Sierra Madre Villa
Pico/Aliso
Mariachi Plaza
Soto
Indiana
Maravilla
East LA Civic Ctr
Atlantic
Pico
Grand
San Pedro
23rd St
Culver City
La Cienga/Jefferson
Expo/La Brea
Farmdale
Expo/Crenshaw
Expo/Western
Expo/Vermont
Expo Park/USC
Jefferson/USC
Washington
Vernon
Slauson
Florence
Firestone
103rd St
Hawthorne/Lennnox
Aviation/LAX
Mariposa
El Segundo
Douglas
Redondo Beach
Crenshaw
Vermont
Harbor Freeway
Avalon
Imperial/Wilmington
Long Beach
Lakewood
Norwalk
Compton
Artesia
Del Amo
Wardlow
Willow
Pacific Coast Highway
Anaheim
Pacific
5th Street
Transit Mall
1st Street
Pacific Ocean
405
5
170
101
134
210
2
110
10
710
60
90
1
42
105
19
91
605
103

Overview

An estimated 10 million souls inhabit the 4,084 miles of Los Angeles County (in case you wonder why this NFT guide is so much bigger than its siblings), and although a railway system does exist, the public transit network is mostly about buses. Most, but not all, of the 300 bus routes through the city are run by the Metropolitan Transportation Authority (MTA). Fares and procedures vary between services. The websites for the services are excellent resources for route and schedule information, as well as trip planning. Fares for seniors, the disabled, and students can be as low as 25% of the full fare and differ for each service. Monthly passes offer regular riders a smaller discount. Up to two children (5 and under on MTA services, 4 and under on LADOT services) ride free with each fare-paying adult. Most buses don't give change, so be sure to carry exact change when boarding a bus. Fare machines take $1 bills, but they don't give change. If you're planning a multi-stage trip that involves bus, rail, or even Amtrak travel, the Metro Trip Planner website will get you from point A to point B to point Z; it conveniently details times, fares, and directions. (Check the Metro Trip Planner section on the next page.) You'll need exact change, for real.

Metropolitan Transportation Authority (MTA)

800-266-6883; www.metro.net

MTA buses are distinguished by their white color and distinctive orange stripes. Bus stops have a big black M on a white, rectangular sign. A single fare on an MTA bus costs $1.50 (55¢ for seniors/disabled). A transfer to a municipal bus costs 30¢ (10¢ for seniors/disabled)—ask your driver for one when you board. If you're changing buses again, buy another transfer from the driver when you hand in the first transfer. Transfers are good for an hour after you receive them. If you plan to switch to the Metro Rail, however, you'll have to pay $1.25 again; at this point, it might be cheaper to purchase a Day Pass, which allows you to board unlimited times for $5.

Frequent riders can save money by purchasing bags of ten tokens at local stores or supermarkets for $15 (which brings down your per-trip cost to $1.50). If you're a regular bus commuter, you might consider buying a weekly pass ($20) or regular monthly pass ($75, and $14 for seniors/disabled). Prepaid passes are sold in advance on TAP cards and can be purchased at Metro Customer Centers and at hundreds of sales outlet locations. Tokens can also be purchased at the same locations. MTA passes are valid on Commuter Express, DASH Downtown LA, Community Connection Routes 142, 147, 203, 208, and all Metro MTA rail and bus routes. LADOT passes are not valid on MTA services.

Los Angeles Department of Transportation (LADOT)

(213, 310, 323, or 818) 808-2273; www.ladottransit.com

DASH (Downtown Area Short Hop) shuttle system operates buses A, B, C, D, E, and F throughout downtown LA. The reliable service runs every five to twelve minutes, depending on the time of day and route, and costs only 50¢. The buses service downtown and also stop at the city's major landmark sites, including Union Station, the Convention Center, USC, Exposition Park and the Garment District. DASH also runs services to many parts of west LA, including Venice, Hollywood West Hollywood, and Beverly Hills, south to Watts Wilmington, and Crenshaw, and north to Studio City Northridge, and Chatsworth.

The **Commuter Express** is mainly a commuter service for people living in suburbs such as Culver City, Westwood Brentwood, Encino, Glendale, Burbank, Redondo Beach and the San Fernando Valley, who work in downtown LA. The fare costs between $1.50 and $4.25. Seniors disabled pay half the regular fare.

Community Connection serves the needs of city neighborhoods including San Pedro, Terminal Island Long Beach Transit Mall, Griffith Park, and Beachwood Canyon. LADOT also operates a battery-powered trolley in San Pedro, which departs every 15 minutes. A one way fare on the regular bus routes costs 90¢, and 45¢ for seniors/disabled, and the electric trolley costs 25¢ per ride.

The new **Holly Trolley** implements the Bunker Hill buses to carry club hoppers, diners, and other Hollywood explorers between Highland and Vine. For just a dollar you can catch a ride until 4 am.

Municipal Buses

'he **Big Blue Bus** serves Santa Monica, Malibu, and 'enice, and it costs one dollar to race between the beach owns. They also operate an express bus (Line 10) to lowntown LA that costs $1.75 (50¢ seniors/disabled). If 'ou buy a Little Blue Card, you'll save a couple of pennies)er ride. The blue buses are instantly recognizable, and he stops are identified by a blue triangle on a light pole narked "Big Blue Bus." Even Paris Hilton and her little)rown dog could figure this one out—that is, if she ever ode the bus. www.bigbluebus.com, 310-451-5444.

'he **West Hollywood CityLine/DayLine** is a shuttle ervice that covers 18 locations in West Hollywood ind costs 25¢ per ride. **West Hollywood Dollar Line** is free shuttle service available only to seniors and the lisabled, 800-447-2189.

'**oothill Transit** serves primarily the San Gabriel and 'omona Valleys, and fares cost between $1.00 for local rips and $4.40 for express service. Monthly passes cost)etween $66 for a local pass and up to $160 for a joint 'oothills/MTA pass on the most expensive express route; vww.foothilltransit.org, 626-967-3147.

:ulver CityBus costs one dollar (50¢ for students, 35¢ for eniors/disabled) and travels between Culver City, Venice, Aar Vista, LAX, and Westwood/UCLA. www.culvercity.org/)us

)range County Transit Authority (OCTA)
vww.octa.net, 714-636-7433
legular fare on OCTA buses costs $1.50; senior and lisability fares are a mere 60¢. A day pass entitles you o unlimited use of all local routes (excluding express outes 701 & 721) on the day it is purchased and costs 3 ($1 for seniors/disabled). A local monthly pass for)CTA services costs $55 ($18 for seniors/disabled). he express monthly pass (includes daily service to os Angeles aboard routes 701 and 721) costs $150. ndividual journeys on the 701 and 721 express routes o LA cost $3.75 and $2.50 if you have a day pass. Metrolink monthly passes are now valid on local OCTA ervices.)

'entura Intercity Service Transit Authority (VISTA)
vww.goventura.org, 800-438-1112
ixed bus routes will set you back $1.25 per ride (60¢ or seniors/disabled). Santa Paula and Fillmore dial-a-ides cost $1.50 (75¢ senior/disabled), and the Conejo Connection/Coastal Express is $3 ($1 senior/disabled). Monthly passes vary between $50 and $105, depending n the routes included in your package.

Metro Trip Planner

Search Engine: *www. socaltransport.org*
This search engine website is one of the best public transport facilities we've ever seen. It covers more than 45 of Southern California's transport networks including MTA buses and trains, OCTA and VISTA buses, Amtrak, Metrolink, MAX, and dozens of municipal services across Southern California.

The search facility prompts you to enter your start point, end point, the day you'd like to travel, the time you need to arrive at your destination, fare category, and special accommodations such as wheelchairs and bicycles. What you get in return is a detailed itinerary, including the type of transport, where it leaves from, the times it departs and arrives, the fare for each sector, and where you need to transfer. For example, if you were going from Universal Studios to Disneyland, leaving your departure point at noon, you would take the Red Metro Line at Universal City Station (12:05 pm—$1.25, get MTA transfer), get off at 7th Street Metro Center (12:25 pm) and take MTA Bus 460 Anaheim/Disneyland (12:32 pm, show driver transfer and pay $2.25). Get off at Disneyland at 2:22 pm and the entire journey will have cost you $3.50. The site even tells you that you should consider buying a Metro Day Pass for $5.00. Always check the return trip separately – it's not always the first trip backwards.

Start and end points can be addresses (including residential), intersections, or landmarks, and you can also decide whether you want the fastest itinerary, fewest transfers, or shortest walking distance. It's a good idea to try all three, as the travel times are often similar, and the cost difference can be significant. If it doesn't recognize an intersection, reversing the street names sometimes helps. All in all, it's a terrific resource for public transportation users—it's more clever and efficient, in fact, than the public transport system it tries to decode.

The relentless controversy surrounding LA transit fuels a broad network of feisty, entertaining transit blogs. To dip in, start with http://la.streetsblog.org and sample the links.

Overview

When you're driving in Los Angeles, it's always high noon. But geography is destiny, and our mass transit options still aren't what they could be, so we do what we must. Features peculiar to Los Angeles's paved circulatory system include "Sigalerts" (legacy of the radio announcer Loyd C. "Sig" Sigmon, these reports warn of unusual or hazardous freeway conditions and generally mean traffic is frozen) and a rush hour that goes from 7 am to 10 am, then returns for a hydrocarbons happy hour at 3 pm and stays busy until at least 8 pm. Even as gas prices regularly scrape $4 a gallon, and commutes get longer, no one seems to be driving any less, or any better, and people haven't stopped moving here.

The Ground Rules

1. The best offense is a good defense.
When the law says you have the right of way, don't be so presumptuous as to expect it will be yielded to you. Driving defensively in LA is like a modern basketball game: it's a full-on contact sport—but it's not supposed to be. LA drivers don't do the following: use turn signals, stay within the solid road lines, wait their turn, or concede that a few tons of steel in their way is any kind of a deterrent. Judging by the sense of urgency Los Angeles drivers often exhibit, you'd think they were all carrying transplant organs or plasma for the trauma ward in their back seats. No, they are just completely self-absorbed. Using a cell in traffic is illegal unless it's hands-free, but it doesn't seem to be rigorously enforced. And it's still permissible to eat a burger, apply makeup, or engage in PDA behind the wheel. (We've seen it.) So keep your guard up. Accept that it's a mess, assume that the other driver is reckless and crazy, and make defensive driving your paranoid knee-jerk reaction of choice. Knowing that the other guy was in the wrong is not going to make the call to your insurance company any sweeter.

2. Plan a route. And then prepare to abandon it.
For any given drive, there is the logical route—the shortest distance between two points, the freeway, whatever. Much like the mythical beast that is "right of way," logic doesn't necessarily prevail. Accidents, roadwork, gawkers, Academy Award festivities, a refrigerator in the far right lane of the highway—these can all wreak havoc on your route of choice. Just as flight attendants instruct you to locate the emergency exit nearest you, we warn you to be aware of where you are at all times as you may need to bail out quite suddenly.

The road less traveled is often a glorious alternative, stop signs or not. However, beware the inherent gamble. These options are often two-lane roads. So all it takes is a Sunday driver, or enough people willing to gamble on the same alternative, and your plan is shot. LA traffic is the Las Vegas of American gridlock. Big money—be brave.

3. Traffic reports are your holy grail.
Gone are the days of watching the morning news. No one has the time. To help with the Sigalerts, we have www.sigalert.com. That's instant traffic updates the second before you're out the door. For on-the-go info, the radio is key. The young might lay claim to their indie rock stations and the post-graduates and middle-aged might have faith in NPR, but the truly erudite LA driver always switches over to the AM for traffic. 1070 AM ha upwards of 6 traffic reports an hour. Yes, it may sound like th signal has traveled forward in time from the seventies, but thei reports are comprehensive. They're not just aimed at thos commuting from outside of LA and they're actually helpfu So get ready to multi-task and embrace the wonder of mixe media. You're not in Kansas anymore.

4. Keep your Thomas Guide within reach.
If you've been driving that old hunk o' junk since before th advent of smartphones and Google Maps, you might sti have a trusty Thomas Guide trapping crumbs on the floor o your back seat. That said, the Thomas Guide is undeniably a incredible resource, especially when driving in the hills, wher reception can be spotty. It's extremely detailed, and if it isn' in the guide, it's not in LA. However, this bulky book looks an feels like a city schematic, and it might as well be a life-siz map of LA that has been cut into little rectangles and boun together in no particular order. While it's not difficult to use, i doesn't possess any definite logic. The old adage that you know you're an Angeleno when you can drive and use your Thoma Guide at the same time is truly the motto of the reckless, law breaking, and accident-prone LA driver. So, if you want to kee your insurance rates down, plan ahead, keep the Thomas Guid at home, and find something more manageable for the ca Like, I don't know…your NFT guide? Or at least pull over befor you break out that giant tome.

5. Make your left turns, do not let the left turns make you.
Nothing can mess up your progress across town—o seemingly, in life—quite like waiting to make a left. You'd thin you were on an organ transplant waiting list. Two problem here: not enough left turn arrows to go around (on som kind of endangered species list, apparently), and the majo thoroughfares are functioning at 110% capacity (with n arrow, you ain't getting across). How many thousands of hour are lost collectively every day by drivers in Los Angeles waitin to go left onto Third Street from Normandie? From Fairfa onto Wilshire (and that's *with* an arrow)? From Cahuenga ont Sunset? We may never know. Though it does explain why th unwritten Law of LA Left Turns that says that 'two cars get t turn on yellow.

Take control of the turns by taking advantage of other traffi lights. For example: say you're heading west on Sixth Stree and need to make the left onto La Brea. This is a sad tas particularly in the morning. Knowing there are traffic light to assist you, you could instead make a left on Sycamore (on block before La Brea), cross Wilshire at the light, turn right o Eighth Street, and then make your left onto La Brea with the ai of yet another light. By not trying to wait out La Brea and Sixt you have also avoided having to pass through the dense mas of vehicles at La Brea and Wilshire. If you can turn left onto side street without a light and return to your desired street fo a left turn with less congestion, this will also help. Also, if yo can pass your street and turn left into a side street or parkin lot, you can turn around, make two easy rights and be on you street as the line builds at the left turn signal you left far fa behind. Repeat these often enough and you will find yourse early to appointments and with more free time than you know what to do with. Think like a champ.

Mind those yellow lights going red.

Simple, but true. First, there's the obvious risk of injury or death to you or your vehicle. But even worse, these days, your chances of getting caught by the law are increasing. More and more intersections are monitored by cameras, which take surprisingly clear photos of you smiling like the cat that caught the canary. The good thing is that they're required to post signs warning you of the cameras. The bad thing is that the ticket arrives in the mail a few days later; the fine varies depending upon which city's law you've violated. But if you do get popped, fear not: since being overwhelmed with derelict red light tickets, LA County is no longer pursuing unpaid photo tickets. It's only a matter of time before they send an embossed sleeve for your pic, as if the light at Sunset & La Cienega might as well be the newest coaster at Magic Mountain.

You're never really lost in LA.

As long as you know where the hills are, you'll always be able to orient yourself and drive in the right direction. If you're in the Valley, the hills can always be found to the south. On the LA side of Mulholland, the hills are always to your north.

All bets are off when it rains.

Even with all the rain LA got last winter, a mere sprinkle still sends LA drivers into a tailspin, leaving accidents in its wake and taking the lead story on the nightly news. You'd think they hadn't seen rain in 20 years, but apparently a dry LA summer does the trick. Santa Anas can make a light shower out of large-scale sprinkler systems, too. Proceed with extreme caution.

Shortcuts

Everybody has discovered at least one shortcut, of which they're extremely proud. Often, they keep these shortcuts even from their children and spouses. The discovery of a shared shortcut can develop a bond that no frat or Masons lodge could ever hope to match. Like knowing where the traffic lights are, there is no way to function in LA without them. Here are a few recommendations. Keep them more secret than we did.

Downtown

Avoid the most congested part of the 110: Beaudry to the west and Figueroa to the east offer good alternatives.

When heading east into downtown, try a more peripheral approach via Second Street or Olympic Boulevard.

Across Town

Pico is better than Wilshire. Olympic is better than Pico. Venice is better than Olympic. Washington trumps all of them.

Strangely, when going through Hollywood, Hollywood Boulevard itself is preferable to Sunset and can be preferable to Franklin, which backs up at Highland.

Wilshire Boulevard through Beverly Hills into Westwood can coagulate badly. San Vicente-to-Sunset, and Burton-to-Little Santa Monica-to-Beverly Glen work well as alternates.

Though Santa Monica Boulevard is actually a highway (the 2), it is not for cross-town trips, particularly through Hollywood/West Hollywood. Years ago, when asked what advice she had for young actors in Hollywood, Bette Davis is said to have replied, "Take Fountain, dahhling." And what do you know? She's still right—even with the stop signs and the zig-zag around LeConte Junior High.

North–South

- Normandie moves pretty well between Koreatown and Los Feliz, as does Hillhurst/Virgil. When these are bad, a good short cut is Wilton/Arlington/Van Ness. Wilton hits Arlington at Olympic and then Van Ness at Slauson. This covers a lot of territory with fewer conniptions.
- Hauser and Cochran move way faster than La Brea, Fairfax, and Crescent Heights. Hauser can be used with Martel and then a short jog west to Gardner at Willoughby to get all the way to Franklin.
- Robertson is preferable to La Cienega. Just about everything is preferable to La Cienega.

Westside/Santa Monica

- 23rd Street morphs into Walgrove, getting you to Venice and points south in no time.
- Unfortunately, Santa Monica is something of a fox hole. Getting out is never easy. The 10 east is always bad, and Century City just makes things difficult with the larger buildings and shopping center drawing more traffic. Pico at times feels begrudgingly like your best bet. If you can jog south, try Palms. You'll be surprised.
- If you're trying to head north out of Santa Monica to the Valley, good luck. Head east on Montana, take that to Westgate just past San Vincente and head up to Sunset. Sunset takes you over the 405. This way you can check it out and see how bad it is. If necessary, turn around and head back to Sepulveda.
- Heading south from Beverly Hills, Beverwil to Castle Heights to Palms to Walgrove comes in handy.
- Carmelita in Beverly Hills is amazing. It picks up by Melrose and drops off at Wilshire. Even with the stop signs it will save you a lot of time, or at the bare minimum will get you away from Santa Monica. You can also jump on it heading south on Beverly to get to Wilshire and skip the Wilshire/Santa Monica intersection.
- National Boulevard is a strange and beautiful thing. Almost as strange as San Vicente. If you figure it out, drop us a note.

The Valley

- Moorpark and Riverside can pull through for you when the 101 and Ventura Boulevard fail you (and oh, they will).
- You'll save a lot of time by taking north-south roads that don't provide access to the 101. Whitsett and Colfax are underappreciated wonders–and usually allow easier left turns as well.

- When coming into the Valley on Beverly Glen and planning on heading back east, you can avoid the back up leading up to and on Ventura by taking Valley Vista. You can cut back to Ventura at several points or reconnect with it just before Coldwater Canyon.
- The Hollywood Freeway (the 170) can also help you, particularly if the 101/134 split is heavy.

Getting To and From the Valley

There are several options when traveling between the San Fernando Valley and points south, and none of them are especially attractive.

- The 405 too often turns into a parking lot. You might try Sepulveda Boulevard instead. NIce slalom effect on light days. When used in conjuction with the 405, this nice tag-team effort can sometimes save you some time.
- The 101 can be a terror in its own right. If you get on at Highland, as is the case when coming from Hollywood, Hancock Park, and the surrounding areas, you find yourself in the left-hand lane—with the rest of traffic moving at the speed of the Autobahn. If Burbank is your destination, you suddenly find yourself with only about 500 yards to cross no fewer than five lanes of traffic to exit at Barham Boulevard—a true test of one's driving mettle. Screenwriter/playwright Roger Kumble wrote in his play *Pay or Play* that there are two kinds of Angelenos, "101 People" and "Cahuenga People." Cahuenga people shy away from this act of bravado and prefer to drive the service road over the hill. Funny enough, he doesn't bother to categorize those smart enough to take whichever will get them to Point B faster.
- The Canyon roads all have their supporters and detractors. Those who opt for these routes over the highways are steadfast in their beliefs and stay true to their Canyon road of choice, but still, one must cop to the fact that the east/west positioning of the roads will often determine which one would be the best for you to use. That said: Laurel Canyon becomes less viable daily and recently has been partially rerouted due to mudslides. Coldwater Canyon backs up just about as easily. Benedict Canyon requires a little finessing. Beverly Glen is the user-friendliest of the four (Tyrone in Sherman Oaks runs into it at Ventura). Just like the highways, these roads improve greatly the earlier you can get to them. The increase in traffic from 7 am to 7:15 am is astounding.

The Freeways

When the freeway is moving and the weather is dry, Los Angeles is a beautiful place, and you never want to leave. The other 90% of the time, you fantasize about moving to San Francisco. Or about hurting someone. Where is the flashing highway marquee from *LA Story* when you need it? "LA wants to help you." If only…

Here's the thing: all freeways are not created equal and the 405 is the most unequal of all. Avoid it whenever possible, at least within a ten-mile radius of LAX. If it's at all convenient, La Cienega Boulevard is preferable as a north-south route. Heading south from Hollywood, La Cienega will actually lead you directly onto the 405, south of the airport, allowing you to overshoot the most common delays.

The 101 is also confusing. It's a north/south road, because it ultimate destination is Northern California, yet it crosses th San Fernando Valley in an east/west direction. The 101 is know as the Hollywood Freeway, at least while you're in Hollywoo and Downtown. Once you reach the Valley, the 101 splits o toward Santa Barbara and becomes the Ventura Freeway. you want to continue on the Hollywood Freeway, you must op for the 170. Confused yet? Meanwhile, the 134 is known as th Ventura Freeway between I. 5 and I. 2, until it hooks up with th 101, which then becomes the Ventura Freeway. This is the bes illustration we know for why the names of freeways are relativel meaningless here in LA.

Though not technically a freeway, the Pacific Coast Highwa deserves special mention here. It's one of the most picturesqu thoroughfares in LA, running—as its name implies—alongsid the Pacific Coast. However, the PCH is plagued by mudslide brushfires, and floods during the rainy season and ofte closed to traffic, stranding Malibu residents or forcing ther to backtrack inland to pick up the 101. We guess that's th price you pay for beachfront property. (Speaking of beach: th shortest distance between Hollywood and Malibu is the 101 t Malibu Canyon. Period.)

Depending on where you are starting from and where you ar going, the 2 and 210 Freeways may save you a lot of time b keeping you out of more congested parts of the city. Just bewar of the 2 as it crawls through Echo Park on Alvarado Street.

A note on the freeway on-ramps: while most on-ramps ar clearly mapped out, LA is rather fond of sketching out th path to a few of their ramps in a circuitous, unclear route that less turn-left-for-north-and-right-for-south and more Where Waldo? Just breathe. You'll figure it out, and make a ment note for next time.

DMV Locations

800-777-0133; www.dmv.ca.gov; Hours: Mon–Tues: 8 am–5 pn Wed: 9 am–5 pm; Thurs–Fri: 8 am–5 pm. Many DMV offices ar open the third Saturday each month from 8 am–12 pm. Check th website for details.

The Department of Motor Vehicles in California handle vehicle registrations, driving records, identification cards, an everything to do with driver's licenses—as well as a cornucopi of other logistical, vehicle-related things almost equally a fascinating as the ones listed here. Thanks to our complet dependency on our vehicles, the department manages t dredge up a whopping $5.9 billion in revenue every year. (Mayb we're in the wrong business…) Much like the freeways the help populate, the DMV always involves long lines and muc waiting. The DMV may be the LCD that LA needs; no amour of glam factor will ingratiate you with the broken-yet-stil somehow-not-wretched clerks. You can make an appointmer via phone or their website and we highly recommend that yo do. Some locations don't process registration issues, so mak sure to check before you have to give up a great parking spc only to have to schlep to a sister location. We'd say that multip trips to the DMV is like salt in the wounds, but, really, nothing like multiple trips to the DMV.

urn the world over on its side and everything loose will land in Los Angeles. —Frank Lloyd Wright

Useful Phone Numbers

mergencies	911
os Angeles City Hall	213-473-3231
:alTrans	916-654-5266
)epartment of Water & Power	800-342-5397
outhern California Edison	800-655-4555
he Gas Company	800-427-2200

Vebsites

vww.notfortourists.com • The most comprehensive LA site there is. (And no, we weren't paid to say that.)

vww.lacity.org • The city's official home on the web.

vww.losangeles.com • From buying real estate to planning a night out on the town, this website has it all.

vww.sigalert.com • Real-time traffic updates with an easy, snazzy interface.

vww.losangeles.citysearch.com • Ultimate insider guide with reviews on shopping, dining and services.

vww.laalmanac.com • It's loaded with everything you could ever want to know about LA.

vww.lacantdrive.com • Maintain a sense of humor.

vww.lapl.org • LA Public Library's handy website—e.g., use the hold system to get a book sent to your library if you're not satisfied with your local branch.

vww.lausd.k12.ca.us • Contact information and report cards for schools in your neighborhood.

vww.blacknla.com • Online resource for LA-based African Americans featuring news articles, business listings, and local events.

vww.la.com • Online resource for Angeleno luxuries, shopping, events, and nightlife.

Essential LA Songs

Hooray for Hollywood" — Various, written by Johnny Mercer & Richard A. Whiting (1937)
There's No Business Like Show Business" — Ethel Merman, written by Irving Berlin (1954)
California Sun" — Rivieras (1964)
California Girls" — The Beach Boys (1965)
California Dreamin'" — The Mamas & The Papas (1966)
Ladies of the Canyon" — Joni Mitchell (1970)
L.A. Woman" — The Doors (1971)
California" — Joni Mitchell (1971)
Am, I Said" — Neil Diamond (1971)
You're So Vain" — Carly Simon (1972)
Ventura Highway" – America (1972)
Eggs and Sausage" — Tom Waits (1975)
Hotel California" — The Eagles (1976)
The Pretender" — Jackson Browne (1976)
Wasted" – Black Flag (1978)
Runnin' With the Devil" – Van Halen (1978)
Los Angeles" — X (1980)
Walkin' in LA" – Missing Persons (1982)
Valley Girl" — Frank and Moon Unit Zappa (1982)
I Love L.A." — Randy Newman (1983)
My Life is Good" — Randy Newman (1983)
Sunset Grill" — Don Henley (1984)
Paradise City" — Guns N Roses (1987)
Jane Says" — Jane's Addiction (1988)
Fallen Angel" — Poison (1988)
F— Tha Police" — N.W.A. (1988)
Free Fallin'" — Tom Petty (1989)
Neighborhood" — Los Lobos (1990)
Under the Bridge" — Red Hot Chili Peppers (1991)
All I Wanna Do" — Sheryl Crow (1993)
Los Angeles" – Frank Black (1993)
LA Song" — Deconstruction (1994)
California Love" — Tupac Shakur (1995)
This Is How We Do It" – Montell Jordan (1995)
Angeles" — Elliot Smith (1996)
Malibu" — Hole (1998)
Californication" — Red Hot Chili Peppers (1999)
California" — Phantom Planet (2002)
Beverly Hills" —Weezer (2005)
Dani California" — Red Hot Chili Peppers (2006)

Less Practical Information

- Los Angeles averages 329 days of sunshine each year. Yet we still whine about the other 36.
- The longest street in Los Angeles is Sepulveda Boulevard, which runs 76 miles from the San Fernando Valley to Long Beach.
- With few exceptions, LA bars are legally prohibited from serving alcohol between the hours of 2 am and 6 am.
- The U.S. Bank Tower (633 W Fifth St) is Los Angeles's tallest building (and was spectacularly taken out by aliens in the 1997 blockbuster *Independence Day*).
- The city boasts more stage theaters (80+) and museums (300) than any other city in the US. And New Yorkers say we have no culture.
- There are 527 miles of freeway and 382 miles of conventional highway in Los Angeles County. Bette Midler is determined to clean up all of them.
- Angelenos drive 92 million vehicle miles every day. This gives them ample time to admire the amber hues of our smog-riddled sunsets.
- Annually, LA residents consume over one billion pounds of red meat, over 300 billion pounds of ice cream, and absolutely no carbs whatsoever.

Essential LA Movies

The Big Sleep (1946)
Sunset Boulevard (1950)
Singin' in the Rain (1952)
Rebel Without a Cause (1955)
Chinatown (1974)
Shampoo (1975)
Big Wednesday (1978)
Grease (1978)
10 (1979)
Blade Runner (1982)
Fast Times at Ridgemont High (1982)
Valley Girl (1983)
Repo Man (1984)
To Live and Die in LA (1985)
Down and Out in Beverly Hills (1986)
Born in East LA (1987)
Less Than Zero (1987)
Who Framed Roger Rabbit (1998)
Pretty Woman (1990)
L.A. Story (1991)
Grand Canyon (1991)
The Player (1992)
Menace II Society (1993)
Short Cuts (1993)
Pulp Fiction (1994)
Heat (1995)
Clueless (1995)
Devil in a Blue Dress (1995)
Get Shorty (1995)
Swingers (1996)
Jackie Brown (1997)
L.A. Confidential (1997)
Volcano (1997)
Slums of Beverly Hills (1998)
Magnolia (1999)
The Muse (1999)
Dancing at the Blue Iguana (2000)
Mulholland Dr. (2001)
Laurel Canyon (2002)
Collateral (2004)
Crash (2005)
Lords of Dogtown (2005)
The Black Dahlia (2006)
The TV Set (2006)
Battle: Los Angeles (2011)

Los Angeles Timeline—a timeline of significant events in the history of Los Angeles (by no means complete)

1781: El Pueble de Nuestra Senora de la Reina de Los Angeles de Porciuncula—a.k.a. Los Angeles—is founded.
1822: Los Angeles becomes a Mexican City when Mexico wins its independence from Spain.
1842: Gold rush hits Southern California.
1850: LA County is established, City of LA is incorporated.
1880: USC is founded.
1881: Rail lines between LA and the East Coast are completed.
1881: *LA Times* begins printing.
1882: Electricity comes to downtown LA.
1887: The land is purchased for Hollywood: a church community planned to promote prohibition and clean living.
1890: First Tournament of Roses Parade.
1891: CalTech opens its doors.
1892: Abbott Kinney stakes his claim in Venice.
1894: Labor rioting breaks out in LA during national railroad strike.
1896: Griffith J. Griffith donates land that will become Griffith Park.
1899: LA Stock Exchange opens.
1902: City's first movie theater opens for business.
1909: Construction on LA aqueduct begins.
1910: Alice Stebbins Wells appointed to LA police force as the nation's first female policewoman.
1913: The Los Angeles Aqueduct brings water from the Owens Valley.
1915: Universal Studios opens.
1915: San Fernando Valley annexed by City of LA.
1919: UCLA is formed.
1922: Hollywood Bowl opens.
1923: The Hollywood Sign is erected.
1932: Tenth Olympic Games are held in LA.
1939: Union Station opens.
1940: Pasadena Freeway (later the 110) is LA's first freeway.
1946: KTLA is LA's first commercial television station.
1947: Black Dahlia murder. The case is never solved.
1953: The famed "four-level" opens, linking the 101 and 110 freeways.
1954: Completion of the Watts Towers.
1955: Disneyland opens.
1958: The Dodgers relocate from Brooklyn.
1960: The Lakers leave Minneapolis for LA.
1964: The Music Center opens Downtown.
1965: LACMA opens its doors.
1965: The Watts Riots.
1968: Robert Kennedy assassinated at Ambassador Hotel.
1969: Manson Murders.
1971: Sylmar Earthquake.
1974: J. Paul Getty Museum opens in Pacific Palisades.
1978: The Hollywood Sign is rebuilt with local celebs donating $27,700 per letter.
1980: Screen Actors Guild strike.
1984: The 23rd Olympics are held in LA.
1985: LA Lakers finally beat the Boston Celtics to take out NBA honors after losing nine finals to them previously.
1989: Mayor Tom Bradley elected to an unprecedented fifth term.
1991: Rodney King is beaten by four police officers.
1992: Verdict in King case leads to citywide rioting.
1992: Landers earthquake.
1993: Menendez murder trial #1.
1993: LA officially opens its first subway line.
1994: O.J. Simpson arrested after slow-speed chase down the 405.
1994: Northridge earthquake.
1995: Menendez murder trial #2.
1995: If it doesn't fit, you must acquit: O.J. found not guilty.
1995: Departure of Rams and Raiders leaves LA without a football team.
1997: The Getty Center opens in Brentwood.
2000: LA Lakers defeat Indiana Pacers for NBA title.
2001: Back-to-back NBA Championships for the LA Lakers.
2001: First championship for the WNBA's LA Sparks.
2002: Three-peat for the LA Lakers and Phil Jackson.
2002: Back-to-back WNBA Championships for the LA Sparks.
2002: Anaheim Angels win their first World Series.
2003: Famed Austrian-bodybuilder-turned-Hollywood-action-star adds another hyphenate. Arnold Schwarzenegger runs for the position of Governor of California during the recall election and wins.
2005: Actor and former child star Robert Blake found not guilty of his wife Bonnie Lee Bakley's murder.
2005: The city elects its first Latino mayor in 130 years.
2006: The WB and UPN merge to form the CW.
2006: LA serves as a focal point for the demonstrations and boycotts over the contentious proposed immigration legislation.
2007: USC beats Michigan in the Rose Bowl 32-18.
2007: Fire in Griffith Park burns over 600 acres.
2008: Southern California faces its worst economic turf-out in decades. In lieu of tax refunds, the state issues IOUs
2009: One-gloved pop-star eccentric Michael Jackson dies of a drug overdose. His back-catalogue resonates from car windows throughout the city.
2012: The Expo Line opens, and the Kings win their first Stanley Cup. Yes, Virginia, LA can have public transit and good hockey.

January

January	Location	Description
Tournament of Roses Parade	Pasadena. Just follow the crowds.	A Southern California tradition. 117 years and counting. (Jan 1)
Rose Bowl	The Rose Bowl, of course	"The Granddaddy of All Bowl Games." (Jan 1)
Japanese New Year "Oshogatsu"	Little Tokyo	Soothe your New Year's hangover with the sound of Taiko drums. (Jan 1)
Golden Globe Awards	Beverly Hilton Hotel	Unlike at the Oscars, the stars are allowed to drink, which leads to occasional embarrassing moments. (mid Jan)
Kingdom Day Parade	Martin Luther King Blvd, at Crenshaw, at Grevillea Park	Parade commemorating the life of MLK, Jr. (mid Jan)

February

February	Location	Description
Lunar New Year Parade & Festival	Pasadena	Parade along Colorado Blvd. (mid Feb)
Firecracker Run 5K/10K	N Broadway & College St, Chinatown	Race celebrating Chinese New Year. (Mid Feb)
Pan African Film & Arts Festival	Magic Johnson Theaters, 3650 Martin Luther King Jr Blvd	One of America's largest festivals of black films and fine arts. (Mid Feb)
Chinese New Year	Chinatown & various locations	Features a parade, a street fair, and even a golf tournament. (mid Feb)
Brazilian Carnaval	Queen Mary, Long Beach	Samba your way down the Walk of Fame. (Feb)
Nissan Open	Riviera Country Club, Pacific Palisades	The PGA championships come to the Westside. (mid Feb)
Queen Mary Scottish Festival	Long Beach	Wear your tartan, eat your haggis!
Ragga Muffins Festival	Long Beach Arena	Bob Marley's b-day celebration.
Black History Parade & Festival	Jackie Robinson Center, Pasadena	Food, kids' play area, and the Black Inventions Museum. (mid Feb)

March

March	Location	Description
Mardi Gras	El Pueblo Historical Monument, 125 Paseo de la Plaza	Celebrate Fat Tuesday on Olvera Street. (March).
LA Times Travel Show	Long Beach Convention Center	Get outta town—at least in your head. (March)
Los Angeles Marathon	Throughout LA	The one day a year we choose not to drive. (early Mar)
Academy Awards	Kodak Theatre, Hollywood Blvd & Highland Ave	More revered as an LA holiday than Presidents' Day. (late Feb-early Mar)
WestWeek	Pacific Design Center, WeHo	An interior design fest! (Mar).
Big Bunny's Spring Fling	LA Zoo	Kiddie crafts and photo ops with "Big Bunny." (late Mar)
Art & Design Walk	West Hollywood	Walk into 300+ showrooms, galleries, and boutiques. (Mar)
Cesar E. Chavez Day	Olvera St	Honors the Mexican-American farm labor leader. (Mar 31)

April

April	Location	Description
Pasadena Cherry Blossom Festival	Rose Bowl	Japanese culture, great food, cool fighting. (first weekend in Apr)
Blessing of the Animals	Olvera St	Check out the parade of house pets and wild animals. (Apr)
Bunka Sai Japanese Cultural Festival	Ken Miller Rec Center, Torrance	Japanese culture, from judo to origami. (mid Apr)
Garifuna Street Fest	Avalon Blvd, South Central LA	Celebrates largest Black ethnic group in Central America. (Apr)
Jimmy Stewart Relay	Griffith Park	Like running a marathon, but with help. (Apr)
Eco Maya Mother Earth Day Festival	Los Angeles City College	Ecology and the cooking of the Largest Tamal in the World (last week in Apr).
50+ Fitness Jamboree & Health Expo	Griffith Park	Includes 1K and 5K walks with celebrity seniors. (Last week in Apr)
Toyota Grand Prix of Long Beach	Downtown Long Beach	Auto racing. (mid Apr)
Los Angeles Times Festival of Books	UCLA campus	The city's biggest and coolest literary event (because we usually have a table). (late Apr)
Blooming of the Roses	Exposition Park Rose Garden	Stop and smell the roses. Literally. (Last week in Apr)
Annual Arbor Day Festival	Cheviot Hills Park & Recreation Center	Trees aren't just for hugging. (Last week in Apr)
Dolo Coker Scholarship Benefit Jazz Concert	Founder's Church, 3281 W 6th St	Supports young jazz hopefuls. (mid Apr)
Santa Anita Derby	Santa Anita Racetrack, Arcadia	Big pre-Kentucky Derby race and festival. (Apr)
Renaissance Pleasure Faire	Santa Fe Dam Recreation Area, Irwindale	Maidens, meade, and minstrels. (Apr–May)
LA Zoo Earth Day Expo	LA Zoo	Meet Rascal the Recycling Raccoon. (Apr 22)
Los Angeles Antiques Show	Santa Monica Air Center, Barker Hangar	Antiques galore. (late Apr)
Indian Film Festival	ArcLight Cinemas, Hollywood	Go beyond Bollywood. (Apr)
Feria de los Ninos Celebration	Hollenbeck Park, East LA	Ethnic food and entertainment with an emphasis on family-friendly activities. (late Apr)

May

May	*Location*	*Description*
• Pasadena Doo Dah Parade	Colorado Blvd, Pasadena	Irreverent spoof of the more stately Rose Parade. Recommended, but extremely subject to change – check the web (Early May)
• Fiesta Broadway	Downtown LA	The largest Cinco de Mayo celebration in the world. (First weekend of May)
• Cinco de Mayo Celebration	Olvera St	Celebrate Mexico's victory over the French. Que bueno! (May 5)
• LA Asian Pacific Film & Video Festival	Various locations	Showcases works by Pacific-American and international artists. (late April–early May)
• Revlon Run/Walk for Women	LA Memorial Coliseum, Exposition Park	5K race raises money to fight women's cancer. (May)
• Family FunFest and Kodomo-no-Hi	Japanese American Cultural & Community Center, Little Tokyo	Celebrate kids the Japanese way. (May)
• Silver Lake Film Festival	Silver Lake	Thinks it's the coolest film fest in town. (mid May)
• Affaire in the Gardens Art Show	Beverly Gardens Park, Beverly Hills	Art show. (mid May and mid Oct)
• Huntington Gardens Annual Plant Sale	San Marino	Let your garden grow. (mid May)
• Festival Dia de Las Madres	Vermont Ave & 8th St Downtown	Mother's Day street fair with food from Mexico, the Caribbean, and Latin America. (early May)
• E3 Electronic Entertainment Expo	LA Convention Center	Boys, their toys, and the nation's most in-demand girls.
• Old Pasadena Summer Fest	Rose Bowl	Five fests in one range from eating to sports. (Memorial Day weekend)
• Silver Lake Jubilee	Sunset Junction	Multi-stage street festival focusing on live music (Memorial Day Weekend).

June

June		
• Life Cycle	San Francisco to Los Angeles	585-mile bicycle ride for AIDS-related charities. (early June)
Los Angeles Film Festival	Hollywood	A breath of cinematic fresh air. (June)
• Great American Irish Fair & Music Festival	Irvine	St. Patrick's Day in the summer. (mid June)
• Playboy Jazz Festival	Hollywood Bowl	Almost more jazz than you can handle. (mid June)
• Mariachi USA Festival	Hollywood Bowl	Traditional mariachi music, as well as Ballet Foklorico. (mid June)
• LA Pride	West Hollywood Park	Celebrates gay pride. (mid June)
• Long Beach Chili Cook-off	Long Beach Marina Green	The competition really heats up (bad pun intended). (mid June)

July

July		
• At the Beach, LA Black Pride Festival	Westin Airport Hotel, Point Dume Beach in Malibu	Largest annual gathering of African-American lesbians and gay men in the world. (early Jul)
• Farmers Classic	LA Tennis Center, UCLA	Tennis tournament. Used to be Mercedes Benz Cup. (last week in Jul)
• Outfest	DGA, 7920 Sunset Blvd	Gay and lesbian film festival. (early to mid Jul)
• Lotus Festival	Echo Park Lake	Celebrates Asian and Pacific cultures. (mid Jul)
• Central Avenue Jazz Festival	Central Ave b/w 42nd & 43rd Sts	Remembers Central Avenue as the hot spot it was in the 1920s–'50s. (late Jul)
• Twilight Dance Series	Santa Monica Pier	Dance away every Thursday from July to September.

August

August		
• Long Beach Jazz Festival	Long Beach	Jazz by the sea. (mid Aug)
• Nisei Week Japanese Festival	Little Tokyo	Celebrating Asian culture and community. (mid Aug)
• Marcus Garvey Day Parade & Festival	Elegant Manor, 3115 W Adams Blvd	Invites all to celebrate "Africa for the Africans at home or abroad." (mid Aug) (late Aug)

September

September		
• LA International Short Film Festival	ArcLight Cinemas, Hollywood	For movie lovers with short attention spans. (mid Sept)
• LA Greek Fest	St. Sophia Cathedral	Eat a gyro, break a plate. (early to mid Sept).
• Emmy Awards	Shrine Auditorium	TV's night to shine. (mid Sept)

eptember	Location	Description
obster Festival	Location varies	Great food, good music, family fun, and cheap Maine Lobster. (mid Sept)
os Angeles City Birthday Celebration	El Pueblo Historical Monument, 125 Paseo de la Plaza	Happy Birthday, dear LA-ay, Happy Birthday to you! (Sept 4)
alvadoran Parade & Festival	LA City College	All things Salvadoran. (mid Sept)
Mexican Independence Celebration	Olvera St	Traditional Mexican foods and entertainment. (mid Sept)
A County Fair	Fairplex in Pomona	Livestock, rides, and food on a stick. (Sept–Oct)
razilian Street Carnival	La Brea Tarpits	Rio Brazilian fun.
hai Cultural Day	Location varies	Day-long celebration of Thailand. (mid Sept)
aste of Santa Monica	Santa Monica Pier	40 of the area's top restaurants participate. (mid Sept)
bbot Kinney Boulevard Festival	Abbot Kinney Blvd, Venice	Over 200 local arts & crafts vendors unite. (late Sept)
ong Beach Blues Festival	Cal State Long Beach	Spend Labor Day weekend with blues heavyweights.

Dctober		
Vest Hollywood Halloween & Costume Carnival	West Hollywood	Fabulous costumes make this the biggest bash in the nation. (Oct 31)
IDS Walk	West Hollywood Park	10K walkathon raises money for AIDS-related organizations.
Affaire in the Gardens	Beverly Gardens Park, Beverly Hills	Twice-yearly art show. (mid Oct)
Oktoberfest	Alpine Village, Torrance	German music, German beer, American hangover.
Echo Park Arts Festival	Various	One of LA's artiest communities' time to shine.
NOHO Theater & Arts Festival	Lankershim Blvd & Magnolia, North Hollywood	Performances scattered throughout the NOHO arts district. (early October)
Harvest Festival of the ARTS	Pico Union Alvarado Terrace Park	Raising children's self-esteem through art. (late Oct)
KTLA KIDS Day LA Celebration	Exposition Park and Recreation Center	Forget the kids. We want to hang out with Jennifer York. (mid Oct)
Autumn in the Japanese Garden	Japanese Garden, 6100 Woodley Ave, Van Nuys	Learn origami or just stroll through the garden.
hipwreck Halloween Terrorfest	Queen Mary, Long Beach	Mazes and monsters on a real haunted boat! (weekends throughout Oct)
all Festival at the Farmer's Market	Farmer's Market, Los Angeles	Carve a pumpkin, watch the leaves turn. (mid Oct)
ong Beach Marathon	Long Beach	In case the LA Marathon didn't wear you out. (mid Oct)
Day of the Dead	Hollywood Forever Cemetery	A true dead man's party. (late Oct)

November		
Dia de los Muertos Celebration	Olvera St	Traditional celebration of Mexico's Day of the Dead. (Nov 1)
Arroyo Arts Collective Discovery Tour	Tour begins at Lummis Home, 200 E Ave 43	Local artists kindly open up their homes and studios. (mid Nov)
Three Stooges Big Screen Event	Alex Theatre, 216 Brand Blvd, Glendale	Of interest to silly cinephiles. Bring a date! (late Nov)
Beverly Hills Flower & Garden Festival	Greystone Estate	Designer gardens, lectures, and tours. (mid Nov)
Downtown on Ice, Winter Wonderland Skating Rink	Pershing Sq	Pretend you're at a tiny version of Rockefeller Center. (Nov–Dec)
Griffith Park Holiday Light Festival	Crystal Springs Rd, Griffith Park	Drive-through tour of impressive lighting displays. (Nov–Dec)
Mariachi Festival	Boyle Ave,/1st St.	Behatted, besuited entertainers convene (Mid Nov.)

December		
KROQ Acoustic Christmas	Universal Amphitheatre	Hot alternative bands feel the spirit of the season. (mid Dec)
Marina del Rey Holiday Boat Parade	Main Channel, Marina del Rey	Imaginatively lit boats by crazy locals. (mid Dec)
Navidad en la Calle Ocho	8th St at Normandie Ave	8th Street's answer to the Hollywood Christmas Parade. (late Dec)
as Posadas	Olvera St	Candlelit reenactment of Mary and Joseph's journey to Bethlehem. (Dec 16-24)
Reindeer Romp	Los Angeles Zoo	Where Santa parks his reindeer (Dec)
ong Beach Christmas Boat Parade of the Thousand Lights	Long Beach Downtown Marina	That's a lotta lights! (Late Dec)

Often, while trapped in LA traffic, it seems that your only options for coping are books-on-CD or trading in your car fo a motorcycle. But never fear, the good news is that LA offers some of the most diverse radio programming anywhere so there's always something to fit your mood—even if it involves a case of road rage. Of course, many of these station now stream their music so you can listen at home, too—check out KPCC's and KCRW's podcasts, archives, and streams

AM Stations			*Noteworthy Programs*
570	KLAC	Talk	Fox Sports , Games and sports talk.
600	KOGO	Talk	Talk with a conservative slant. Home of Dr. Laura, George Noory and, of course, Rush.
610	KAVL	Fox Sports	Lots of games, plus sports talk.
640	KFI	Talk	"More stimulating talk radio" that'll push your buttons, from Rush Limbaugh to acidic tax protestors John and Ken.
690	XEWW	Spanish/Talk	
710	KSPN	ESPN Radio	Sports, sports, sports.
740	KBRT	Religious	The Word from Above broadcast from…Catalina Island!
790	KABC	News/Talk	Larry Elder, Sean Hannity, et al.
830	KMXE	Spanish	
870	KRLA	Talk	Lots of shows about health.
900	KALI	Spanish/Religious	
930	KHJ	Spanish/News	Regional Mexican music.
980	KFWB	News	News, Dodgers games, and traffic on all the ones (:01, :11, :21. . .)
1020	KTNQ	News/Talk (Spanish)	Galaxy soccer games.
1070	KNX	News	A poor man's NPR it might be, but they have fantastic traffic reports—and Food News is transfixing. . .
1110	KDIS	Radio Disney	Mickey Mouse, squeaky-clean pop tunes, and, of course, death metal.
1150	KXTA	Talk	Fox's radio affiliate.
1190	KXMX	Variety/Foreign Language	
1230	KYPA	Korean	Radio Korea.
1260	KMZT	Classical	The call letters stand for Mozart!
1280	KFRN	Religious	"Family Radio."
1300	KAZN	Chinese	
1330	KWKW	Talk (Spanish)	News, talk, sports, and Laker games en español.
1390	KLTX	Spanish/Religious	
1430	KMRB	Chinese	
1460	KTYM	Religious	
1480	KVNR	Vietnamese	Little Saigon radio from Santa Ana.
1510	KSPA	Talk	Business and finance talk radio.
1540	KMPC	Korean	
1580	KBLA	Spanish	
1650	KFOX	Korean	

FM Stations			*Noteworthy Programs*
88.1	KKJZ	Jazz & Blues	Your saturday night soundtrack on United Groove.
88.5	KCSN	Eclectic/NPR	College radio.
88.7	KSPC	Alternative	College radio at its most bizarre.
89.3	KPCC	Eclectic/NPR	Straight up NPR, with *Morning Edition*, *All Things Considered*, *Car Talk*, and *This American Life*.
89.9	KCRW	Eclectic/NPR	*Morning Becomes Eclectic* breaks new bands; clever programming gives your brain a workout, too.
90.7	KPFK	Eclectic/Political	Talk radio with a very liberal slant.
91.5	KUSC	Classical	Relaxing classical, even in horrible traffic.
92.3	KHHT	R&B Oldies	Legendary Art Leboe knows how to get you in the mood.
92.7	KLIT	Adult Contemporary	
93.1	KCBS	Classic Rock/Pop	Some classic rock and a lotta hits make "Jack FM" a good deal.
93.5	KDAY	Hip-hop/R&B	Old and new hip-hop; features Dr. Dre—both of them!
94.3	KBUA	Spanish	
94.7	KTWV	Smooth Jazz	"The Wave" is for fans of Kenny G and John Tesh.
95.1	KFRG	Country	"K-Frog" takes its amphibious theme very seriously.
95.5	KLOS	Classic Rock	Classic rock with Mark & Brian in the morning as a baby-boomer-funny alternative.
95.9	KFSH	Contemporary Christian	Ultra-clean-cut Christian pop and rock music.
96.3	KXOL	Spanish	Spanish pop and dance music.
96.7	KWIZ	Mexican	Regional Mexican.
97.5	KLYY	Spanish Pop/Rock	Modern Spanish hits.
97.9	KLAX	Mexican	Regional Mexican.
98.3	KRCV	Spanish	
98.7	KYSR	Adult Contemporary	AC in the OC
99.1	KGGI	Top 40	
99.5	KKLA	Religious	Religious talk radio.
99.9	KOLA	Rock Oldies	Plenty of '60s and '70s tunes, plus Beatles Brunch on Sundays.
100.3	KKBT	Urban Contemporary	Steve Harvey handles the morning shift; the mix shows are amazing.
101.1	KRTH	Oldies	It's always a kinder, gentler time on K-Earth.
101.9	KSCA	Mexican	Regional Mexican.
102.3	KJLH	Urban Contemporary	Owner Stevie Wonder keeps this smooth station on track.
102.7	KIIS	Top 40	Find Ryan Seacrest here, plus more pop than you can handle.
103.5	KOST	Adult Contemporary	Dedications all night with "Love Songs on the KOST."
103.9	KRCD	Spanish	Shares a signal with 98.3 KRCV.
104.3	KBIG	Adult Contemporary	Music from the '70s, '80s, and '90s. And occasionally the '00s.
105.1	KMZT	Classical	"K-Mozart" will have you "air-conducting" in you car.
105.9	KPWR	Dance/Urban	Big Boy's morning show cracks us up; the beats bounce the rest of the day.
106.3	KALI	Vietnamese	
106.7	KROQ	Modern Rock	Heavy on the hard stuff, this influential station breaks new bands all the time.
107.1	KSSE	Spanish	
107.5	KLVE	Spanish	Spanish adult contemporary.
107.9	KWVE	Religious	

Before children (BC), a day with nothing to do was just that. Or, as we liked to think of it, heaven. But when you have kids you have to have a plan—a series of them, actually. Plans for at-home, plans for being on-the-go. Rainy-day plans, too-hot-to-be-outside plans. Because this is LA, your plans have to be better than everybody else's plans or your kids will be doomed from the get-go. There are, of course, some bright spots to parenting in LA. Our endless summer means that you very rarely have to worry about lost jackets, mittens, or umbrellas. We also drive almost everywhere, making our choice of stroller far less important than our choice of black SUV, the preferred automobile of hip LA parents.

Essentials

Kids come into the world with nothing, yet by their first birthday their stuff fills up at least half the rooms in your house. Where does all of this accoutrement come from? Well, we can name a few of the culprits. Here are some of our favorite places for both the necessities and the more frivolous (but no less fun) purchases.

Map	*Store*	*Address*	*Phone*	*Description*
1	Auntie Barbara's	238 S Beverly Dr, Beverly Hills	310-285-0873	Vintage children's furnishings.
3	Flicka	204 N Larchmont Blvd	323-466-5822	Upscale kids' clothes.
15	Petite Ami	15301 Antioch St, Pacific Palisades	310-459-0011	Fancy children's apparel.
15	Ivy Greene for Kids	1020 Swarthmore Ave, Pacific Palisades	310-230-0301	Kids' formal wear.
15	Puzzle Zoo	1041 Swarthmore Ave, Pacific Palisades	310-454-8648	Toys galore.
16	Bellini Juvenile Designer Furniture	114 S Beverley Dr, Brentwood	310-859-7133	Nursery furniture.
18	The Acorn Store	1220 5th St, Santa Monica	310-451-5845	Wooden toys.
18	The Pump Station	2415 Wilshire Blvd, Santa Monica	310-998-1981	For nursing moms & tots.
18	Puzzle Zoo	1413 Third St Promenade, Santa Monica	310-393-9201	Awesome toy store.
18	This Little Piggy Wears Cotton	309 Wilshire Blvd, Santa Monica	310-260-2727	Comfy kids' clothes.
18	Every Picture Tells A Story	1311C Montana Ave, Santa Monica	310-451-2700	Art gallery & bookstore.
18	Mom's The Word	910 Montana Ave, Santa Monica	310-451-9604	Maternity & nursing wear.
19	Malina Children's Store	3304 Pico Blvd, Santa Monica	310-395-5965	High-end clothes.
20	Riginals	Century City Mall, 10250 Santa Monica Blvd, Century City	310-557-2532	High-end clothes.
20	Peanut Butter Playground	2042 Westwood Blvd, Westwood	310-475-5354	Upscale clothes & toys.
20	Traveling Tikes	10461 Santa Monica Blvd, Century City	310-234-9554	Strollers, bikes, & more.
23	Needles N'Tees	9223 W Pico Blvd	310-276-2531	Personalized items.
25	Sid & Me	8338 Lincoln Blvd, Westchester	310-670-5550	Everything for baby's room.
27	Baby A	1108 Manhattan Ave, Manhattan Beach	310-798-8086	Upscale gifts for tikes.
27	Babystyle	3200 Sepulveda Blvd, #C5, Manhattan Beach	310-802-0224	Website comes to life.
31	Little Moon	1813 S Catalina Ave, Redondo Beach	310-373-3766	Fancy frocks & the like.
34	Saturday's Child	2529 Mission St, San Marino	626-441-8888	High-end kids' stuff.
45	Babyland	7134 Topanga Canyon Blvd, Can Pk	818-704-7848	Affordable kids' furniture.
49	Gregory's Toys	16101 Ventura Blvd, Encino	818-906-2212	Toys, toys, toys.
49	A Mother's Haven	15928 Ventura Blvd, Encino	818-380-3111	Nursing products & support.
50	Juvenile Shop	13356 Ventura Blvd, Sherman Oaks	818-986-6214	One-stop baby shopping.
50	Burgundy Blue Outlet	4818 Fulton Ave, Sherman Oaks	818-981-7446	High-end, low-cost clothes.
50	Doll Shoppe	13300 Riverside Dr, Sherman Oaks	818-784-3655	Dolls & their accessories.
51	Safer Baby	13215 Ventura Blvd, Studio City	818-784-6628	One-stop baby-proofing.
51	Storyopolis	12348 Ventura Blvd, Studio City	818-509-5600	Children's literature & art.
51	M Fredric Kids	12128 Ventura Blvd, Studio City	818-985-9445	Cute & comfy clothes.
53	Harry Harris Children's Shoes	16744 Ventura Blvd, Encino	818-981-2641	First footwear.
53	Encino Kid	17157 Ventura Blvd, Encino	818-990-4510	Kids' clothing.
57	Wound & Wound Toy Co	1000 Universal Studios Blvd	818-509-8129	All things wind-up.

The Bestest of the Best

- **Most Kid-Friendly Mall:** The Grove, 189 The Grove Dr, 888-315-8883 (Map 2). They've got a trolley, a musical water fountain, and events for children such as puppet shows, arts, and crafts every Thursday morning. There's even a huge central lawn where you can catch a live band and eat ice cream. Oh, and there are shops and restaurants for parents, too.
- **Coolest Bookstore:** Storyopolis, 12348 Ventura Blvd, Studio City, 818-509-5600 (Map 51). Looking for *The Da Vinci Code*? Look somewhere else. This store sells only the most beautiful and beloved children's books, along with the artwork found within. Go for the story time, every day at 11 am.
- **Best Playground:** Shane's Inspiration, Griffith Park (Map 5). The playground was designed to allow handicapped children to play alongside their able-bodied peers on equipment that is colorful, innovative, and appealing to all. For a similar playground, check out Aidan's Place in Westwood Park, on Sepulveda Boulevard just south of Wilshire Boulevard.
- **Most Surprising Place for Parents to Network:** Petting Zoo, Studio City Farmers Market, Ventura Pl b/w Laurel Canyon & Ventura Blvd; Sundays, 8 am–1 pm (Map 56). Overall, the Studio City Farmers Market is a kids' paradise on Sunday mornings. It features pony rides, a moon bounce, face painting, and a small train. Stand in the petting zoo long enough and you will encounter every person you have ever met in LA who has a child under the age of five. The animals are docile and the pen is kept as clean as is realistically possible. And the pig loves to have his belly rubbed.
- **Best Resource for New Mothers:** The Pump Station, 2415 Wilshire Blvd, Santa Monica, 310-998-1981 (Map 18). From breast pumps to nursing bras to high-end baby clothes, the Pump Station carries everything you need to get through the first few months of mommyhood. Even more useful, however, are the new-mother support groups, where lactation consultants/RNs can talk any nervous new mother down from the ledge.

Parks for Playing

What makes for an excellent public park? In our opinion, any combination of the following: ample shade, well-maintained (and appealing or innovative) equipment, and an indefinable, overall good vibe. Most LA neighborhood parks feature at least a strip of grass and a slide or two, but these are some of the parks that are worth venturing out of your own neighborhood to explore:

- **Coldwater Canyon Park**, Coldwater Canyon Dr & N Beverly Dr, Beverly Hills (Map 1). The signs may say "No wading," but on any given day, dozens of kids splash through the man-made stream that runs through this park.
- **Roxbury Park**, Olympic Blvd & Roxbury Dr, Beverly Hills (Map 1). Not one, but two sizeable playgrounds with a wide variety of obstacles to climb on or slide down. Steam emanates from the dinosaur area every ten minutes or so.
- **West Hollywood Park**, San Vicente Blvd b/w Melrose Ave & Santa Monica Blvd, West Hollywood (Map 2). Run of the mill equipment, but a shady canopy covers the toddler play area. Great weekday "Tiny Tots" program.
- **Shane's Inspiration**, Griffith Park (Map 5). This colorful playground was designed to accommodate handicapped and able-bodied children alike.
- **Echo Park**, b/w Glendale Blvd & Echo Park Ave, just south of Sunset Blvd (Map 5). Lively crowds and a small lake, with paddleboats available for rent.
- **La Cienega Park**, La Cienega Blvd & Olympic Blvd (Map 6). Excellent music and dance classes for the smallest kids; colorful playground and chess players almost all day.
- **MacArthur Park**, 6th St & Alvarado St (Map 8). Small lake with paddleboats, as well as the chance to visit the park that inspired the epic '60s song.
- **Kenneth Hahn State Recreational Area**, La Cienega Blvd south of Rodeo Rd (Map 10). Hiking trails and a terrific play area for kids.
- **Douglas Park**, Wilshire Blvd & 25th St, Santa Monica (Map 19). Lots of grass and a water area that is home to several ducks.
- **Westwood Park**, Sepulveda Blvd b/w Wilshire Blvd & Santa Monica Blvd (Map 20). Features Aidan's Place, a playground designed to accommodate both handicapped and able-bodied children.
- **Penmar Playground**, Rose Ave & Penmar Ave, Venice (Map 21). Brand new playground and piñata pole, great for kids' birthday parties.

- **Culver City Park**, Jefferson Blvd & Duquesne Ave (Map 24). Features a 5000-square-foot skateboard park. Helmets required.
- **Polliwog Park**, N Redondo Ave & Manhattan Beach Blvd (Map 27). Park contains a pond as well as a playground area featuring a large, wooden, sunken galleon.
- **Seaside Lagoon**, 200 Portofino Wy, Redondo Beach (Map 31). Beach playground with a large, heated, saltwater swimming pool.
- **Garfield Park**, Stratford Ave & Mission Aly, South Pasadena (Map 34). Lots of shade and rolling green hills.
- **Lacey Park**, Monterey Rd & Virginia Rd, San Marino (Map 35). Includes a stroller/bicycle loop for fitness-minded moms and traveling tykes.
- **Lake Balboa Park**, Balboa Blvd & Victory Blvd (Map 46). Ducks to feed, a lake to walk around, and a great play-ground to boot.
- **Johnny Carson Park**, 400 S Bob Hope Dr & Riverside Dr (Map 50). Picturesque park home to numerous community events and festivals.
- **Encino Park**, Ventura Blvd & Genesta Ave (Map 53). Two shady playgrounds, at least one of which keeps the little ones fenced in.
- **Studio City Recreation Center (AKA Beeman Park)**, Beeman Ave & Rye St (Map 56). Lively, well-lit park serves as a community hub with large festivals for Halloween and Easter.

Rainy Day Activities—Indoor Playgrounds

Because wet weather is such an anomaly in Southern California, LA parents tend to lose it a little when forced to seek shelter indoors with the kids for a day or two. The kids, however, are perfectly happy, especially with a trip to some of LA's indoor playgrounds, where the temperature is always a pleasant 72 degrees and there's plenty of padding and cushions to break their fall.

- **Amy's Indoor Playground,** 1115 Mission Street, South Pasadena, 626-799-0304 (Map 34)
- **Gymboree Play & Music**, Westside Pavilion, 10800 W Pico Blvd, West LA, 310-470-7780 (Map 23)
- **Gymboree Play & Music**, 14801 Ventura Blvd, Sherman Oaks, 818-905-6225 (Map 49)
- **Gymboree Play & Music**, 443 E Irving Dr, Suite F, Burbank, 818-955-8964 (Map 50)
- **Gymboree Play & Music**, 435 S Fair Oaks Ave, South Pasadena, 626-445-1122 (Map 34)
- **Under the Sea**, 2424 W Victory Blvd, Burbank, 818-567-9945 (Map 45)

Classes

Most of the play facilities listed above emphasize open play, allowing for parental spontaneity and the fickle nature of young children. However, with a little planning and structure (as counterintuitive as that might be), LA kids have a variety of classes available to them rivaling those of most Ivy League universities.

- **My Gym**, numerous locations around the LA area, visit www.my-gym.com for addresses. Gymnastics, circle time, and other traditionally kid-like activities.
- **Creative Kids**, 11301 W Olympic Blvd, West LA, 310-473-6090 (Map 19). Their diverse schedule includes art classes for toddlers, dance and cooking for slightly older kids, and children's theater for ages 3–18.
- **Dance & Jingle**, 1900 W Mountain St, Glendale 818-845-3925 (Map 46). Highly sought-after music and movement class.
- **LA Zoo**, Zoo Dr, Griffith Park, 323-644-4200 (Map 51). The zoo's classes range from Toddler Totes, which involves singing, an animal guest, and a backpack filled with edu-cational goodies, to Wild Planet, a more sophisticated program for adolescent zookeepers-in-training.
- **Music Together**, numerous locations around LA. Visit www.musictogether.com for more information. Teaches young children the fundamentals of rhythm and music through the modeling of parents and caregivers while exposing them to a wide array of music from diverse cultures and time periods.
- **Family Gallery Kits**, Skirball Cultural Center, 2701 N Sepulveda Blvd, 310-440-4500 (Map 49). Along with the center's ongoing arts and cultural exhibition, the organization provides an interactive kit packed with games, puzzles, and activities for 4–8 year olds.

Where to Go for More Information

Where to go for additional information:

- www.gocitykids.com
- www.at-la.com/@la-kid.htm
- *Fun and Educational Places to Go With Kids and Adults in Southern California* by Susan Peterson, Sunbelt Publications, 2001.

For the seriously ill or the terminally addicted to cosmetic surgery, Los Angeles boasts some of the most sought-after physicians and medical centers in the United States. The **UCLA Medical Center (Map 20)**, **Saint John's Medical Center (Map 18)**, and **Cedars-Sinai (Map 2)** are three of the best treatment facilities in the world. All have extensive networks of clinics and affiliated physicians around the city and county. Of the three Cedars has perhaps seen the longest list of celebrity births, deaths, and hospitalizations; Saint John's was the hospital that ushered adversaries Tom Cruise's and Brooke Shields's babies into the world. If not, keep in mind that the entire staff of Cedars-Sinai appears to be on loan from a modeling agency.

Emergency Rooms	*Address*	*Phone*	*Map*
Alhambra	100 S Raymond Ave	626-570-1606	39
Brotman	3828 Delmas Ter	310-836-7000	24
Cedars-Sinai Medical Center	8700 Beverly Blvd	310-423-8780	2
City of Angels	1711 W Temple St	213-989-6100	9
Encino-Tarzana Regional Medical Center-Encino Campus	16237 Ventura Blvd	818-995-5000	54
Encino-Tarzana Regional Medical Center-Tarzana Campus	18321 Clark St	818-881-0800	46
Estelle Doheny Eye Hospital	1450 San Pablo St	323-442-7100	40
Glendale Adventist	1509 Wilson Terr	818-409-8000	51
Glendale Memorial	1420 S Central Ave	818-502-1900	51
Good Samaritan	1225 Wilshire Blvd	213-977-2121	9
Hollywood Presbyterian	1300 N Vermont Ave	213-413-3000	4
Huntington Memorial	100 W California Blvd	626-397-5000	34
LA County USC Medical Center	1200 N State St	323-226-2622	40
Little Company of Mary	4101 Torrance Blvd	310-540-7676	31
Los Angeles Community	4081 E Olympic Blvd	323-267-0477	41
Miracle Mile	6000 San Vicente Blvd	323-930-1040	6
Mission Community	14850 Roscoe Blvd	818-787-2222	47
Northridge - Roscoe Campus	18300 Roscoe Blvd	818-885-8500	46
Olympic Medical Center	5900 W Olympic Blvd	310-657-5900	6
Pacific Alliance	531 W College St	213-624-8411	9
Promise Hospital of East LA	443 S Soto St	323-261-1181	40
Santa Monica UCLA Medical Center	12225 15th St	310-319-4000	18
Sherman Oaks	4929 Van Nuys Blvd	818-981-7111	55
St. Vincent	2131 W 3rd St	213-484-7111	9
Temple Community	225 N Hoover St	213-382-7252	8
Torrance Memorial	3330 Lomita Blvd	310-325-9110	32
UCLA Medical Center	10833 Le Conte Ave	310-825-7271	20
USC University Hospital	1500 San Pablo St	888-700-5700	40
White Memorial	1720 East Cesar E Chavez Ave	323-268-5000	40

Other Hospitals	*Address*	*Phone*	*Map*
California Hospital Medical	1401 S Grand Ave	213-748-2411	9
Centinela	555 E Hardy St	310-673-4660	13
Children's	4650 W Sunset Blvd	323-660-2450	4
East LA Doctors	4060 Whittier Blvd	323-268-5514	41
Kaiser Foundation	4867 W Sunset Blvd	323-783-4011	4
Kaiser Foundation	6041 Cadillac Ave	323-857-2201	6
LA County Women's	1240 N Mission Rd	323-226-3221	40
Life Well Institute	5835 Washington Blvd	323-857-0800	10
Providence St Joseph Medical	501 S Buena Vista St	818-843-5111	50
St John's	1328 22nd St	310-829-5511	18
Valley Presbyterian	15107 Vanowen St	818-782-6600	47

Borrow a book from a friend and it sits on your nightstand for two years. Borrow that same book from the library and you have a deadline to meet—or a fine in your future. If it's instant gratification you seek, the Los Angeles Public Library stinks; but if you think of it as a kind of Amazon.com without shipping fees, it's a phenomenal service. The system works like Netflix: go online, find a book, select the branch to which you'd like your book sent, and—*voila!*—the library emails when said book is ready for pick-up. The drag is that you sometimes end up waiting months for the hottest bestsellers, but the price is right and the selection is vast.

The Library system offers more than just books—DVDs, CDs, and books-on-tape are all available to borrow. Computers are available, free of charge, for up to two hours a day at all branches. The Grandparents and Books program pairs senior citizens and kids for story time and games. This program is also available at most neighborhood branches. **The Los Angeles Central Library (Map 9)**, downtown, is worth a special trip. Its diverse collection of art includes the Children's Court, which features whimsical marble panels of kid-lit images like Alice in Wonderland and Mother Goose, and a breathtaking eight-story atrium.

Library	Address	Phone	Map
Alhambra	101 S 1st St	626-570-5008	39
Allendale	1130 S Marengo Ave	626-744-7260	34
Angeles Mesa	2700 W 52nd St	323-292-4328	11
Anthony Quinn	3965 E Cesar Chavez Ave	323-264-7715	41
Arroyo Seco Regional	6145 N Figueroa St	323-255-0537	33
Atwater Village	3379 Glendale Blvd	323-664-1353	5
Balch Art Research Library	5905 Wilshire Blvd	323-857-6000	6
Baldwin Hills	2906 S La Brea Ave	323-733-1196	10
Benjamin Franklin	2200 E 1st St	323-263-6901	40
Beverly Hills	444 N Rexford Dr	310-288-2220	1
Buena Vista	300 N Buena Vista St	818-238-5620	50
Burbank Central	110 N Glenoaks Blvd	818-238-5600	50
Cahuenga	4591 Santa Monica Blvd	323-664-6418	4
Canoga Park	20939 Sherman Wy	818-887-0320	45
Central	630 W 5th St	213-228-7000	9
Chatsworth	21052 Devonshire St	818-341-4276	42
Chinatown	639 N Hill St	213-620-0925	9
City Terrace	4025 City Terrace Dr	323-261-0295	41
Crenshaw-Imperial	11141 Crenshaw Blvd	310-412-5403	28
Crowell Public Library	1890 Huntington Dr	626-300-0777	39
Culver City Julian Dixon	4975 Overland Ave	310-559-1676	24
Cypress Park	1150 Cypress Ave	323-224-0039	36
Donald Bruce Kaufman	11820 San Vicente Blvd	310-575-8273	16
Eagle Rock	5027 Caspar Ave	323-258-8078	33
East Los Angeles	4837 E 3rd St	323-264-0155	41
Echo Park	1410 W Temple St	213-250-7808	9
Edendale	2011 W Sunset Blvd	213-207-3000	5
El Camino Real	4264 E Whittier Blvd	323-269-8102	41
El Retiro	126 Vista Del Parque	310-375-0922	31
El Segundo	111 W Mariposa Ave	310-524-2722	27
El Sereno	5226 Huntington Dr	323-255-9201	38
Encino-Tarzana	18231 Ventura Blvd	818-343-1983	53
Exposition Park	3900 S Western Ave	323-290-3113	11
Fairfax	161 S Gardner St	323-936-6191	2
Felipe De Neve	2820 W 6th St	213-384-7676	8
Frances Howard Goldwyn	1623 N Ivar Ave	323-856-8260	3
Glendale Central	222 E Harvard St	818-548-2030	51
Goethe Institute	5750 Wilshire Blvd	323-525-3388	6
Granada Hills	10640 Petit Ave	818-368-5687	44
Grandview Library	1535 5th St	818-548-2049	50
Harbor Gateway Branch	24000 S Western Ave	310-534-9520	32
Hawthorne	12700 Grevillea Ave	310-679-8193	28
Henderson	4805 Emerald St	310-371-2075	31
Hermosa Beach Public Library	550 Pier Ave	310-379-8475	29
Hill Avenue Branch	55 S Hill Ave	626-744-7264	35
Hyde Park-Miriam Matthews Branch	2205 W Florence Ave	323-750-7241	14
Inglewood Public Library	101 W Manchester Blvd	310-412-5380	13
Jefferson Branch	2211 W Jefferson Blvd	323-734-8573	11
John C Fremont Branch	6121 Melrose Ave	323-962-3521	3
John Muir Branch	1005 W 64th St	323-789-4800	14
Junipero Serra Branch	4607 S Main St	323-234-1685	12
Katy Geissert Civic Center Library	3301 Torrance Blvd	310-618-5959	32
LA County Law Library-Santa Monica	1725 Main St	310-260-3644	18
LA County Law Library-Torrance	825 Maple Ave	310-222-8816	30
LA County Law Library-Van Nuys	6230 Sylmar Ave	818-374-2499	47

LA Law Library	301 W 1st St	213-785-2529	9
La Pintoresca Branch	1355 N Raymond Ave	626-744-7268	34
Lamanda Park Branch	140 S Altadena Dr	626-744-7266	35
Lawndale Library	14615 Burin Ave	310-676-0177	28
Lennox	4359 Lennox Blvd	310-674-0385	13
Lincoln Heights Branch	2530 Workman St	323-226-1692	37
Linda Vista Branch	1281 Bryant St	626-744-7278	34
Little Tokyo Branch	203 S Los Angeles St	213-612-0525	9
Lloyd Taber Marina del Rey	4533 Admiralty Wy	310-821-3415	25
Lomita	24200 Narbonne Ave	310-539-4515	32
Los Angeles Central Library	630 W 5th St	213-228-7000	9
Los Angeles Main Branch-Braille Institute Library	741 N Vermont Ave	800-808-2555	4
Los Feliz Branch	1874 Hillhurst Ave	323-913-4710	4
Malabar Branch	2801 Wabash Ave	323-263-1497	40
Malaga Cove Library	2400 Via Campesina	310-377-9584	31
Manhattan Beach	1320 Highland Ave	310-545-8595	27
Mar Vista Branch	12006 Venice Blvd	310-390-3454	22
Mark Twain Branch	9621 S Figueroa St	323-755-4088	14
Memorial Branch	4625 W Olympic Blvd	323-938-2732	7
Mid-Valley Regional Branch Library	16244 Nordhoff St	818-895-3650	44
North Hollywood Regional	5211 Tujunga Ave	818-766-7185	56
North Torrance Branch	3604 Artesia Blvd	310-323-7200	30
Northridge Branch	9051 Darby Ave	818-886-3640	43
Northwest Branch	3323 W Victory Blvd	818-238-5640	49
Nursing Library	1237 N Mission Rd	323-226-6521	40
Pacific Park Branch	501 S Pacific Ave	818-548-3760	51
Palisades Branch	861 Alma Real Dr	310-459-2754	15
Palms-Rancho Park Branch	2920 Overland Ave	310-840-2142	23
Panorama City Branch	14345 Roscoe Blvd	818-894-4071	47
Pasadena Central	285 E Walnut St	626-744-4066	34
Pico Union Branch	1030 S Alvarado St	213-368-7545	8
Pio Pico Koreatown Branch	694 S Oxford Ave	213-368-7647	8
Playa Vista Branch	6400 Playa Vista Dr	310-437-6680	25
Porter Ranch Branch	11371 Tampa Ave	818-360-5706	43
Redondo Beach North Branch	2000 Artesia Blvd	310-318-0677	29
Redondo Beach Public Library	303 N Pacific Coast Hwy	310-318-0675	31
Robert Louis Stevenson Branch	803 Spence St	323-268-4710	40
Robertson Branch	1719 S Robertson Blvd	310-840-2147	6
San Pedro Regional	931 S Gaffey St	310-548-7779	p172
San Rafael Branch	1240 Nithsdale Rd	626-744-7270	34
Santa Catalina Branch	999 E Washington Blvd	626-744-7272	35
Santa Monica Montana Avenue Branch	1704 Montana Ave	310-458-8682	18
Santa Monica Ocean Park Branch	2601 Main St	310-458-8683	18
Santa Monica Public Library	601 Santa Monica Blvd	315-458-8600	18
Santa Monica Public Library (temporarily closed)	1343 6th St	310-458-8600	18
Sherman Oaks Library	14245 Moorpark St	818-205-9716	55
Silver Lake Branch	2411 Glendale Blvd	323-913-7451	5
Sons of the Revolution Library	600 S Central Ave	818-240-1775	51
South Pasadena Library	1100 Oxley St	626-403-7340	34
Southeast Branch	23115 Arlington Ave	310-530-5044	32
Studio City Branch	12511 Moorpark St	818-755-7873	56
Sun Valley Branch	7935 Vineland Ave	818-764-1338	48
Valley Plaza Branch	12311 Vanowen St	818-765-9251	48
Van Nuys Branch	6250 Sylmar Ave	818-756-8453	47
Venice Abbot Kinney Memorial	501 S Venice Blvd	310-821-1769	21
Vermont Square Branch	1201 W 48th St	323-290-7405	11
Vernon Leon H. Memorial Branch	4504 S Central Ave	323-234-9106	12
View Park	3854 W 54th St	323-293-5371	10
Villa Parke Community Center Branch	363 E Villa St	626-744-6510	34
Walteria Branch	3815 W 242nd St	310-375-8418	31
Washington Irving Branch	4117 W Washington Blvd	323-734-6303	7
West Hollywood	715 N San Vicente Blvd	310-652-5340	2
West Los Angeles Regional	11360 Santa Monica Blvd	310-575-8323	19
West Valley Regional	19036 Vanowen St	818-345-9806	46
Westchester Loyola Village Branch	7114 W Manchester Ave	310-348-1096	25
Westwood Branch	1246 Glendon Ave	310-474-1739	20
Will & Ariel Durant Branch	7140 W Sunset Blvd	323-876-2741	2
Wilshire Library	149 N St Andrews Pl	323-957-4550	7
Wiseburn	5335 W 135th St	310-643-8880	28
Woodcrest	1340 W 106th St	323-757-9373	14

Here's the deal in LA. West Hollywood's pretty-boy ground zero is located at **The Abbey**. Places farther east down Santa Monica Boulevard, like **FuBar** and **Club7969**, trade in the gloss for raw power. FuBar is a little darker, wilder, and more intimate. **7969** is hot and packed on Saturdays with Hot Dog, Mario Diaz's sexy boy party. **O-Bar** is a swanky lounge that is cruising heaven. On Sunday afternoons, there's always Size 9 at **Here Lounge**, where, if you're lucky, the sun won't be the only thing to go down. Far from the reaches of WeHo, Silver Lake's gay scene is decidedly more mellow and friendly. **Akbar** is the place to go for cute, indie, normal-bodied boys, **Faultline** can give you that hot leather daddy moment we all need from time to time, and **The Eagle** is a mixed scene with retro porn playing.

Some of the girl action is mixed in with the male scene in LA; check out nights Wednesday's GirlBar at **The Abbey** or Friday's TruckStop at **Here**. If you're looking for a lady scene coupled with damn good drinks, head to the **Oxwood Inn** in Van Nuys. **Akbar** is mostly guys but some ladies, and the clientele skews younger and more hipster-er than the West Hollywood scene. And you have to visit **The Palms** at least one – this lesbian bar has been open for over 40 years.

Health Center & Support Organizations

LA Gay & Lesbian Center (LAGLC) McDonald Wright Building • 1625 N Schrader Blvd, Los Angeles, CA 90028 • 323-993-7400 • www.laglc.org

LAGLC offers the following services:

- Pedro Zamora Youth HIV Program • 323-993-7571
- Jeffrey Goodman Special Care Clinic • 323-993-7500
  12-Step Program Meetings including AA, Alanon, NA, Marijuana Anon, Crystal Meth Anon, Sexual Compulsives Anon, and Anorexics Anon.
- Counseling services including general, addiction recovery, domestic violence, and HIV/AIDS • 323-993-7500
- HIV Testing • 323-993-7500
- Audre Lorde Lesbian Health Clinic • 323-993-7500
- Sexual Health Program • 323-860-5855

AIDS Project Los Angeles • 213-201-1600 • www.apla.org • Assistance and information hotline for people living with AIDS.

HIV LA • www.hivla.org
An online resource in English and Spanish that helps people with HIV/AIDS find services available in Los Angeles County.

GLAAD Los Angeles • 5455 Wilshire Blvd #1500, Los Angeles, CA 90036 • 323-933-2240 • www.glaad.org

Gay & Lesbian Youth Talkline • 800-246-7743

The Trevor Project • www.trevorproject.org • Support line for LGBT youth.

Websites

- **LA Gay & Lesbian Center • www.laglc.org**
  LA Gay and Lesbian Center is the largest and oldest in the country, and is an invaluable community resource offering legal, medical, outreach, and educational services, among many others.
- **Circuit Noize • www.circuitnoize.com**
  The premier source of circuit party information, parties, events, music, tickets, gay travel, and dancing.
- **Gay.com • www.gay.com**
  If you're looking for love online, this is the place to visit. Gay.com has hundreds of chat rooms for people around the country, with eight devoted to LA, two to Long Beach, and two to Orange County.
- **Gay and Lesbian Community Yellow Pages • www.gmcla.org** • Online version of Yellow Pages distributed through West Hollywood
- **Gay Los Angeles • www.gaylosangeles.com**
  Lesbian and gay directory for gay-owned and gay-friendly places in Los Angeles (bars, clubs, saunas, restaurants, and more).
- **West Hollywood • www.westhollywood.com**
  Comprehensive online guide to gay West Hollywood, featuring music, arts, videos, nightlife, circuits, classifieds, buzz, photos, and shopping.
- **QV Magazine • www.qvmagazine.com**
  Online edition of LA's gay Latino magazine.
- **Power Up • www.powerupfilms.org**
  A group dedicated to promoting the visibility of gay women in film, entertainment, and media.
- **Los Angeles Tennis Association • www.lataweb.com**
  With more than 400 members, this is the largest gay and lesbian tennis club in the world. All skill levels welcome.
- **Greater Los Angeles Softball Association • www.lagaysoftball.com**
  This exclusively gay and lesbian league has more than 30 teams participating in their men's and women's divisions.
- **Gay Men's Chorus of Los Angeles • www.gmcla.com**
  Check out their site for performance dates and a rehearsal schedule.
- **Metropolitan Community Church • www.mccla.org**
  This popular church is gay- and lesbian-friendly and offers multi-denominational services.

Bookstores

- **Circus of Books** (two locations) • 8230 Santa Monica Blvd (b/w Harper & LaJolla Aves), West Hollywood • 323-656-6533; and 4001 Sunset Blvd (at Sanborn Ave), Silver Lake • 323-666-1304 • www.circusofbooks.com • Hours: 6 am–2 am, daily.

Publications

From local news headlines to club listings, these LGBT publications bring you all the news that's gay. Most of these publications can be found in gay-friendly bookstores, cafes, bars, and various shops.

- **A & U** • 888.245.4333 • www.aumag.org
- **Circuit Noize** • 818-769-9390 • www.circuitnoize.com
- **Cybersocket** • 323.650.9906 • www.cybersocket.com
- **Frontiers** • 323-930-3220 • www.frontiersnewsmagazine.com
- **MetroSource LA** • 323-933-2300 • www.metrosource.com
- **POZ Magazine** • www.poz.com
- **QV Magazine** • 702-676-1427 • www.qvmagazine.com
- **The Lesbian News** • 800-458-9888 • www.lesbiannews.com
- **The Advocate** • 323-852-7200 • www.advocate.com
- **In Los Angeles Magazine** • 323.848.2200 • www.inlamagazine.com
- **Odyssey Magazine** • 323-874-8788 • www.odysseymagazine.net

91311
42
43
44
91331
91214
91324
91325
91343
91352
91304
91402
91020
91306
91335
91405
91605
91504
91501
91208
91001
91303
45
46
91406
47
48
91606
49
91207
91371
91411
91401
91502
91201
91367
91202
91103
91104
91316
91607
91601
91505
91506
50
91364
91356
91423
91602
91203
134
91206
91106
91436
91403
91604
91608
91204
91205
91041
H
91101
52
53
54
55
56
51
91105
35
90068
90027
90042
91108
57
2
110
90046
33
90065
91030
90077
90039
90028
90290
90210
90069
4
36
91801
917
90038
90029
90049
17
2
5
90272
1
3
90004
90026
90032
91803
39
F
90048
90036
90020
90012
90031
38
10
16
D
90024
90211
90010
90057
37
20
B
90212
90005
90033
91754
91755
15
90035
90019
90006
90063
90025
90064
6
7
8
A
90013
41
90402
90403
90034
C
19
23
90015
90021
90022
40
18
90404
10
90016
90018
90007
E
9
90640
90401
90405
90232
90008
11
90037
90011
90023
5
90058
90066
10
12
90040
24
22
90230
90062
90270
90291
90056
90043
21
110
90255
710
90292
90302
90001
90201
90047
26
90003
13
14
90240
90293
25
90045
90301
90305
90044
90002
90280
90241
90304
90303
90059
105
90262
90242
90245
90250
90061
90222
28
90249
27
90723
90221
90706
90266
90260
90247
G
90220
90504
90248
90747
90805
405
90278
90254
29
90746
90712
30
90713
90501
90503
90502
90807
90277
90808
90745
90810
31
90505
32
90806
90815
90717
90710
90274
90744
90813
90804
90840
90275
90732
Pacific
Ocean
A 90014
B 90067
C 90071
D 90073
E 90089
F 90095
G 90506
H 91123
I 91521
J 91522
K 91523

Map	Address	Zip
1	312 S Beverly Dr	90212
1	323 N Crescent Dr	90210
1	325 N Maple Dr	90210
2	1125 N Fairfax Ave	90046
2	7610 Beverly Blvd	90048
2	820 N San Vicente Blvd	90069
3	1385 N Western Ave	30027
3	1425 N Cherokee Ave	90028
3	1615 Wilcox Ave	90028
4	1825 N Vermont Ave	90027
5	1525 N Alvarado St	90026
5	3370 Glendale Blvd	90039
6	1270 S Alfred St	90035
6	4960 W Washington Blvd	90016
6	5350 Wilshire Blvd	90036
7	4040 W Washington Blvd	90018
8	2390 W Pico Blvd	90006
8	265 S Western Ave	90004
8	3171 W Olympic Blvd	90006
8	3751 W 6th St	90020
8	928 S Western Ave	90006
9	100 W Olympic Blvd	90015
9	1055 N Vignes St	90012
9	1808 W 7th St	90057
9	201 N Los Angeles St	90012
9	2005 W 6th St	90057
9	300 N Los Angeles St	90012
9	350 S Grand Ave	90071
9	406 E 2nd St	90012
9	505 S Flower St	90071
9	506 S Spring St	90013
9	750 W 7th St	90017
9	818 N Hill St	90012
9	900 N Alameda St	90012
10	3894 Crenshaw Blvd	90008
11	1515 W Vernon Ave	90062
11	5472 Crenshaw Blvd	90043
11	5832 S Vermont Ave	90044
12	4352 S Central Ave	90011
12	5115 S Figueroa St	90037
12	819 W Washington Blvd	90015
13	300 E Hillcrest Blvd	90301
14	2200 W Century Blvd	90047
14	3212 W 85th St	90305
14	8200 S Vermont Ave	90044
15	15209 W Sunset Blvd	90272
15	15243 La Cruz Dr	90272
16	200 S Barrington Ave	90049
18	1025 Colorado Ave	90401
18	1217 Wilshire Blvd	90403
18	2720 Neilson Wy	90405
19	11270 Exposition Blvd	90064
19	11420 Santa Monica Blvd	90025
19	3010 Wilshire Blvd	90403
20	11000 Wilshire Blvd	90024
21	313 Grand Blvd	90291
22	3826 Grand View Blvd	90066
23	10850 W Pico Blvd	90064
23	3751 Motor Ave	90034
24	11111 Jefferson Blvd	90230
24	9942 Culver Blvd	90232
25	215 Culver Blvd	90293
26	7381 La Tijera Blvd	90045
26	9029 Airport Blvd	90009
27	1007 N Sepulveda Blvd	90266
27	425 15th St	90266
28	12700 Inglewood Ave	90250
28	4320 Marine Ave	90260
29	565 Pier Ave	90254
30	18080 Crenshaw Blvd	90504
31	1201 N Catalina Ave	90277
32	1433 Marcelina Ave	90501
32	2510 Monterey St	90503
32	25131 Narbonne Ave	90717
32	291 Del Amo Fashion Sq	90503
33	5132 York Blvd	90042
33	5930 N Figueroa St	90042
33	7435 N Figueroa St	90041
34	1001 Fremont Ave	91030
34	281 E Colorado Blvd	91101
34	600 Lincoln Ave	91109
34	99 W California Blvd	91105
35	2609 E Colorado Blvd	91107
35	2960 Huntington Dr	91108
35	967 E Colorado Blvd	91106
36	3950 Eagle Rock Blvd	90065
37	3001 N Broadway	90031
38	4875 Huntington Dr	90032
39	1603 W Valley Blvd	91803
40	2016 E 1st St	90033
40	3641 E 8th St	90023
41	3729 E 1st St	90063
41	975 S Atlantic Blvd	90022
42	21606 Devonshire St	91311
43	18039 Chatsworth St	91344
43	19300 Rinaldi St	91326
43	9534 Reseda Blvd	91324
45	21801 Sherman Wy	91303
45	7655 Winnetka Ave	91306
45	8201 Canoga Ave	91304
46	5609 Yolanda Ave	91356
46	5805 White Oak Ave	91316
46	7320 Reseda Blvd	91335
47	15701 Sherman Wy	91406
47	6200 Van Nuys Blvd	91401
48	6535 Lankershim Blvd	91606
48	7035 Laurel Cyn Blvd	91605
49	2140 N Hollywood Wy	91505
50	135 E Olive Ave	91502
50	6444 San Fernando Rd	91201
51	1009 N Pacific Ave	91202
51	101 N Verdugo Rd	91206
51	120 E Chevy Chase Dr	91205
51	313 E Broadway	91205
52	22121 Clarendon St	91367
53	4930 Balboa Blvd	91316
54	14900 Magnolia Blvd	91403
56	11304 Chandler Blvd	91601
56	12450 Magnolia Blvd	91607
56	3950 Laurel Cyn Blvd	91604
57	10063 Riverside Dr	91602

Important Phone Numbers

Life-Threatening Emergencies:	911
Citywide Services Directory:	311
Non-Emergency Information Line:	877-ASK-LAPD (275-5273)
Rape Victims Hotline:	626-793-3385
Suicide Hotline:	213-381-5111
Crime Victims Hotline:	213-485-6976
Domestic Violence Hotline:	800-978-3600
Missing Persons Unit:	213-485-5381
Sex Crimes Report Line:	213-485-2883
Legal Aid:	213-385-2202
Lights & Noise Complaints:	888-524-2845
California Highway Patrol:	323-906-3434
Terrorist Threats:	877-A-THREAT (284-7328)
Website:	www.lapdonline.org

Statistics

Statistics	2009	2008	2007	2006	2005
Homicides	315	385	394	480	487
Rapes	771	840	867	1059	928
Robberies	12,144	13,386	13,445	14,353	13,453
Aggravated Assaults	10,549	12,037	12,831	14,634	15,502
Burglaries	18,161	19,675	19,415	20,359	21,543
Grand Thefts Auto	18,033	22,417	23,148	25,389	26,573

Police Stations

Alhambra Police Dept	211 S 1st St	626-570-5168	39
Beverly Hills Police	464 N Rexford Dr	310-550-4951	1
Burbank Police Dept	200 N 3rd St	818-238-3000	50
CSU Northridge Dept of Police Services	18111 Nordhoff St	818-677-2111	43
Culver City Police Dept	4040 Duquesne Ave	310-837-1221	24
East Los Angeles County Sheriff's Dept	5019 E 3rd St	323-264-4151	41
El Segundo City Police Dept	348 Main St	310-524-2760	27
Glendale Police Dept	131 N Isabel St	818-548-4840	51
Hawthorne Police Dept	12501 S Hawthorne Blvd	310-675-4443	28
Hermosa Beach Police Dept	540 Pier Ave	310-318-0360	29
Inglewood Police Dept	1 W Manchester Blvd	310-412-5207	13
Lawndale Sheriff Service Center	15331 Prairie Ave	310-219-2750	28
Los Angeles Central Police Dept	251 E 6th St	213-485-3101	9
Los Angeles County Sheriff's Dept-Marina del Rey Station	13851 Fiji Wy	310-482-6000	25
Los Angeles County Sheriff's Dept-Universal Citywalk	1000 Universal Studios Blvd	818-622-9539	57
Los Angeles County Sheriff's Dept-West Hollywood Station	780 N San Vicente Blvd	310-855-8850	2
Los Angeles Police Dept Headquarters	100 W 1st St	213-485-2121	9
Los Angeles Police Dept-Devonshire	10250 Etiwanda Ave	818-832-0633	43
Los Angeles Police Dept-Hollenbeck	1936 E 1st St	323-342-4100	40
Los Angeles Police Dept-Hollywood	1358 N Wilcox Ave	213-972-2971	3
Los Angeles Police Dept-Newton	3400 S Central Ave	310-846-6547	12
Los Angeles Police Dept-North Hollywood	11640 Burbank Blvd	818-623-4016	48
Los Angeles Police Dept-Northeast	3353 San Fernando Rd	213-485-2563	51
Los Angeles Police Dept-Pacific	12312 Culver Blvd	310-482-6334	22
Los Angeles Police Dept-Rampart	1401 W 6th St	213-484-3400	9
Los Angeles Police Dept-Southwest	1546 W Martin Luther King Jr Blvd	213-485-2582	11
Los Angeles Police Dept-Van Nuys	6240 Sylmar Ave	818-374-950	47
Los Angeles Police Dept- West LA	1663 Butler Ave	310-444-0701	19
Los Angeles Police Dept-West Valley	19020 Vanowen St	818-374-7611	45
Los Angeles Police Dept- Wilshire	4861 Venice Blvd	213-473-0476	7
Manhattan Beach Police Dept	420 15th St	310-802-5140	27
Pasadena Police Dept	207 N Garfield Ave	626-744-4501	34
Redondo Beach Police Dept Main Station	401 Diamond St	310-379-2477	31
San Marino Police Dept	2200 Huntington Dr	626-300-0720	35
Santa Monica Police Dept	333 Olympic Dr	310-395-9931	18
South Pasadena Police Dept	1422 Mission St	626-403-7270	34
Torrance Police Dept	3300 Civic Center Dr	310-328-3456	30

Many of Los Angeles's landmarks double as a tangible histories of the city. From elegant Art Deco and Spanish architecture to gooey bogs of tar, to the ubiquitous Angelyne and everything in between, a cruise around Los Angeles is more educational—and (gas prices permitting) much cheaper—than a day spent at Disneyland.

So go ahead and be a tourist in your own backyard! Go mural sighting in Echo Park and East LA; compare your shoe size with Marilyn Monroe's at **Grauman's Chinese Theater (Map 3)** and have a drink at the historical **Pig n Whistle (Map 3)**; spend an afternoon of browsing in the downtown **LA Central Library (Map 9)** and stroll the surrounding Maguire Gardens before grabbing a bite at **Clifton's Cafeteria (Map 9)**; or take a train ride in **Griffith Park (Map 51)**, go for a round or two of golf (you've got four courses to choose from) and shuttle up to the Observatory to watch the sunset over a twinkling LA skyline.

Historical LA

Grand Central Market (Map 9) in downtown Los Angeles has been operating since 1917 and is still a great place to buy meat, produce, ice cream and your favorite Mexican delicacies. Just across the street is **Angel's Flight (Map 9)**, a relic from old LA's ancient trolley system. For you beachcombers out there, do what Angelenos have done for decades and ride the roller coaster at **Santa Monica Pier (Map 18)** after a day of surf and sand. Just south of Santa Monica, the remaining four **Venice Canals (Map 21)** (between Venice Boulevard and Sherman Canal Court) give you a sense of Abbot Kinney's original 1904 Italian vision for this beach community…give or take a million-dollar home or two.

Buildings

It's disgustingly easy to tear down buildings in LA and a good number of the city's legendary landmarks have long been razed (the Brown Derby, Coconut Grove). But those that do remain are quite extraordinary. Hollywood's cylindrical **Capitol Records Building (Map 3)** is evocative of a pile of vinyl on a spindle. Down the street is **Grauman's Chinese Theatre (Map 3)**, open since 1927, which can rightly claim to be the most famous movie theater in the world, thanks to its cement welcome mat. The Emerald City-like green **Wiltern Theater (Map 7)**, named for the intersection where it sits at Wilshire and Western, is a stunning example of Art Deco architecture. Downtown Los Angeles is home to a bevy of historical landmarks, among them the grand **Union Station (Map 9)**, built in 1939 in the Spanish-mission style, the **Bradbury Building (Map 9)** (of *Blade Runner* fame) is Victorian opulence and ingenuity at its finest, and the **Eastern Columbia Buildings (Map 9)** are dynamic by day and blaze the downtown skyline by night. The Persian-inspired **Shrine Auditorium (Map 12)**, former home of the Oscars, now hosts concerts and lesser award shows. And as a convergence of the holy and the postmodern, there is the impressive strength and serenity of the **Cathedral of Our Lady of the Angels (Map 9)**, fascinating regardless of religious affiliation.

Outdoor Spaces

For all its freeways and urban sprawl, Los Angeles is no concrete jungle. There are some terrific places to have a picnic, go for a hike, hear music, cheer for your team, or just laze in the California sunshine. The athletic flock to **Pan Pacific Park (Map 2)** near the Miracle Mile for softball and basketball; families, hikers, golfers, and horseback riders recreate in rustic **Griffith Park (Map 51)**; golfers and sun worshippers head to the vast **Rancho Park (Map 23)** in Cheviot Hills; and those seeking a refreshing hike in the hills visit the **Hollywood Reservoir (Map 57)** or the ever-popular **Runyon Canyon (Map 2)**. And absolutely nothing can match an outdoor summertime concert at the **Hollywood Bowl (Map 3)** or the **Greek Theatre (Map 4)**—both boast awesome acoustics and make for a lovely evening of food, wine, and music. Much cherished by Angelenos and a fine example of mid-century modern architecture, **Dodger Stadium (Map 5)** opened in 1962 and still remains free of an annoying corporate sponsor moniker. An enduring celebration of LA's Mexican heritage is **Olvera Street (Map 9)** off Cesar Chavez downtown, where traditional dances and mariachis are the backdrop to some authentic Mexican dining.

Architecture

Always a forward-thinking city, Los Angeles has been attracting the funky and the innovative with its municipal reputation for starting trends. The results are evident in the colorful shapes of the **Pacific Design Center (Map 2)**, housing furniture, art galleries, and design offices. Two famous Frank Lloyd Wright–designed homes near Hollywood—the ailing **Ennis-Brown House (Map 4)** and the **Hollyhock House (Map 4)**— offer tours frequently; check to make sure the buildings are not currently under construction. LA's early 20th century explosion makes it an Art Deco heaven, boasting dozens of striking examples of the movement from the soaring **City Hall (Map 9)** to the opulent movie palaces that crowd Broadway, particularly the triumphant **Orpheum (Map 9).** The most recent architectural wonder in Los Angeles is, of course, Frank Gehry's **Walt Disney Concert Hall (Map 9)**. Resembling a carefully wadded crumple of metal, the building is quite impressive both inside and out. Running a close second to Gehry's LA opus is the new, expressively modern **Caltrans District 7 Headquarters (Map 9)** downtown.

Lowbrow Landmarks

Nobody did lowbrow better than the late great drunken saint of Los Angeles: Charles Bukowski. To relive the poetic debauchery, drop a few bucks and bet on the ponies at **Hollywood Park (Map 13)** near LAX; afterwards, take your winnings to tip the dancers at the seedy (yet historic) **Jumbo's Clown Room (Map 4)** in Hollywood, where the performers (like Courtney Love before them) gyrate to Tom Waits and The Clash. **Whisky A Go Go (Map 2)** is a distinct musical landmark surrounded by the garish cultural wasteland of the Sunset Strip. Once the home of legendary rock bands like The Doors, Love, Van Halen, and X, the Whisky has since lost its luster to a never ending line-up of wanna-be bands. However, it's still worth a look, for posterity's sake.

Lame, Bad, & Overrated Landmarks

If **Rock Walk (Map 2)** doesn't prove as rockin' as you had hoped, cross the street and head to **El Compadre (Map 2)** for a kick-ass flaming margarita to tame those blues. Farther down Sunset you'll find the **Sunset Strip (Map 2)**. Crowded with hordes of suburban drunk kids, gridlocked traffic, and cops at every corner, the Strip is best done once (before night falls) and left to the tourists thereafter. Many of the tourist traps on Hollywood Boulevard are a waste of traveler's checks; avoid the **Hollywood Wax Museum (Map 3)** at all costs, and the new **Hollywood & Highland Mall (Map 3)** is sterile and soulless. Also overrated are the **La Brea Tar Pits (Map 6)** – smelly and boring, although the nearby Page Museum and food trucks are worth a look/bite. Skip eating at **Pink's (Map 2)**—a hot dog is, after all, only a hot dog and doesn't justify the wait in line. If you must, start your day (or end your night) with a Chicago Dog right as they open up at 9:30 am.

Underrated Landmarks

The **Silent Movie Theatre (Map 2)** on Fairfax was silenced for a number of years following the murder of its second owner, Lawrence Austin, in 1997, but now it's up and running again and definitely worth a visit. Continuing in the macabre vein of the dead and the silent, the oddly festive **Hollywood Forever Cemetery (Map 3)** is the final resting place of stars both famous (Douglas Fairbanks, Cecil B DeMille, Dee Dee Ramone) and infamous (Bugsy Siegel!). Old films are frequently shown al fresco in the graveyard to a fun, hip crowd—check www.cinespia.org for details. For a little more Hollyweird, check out the **Magic Castle (Map 3)**—you can book a room here or go for dinner and a show put on by some of the world's premier smoke-and-mirror masters. Sticking with the weirdly metaphysical, head on over to the **Museum of Jurassic Technology (Map 24)** on Venice Boulevard for a peek into a cabinet of curiosities that will surely leave you dumbstruck.

Los Angeles offers just a few too many hotel choices—so many, in fact, that it can easily induce a case of option paralysis. If you have money to spend, we offer this cheat-sheet to aid your decision-making. The **Chateau Marmont (Map 2)**: legendary, low-key, timeless. The **Four Seasons (Map 1)**: beautiful rooftop pool, excellent location, and with press junkets held year-round here, you never know who you might encounter on the elevator. Need a place to hide out while you recover from a "procedure?" The **Peninsula (Map 1)**, definitely. **Maison 140 (Map 1)** and the **Avalon Hotel (Map 1)** are stylish, sexy, and lighter-hearted than the more Baroque stuff you'd otherwise find in Beverly Hills. Similarly style-conscious is their sibling property, the **Chamberlain (Map 2)** in West Hollywood. The **Sunset Marquis (Map 2)** has a famously fabulous scene at the Whiskey Bar on premises—though you must be a hotel guest, or a bold-faced name, to belly-up.

Feeling architecturally significant? The **Sunset Tower Hotel (Map 2)**, an Art Deco gem, is back in business after extensive renovations and offers a substantially lower profile than Sunset Boulevard skyline hogs the **Standard (Map 9)** and the **Mondrian (Map 2)**. Out at the beach, within sight of the Santa Monica Pier but far from the maddening crowd, is the delicious **Hotel Casa Del Mar (Map 18)**. Next door is the famous **Shutters on the Beach (Map 18)**, a more rustic stay with five-star restaurants and service. If you are planning to spend a longish evening in Hollywood, book a room at the **Hollywood Roosevelt Hotel (Map 3)**—a landmark within stumbling distance of all of the star-studded clubs. And finally, when headed downtown, say, for an oversized night at the STAPLES Center or for your company's Christmas blow-out, book one of the Moroccan Suites at the **Figueroa Hotel (Map 9)**. It's a quirky, mysterious beauty, and once you've time-traveled through the well-decorated lobby, and sat down for a nightcap by the pool, you will wonder why it took you so long to find the place. **Farmer's Daughter Hotel (Map 2)** is lovely, convenient to everything, and also directly across the street from the Farmer's Market.

As with so many things, the best rates are always found online; comparison-shopping is the cowboy way.

Map 1 • Beverly Hills

The Beverly Hills Hotel	9641 W Sunset Blvd	310-276-2251	$$$$$$
Four Seasons Beverly Wilshire	9500 Wilshire Blvd	310-275-5200	$$$$$
Maison 140	140 S Lasky Dr	310-281-4000	$$$$
Peninsula Beverly Hills	9882 S Santa Monica Blvd	310-551-2888	$$$$$

Map 2 • West Hollywood

Chamberlain Hotel	1000 Westmount Dr	310-657-7400	$$$
Chateau Marmont	8221 W Sunset Blvd	323-656-1010	$$$$$
Farmer's Daughter Hotel	115 S Fairfax Ave	323-937-3930	$$
Four Seasons Los Angeles	300 S Doheny Dr	310-273-2222	$$$$$
Mondrian	8440 W Sunset Blvd	323-650-8999	$$$$
The Standard Hotel Hollywood	8300 W Sunset Blvd	323-650-9090	$$$
Sunset Marquis Hotel	1200 Alta Loma Rd	310-657-1333	$$$$
Sunset Tower Hotel	8358 W Sunset Blvd	323-654-7100	$$$$

Map 3 • Hollywood

Hollywood Roosevelt Hotel	7000 Hollywood Blvd	323-466-7000	$$

Map 9 • Downtown

Figueroa Hotel	939 S Figueroa St	213-627-8971	$$
The Standard Hotel Downtown	550 S Flower St	213-892-8080	$$$

Map 18 • Santa Monica

Hotel Casa Del Mar	1910 Ocean Way	310-581-5533	$$$$$
Shutters on the Beach	1 Pico Blvd	310-458-0030	$$$$$

As a local, you know of the many advantages to living in Los Angeles. Right up there with the ability to get a burger with avocado on every corner and the possibility of Christmas tree shopping in flip-flops is the abundance and proximity of neighborhood Farmers Markets. Sure, most places have Farmers Markets these days, but not like us Angelenos. Every day there is a market happening somewhere in the city, and each market has its own flavor and cultural or ethnic twist.

Vendors at the **Alhambra Farmers Market (Map 39)**, which caters to a predominantly Chinese population, carry vegetables and fruits you won't see on the Westside; the **Silver Lake (Map 4)** market is younger and funkier, offering Guatemalan crafts and leather goods. **Venice (Map 21)** is about food, but also features live music and pony rides for the kids (the latter occasionally picketed by local PETA activists). Both **South Pasadena (Map 34)** and **West Hollywood (Map 2)** are laid-back and small-town. The motherlode is to be found in **Hollywood (Map 3)**. On Sunday mornings, the intersection of Selma and Ivar explodes with orchids, the freshest veggies, and lively drum circles. Make sure to save time for the pupusas.

As the grandmama of them all, the **Santa Monica Wednesday Farmers Market (Map 18)**, is almost as impressive, where you can buy organic Heritage tomatoes a half a block from the Pacific Ocean. Chances are you'll also be rubbing shoulders with area chefs and celebrities. This market carries the largest selection of organic foods in the LA area and is worth the trip for the atmosphere and location alone. Check out what's in season before you go by tuning into KCRW's *Good Food*—they broadcast live reports from the market every weekend. Bon appetit.

Farmers Markets	*Address*	*Map*
Beverly Hills (Sun, 9 am–1 pm)	9300 Civic Center Dr	1
Melrose Place (Sun, 9 am–2 pm)	8400 Melrose Ave	2
The Original Farmers Market (Mon–Fri, 1 pm–6 pm; Sat, 9 pm–8 pm; Sun, 10 am–7 pm)	6333 W 3rd St	2
West Hollywood (Mon, 9 am–2 pm)	N Vista St & Fountain Ave	2
Hollywood (Sun, 8 am–1 pm)	Ivar Ave & Selma Ave	3
Silver Lake (Sat, 8 am–1 pm)	3700 W Sunset Blvd	4
Atwater Village (Sun, 10 am–2 pm)	3250 Glendale Blvd	5
La Cienega (Thurs, 3 pm–7 pm)	1801 S La Cienega Blvd	6
Larchmont Village (Sun, 10 am–2 pm)	209 N Larchmont Blvd	7
Little Tokyo (Tues, 10 am–2 pm)	1st St & Main St	9
Los Angeles - Figueroa at 7th (Thurs, Fri, Sat, 10 am–4 pm)	735 S Figueroa St	9
Los Angeles - Chinatown (Thurs, 4 pm–8 pm)	727 N Hill St	9
Crenshaw	3650 W Martin Luther King Jr Blvd	11
Leimert Park Village (Sat, 9 am–2 pm)	W 43rd St & Degnan Blvd	11
Los Angeles - Harambee (Sat, 10 am–4 pm)	Crenshaw Blvd & W Slauson Ave	11
Los Angeles - Adams & Vermont (Wed; Jun–Aug, 1 pm-6 pm; Sept–May, 2 pm–5 pm)	1432 W Adams Blvd	11
Los Angeles - Central Ave (Sat, 9 am–1 pm)	43rd St & Central Ave	12
Pacific Palisades (Sun, 8 am–1:30 pm)	1037 Swarthmore Ave	15
Brentwood (Sun, 9 am–1 pm)	741 S Gretna Green Way	16
Santa Monica Organic Farmers Market (Sat, 8:30–1 pm)	Arizona Ave & 3rd St	18
Santa Monica (Sun, 9:30 am–1 pm)	2640 Main St	18
Santa Monica Virginia (Sat, 8 am–1 pm)	2200 Virginia Ave	19
West Los Angeles (Sun, 9 am–2 pm)	1645 Corinth Ave	19
Century City (Thurs, 11:30 am–3 pm)	1800 Avenue of the Stars	20
Westwood (Thurs, 1 pm–7 pm)	Weyburn Ave & Westwood Blvd	20
Venice (Fri, 7 am–11 am)	Venice Blvd & Venice Wy	21
Culver City (Tues, 2 pm–7 pm)	Culver Blvd & Main St	24
Westchester (Wed, 8:30 am–1 pm)	W 87th St & Truxton Ave	26
El Segundo (Thurs, 3pm–7pm)	Main St & E Pine Ave	27
Hermosa Beach (Fri, 12 pm–4 pm)	Valley Dr b/w 10th St & 8th St	29
Redondo Beach - Harbor Dr (Thurs, 8 am–1 pm)	N Harbor Dr & W Torrance Blvd	31
Torrance (Tues, 8 am–12 pm; Sat, 8 am–1 pm)	2200 Crenshaw Blvd	32
Eagle Rock (Fri 5 am–8:30 pm)	2100 Merton Ave	33
Pasadena Villa Park (Tues, 9 am–1 pm)	363 E Villa St	34
South Pasadena (Thurs 4 pm–8 pm)	Meridian Ave & El Centro St	34
Pasadena Victory Park (Sat, 8:30 am–1 pm)	Paloma St & E Sierra Madre Blvd	35
Alhambra (Sun, 8:30 am–1 pm)	S Monterey St b/w E Main St & E Bay State St	39
Chatsworth (Sat, 8 am–1 pm)	Devonshire St & Canoga Ave	42
Northridge (Wed, 5 pm–9 pm)	9301 Tampa Ave	43
Encino (Sun, 8 am–1 pm)	17400 Victory Blvd	46
Burbank (Sat, 8 am–12:30 pm)	E Olive Ave & S Glenoaks Blvd	50
Woodland Hills (Sat, 8 am–4 pm)	6200 block of Topanga Cyn Blvd	52
Studio City (Sun, 8 am–1 pm)	Ventura Blvd & Radford Ave	56

Overview

These days, Los Angeles has a good number of dog parks in which your beloved pooch can romp and play, and the list is growing—you can even find areas for the big bow-wows like German Shepherds and Mastiffs. For the little guys, like the feisty Yorkies or the ever-snorting pugs, there's the small dog park. If you and your canine buddy are making your way out to a fenced grassy area for a play date, consider a few rules to make everyone's life easier:

1. Make sure your four-legged child plays nice with the other kids.
2. If your dog drops the poop, you get to scoop. (Heck, most dog parks provide you with a poop bag and trashcan to make it even easier on you.)
3. If your dog is in heat, keep her at home.
4. If your dog generally snarls, snaps, and likes to sink his teeth into live meat, that means he shouldn't be socializing at a dog park.
5. If the sign says "for dogs up to 30 pounds" don't bring your Great Dane in—even if you swear she's well trained.
6. If your dog isn't spayed, neutered, or current with his vaccinations, it's best not to bring him.
7. If you can't get laid here, you may as well give up.

We've compiled our own list of dog parks for you to scour. Each park has its own set of specific rules, so remember to read the signs when you enter.

For more information online, a great website to check is www.dogfriendly.com. It provides loads of information on dog-friendly parks, accommodations, attractions, restaurants, and retail stores. If you're into inflicting tutus upon your dog and parading her around on Halloween, they have information on that, too. Two other helpful websites can be found at www.laparks.org and www.dogpark.com.

The Boneyard, Culver City Dog Park

End of Duquesne in Culver City Park (South of Jefferson Blvd), Culver City

This place has been in the works since 2001, and as of April 2006, it has officially opened for public use. Just over an acre in size, this dog park has space designated for both big and little dogs. It's open every day of the week with no official hours except dawn to dusk. Bring your tennis balls and doggy bags, but leave the cigarettes at home. Water is provided at the doggie drinking fountains.

El Segundo Dog Park

600 E Imperial Ave, El Segundo

Located near LAX, you and Buster can fling Frisbees while watching the planes go by. Just be careful where you're walking while you're looking up. There are two areas: one for the little guys, 30 pounds and under, and one for the big boys, 31 pounds and up. Parking is a sure bet on the street adjacent to the park. Poop bags are provided for your convenience, along with trash receptacles. And don't worry al[l] the bonding and frolicking will give you cotton mouth: they provide public drinking fountains for us two-legged folks and a lower model for the four-legged ones.

Long Beach Recreation Dog Park

5201 E 7th St (Cross Street is Park Ave), Long Beach

Ah, Long Beach: your dog finally has nearly two acres of fenced-in area in which to play. With separate areas for big dogs and little dogs, there's room for everyone's ego. The park is open from 6 am until 10 pm, and you and your canine can make a drink pit stop at the watering stations. Everyone's jonesing to get into this park, so if you're hard up for play buddies for your dog (or, hey, for yourself) and you're in the area, do yourself a favor and stop here. Want to strike up a convo with the hottie toting the Italian Greyhound? You can mention that this park was a set location for the 2005 Diane Lane and John Cusack film, *Must Love Dogs.*

Laurel Canyon Park

8260 Mulholland Dr (near Laurel Canyon Blvd), Studio City
818-769-4415

Laurel Canyon Park boasts three acres of off-leash space in a fenced-in area. Dogs must be leashed between 10 am and 3 pm, but it's doggie anarchy between 6 am and 10 am and again from 3 pm until dusk. Other amenities include free parking, a small fenced-in children's play area, and a hot dog stand!

This is a spacious dog park, but it has drainage problems, so keep the towels handy, because your dog's going to come home fairly filthy; nonetheless, Laurel Canyon Park remains a popular place for dog lovers, and it attracts a healthy clot of celebrity pet owners. You're more likely to have a star sighting here than at the Chateau Marmont.

Silver Lake Recreation Center

850 W Silver Lake Dr, Los Angeles, 323-644-3946

Open from 6 am until 10 pm, the Rec Center features 1.25 acres of off-leash running room. The only parking available is on the street. Silver Lake Recreation Center is a well-known meeting place for pooch owners, so if you're new to town and looking to make new friends with excellent fashion and intimidating scenester associations, take your dog down for a run. Just be mindful—the fastidious regulars here will be quick to bark at you if you don't securely shut the gates. Traffic tends to pick up around the curves, and it'd take only seconds for someone's beloved to leap from sanctuary to tragedy. No grass, just dirt, which makes for some muddy K-9s on those ten days of rain.

Runyon Canyon Park

2000 N Fuller Ave (north of Franklin Ave), Hollywood, 323-666-5046

Located in Hollywood, Runyon Canyon Park is almost completely undeveloped. While it doesn't have a fenced-in dog play area, dogs are permitted to roam the hiking trails unleashed, as long as they're with their owners. Within the 160-acre park, there are several hiking trails of varying difficulty with amazing views. You and your pooch can break a sweat together and enjoy the scenery next to a host of celebrities and their own canine buddies.

Westminster Dog Park

1234 Pacific Ave, Venice, 310-396-1615

This park features a fenced-in area with off-leash space for both large dogs and small dogs (under 25 lbs). Open from 6 am until 10 pm, you can usually find a spot in the lot adjacent to the dog park.

Barrington Dog Park

333 S Barrington Ave, Los Angeles, 310-476-4866

This 1.5-acre dog park located in Brentwood is open daily from 5 am to 10:30 pm and closes for maintenance on Tuesday mornings from 6 am to 10 am. The park is off-leash, fenced-in, and features separate sections for dogs big and small. The Friends of Barrington Dog Park maintain a website at www.fobdp.org that lists doggie resources, park news and events, as well as a photo gallery of the furry friends who frequent the park.

Sepulveda Basin Off-Leash Dog Park

17550 Victory Blvd, Encino, 818-756-7667

Featuring a five-acre off-leash area with half an acre for small pooches, Sepulveda Basin Dog Park is open daily from sunrise to sunset, except Friday mornings when it opens at 11 am. On-site parking can accommodate up to 100 cars. Whatever you do, avoid parking on White Oak Avenue or Victory Boulevard at all times, as ticketing agents here are eagle-eyed and vigilant. (Getting a ticket is a matter of "when," not "if.")

Griffith Park Dog Park

North end of John Ferraro Soccer Field on North Zoo Dr, Los Angeles, 323-913-4688

Griffith Park has its own dog park with compartmentalized areas for dogs big and little to roam off-leash. Open from 5 am to 10:30 pm every day of the week, the park has troughs to keep the dogs well-hydrated and a parking area for 40 cars. If you can't get enough outdoor space for your dog, explore the rest of Griffith Park. The trails across from the observatory are pro-dog, and you can even take your dog to the roof of the observatory via the outside stairs (though the dog's got to be on a leash). The one-mile train ride off Crystal Springs allows dogs onboard (accompanied by an adult, of course). We suggest that you pick up a map at the Ranger's Station (Crystal Spring and Griffith Park Drive) to check which trails allow dogs.

Beaches

While dogs, leashed or not, are prohibited from places like Venice Beach and the Ocean Front Walk, there are still some dog-friendly beaches and a core group of volunteer vigilantes fighting to keep it that way. Huntington Dog Beach (PCH and Golden West Street, www.dogbeach.org) is a beautiful one-mile stretch of beach that allows dogs on leashes, providing their owners pick up after them. The only place dogs are allowed off-leash is in the water, under supervision. Leo Carrillo State Beach (PCH 28 miles north of Santa Monica) also allows leashed dogs, but there are restrictions about where dogs can play—check the signs carefully before embarking on a beach adventure with your dog. Redondo Beach Dog Park is located away from the foreshore next to Dominguez Park (200 Flagler Lane and 190th Street, www.rbdogpark.com). A fenced-in area, Redondo Beach Dog Park has play spaces for large and small dogs. Long Beach has almost three acres of leash-free beach fun for dogs, located in the revitalized Belmont Shore area. Look for the signs marking the designated areas between Roycroft and Argonne Avenues.

General Information

NFT Maps:	2 & 9
Main Address:	250 S Grand Ave Los Angeles, CA 90012
Phone:	213-626-6222
Website:	www.moca.org
Hours:	Mon & Fri: 11 am–5 pm; Thurs: 11 pm–8 pm; Sat & Sun: 11 am–6 pm; closed Tuesdays, Wednesdays, and major holidays
Admission:	adults: $12 (valid for all locations on the date of purchase); seniors & students: $7; children under 12: free; Thursdays after 5 pm: free

Overview

In a city where modern and contemporary generally refer to the latest plastic surgery or BMW, Los Angeles's Museum of Contemporary Art is a surprisingly refreshing destination. Located downtown in the shadow of the towering California Plaza, the museum sits catty-corner to Frank Gehry's Walt Disney Concert Hall. It is the only LA museum devoted exclusively to contemporary art (post-WWII)—if you're looking for Cézanne or Klimt, head to LACMA. This main building houses selections from the impressive permanent collection and various special exhibitions, while the two satellite locations—in Little Tokyo and West Hollywood—display large installations and design-focused exhibits, respectively.

Between its three locations, MOCA offers a substantial survey of the art that shaped the latter half of the 20th century, as well as artists of the '00s that built reputations in places like the adjacent Chinatown art scene and those experimenting with interactive and digital media. While the museum is often lauded by critics and laymen alike, it was hit hard by the Great Recession and has struggled financially in recent years.

The entrance plaza of MOCA at Grand Avenue sports a massive sculpture by Nancy Rubins, composed mainly of stainless steel airplane parts. Down below, MOCA's main location is a cavernous space featuring, in part, exhibits culled from its more than 5,000 permanent works, courtesy of art world phenoms like Frank Stella, Roy Lichtenstein, Jackson Pollock, Lee Friedlander, Cindy Sherman, Tracy Emin, and Steve McQueen.

It's also host to larger, traveling exhibitions, many of which include pieces loaned by the museum. MOCA has gained a reputation for mounting innovative retrospectives on contemporary artists and movements that have rarely been explored in such depth. While the museum's recent Basquiat and Rauschenberg retrospectives were well received, its 2011 show Art in the Streets courted controversy with its focus on graffiti. In 2009-2010, MOCA celebrated its 30th Anniversary with Collection: MOCA's First Thirty Years, the "largest-ever exhibition of the museum's world-renowned permanent collection."

MOCA at the Geffen Contemporary

152 Central Ave, 213-626-6222
Hours & Admission same as Grand Avenue location.

MOCA at the Geffen Contemporary—known as the "Temporary Contemporary" until a cool five mil from namesake David Geffen made it permanent—is a cavernous former police car garage in the heart of Little Tokyo. Past shows have included a 30-year retrospective on installation art in which many of the installations inhabited room-sized areas, and Gregor Schneider's *Dead House Ur* in which the artist reconstructed the entire interior of his childhood home. MOCA also uses this space in collaboration with other arts organizations to host gala events; in 2005 it co-hosted the GenArt independent designer runway shows that kicked off LA's Fashion Week.

Don't look for prototypical art exhibits here—the Geffen prides itself on wide-open industrial space and is decidedly anti-establishment. In 2007, WACK! Art and the Feminist Revolution explored the foundation of feminist art from 1965-80. More recently, 2010's Mi casa es tu casa examined the contemporary themes of illegal immigration and ethnic identity.

MOCA at the Pacific Design Center

8687 Melrose Ave, 310-289-5223

Hours: Tues–Fri: 11 am–5 pm; Sat & Sun: 11 am–6 pm; closed Mondays & major holidays

Admission: Free

This smaller satellite location in West Hollywood opened in 2001 and is mainly used for exhibits that focus on one artist, architect, designer, or art collective. The museum's lot at the Pacific Design Center is a separate structure that's set away from the PDC's home-décor shops and across an expansive plaza where MOCA loves to throw its big fundraiser parties. This little gallery-like space allows you to cruise through its two floors in about 20 minutes.

How to Get There—Driving

MOCA Grand Avenue: From the 110, exit at 4th Street. Turn left on Grand Avenue. The museum will be on your right.

MOCA at Geffen Contemporary: From the 101, exit at Los Angeles Street. Turn right on Los Angeles Street, then turn left on 1st Street. The museum will be on your left.

MOCA at the Pacific Design Center: From the 10, exit at Robertson Boulevard going north. Turn right on Melrose Avenue, then turn left on San Vicente Boulevard. The Design Center will be on your right. From the 101, exit west on Melrose Avenue. Turn right on San Vicente Boulevard. The Design Center will be on your right.

How to Get There—Public Transit

The MOCA and MOCA at the Geffen Contemporary locations are both accessible from the Silver, Red, or Purple Metro Lines at Civic Center Station. The Station is located at North Hill Street & West 1st Street—one block northeast of MOCA and 6 blocks west of the Geffen Contemporary.

Parking

MOCA Grand Avenue: Parking is available for $9 in the Walt Disney Concert Hall parking garage on Grand Avenue ($20 deposit, $11 refund with MOCA validation). On the weekends, museum members can park in the California Plaza parking garage on Olive Street for a reduced rate of $7.50. Metered street parking is also available on Grand Avenue, 3rd Street, and Hope Street, but you'll only have two hours, max.

MOCA at Geffen Contemporary: Parking is available at the Advanced Parking Systems garage on Central Avenue for a daily flat rate of $6.50. The public parking lot on Judge John Aiso Street offers an $8 flat rate on weekdays, or $7 after 4 pm and on weekends.

MOCA at the Pacific Design Center: Parking is available in the Pacific Design Center's lot on Melrose. The first 20 minutes are free, then it's $1.50 for each block of 15 minutes thereafter with a $13.50 maximum charge per day. Flat rates are available after 6 pm ($6 on Mon-Wed, $9 on Thurs, and $10 Fri-Sat) and on weekends ($7 on Sat from 10 am to 6 pm and all day Sun).

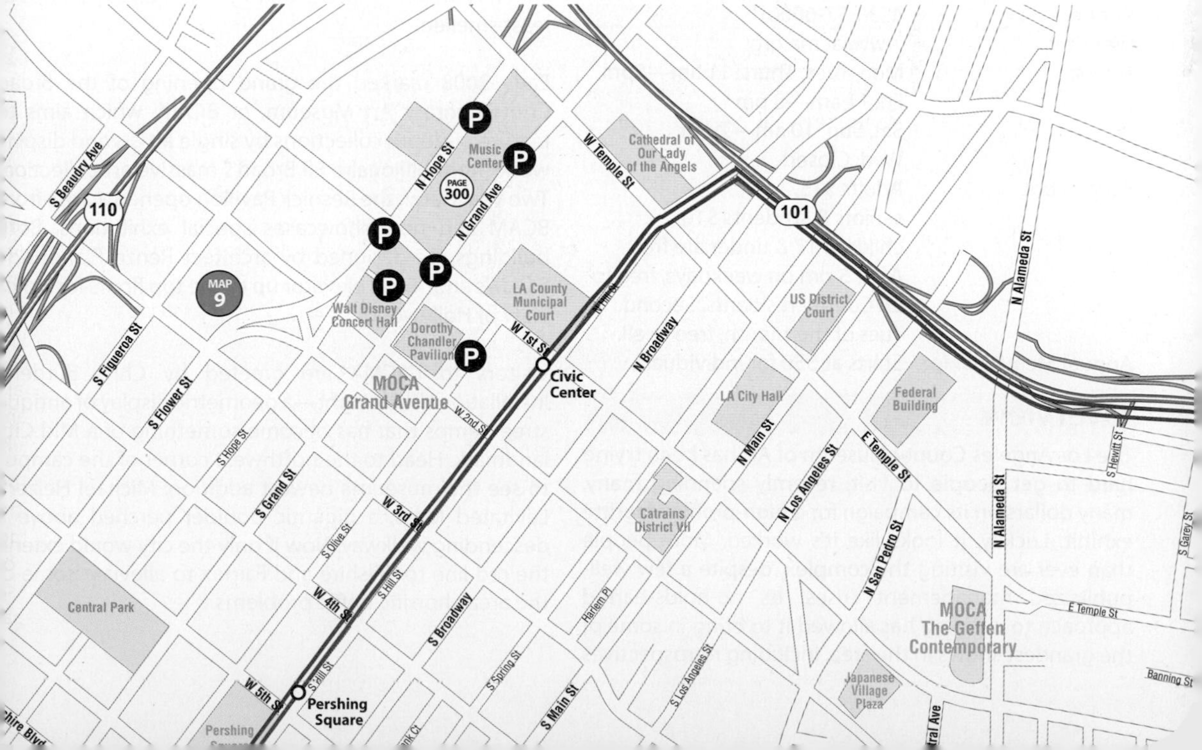

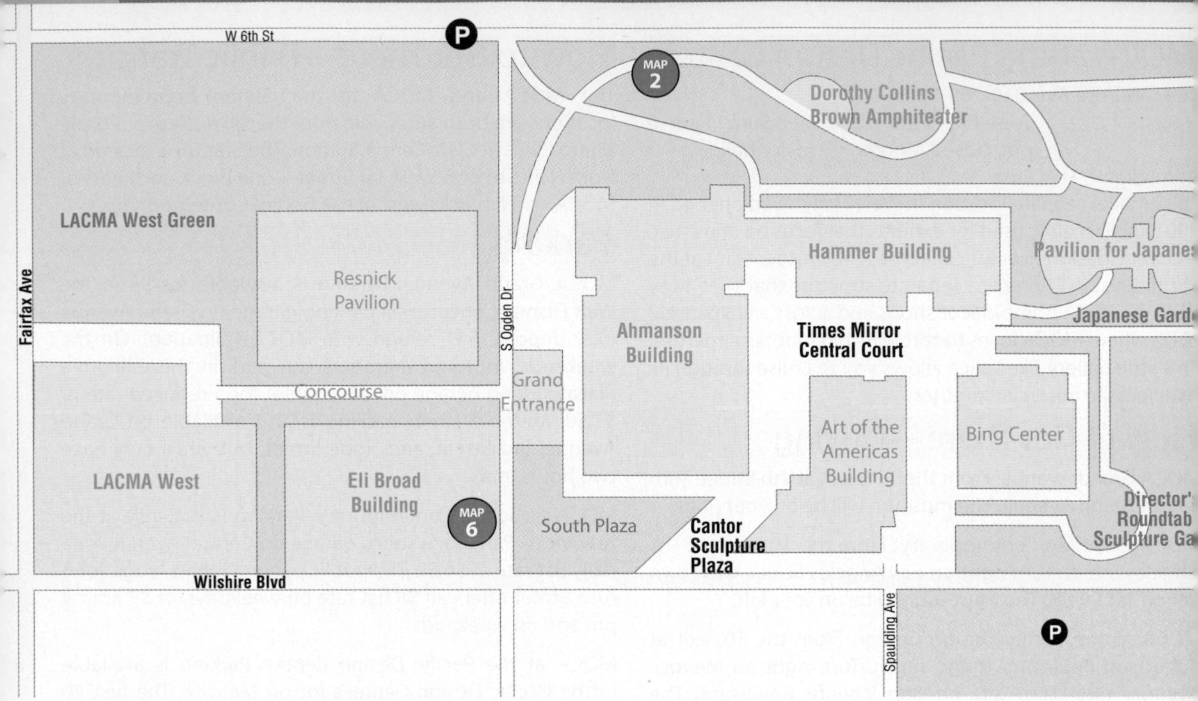

General Information

NFT Maps:	2 & 6
Address:	5905 Wilshire Blvd Los Angeles, CA 90036
Phone:	323-857-6000
Website:	www.lacma.org
Hours:	Mon, Tues, Thurs: 11 am—5pm Fri: 11 am—8 pm Sat, Sun: 10 am—7 pm Wed: Closed
Admission:	Adults $15, seniors & students $10, children 17 & under are free After 3 pm on weekdays, free to LA County residents. Second Tues of the month, free to all.
Annual Membership:	Starts at $50 for individuals.

Overview

The Los Angeles County Museum of Art has been trying hard to get people to visit, recently spending many, many dollars on its campaign for a high-profile Magritte exhibit. Luckily, it looks like it's worked. More people than ever are visiting the complex, despite a few well-publicized management crises. Its no-holds-barred approach to curating has allowed it to bring in some of the grandest shows in the area, including retrospectives of Klimt, Rivera, and the French Masters. A day is easil lost here; in addition to the Art Museum, the LACM grounds are also home to a lovely park, the Pag Museum, and the rather anticlimactic La Brea Tar Pits which Angelenos have probably heard of, or perhaps a least smelled.

Early 2008 marked the grand opening of the Broa Contemporary Art Museum, or BCAM, which aims t feature in-depth collections by single artists and displa works from billionaire Eli Broad's massive art collectio Two years later, the Resnick Pavilion opened across fron BCAM and now showcases special exhibitions. Bot buildings are designed by architect Renzo Piano; rid BCAM's enormous elevator up to the top floors for a nic view of Hollywood.

Visitors to LACMA are greeted by Chris Burden' installation Urban Light—a geometric display of antiqu street lamps that has become something of a Mid Cit landmark. Head to the northwest corner of the campu to see the museum's newest addition: Michael Heizer' Levitated Mass, a gigantic boulder perched above descending walkway. Now if only the city would exten the red line to Wilshire and Fairfax to alleviate some o the area's horrific traffic problems.

LACMA East

The buildings on the east end of the LACMA campus may not be as flashy as the new Renzo Piano structures, but they are home to some fantastic art. The Ahmanson Building is perhaps the most varied, displaying everything from Islamic art to German Expressionism. The Boone Children's Gallery, as well as the museum's collection of Korean art, can be found in the Hammer Building. The Art of the Americas Building displays art from the New World, while the Pavilion for Japanese Art is a freestanding building that holds Japanese works from 3000 B.C. to the 20th century.

LACMA is also a great destination on weekend evenings. On Fridays, the museum is open late—until 8 pm—and there's live jazz in the Times Mirror Central Court starting at 6 pm. You can also hear live chamber music every Sunday at 6 pm in the Bing Theater. Both of these weekly concerts are free. The Bing Theater is also home to regular screenings of classic films, occasionally with a guest speaker. Movie tickets include admission to all of the galleries and cost $10 for the public and $7 for members, seniors, and students. Screenings are every Friday and Saturday at 7:30 pm.

LACMA West

In 1998, the Art Deco May Company department store reopened as LACMA West. For a time, the building was home to the museum's collection of Latin American art, but it is now closed for renovations. The LACMA Board has announced plans to work with the Academy of Motion Picture Arts and Sciences to transform the space into a museum dedicated to the art of movies.

The George C. Page Museum

Located just east of LACMA, the Page Museum is best known as the home of the La Brea Tar Pits. Almost everyone who moves to Los Angeles has heard of the Tar Pits in some context, and most make a pilgrimage at some point, hoping to see something dynamic, something bubbling, something interesting. What you end up seeing, however, is a large pool of tar. It's about as anticlimactic as it gets. The Tar Pits become exponentially more interesting during an eight-to-ten-week period, usually in July and August, when excavation takes place. It's during this time that museum-goers can watch paleontologists sift through the tar. The process is painstaking and oddly fascinating, even if it's hard to escape the feeling that everything cool has already been unearthed.

Inside the Page Museum, it's possible to view over one million specimens of fossils recovered from the Tar Pits. Among them are saber-toothed cats and mammoths. Sadly, there are no dinosaurs, but many a child has been riveted by the exhibit of the 9,000-year-old La Brea Woman, whose fossil is still the only human remains ever found in the Tar Pits.

Open everyday from 9:30 am until 5 pm. Adults $11, seniors & students $8, and children 5-12 $5. Admission is free on the first Tuesday of every month, excluding July and August.

How to Get There—Driving

From the 10, exit at Fairfax Avenue and drive north. Turn right at Wilshire Boulevard. The museum will be on your left. From the 101 S, exit at Highland and head south to Franklin. Turn right and take Franklin to La Brea. Make a left onto La Brea, and continue south to Wilshire Boulevard. Turn right on Wilshire, and the museum will be on your right.

Parking

There are parking lots on Wilshire, just across from the museum at Spaulding Avenue and at Ogden Drive. These lots charge a flat rate of $10 during the day, but they are free after 7 pm. If you're lucky, you'll nab one of the metered spots behind the museum (along 6th Street) that allow 4-hour parking from 8 am until 6 pm. Take lots of quarters with you. If you park in the parking structure, take a moment of silence for the previous parking structure, which featured historically significant murals by Margaret Kilgallen that were torn down. You can imagine what we think of that decision…

How to Get There—Mass Transit

MTA buses 20, 21, 217, and 720 all stop near the museum, on either Wilshire Boulevard or Fairfax Avenue.

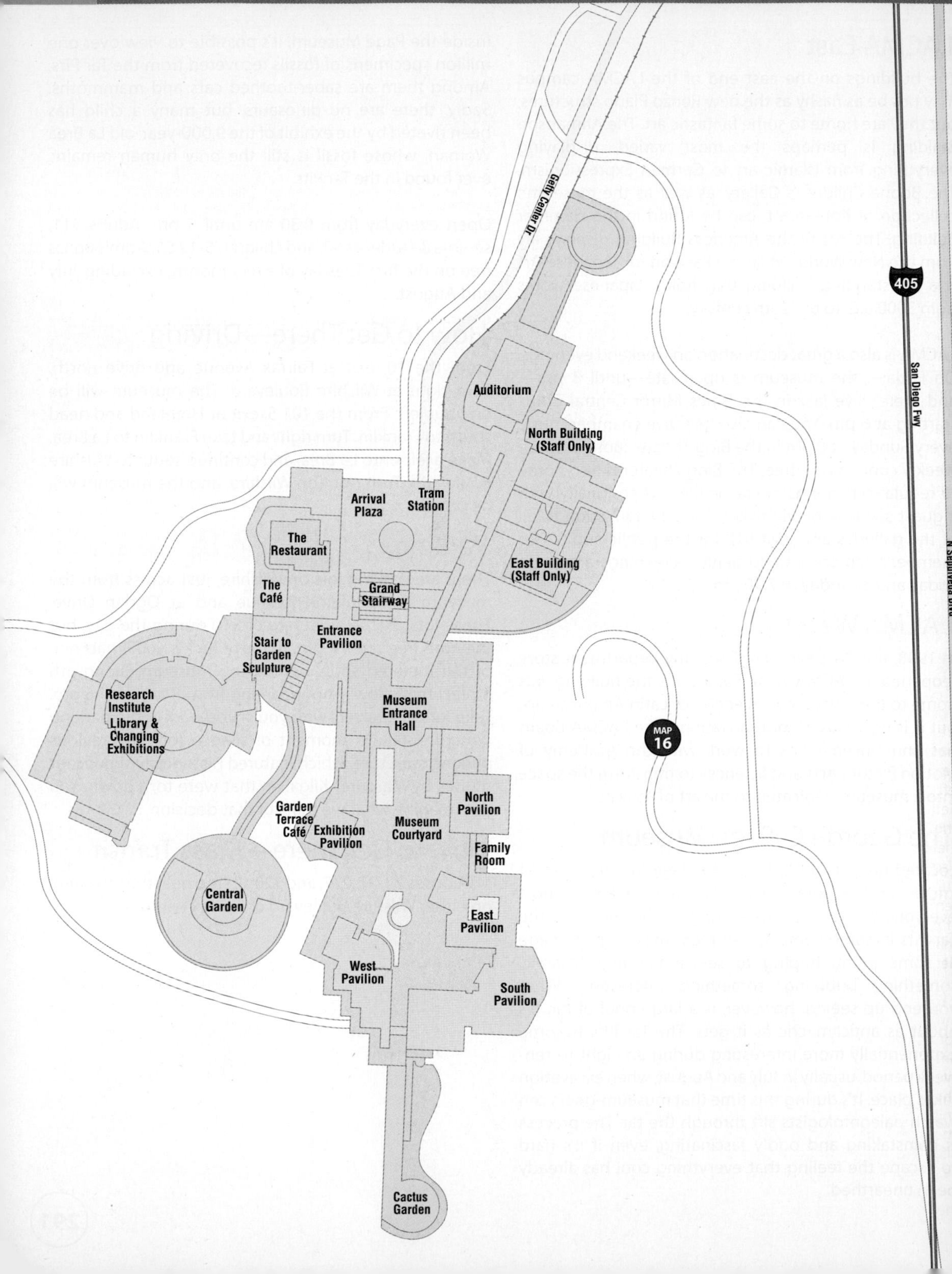
Getty Center Dr
405
San Diego Fwy
N Sepulveda Blvd
Auditorium
North Building
(Staff Only)
Arrival
Plaza
Tram
Station
The
Restaurant
East Building
(Staff Only)
The
Café
Grand
Stairway
Entrance
Pavilion
Stair to
Garden
Sculpture
Research
Institute
Library &
Changing
Exhibitions
Museum
Entrance
Hall
MAP
16
North
Pavilion
Garden
Terrace
Café
Exhibition
Pavilion
Museum
Courtyard
Family
Room
Central
Garden
East
Pavilion
West
Pavilion
South
Pavilion
Cactus
Garden

General Information

NFT Map:	16
Address:	1200 Getty Center Dr Los Angeles, CA 90049
Phone:	310-440-7300
Website:	www.getty.edu
Hours:	Tues–Fri & Sun: 10 am–5:30 pm Sat: 10 am–9 pm; Summer Fridays: 10 am–9 pm Closed Mondays and major holidays
Admission:	free, but parking is $15

Overview

Although the Getty stands as one of the most expensive museums in the world to build, it's free for visitors. Even the $15 parking is a steal by LA standards (if you park in the residential areas you can just walk up to avoid the parking fee). Get in early, get a parking spot, and ride that tram up the hill to one of the most gorgeous places in Southern California. You don't even need to see one piece of official art to be blown away.

Designed by Richard Meier, the J. Paul Getty Center is a multi-sensory experience. From the building's amazing architecture to the Robert Irwin garden, which demands but afternoon stroll (or better yet, joining on one of the docent-led tours), the place is a work of art in itself.

Hip programs such as "Saturday Nights at the Getty" offer coolly eclectic music, readings, and screenings. Again, all of which are free. So what are you waiting for?

What to See

Oh, and there's art, too. The original Getty Museum began as a place for oilman J. Paul Getty to hang his large collection of art. Most art critics agree that although Getty's collecting habits proved prolific, his purchases were somewhat naïve. Though he never lived to see the museum's current incarnation, he left behind a staggering trust fund that has allowed the Getty to aggressively add to the collection over the years. The permanent collection includes several Van Goghs, among them the Getty's highest-profile acquisition, *Irises*. There are also Rembrandts, Cézannes, and a rare collaboration between Rubens and Brueghel. In addition to the mostly pre-20th-century paintings, the Getty boasts an impressive collection of photography from the late 1830s to the present. The ever-changing special exhibitions are a highlight of any visit to the Getty Center.

It may be impossible to see the entire collection in one visit—three hours is the absolute minimum you should plan on spending at the museum—and then there is the rest of the Getty Center. The Central Garden designed by Robert Irwin is intended to be (and most definitely is) a work of art on its own. The garden's benches and chairs invite visitors to relax and enjoy the view, which includes the entire Santa Monica Bay. Pay attention to the sound of the stream; Irwin placed rocks from different parts of the world to create different sounds as you descend into the garden. Meier's building design is also worth much more than a cursory look. The travertine marble used in the construction comes from the same source as that used to build the Coliseum in Rome and, if you look closely, you can sometimes spot fossils trapped inside the stone. Both highly trained aesthetes and novice admirers of beauty and design will notice and appreciate the sparseness and order of Meier's main buildings in contrast with Irwin's controlled chaos in the garden, which he re-landscapes seasonally.

If you can score yourself a library card to the research library (good luck!), you'll have access to one of the most amazing libraries in Los Angeles—from old optical toys like kaleidoscopes to Allan Kaprow's writings. There's an eclectic array of magical things here.

Where to Eat

The remote location means that you're basically limited to the Getty Center's dining facilities, but luckily the options here are many and all quite good. At the high end, The Restaurant is open for lunch every day and serves dinner from 5 pm until 9 pm on Saturdays. Their menu is market-driven, so it changes frequently and serves healthy, California-style fare. Reservations are suggested and can be made online or by calling 310-440-6810. Same-day reservations are sometimes available through the Visitor Information Desk.

The Café is run by the same management as The Restaurant, making the same high-quality food available in a more casual self-service setting. The Café is open Tuesday—Friday from 11:30 am to 3 pm, Saturdays 11:30 am to 6 pm, and Sundays from 11:30 am to 3:30 pm. Additionally, the Garden Terrace Café is a seasonal self-serve dining facility that overlooks the Central Garden.

There are also several coffee carts around the complex that carry lunch items and snacks. Should you opt to brown-bag it, a picnic area is located at the lower tram station and is open until 30 minutes before closing time.

How to Get There—Driving

Since local streets are often blocked, the best way to get to the Getty is to make your way to the 405 and exit at Getty Center Drive. Follow the signs into the parking garage. Parking is $15, but students with ID park for free. Elevators for the parking garage are all color-coded, making it easy to remember where you've parked. Bonus points for Al Gore-lovin' hybrid drivers: The Getty now has plug-ins for electric cars, so you can juice up your ride while checking out the art.

Once you park your car, you have two options for getting to the Getty Center. You can take the tram, which runs frequently, or you can walk to the top of the hill. Bear in mind that the walk is about a mile and at a very steep incline.

How to Get There—Mass Transit

MTA Bus 761 will drop you off right at the Getty's entrance on Sepulveda Boulevard.

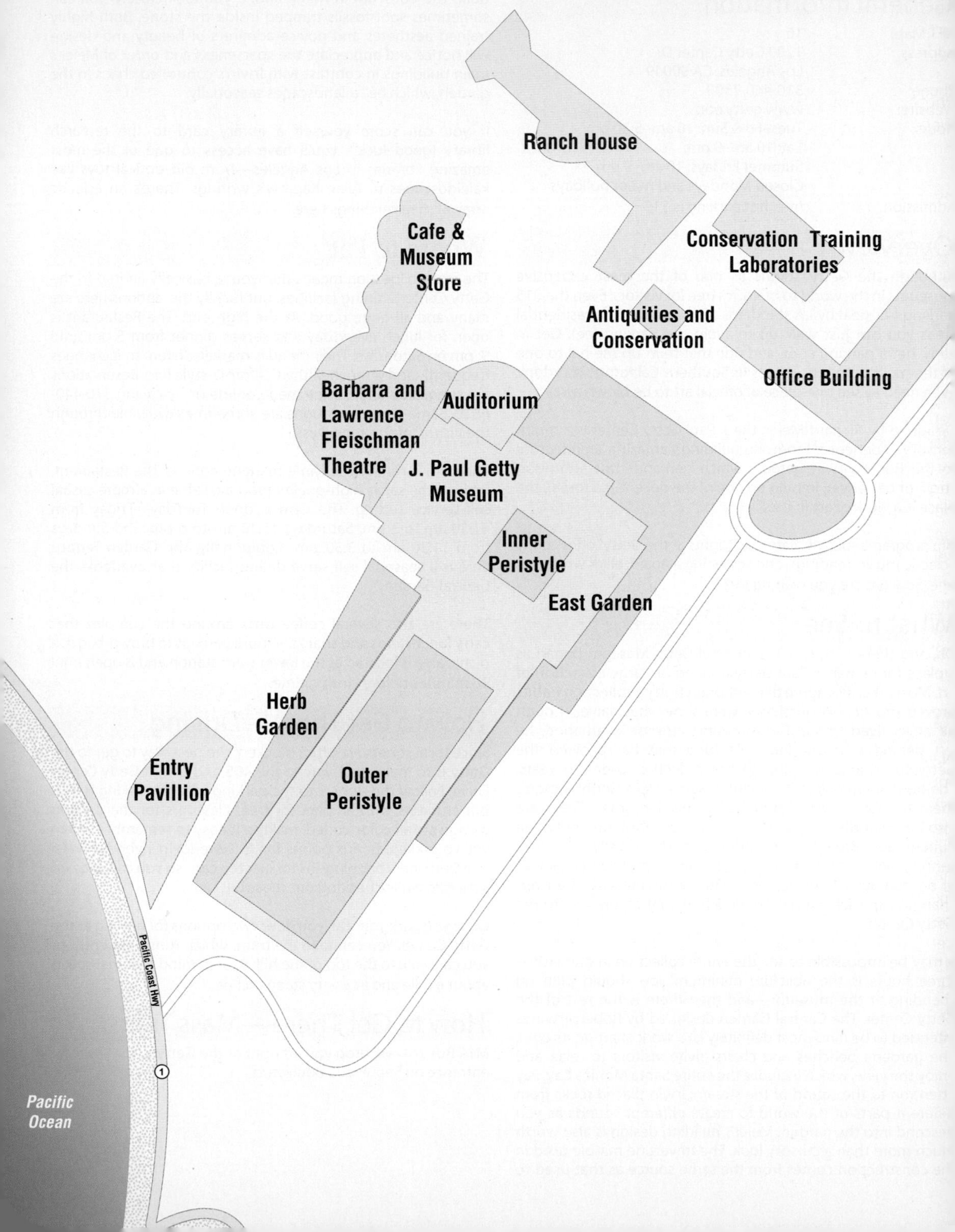
Ranch House
Cafe &
Museum
Store
Conservation Training
Laboratories
Antiquities and
Conservation
Office Building
Barbara and
Lawrence
Fleischman
Theatre
Auditorium
J. Paul Getty
Museum
Inner
Peristyle
East Garden
Herb
Garden
Entry
Pavillion
Outer
Peristyle
Pacific Coast Hwy
1
Pacific
Ocean

General Information

NFT Map:	15
Address:	17985 Pacific Coast Hwy Pacific Palisades, CA 90272
Phone:	310-440-7300
Website:	www.getty.edu
Hours:	Wed–Mon 10 am–5 pm Closed Tuesdays and major holidays.
Admission:	Free (advanced, timed tickets required); Parking is $15, or $10 after 5 pm for any evening programs.

Overview

Here's some rare truth in advertising. The Getty Villa actually feels like a real villa. Built in the '70s, it was the home of the J. Paul Getty Museum before it made its jump to the hilltop structure off the 405. After some remodeling, it's a it was transformed into a vivid reproduction of the 1st-century Villa del Papiri at Herculaneum in Italy. That means the main building surrounds a massive reflecting pool–filled peristyle (essentially a fancy courtyard with kick-ass columns; don't worry, we had to look it up too), with gorgeous gardens and plenty of places to take a nice stroll. Inside said column-lined buildings there's art from ancient Greece, Rome, and Etruria. An outdoor café and grassy areas that are just begging for a picnic or some lounging add to the whole leisurely Roman vibe. It's almost like you're part of the ruling empire all over again. Just don't get too comfy; we all know what happened to them.

What to See

Naked statues with broken arms, of course. Okay, and much more. The Villa is home to nearly 44,000 antiquities with about 1,200 on display at any time. Beyond the permanent collections, which are arranged by theme to better communicate their history, the Villa's exhibitions have included studies of glassmaking and architecture. Exhibitions are complemented by play readings, musical performances, demos, and other programs in a 250-seat auditorium or the old-school-like-a-Socratic-fool 450-seat outdoor classical theater. You don't have to be classically inclined to drop some cash in the gift shop, which sells everything from 24k gold replicas of Roman jewelry to full gladiator getup for the 10-and-under set.

Where to Eat

Naturally, the Café at the Getty Villa specializes in Mediterranean fare: panini, pizzas, pastas, you know the drill. It's open from 11 am to 3 pm on weekdays and 11 am to 4 pm on Saturday and Sunday.

If you just need a little nosh, the Espresso Cart near the Café entrance serves up coffee, cold drinks, and quicker food such as sandwiches and to-go salads. Why not get the most out of the great weather? See the Getty website for more information.

How to Get There—Driving

Sorry, you're going to have to fight your way down the Pacific Coast Highway for this one. Even trickier, you can only enter the Getty Villa by going northbound and being in the right-hand lane of PCH. Just hang on tight and make the turn into the Getty's parking lot (if you turn into the ocean, you went the wrong way). After that, the on-site parking structure is a snap.

How to Get There—Mass Transit

Los Angeles Metro Bus 534 stops near the Getty Villa entrance on Pacific Coast Highway. Potential Villa visitors should know that walk-ups are not permitted, and if you do take the bus, you must have your ticket to the Getty Villa hole-punched by the driver in order to be admitted. We're not sure how stringent they are about this policy...but don't say we didn't warn you.

General Information

NFT Map: 4
Address 2700 N Vermont Ave
(in Griffith Park)
Los Angeles, CA 90027
Hotline: 323-665-1927
Administration: 323-665-5857
Ticketmaster: 213-480-3232
Website: www.greektheatrela.com

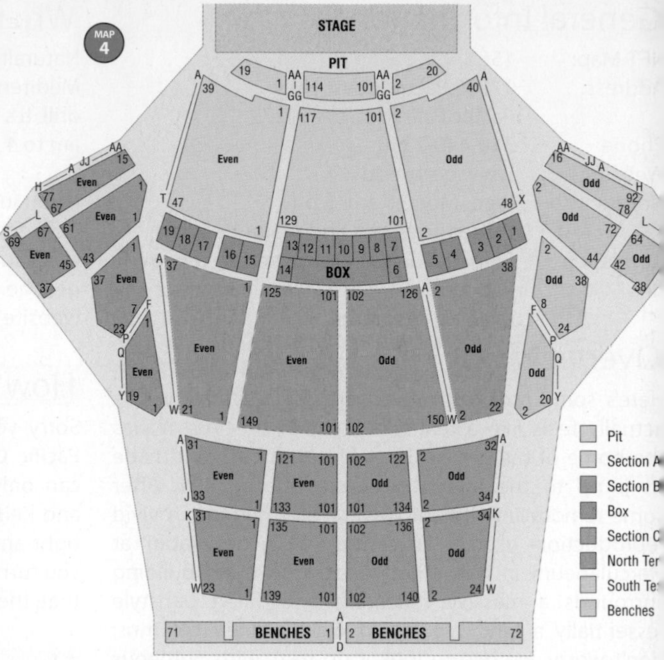

Overview

While the Hollywood Bowl will always be LA's premier outdoor venue, the Greek Theatre is a close second, thanks largely to its gorgeous location. The Greek still leans heavily on safe nostalgia acts, but in recent years, it's booked more music that those under 30 can appreciate without irony. Tom Jones still plays here, but so do the Flaming Lips, the Yeah Yeah Yeahs, and others who aren't pulling down Social Security.

Nestled up in Griffith Park, this sylvan amphitheater always feels cooler and less smoggy than the rest of the city. The Greek Theatre is about a third of the size of the Bowl, and twice as bucolic. If the weather's right, the sky can be so clear that you might actually be able to impress your date by pointing out Orion and Polaris—forgetting that you're in LA all together. No wonder the Coachella set is getting hip to the place. The Arcade Fire, Radiohead, Death Cab for Cutie, even Ashlee Simpson have all decided to go Greek during recent tours. None have trashed the place—yet.

How to Get There—Driving

From the 10, exit at Vermont and drive north to Griffith Park. From the 101 heading north, exit at Vermont Avenue. Turn right onto Vermont and follow it into Griffith Park. From the 101 heading south, exit at Vine Street. Go straight under the underpass, and you will be going east on Franklin Avenue. When you reach Western Avenue, turn left. Western will curve to the right and turn into Los Feliz Boulevard. Turn left at Vermont, and follow it into Griffith Park.

Parking

$15 at the Greek Theatre will buy you the stacked parking option (read: you can't leave until everyone arounc you does). For $50 you can get valet, allowing you tc leave whenever the heck you want. Call 323-665-585 to make advance reservations 10 am to 6 am Monday through Friday. The Greek has also partnered up witl several Los Feliz restaurants to offer "Dine and Ride, which offers concert-goers parking, dinner, and a shuttle to the show for around $55. Check out the dining options and availability at www.dineandride.com. If you're really sly, you can score parallel parking along the many side roads around the Greek. This option costs $10 anc you can leave whenever you want. Free shuttles will take you from your parking spot to the venue. If you're making a date of it and you're game for a stroll, parking o lively, venue-packed Hillhurst is also an option.

How to Get Tickets

The Greek Theatre's box office only sells tickets ir person. They are open Mon-Fri, 12 pm to 6 pm, Saturday 10 am to 4 pm, and are closed on Sunday. Tickets to a events are also available through Ticketmaster: www ticketmaster.com, 800-745-3000.

General Information

NFT Map:	3
Address:	2301 N Highland Ave Hollywood, CA 90068
General Information:	323-850-2000
Website:	www.hollywoodbowl.com
Ticketmaster:	213-480-3232

Overview

You know the final scene in *Beaches*, where the divine Miss M sings *Wind Beneath My Wings* in that amazingly panoramic concert setting with impeccable acoustics? Yup, that's the Hollywood Bowl. This historic and beloved concert venue is another wonder of that sweet Hollywood magic. It's mere yards away from the 101 freeway, yet it feels like another world. Pack up your own food (and booze) take the hike up to the amphitheater seats, and soak up the sounds of Beethoven, something tasty from the Playboy Jazz Festival, or—if you prefer the hipper route—a mature mash-up such as The Decemberists with the Los Angeles Philharmonic.

The bowl originally opened in 1922, although its signature "shell" recently endured a much-needed face-lift and debuted with improved acoustics in 2004. The official season runs from June through mid-September when fireworks light up the weekend and some twists on classical tunes (how about Bugs Bunny on Broadway?) make it a welcome event even for the uninitiated. In other words, it's the place to bring anyone you want to impress—from your parents to that special someone. The program is varied and less expensive than you might think. So much so, it's almost amazing how many Angelenos *haven't* been to the Bowl. Don't let yourself be one of them.

How to Get There—Driving

The Hollywood Bowl is located on Highland Avenue, just north of Franklin Avenue. From the 10, exit at La Brea, and drive north. Turn right at Franklin Avenue, and head east until you reach Highland Avenue. Make a left turn, and the Bowl will be just ahead on your left. From the 101, exit at Highland Avenue and follow the signs to the Bowl.

Parking

There are a stingy 2,800 on-site parking spaces for an 18,000-seat amphitheater. If that doesn't stop you from wanting to park, you have to deal with pricey stacked parking lots operated by the Bowl. Parking rates range from $17 to $35. There are many privately run lots open for business when there's a concert, but skip those rip-offs. The way to do it is by parking at the Hollywood & Highland lot, validating your ticket at mall customer service (or picking up a quick snack), and walking up the hill with your picnic basket. You definitely won't be alone. It's cheaper, less difficult for the return trip home, and besides, a little exercise never killed anyone.

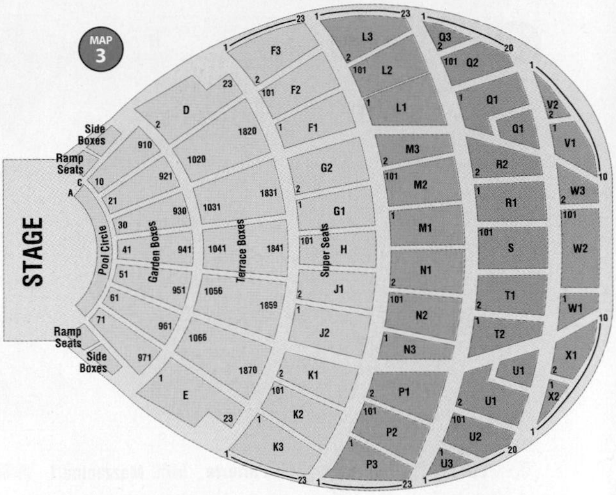

How to Get There—Mass Transit

The Park & Ride service, available for all "LA Phil Presents" concerts, lets you park at one of 14 lots around town and ride a shuttle to the Bowl for $5, round-trip (when purchased in advance; on-board purchases cost $10). The Bowl Shuttle service offers free parking at four different locations and a $5 round-trip shuttle every 15 minutes or so starting 2.5 hours before show time. For Park & Ride and Bowl Shuttle information, visit the "Getting to the Bowl" section of www.metro.net.

The MTA Hollywood Bowl Shuttle (line 163) offers non-stop service to and from the Bowl when there's a concert. Catch the bus at Hollywood and Argyle, steps away from the Hollywood/Vine Metro Rail Red Line stop. The shuttle is free with a round-trip Metro Rail ticket. You can also take the 156 bus from the San Fernando Valley or downtown. 800-266-6883; visit www.mta.net.

Where to Eat

Fill your basket with Trader Joe's Camembert, dry salami, and a bottle of two-buck-Chuck and join the thousands munching *en plein air* before the concert. Picnic areas open up to four hours before the concert, and tables are first come-first serve. If DIY is not your thing, the Hollywood Bowl offers a variety of overpriced dining choices, all owned and operated by Patina at the Bowl, part of chef Joachim Splichal's catering and restaurant empire. Whether it's lobster and Veuve Clicquot at the exclusive Pool Circle or popcorn from a concession stand, you will find something to simultaneously ease your hunger pangs and the weight of your wallet. The Rooftop Grill offers sit-down service pre-concert, and the two Marketplace outlets sell sushi and other foodie nibbles to go.

Tickets

Subscription series go on sale earlier than individual seats for all "LA Phil Presents" concerts, and subscribers can add individual tickets to their orders before the general public. Individual tickets go on sale in May. Prices in those coveted box seats can approach $100 per person most nights, but the Bowl still offers their famous $1 seats for many concerts. Call the box office at 323-850-2000 or visit www.hollywoodbowl.com. Tickets are also available through Ticketmaster.

MAP 3

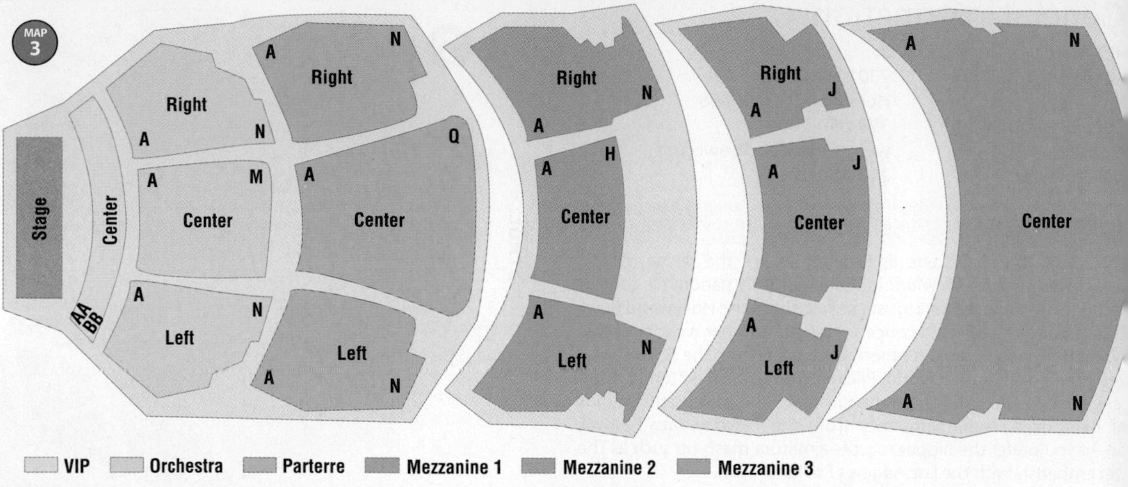

General Information

NFT Map:	3
Address:	6801 Hollywood Blvd Hollywood, CA 90028
Box Office:	323-308-6300
Ticketmaster:	213-480-3232
Website:	www.dolbytheatre.com

Overview

The Dolby Theatre (formerly the Kodak Theatre) hosts two of Hollywood's most important events: the Academy Awards and the American Idol finale. It's location right in the heart of the Hollywood & Highland entertainment complex means that visitors can also engage in another quintessential LA activity: shopping.

Not everything that takes place on its hallowed stage is Oscar-worthy. Kathy Griffin regularly slags on Hollywood phonies in her one-woman shows, and Sesame Street Live is a more typical Dolby attraction. But that's Hollywood for ya—sometimes you get an Oscar, and sometimes you get Elmo.

Drawbacks that lessen the venue's cred include seats in the upper levels (the only ones that you can usually afford) raked at an alarmingly high angle and the fact that the red carpet for the Academy Awards actually rolls out through a mall. Those looking for some Hollywood magic are advised to shell out the money for a guided tour (adults $17, students & seniors $12).

The good news? The Hollywood & Highland entertainment complex, which houses the Dolby, is slowly improving with more shops and eateries like the ubiquitous California Pizza Kitchen. And if you want to balance a night of theater with a little trashiness, there's always Hooters across the street.

How to Get There—Driving

The Dolby Theatre is part of the Hollywood & Highland complex, found—*surprise!*—at the corner of Hollywood & Highland. From most parts of Los Angeles, the easiest way to reach this behemoth is via the 101 Freeway. Avoid the Highland Avenue exit if you can—it's always congested. Try the Cahuenga exit and head west on Hollywood Blvd, followed by a right onto Highland. Enter the parking garage via Highland next to the Renaissance Hollywood Hotel. From the south you may want to avoid significant traffic by taking the 10 to La Brea Avenue and heading north. Take La Brea all the way up to Franklin Avenue and turn right, then make another right onto Highland Avenue. Drive south until you reach the entrance for the parking garage.

Parking

The closest parking facility for the Dolby is the Hollywood & Highland parking garage. Escalators from said garage will deliver you virtually to the Dolby Theatre's doorstep and any merchant in the mall will validate your parking, making it a bargain at just $2 for two hours. (Valet parking is also available for an additional $6.) The parking garage is undoubtedly your best bet, as long as you don't forget to get validated and you don't mind the deep, cavernous, and impossibly designed structure.

If you've got a little extra time, however, there are several lots that can be entered from Hollywood Boulevard that cater to the tourists who have come to see the Walk of Fame. Rates vary and tend to get more expensive as night falls and nightclub-bers come out to play.

How to Get There—Mass Transit

The Metro Red Line stops at the Hollywood/Highland Station. This may actually be the easiest option for people coming from the Valley, especially when Highland Avenue backs up during Hollywood Bowl season. The 156, 212, 217, 312, and 717 buses also stop in the immediate vicinity of the Dolby. Once there, the convenient Holly Trolley can shuttle you around Hollywood between Highland and Vine for a mere dollar (free for LADOT Pass Holders).

How to Get Tickets

The box office at the Dolby Theatre, located on level one of the Hollywood & Highland center, is open Monday through Saturday from 10 am to 6 pm, and on Sundays from 10 am until 4 pm. Tickets are also available through Ticketmaster.

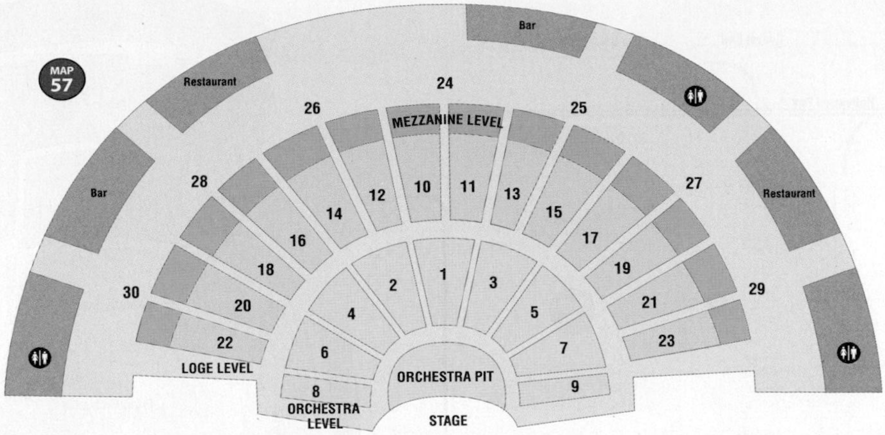

General Information

NFT Map:	57
Address:	100 Universal City Plz Universal City, CA 91608
Box Office:	818-622-4440
Ticketmaster:	213-252-8497
Website:	www.citywalkhollywood.com/concerts.php

Overview

You may not see it at first blush, but the lengthily titled Gibson Amphitheatre at Universal CityWalk has a pretty rich history. It was originally an outdoor stunt stage for Universal Studios, then it was turned into an outdoor amphitheater hosting the likes of the Grateful Dead and Frank Sinatra before getting a roof in 1982, then a name change and new decor.

After all of that, the 6,000-seat Gibson stands as a medium-sized venue for medium-sized bands (either on their way to stardom or on their way, uh, down). In other words, this is the best place to catch everything from a packaged metal or reggaeton tour to any band that "VH1 Classic Presents" would get behind (think The O'Jays to Ringo Starr). The best thing about the place? Location, location, location. The adjoining Universal CityWalk is bigger than ever, offering plenty of places to eat and drink beforehand, making that whole dinner-and-a-show thing all the easier.

How to Get There—Driving

The Gibson Amphitheatre is located right outside the gates of the Universal Studios Hollywood theme park, just off the 101 Freeway. If you are coming from the north, take the 101 S and exit at Lankershim Boulevard. Turn left onto Cahuenga Boulevard and make a left onto Universal Center Drive. From there, head up the hill to the parking facilities. From the south, take the 101 N and exit at Universal Center Drive. Turn right at the first traffic light and drive up the hill to the parking facilities.

Parking

General parking at Universal CityWalk is $15 before 3 pm and $10 thereafter, while preferred parking ranges from $20-$25. Validated valet parking costs $3 for the first hour, $8 for the first 90 minutes, and $3 per half hour thereafter. Without validation, valet parking is $14 for the first half hour and $3 for each half hour after that. Restaurants at Universal CityWalk provide validation for parking, but concession stands inside the Amphitheatre do not. Or, park for free at the Kiss & Ride lot adjacent to the Metro Red Line. Walk across the street from the subway station and get on the free shuttle up the hill to CityWalk, the theme park and Amphitheatre. Make sure to note what time the last shuttle leaves!

How to Get There—Mass Transit

The Universal City Metro Red Line stop is located just across Lankershim Boulevard from the Universal Studios entrance. If you cross the street from the subway station, the free shuttle mentioned above will take you up the hill to CityWalk, the theme park and Amphitheatre.

MTA buses 96, 150, 152, 156, 166, 240, and 750 also run to the Universal City Station.

How to Get Tickets

You can call the box office hotline at 818-622-4440 to hear what shows are playing. Tickets for most events are available through Ticketmaster, the Gibson Amphitheatre Main box office, or the CityWalk box office. The Gibson box office is open Thurs-Mon, 1 pm to 9pm and is closed Tues-Wed. The Universal CityWalk box office is open Sun-Thurs, 1 pm to 8:45 pm and Fri-Sat, from 1 pm to 10:30 pm.

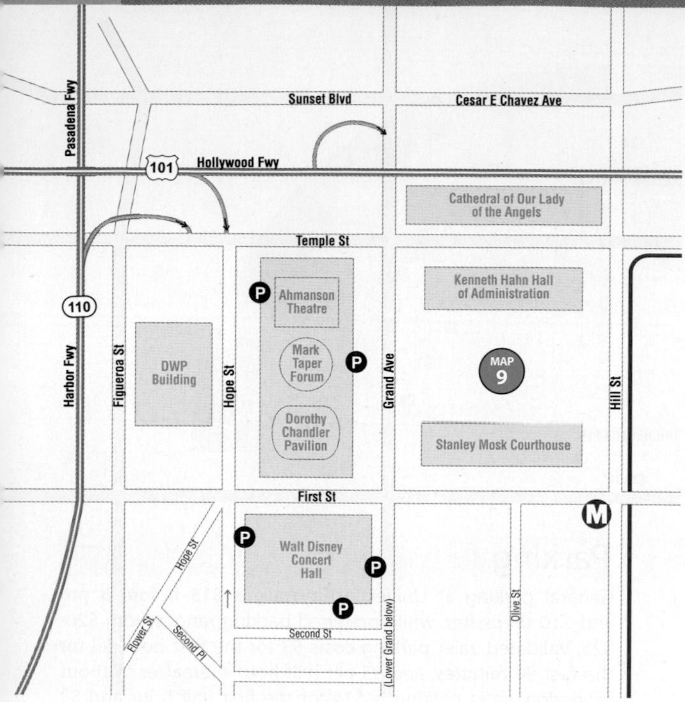

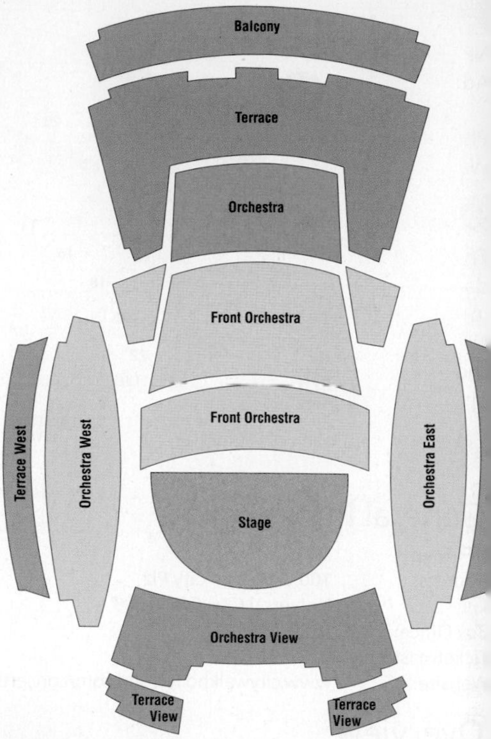

Walt Disney Concert Hall

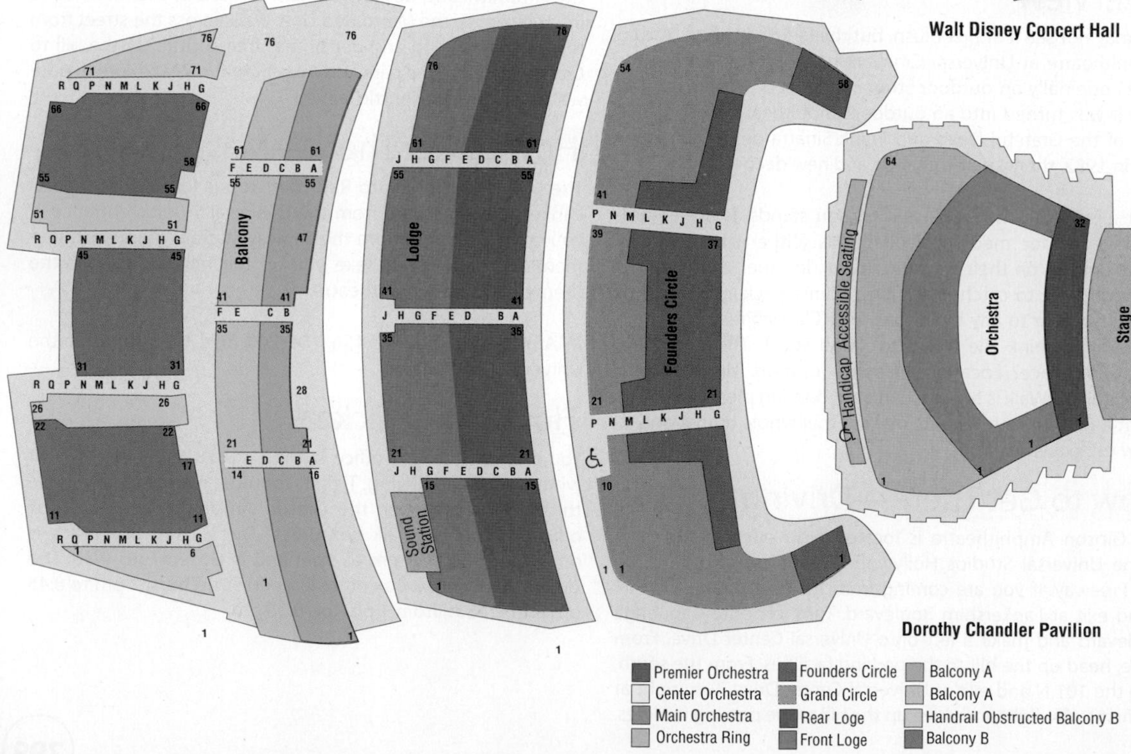

Dorothy Chandler Pavilion

General Information

NFT Map: 9
Address: 135 N Grand Ave
Los Angeles, CA 90012
Phone: 213-972-7211
Website: www.musiccenter.org

Overview

The Music Center brings world-renowned actors, dancers, and classical musicians to its four main venues in downtown LA. Whether it's a classic production of La Bohème or a new composition by John Adams, the Music Center's resident companies add much-appreciated artistic gravitas to the city.

Walt Disney Concert Hall

The curving stainless-steel exterior of Frank Gehry's Walt Disney Concert Hall, erected October 2003, is now an iconic Southland image. The Los Angeles Philharmonic, infused with new energy by its young music director Gustavo Dudamel, routinely sells out the house. Catching a concert in the state-of-the-art auditorium is something everyone in LA should experience at least once. Steep tickets prices are a paltry excuse: $17 can buy you a seat in the choral bench section, where you can look over the musicians' shoulders and follow along with their scores. These cheap seats are available by phone or at the Grand Avenue box office starting at noon on the Tuesday two weeks before the week of the concert. They sell out within 30 minutes and are not available for all performances. For more information on the Los Angeles Philharmonic and Walt Disney Concert Hall, including schedules and tickets, visit www.laphil.com, or call 323-850-2000.

Under the baton of musical director Grant Gershon, the Grammy-nominated Los Angeles Master Chorale sings everything from avant-garde opera such as 2007's wildly popular, multimedia "Tristan Project," to Handel's Messiah (yes, you can sing along) in a hall that gives new meaning to "surround sound." $10 Student Rush seats (obstructed view) are available to students with valid ID at the box office two hours before every performance on a cash-only, one-ticket-per-person basis. For Master Chorale schedules and tickets, visit www.lamc.org, or call 213-972-7282.

REDCAT

Short for the Roy and Edna Disney/CalArts Theater & Gallery, REDCAT is a slick black-box theater and art gallery operated by the California Institute of the Arts. REDCAT boasts an impressively diverse season of live performances and films highlighting innovative up-and-comers and cutting-edge performance artists from around the world. $10 Student Rush tickets are available at the box office 30 minutes before most performances on a cash-only, one-per-person (with ID) basis. The lobby houses a nice café/bookstore as well as an open gallery space that shows a range of innovative installations. For REDCAT schedules and tickets, visit www.redcat.org, or call 213-237-2800.

Dorothy Chandler Pavilion

The 3,197-seat Chandler, located on the southern end of the Music Center plaza, is home to the Los Angeles Opera and Music Center Dance programs. LA Operà, led by Plácido Domingo and music director James Conlon, presents greatest hits, new works, and intimate vocal recitals with stars like Renée Fleming. $25 Student and half-price Senior Rush Tickets go on sale from 10–Noon for matinees and 4-6 pm for evening performances on a cash-only, one-per-person basis (with valid ID only). Visit www.laopera.com, or call 213-972-8001 for LA Opera tickets and schedules. The company drew international attention in 2010 when it mounted an innovative production of Wagner's Ring cycle.

Dance at the Music Center is the organization responsible for bringing famed troupes such as the Alvin Ailey American Dance Theater and the American Ballet Theatre to the Chandler's stage. Student and Senior Rush Tickets priced $10–$15 are available at the Chandler box office two hours prior to curtain on a cash-only, one-per-person basis (with valid ID only). For more information, visit www.musiccenter.org, or call 213-972-0711.

Mark Taper Forum & Ahmanson Theatre

Center Theatre Group produces high-profile musicals, dramas, and comedies on the stages of the Mark Taper Forum and Ahmanson Theatre, most of which are on their way to or from Broadway. Purchase tickets for either venue at the Ahmanson's box office, located on the north end of the Music Center plaza, or buy online. $12 rush tickets (balcony level) are available two hours before most performances on a cash-only, two-per-

person basis. The Hot Tix! discount offers a certain percentage of tickets to each show for only $20. For more information on Center Theatre Group, including schedules and tickets, visit www.centertheatregroup.org or call 213-628-2772. Non-affiliated, half-priced ticket consolidators abound, too. Check out Plays411.com or LAStageTix.com for discounts.

Where to Eat/Shop

The Patina Group operates all Music Center restaurants and concessions. Kendall's Brasserie & Bar, located on N Grand Avenue under the Chandler, has an impressive selection of imported beers and tasty French fare. Both the casual grab-and go Spotlight Café and the sit-down burger spot Pinot Grill are centrally located between the Dorothy Chandler Pavilion and the Mark Taper Forum. Across First Street, the Walt Disney Concert Hall has a ho-hum sandwich shop in the lobby, so instead we recommend visitors try the wonderfully inventive and delicious meals prepared by super chef Joachim Splichal's fine-dining flagship, Patina. For more information on Patina's restaurants, visit www.patinagroup.com. REDCAT's minimal-yet-cozy Lounge is independently operated and serves snacks, coffee drinks, and cocktails.

The LA Phil Store is located in the Walt Disney Concert Hall lobby and sells gifts for music aficionados and architecture buffs, including T-shirts, jewelry, music recordings, and books. REDCAT, too, has a tiny giftshop specializing in art theory and biographies.

How To Get There—Driving

The Music Center is located in downtown Los Angeles near the intersection of the 110 and the 101 freeways.

Chandler/Ahmanson/Taper (135 N Grand Ave)
110 N and 110 S: Exit Temple, turn left on Temple, right on Grand, then turn right into the Music Center garage.

101 N: Exit at Grand, turn right on Grand, and turn right into the Music Center garage.

101 S: Exit on Temple, turn left on Temple, right on Grand, and turn right into the Music Center garage.

Walt Disney Concert Hall (111 S Grand Ave)
From 110 N: Exit on Fourth, continue straight, turn left on lower Grand, pass Kosciuszko, and turn left into the WDCH parking garage.

From 110 S: Exit at Hill, continue past Temple, turn right on First, left on Olive, right on Kosciuszko, right on lower Grand, and left into the WDCH parking garage.

From 101 N: Exit on Grand before the 110 interchange, turn right on Grand, right on Second, and right into the WDCH parking garage.

From 101 S: Exit at Temple, go straight onto Hope, turn left at Second Place, merge onto Kosciuszko from the middle lane, turn left on lower Grand, and turn left into the WDCH parking garage.

Parking

For self-parking at the Chandler, Ahmanson, or Taper, use the Music Center garage located on Grand Avenue between Temple and 1st Streets. Daytime parking costs $3.50 for every 15 minutes with a $20 maximum, while the evening/event rate (after 4:30 pm for evening performances, two hours prior to matinee performances, and weekends all day) costs $9. Valet parking is available on Hope Street for $23.

The parking area located directly beneath WDCH has two entrances; one on 2nd Street and one on lower Grand Avenue. Valet parking is available on Hope Street for $23.

If you're buying or picking up tickets for any venue, the box office will validate for 30 minutes of free parking.

Additional parking options are within walking distance. County Lot 17 on Olive Street has parking for $8, DWP charges $5 (enter on Hope Street or 1st Street), or cruise through County Mall Parking VIP-style, with their underground tunnel to the Music Center Garage (enter on Grand Avenue) for $8.

How To Get There—Mass Transit

The Metro Red Line stops at the Civic Center/Tom Bradley Station at First & Hill Streets, two blocks east of the Music Center. Metro Blue, Green, and Gold Lines connect with the Red Line.

Many bus lines stop near the center—consult the service providers listed below for routes and schedules.

MTA: 800-266-6883, www.metro.net
Foothill Transit: 800-743-3463, www.foothilltransit.org
Metrolink: 800-371-5465, www.metrolinktrains.com
Big Blue Bus: 310-451-5444, www.bigbluebus.com

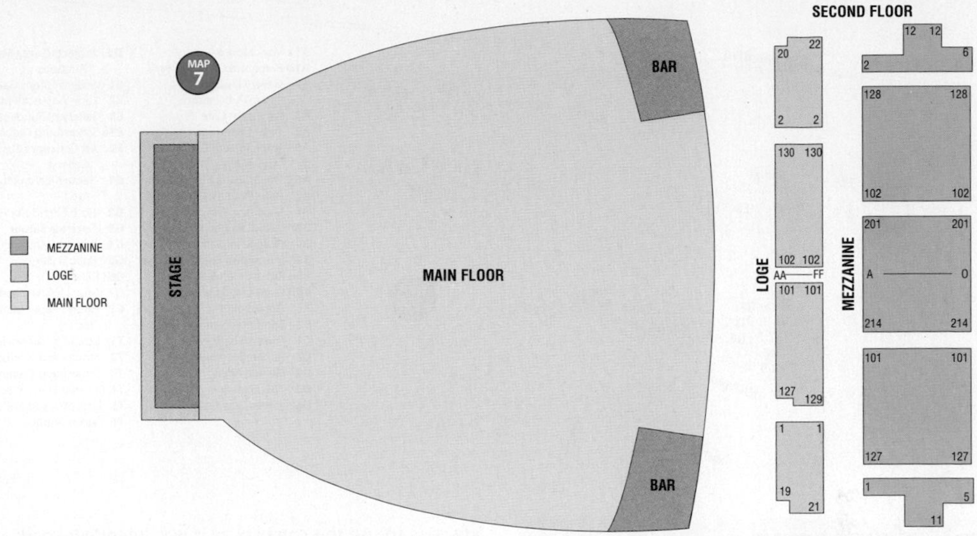

General Information

NFT Map:	7
Address:	3790 Wilshire Blvd Los Angeles, CA 90010
Phone:	213-388-1400
Box Office:	213-380-5005
Ticketmaster:	213-480-3232
Website:	www.livenation.comvenues/14361/ the-wiltern

Overview

The Wiltern is undeniably one of LA's most beloved landmarks, with its trademark blue neon sign and imposing marquee watching over Wilshire Boulevard. With its omnipresent line snaked around the building, the Wiltern looks like the hottest concert venue in town. A $1.5 million renovation in 2002 knocked out the lower level's 1,200 permanent seats to make room for a first-come, first-served general admission area. So when Death Cab for Cutie or Feist come to town, you can guarantee every indie-loving teenager from LA to the OC will be lined up for that prime pit spot. Don't worry, there is permanent seating available in the balcony for those who prefer to rock from their chairs.

The building's Art Deco architecture is so snazzy that the place was declared an official City of Los Angeles Historic-Cultural Monument, and its moderate size makes it a great place to catch a band before they hit arena status. As the Wiltern is located in the heart of K-town, you can follow up that perfect Black Keys show with some delicious Korean barbeque and raucous karaoke.

How to Get There—Driving

Any number of east-west streets will take you to Western Avenue. The Wiltern is at the corner of Western and Wilshire. From the 10, exit at Western Avenue and drive north until you reach Wilshire Boulevard. The venue will be on your right. From the 101, use the Santa Monica Boulevard/Western Avenue exit and take Western south to Wilshire.

Parking

There are a number of parking lots in the area and limited street parking on and around Wilshire Boulevard. A large parking structure is available right behind the theater, which can be accessed from Oxford or Western. Lots generally charge between $8 and $20.

How to Get There—Mass Transit

The Metro Red Line is a convenient and inexpensive way to reach the Wiltern and avoid paying for parking. The Wilshire/Western station is just across Wilshire from the theatre. A number of buses also access the Wiltern. Bus 720 runs along Wilshire Boulevard, while buses 207 and 357 run on Western Avenue. Routes 18 and 209 also stop near the theater.

How to Get Tickets

Buy tickets online or by phone through Ticketmaster. Or, skip the exorbitant fees and go straight to the box office—it's open three hours prior to showtimes.

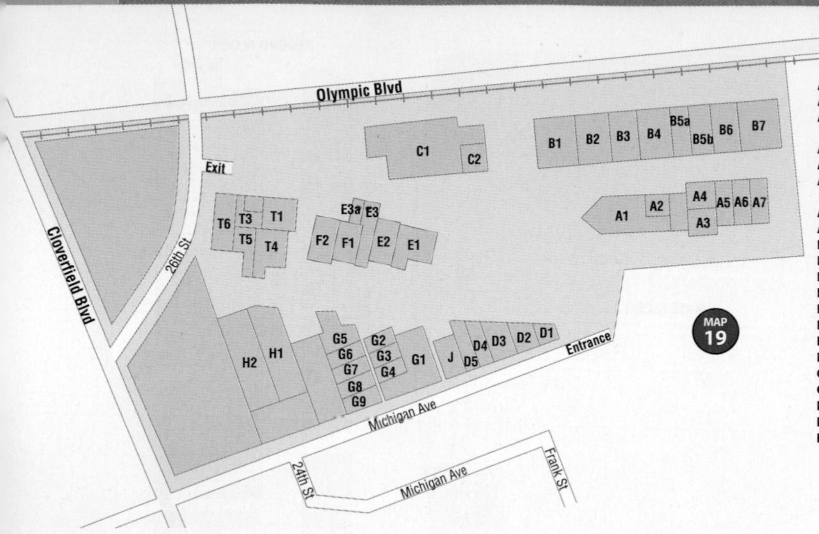

A1a Mark Moore Gallery
A1b Bergamot Café Gallery
A2 Gallery Luisotti/ Ram Publications
A3 Bergamot Cafe
A4 Peter Fetterman Gallery
A5 Frank Picture Gallery at OFF MAIN
A6 The Sculpture Foundation
A7 Peter Fetterman Gallery
B1 Shoshana Wayne Gallery
B2 Patrick Painter Inc.
B3 Craig Krull Gallery
B4 Rosamund Felsen Gallery
B5a Richard Heller Gallery
B5b Frank Lloyd Gallery
B6 Greenfield Sacks Gallery
B7 Samuel Freeman Gallery
C1 Track 16 Gallery
C2 Robert Berman Gallery
D2 Galerie Anais
D3 TAG Gallery
D4 James Gray Gallery
D5 Projects/Santa Monica Auctions
E1 William Turner Gallery
E2 Latin American Masters
E3 Gallery of Functional Art
E3a Schomburg Gallery
F2 Art Concepts Custom Framing Gallery
G1 Santa Monica Museum of Art
G2 Ruth Bachnofer Gallery
G3 Suzanne Felsen
G4 Ikon Ltd/Kay Richards
G5 Rose Gallery
G6 F.I.G.
G7 Grey McGear Modern, Inc.
G8 Hiromi Paper International Inc
T1 Sarah Lee Artworks & Projects
T2 Tamburello Productions
T3 Schlesinger Gallery
T4 Montalba Architects, Inc.
T5 Lopro/Nason Gallery
T6 Sulkin Studio

General Information

NFT Map:	19
Address:	2525 Michigan Ave Santa Monica, CA 90404
Bergamot Website:	www.bergamotstation.com
Hours:	Tues-Fri: 10 am—6pm, Sat: 11 am—5:30 pm, Closed Sun & Mon
Admission:	Free

Overview

Though one of the older fixtures of contemporary art in Los Angeles, Bergamot Station is still its own little "art walk" offering an interesting one-stop artistic experience. Originally a stop on the now nonexistent Red Car trolley system in the early twentieth century. Bergamot Station spent most of the last fifty years in a variety of incarnations from celery-packing facility to ice-making plant. After it was abandoned, the City of Santa Monica wisely saw the area's potential and asked developer Wayne Black to find an artistic use for the property. Boy, did he. By 1994, Bergamot Station was up and running as the largest art gallery complex and cultural center in Southern California. It now stands as eight acres of ideas, hopes, inspiration, and gratis wine and cheese (when you pop in for one of the many openings, that is).

What to See

Bergamot Station is home to almost forty galleries, each with its own personality. Rose Gallery deals in photographs and has shown a diverse line-up of artists from Manuel Alvarez Bravo to Wim Wenders. Patrick Painter, who shows Bas Jan Ader, is known for posthumously creating "new" works by deceased artists for profit's sake (undeniably unethical, but money does run the art-world). Track 16 focuses on modern and contemporary art and has featured artists like Karen Finley and Man Ray. The Gallery of Functional Art definitely shows art—but art that often doubles as furniture or lighting. Suzanne Felsen's unique jewelry is art by any definition of the word. One of the first Bergamot Galleries, the Shoshana Wayne Gallery, showcases artists such as Yoko Ono and Philip Argent. There is an eclectic variety to be seen at Bergamot Station and our advice is to use the complex as it was intended—park and stroll from one gallery to the next. If you keep a brisk pace, you can get through everything in an hour or two, but to get the most out of Bergamot Station, we would suggest spending an entire afternoon.

In addition to the galleries, Bergamot Station has several other tenants of note, including the Santa Monica Museum of Art. This non-collecting museum always features truly unique exhibits. Santa Monica Auctions features live art auctions of works by major artists. Hiromi Paper International is a retail shop that sells just one thing—paper. Hiromi's papers range from offbeat to exquisite, and most are so gorgeous that it would be a shame to write on them.

Where to Eat

Bergamot Café remains the complex's only option for breakfast or lunch. It's open Monday from 9 am until 4 pm, Tuesday through Friday from 9 am until 5 pm, and on Saturday from 10 am until 5 pm. They mainly serve sandwiches and salads. www.bergamotcafe.com. There are also some excellent restaurants in the area for a more leisurely lunch or a post-gallery dinner.

- **Il Moro**, 11400 W Olympic Blvd, 310-575-3530. Delicious pastas and Italian entrees.
- **LA Farm**, 3000 W Olympic Blvd, 310-449-4000. California-style cuisine in a beautiful patio setting.
- **Hop Li**, 11901 Santa Monica Blvd, 310-268-2463. Your favorite Chinese dishes, with an emphasis on fish and seafood.

How to Get There—Driving

Located on Michigan Avenue in Santa Monica, just east of Cloverfield Boulevard, Bergamot Station is easily accessed from the 10 by exiting at Cloverfield/26th Street. Turn right at the first traffic light, Michigan Avenue, and stay on Michigan until it dead ends. The entrance to Bergamot Station will be on your left.

If you're taking surface streets, Olympic Boulevard is usually the best bet. Take Olympic to Cloverfield and turn left, then turn left again on Michigan Avenue. Bergamot Station is at the end of the street on the left-hand side.

Los Angeles, the world's other film capital (we tip our hats to prolific Bollywood with awe and respect), is a movie-goer's paradise, offering a huge assortment of theaters playing old, new, revival foreign, indie, gay, and silent films (and, of course, the rare gay-foreign-silent trifecta). The sprawling range of genres and theaters that cater to the movie-obsessed ensures that whatever your passion, you're bound to find something in this town to sate your cinematic tastes.

Palaces

Once you make it past the costumed Jack Sparrow and Spider-Man, **Grauman's Chinese Theatre (Map 3)** really is a sight to be seen, having recently been remodeled and featuring state-of-the-art everything. The **ArcLight Hollywood (Map 3)** is civilized movie-going at its best with assigned seating, one of the best sound and picture systems in the world, and alcohol friendly 21-and-over screenings (but at a cost: $16 on Friday and Saturday nights; $13.75 otherwise). While the Hollywood location features the historic Cinerama Dome, ArcLight also has branches in Pasadena, Sherman Oaks, and El Segundo. **The Bridge: Cinema de Lux (Map 26)** offers similar amenities to the Arclight but on the Westside. **Pacific's The Grove Stadium 14 (Map 2)** is big on swank and style and the new **AMC Century 15 (Map 20)** is satisfyingly super-sized, though the Saturday-night crowds tend to be, as well. The **Vista Theatre (Map 4)** in Silver Lake has leg-room galore and a beautiful, if kitschy, Egyptian theme. The **AMC Magic Johnson Theatre 15 (Map 10)** in Baldwin Hills is also pleasingly palatial.

Jewel-Boxes

If you are of a certain age, it's possible that your love of film was born in a real theater—not at home in front of the VCR—watching something by Bergman, de Sica, or Renoir. If so, there are a handful of movie houses in LA where you can recapture some of that delicate, old-school thrill—regardless of what contemporary film might be playing. In this category we place **the Landmark Regent (Map 20)**, **NuArt (Map 19)**, and **Rialto (Map 34)** theatres. The **Laemmle Music Hall 3 (Map 6)** and **Royal (Map 19)** theaters, as well as the intimate **Aero Theater (Map 18)** in Santa Monica, are also excellent in that capacity. Many of these old theaters do not have parking lots, so give yourself extra time.

Shoe Boxes

At $10 or more per ticket, we felt it irresponsible not to mention that some theaters are inherently disappointing in their size or layout. We cast no aspersions on their programming (most of which is beyond reproach), but want you to be prepared for smallish screens and/or unusual spatial configurations at **Westside Pavilion Cinemas (Map 23)**, the **Five Star Theaters Los Feliz 3 (Map 4)**, and the **Loews Beverly Center 13 (Map 2)**.

Independent

Laemmle and Landmark theaters are located throughout the city and can be counted on to play the low-budget, independent, foreign, or controversial film that you've been waiting to see. The **Five Star Theaters Los Feliz 3 (Map 4)** on Vermont screens a nice mix of indie and big-budget pictures, with a Wednesday "Mommy and Me" matinee at 10:30 am.

Bargains

The **Academy 6 (Map 35)** in Pasadena gives you a second chance to see first-run films you missed a month or so ago, as well as independent/foreign films that you might not have seen at all—tickets are as low as $2 if you go before six o'clock. Seven dollars will buy you admission to a double feature of second-run movies at the somewhat sketchy **Vine Theatre (Map 3)** (enter at your own risk); the two films are often oddly paired, though—an R-rated thriller and a G-rated animated feature, for instance. Also billing double features—although this movie match-up is strictly revival—is the enduringly popular **New Beverly Cinema (Map 2)**, where for $8 , or $6 for seniors and children under 12. You can see two by Godard or a couple of spaghetti westerns.

Specialty

Every summer, the Los Angeles Conservancy presents classic films (*Roman Holiday*, anyone? *North by Northwest*?) in the historic theaters downtown on Broadway as part of their "Last Remaining Seats" program (on the web at www.laconservancy.org). For art films, with or without a narrative, check out the current listings at **REDCAT (Map 9)** at Disney Hall. he Bing Theater at LACMA frequently shows films that correspond to the museum's many exhibits. LACMA also hosts the occasional film series as well as talks with legendary actors and directors.

Grauman's Egyptian Theater (Map 3) has been carefully restored to its 1922 grandeur by the folks of American Cinematheque, who also call this famous landmark their home; the theater features a veritable feast of film-geek favorites—director's cuts, anniversary specials, and films not on video. Summer screenings at **Hollywood Forever Cemetery (Map 3)** allow film buffs to actually sit on the grave of the matinee idol projected on the screen while enjoying wine and cheese with hundreds of fellow Angelenos (check www.cinespia.org for details). While not technically a theater, **Cinespace (Map 3)**, a bar and restaurant in Hollywood, shows films nightly. **Pacific El Capitan (Map 3)** theater across from Grauman's Chinese is a grand old palace owned by Disney and presents Disney films exclusively. Last, but certainly not least, is the historic **Silent Movie Theatre (Map 2)** on Fairfax. The Bing Theater at LACMA is the only remaining silent theater in the world and has drawn in curious audiences for over sixty years with a bill of pre-talkie films and the murderous legend surrounding the theater. Its programming has been gloriously and eclectically revitalized by the non-profit group Cinefamily; Silent Wednesdays now co-exist with Dennis Hopper marathons and a screening of Beat Street (with original NWA DJ Arabian Prince on the ones and twos during intermission).

Movie Theaters	Address	Phone	Map	
Aero Theatre	1328 Montana Ave	310-260-1528	18	Classic and under-appreciated films on the big screen.
AMC Burbank 16	125 E Palm Ave	818-953-2932	50	Burbank's premiere multiplex—and it's got the crowds to prove it.
AMC Burbank Town Center 6	770 N 1st St	818-562-1401	50	The popular locale can make a Friday night movie quite an ordeal.
AMC Burbank Town Center 8	201 E Magnolia Blvd	818-563-4901	50	The fraternal twin of Media Center 6—this one is inside the mall.
AMC Century 15	10250 Santa Monica Blvd	310-277-2262	20	Great location makes this multiplex worth the trip.
AMC Del Amo 18	3525 W Carson St	310-921-2046	32	Standard mall mega-plex.
AMC Loews Broadway 4	1441 3rd St Promenade	310-458-3924	18	In the heart of the Promenade, the Broadway is a long time favorite.
AMC Marina Pacifica 12	6346 E Pacific Coast Hwy	562-430-8790	100	First-run theatre with decent screens and sound.
AMC Promenade 16	21801 Oxnard St	818-883-0706	45	The location is right, even if the prices aren't.
AMC Rolling Hills 20	2591 Airport Dr	310-326-5011	32	Go in with low expectations and…you won't be disappointed.
AMC Santa Monica 7 Plex	1310 3rd St Promenade	310-451-9440	18	Convenient for promenade shoppers, but the theatre could do with an update or two.
AMC South Bay Galleria 16	1815 Hawthorne Blvd	310-793-7477	30	It's in a mall, but manages to be decent despite the largely teenage demographic.
AMC Universal Citywalk Stadium 19 with IMAX	100 Universal City Plaza	818-508-0711	57	Recently underwent a massive (and dearly needed) refurbishment.
ArcLight Beach Cities	831 S Nash St	310-607-9630	27	Ritzy and pricey but great for impressing a date.
ArcLight Hollywood	6360 W Sunset Blvd	323-464-1478	3	The crème de la crème of LA cinemas. No one does it better.
ArcLight Pasadena	336 E Colorado Blvd	626-568-9651	34	Big and pricey. Just like the movies it shows.
Art Theater	2025 E 4th St	562-438-5435	p. 178	Long Beach's oldest single-screen cinema features a variety of indie fare.
Billy Wilder Theater at the Hammer Museum	10899 Wilshire Blvd	310-206-3456	20	The UCLA Film & TV Archive's brand new home!
Bing Theater at LACMA	5905 Wilshire Blvd	323-857-6010	6	LACMA's huge variety of films varies monthly.
California Science Center IMAX	700 State Dr	213-744-2019	11	Impressive IMAX venue featuring family-friendly fare.
The Cinefamily	611 N Fairfax Ave	323-655-2510	2	A delightful one of a kind gem featuring pre-talkie films and live music accompaniment.
Cinemark at the Pike	99 S Pine Ave	562-435-5754	p. 178	Fun and friendly stadium-style cinema.
Cinemark Century 8	12827 Victory Blvd	818-508-1943	48	Friendly valley theater.
Downtown Independent Theater	251 S Main St	213-617-1033	9	Budding cinefiles flower here.
Echo Park Film Center	1200 N Alvarado St	213-484-8846	5	LA's DIY film hang out.
Edwards Long Beach Stadium 26 & IMAX	7501 Carson Blvd	562-429-3321	n/a	IMAX!
Edwards Renaissance Stadium 14 & IMAX	1 E Main St	626-300-8312	39	Excellent multiplex that's clean, comfortable and cute. (Yes, cute.)
Egyptian Theater	6712 Hollywood Blvd	323-461-2020	3	The beautiful home of American Cinematheque features an eclectic variety of features, shorts, and documentaries.
El Capitan Theatre	6838 Hollywood Blvd	818-845-3110	3	Elegant movie palace with an all-Disney bill. (At least it's cheaper than Disneyland.)

Movie Theaters	Address	Phone	Map	
Grauman's Chinese Theatre	6925 Hollywood Blvd	323-464-6266	3	The most famous movie theatre in the world, and rightly so.
Highland Theater	5604 N Figueroa St	323-256-6383	33	Good size, good sound, great prices: $3 on Tuesdays and Wednesdays!
Hollywood Forever Cemetery	6000 Santa Monica Blvd	323-469-1181	3	Watch a Jayne Mansfield film while sitting near her grave. Only in LA.
Laemmle Monica 4	1332 2nd St	310-478-3836	18	Low-key and intimate indie arthouse theatre.
Laemmle Music Hall 3	9036 Wilshire Blvd	310-478-3836	6	A comfortable (and clean) arthouse theatre.
Laemmle Playhouse 7	673 E Colorado Blvd	310-478-3836	34	State-of-the-art facilities in an old-world gem.
Laemmle Royal	11523 Santa Monica Blvd	310-478-3836	19	You gotta dig the Royal--as unpretentious as the films it showcases.
Laemmle Town Center 5	17200 Ventura Blvd	310-478-3836	53	One of the Valley's few arthouse options, which means it should be a lot better than it is.
Landmark Nuart Theatre	11272 Santa Monica Blvd	310-281-8223	19	The eclectic Nuart is the consummate arthouse experience. Awesome flicks, atmosphere galore, and midnight movies!
Landmark Regent Theatre	1045 Broxton Ave	310-281-8223	20	It's impossible not to love the Regent--everything that going to the movies is meant to be.
New Beverly Cinema	7165 Beverly Blvd	323-938-4038	2	Revival theater and a true LA original. The double features are legendary.
Old Town Music Hall	140 Richmond St	310-322-2592	27	Silent films + Wutlitzer pipe organ = truly awesome stuff.
Pacific Fashion Center 10	9400 Shirley Ave	818-501-5121	43	It's hard to fault a theater with bathrooms cleaner than your Mom's.
Pacific Sherman Oaks 5	14424 Milbank St	818-501-5121	55	Average and otherwise unimpressive if it weren't for the balconies--they're kinda cool.
Pacific Theaters at the Grove	189 The Grove Dr	323-692-0829	2	Gorgeous cinema is big on swank and style, but its popularity is a problem come weekends.
Pacific Winnetka 21	9201 Winnetka Ave	818-501-5121	42	An enormous 21 screen movie palace.
REDCAT	631 W 2nd St	213-237-2800	9	Features film screenings, live performances, and a cracking good coffee lounge.
Regency Academy Cinemas	1003 E Colorado Blvd	626-229-9400	35	With $6 ticket prices and a great indie lineup, it's hard not to love the Academy.
Regency Commerce 14	950 Goodrich Blvd	323-726-8022	n/a	New releases at Goodrich and Whittier.
Regency Granada Hills 9	16830 Devonshire St	818-363-3679	44	Nothing fancy.(Not that you'd expect it anyway.)
Regency Van Nuys Plant 16	7876 Van Nuys Blvd	818-779-0323	47	Just your average run of the mill multiplex.
Regency Village Theatre	961 Broxton Ave	310-208-5576	20	Westwood's iconic theatre delivers the ultimate movie-going experience.
United Artists Long Beach 6	6601 E Pacific Coast Hwy	562-430-2228	p. 178	So-so movie theatre with so-so movies.
Vintage Los Feliz 3	1822 N Vermont Ave	323-664-2169	4	Single-screen venue bursting with personality and to-die-for popcorn. We kid you not.
Vista Theatre	4473 W Sunset Blvd	323-660-6639	4	A wildly gaudy movie palace shows first runs and indie flicks.
Warner Grand Theatre	478 W 6th St	310-548-7672	p. 172	Lavish art deco movie palace hosts special screenings and live performances.

LA's cultural diversity is reflected by its tremendous array of museums scattered through the city. From dinosaur bones to fairy skeletons, Andy Warhol to Uta Barth, the Abstract Expressionism to Japanese prints, there are plenty of ways to get your 'edu-tainment' fix.

Large/City

At the heart of the Miracle Mile is the **Los Angeles County Museum of Art (Map 6)**, or LACMA, with its comprehensive collection including Renaissance masterpieces, costumes and textiles, and African beadwork. The museum hosts weekly jazz and chamber music concerts and its Bing Theater shows documentaries and revival films. The **Page Museum (Map 6),** part of the LACMA campus, showcases fossils recovered from the La Brea Tar Pits that bubble nearby. In Brentwood, escape the hellish 405 and ascend by computer-operated tram to the **Getty Center (Map 16)**, a heavenly museum complex perched on a hilltop. The permanent collection includes works by Van Gogh, Cézanne, and Rembrandt, but the museum's spectacular views, gardens, and architecture steal the show. As it's one of the city's few free museums, all you'll pay for is parking. The Getty's sister museum, the **Getty Villa** in Malibu, re-opened its collection of antiquities in the winter of 2006. Downtown's **Museum of Contemporary Art (MOCA) (Map 9)** owns works by Lichtenstein, Rauschenberg, and Rothko and hosts hip opening-night parties. The **The Autry National Center** in Griffith Park mounts fascinating exhibits on subjects like the art of rawhide braiding and Jewish life along the Santa Fe Trail. Kids love to visit the creepy-crawly insect zoo at the **Natural History Museum of Los Angeles (Map 11)** in Exposition Park. In San Marino, bask in the glorious gardens at the **Huntington (Map 35)**, but don't miss the institution's world-renowned art and rare manuscript collections.

Small Collections

The **Norton Simon Museum (Map 34)** in Pasadena houses a fine private collection of European, American, and Asian art, including many of the bronze sculptures in Edgar Degas's *Dancer* series. Work by famed Harlem Renaissance artist Palmer C. Hayden is on display at the **Museum of African American Art (Map 10)** in Crenshaw. UCLA's recently remodeled **Hammer Museum (Map 20)** shows this year's cutting-edge artwork alongside last century's masterpieces. For a family field trip, try the **Craft & Folk Art Museum (Map 6)** or the **Zimmer Children's Museum (Map 6)** on Wilshire's Museum Row.

Specialty

Confront the past at the **Museum of Tolerance (Map 23)**, where interactive exhibits focus on the Holocaust and the American civil rights movement. The **Japanese American National Museum (Map 9)** in Little Tokyo hosts taiko drummers, sumi-e lessons, and special exhibitions such as the recent Isamu Noguchi retrospective. Indulge your favorite hot-rod historian at the **Petersen Automotive Museum (Map 6)** near LACMA. The **Los Angeles Police Historical Society (Map 33)** displays bullets older than your grandfather, and the photos at the **African American Firefighter Museum (Map 9)** reveal the role played by black firefighters in the history of Los Angeles. Complete with its very own exit off the 405, the **Skirball Cultural Center (Map 54)** is a premier Jewish cultural organization that offers socially relevant exhibitions along with regular musical and literary events.

Oddities

Culver City's **Museum of Jurassic Technology (Map 24)** is one of the most unique places in the city and home to those aforementioned fairy skeletons and other peculiarities. Next door to the MJT is **CLUI (Center for Land Use Interpretation) (Map 24)**, a great exhibition space dedicated to the theme of land usage across the country. While not technically a museum, the LA County Coroner's Gift Shop, Skeletons in the Closet (**See Shopping, Map 40**), is a must-shop experience for the macabre or anyone looking for a chalk body outline beach towel. **The Paley Center for Media (Map 1)**, as implied by the name, is a must see for media fanatics. The **Museum of Neon Art (Map 9)** is just what it sounds like and expectedly trippy.

Museums	Address	Phone	Map
A+D Museum	900 E 4th St	323-932-9393	9
African American Firefighter Museum	1401 S Central Ave	213-744-1730	9
Alhambra Historical Society Museum	1550 W Alhambra Rd	626-300-8845	39
Armory Center for the Arts	145 N Raymond Ave	626-792-5101	34
The Autry	4700 Western Heritage Way	323-667-2000	n/a
Blitzstein Museum of Art	428 N Fairfax Ave	310-910-1938	2
Cabrillo Marine Aquarium	3720 Stephen M White Dr	310-548-7562	p. 172
California African American Museum	600 State Dr	213-744-7432	11
California Heritage Museum	2612 Main St	310-392-8537	18
California Science Center	700 Exposition Park Dr	323-724-3623	12
Chinese American Museum	425 N Los Angeles St	213-485-8567	9
The Center for Land Use Interpretation	9331 Venice Blvd	310-839-5722	24
Craft & Folk Art Museum	5814 Wilshire Blvd	323-937-4230	6
El Pueblo de Los Angeles Historical Monument	200 N Main St	213-485-6855	9
Fowler Museum	Sunset Blvd & Hilgard Ave	310-825-4361	17
Geffen Contemporary	152 N Central Ave	213-626-6222	9
Getty Center	1200 Getty Center Dr	310-440-7300	16
Getty Villa Pacific Palisades	17895 Pacific Coast Hwy,	310-440-7300	n/a
Grier Musser Museum	403 S Bonnie Brae St	213-413-1814	9
Guinness World Records Museum	6764 Hollywood Blvd	323-463-6433	3
Hammer Museum	10899 Wilshire Blvd	310-443-7000	20
Hermosa Beach Historical Society	710 Pier Ave	310-318-9421	29
The Hollywood Heritage Museum	2100 N Highland Ave	323-874-2276	3
Hollywood Museum	1660 N Highland Ave	323-464-7776	3
Hollywood Wax Museum	6767 Hollywood Blvd	323-462-5991	3
Holyland Exhibition (by appointment only)	2215 Lake View Ave	323-664-3162	5
The Huntington	1151 Oxford Rd	626-405-2100	35
Japanese American National Museum	369 E 1st St	213-625-0414	9
Kidspace Children's Museum	480 N Arroyo Blvd	626-449-9144	34
Korean American Museum	3727 W 6th St	213-388-4229	8
L. Ron Hubbard Life Exhibition	6331 Hollywood Blvd	323-960-3511	3
Los Angeles County Museum of Art	5905 Wilshire Blvd	323-857-6000	6
Los Angeles Museum of the Holocaust	100 The Grove Dr	323-651-3704	6
Los Angeles Police Museum	6045 York Blvd	323-344-9445	33
MAK Center	835 N Kings Rd	323-651-1510	2
Manhattan Beach Historical Society	1601 Manhattan Beach Blvd	310-374-7575	27
MOCA at the Pacific Design Center	8687 Melrose Ave	310-657-0800	2
Museum of African American Art	4005 Crenshaw Blvd	323-294-7071	10
Museum of Contemporary Art (MOCA)	250 S Grand Ave	213-626-6222	9
Museum of Jurassic Technology	9341 Venice Blvd	310-836-6131	24
Museum of Neon Art	216 S Brand Blvd, Glendale	213-489-9918	51
Museum of Tolerance	9786 W Pico Blvd	310-553-8403	23
Natural History Museum of Los Angeles County	900 Exposition Blvd	213-763-3466	11
Norton Simon Museum	411 W Colorado Blvd	626-449-6840	34
Pacific Asia Museum	46 N Los Robles Ave	626-449-2742	34
Pacific Design Center	8687 Melrose Ave	310-657-0800	2
Page Museum at the La Brea Tar Pits	5801 Wilshire Blvd	323-934-7243	6
Paley Center for Media	465 N Beverly Dr	310-786-1091	1
Pasadena Museum of California Art	490 E Union St	626-568-3665	34
Pasadena Museum of History	470 W Walnut St	626-577-1660	34
Petersen Automotive Museum	6060 Wilshire Blvd	323-930-2277	6

Psychiatry: An Industry of Death Museum	6616 W Sunset Blvd	323-467-4242	3
Redondo Beach Historical Museum	302 Flagler Ln	310-318-0684	29
Roundhouse Marine Studies Lab and Aquarium	2 Manhattan Beach Blvd	310-379-8117	27
Ripley's Believe It or Not	6780 Hollywood Blvd	323-466-6335	3
Santa Monica History Museum	1350 7th St	310-395-2290	18
Santa Monica Museum of Art	2525 Michigan Ave	310-586-6488	19
Skirball Cultural Center	2701 N Sepulveda Blvd	310-440-4500	54
South Pasadena Historical Museum	913 Meridian Ave	626-799-9089	34
Southwest Museum of the American Indian	234 Museum Dr	323-221-2164	36
Torrance Historical Society	1345 Post Ave	310-328-5392	32
Travel Town Museum	5200 Zoo Dr, Los Angeles	323-662-5874	n/a
Western Museum of Flight	3315 Airport Dr	310-326-9544	32
Zimmer Children's Museum	6505 Wilshire Blvd	323-761-8984	6

General New/Used

LA's humongous selection of bookstores makes it easy to blow your grocery money on hard covers, even without a visit to the local **Barnes & Noble**. As the state's economy ails, Southern California has seen some of its most beloved bookstores go out of business, including the small independent chain Dutton's and the legendary Acres of Books in Long Beach. If you love rummaging used book shops, this is a terrific time to spend some scratch in them.

Vroman's (Map 34) in Pasadena is over a century old, but its collection is as large and current as those of the big chains. **Brand Bookshop (Map 51)** in Glendale lures customers with its eccentric window display (edible insect cookbook, anyone?) and keeps them turning the pages with over 100,000 used and out-of-print titles in every category imaginable. Across the street, you'll find **Bookfellows**, a/k/a **Mystery of Imagination (Map 51)**, which specializes in collectable genre paperbacks (Thrills! Horror! Here and there, unintentionally hilarious smut!) but runs the pulp gamut.

Small New/Used

Skylight Books (Map 4) in Los Feliz has a well-edited collection of literary fiction, travel, local-interest, and film books, a resident kitty cat dozing in the window, and an impressive monthly lineup of literary events. **Small World Books (Map 21)** in Venice combines a fine selection of new titles with an ideal beachfront location. Downtown's **Caravan Bookstore (Map 9)**, the last of the old Bookseller's Row shops, carries rare and out-of-print works. Also downtown, the Last Bookstore attracts a hip clientele by offering coffee and vinyl LPs alongside its large collection of used books. Not ready to buy? Libros Schmibros in Boyle Heights doubles as a lending library.

Specialty

If you're into something, odds are there's a bookshop that'll suit your interests. An intriguing selection of maps, travel guides, and photography books at **Distant Lands (Map 34)** in Pasadena inspires journeys by plane, train, or armchair. Likewise, West Hollywood's **Traveler's Bookcase (Map 2)** shelves over 14,000 books to stimulate your wanderlust. **Eso Won Books (Map 11)** in Baldwin Hills specializes in African-American literature and hosts frequent signings. **Dawson's Book Shop (Map 3)** in Hollywood is the source for antiquarian books on California history, Western Americana, and photography, and its gallery exhibits the likes of Ansel Adams, Edward Weston, and Eadweard Muybridge. The sleek **Equator Books (Map 21)** on Venice's trendy Abbot-Kinney strip specializes in rare and collectible coffee table tomes on surfing, call girls, and circus freaks.

West Hollywood is a microcosm of LA's literary scene, supporting a mind-boggling range of special interest bookstores. **Cook's Library (Map 2)** on 3rd Street stocks thousands of cookery books for Ferran Adria wannabes. **Mystery Pier (Map 2),** located on the Sunset Strip, is an antiquarian shop of the highest caliber, stocking first editions of American and British literature with an impressive collection of mystery and true crime titles. You can spend a day meditating in the stacks at the **Bodhi Tree Bookstore (Map 2)** on Melrose, purveyor of metaphysical titles both new and recycled. Check out the collection of dried herbs and crystal pendants along with the ethereal tomes. On Santa Monica, **A Different Light (Map 2)** caters to the area's gay, lesbian, bisexual, and transgender communities. **Circus of Books** in Silver Lake **(Map 4)** and West Hollywood **(Map 2)** has a large collection of gay erotica and pornography as well as zines and more mainstream gay and lesbian books. **Storyopolis (Map 56)** on Ventura specializes in children's literature, including rare and collectible titles from the turn of the 20th century. The store's readings, nifty lithograph collection, art classes, and sock hops (yes, sock hops!) keep kids and parents coming back for more.

Art/Film Books

LA is where art and entertainment collide, and the city's bookstores gather up the pieces. The eye-popping **Taschen (Map 1)** store in Beverly Hills, and the newer branch at the Grove, stock the iconoclast publisher's brand of luxe art tomes and naughty coffee table books. **Arcana (Map 18),** nuzzled in the ever-gentrifying 3rd Street Promenade, carries a staggering collection of art books dating from Abstract Impressionism to the present, organized by artist and theme. Where Arcana leaves off, **Hennessey + Ingalls (Map 18)** picks up. With an impressive collection of Renaissance monographs and architecture books, the store has as large a visual-arts collection as you'll find anywhere. **LACMA (Map 6)** and the **Getty (Map 16)** both carry exhibition catalogues and academic art books, and the **MOCA bookstore** has three locations in addition to its primary downtown residence **(Map 9)**: one at the Pacific Design Center **(Map 2)**, one at Main Street in Santa Monica **(Map 12)**, and another at the Geffen Contemporary **(Map 9)**. **Meltdown (Map 2)** in West Hollywood is famous for comics and collectibles, but its selection of graphic novels is equally strong. **Golden Apple (Map 2)** is a sci-fi/comic geek's private Valhalla— and girls are most definitely allowed. **Book Soup (Map 2)** on the Sunset Strip boasts the best lineup of readings in the city and floor-to-ceiling shelves stocked with art, photography, film, and music-oriented titles.

Map 1 • Beverly Hills

TASCHEN	354 N Beverly Dr	310-274-4300	Art and photo books.

Map 2 • West Hollywood

Automobile Books	8980 Santa Monica Blvd	310-657-9699	Books about cars.
Barnes & Noble	189 Grove Dr	323-525-0270	Chain.
Book Soup	8818 W Sunset Blvd	310-659-3110	Great independent bookstore.
Circus of Books	8230 Santa Monica Blvd	323-656-6533	Gay/lesbian; general interest art/photo books.
Golden Apple Comics	7018 Melrose Ave	323-658-6047	Shangri-la for comic book lovers.
Heaven Books	7740 Santa Monica Blvd	323-654-5486	Russian books.
Houle Rare Books & Autographs	7260 Beverly Blvd	323-937-5858	Used and rare.
Interbook	7513 Santa Monica Blvd	323-882-6160	Russian books.

Kovcheg Russian Bookstore	7508 W Sunset Blvd	323-876-2749	Russian books.
Meltdown Comics & Collectibles	7522 Sunset Blvd	323-851-7223	Largest comic book store on the West Coast! Or whatever.
Michael R Thompson Booksellers	8242 W 3rd St	323-658-1901	Fine antiquarian and scholarly books.
MOCA at the Pacific Design Center	8687 Melrose Ave	310-289-5223	Contemporary art books and magazines.
Mystery Pier Books	8826 W Sunset Blvd	310-657-5557	First edition and rare books.
Samuel French Bookstore	7623 W Sunset Blvd	323-876-0570	Theater and film books.
Traveler's Bookcase	8375 W 3rd St	323-655-0575	Excellent shop for travelers.

Map 3 • Hollywood

Cosmopolitan Book Shop	7017 Melrose Ave	323-938-7119	General new and used.
Counterpoint Records and Books	5911 Franklin Ave	323-957-7965	Wide selection of gently used books and music.
Daily Planet Book Store	5931 Franklin Ave	323-957-0061	New fiction.
Dawson's Book Shop	535 N Larchmont Blvd	323-469-2186	Rare books on the American West.
Edmund's Bookshop	6644 Hollywood Blvd	323-463-3273	Cinema and theatre books.
Opamp Technical Books	1033 N Sycamore Ave	323-464-4322	Technical books.

Map 4 • Los Feliz

Circus of Books	4001 W Sunset Blvd	323-666-1304	Gay books and magazines.
Philosophical Research Society Bookstore	3910 Los Feliz Blvd	323-663-2167	Philosophy and spirituality.
Siam Books	5178 Hollywood Blvd	323-665-4236	Thai books.
Skylight Books	1818 N Vermont Ave	323-660-1175	Independent general interest.
Soap Plant / Wacko	4633 Hollywood Blvd	323-663-0122	Eclectic selection.

Map 5 • Silver Lake/Echo Park/Atwater

Aldine Books	1498 Sunset Blvd	323-666-2690	Used.
Libreria Mexico de Echo Park	1632 W Sunset Blvd	213-250-4835	Hispanic general interest.

Map 6 • Miracle Mile/Mid-City

Ahmanson Bookstore at LACMA	5905 Wilshire Blvd	323-857-6146	Eclectic art books.
New Mastodon German Books	5820 Wilshire Blvd	323-525-1948	New and used German books.

Map 7 • Hancock Park

Chevalier's Books	126 N Larchmont Blvd	323-465-1334	General interest, new books.
Educational Bookstore	3959 Wilshire Blvd	213-387-3184	Educational books and school supplies.

Map 8 • Korea Town

Dong-A Book Plaza	3460 W 8th St	213-382-7100	Korean books.
Kachi	401 S Vermont Ave	213-487-6921	Comics.
Libreria Hispanoamerica	2502 W 6th St	213-384-6084	Spanish books.
Orange Comics	3500 W 8th St	213-383-5250	Comics.
Seojong Bookstore	3250 W Olympic Blvd	323-735-7374	Korean books.
Student Books	244 S Oxford Ave	213-387-1582	K-7 textbooks.
Sung Ji Book Center	2837 W Olympic Blvd	213-388-2839	Korean books.
Western Comics	730 S Western Ave	213-385-7025	Korean comics.

Map 9 • Downtown

Caravan Bookstore	550 S Grand Ave	213-626-9944	Out of print books.
China Bookstore	652 N Broadway	213-680-9230	Chinese books.
Great Wall Books & Art	970 N Broadway	213-617-2817	Chinese and medical books.
International Fashion Publications	110 E 9th St	213-622-5663	Fashion-related books.
Kinokuniya Bookstore	123 Astronaut Ellison S Onizuka St	213-687-4480	Japanese books, some English.
Libros Revolucion	312 W 8th St	213-488-1303	Spanish and English books.
MOCA at the Geffen Contemporary	152 N Central Ave	213-633-5323	Contemporary art books and magazines.
MOCA Store	250 S Grand Ave	213-621-1710	Contemporary art books and magazines.
Niming Books	969 N Hill St	213-687-9817	Chinese books.
Thai Books & Music Dokya	1100 N Main St	323-342-9982	Thai books.

Map 11 • South Central West

Eso Won Books	4331 Degnan Blvd	323-290-1048	African-American books.
Libreria Azteca	1429 W Adams Blvd	323-733-4040	Spanish books.
University of Southern California Bookstore	840 Childs Wy	213-740-0066	Text and trade books.

Map 12 • South Central East

Theosophy Co.	246 W 33rd St	213-748-7244	Theosophy books.

Map 13 • Inglewood

Zahra's Books & Things	900 N La Brea Ave	310-330-1300	African-American books.

Map 14 • Inglewood East/Morningside Park

Bright Lights Children's Books	8461 S Van Ness Ave	323-971-1296	Multicultural children's books—Saturday only.
Express Yourself Books	1425 W Manchester Ave	323-750-4114	General interest books.

Map 16 • Brentwood

The Getty Museum Store	1200 Getty Center Dr	310-440-7300	Getty publications.
Iliad Bookshop	5400 Cahuenga Blvd	818-509-2665	Used literature, cinema, and arts.

Map 17 • Bel Air/Holmby Hills

UCLA BookZone	308 Westwood Plz	310-206-4041	Very large college bookstore

Map 18 • Santa Monica

A&R Textbooks	1703 Pico Blvd	310-314-4361	Textbooks.
Angel City Books & Records	218 Pier Ave	310-399-8767	Used art and literature.
Arcana Books on the Arts	1229 3rd St Prom	310-458-1499	Excellent art and architecture. Hard to find.
Barnes & Noble	1201 3rd St Prom	310-260-9110	Chain.
Barry R Levin Science Fiction	720 Santa Monica Blvd	310-458-6111	Science fiction, fantasy, and horror.
Hennessey + Ingalls Art Books	214 Wilshire Blvd	310-458-9074	Superb art and architecture.
HI de Ho Comics & Books With Pictures	525 Santa Monica Blvd	310-394-2820	Comics.

Map 19 • West LA/Santa Monica East

Alias Books	1650 Sawtelle Blvd	310-473-4442	Rare and out-of-print.
Asahiya Bookstore	2130 Sawtelle Blvd	310-375-3303	Japanese Books.
Collectors Exchange	3126 S Sepulveda Blvd	310-996-8811	Comic books.
Sawtelle Books & Music	11301 W Olympic Blvd	310-477-8686	Japanese books.

Map 20 • Westwood/Century City

Dehkhoda Persian Bookstore	1387 Westwood Blvd	310-477-0044	Persian books.
Text Book Plus	927 Westwood Blvd	310-824-1155	College books.

Map 21 • Venice

Beyond Baroque Foundation	681 Venice Blvd	310-822-3006	Literary arts.
Mystic Journey Bookstore	1319 Abbot Kinney Blvd	310-399-7070	An enchanted place for spiritual exploration and metaphysical wonder!
Small World Books	1407 Ocean Front Wk	310-399-2360	General and mystery.

Map 22 • Mar Vista

Sam Johnson's Bookshop	12310 Venice Blvd	310-391-5047	Rare and out-of-print.

Map 23 • Rancho Park/Palms

Children's Book World	10850 W Pico Blvd	310-559-2665	Children's books.

Map 24 • Culver City

Abba Padre Bikes and Books	4219 Sepulveda Blvd	310-390-5203	Main dish of bicycles, with a side of Christian tomes.
The Center for Land Use Interpretation	9331 Venice Blvd	310-839-5722	Fabulous selection of books on land use, energy issues, Americana, etc.
Comics Ink	4267 Overland Ave	310-204-3240	Comic books.

Map 25 • Marina Del Rey/Westchester West

Barnes & Noble	13400 Maxella Ave	310-306-3213	Chain.

Map 26 • Westchester/Fox Hills/Ladera Heights

Pepperdine U Bookstore-West LA Campus	6100 Center Dr	310-568-5741	College textbooks.

Map 27 • El Segundo/Manhattan Beach

Barnes & Noble	1800 Rosecrans Ave	310-725-7025	Chain.
Comic Bug	1807 Manhattan Beach Blvd	310-372-6704	Comic books.

Map 28 • Hawthorne

A Baseball Clubhouse and Comic Books	13308 Inglewood Ave	310-675-3333	Mostly baseball cards, some comic books.

Map 29 • Hermosa Beach/Redondo Beach North

Dave's Olde Bookshop	2123 Artesia Blvd	310-793-1300	Used indie fiction.
Mysterious Galaxy	2810 Artesia Blvd	310-542-6000	Sci-fi, fantasy and mystery; also known for great book signings.

Map 30 • Torrance North

Stuart Ng Books	20655 Western Ave	310-909-1929	A rarity, only sells books on comic art and illustration.

Map 31 • Redondo Beach

Barnes & Noble	21500 Hawthorne Blvd	310-370-5552	Chain.
Book Again	5039 Torrance Blvd	310-542-1156	Used fiction.
Psychic Eye Bookshop	3902 Pacific Coast Hwy	310-378-7754	Metaphysical, self-help.
Sandpiper Books	4665 Torrance Blvd	310-371-2002	Used.

Map 32 • Torrance South

Barnes & Noble	21400 Hawthorne Blvd	310-370-5552	Chain.
Book Off	21712 Hawthorne Blvd	310-214-4800	Used books, DVDs, CDs and games at rock-bottom prices.
The WWII Store	1422 Marcelina Ave	310-533-4992	WWII…period.

Map 33 • Highland Park

Another World Comics & Books	1615 Colorado Blvd	323-257-7757	Comics, sci-fi.
Appleby Books	1007 N Ave 51	323-478-0655	Children's collectibles.
Pop Hop Books & Print	5002 York	323-259-2490	Friendly used bookstore and print studio filled with hidden gems.

Map 34 • Pasadena

Alexandria Metaphysical Bookstore II	170 S Lake Ave	626-792-7885	Metaphysical books.
Barnes & Noble	111 W Colorado Blvd	626-585-0362	Chain.
Book Alley	1252 E Colorado Blvd	626-683-8083	Used art, literature, philosophy.
Book 'em Mysteries	1118 Mission St	626-799-9600	Mystery.
Cliff's Books	630 E Colorado Blvd	626-449-9541	Used.
Comic Odyssey	319 S Arroyo Pkwy	626-577-6696	Comic books.
Distant Lands Travel Bookstore & Outfitter	56 S Raymond Ave	626-449-3220	Maps and travel books.
Gamble House	4 Westmoreland Pl	626-449-4178	Design, art, and architecture.
Norton Simon Museum of Art	411 W Colorado Blvd	626-449-6840	Museum shop.
Vroman's Bookstore	695 E Colorado Blvd	626-449-5320	Great independent bookstore.

Map 35 • Pasadena East/San Marino

Archives Bookshop	1396 E Washington Blvd	626-797-4756	Academics, philosophy, religious.
Comics Factory	1298 E Colorado Blvd	626-585-0618	Comics.
Cook Books	1388 E Washington Blvd	626-296-1638	Cook books.
Crossroads Books	1196 E Walnut St	626-795-8772	Rehab books.
San Marino Toy & Book Shoppe	2424 Huntington Dr	626-309-0222	Children's books.

Map 38 • El Sereno

Legal Books Distributing	4247 Whiteside St	323-526-7110	Legal books warehouse.
Student Book Mart & Copy Center	1725 N Eastern Ave	323-262-5511	Textbooks for Cal-State.

Map 39 • Alhambra

Jilie	1283 E Valley Blvd	626-308-1466	Chinese books.
Ng Hing Kee of Los Angeles	29 E Valley Blvd	626-943-9933	Chinese general interest.

Map 40 • Boyle Heights

Libros Schmibros	1711 Mariachi Plaza de Los Angeles	323-302-9408	Hire a mariachi outside this used bookstore and lending library.
Sears Book Center	2650 E Olympic Blvd	323-265-3153	Spanish books.

Map 44 • Mission Hills / North Hills

Bookhouse	17048 Devonshire St	818-832-0976	Children's, biography.
Continental Comics	17032 Devonshire St	818-368-8909	Comics.

Map 45 • Canoga Park / Woodland Hills

Barnes & Noble	6100 Topanga Canyon Blvd	818-704-3850	Chain.
Builder's Bookstore	8001 Canoga Ave	818-887-7828	Construction books.
Collector's Paradise	7131 Winnetka Ave	818-999-9455	Comic books, graphic novels.
The Flip Side	19950 Ventura Blvd	818-883-9550	Comics and videos.
Pierce College—Bookstore	6201 Winnetka Ave	818-347-0313	Text and trade books.

Map 46 • Reseda

Imagine Center	18635 Ventura Blvd	818-345-1100	New age, spiritual.
Russian Gifts & Books	5424 Reseda Blvd	818-342-1668	Russian books.

Map 47 • Van Nuys

Bargain Books	14426 Friar St	818-782-2782	General used.
Comics & Fun	6411 Sepulveda Blvd	818-779-7643	Comic books, posters, magazines.
Libreria El Quijote	14534 Victory Blvd	818-989-2411	Spanish books.
Russian Books	13757 Victory Blvd	818-781-7533	Russian books.
Theodore Front Musical Literature	16122 Cohasset St	818-994-1902	Books about music.

Map 49 • Burbank

American Opinion Books & Flags	5653 Cahuenga Blvd	818-769-4019	Right-wing books.
Autobooks/Aerobooks	3524 W Magnolia Blvd	818-845-0707	Auto and air.
Dark Delicacies	4213 W Burbank Blvd	818-556-6660	Horror books.
Woodbury University Book Store	7500 N Glenoaks Blvd	818-767-0888	College books.
The Writers Store	3510 W Magnolia Blvd	800-272-8927	Should be 'The Screenwriters Store.' Resource for industry aspirants.

Map 50 • Burbank East/Glendale West

Barnes & Noble	731 N San Fernando Blvd	818-558-1383	Chain.
Book Castle's Movie World	212 N San Fernando Blvd	818-846-0459	Books on movies, theatre, dance, TV.

Map 51 • Glendale South

Abril Armenian Bookstore	415 E Broadway	818-243-4112	Armenian books.
Barnes & Noble	210 Americana Way	818-545-9146	Store at the Americana.
Berj Armenian Bookstore	422 S Central Ave	818-244-3830	Armenian books.
Bookfellows/Mystery & Imagination	238 N Brand Blvd	818-545-0121	Rare books.
Brand Bookshop	231 N Brand Blvd	818-507-5943	Used books.
Legacy Comic Books & Sportscards	123 W Wilson Ave	818-247-8803	Comics.
Sardarabad Books	1111 S Glendale Ave	818-500-0790	Iranian books.

Map 54 • Sherman Oaks West

Earth-2 Comics	15017 Ventura Blvd	818-386-9590	Comics.

Map 55 • Sherman Oaks East

Books on the Boulevard	13551 Ventura Blvd	818-905-0988	Hardcover non-fiction.
Dragon Books	2954 N Beverly Glen Cir	310-441-8545	Rare and antiquarian.
Psychic Eye Bookshop	13435 Ventura Blvd	818-906-8263	Metaphysical, self-help.
Storyopolis	12945 Ventura Blvd	818-990-7600	Great children's bookstore.

Map 56 • Studio City/Valley Village

Bookstar	12136 Ventura Blvd	818-505-9528	Owned by B&N—chain.
Comicsmash	11824 Ventura Blvd	818-761-3753	Comic books.
DJ'S Universal Comics	11038 Ventura Blvd	818-761-3465	Comic books

Map 57 • Universal City/Toluca Lake

Last Grenadier	820 N Hollywood Wy	818-848-9144	Military topics; role-play gaming books.
Upstart Crow	1000 Universal Center Dr	818-763-1811	General interest.

Overview

Anybody who tells you that nightlife in LA sucks has just been to the wrong places. The city reflects its melting pot populous, and there are bars and clubs for *everyone*—people who love people and people who hate people, people with bottle service $ and people with a few bucks for a shitty beer, people who love dancing to shitty music and people who love dancing to good music. Hell, there are even bars that cater to people from other American cities, so you can always know where to watch your hometown football team.

Los Angeles is less a single entity than the sum of fifty or so distinct mid-sized cities that can seem neigh impossible to unravel. Neighborhoods and "scenes" rarely twain, unless you're say, looking for a skinny jean, PBR-and-Modelo hipster haven (Echo Park) or an ear-splitting club to grab an overpriced shit cocktail and dumb drugs (Hollywood). But despite the geographic disparity Angelenos cut through the Gordian Knot bar culture and excitedly dig out, share, and champion their faves, eventually identifying with their boozeholes of choice with the same seriousness as their political or religious convictions.

Keeping track of dance nights, comedy, live music, and all of the other weird shit that makes up LA nightlife can get complicated. **LA Weekly**, LA's premier free paper, is a good place to check for what's going on, and the **LA Times** has its **Calendar Live** section. (Each has an online counterpart, in case you think **Craigslist** is a fad.) There's also a honking traffic jam of sites like **www.la.com**. One namecheck on **Daily Candy** means your corner bar just got drafted—that's how hungry everyone is for the next big, pre-approved thing. Is this sounding like finding a needle in a haystack? Well, it is and it isn't. Consider all of this a childproof toolbox. Rummage, experiment, and find your favorites. Remember: in LA, word of mouth is king, and whatever advice you bought from your guerrilla marketing guru, there's no faking that funk. But here are some of our suggestions to get things rolling…

LA is a brilliant, weird place, so no matter where you go, you'll have a story. But if you're looking for some guidance, here are our suggestions…

Best Dive Bars

If we need to explain what a dive bar is to you, that means that you probably won't like dive bars. Think cash only, cheap drinks, bad wine, a pool table, karaoke, a cast of grizzled regulars, and if you're really lucky, a MegaTouch machine loaded up with dirty photo hunt. Los Feliz has two of the greats, **Ye Rustic Inn (Map 4)** and the **Drawing Room (Map 4)**. If you're a dive bar collector of sorts, the **Frolic Room (Map 3)** is a must-Bukowski drank there, after all. **Frank 'n Hank (Map 8)** is dive-bar sparse to the point that has only one piece of art; a large painting of a naked lady. **The Roost (Map 5)** is your dive bar in Atwater Village, and **Gold Room (Map 5)** is your must in Echo Park (there are free tacos, too). It feels weird calling **Jumbo's Clown Room (Map 4)** a dive, because the pole dancers are insanely talented. But the weird clown pictures and cheap beer are 100% dive. More westerly, **Cozy Inn (Map 24)** has shuffleboard, a good jukebox, and pool. Up in the valley, there's the **Foxfire Room (Map 56)**, with a sweet-ass jukebox, and the dangerously strong tiki stylings of **Tonga Hut (Map 48)**.

Best Outdoor Spaces

Constant sun and an average outdoor temperature of 72 degrees mean that many LA bars drag their tables outside. One of the best places is **Golden Road Brewing (Map 51)**, where the indoor/outdoor space has plenty of games and lots of delicious brews. The trÃ¨s rive gauche **Figaro Bistrot (Map 4)** on Vermont in Los Feliz lines up 'round marble tables to squeeze in thirsty hipsters. **Malo (Map 4)** on Sunset has an industrial-looking, surprisingly intimate outdoor seating area with heating lamps. For stargazing through your beer goggles, the rooftop bar at **The Standard (Map 9)** needs to be experienced once. The **Red Lion Tavern (Map 5)** does the German beer garden thing right, while **Idle Hour (Map 56)** gives you fancy outdoor cocktails on the edge of NoHo. And for those down near the beaches, **Abigaile (Map 29)** is a must-the former brewer of Stone is cookin' up beer there.

Best Lounges

In a city where image is reality, the larger-than-life style of LA's clubs tends to squash the urban reign of the almighty bar. Dives often seem a bit lost amid the velvet rope-gawking, and the current Cahuenga fascination distracts from simpler watering holes. What emerges is LA's answer to compromise: the lounge. What passes for a stylish alternative in other cities is the modest choice in LA. But a solid lounge is a beautiful thing no matter what city it's in, and LA has some truly solid ones. Many lounge-prone Angelenos migrate from the velvet ropes of Hollywood Boulevard to Sunset, where they stumble into **The Well (Map 3)**. Modish warmth is key to this lounge's hip brown-and-black design and tall leather banquettes; with a killer juke mix and a smooth transition from lowkey hangout to loud and lively late night spot, it's a big draw. **The Brig (Map 21)** on Abbot Kinney in Venice is a chic, sleekly illuminated mod dream. As swanky as it is (down to the bathrooms), it's still a laid-back lounge where the cocktails and pool, not the celebrities, pull rank. If you're looking for something dressed up with a touch of seedy, **Jones (Map 2)** in WeHo is a good bet. The elegant wraparound bar gives way to bathrooms plastered in inelegant Polaroids of naughty-bit flashing patrons. Probably the most well known local lounge, **The Dresden Room (Map 4)** solidified its fame with a cameo in 1996's prerequisite LA film *Swingers*, and comes with its very own lounge act. Say hi to Marty and Elayne when you go. They're sweethearts.

Best Beer Selection

If you scoff at light lager swill, there are plenty of options. If you're a beer cynic, places such as **Father's Office (Map 18, 24)**, with 30 microbrews on tap, and **The Library Alehouse (Map 18)**, coming in right behind with 29 on tap, are all the conversion you'll need. Oh, and don't worry if you're stuck in Hollywood, it's not all clubs and vodka tonics—**Blue Palms Brewhouse (Map 3)** keeps you wells-sudsed along the Walk of Fame. Burbank has made a worthy addition to the beer snob scene with **Tony's Darts Away (Map 49)**, serving a wide array (and only) beers brewed in California, with a heavy IPA bias. But their sister restaurant, **Mohawk Bend (Map 5)**, has a wider selection. For a bottle shop where you can take away or drink on the premises, we'll direct you to another Echo Park spot—**Sunset Beer (Map 5)**. For local breweries, there's the big, outdoor-game laden **Golden Road Brewing** **(Map 51)**, smaller-but-tasty **Eagle Rock Brewery (Map 51)**, **Angel City (Map 9)**, and Craftsman Brewing, which is your local brewery for sours. It doesn't have its own tap room, but pretty much rules the beer selection at pizza joint **Maximiliano (Map 33)**.

Best Milieu

Decor varies greatly among LA's proud gin joints. Drop by the **Bigfoot Lodge (Map 5)** in Atwater to swig down a few beers while you cozy up to Smokey the Bear. The owner of **Tiki-Ti (Map 4)** in Los Feliz is so dedicated to keeping up his mini-Polynesian paradise that patrons will find the bar closed when he's in the islands "doing research." Try **Oldfields (Map 24)** for a retro-speakeasy vibe and killer scotchy-scotchscotch. For upscale chic, **Casa del Mar (Map 18)** in Santa Monica delivers with a grand lobby/bar serving drinks with grand price tags. Of all the bars doing that "look at our immaculate old-timey interior" thing, **Melrose Umbrella Company (Map 2)** is possibly our favorite-it's just enough without being too much. Or if "too much" is your preference, you should see **No Vacancy (Map 3)** at least once-it can get douchey thanks to the H-wood location, but you enter through a goddamn hidden staircase under a bed. **The Edison (Map 9)** downtown takes boiler-room chic to a new, drunken level with its historically accurate industrial vibe—just beware of the gate-keeping bouncers who hold a staunch no-tennis-shoes policy. Or, just get with the program, you slob.

Best Dancing

So you think you can dance? Whether you shake your moneymaker to salsa, hip-hop, techno, or reggae, there is someplace for everyone to get down in Los Angeles. For hot and sweaty Havana nights, it doesn't get more authentic than Hollywood's **El Floridita (Map 3)** salsa club, located in a shady strip mall on Fountain and Vine. Downtown's legendary **Mayan (Map 9)** doubles as a concert venue and an exclusive salsa club with a strict dress code—call ahead for details. Over in the 90069, Boys Town boasts a plethora of gay dance clubs known for, um, stiff drinks, um, throbbing music, and Schwarzenegger-esque bartenders. Some of the most popular include **Factory (Map 2)**, **The Abbey (Map 2)**, **Micky's (Map 2)**, and **Rage (Map 2)**. For less hype, head to Los Feliz's **Akbar (Map 4)** to find a LGBT-friendly crowd and a chill Eastside vibe. Central Hollywood has replaced the Strip as the hotspot for club-hopping millennials, short-run celebrities, and indie fauxhemians. **Cinespace (Map 3)**, **Avalon (Map 3)**, and **Bardot (Map 3)** are all popular dance spots within one two-block radius. If electro and dub are your style, **The Echo**'s **(Map 5)** hipster-attracting Dub Club on Wednesdays in Silver Lake is a plaid-flaunting good time. For a wild night out on the cheap, check out **La Plaza (Map 2)** on La Brea, with DJs spinning ranchero music and fabulous Latino drag-queen performances at 10 pm and midnight on the weekends.

Best Music

Out-of-work musicians are almost as plentiful in Los Angeles as out-of-work actors. Lucky for them, LA draws more than enough stadium-filling performances to help them keep the dream alive while offering plenty of smallish venues where they can showcase their talent. If you want your music grand, orchestral, and outdoors, then head to **The Hollywood Bowl (Map 3)**. Pack a picnic, a blanket and your significant other and head on up for a stunning view and some outstanding acoustics. The Bowl plays host to rock shows, classic bands, an impressive Independence Day fireworks show, and the occasional Garrison Keillor radio performance. Another panoramic outdoor attraction is the **Greek Theatre (Map 4)**, a gorgeous venue in Griffith Park showcasing a lot of nostalgia acts and a recent current of freshness. On the Sunset Strip, the dependable **House of Blues (Map 2)** draws in big names. Local institutions like the **Whisky A Go-Go (Map 2)** and the **Viper Room (Map 2)** draw crowds for their reputations alone, while offering a mix of both established and undiscovered bands. Some adventurous performers and voyeurs take their chances at **Mr. T's Bowl (Map 33)**, a seedy former bowling alley in Highland Park. For the freshest indie bands and underground rock, try the **Troubadour (Map 2)**. **The Wiltern (Map 7)** and the **El Rey Theatre (Map 6)** in mid-Wilshire are local favorites for catching bigger bands at a smaller venue, while **The Satellite (Map 5)** in Silver Lake and **The Echo (Map 5)** in Echo Park bring in locals and music insiders with more alternative live music. **The Hotel Cafe (Map 3)** is undoubtedly LA's best loved acoustic venue, with a cozy New York vibe and some impressive names performing nightly. For live music that doesn't overpower the pub atmosphere, **Molly Malone's (Map 2)** is a deservedly popular spot. It's a great place to see a wide range of great bands (from alt rock to reggae) and then shoot some darts. Those with more, ahem, evolved tastes can often be caught taking in a Friday night performance at the **Getty (Map 16)**, or a live music-silent film combo at **The Cinefamily (Map 2)**. The famous, cavernous **Amoeba Music (Map 3)** packs in locals with (free!) live in-store performances—check their marquee for upcoming shows from surprisingly big names. DJs are people too. Some people even consider them musicians. The most eclectic slate of DJs spins at **Verdugo (Map 36)** and the crowd is wildly different from night to night

Overview

When it's feedin' time, Los Angeles is a city of many juxtapositions. Hence, some genius invented "fusion" to please every palate and satisfy the giant melting pot that makes up this town. LA is also where "Californian" cuisine was born, and it involves a lot more than avocado, trust. The city borrows many of its flavors from the neighbors. With Mexico next door, sliding-scale "authentic" south-of-the-border dishes are served up in hundreds of restaurants citywide. The Pacific lapping at our sandy shores brings with it a strong Asian influence. Dim sum palaces, Korean barbecue joints, and hidden Thai gems are daily adventures here. And the sushi—it's the best in (dare we say) the world. In addition, California's abundant agriculture provides us with loads of fresh produce year-round from local purveyors. Many restaurants have made their name on having the freshest and localest. Not to worry, there's plenty of meat. Angelenos don't eat? Please. Ever heard of bacon?

Eating Old

Taix (Map 5) on Sunset in Echo Park has been serving up French country cuisine at peasant prices since 1927; now with hipster background music. Down the road is **Langer's (Map 8)**, putting New York pastrami to shame since 1947. **Philippe the Original (Map 9)** still serves its famous French dip sandwiches at long tables on a sawdust-covered dining room floor. During the inevitable exodus from a Staples Center event, don't pass up the **Original Pantry Café (Map 9)**, a 24-hour diner that claims to have never closed its doors since opening more than 80 years ago, a feat that includes changing locations. **Musso & Frank Grill (Map 3)** has been operating since Hollywood was a thumb-sucking infant (1919), serving some of the city's best martinis—the food's no good, but you're there to Bukowski it up. The paper-hatted staff behind the counter at **Apple Pan (Map 23)** has been dishing out hickory burgers and pie since 1947. **The Galley (Map 18)** is supposedly Santa Monica's oldest restaurant, serving steaks and seafood since 1934. Legend has it that Orson Welles once ate 18 hot dogs in one sitting at **Pink's (Map 2)** on La Brea—it's not true, but hundreds line up daily to challenge the portly auteur's record.

Eating Cheap

Why make the drive down south when there are so many independent taquerias throughout LA? Many starving actors quell the hunger pangs at a number of hole-in-the-wall restaurants. Some of our favorite eats are the **¡Loteria! Grill (Map 2)** and **Poquito Mas (Maps 49, 50)**. If neither of these do it for you, just drive around for a while, peeling your eyes for the ubiquitous taco truck. There are blogs dedicated to tracking these mobile coches saborosos, and you won't find a cheaper meal north of the border. If you are so stuffed that you think you're not seeing the bill correctly following a filling, yet inexpensive meal, you're most likely at one of the several **Versailles (Maps 6, 24, 27, 53)** restaurants serving up authentic Cuban food: go pork or go home. Still, our hands-down favorite for cheap eats is **Zankou Chicken (Maps 4, 47, 51)**, an Armenian, cash-only mini-chain with the most delectable poultry you will ever taste served with garlic sauce and pita, fast.

Eating Hip

If any city does hip, it's Los Angeles, though unfortunately the style sometimes seems to weaken the food. Recommended here are restaurants that are both hip and delicious. Head to **Lazy Ox (Map 9)** Downtown to enjoy scrumptious and hearty food from around the world, on plates both small and large. **Barbrix (Map 5)** in Silver Lake has so many tiny menu items to sample (along with a large selection of unusual wines by the glass) that you may have to be carried to your Prius. **Bouchon (Map 1)** in Beverly Hills is for those who've already arrived, or who are pretending very well. If you're still on your way, West Hollywood's **Lucques (Map 2)** is an excellent compromise. **Animal (Map 2)** has rock stars in the kitchen and the dining room, and brunch on the outdoor patio at **Malo (Map 4)** is quite cool. Also still fashionable and delicious is **Pizzeria Mozza (Map 3)**, a hive of fabulosity and actual eating of carbs. If you're down Beach Cities way, **MB Post** is the place to be **(Map 27)**.

Eating Late

In a city that needs its beauty sleep, only a few of LA's restaurants stay open for the late-night pangs. **Fred 62 (Map 4)** on Vermont serves starving hipsters burgers, Asian noodles, gooey desserts, and damned good coffee 24 hours a day. For a late-night diner experience, head to the pop-art fabulous **Swingers (Map 2)** on Beverly Boulevard or the historic **Canter's Deli (Map 2)** on Fairfax and bag some cheesecake for the morning after. If you've just returned from Paris and are used to eating bistro-style at midnight, drive over the hill to Studio City's **Firefly (Map 56)** for très magnifique, if pricey, food and a lovely outdoor seating area.

Eating Ethnic

Often, but not always, the best ethnic restaurants are situated in the corresponding ethnic neighborhoods. A wealth of Ethiopian restaurants line Fairfax, just south of Olympic Boulevard; our favorite is **Nyala Ethiopian Cuisine (Map 6)**, wherein dishes like doro wat and injera can be sampled for less than $7 during the daily lunch buffet. The affordable four-course dinner at Armenian restaurant **Carousel (Map 51)** in East Hollywood is not to be missed. South Los Angeles is home to some of the city's best soul and Cajun food; for gumbo try **Harold & Belle's (Map 11)** on Jefferson. Our tummies rumble just thinking about Koreatown. For an interactive and highly satisfying group dining experience, try one of the many Korean barbecue restaurants—we like **Soot Bul Jeep (Map 8)** on the cheap side and **Dong Il Jang (Map 8)** on the posh end. Don't worry if you can't read Korean; the menus have pictures that you can point to for ordering ease. In Little Tokyo, **Sushi-Gen (Map 9)** can't be beat.

Eating Meat

From duck to filet mignon, from free-range chicken to, like we said, bacon, we love to eat meat in the US of A. And California is an absolute hotbed of it: foie gras may technically be illegal, but we absolutely still know where to find it (but you'll have to find out for yourself). For beef, try old-school **Taylor's (Map 8)** in Koreatown, schmoozy **Mastro (Map 1)** in Beverly Hills, or over-the-top British **Tam O'Shanter (Map 5)** in Atwater for prime rib. For strictly German-style brats, give the **Red Lion Tavern (Map 5)** in Silver Lake a try, or go to **Wurstkuche (Map 9)** downtown if fillings like rattlesnake and apple are more your speed. Let's not forget fish: Downtown's **Water Grill (Map 9)** is an upscale seafood destination, as is **Crustacean (Map 1)** in Beverly Hills. And for some pork, Asian-style? Get pork broth ramen, with a side of pork, at **Santouka** (multiple locations).

Eating Meatless

With an abundance of fresh vegetables and fruits in California, we like to go meatless once in a while. For this crunchy dining experience we'll head to **Real Food Daily (Map 2)**, a chain of organic, vegan restaurants serving a huge menu of tempeh, tofu, and stunning weekly specials. **A Votre Sante (Map 16)** in Brentwood has been dishing up vegetarian specialties since the 1980s, and they've managed to plump up their menu without resorting to imitation meat. To really own your veggie roots at **Home (Map 4)** in Los Feliz, order the yogurt, fruit, and granola concoction titled "My Sister the Tree Hugger." For the culturally adventurous yank, **Paru's (Map 4)** is a bounty of all-veggie Indian fare.

Editor's Favorites

When it's feedin' time, Los Angeles is a city of many juxtapositions. Hence, some genius invented "fusion" to please every palate and satisfy the giant melting pot that makes up this town. LA is also where "Californian" cuisine was born, and it involves a lot more than avocado, trust. The city borrows many of its flavors from the neighbors. With Mexico next door, sliding-scale "authentic" south-of-the-border dishes are served up in hundreds of restaurants citywide. The Pacific lapping at our sandy shores brings with it a strong Asian influence. Dim sum palaces, Korean barbecue joints, and hidden Thai gems are daily adventures here. And the sushi—it's the best in (dare we say) the world. In addition, California's abundant agriculture provides us with loads of fresh produce year-round from local purveyors. Many restaurants have made their name on having the freshest and localest. Not to worry, there's plenty of meat. Angelenos don't eat? Please. Ever heard of bacon?

Overview

It's been said there are four seasons in Los Angeles: spring, summer, fall, and awards season. With an intimidating index of outdoor malls and boutique-rich neighborhoods, Angelenos take full advantage of their city's balmy shopping weather. Although the fashion vanguard of New York, London, and Milan tend to condescend to LA designers, Los Angeles has long been the birthplace of trends thanks to the influence of film and television. The relationship is symbiotic, with celebrities moonlighting as designers and local stylists and designers achieving star status. People around the world can open a magazine on any given day and see what Paris, Kim, or Miley is wearing as she schleps shopping bags and a triple non-fat macchiato down Robertson Boulevard and understand: They're just like us! Shop on.

Shopping Districts

Los Angeles has wonderful shopping malls, but thankfully they're not a credit card-wielder's only option. In fact, LA has a surprising number of neighborhood shopping drags that feature lively, locally owned businesses, should the whole "United States of Generica" thing get you down.

Downtown: Whether you're looking for flowers, textiles, toys, or jewelry, downtown has a district devoted to whatever your pleasure (i.e., poison) may be. The LA Fashion District (formerly called the "Garment District") is home to more than Santee Alley's knock-off handbags and shoes: it serves as the city's nucleus of showrooms, distributors, designers, and working fashion professionals. You'll also find an overwhelming assortment of fabrics for fashion or home design, flowers, produce, and housewares. This merchandise Mecca is located between 6th Street to the north, the 10 Freeway to the south, Main Street to the west, and San Pedro Street to the east. Good luck finding parking.

East on **Sunset Boulevard** from Los Feliz to Echo Park, a flotilla of stores has begun to form. The furniture and decor options range from proper antiques through vintage to just plain old junk, but prices are still better than what you'd find in similarly themed venues to the west (how ya doin', La Brea). You'll also find several indie clothing boutiques that allow Eastside hipsters access to their designer duds without the fatal indignity of being seen at Fred Segal.

Los Feliz Village is the square mile (or so) delineated by Los Feliz Boulevard, Hillhurst Avenue, Vermont Avenue, and Hollywood Boulevard. In recent years, a rash of press excitement turned it from "America's hippest neighborhood" into its most-hyped. The din has died down a bit, though new cafés and boutiques still open. There are still enough family-owned restaurants and beloved local landmarks to keep it grounded.

Larchmont Boulevard, between Beverly and 1st Streets, is Hancock Park's friendly, low-key commercial area. A delightful place to shop for books, gifts, wine, and women's clothing, it is made all the more pleasant by the number of restaurants offering sidewalk seating for proper people-watching. Not to be missed, the farmers market on Sundays always draws a crowd.

Fairfax High School is an appropriate buffer between the two cliques that make up the shopping district known as **Melrose Avenue**. Stretching from La Brea to Fairfax, the eastern portion of Melrose is a nexus of tourists, tattoo shops, Harley riders, and vintage t-shirt outlets. West of Fairfax and until La Cienega, however, Melrose beckons the rich, the popular, and the unrepentant with the siren call of posh boutiques including **Tarina Tarantino (Map 2)** and **Fred Segal (Maps 2, 18)**.

Running parallel to Melrose to the south are two of LA's most established shopping districts: **West 3rd Street** and **Beverly Ave. 3rd Street** has attracted fashion-forward boutiques like **Milk (Map 2)** and **EM & Co. (Map 2)**, which have made a home alongside LA pioneer **Trina Turk (Map 2)**. On Beverly, cool furniture shops accompany the cutting-edge fashion of boutiques like **Beige (Map 2)**. Both streets lead into the city's gargantuan shopping cartel that is the Grove, meaning you can shop the hippest undiscovered designers and still lunch at Johnny Rockets if you want.

Just past the once-popular, now obsolete Beverly Center is the played-out Robertson Boulevard, a shopping area killed by the hubris of one too many Hilton & co. sightings at Kitson. Home to an **American Apparel (Map 2)** and the still-trendy **Madison (Map 2)**, Robertson maintains its status in part due to its paparazzi mainstay, the Ivy restaurant.

No survey of Los Angeles shopping would be complete without at least a mention of the venerable **Rodeo Drive**. Known perhaps best for its cameo alongside Julia Roberts in Pretty Woman, Rodeo is home to the old guard: **Giorgio Armani (Map 1)**, **Gucci (Map 1)**, and **Chanel (Map 1)** all have boutiques here. You may not be able to buy anything, but you're guaranteed to see at least one celebrity (someone like Larry King), a handful of expensive sports cars, and a constant stream of gaping tourists.

On the West Side, shopping feels like a birthright (or part of the 401K), with areas like **Montana Avenue** accommodating Santa Monica's upper crust. The blocks between 7th and 17th Streets feature upscale boutiques selling sweaters, chic clothes for men and women, children's apparel and jewelry. If you don't mind the myriad homeless population, throngs of teens on first dates, or the dodgy street performers (and, really, they're not trying to bug you), the **3rd Street Promenade (Map 18)** in Santa Monica is a popular outdoor shopping area with pretty much anything you're looking to buy. For an artsy and laid-back shopping day, head to **Abbot Kinney** in Venice, where fancy furniture stores vie with surf shops and galleries for your attention and your dollar.

Over the hill in **Studio City**, Tujunga Avenue south of Moorpark keeps it real and local; it's another good spot for shoes, gifts, cards, and lazy weekend meals. Originally made famous by musicians Frank Zappa and Tom Petty, **Ventura Boulevard** isn't just for Valley Girls anymore. It's quickly become the SFV's answer to its popular West Hollywood and Beverly Hills counterparts with some of the hippest boutiques, cafés, and spas in Los Angeles.

Clothing

Fred Segal (Maps 2, 18) (with stores on Melrose and on Broadway in Santa Monica) is, for many, the arbiter dicta of Los Angeles style. Even those who don't wear their high-end threads have to admit that their cosmetics and apothecary departments are exceptional. The store is actually a collection of boutiques, with the notable **Ron Herman (Maps 1, 2, 16)** carrying everything from Earnest Sewn jeans to C&C California tanks. Aside from the longstanding hegemony of Fred Segal, LA is home to countless intriguing boutiques and retail outlets.

All of the standard department stores have outposts in Los Angeles, including **Saks Fifth Avenue (Map 1)**, **Nordstrom (Map 2)**, **Bloomingdale's (Map 55)**, **Barney's (Map 1)**, and **Neiman Marcus (Map 1)**, among countless others. Many locals hit up the the **Grove at Farmers Market (Map 2)** for a mix of department-store looks and shabby-chic trends from **Anthropologie (Map 1)** and **Michael Stars (Maps 2, 18, 27)**. The neighboring **Beverly Center (Map 2)** offers shoppers an eight-level behemoth mall with retail favorites like **Politix (Map 2)** and **Ben Sherman (Map 2)**.

Although not a shopping district in its own right, the Hollywood stretch of La Brea is home to some of LA's most popular stores, including **Jet Rag (Map 2)**, a vintage landmark, and **American Rag (Map 2)**, featuring both vintage and new designer finds. Also on La Brea, **Buffalo Exchange (Map 54)** lets you buy and sell fashionable cast-offs and trendy accessories. Just remember to stay off La Brea after 4 pm They'll tow you, stat.

It can be said that Angelenos are just as preoccupied with their underclothing, and what better way for a girl to show off her Pilates-toned bod and year-round tan (or spray tan) than with sexy offerings from **Agent Provocateur (Map 2)** on Melrose or **Trashy Lingerie (Map 2)** on La Cienega. Or replicate the designer look with a Pussycat Dolls getup from the flagship **Frederick's of Hollywood (Map 3)** on Hollywood Blvd.

Housewares

Face-lifts are not relegated to bodily makeovers in Los Angeles—locals are constantly updating their pricey digs with furnishings from the city's many houseware and furniture shops. And there is no one dominant style in architecture—or interior design—so finding stuff that looks like "you" isn't too difficult a task. Finding it at a reasonable price is another matter entirely.

Those with fat wallets will enjoy their visit to **H.D. Buttercup (Map 24)** at the Helms Bakery. It's got tens of thousands of square feet filled with beautiful furniture and other elegant household items, from the spatial geniuses who brought you ABC Carpet in New York. **Berbere Imports (Map 10)**, also in the neighborhood, is a one-stop shop for teak furniture, Moroccan lamps, stone Buddhas, and terra cotta urns. On La Brea between Melrose and Wilshire are funky yet elegant furniture shops.

The folks at **Liz's Antique Hardware (Map 2)** can locate or recreate any doorknob or hinge you show them. **Koontz Hardware (Map 2)** in West Hollywood has everything from dishtowels to chainsaws packed into its Santa Monica Boulevard store. **Rehab Vintage (Map 2)** on Beverly is the go-to shop for lovers of steel furniture and clean lines. Yuppie professionals pass lazy Sundays shopping for furniture and housewares at local favorites **Crate & Barrel (Map 2)** at the Grove. Meanwhile, over the hill, Studio City's **Bedfellows (Map 56)** offers swanky furnishings for the boudoir.

The western stretch of Melrose is home to pure houseware porn; with designer bathtubs and tiles cozying up next to lush carpets, you'll need a second mortgage to finance your new lifestyle. The **Pacific Design Center (Map 2)** houses the crème de la crème of home furnishings, featuring top designers and avant-garde flourishes.

Music

The enormous **Amoeba Music (Map 3)** on Sunset and Cahuenga has two floors of every type of music, DVD, and band-related geegaw you can imagine. Don't be intimidated by the long line—Amoeba is a well-oiled machine, with 20+ clerks and seasoned locals who know the drill. **Counterpoint Records and Books (Map 3)** is a local indie favorite. **Canterbury Record Shop (Map 34)** in Pasadena and Silver Lake's **Rockaway Records (Map 5)** also offer inspired rummaging along the new-used continuum.

Food

Surfas (Map 24) in West LA has an impressive wholesale stock of imported gourmet food and restaurant supplies that is open to the public (but let's just keep that between us, capiche?). Wildly popular and tasty is the French-style take-home deli and catering at **Joan's on Third (Map 2)**.

The final proof of a neighborhood's gentrification comes in the form of a gourmet cheese store. Thus, the **Cheese Store of Silver Lake (Map 4)** joins **Say Cheese (Map 5)**, **Bristol Farms (Maps 2, 20)**, and the **Cheese Store of Beverly Hills (Map 1)** in carrying everything from Abbaye to Humboldt Fog along with wine, gourmet foods, and other ways of impressing your to-good-for-you date. For those exalted occasions when Two Buck Chuck simply will not do, **Silver Lake Wine (Map 5)** and **Larchmont Village Wine & Cheese (Map 7)** are invaluable resources for good grape. **The Oaks Gourmet (Map 3)** on Bronson is two-fold as a source for great meats, wines, and cheeses alongside an amazing sit-down restaurant that's been there for years.

Home to the aforemocked Two Buck Chuck, **Trader Joe's** is a Southern California institution with numerous locations wherein each and every item on the shelf is handpicked, sampled, and sold at a no-kidding reasonable price.

The Hollywood/Ivar Farmers Market (Map 3) is a Sunday tradition, where locals stock up on organic veggies and fresh hummus while enjoying live music from Rastafarians and other performers. Last, but certainly not least (if we said it was least, it would beat us up), is downtown's **Grand Central Market (Map 9)**, located on Broadway near 4th Street, which has been bustling with a diverse crowd ever since it opened in 1917.

Flea Markets & Sample Sales

Call it a flea market and you're likely to give away your East Coast roots. True Southern Californians refer to this Sunday afternoon activity by its regional name: swap meet. Call it what you will; there is no shortage of options to keep everyone from eBay dweebs to vintage-furniture hounds happy. Perhaps the biggest and best known local swap meet, Pasadena's **Rose Bowl Flea Market (Map 34)** isn't for amateurs. Every second Sunday of the month (rain or shine), the flea market opens at 5 a.m. for large crowds eager to stock up on antiques, vintage clothes, and plenty of beef jerky. If you want to start smaller, Fairfax High School hosts the **Melrose Trading Post (Map 2)** every Sunday at the corner of Fairfax and Melrose. For just a $2 entrance fee, it's less pressure than the Rose Bowl, and you're more likely to find locals hocking new designer duds they can't fit in their closet anymore, or their burgeoning jewelry or t-shirt lines. And you can hit up **Jet Rag (Map 2)** on your way home—the vintage store holds a $1 parking-lot sale every Sunday, for those about to get down on the cement and dig for bargains. The **Venice Beach Boardwalk (Map 21)** is a standard tourist trap, complete with street performers, beggars, ripoff souvenir shops and ribald t-shirts, but you've got to see it at least once.

Sample sales may seem a tad intimidating for the non-fashion-industry population, but can be well worth the time if you keep your ear to the ground and your cash at the ready. Some sample sales live up to the name and only offer sample sizes (usually a teeny size 2 or 4 and a size 6 shoe), but this isn't always the case. Some of the most popular local organizers are **Sassy City Chicks (www.sassycitychicks.com)**, **Fashion Co-Op (www.fashioncoop.com)**, and **Billion Dollar Babes (www.bdbshop.com)**, each hosting a number of events locally. Consult their websites for more information about dates, times, and tickets.

As home to many designer showrooms, factories, and distributors, downtown Los Angeles is an excellent source for impromptu sample sales and designer co-ops. Check the **California Market Center (Map 9) (www.californiamarketcenter.com)** where some showrooms sell to the general public on the last Friday of the month.

FYI: Some sample sales have dressing rooms and accept credit cards, and some do not—so if you really want those half-price Chip & Pepper jeans, leave your modesty at home and pack the cashola.

Key to City Abbreviations

AL Alhambra
BH Beverly Hills
BU Burbank
CH Chatsworth
CP Canoga Park
CU Culver City
EN Encino
ES El Segundo
GA Gardena
GH Granada Hills
GL Glendale
HA Hawthorne
HB Hermosa Beach
HC Harbor City
IN Inglewood
LA Los Angeles
LO Lomita
LW Lawndale
MA Marina Del Rey
MB Manhattan Beach
MH Mission Hills
MP Monterey Park
NH North Hollywood
NO North Hills
NR Northridge
PA Pasadena
PP Pacific Palisades
PV Palos Verdes Estates
RB Redondo Beach
RE Reseda
SC Studio City
SG San Gabriel
SM Santa Monica
SO Sherman Oaks
SP South Pasadena
SV Sun Valley
TO Torrance
TP Topanga
TZ Tarzana
VE Venice
VN Van Nuys
WH Woodland Hills

Street Index

Street Index

Street Index

Street Index

Street Index

Street Index